THE ✤ TIMES

Good University Guide 2009

John O'Leary

with
Patrick Kennedy
Dr Nicki Horseman

TIMES BOOKS

Published in 2008 by Times Books

HarperCollins Publishers
77–85 Fulham Palace Road
Hammersmith
London
W6 8JB

www.collins.co.uk

First published in 1993 by Times Books. Fifteenth edition 2008

The main university league table (pages 40–45) and subject tables (pages 49–170)
© HarperCollins Publishers and Times Newspapers Ltd 2008
All other material © John O'Leary 2008

The Times is a registered trademark of Times Newspapers Ltd

Please see chapter 2 for a full explanation of the sources of data used in the
ranking tables. The data providers do not necessarily agree with the data
aggregations or manipulations appearing in this book and are also not
responsible for any inference or conclusions thereby derived.

ISNB 978-0-00-727353-9

Printed and bound in Great Britain by Clays Ltd, St Ives plc.

Contents

About the Author

John O'Leary is a freelance journalist and education consultant. He was the Editor of *The Times Higher Education Supplement* from 2002 to 2007 and was previously Education Editor of *The Times,* having joined the paper in 1990 as Higher Education Correspondent. He has been writing on higher education for nearly 30 years and established the World University Rankings, published by *Times Higher Education* and QS. He has a degree in politics from the University of Sheffield.

Acknowledgements
We would like to thank the many individuals who have helped with this edition of *The Times Good University Guide.* We are particularly indebted to Alexandra Frean, Education Editor of *The Times,* for her support; to Patrick Kennedy and Dr Nicki Horseman, the lead consultants for Exeter Enterprises Limited, which has compiled the main university league table and the individual subject tables for this Guide on behalf of *The Times* and HarperCollins Publishers; to the members of *The Times Good University Guide* Advisory Group for their time and expertise: Alexis Cornish, Director of Planning, University of Edinburgh, Carole Hobden, Senior Strategy and Planning Officer, Imperial College London, Sue Hybart, Director of Planning, Cardiff University, Fidelma Hannah, Director of Planning, Loughborough University; Janet Isaac, Head of Corporate Information, University of Plymouth, and Richard Messer, Director of Planning Support, University of Reading; Jonathan Waller and Louise Bamford of HESA for their technical advice; Susannah Attwell of University and College Sport and Kit Martin for the provision of the table of sports facilities in chapter 6; and Tony Tysome, Murad Ahmed and Patrick Foster for their contributions to the book. We also wish to thank UNITE, the UK's largest provider of student accommodation, for access to the results of their Student Experience Report 2007 compiled by TNS Consumer (to find out more about UNITE visit **www.unite-students.com**); and all the university staff who assisted in providing information for this edition.

How to Use this Book

The Times Good University Guide 2009 will help you to select the subject and university of your choice and to guide you through the whole process of getting to university. The answers to the questions below will help you to get the most out of the information we offer.

How do I choose a course?
- The first half of chapter 1 provides advice on what you should consider when choosing a subject area and relevant courses within that subject.
- Chapter 3 provides details for 61 different subject areas (as listed on page 48).
- For each subject there is a league table that provides our assessment of the ranking of all universities offering courses in the particular subject area.
- For each subject we also provide some background information, details of employment prospects and selected websites where you can find out more about the subject.
- Specific advice for international students is given in chapter 9.

How do I choose a university?
- The second half of chapter 1 provides advice on choosing a university.
- Central is the main *Times League Table* on pages 40–45. This ranks the universities by assessing their quality not just according to student satisfaction (drawn from the National Student Survey) but also through seven other factors, including research quality, the spending on services and facilities, and graduate employment prospects. This table gives an indication of the overall performance of each university.
- The second half of the book contains two pages on each university, giving a general overview of the institution as well as data on student numbers, how to contact the university, the accommodation provided by the university, and the fees payable and the bursaries available.
- In addition, chapter 6 provides information on sport and sporting facilities across all the universities.
- For those considering Oxford or Cambridge, details of admission processes and of all the colleges can be found in chapter 10.
- Specific advice for international students is given in chapter 9.

How do I apply?
- Chapter 4 outlines the application procedure for university entry.
- It starts by advising you on how to complete the UCAS application, and then takes you step-by-step through the process that we hope will lead to your university place for autumn 2009.
- Specific information about applying to Oxford and Cambridge is given in chapter 10.

Can I afford it?
- Chapter 7 outlines the costs of studying at university (including the payment of fees) as well as sources of funds (including student loans, grants and bursaries).
- Chapter 5 provides advice on where to live while you are there.
- Accommodation charges for each university are given in the university profile in chapter 11.

How do I find out more?

- *The Times Good University Guide* website **www.timesonline.co.uk/gug** will keep you up to date with developments throughout the year and contains further information and online tables.
- In each university profile (chapter 11) contact details are given (including e-mail addresses and websites), so you can obtain more information on any university you are interested in.
- At the end of each chapter, a selection of useful websites is given.
- A further listing (pages 515–17) provides contact details for Higher Education Institutes and Colleges that are not covered elsewhere within the book.

We hope you find the information useful in planning for your university career. If you have any suggestions for further information you would like to see, please send them to:
The Times Good University Guide
Collins Reference
HarperCollins Publishers
77–85 Fulham Palace Road
Hammersmith
London W6 8JB
or contact us at: **gooduniguide@harpercollins.co.uk**

Introduction

Normal service has been resumed in higher education, after two years of turmoil for anyone contemplating a degree, and the signs are that competition for places in 2009 will be as fierce as ever. The decline in demand for a university education in the year that top-up fees were introduced now appears to have been no more than a predictable blip. The numbers applying – and actually starting courses – in 2007 showed a healthy increase, which has accelerated since.

International surveys continue to show the salary premium enjoyed by UK graduates over those who choose not to go to university as among the highest in the world. And with more and more jobs requiring a degree, the financial case for going to university remains compelling, even without the wider benefits of an undergraduate education. But national averages conceal big differences in the advantages conferred by different subjects and different universities. Making the right choice of course has never been more important.

Universities and league tables

This *Guide* – identified by a Government-funded review as the most influential of its type – is not designed to make that choice for prospective applicants. Everyone has their own priorities, both academic and social. But it will provide much of the information necessary to narrow down the possibilities and present it in a way that offers valid comparisons.

League tables are seldom popular with those being measured, and the review contained criticisms of all university rankings. But the rankings at the heart of this *Guide* have stood the test of time, after 15 years of publication, and are quoted frequently by universities themselves and by those with an interest in higher education, both at home and abroad.

Indeed, favourable results invariably appear prominently on universities' websites. Professor David Eastwood, chief executive of the Higher Education Funding Council for England, which commissioned the review, reminded universities at a conference to discuss its findings that they often "deplore league tables one day and deploy them the next". He said the tables had become part of the higher education landscape and one of the sources to which prospective students would refer when choosing where and what to study.

However, this *Guide* contains far more than league tables. There are chapters on choosing a course and a university, the application process, managing your money as a student, where to live and what to expect in terms of sport. There are also special sections for overseas applicants and for parents, as well as profiles of every university.

This year's outlook

Top-up fees may not have brought about the collapse in recruitment that many predicted, but they have certainly added to the turbulence and uncertainty that has become a regular feature of higher education. Students are more conscious of the need for a marketable qualification to service growing levels of debt among graduates. However, the initial rush away from pure academic subjects towards the vocational has not persisted. While some job-related degrees, including most branches of engineering, continue to prove attractive, the pattern is now much more mixed. Subjects such as politics, with no direct link to employment, have maintained their popularity in 2008, while others such as business studies and computing have struggled.

Similarly, while there is still a trend for more students to stay at or near home to cut down costs, it appears to be less marked than in the first year of top-up fees. A number of high-quality universities without large centres of population on which to draw saw applications drop alarmingly in that first year, but most have recovered now. The longstanding British preference for studying away from home has begun to reassert itself among those who can afford it.

What has not changed in 2008 is the growing tendency for UK students to remain within national borders. More Scots have applied to Scottish universities, where they will no longer pay the graduate endowment; more Welsh are applying to study in Wales, where they are eligible for reduced fees; and more English are chasing places at universities in England, with fewer looking further afield.

The new incentive for English students is a Government grant of almost £3,000, available in full to those from families with a combined income of less than £25,000, and in part where family income reaches £60,000. Ministers hope that, combined with university bursaries, the new scheme will boost participation among working-class students, but the threshold is high enough to benefit many from middle-class backgrounds as well.

So far, top-up fees have seen a slight increase in working-class participation in higher education, although far less than the Government is seeking. Indeed, the fee changes have not all been bad news for students: the requirement to pay fees of £1,000-plus upfront has gone and grants, bursaries and scholarships made available to bring down the cost for those from poor backgrounds. The institutional profiles in this year's *Guide* include a section detailing the (sometimes complex) arrangements at each university.

The hunt for places

Competition for places on popular courses is unlikely to falter in 2009. The number of 18-year-olds is still increasing for the moment, A-level pass rates are improving, and the range of qualifications accepted by universities has expanded. In addition, the number of applicants from the accession countries of the European Union is growing and universities have stepped up their efforts to recruit students from other parts of the world, who pay even higher fees.

Nevertheless, in 2009, as in previous years, there will be a place somewhere in the higher education system for virtually every candidate with the basic qualifications for a course at this level, whether those are A levels, Highers or relevant vocational qualifications. More than 90 per cent of those with two A-level passes go on to higher education each year, and almost all of the remainder choose a different career path, rather than being rejected. But the most popular courses will be heavily oversubscribed, and that is where the *Guide* comes in.

Commentators on higher education distinguish between "selecting universities" and "recruiting universities", but these labels underestimate the complexity of the choices facing today's applicants. There are very few universities where all the courses are heavily selective – there are simply not enough well-qualified candidates to go around in some subjects – and most so-called recruiting universities have areas in which they excel and can attract a strong field of applicants. The *Guide* uses the ratings of academics and students, plus entry standards and graduate employment rates, to differentiate between universities in 61 different subject areas.

When *The Times Good University Guide* first appeared almost 15 years ago, it helped to explode the myth that any British degree was as good as any other. Since then, the statistics behind the tables have confirmed significant variations in performance within British higher education. Charles Clarke, Labour's former Education Secretary, was prepared to cite this *Guide* as evidence to demolish what he termed the "emperor's clothes idea that all universities are broadly the same".

The changes that Mr Clarke was advocating and that his successors have pursued – chiefly the introduction of variable tuition fees, but also the encouragement of greater specialisation – are creating a new pecking order in higher education, albeit one with familiar names at the top. Employers already distinguish between universities as well as individuals. The need to know the standing of a university, both as an institution and in the various subjects it offers, can only become more important as time goes on.

This year's tables

Unlike most of the rankings that have sprung up in recent years, *The Times Good University Guide* has maintained as much consistency as possible in the methods used to compare universities. The indicators and weightings used in the overall ranking of universities are the same as last year, when the *Guide* was published exclusively online. Apart from a minor alteration in the way that student satisfaction scores are calculated, the only change has been to revert, for one year only, to compiling entry scores from A levels and Highers alone. This was done to maintain a fair basis for comparison when it emerged that the scores of some Scottish universities contained UCAS tariff points for qualifications that were not included in the returns of other institutions.

The biggest development this year is in the subject tables, which for the first time incorporate results from the National Student Survey. Student satisfaction was already a feature of the main table, but we have waited for three editions of the survey to ensure that the data are reliable at subject level. Many departments do not appear because the rules of the survey restrict the publication of scores to those with a 50 per cent response rate from at least 30 students. Where necessary, scores are generated from universities' performance on the other measures in the relevant table. The change inevitably renders comparisons with last year's *Guide* unreliable.

The other change that seems to occur every year is in the number of universities: two more have been created since the last edition was published. Buckinghamshire New University makes its debut two years after several of its fellow colleges of higher education were promoted. Like many debutants before it, Bucks starts near the foot of the table, but by no means right at the bottom. The other new university this year – Swansea Metropolitan – does not appear in the tables because it instructed the Higher Education Statistics Agency not to release its data. Had it not done so, the indications are that it would have been in a similar position to Bucks.

Swansea Met has joined London Metropolitan and Liverpool Hope universities in blocking the release of data in order to avoid appearing in league tables. London Met originally argued that statistics relating to its two predecessor institutions (London Guildhall and North London) would create a misleading impression of the merged institution. Although this objection no longer holds good, the university has maintained its stance and, regrettably for those seeking information on one of the capital's largest universities, it still cannot be included in the main table, or in the many subject rankings for which it is eligible. London Met was 98th out of 100 universities in its one appearance in the ranking, while Liverpool Hope was last of the 113 universities in last year's table.

The first *Times* League Table effectively produced a dead heat between Oxford and Cambridge, with the light blues a fraction of a point ahead. After several years of Cambridge domination, changes in methodology saw the roles reversed in the 2003 edition and Oxford subsequently extended its lead. The current table sees Oxford maintain its leadership, despite playing second fiddle to Cambridge in most of the subject tables. Cambridge has the better record on research, entry standards and graduate destinations, but Oxford's lead in staffing levels, degree classifications, completion rates and particularly in spending on libraries and other student facilities makes the difference. Oxford also boasts the top student satisfaction rating, while Cambridge undergraduates still did not respond to the National Student Survey in sufficient numbers to produce a score. Accurate comparisons of the two are difficult because of the mix of college and central university responsibilities, but Oxford appears to include more college spending in its submission. Cambridge remains well ahead of Imperial College and the London School of Economics, while St Andrews remains the top university in Scotland and Cardiff is well clear in Wales.

For most readers, however, the scramble over a handful of points at the top of the overall ranking of universities will be literally academic. The key information is contained in the subject tables, which now cover every area of higher education. One of the strengths of this *Guide*, and others like it, has been to highlight the quality of previously underestimated universities such as York and Bath, and to celebrate the achievements of centres of excellence such as the social sciences at Essex.

Universities' own research suggests that well over half of all applicants use newspaper guides, and this year's review predicts that league tables will become increasingly influential as fees rise further. Candidates have already become more selective about the courses they choose, as top-up fees have been introduced and the financial pressures on students and their families have grown.

The new hierarchy

Higher education has seen other important changes with the introduction of incentives to extend access to a wider share of the population, and much more selective allocation of research funds. The Government wants half of all young people to experience higher education by the time they are 30, many of them taking two-year Foundation degrees rather than the traditional honours. The result is a gradual return to the hierarchical system that seemed to have been abandoned when the polytechnics acquired university status; only this time there are more than two tiers. This year's table sees as stark a division between old and new universities as there has been since the *Guide* was first published.

At the top of the pile, in terms of funding and prestige, is a group of perhaps 20 universities, which attract 90 per cent of the resources available for research and also take the lion's share of money for teaching, partly because they offer expensive subjects such as medicine and engineering. A middle group, composed mainly of traditional universities, has been recruiting more undergraduates – especially overseas – while trying to compete on research. The remainder are having to survive mainly by expanding, or at least maintaining, student numbers and interacting with local companies.

Universities in the last group have been feeling the squeeze since several of the most popular institutions have taken advantage of a relaxation in recruitment controls to expand their numbers. But fears have also been expressed for some of those in the middle, which miss out not only on the Government's boost for leading research but also on the rewards for widening access to higher education. Applicants with the necessary qualifications will no doubt continue to migrate towards the more prestigious institutions.

Uncertainty over sixth–form qualifications continues to complicate the picture. The future of A levels is uncertain, with the Government championing a new range of vocational (and eventually academic) diplomas. And even the current range of qualifications is treated differently by different types of university. Most of the leading institutions continue to frame their offers in terms of A-level grades, but the majority of others now use the UCAS tariff to set a points requirement. Whichever system is used, every grade may help in the race for selection. And the right choice of course remains vital. This book should help in the process of choice for, unlike other guides, its emphasis is on the quality of education.

The university explosion

At first sight, choosing a university appears to have become simpler over the past decade. The distinction between universities and polytechnics was swept away in 1992, and the number of places expanded to the point where far more young (and not-so-young) people could benefit from higher education. Although the parties differed in the 2005 election about the scale of expansion, consensus has grown among politicians and business leaders that, quite apart from the benefits to the individual, a modern economy needs mass higher education. Countries such as the United States and Japan reached the same conclusion long ago but a combination of factors – not all of them planned – has seen Britain making up for lost time at a rate that has prompted concerns about the quality of some courses.

More than a third of 18-year-olds are now going on to higher education, compared with one in seven in 1980, while a much higher proportion will take a higher education course at some point in their life. Yet, paradoxically, by ridding Britain of its elite university system, the last Conservative Government sowed the seeds of a different form of elitism. The very process of opening up higher education ensured the creation of a new hierarchy of institutions. The old certainties could not survive in a nation of more than 100 diverse universities and a growing number of degree-providing colleges.

As student numbers have gone through the roof, however, general higher education budgets have been squeezed and the funding gap has widened. Beneath the veneer of a unified higher education system, it was inevitable that greater specialisation would arrive eventually. There is no need for formalised divisions like the American Ivy League because the market – and now Government policy – is already taking the university system in that direction.

The need for information

There always was a pecking order of sorts. Oxford and Cambridge were world leaders long before most British universities were established, and parts of London University have always enjoyed a high status in particular fields. But few outside the higher-education world could discriminate between Aberdeen and Exeter, for example.

Employers, careers advisers, even academics, had their own ideas of which were the leading universities, but there was little hard evidence to back their conclusions. Often they were based on outdated, inaccurate impressions of distant institutions. The expanded higher education system has made such judgements more scientific as well as more necessary. Employers of graduates and those who commit their money to student sponsorship or funding research are comparing institutions department by department. This has become possible because of a new transparency in what a former Higher Education Minister described as the "secret garden of academe". Official demands for more and more published information may have taxed the patience of university administrators, but they have also given outsiders the opportunity to make more meaningful comparisons. The unistats.com website represents the latest attempt to bring together the statistics relevant to applicants. But many readers value the more concise nature of guides such as this one, which distil the information displayed on such sites into a more manageable form.

Why university?

Doubtless some will be tempted, once the cost of living has been added to the fees burden and the attractions of university life balanced against loss of potential earnings, to write off higher education. There are plenty of self-made millionaires who still swear by the University of Life as the only training ground for success. Yet even by narrow financial criteria it would be rash to dismiss higher education. With so many more competing for jobs, a degree will never again be an automatic passport to a fast-track career. But graduates' financial prospects remain much brighter than school leavers', as do their prospects in other important areas, such as health.

Even for those who cannot or do not wish to afford three or more years of full-time education after leaving school, university remains a possibility. The modular courses adopted by most universities enable students to work through a degree at their own pace, dropping out for a time if necessary, or switching to part-time attendance. Distance learning is another option, and advances in information technology now mean that some nominally full-time courses are delivered mainly via computers.

For many – perhaps most – students, therefore, the university experience is not what it was in their parents' day. There is more assessment, more crowding, more pressure to get the best possible degree while also finding gainful employment for at least part of the year. The proportion of students achieving first-class degrees has risen significantly, while an upper second (rather than the previously ubiquitous 2:2) has become the norm. Research shows that the classification has a real impact in the labour market.

Into the future

The 2004 Higher Education Act and the White Paper that preceded it ensured that the pace of change in universities would accelerate. In the future it is likely that more students will begin their degrees at further education colleges, more will opt initially for two-year courses and the range both of subjects and teaching methods will grow still further. Some predict the rise of the "virtual university" or the demise of the conventional higher-education institution, as companies customise their own courses. However, universities have demonstrated enduring popularity and show every sign of weathering the current turbulence.

Overall competition for places will ease over the coming decade, as the population of 18-year-olds begins to decline. But numbers will remain more buoyant among the socio-economic groups that provide the bulk of university students than in the population as a whole, so the effects may be less dramatic than many commentators have predicted. Especially in traditional universities, many arts and social science courses will remain oversubscribed and some science degrees, too, will continue to command high entrance requirements. There may be institutional casualties, particularly if public spending is tightened to the extent that many in universities predict. However, the value of higher education to society and to the economy is now generally acknowledged. There may be difficult times ahead for universities, but most are strong enough to survive.

1

What and Where to Study

Choosing where and what to study are life-shaping decisions. The outcome will help determine your career and personal life far beyond the next three or four years (and they are important enough). Many graduates end up living and working near their university; they may make their closest friends in their student days and may even meet their future partner there. So finding the right university demands serious thought and research, and this *Guide* may play an important part.

Is higher education for you?

Before you start, there is one important question to ask yourself: what do you want out of higher education? The answer will make it easier to choose where (and whether) to be a student. With more than a third of school-leavers going on to university, it is easy to drift that way without much thought, opting for the subject in which you expect the best grades and looking for a university with a reasonable reputation and a good social life. Your career will look after itself – you hope.

With graduate debt soaring, however, and job prospects varying widely between subjects, now is the time to look at your own motivation. Love of a subject is perhaps the best reason for taking a degree, and one that allows you to focus almost exclusively

UNITE Student Experience Report 2007	
Why did you decide to go to university?	
To gain qualifications	73%
Improve my chances of getting a job	65%
Improve my earning potential	44%
For the experience	44%
To learn more about interesting subjects	43%
I have always wanted to go	38%
Natural progression	37%
To stretch me intellectually	36%
To mix with different people	34%

on the search for a course that corresponds with your passions. If, on the other hand, higher education is a means to an end, you need to think about career ambitions and look carefully at employment rates for any courses you might consider.

Many graduates look back on their student days as the best years of their lives, and there is nothing wrong with wanting to have a good time. Remember, though, that you will be paying for it later (literally) and there will be more studying than partying. If you have not enjoyed sixth-form or college courses, you may be better off in a job and possibly becoming one of the hundreds of thousands each year who return to education later in life.

Narrowing down the choices

Once you have decided that higher education is for you, the good news is that, as long as you start early enough, finding the right university need not be stressful. Media attention focuses on the scramble for places on a relatively small proportion of courses where competition is intense, but there are plenty of places at good universities for candidates with the basic qualifications – it's just a matter of finding the one that suits you best. For older applicants, relevant work experience and demonstrable interest in a subject may be enough to win a place.

If anything, the problem is that of too much choice. Students prepared to move away from home will have more than 100 universities and numerous specialist colleges to consider, most with hundreds – even thousands – of course combinations on offer. Institutions come in all shapes and sizes, so there is work to do at the outset narrowing down your options.

Deciding what you want to study may reduce the field considerably – only seven institutions offer veterinary medicine for example, although the total is closer to 100 in subjects such as law and English. By the time you have factored in personal preferences about the type or location of your ideal university, the list of possibilities may already be reduced to manageable proportions.

After that, you can take a closer look at what the courses contain and what life is really like for students. Prospectuses and university websites will give you an accurate account of course combinations, and important facts like the accommodation available to new students, but it is their job to sell the university. To get a true picture, you need more – preferably a visit not just to the university, but the department where you would be studying. If that is not possible, there are plenty of other sources of objective information, such as the National Student Survey (which is available online, with a range of additional data about each institution, at www.unistats.com).

Many students' unions publish alternative prospectuses, giving a "warts and all" view of the university, and those that do not provide this service may be able to arrange a brief discussion with a current student, either by phone or email. Your school or college may put you in contact with someone who went to a university that you are considering. Guides and collections of statistics may give you valuable information about a course or a university, but there is no substitute for personal experience.

What to study?

Most people seeking a place in higher education start by choosing a subject and a course, rather than a university. If you take a degree, you are going to spend at least three years immersed in your subject. It has to be one you will enjoy and can master – not to mention one that you are qualified to study. Many economics degrees require maths, for example, while some medical schools demand chemistry or biology. The UCAS website (www.ucas.com) contains course profiles, including entrance requirements, which are a good starting point, while universities' own sites contain more detailed information. In chapter 3, we describe 61 subject areas and provide league tables for each of them.

Top Ten Most Popular Subjects by Applications		Highest Applications to Places		
1	Business and Administration	84,399	1	Medicine	9.4
2	Law	77,459	2	Dentistry	9.4
3	Pre-clinical Medicine	70,377	3	Nursing	9.4
4	Psychology	70,295	4	Aural and Oral Sciences	8.4
5	English Studies	50,251	5	Anatomy and Physiology	8.2
6	Management Studies	49,447	6	Pharmacology and Pharmacy	7.5
7	Nursing	47,051	7	Economics	7.4
8	Training Teachers	43,896	8	Dance	7.4
9	History	41,917	9	Architecture	7.3
10	Sports Science	39,242	10	Drama	7.3

UCAS 2008 (number of applications to 15 January 2008)   UCAS 2007 (refers to subjects with 500 or more places)

Your school subjects and the UCAS tariff

The official yardstick by which your results will be judged is the UCAS tariff (see page 18), which gives a score for each grade of every type of UK qualification considered relevant for university entrance, as well as for the International Baccalaureate (IB). This tariff has become more controversial as more subjects and types of qualifications have been included in it. It is proposed that top scores in new vocational diplomas will attract more points than a full set of A grades at A level, while the most successful IB students already earn considerably more points. If this process continues, it is less likely that the leading universities will use the tariff.

There is a separate issue for some of the top universities about subjects studied at A level. The variety of A level courses studied contains many subjects that they do not consider on a par with traditional academic subjects. For many years, a minority of universities have refused to accept General Studies as a full A level for entrance purposes (although even some in the Russell Group of top universities do). The growth of supposedly "soft" subjects, such as media studies and photography, has prompted a few to produce lists of subjects that will only be accepted as a third, or fourth, A level. The Cambridge list (see below) includes no fewer than 20 A levels, including business studies, dance and home economics, and five International Baccalaureate (IB) subjects.

For most courses at most universities, there are no such restrictions, although those choosing A levels would be wise to bear the list in mind in case more of the leading universities move in this direction. At the very least, it is an indication of the subjects that admissions tutors may take less seriously than the rest.

While the majority of universities use the tariff to make offers of places, those that are heavily oversubscribed will tend to demand particular grades, often naming the subjects in which the highest grades are required. There are no set rules about using the tariff. Some universities will give credit for qualifications in key skills, for example, while others exclude them from candidates' points totals. In certain universities, some departments, but not others, will use the tariff to set offers. The university's prospectus or website should show which does what. In addition some universities now require applicants to take an entrance test. The details are listed on page 19.

Cambridge List of Subjects only Acceptable as a Third or Fourth Subject

A levels		IB
• Accounting	• Information and	• Travel and Tourism
• Art and Design	Communication Technology	• Business and Management
• Business Studies	• Leisure Studies	• Design and Technology
• Communication Studies	• Media Studies	• Information Technology in a
• Dance	• Music Technology	Global Society
• Design and Technology	• Performance Studies	• Theatre Arts
• Drama/Theatre Studies	• Performing Arts	• Visual Arts
• Film Studies	• Photography	
• Health and Social Care	• Physical Education	
• Home Economics	• Sports Studies	

General Studies and Critical Thinking A levels will only be considered as fourth A level subjects and will not therefore be accepted as part of a conditional offer.

Making a choice

Choosing a subject to study at university is not always as straightforward as it sounds. Your A levels, or Scottish Highers, may have chosen themselves, but the range of subjects across the whole university system is vast. Even subjects that you have studied at school may be quite different at degree level – some academic economists actually prefer their undergraduates not to have taken economics A level because they approach the subject

The UCAS Tariff

GCE/VCE Qualifications				Points	Scottish Qualifications		
GCE AS/ AS VCE	GCE AS Double Award	GCE A level/ AVCE	GCE/AV CE Double Award		Advanced Higher	Higher	Int 2
			AA	240			
			AB	220			
			BB	200			
			BC	180			
			CC	160			
			CD	140			
	AA	A	DD	120	A		
	AB			110			
	BB	B	DE	100	B		
	BC			90			
	CC	C	EE	80	C		
				72	D	A	
	CD			70			
A	DD	D		60		B	
B	DE			50			
				48		C	
				42		D	A
C	EE	E		40			
				35			B
D				30			
				28			C
E				20			

International Baccalaureate

Points for the International Baccalaureate (IB) are awarded to candidates who achieve the IB Dip

IB Dip	Points	IB Dip	Points	IB Dip	Points	IB Dip	Points
45	768	39	628	33	489	27	350
44	744	38	605	32	466	26	326
43	722	37	582	31	442	25	303
42	698	36	559	30	419	24	280
41	675	35	535	29	396		
40	652	34	512	28	373		

so differently. Other students are disappointed because they appear to be going over old ground when they continue with a subject that they enjoyed at school. Universities now publish quite detailed syllabuses, and it is a matter of going through the fine print.

The greater difficulty comes in judging your suitability for the many subjects that are not on the school or college curriculum. Philosophy and psychology sound fascinating (and are), but you may have no idea what degrees in either subject entail – for example, the level of statistics that may be required. Forensic science may look exciting on television – more glamorous than plain chemistry – but it may open fewer doors if the type of work portrayed in *Silent Witness* or *Raising the Dead* is not available.

Vocational subjects

The introduction of top-up fees has encouraged more students into job-related subjects, rather than traditional academic disciplines, in the hope of improving their employment prospects. This is understandable and, if you are sure of your future career path, possibly also sensible. But much depends on what that career is – and whether you are ready to make such a long-term commitment. Some of the programmes that have attracted public ridicule, such as surf science or golf course management, may narrow graduates'

Admissions Tests

Some of the most competitive courses now have additional entrance tests. Test dates and other details are available on the UCAS website.

BioMedical Admissions Test (BMAT): for medicine and veterinary medicine at Cambridge, Oxford, Royal Veterinary College, University College London, Imperial College London (www.bmat.org.uk)

English Literature Admissions Test (ELAT): for English at Oxford

Graduate Medical School Admissions Test (GAMSAT): for graduate entry to medicine and dentistry at St. Georges Hospital Medical School, Nottingham, Peninsula College of Medicine and Dentistry, Swansea, Keele (www.gamsatuk.org)

History Aptitude Test (HAT): for modern history at Oxford

National Admissions Test for Law (LNAT): for entry to law at Birmingham, Bristol, Cambridge, Durham, Exeter, Glasgow, King's College London, Nottingham, Oxford, University College, London (www.lnat.ac.uk)

Modern and Medieval Languages Test (MML): for modern and medieval languages at Cambridge

Philosophy, Politics and Economics (PPE) Admissions Test: for philosophy, politics and economics course at Oxford

Sixth Term Examination Papers (STEP): for mathematics at Cambridge

Thinking Skills Assessment (TSA): mainly for computer science, natural sciences, engineering and economics at most Cambridge colleges

UK Clinical Aptitude Test (UKCAT): for medicine and dentistry at Aberdeen, Brighton and Sussex Medical School, Cardiff University, Dundee, Durham, East Anglia, Edinburgh, Glasgow, Hull York Medical School, Keele, King's College London, Imperial College London (graduate entry), Leeds, Leicester, Manchester, Newcastle, Nottingham, Oxford (graduate entry), Peninsula College of Medicine and Dentistry, Queen Mary University of London, Queen's University Belfast, Sheffield, Southampton, St Andrews, St George's University of London, Warwick (graduate entry) (www.ukcat.ac.uk)

options to a worrying extent, but there is nothing wrong with their employment records. Jibes about so-called "Mickey Mouse" courses have become less frequent, although there are some who are yet to accept that the higher education curriculum has moved into new areas since they were students. Many vocational courses are tailored to particular professions. If you choose one of these, make sure that the degree is recognised by the relevant professional body (such as the Engineering Council or one of the institutes) or you may not be able to use the skills that you acquire. Most universities are only too keen to make such recognition clear in their prospectus; if no such guarantee is published, contact the university department running the course and seek assurances.

Even where a course has professional recognition, bear in mind that a further qualification may be required to practise. Both law and medicine, for example, demand additional training to become a fully qualified solicitor, barrister or doctor. Nor is either degree an automatic passport to a job: only about half of all law graduates go into the profession and the UK is now training more medical students than the National Health Service can afford. Both law and medicine also provide a route into the profession for graduates who have taken other subjects. Law conversion courses, though not cheap, are increasingly popular, and there is a growing number of graduate-entry medical degrees.

One way to ensure that a degree is job-related is to take a "sandwich" course, which involves up to a year in business or industry. Students often end up working for the organisation which provided the placement, while others gain valuable insights into a field of employment – even if only to discount it. The drawback with such courses is that, like the year abroad that is part of most language degrees, the period away from university inevitably disrupts living arrangements and friendship groups. But most of those who take this route find that the career benefits make this a worthwhile sacrifice.

Academic or vocational courses?
Employers' organisations calculate that more than half of all graduate jobs are open to applicants from any subject, and recruiters for the most competitive graduate training schemes often prefer traditional academic subjects to apparently relevant vocational degrees. Newspapers, for example, often prefer a history graduate to one with a media studies degree; computing firms take a disproportionate number of classicists. A good degree classification and the right work experience are more important than the subject for most non-technical jobs. But it is hard to achieve a good result on a course that you do not enjoy, so scour prospectuses, and email or phone university departments to ensure that you know what you are letting yourself in for. Their reaction to your approach will also give you an idea of how responsive they are to their students.

If you are not sure whether you will be suited to a particular subject, you can take an online aptitude test through the UCAS website. The "What to study" section gives you access to the Stamford Test, which uses an online questionnaire to match your interests and strengths to possible courses and careers (www.ucas.com/students/beforeyouapply/whattostudy/stamfordtest).

Studying more than one subject
You may find that more than one subject appeals, in which case you could consider Joint Honours – degrees that combine two subjects – or even Combined Honours, which will cover several related subjects. Such courses obviously allow you to extend the scope of your studies, but they should be approached with caution. Even if the number of credits

suggests a similar workload to Single Honours, covering more than one subject inevitably involves extra reading and often more essays or project work.

However, there are advantages. Many students choose a "dual" to add a vocational element to make themselves more employable – business studies with languages or engineering, for example, or media studies with English. Others want to take their studies in a particular direction, perhaps by combining history with politics, or statistics with maths. Some simply want to add a completely unrelated interest to their main subject, such as environmental science and music, or archaeology and event management – both combinations that are available at UK universities.

At most universities, however, it is not necessary to take a degree in more than one subject in order to broaden your studies. The spread of modular programmes ensures that you can take courses in related subjects without changing the basic structure of your degree. You may not be able to take an event management module in a single-honours archaeology degree, but it should be possible to study some history, or a language. The number and scope of the combinations offered at many of the larger universities is extraordinary. Indeed, it has been criticised by academics who believe that "mix-and-match" degrees can leave a graduate without a rounded view of a subject. But for those who seek breadth and variety, close scrutiny of university prospectuses (whether online or on paper) is a vital part of the selection process.

What type of course?

Once you have a subject, you must decide on the level and type of course. Most readers of this guide will be looking for full-time degree courses, but higher education is much broader than that. You may not be able to afford the time or the money needed for a full-time commitment of three or four years at this point in your life. Tens of thousands of people each year opt for a part-time course – usually while holding down a job – to continue learning and improve their career prospects. It can be exhausting, unless your employer gives you time off to study, and any financial support you receive from the Government will not be the same as that provided for full-time students. However, if you have the stamina for a course that will usually take twice as long as the full-time equivalent, this route may make a degree more affordable. Part-time students tend to be highly committed to their subject, and many claim that the quality of the social life associated with their course makes up for the quantity of leisure time enjoyed by full-timers.

Another option, if you are confident that you can manage without regular face-to-face contact with teachers and fellow students, is distance learning. Courses are delivered mainly or entirely online or through correspondence, although some programmes offer a certain amount of local tuition. The process might sound daunting and impersonal, but students of the Open University (OU), all of whom are educated in this way, are the most satisfied in the country, according to the results of the annual National Student Survey. Attending lectures or oversized seminars at a conventional university can be less personal than regular contact with your tutor at a distance. Of course, not all universities are as good at communicating with their distance-learning students as the OU, or offer such high-quality course materials, but this mode of study does give students ultimate flexibility to determine when and where they work. Distance learning is becoming increasingly popular for the delivery of professional courses, which are often needed to supplement degrees. The OU now takes students of all ages, not just mature students.

Even if you are set on a full-time course, you might not want to commit yourself for three years. Growing numbers are taking two-year Foundation degrees – vocational courses which the Government would like to be the main source of expansion in universities and colleges. Even more students take longer-established two-year courses, such as Higher National Diplomas or other diplomas tailored to the needs of industry or parts of the health service. Those who do well on such courses usually have the option of converting their qualification into a degree with further study, although many achieve their goal without immediately staying on for a further two or more years.

A number of universities have experimented with two-year degrees, squeezing more work into an extended academic year. The so-called "third semester" makes use of the summer vacation for extra teaching, so that mature students, in particular, can reduce the length of their career break. But the pattern has really only caught on at the University of Buckingham, the UK's only established private university, where it has had a small but enthusiastic following for more than 30 years.

Other short courses – usually lasting a year – are designed for students who do not have the necessary qualifications for a degree in their chosen subject. Foundation courses in art and design have been common for many years, and are the chosen preparation for a degree at leading departments, even for many students whose A levels would win them a degree place elsewhere. Access courses perform the same function in a wider range of subjects for students without A levels, or for those whose grades are either too low or in the wrong subjects to gain admission to a particular course. Entry requirements are modest, but students have to reach the same standard as regular entrants if they are to progress to a degree.

Yet more choice

No single guide can allow for personal preferences in choosing a course. You may want one of the many degrees that incorporate a year at a partner university abroad, or to try a six-month exchange on the Continent through the European Union's Erasmus Programme. Either might prove a valuable experience and add to your employability. You might prefer a January or February start to the traditional autumn introduction – there are plenty of opportunities for this, mainly at new universities. In some subjects – particularly engineering and the sciences – the leading degrees may be Masters courses, taking four years rather than the norm (in England) of three.

Top Ten Universities for Female Students		Top Ten Universities for Male Students	
1 Manchester Metropolitan	12,355	1 Manchester	11,175
2 Leeds	12,040	2 Manchester Metropolitan	9,705
3 Manchester	11,650	3 Leeds	9,625
4 Cardiff	9,440	4 Nottingham	8,925
5 Ulster	9,275	5 Sheffield	7,710
6 Edinburgh	9,175	6 Nottingham Trent	7,620
7 Birmingham	9,055	7 Sheffield Hallam	7,445
8 West of England, Bristol	8,435	8 Birmingham	7,300
9 Nottingham	8,420	9 Edinburgh	7,210
10 Glasgow	8,345	10 West of England, Bristol	7,155
HESA (2007)		HESA (2007)	

Job prospects

For many – perhaps most – students, job prospects are the key element in choosing a subject. The tables on pages 24–25 are the obvious starting point in assessing whether your prospective course will pay off in career terms. The Higher Education Statistics Agency (HESA) collects data both on what graduates do straight after graduation (sometimes called graduate destinations) and their average salaries. But the results are to be treated with caution because they represent only the first six months of a graduate's career – not even that if he or she has gone on to postgraduate study – and they make no allowances for the variety of entry routes into different areas of employment. Dentists, for example, have been virtually guaranteed a job if they complete a degree successfully, whereas those going into art and design know that periods of freelance and/or casual work may be an occupational hazard at the start of their career.

This type of table can mislead. We use classifications developed at the universities of Warwick and the West of England to distinguish between "graduate-level" work and jobs that do not normally require a degree. Subjects are ranked on "positive destinations", which include postgraduate study and other forms of training, whether or not they are combined with a job. Some similar tables do not make a distinction between different types of job – thus giving universities and subjects uniformly high employment rates.

The second table, on pages 26–27, gives average earnings six months after graduation. It contains interesting – and in some cases surprising – information about early career pay levels. Few would have placed social work and nursing among the top dozen fields for graduate pay, for example, while business studies and accounting do not make the top 20. Those positions underline the differences between starting salaries and long-term prospects in different jobs.

By three years after graduation, the figures are significantly different, according to recent research. HESA found that by then, overall unemployment had dropped from 5 per cent, six months after graduation, to 2 per cent, while 80 per cent were in graduate occupations, compared with 71 per cent in the initial survey of the same group. Corresponding differences emerged when the sample was broken down by subject.

Where to study

Once you have decided what to study, there are still several factors that might influence your choice of university or college. Obviously, you need to have a reasonable chance of getting in, you may want reassurance about the university's reputation, and its location will probably also be important to you. On top of that, most applicants have views about the type of institution they are looking for – big or small, old or new, urban or rural, specialist or comprehensive. You may surprise yourself by choosing somewhere that does not conform to your initial criteria, but working through your preferences is another way of narrowing down your options.

Entry standards

Unless you are a mature student or have taken a gap year, your passport to your chosen university will be a conditional offer based on your predicted grades, previous exam performance, personal statement and school or college reference. A lucky few may get an offer that is so low that success is a foregone conclusion – because the university considers them outstanding and needs no further evidence of their potential. But only those who already have their grades receive unconditional offers.

What Graduates Do by Subject Studied

	Times **Subject** (ranked by the total of the first three columns on the right)	Employed in Graduate Job	Employed in Graduate Job and Studying	Studying and Not Employed	Employed in Non-Graduate Job and Studying	Employed in Non-Graduate Job	Unemployed
1	Dentistry	84%	16%	0%	0%	0%	0%
2	Medicine	88%	6%	6%	0%	0%	0%
3	Veterinary Medicine	81%	4%	13%	0%	1%	2%
4	Nursing	87%	7%	1%	0%	3%	2%
5	Pharmacology and Pharmacy	68%	17%	8%	0%	4%	2%
6	Architecture	58%	20%	14%	1%	5%	3%
7	Building	72%	16%	3%	1%	5%	3%
8	Civil Engineering	72%	11%	7%	0%	7%	3%
9	Chemical Engineering	59%	6%	18%	2%	9%	6%
10	Land and Property Management	42%	35%	4%	2%	13%	4%
11	Town and Country Planning and Landscape	48%	13%	19%	2%	13%	4%
12	Education	64%	4%	10%	2%	16%	3%
13	Chemistry	34%	6%	39%	1%	14%	6%
14	Celtic Studies	30%	8%	37%	4%	16%	5%
15	Mechanical Engineering	60%	7%	10%	1%	15%	7%
16	Social Work	66%	6%	5%	2%	16%	6%
17	Law	21%	5%	47%	5%	19%	4%
18	Other Subjects Allied to Medicine	63%	7%	7%	1%	16%	6%
19	General Engineering	54%	9%	14%	1%	16%	7%
20	Mathematics	34%	13%	26%	3%	18%	5%
21	Physics and Astronomy	30%	8%	36%	2%	16%	7%
22	Geology	41%	4%	28%	2%	19%	7%
23	Economics	42%	14%	15%	3%	20%	6%
24	Aeronautical and Manufacturing Engineering	50%	6%	13%	2%	20%	8%
25	Theology and Religious Studies	31%	5%	29%	5%	24%	5%
26	Electrical and Electronic Engineering	51%	5%	13%	2%	19%	10%
27	French	40%	5%	21%	3%	26%	4%
28	Music	35%	6%	26%	3%	25%	5%
29	Anatomy and Physiology	25%	4%	36%	3%	25%	6%
30	German	40%	5%	20%	3%	26%	5%
31	Food Science	48%	4%	14%	2%	24%	8%
32	East and South Asian Studies	47%	5%	15%	1%	23%	9%
33	Computer Science	52%	4%	9%	2%	22%	10%
34	Accounting and Finance	31%	23%	8%	6%	27%	6%
35	Middle Eastern and African Studies	37%	9%	20%	1%	20%	13%

	Times Subject (ranked by the total of the first three columns on the right)	Employed in Graduate Job	Employed in Graduate Job and Studying	Studying and Not Employed	Employed in Non-Graduate Job and Studying	Employed in Non-Graduate Job	Unemployed
36	Materials Technology	43%	5%	16%	3%	26%	7%
37	Iberian Languages	43%	4%	17%	3%	28%	6%
38	Biological Sciences	29%	5%	30%	3%	27%	7%
39	Italian	42%	5%	15%	4%	28%	7%
40	Russian	38%	4%	18%	5%	30%	5%
41	Geography and Environmental Sciences	34%	5%	22%	3%	30%	5%
42	Classics and Ancient History	28%	5%	26%	4%	30%	6%
43	Politics	35%	5%	20%	4%	30%	7%
44	Business Studies	47%	7%	7%	3%	31%	6%
45	Philosophy	30%	5%	23%	4%	31%	6%
46	Archaeology	32%	4%	21%	5%	31%	8%
47	English	30%	3%	23%	5%	33%	6%
48	History	27%	4%	24%	4%	34%	6%
49	Anthropology	32%	4%	18%	4%	33%	9%
50	Art and Design	44%	3%	7%	4%	33%	9%
51	Linguistics	27%	5%	21%	4%	35%	7%
52	Librarianship and Information Management	44%	3%	7%	2%	34%	9%
53	Agriculture and Forestry	39%	7%	8%	3%	37%	6%
54	Hospitality, Leisure, Recreation, Sport and Tourism	34%	4%	13%	4%	39%	5%
55	American Studies	32%	4%	14%	5%	38%	6%
56	Psychology	29%	5%	17%	5%	39%	6%
57	Social Policy	30%	4%	15%	5%	38%	7%
58	History of Art, Architecture and Design	28%	4%	19%	4%	39%	6%
59	Sociology	30%	4%	14%	4%	41%	6%
60	Communication and Media Studies	41%	3%	6%	3%	39%	8%
61	Drama, Dance and Cinematics	36%	4%	9%	4%	39%	8%
	Grand Total	**43%**	**6%**	**16%**	**3%**	**26%**	**6%**

The table is ranked by the sum of "positive" destinations – Employed in Graduate Job, Employed in Graduate Job and Studying, and Studying and Not Employed – that is, activities that require a degree.
Source: HESA 2005–06 DLHE return

What Graduates Earn by Subject Studied

	Subject	Graduate Employment or Self Employment	Non-graduate Employment or Self Employment
1	Medicine	£30,520	*
2	Dentistry	£28,030	*
3	Chemical Engineering	£25,136	£20,364
4	Economics	£24,466	£16,587
5	Veterinary Medicine	£23,437	*
6	Physics and Astronomy	£22,624	£14,054
7	Social Work	£22,566	£15,418
8	General Engineering	£22,488	£17,120
9	Mechanical Engineering	£22,378	£15,721
10	Civil Engineering	£22,364	£17,045
11	Building	£21,914	£15,638
12	Land and Property Management	£21,769	*
13	Mathematics	£21,760	£15,081
14	Electrical and Electronic Engineering	£21,656	£17,335
15	Aeronautical and Manufacturing Engineering	£21,527	£16,623
16	East and South Asian Studies	£21,311	£15,909
17	German	£20,942	£14,481
18	Computer Science	£20,935	£15,742
19	Nursing	£20,763	£17,145
20	Politics	£20,423	£14,863
21	Town and Country Planning and Landscape	£20,124	£15,705
22	Business Studies	£20,080	£15,486
23	Middle Eastern and African Studies	£19,984	*
24	Classics and Ancient History	£19,938	£14,263
25	Russian	£19,934	£16,716
26	Chemistry	£19,904	£13,886
27	Accounting and Finance	£19,713	£15,691
28	Geology	£19,642	£12,823
29	Philosophy	£19,611	£14,149
30	Education	£19,585	£13,143
31	Librarianship and Information Management	£19,469	£13,614
32	Italian	£19,325	£14,365
33	History	£18,957	£13,932
34	Other Subjects Allied to Medicine	£18,937	£13,868
35	Food Science	£18,781	£14,507
36	History of Art, Architecture and Design	£18,758	£15,032
37	Anthropology	£18,694	£14,407
38	Materials Technology	£18,661	£14,429
39	Geography and Environmental Sciences	£18,650	£14,431
40	French	£18,644	£14,966
41	Law	£18,592	£14,499
42	Theology and Religious Studies	£18,496	£13,093

Subject	Graduate Employment or Self Employment	Non-graduate Employment or Self Employment
43 Pharmacology and Pharmacy	£18,491	£15,083
44 Anatomy and Physiology	£18,435	£13,862
45 American Studies	£18,296	£14,025
46 Biological Sciences	£17,902	£13,664
47 Social Policy	£17,897	£14,140
48 English	£17,803	£13,794
49 Architecture	£17,778	£15,073
50 Iberian Languages	£17,704	£15,362
51 Sociology	£17,693	£14,096
52 Hospitality, Leisure, Recreation, Sport and Tourism	£17,456	£13,968
53 Linguistics	£17,441	£14,089
54 Psychology	£17,374	£13,597
55 Agriculture and Forestry	£17,229	£14,654
56 Archaeology	£17,226	£13,376
57 Communication and Media Studies	£16,947	£13,972
58 Art and Design	£16,829	£13,439
59 Music	£16,809	£13,344
60 Drama, Dance and Cinematics	£16,563	£13,874
61 Celtic Studies	£15,652	*
Total	**£20,113**	**£14,402**

*Too few students to calculate a meaningful average (7 or less).
 Source: HESA 2005–06 DLHE return

Supply and demand dictate whether you will receive an offer, and that is influenced both by the university and the subject. A few universities (but not many) at the top of the league tables are heavily oversubscribed in every subject; others will have areas in which they excel, but may make relatively modest demands for entry to other courses. Even in many of the leading universities, the number of applicants for each place in languages or engineering is not high. Conversely, three As at A level will not guarantee a place on one of the top English or law degrees, but there are enough universities running courses to ensure that three Cs will put you in with a chance somewhere.

University prospectuses and the UCAS website will give you the "standard offer" for each course, but in some cases this is pitched deliberately low in order to leave admissions staff extra flexibility. The standard A-level offer for medicine, for example, is usually two As and a B, but nearly all successful applicants have three As or more. The average entry scores in our subject tables give the actual points obtained by successful applicants – many of which are far above the offer made by the university, but which give an indication of the pecking order at entry. The subject tables (in chapter 3) are, naturally, a better guide than the main table (in chapter 2), where average entry scores are influenced by the range of subjects available at each university.

Location

The most obvious starting point is the country you study in. Most degrees in Scotland take four years, rather than the UK norm of three. It is possible, but not normal, for A-level candidates to go straight into the second year of a Scottish degree course. Otherwise, four years obviously cost more than three, especially given the loss of the year's salary you might have been earning after graduation. A later chapter will go into the details of the system, but suffice to say that students from Scotland pay no fees, while those from the rest of the UK do. Nevertheless, Edinburgh and St Andrews remain particularly popular with English students and more than 1,000 students from Northern Ireland entered Scottish universities in 2007.

Far from crossing national boundaries, however, growing numbers of students choose to study near home, whether or not they continue to live with their family. This may be to cut costs or for personal reasons, such as family circumstances, a girlfriend or boyfriend, continuing employment, or religion. Some simply want to stick with what they know. But the trend for full-time students who do go away to study, is to choose a university within about two hours' travelling time. The assumption is that this is far enough to discourage parents from making unannounced visits, but close enough to allow for occasional trips home to get the washing done and have a decent meal. The leading universities recruit from all over the world, but most still have a regional core.

The most popular universities, in terms of total applications, are nearly all in big cities – generally with other major centres of population within that two-hour travelling

UNITE Student Experience Report 2007
Which of these were important to you in your selection of university?

Overall reputation	51%
Academic reputation	49%
Quality of teaching	41%
Town/city reputation for social life	39%
Quality of learning	34%
University league tables	29%
University reputation for social life	29%
Guarantee of place in halls	27%
Social facilities in town	26%
Availability of good halls	23%
Social facilities in university	22%
Availability of accommodation	20%
Sports facilities	17%
Facilities not important	15%
Teaching assessments	12%
Research assessments	12%
Value for money	9%

Top Universities for Graduate Salaries			Top Universities for Applications		
1	London School of Economics	£27,694	1	Manchester	48,034
2	Imperial College	£26,822	2	Leeds	46,475
3	St George's, London	£26,655	3	Edinburgh	42,895
4	Cranfield	£26,132	4	Bristol	40,629
5	King's College London	£23,782	5	Nottingham	35,448
6	University College, London	£23,614	6	Birmingham	33,089
7	The Royal Veterinary College	£23,544	7	Manchester Metropolitan	32,015
8	Queen Mary, London	£23,491	8	Warwick	31,729
9	City	£23,117	9	Cardiff	28,348
10	Cambridge	£22,910	10	University College London	27,893

HESA (2007); refers to 2005–06   UCAS 2008 (data to 15 January 2008)

window. For those looking for the best nightclubs, top sporting events, high-quality shopping or a varied cultural life – in other words, most young people, and especially those who live in cities already – city universities are a magnet. The big universities also, by definition, offer the widest range of subjects, although that does not mean that they necessarily have the particular course that is right for you. Nor does it mean that you will actually use the array of nightlife and shopping that looks so alluring in the prospectus, either because you cannot afford to, because student life is focused on the university, or even because you are too busy working.

City universities are the right choice for many young people, but it is worth bearing in mind that the National Student Survey shows that the highest satisfaction levels tend to be at smaller universities, often those with their own self-contained campuses. It seems that students identify more closely with institutions where there is a close-knit community and the social life is based around the students' union rather than the local nightclubs.

Few UK universities are in genuinely rural locations, but some – particularly among the latest group to be promoted from college status – are in relatively small towns. Several longer-established institutions in Wales and Scotland also share this type of setting, where the university dominates the town. The only way to be certain if this, or any other type of university, is for you is to visit. Schools often restrict the number of open days that sixth-formers can attend in term-time, but some universities offer a weekend alternative. The full calendar of events is available at www.opendays.com and on universities' own websites. Bear in mind, if you only attend one or two, that the event has to be badly mismanaged for a university not to seem an exciting place to someone who spends his or her days at school, or even college. Try to get a flavour of several institutions before you make your choice.

How many universities to pick?

When that time comes, of course, you will not be making one choice but five; four if you are applying for medicine, dentistry or veterinary science. (Full details of the application process are given in chapter 4.) Tens of thousands of students each year eventually go to a university that did not start out as their first choice, either because they did not get the right offer or because they changed their mind along the way. UCAS rules are such that applicants do not list universities in order of preference anyway – indeed, universities

Top Universities for Students Living at Home			Top Universities for Ethnic Minorities		
1	Manchester Metropolitan	5,710	1	Westminster	6,045
2	Wolverhampton	5,485	2	Kingston	5,730
3	Glasgow Caledonian	5,230	3	Middlesex	5,615
4	Glasgow	5,115	4	Hertfordshire	5,105
5	Westminster	4,925	5	De Montfort	4,605
6	Ulster	4,175	6	Greenwich	4,590
7	Hertfordshire	4,020	7	Brunel	4,580
8	Queen Mary, London	3,990	8	Manchester Metropolitan	4,420
9	Queen's University, Belfast	3,975	9	Queen Mary, London	4,400
HESA (2007)			HESA (2007)		

are not allowed to know where else you have applied. So do not pin all your hopes on one course; take just as much care choosing the other universities on your list.

Until recently, it was normal for applicants to include at least one "insurance" choice on that list – a university or college where entry grades were significantly lower than at their preferred institutions. This practice has been in decline, presumably because candidates expecting high grades think they can pick up a lower offer either in Clearing or through UCAS Extra, the service that allows applicants rejected by their original choices to apply to courses that still have vacancies after the first round of offers.

The recent switch from being able to choose six courses to only being able to apply for five may cement this change but, if you are at all uncertain about your grades, including an insurance choice remains a sensible course of action. The main proviso, as with all your choices, is that you must be prepared to go and take up that place. If not, you might as well go for broke with courses with higher standard offers and take your chances in Clearing, or even retake exams if you drop grades.

Reputation

The reputation of a university is something intangible, usually built up over a long period and sometimes outlasting reality. Before universities were subject to external assessment and the publication of copious statistics, reputation was rooted in the distant past. League tables are partly responsible for changing that, although employers are often influenced by what they remember as the pecking order of higher education when they were students.

Going Abroad

While most British students stay in their own country, a small, but steadily increasing, band is venturing overseas – mainly to the United States, but also to Australia and some parts of Europe. This trend is being actively encouraged by American "Ivy League" universities, such as Harvard and Yale, which promote generous scholarships on recruiting visits to independent schools, and it may well accelerate if UK tuition fees are allowed to rise significantly.

For the moment, however, travel costs and longer degree courses make the American experience an expensive one at most universities. The Fulbright Commission runs "College Day" in London and Edinburgh for those who would like to talk through the possibilities.

Fees are still low, or non-existent, in most of Europe, although British students tend to be nervous of the language barrier. A halfway house is to choose a course at a British university with the option of a year at a partner university overseas, or to apply for a six-month exchange under the European Union's Erasmus Programme.

Further information is available from the web:

Association of Commonwealth Universities	www.acu.ac.uk
College Board (USA)	www.collegeboard.com
Education Ireland	www.educationireland.ie
Finaid (USA)	www.finaid.org
Fulbright Commission (USA)	www.fulbright.co.uk
Study in Australia	www.studyinaustralia.gov.au
Study in Canada	www.studyincanada.com

The fragmentation of the British university system into groups of institutions is another factor: the Russell Group (www.russellgroup.ac.uk) represents 20 research-intensive universities, nearly all with medical schools; the 1994 Group (www.1994group.ac.uk) a similar number of smaller research universities; and the Million Plus Group containing many of the former polytechnics and newer universities. In addition there is Guild HE (www.guildhe.ac.uk), an organisation mainly for specialist colleges, but including five of the newest universities.

Many of you will barely have heard of a polytechnic, let alone be able to identify which of today's universities had that heritage, but you will know which of two universities in the same city has the higher status. While that should matter far less than the quality of a course, it would be naïve to ignore institutional reputation entirely if that is going to carry weight with a future employer. Some big firms restrict their recruitment efforts to a small group of leading universities, for example, and, however shortsighted that might be, it is something to bear in mind if a career in the City or a big law firm is your ultimate aim.

Cost

Critics of top-up fees feared that the fees, introduced in 2006, would add cost to the list of factors driving students' choice of university. But only Leeds Metropolitan University pitched its fees significantly below the original £3,000 maximum, opting for £2,000 and leaving them at that level subsequently. Other than in Oxford and Cambridge, where there is an additional college fee (not paid by those paying the standard UK tuition fee), cost differences are restricted to rents and the general cost of living in different parts of the country. Some cities – notably London – are notoriously expensive for students and non-students alike. But even these comparisons can be complicated by the availability of part-time employment – an important factor for a growing number of students today. One survey rated London as one of the cheapest places in the UK to study once earning opportunities were taken into account. If you intend to take part-time employment while studying, check that your chosen university has a "job shop", or some other organisation to help students find reasonably paid work.

Accommodation costs listed alongside the university profiles in this *Guide* are probably the nearest proxy for a cost-of-living indicator. The *Guide* also includes a summary of the bursaries available at each university. The size of bursaries varies enormously, as do the rules governing eligibility. Most bursaries are available only to

Top Universities for Mature Students		Top Universities for Students with a Disability	
1 Manchester Metropolitan	8,720	1 De Montfort	1,725
2 Middlesex	7,220	2 Plymouth	1,515
3 Manchester	6,910	3 Manchester Metropolitan	1,455
4 UWE, Bristol	6,455	4 Ulster	1,405
5 Edinburgh	6,155	5 Leeds	1,405
6 Ulster	6,135	6 Manchester	1,395
7 Greenwich	5,945	7 University of the Arts, London	1,315
8 Leeds	5,935	8 Nottingham	1,215
9 Northumbria	5,800	9 Edinburgh	1,190
HESA (2007)		HESA (2007)	

students who qualify for at least some Government support, but scholarships are awarded for other achievements, regardless of family income.

Facilities

Universities compete for the best students not only through their courses but, increasingly, also through non-academic facilities. Accommodation is the main selling point for those living away from home, but sports facilities, libraries and computing equipment also play an important part. Even campus nightclubs have become part of the facilities race that has coincided with the introduction of top-up fees.

Many universities guarantee first-year students accommodation in halls of residence or university-owned flats. But it is as well to know what happens after that. Are there enough places for second or third-year students who want them, and if not, what is the private market like? Rents for student houses vary quite widely across the country and there have been tensions with local residents in some cities. All universities offer specialist accommodation for disabled students – and are better at providing other facilities than most public institutions. Their websites give basic information on what is provided, as well as contact points for more detailed inquiries.

Special-interest clubs and recreational facilities, as well as political activity, tend to be based in the students' union – sometimes knows as the guild of students, especially in Scotland. In some universities, the union is the focal point of social activity, while in others the attractions of the city seem to overshadow the union to the point where facilities are underused. Students' union websites are included with the information found in the university profiles (chapter 11).

Sources of information

With more than 100 universities to choose from, the Unistats and UCAS websites, as well as guides such as this one, are the obvious places to start your search for the right course. But once you have narrowed down the list of candidates, you will want to go through undergraduate prospectuses. Most are available online, where you can select the relevant sections rather than waiting for an account of every course to arrive in the post. Beware of generalised claims about the standing of the university, the quality of courses, friendly atmosphere and legendary social life. Stick, if you can, to the factual information, which is generally accurate.

Top Universities for Student–Staff Ratios		Top Universities for Services & Facilities/Student	
1 University College London	9.1	1 Imperial College	£3,218
2 Imperial College	10.4	2 Oxford	£2,884
3 School of Oriental & African Studies	10.5	3 Cambridge	£2,299
4 Oxford	11.6	4 Warwick	£1,881
5 King's College London	11.9	5 School of Oriental & African Studies	£1,746
6 Cambridge	12.2	6 University College London	£1,702
7 London School of Economics	12.6	7 King's College London	£1,696
8 St Andrews	12.6	8 Bedfordshire	£1,685
9 Lancaster	12.7	9 Abertay	£1,671
10 Manchester	12.8	10 Aston	£1,607

The Times League Table 2009 — *The Times* League Table 2009

If the material that the universities publish about their own qualities is less than objective, much of what you will find on the internet is equally unreliable, for different reasons. A straightforward search on the name of a university will turn up spurious comparisons of everything from the standard of lecturing to the attractiveness of the students. These can be seriously misleading and are usually based on anecdotal evidence, at best. Make sure that any information you may take into account comes from a reputable source and, if it conflicts with your impression of a university, try to cross-check it with this *Guide* and the institution's own material.

Checklist

Choosing a subject and a place to study is a major decision. Make sure you can answer these questions:

Choosing a course:
- What do I want out of higher education?
- Which subjects do I enjoy studying at school?
- Which subject or subjects do I want to study?
- Do I have the right qualifications?
- What are my career plans and does the subject and course fit these?

Choosing a university:
- What type of university do I wish to go to: campus, city or smaller town?
- How far is the university from home?
- Is it large or small?
- Is it specialist or general?
- Does it offer the right course?
- How much will it cost?
- Have I arranged to visit the university?

Useful websites

The following websites will help you find out more about the topics discussed in this chapter. The best starting point is the UCAS website. On the site there's lots of information on courses, universities and the whole process of applying to university.

www.ucas.com
Within the UCAS site, useful but not immediately obvious pages include:
The Stanford Test
www.ucas.com/students/beforeyouapply/whattostudy/stamfordtest
The UCAS tariff (and especially its use with vocational courses)
www.ucas.com/students/ucas_tariff/tarifftables/

As a source of statistical information (and for full details of the National Student Survey), visit: **www.unistats.com**

Course Discover Database
www.coursediscoveronline.co.uk
Foundation degrees: Foundation Degrees Forward
www.fdf.ac.uk/
HERO, an official site covering many aspects of higher education,
from applying to research.
www.hero.ac.uk
UK Course Finder
www.ukcoursefinder.co.uk
Unofficial Guides to universities
www.unofficial-guides.com
Woody's Web-Watch, an independent website for students, parents
and careers advisers, with a wide selection of useful links.
www.woodyswebwatch.com
Open days, for a full calendar
www.opendays.com

Students with disabilities
www.bbc.co.uk/ouch/lifefiles/student
SKILL National Bureau for Students with Disabilities
www.skill.org.uk

Studying overseas
Association of Commonwealth Universities
www.acu.ac.uk
College Board (USA)
www.collegeboard.com
Education Ireland
www.educationireland.ie
Erasmus Programme (EU)
www.erasmus.ac.uk
Finaid (USA)
www.finaid.org
Fulbright Commission
www.fulbright.co.uk
Study in Australia
www.studyinaustralia.gov.au
Study in Canada
www.studyincanada.com

University groupings
1994 Group, a group of medium and small research-intensive universities
www.1994group.ac.uk
GuildHE, a group of higher education colleges, specialist institutions and
some universities:
www.guildhe.ac.uk
Russell Group: a group of large research-intensive universities:
www.russellgroup.ac.uk

The Top Universities

2

What distinguishes a top university? And who is to say that one course is better than another – especially when the university system is so reluctant to make any such comparison?

Higher education now publishes copious statistics, but resists combining them in a way that might answer applicants' questions. Critics of league tables insist that this is because every university has different priorities, and every course different ways of approaching a subject. Students must choose the one that suits them best.

So they must. However, the sheer range of universities and courses in the UK is such that most applicants need some help paring down the options to create a short list for their five application choices. For 15 years, *The Times Good University Guide* has been assisting students and their parents with that process, using the statistics that universities themselves employ to measure their own performance.

Every element of the table in this chapter has been chosen for the light it shines on the undergraduate experience and a student's future prospects. The selection of these eight measures and the way in which they are combined give a particular view of universities' overall strengths, but it is one that has stood the test of time. Unlike some others, *The Times Good University Guide* has placed a premium on consistency, confident that the measures are the best available for the task.

Some changes have been enforced upon us. Universities stopped assessing teaching quality subject by subject in 2001, and this was the most heavily weighted measure in the table. Spending on libraries, which was a measure in virtually all university league tables, is no longer collected separately from that relating to museums, galleries and observatories. There have been new developments, too, such as the National Student Survey, which could not be ignored.

The basic information that applicants need, however, in order to judge universities and their courses does not change. A university's entry standards, staffing levels, completion rates, degree classifications and graduate employment rates are all vital pieces of intelligence for anyone deciding where to study. And research grades, while not directly involving undergraduates, bring with them considerable funds and enable a university to attract top academics. Leading researchers in any subject may deliver the most inspiring lectures.

Most of the measures in *The Times Good University Guide's* table have been used since it was first published and, while any element can be discounted by the individual, the package has struck a chord with readers. The ranking is the most-quoted of its type both in Britain and overseas, and has built a reputation as the most authoritative arbiter of changing fortunes in higher education.

The measures used in the ranking are kept under review by a group of university administrators and statisticians, which meets annually. All the data are in the public domain and are sent to universities for checking before the table in this chapter and the subject tables in chapter 3 are compiled.

Indeed, while the various official bodies concerned with higher education do not publish league tables, several produce system-wide statistics in a format that encourages comparison. The Higher Education Funding Councils' Research Assessment Exercise was one early example of this, with universities trumpeting their successes almost as soon as the grades had been announced. The Higher Education Statistics Agency (HESA), which supplies most of the figures used in our tables, also publishes annual "performance indicators" on everything from completion rates and research output to the proportion of under-represented social groups at each university.

Any scrutiny of league table positions is best carried out in conjunction with an examination of the relevant subject table – it is the course, after all, that will dominate your undergraduate years and influence your subsequent career.

How *The Times* League Table works

The table is presented in a format that displays the raw data, wherever possible. In building the table, scores for Student Satisfaction and Research Quality were weighted by 1.5; all other measures were weighted by 1. The indicators were combined using a common statistical technique known as Z-scores, to ensure that no indicator has a disproportionate effect on the overall total for each university, and the totals were transformed to a scale with 1000 for the top score.

For Entry Standards, Good Honours and Graduate Prospects the score was adjusted for subject mix. It is accepted that engineering, law and medicine graduates will tend to have better graduate prospects than their peers from English, psychology and sociology courses. Comparing results in the main subject groupings helps to iron out differences attributable simply to the range of degrees on offer. This process makes it impossible to compare universities' scores from one year to the next, although their relative positions in the table are comparable. Individual scores are dependent on the top performer, so a university might drop from 60 per cent of the top score to 58 per cent but still have improved, if the leading university had done better still. This subject-mix adjustment means that it is not possible to replicate the scores in the table from the published indicators because the calculation requires access to the entire dataset.

Only where data are not available from HESA are figures sourced directly from universities. Where this is not possible – for example, in the case of Scottish universities that are not part of the National Student Survey – scores are generated according to a university's average performance on other indicators.

The organisations providing the raw data for the tables are not involved in the process of aggregation, so are not responsible for any inferences or conclusions we have made. Every care has been taken to ensure the accuracy of the tables and accompanying information, but no responsibility can be taken for errors or omissions.

The Times League Table uses eight important measures of university activity, based on the most recent data available at the time of compilation:

- Student satisfaction
- Research quality
- Entry standards
- Student–staff ratio
- Services and facilities spend
- Completion
- Good honours
- Graduate prospects

Student satisfaction

This is a measure of students' views of the quality of their courses. The National Student Survey (NSS) was the source of this data. The NSS is an initiative undertaken by the Funding Councils for England, Northern Ireland and Wales. It is designed, as an element of the quality assurance for higher education, to inform prospective students and their advisers in choosing what and where to study. The survey encompasses the views of final-year students on the quality of their courses. Data from the surveys published in 2006 and 2007 were used.

- The National Student Survey covers six aspects of a course: teaching, assessment and feedback, academic support, organisation and management, learning resources and personal development, with an additional question gauging overall satisfaction. Students answer on a scale from 1 (bottom) to 5 (top) and the measure is the percentage of positive responses (4 and 5) in each section, averaged to produce the final score.
- The survey is based on the opinion of final-year students rather than directly assessing teaching quality. Most undergraduates have no experience of other universities, or different courses, to inform their judgements. Although all the questions relate to courses, rather than the broader student experience, some types of university – notably medium-sized campus universities – tend to do better than others.
- Scottish universities were not automatically included in the survey, although eight out of 14 have so far opted in.
- Cambridge did not have a sufficiently high response rate in either year to have their outcome published. Some other universities did not reach the threshold in one of the two years.

Research quality

This is a measure of the quality of the research undertaken in each university. The information was sourced from the 2001 Research Assessment Exercise, a peer-review exercise used to evaluate the quality of research in UK higher education institutions, undertaken by the UK Higher Education Funding Bodies. The next Research Assessment Exercise will be published in December 2008.

- A rating (5*, 5, 4, 3a, 3b, 2, 1) was given to every university department that took part. A rating of 5* meant that the research was regarded as being of international significance. These quality ratings were then given a score on a linear seven-point scale (7, 6, 5, 4, 3, 2, 1). Universities could choose which staff to include in the assessment exercise, so, to factor in the depth of the research quality, each score has been weighted by the number of staff returned in the assessment exercise as a proportion of all eligible staff.
- If you look at the RAE scores in the subject tables, you will see that the ratings are accompanied by a letter (A, B, C, D, E, F) that indicates the proportion of staff included in the assessment: A signifies that most staff were entered while F signifies that most staff were not entered. As noted above, this has been factored into our score.

Entry standards

This is the average score, using the UCAS tariff (see page 18), of new students under the age of 21 who took A and AS Levels, Highers and Advanced Highers. It measures what new students actually achieved rather than the entry requirements suggested by the universities. The data comes from HESA for 2006–07. The original sources of data for this measure are data returns made by the universities themselves to HESA.

- Using the UCAS tariff, each student's examination results were converted to a numerical score. HESA then calculated an average for all students at the university. This was based on A and AS levels and Scottish Highers and Advanced Highers only; key and core skills were not included. The results have then been adjusted to take account of the subject mix at the university.
- A score of 360 represents three As at A level. Although 27 of the top 30 universities in the table have entry standards above 360, it does not mean that everyone achieved such results. Courses will not ask for more than three subjects and you will need to reach the entry requirements set by the university rather than the scores represented here.

Student–staff ratio

This is a measure of the average number of students to each member of the academic staff, apart from those purely engaged in research. In this measure a low score is better than a high score. The data comes from HESA for 2006–07. The original sources of data for this measure are data returns made by the universities themselves to HESA.
- The figures, as calculated by HESA, allow for variation in employment patterns at different universities. A low value means that there are a small number of students for each academic member of staff, but this does not, of course, ensure good teaching quality or contact time with academics.
- Student–staff ratios are usually low for medicine and this will influence the scores of universities with medical schools.

Services and facilities spend

The expenditure per student on staff and student facilities, including library and computing facilities. The data comes from HESA for 2004–05 and 2005–06. The original sources of data for this measure are data returns made by the universities themselves to HESA.
- This is a measure calculated by taking the expenditure on student facilities (sports, grants to student societies, careers services, health services, counselling, etc.) and library and computing facilities (books, journals, staff, central computers and computer networks, but not buildings) and dividing this by the number of full-time-equivalent students. Expenditure is averaged over two years to even out the figures (for example a computer upgrade undertaken in a single year).

Completion

This measure gives the percentage of students expected to complete their studies (or transfer to another institution) for each university. The data comes from the HESA performance indicators, based on data for 2005–06 and earlier years.
- This measure is a projection, liable to statistical fluctuations.

Good honours

This measure is the percentage of graduates achieving a first or upper second class degree. The results have been adjusted to take account of the subject mix at the university. The data comes from HESA for 2006–07. The original sources of data for this measure are data returns made by the universities themselves to HESA.
- Four-year first degrees, such as an MChem, are treated as equivalent to a first or upper second.

- Scottish Ordinary degrees (awarded after three years rather than the usual four in Scotland) are excluded.
- Universities control degree classification, with some oversight from external examiners. There have been suggestions that the number of good honours degrees are increasing and that this measure may not be as objective as it should be. However, it remains the key measure of a student's success and employability.

Graduate prospects

This measure is the percentage of the total number of graduates who take up graduate-entry employment or further study. The results have been adjusted for subject mix. The data comes from HESA for 2006 graduates.

- HESA surveys graduates six months after graduation to find out what they are doing and the data are based on this survey.

Useful websites

The main League Table is available on *The Times* website **www.timesonline.co.uk/gug.** There is the facility there to compare selected universities. The subject tables are also available to view on this site.

For more information on the data collected by the Higher Education Statistics Agency (HESA) and a detailed explanation of the HEFCE performance indicators, visit the HESA site:
www.hesa.ac.uk

Full information on the 2001 Research Assessment Exercise can be found at:
www.hero.ac.uk/rae/
Information on the 2008 Research Assessment Exercise can be found at:
www.rae.ac.uk/

	Student satisfaction (%)	Research quality	Entry standards	Student–staff ratio	Services and facilities spend per student (£)	Completion (%)	Good honours (%)	Graduate prospects (%)	Total
Max score	100.0	7.0	n/a	n/a	n/a	100.0	100.0	100.0	1000
1 Oxford	84	6.2	502	11.6	2884	98.6	90.1	83.9	1000
2 Cambridge	..	6.5	518	12.2	2299	97.9	85.4	88.4	950
3 Imperial College	76	5.8	473	10.4	3218	96.0	69.1	89.3	865
4 London School of Economics	74	6.3	469	12.6	1562	96.9	75.2	87.7	818
5 St Andrews	82	5.3	446	12.6	1162	94.8	83.9	73.7	791
6 Warwick	76	5.6	448	13.6	1881	96.7	79.4	74.9	775
7 University College London	76	5.5	434	9.1	1702	94.3	75.1	81.5	767
8 Durham	78	5.2	447	15.4	1375	96.4	78.8	75.9	760
9 York	77	5.5	423	13.1	1313	95.2	74.7	70.5	736
10 Bristol	75	5.2	430	14.7	1535	95.8	78.4	81.5	724
11 King's College London	77	4.7	406	11.9	1696	93.2	72.1	80.4	715
12 Loughborough	83	4.3	361	17.1	1293	94.0	67.4	73.2	709
13 Exeter	81	4.7	381	16.8	1183	94.8	79.8	68.5	708
14 Leicester	83	4.5	360	14.5	1329	92.9	69.0	72.3	706
15 Bath	75	5.2	428	16.6	1291	95.3	77.3	81.0	701
=16 Nottingham	75	5.0	403	13.8	1390	96.2	75.7	76.0	696
=16 Southampton	79	5.4	389	16.3	1479	90.7	74.8	71.8	696
18 Edinburgh	73	5.0	430	13.3	1294	92.2	79.9	74.9	682

Rank	University								
19	Lancaster	78	5.4	375	12.7	1227	92.5	68.8	60.9	680
=20	Newcastle	75	4.4	394	14.9	1481	92.3	71.1	75.3	657
=20	Glasgow	78	4.3	396	13.4	1373	85.5	68.4	75.0	657
22	Sheffield	76	4.5	403	14.5	1140	92.4	71.9	73.7	650
23	East Anglia	82	5.0	359	17.9	1127	91.2	67.5	63.0	647
24	School of Oriental and African Studies	71	5.3	368	10.5	1746	84.4	73.4	68.0	646
25	Birmingham	77	4.3	402	15.3	1342	92.4	68.4	70.4	643
26	Aberdeen	80	4.0	350	13.5	1168	78.8	69.7	76.2	640
27	Manchester	73	5.1	412	12.8	1378	92.3	70.5	67.4	638
28	Aston	76	3.9	351	17.4	1607	88.4	65.8	76.4	637
29	Cardiff	77	4.5	381	14.3	1085	90.1	67.6	73.5	628
30	Royal Holloway	74	5.2	361	14.7	1244	88.2	66.4	66.9	626
=31	Leeds	75	4.5	385	14.6	1014	92.1	71.8	67.3	619
=31	Reading	78	4.9	340	16.2	1012	91.7	71.7	63.3	619
=31	Queen's, Belfast	77	4.3	364	15.3	1222	86.6	70.3	76.1	619
34	Liverpool	75	4.6	377	13.3	1013	90.0	67.6	70.7	610
35	Strathclyde	76	3.6	367	16.8	1219	81.8	74.6	76.4	604
36	Kent	79	4.0	307	16.3	1143	87.0	59.7	70.5	601
37	Queen Mary, London	75	4.7	340	12.8	1173	88.5	60.8	75.1	594
38	Sussex	69	5.1	387	15.0	1136	88.3	79.5	62.0	593
39	Surrey	72	4.7	339	16.3	1156	86.8	61.9	77.3	582
40	Stirling	..	3.9	288	15.4	964	89.9	67.9	71.8	581
41	Keele	75	4.0	313	15.3	1048	84.3	64.0	77.6	578
42	Essex	75	4.8	309	14.1	1149	83.4	60.4	62.8	576
43	Aberystwyth	81	4.0	296	19.0	997	89.8	61.8	56.2	560
44	Dundee	78	4.2	373	13.7	971	68.7	66.3	73.9	559
45	Hull	80	3.2	297	18.6	934	83.9	56.4	71.0	550

	Student satisfaction (%)	Research quality	Entry standards	Student–staff ratio	Services and facilities spend per student (£)	Completion (%)	Good honours (%)	Graduate prospects (%)	Total
Max score	100.0	7.0	n/a	n/a	n/a	100.0	100.0	100.0	1000
46 Goldsmiths College	73	4.9	307	15.5	793	82.2	64.8	63.6	546
47 Heriot-Watt	75	4.2	343	16.6	1115	82.3	55.0	72.1	542
48 Swansea	77	4.4	295	15.1	1010	88.3	49.9	61.4	531
49 Bradford	76	3.4	280	15.0	1167	82.2	60.5	73.9	528
50 City	72	3.7	321	18.1	878	85.0	63.7	77.1	509
51 Bangor	77	3.9	279	18.4	1023	77.0	55.6	65.9	502
52 Brunel	69	3.1	313	16.3	1475	85.4	63.7	63.6	498
53 Ulster	75	2.4	278	16.4	1462	77.0	60.1	62.1	487
54 Robert Gordon	..	0.9	321	17.9	1070	79.8	58.8	77.6	480
55 Oxford Brookes	76	1.6	300	18.2	944	84.9	59.1	65.9	471
56 Nottingham Trent	70	1.4	269	18.0	990	89.1	56.4	74.0	460
57 Bournemouth	72	0.7	287	19.5	967	85.2	57.0	70.8	445
58 Gloucestershire	73	1.7	258	17.2	1074	80.5	54.9	60.2	436
59 Chichester	78	1.7	253	19.6	733	88.0	46.7	55.5	434
60 Brighton	73	1.7	288	19.6	806	83.0	58.8	67.7	432
61 Portsmouth	75	1.7	272	19.4	917	81.4	49.3	65.4	428
62 Plymouth	74	1.6	277	16.4	1000	81.2	60.2	55.3	425
63 Central Lancashire	75	0.9	271	17.5	984	76.9	50.9	64.4	421

Rank	University									
64	Napier	..	0.8	257	17.9	915	73.3	60.8	77.9	420
65	West of England	74	1.6	261	18.8	906	80.6	55.9	64.4	415
66	Winchester	75	1.5	267	17.9	796	84.5	57.4	49.7	411
67	Staffordshire	76	1.1	251	17.6	1000	79.8	52.5	53.8	410
=68	Glasgow Caledonian	74	1.2	311	19.8	850	74.8	65.7	60.5	408
=68	Queen Margaret Edinburgh	..	1.5	286	20.2	831	77.7	58.5	69.8	408
70	Lampeter	74	4.4	274	25.0	480	76.9	56.1	58.8	403
71	Birmingham City	71	0.8	268	15.8	1138	77.3	56.6	63.8	401
72	Bath Spa	72	1.5	274	19.5	563	85.7	64.7	55.2	400
73	Northumbria	73	1.1	292	21.0	1010	80.7	49.9	66.4	395
74	Coventry	76	1.0	261	20.2	1004	73.7	60.4	62.0	394
75	University of the Arts, London	62	4.4	304	20.8	870	87.1	58.8	51.5	392
76	Sheffield Hallam	72	1.1	269	19.9	938	85.0	58.1	60.6	391
=77	Glamorgan	75	1.3	237	15.9	1123	69.3	51.8	58.4	388
=77	De Montfort	72	1.4	250	17.4	831	80.6	49.0	64.8	388
79	Hertfordshire	72	1.4	256	15.6	1087	75.9	47.7	62.1	383
80	Canterbury Christ Church	74	1.1	247	17.8	559	83.5	47.0	63.2	382
81	Worcester	76	0.8	245	19.7	814	80.8	45.6	62.7	380
82	Sunderland	73	1.7	249	16.1	737	77.0	47.7	59.3	379
83	Salford	71	2.1	269	18.4	923	73.2	54.1	63.5	377
84	Northampton	76	1.0	225	19.0	786	80.0	55.2	56.3	376
85	UWIC, Cardiff	72	0.8	246	19.9	1112	85.1	48.6	55.3	375
=86	Roehampton	71	1.9	224	21.0	1308	79.5	52.1	56.9	372
=86	Chester	74	0.5	274	17.9	734	76.1	54.3	57.6	372
88	Teesside	77	0.7	253	19.5	750	74.4	50.2	57.3	360
89	Bedfordshire	73	0.6	220	21.2	1685	75.4	47.0	59.6	356
90	Huddersfield	75	0.9	262	19.8	616	78.9	53.3	53.2	353

	Student satisfaction (%)	Research quality	Entry standards	Student–staff ratio	Services and facilities spend per student (£)	Completion (%)	Good honours (%)	Graduate prospects (%)	Total
Max score	100.0	7.0	n/a	n/a	n/a	100.0	100.0	100.0	1000
91 York St John	72	0.4	281	22.3	841	85.4	50.7	55.2	347
92 Manchester Metropolitan	71	1.2	272	20.2	937	75.2	51.3	59.4	345
93 Kingston	71	1.2	236	19.8	966	78.6	50.0	60.2	340
94 Liverpool John Moores	71	1.2	250	19.5	902	77.1	45.1	61.3	336
95 Derby	73	0.9	267	19.8	1054	77.0	47.8	49.5	334
96 UWCN, Newport	71	0.5	219	20.1	890	74.9	50.7	60.4	327
97 Southampton Solent	71	0.5	229	20.5	980	78.2	43.1	55.7	326
98 Edge Hill	76	0.4	250	22.1	597	78.3	44.4	57.0	322
99 Cumbria	68	0.6	267	20.4	685	76.6	47.5	72.8	320
100 Abertay	..	0.7	264	20.3	1671	64.0	47.6	51.4	317
=101 Leeds Metropolitan	68	0.8	264	23.6	984	82.7	53.6	59.4	316
=101 Westminster	68	1.2	254	16.4	763	80.5	49.6	51.0	316
=103 West of Scotland	..	0.7	255	19.4	1099	68.7	46.1	62.3	312
=103 Lincoln	70	0.7	261	23.7	842	83.9	52.9	50.3	312
105 Middlesex	67	1.3	219	22.1	1412	71.9	47.3	61.2	301
106 Anglia Ruskin	70	0.5	256	17.1	647	64.8	52.3	60.6	297
107 Wolverhampton	72	0.6	197	18.6	945	73.9	41.1	56.8	286
108 Buckinghamshire New	68	0.8	203	18.7	999	82.0	44.7	45.2	282

109	East London	70	1.4	187	20.6	1218	68.5	40.6	59.4	280
110	Greenwich	68	1.2	212	23.4	824	79.7	42.4	63.0	263
111	Bolton	74	0.8	203	21.0	772	63.3	52.6	51.8	262
112	Thames Valley	67	0.4	212	20.6	747	69.5	48.4	62.7	256
113	London South Bank	72	1.3	193	25.2	822	72.0	48.4	56.3	245

Liverpool Hope, London Metropolitan and Swansea Metropolitan have refused to allow the release of data, and so do not appear in this year's League Table.

3 The Top Universities by Subject

Knowing where a university stands in the pecking order of higher education is a vital piece of information for any prospective student, but the quality of the course is what matters most. The most modest institution may have a centre of specialist excellence, and even famous universities have mediocre departments. This section offers some pointers to the leading universities in a wide range of subjects.

This year, for the first time, the subject tables include scores from the National Student Survey (NSS). These distil the views of final-year undergraduates on several aspects of their course, including teaching quality, assessment and feedback, and the level of resources. They have been added to the three measures used in previous editions of the *Guide*: research quality, students' entry qualifications and graduate employment prospects. None of the measures has been weighted.

Expert assessors produced official ratings for research quality and, in the Education table, teaching quality. Data supplied by the Higher Education Statistics Agency (HESA) are used to calculate average entry qualifications and the employment prospects of graduates. The prospects information draws a distinction between different types of employment: graduate employment, where a degree is normally required, and non-graduate employment. The tables give the percentage of "positive destinations" by adding those undertaking further study to the total in graduate employment.

Subjects are listed in the categories used by HESA. Many, such as dentistry or sociology, have their own table, but others are grouped together in broader categories, such as subjects allied to medicine, which includes such specialisms as physiotherapy and radiology. To qualify for inclusion in a table, a university has to have data for at least two of the measures. Scores are not published where the number of students is too small for the outcome to be statistically reliable. In the NSS, a 50 per cent response rate is required from a minimum of 30 students.

Cambridge is again by far the most successful university, despite failing to reach the NSS response threshold for the university as a whole. It tops 37 of the 61 tables, two more than on the last occasion that the full range of subjects was covered, two years ago. Oxford has the next highest number of top places with five, followed by Edinburgh, Loughborough and Warwick with three.

The subject rankings demonstrate that there are "horses for courses" in higher education. Thus the London School of Economics is more than a match for its rivals in social science, while Imperial College remains a force in engineering. In their own fields, table-toppers such as Loughborough in sports science (see *Hospitality, Leisure, Sport, Recreation and Tourism*), Warwick in accounting and finance, and Surrey in food science, are equally well-known. But the tables contain less obvious success stories, such as Sheffield in journalism (see *Communication and Media Studies*).

Research quality
This provides a measure of the average quality of research undertaken in the subject area. The first figure gives a quality rating of 5* (top), 5, 4, 3a, 3b, 2 or 1 (bottom). The letter refers to the proportion of staff included in the numerical assessment, with A including

virtually everyone and F hardly anyone. These data are from 2001, when the last Research Assessment Exercise took place.

Entry standards

This is the average score in A and AS Levels, Highers and Advanced Highers for new students under the age of 21, taken from HESA data for 2005–06. Each student's examination grades were converted to a numerical score using the UCAS tariff (A level A = 120, B = 100, etc; Scottish Highers A = 72, B = 60, etc) and added up to give a total score. HESA then calculated an average score for each university.

Student satisfaction

This measure is taken from the National Student Survey results published in 2006 and 2007. A single year's figures are used when that is all that is available, but an average of the two years' results is used in all other cases. The score for each university represents the percentage of final-year undergraduates declaring themselves satisfied or very satisfied with their course, averaged over the seven sections of the survey.

Graduate prospects

This is the percentage of graduates undertaking further study or in a graduate job, in the annual survey by HESA six months after graduation. Two years of data are aggregated to make the data more reliable. A low score on this measure does not necessarily indicate unemployment – some graduates may have taken jobs that are not categorised as graduate work. The averages for each subject are given at the bottom of the relevant subject table in this chapter and in a table in chapter 1 (see pages 24–25).

The Education table uses a fifth measure: teaching quality, as measured by the outcomes of Ofsted inspections of teacher training courses.

Useful websites

Intute is a free online service that provides access to authenticated web resources. The service has been created by a network of UK universities and partners. Subject specialists select and evaluate the websites and provide descriptions of the sites. There are sections for most of the subjects covered by the subject tables, and it is a valuable tool in researching more about subjects that might interest you. It is broken down into four main categories: arts and humanities, science and technology, social sciences and health and life sciences:
www.intute.ac.uk
www.intute.ac.uk/sciences
www.intute.ac.uk/artsandhumanities
www.intute.ac.uk/socialsciences
www.intute.ac.uk/healthandlifesciences

Two other sites for finding out more about the arts and sciences are:

British Academy Directory of UK Subject Associations and Learned Societies in the Humanities and Social Sciences
www.britac.ac.uk/links/uksahss.asp

Royal Society for the Encouragement of Arts, Manufacture and Commerce
www.rsa.org.uk/

The subjects listed below are covered in the tables in this chapter:

Accounting and finance
Aeronautical and manufacturing engineering
Agriculture and forestry
American studies
Anatomy and physiology
Anthropology
Archaeology
Architecture
Art and design
Biological sciences
Building
Business studies
Celtic studies
Chemical engineering
Chemistry
Civil engineering
Classics and ancient history
Communication and media studies
Computer science
Dentistry
Drama, dance and cinematics
East and South Asian studies
Economics
Education
Electrical and electronic engineering
English
Food science
French
General engineering
Geography and environmental sciences
Geology

German
History
History of art, architecture and design
Hospitality, leisure, sport, recreation and tourism
Iberian languages
Italian
Land and property management
Law
Librarianship and information management
Linguistics
Materials technology
Mathematics
Mechanical engineering
Medicine
Middle Eastern and African studies
Music
Nursing
Other subjects allied to medicine
   (see page 145 for included subjects)
Pharmacology and pharmacy
Philosophy
Physics and astronomy
Politics
Psychology
Russian and East European languages
Social policy
Social work
Sociology
Theology and religious studies
Town and country planning and landscape
Veterinary medicine

Accounting and Finance

Warwick has taken over from the London School of Economics at the top of the accounting and finance table. The table was compiled from data extracted from the Business Studies ranking. Although the demand for places was down by 11 per cent at the start of 2008, with the switch from six choices per applicant to five, accounting alone remains among the 20 most popular subjects, attracting more than 26,000 applications. The LSE and third-placed Exeter are both less than a point behind Warwick. Exeter has the most satisfied students, while the LSE has the highest entry standards.

The top two are among four universities with 5* grades from the last Research Assessment Exercise. The others are Manchester, in sixth place, and Lancaster, in ninth. Robert Gordon has the best employment score in the table, with more than nine out of ten leavers finding a graduate-level job within six months of finishing the course for the third year in a row.

At 19th in the table, Robert Gordon is the highest-ranking new university, although almost half of the institutions in the ranking are former polytechnics. The competition for top university in Scotland is unusually close, with Edinburgh only a fraction ahead of Strathclyde and Glasgow. Bangor has overtaken Cardiff for that accolade in Wales.

Entry scores are quite widely spread among the 74 universities in the table. Eight averaged more than 400 points and seven less than 200 points. Employment prospects are better than in many areas of higher education, but in 2006 nearly a third of graduates started their careers in low-level jobs. The unemployment rate of 6 per cent was on the average for all subjects. Starting salaries in graduate jobs are only just in the top 30 for all subjects, at a little more than £19,700.

- Actuarial Profession: **www.actuaries.org.uk/**
- Association of Chartered Certified Accountants: **www.accaglobal.com**
- Careers in accounting: **www.careers-in-accounting.com/**
- Chartered Institute of Public Finance and Accountancy: **www.cipfa.org.uk**
- Institute of Chartered Accountants: **www.icaew.co.uk/students**
- Institute of Chartered Accountants of Scotland: **www.icas.org.uk**
- Institute of Financial Services: **www.ifslearning.ac.uk/**

Accounting and Finance	Research quality/5	Entry standards	Student satisfaction %	Graduate prospects %	Overall rating
1 Warwick	5*B	457	77	85	100.0
2 London School of Economics	5*A	464	72	87	99.8
3 Exeter	5D	370	91	80	99.4
4 Loughborough	4C	397	87	83	98.7
5 Edinburgh	5A	452	78	75	97.9
6 Manchester	5*A	396	80	70	97.8
7 Strathclyde	5C	414	82	82	97.7
8 Glasgow	5C	426	79	86	96.9
9 Lancaster	5*B	386	83	67	96.6
10 City	5C	380	82	81	95.8
11 Queen's, Belfast	4B	389	80	83	95.5

Accounting and Finance cont.

	Research quality/5	Entry standards	Student satisfaction %	Graduate prospects %	Overall rating
12 Nottingham	5B	403	75	85	95.3
13 Birmingham	4D	380	86	73	93.7
14 Dundee	4A	322	83	66	92.2
15 Hull	4C	316	82	79	91.6
16 Bangor	5B	283	82	73	91.3
17 Newcastle	5D	401	76	81	91.0
18 Aberdeen	4B	342		71	90.5
19 Robert Gordon		331		94	90.4
20 Southampton	4B	381	71	83	89.7
21 Bristol	5B	408	68	81	89.6
=22 East Anglia	3aC	330	84	68	89.2
=22 Leeds	5C	396	72	79	89.2
24 Stirling	5B	284		71	89.1
25 Cardiff	5B	366	76	63	88.7
26 Durham	5A	332	69	78	88.0
27 Sheffield	4B	358	75	71	87.9
28 Kent	3aC	327	75	77	85.3
29 Heriot-Watt	4D	346	73	75	84.1
30 De Montfort	3aC	244	83	61	83.8
31 Bradford	4C	223	82	62	83.7
32 Reading		348	78	77	83.4
33 Liverpool	3aA	374	75	49	83.0
34 Central Lancashire	3bE	260	81	70	82.0
35 Ulster	3aD	308	77	65	81.9
36 Portsmouth	4C	244	77	58	80.6
=37 Nottingham Trent	3bD	224	74	84	80.0
=37 West of England	5E	242	77	67	80.0
39 Essex	5C	292	67	71	79.8
=40 Salford	3aB	295	74	54	79.2
=40 Queen Mary, London		323	75	70	79.2
42 Aberystwyth	3bC	286	79	47	78.3
43 Glasgow Caledonian	4F	261	79	60	78.2
44 Liverpool John Moores	3bE	231	78	64	77.5
45 Glamorgan	3bD	236	74	67	77.0
46 Northumbria		330	76	58	76.8
=47 Napier	3bE			67	76.7
=47 Bournemouth		259	80	59	76.7
49 Oxford Brookes		288	77	62	76.6
50 Birmingham City		233	80	61	76.3
51 Keele		284	73	71	75.9
=52 East London		172	81	64	75.4
=52 Gloucestershire		238	77	63	75.4
54 Sheffield Hallam	3aF	260	79	50	75.3

		Research Quality				
55	Wolverhampton		187	81	62	75.2
56	Brighton	3aE	242	75	55	74.5
57	Northampton		224	81	51	74.3
58	West of Scotland	5F	306		50	74.1
59	Kingston		249	78	53	73.8
60	Manchester Metropolitan		246	75	57	72.8
61	London South Bank	3aE	171	79	45	71.4
=62	Coventry		228	75	55	71.3
=62	Huddersfield	3bE	232	73	52	71.3
64	Bedfordshire		159	84	42	71.2
65	Greenwich	3bF	172	78	47	70.5
66	Plymouth	3bE	255	75	38	70.4
67	Lincoln		241	73	53	70.2
68	Hertfordshire		240	72	55	69.9
69	Middlesex	3aE	173	72	50	68.2
70	Derby		207	75	44	67.8
71	UWIC, Cardiff		241	75	36	67.4
72	Southampton Solent		177	72	56	67.3
73	Staffordshire		227	68	53	66.8
74	Leeds Metropolitan		257	64	49	64.1

Employed in graduate job:	31%	Average starting graduate salary:	£19,713
Employed in graduate job and studying:	23%	Average starting non-graduate salary:	£15,691
Studying:	8%		
Employed in non-graduate job and studying:	6%	The letters that appear in the Research Quality column indicate the	
Employed in non-graduate job:	27%	proportion of staff included in the assessment, A showing that	
Unemployed:	6%	almost all staff were included and F showing that hardly any were.	

Aeronautical and Manufacturing Engineering

Most of the courses in this table focus on aeronautical or manufacturing engineering, but it includes some with a mechanical engineering title. To add to the confusion, manufacturing degrees often go under the rubric of production engineering (see General Engineering and Mechanical Engineering). The number of institutions in the ranking has been dropping – there were eight more when it was last published, in 2006.

Cambridge remains well clear of the field, with the highest scores on every indicator, albeit level with Portsmouth on student satisfaction and with three other universities for research. No university comes close to Cambridge's entry grades, but Southampton and Bath (in second and third place respectively) and eighth-placed Liverpool share the distinction of the highest possible research grade. Imperial College, in fourth place, and Queen's, Belfast, in ninth, also have 5* research grades but entered fewer academics for assessment.

Only Nottingham and Kingston, neither of which is in this year's top ten, were awarded maximum points for teaching quality in the 1996–98 assessment. Portsmouth's highly satisfied students have helped it to become the only new university in the top 20, while Glasgow is top in Scotland and Swansea in Wales. Newcastle, in seventh place, has the best jobs record, as the only university where every leaver went straight into graduate-level employment or further study.

Aeronautical and Manufacturing Engineering cont.

Aerospace engineering saw four successive increases in applications, bucking the trend in other branches of engineering. But this had come to a halt at the start of 2008, when the decline associated with the switch from six choices per applicant to five, was much steeper than the average for all subjects. Many graduates go on to further study or training to meet professional requirements and – particularly for aeronautical engineering graduates – employment prospects are bright. The subject is in the top 15 for graduate salaries, with an average of over £21,500 for those in graduate jobs. The unemployment rate has come down, but is still above average for all subjects even though half go straight into graduate jobs. Three Cs at A level (and another at AS level) will secure a place on many courses outside the top ten.

- Manufacturing Institute: **www.makeit.org.uk/**
- Royal Aeronautical Society: **www.aerosociety.com/**
- Why Aeronautical engineering?: **www.science-engineering.net/ aeronautical_engineering.htm**

Aeronautical and Manufacturing Engineering	Research quality/5	Entry standards	Student satisfaction %	Graduate prospects %	Overall rating
1 Cambridge	5*A	536	84	96	100.0
2 Southampton	5*A	436	83	81	91.8
3 Bath	5*A	461	78	85	91.4
4 Imperial College	5*B	494	77	85	90.1
5 Bristol	4B	453	81	87	88.0
6 Sheffield	5A	380	74	85	84.3
7 Newcastle	4B		71	100	83.4
8 Liverpool	5*A	373	75	71	82.9
9 Queen's, Belfast	5*B	350	76	79	82.6
10 Loughborough	5B	385	77	78	82.5
11 Manchester	5A	408	74	67	81.1
12 Nottingham	5B	361	77	72	80.6
13 Swansea	4A	271	77		76.8
14 Surrey	4B	305	78	70	76.7
15 Aston	5C	308	71	77	74.4
16 Glasgow	4A	395	61	74	73.8
17 Brunel	5C	335	72	66	73.1
18 Leeds	5*B	360	66	59	72.5
19 Queen Mary, London	5B	271	72	63	72.2
20 Portsmouth	4D	209	84	59	70.8
21 Ulster		216	74	96	70.0
22 Hertfordshire	3aD	263	78	64	69.7
23 Kingston	3aC	255	69	77	69.4
=24 Strathclyde	4D	352	67	65	68.6
=24 Northumbria	3bD		75	63	68.6
26 Coventry	3aC	230	76	61	68.1
27 West of England	3bD	245	73	71	67.6

	Research Quality				
28 Salford	3aA	231	63	75	67.2
=29 City	4D	268	67	70	66.7
=29 Plymouth	4E		76	56	66.7
31 Staffordshire	3bA		65	60	63.9
32 Sussex		354	70	54	62.9
33 De Montfort	4C		61	60	61.5
34 Liverpool John Moores	3aE	219	73	51	61.3
35 Derby	3aD		67	55	61.1
=36 UWIC, Cardiff		318	68	43	57.9
=36 Buckinghamshire New	2E		64	60	57.9
38 Manchester Metropolitan		247	67	55	57.7
39 London South Bank	3aD		62	52	56.6

Employed in graduate job:	50%	Average starting graduate salary:	£21,527
Employed in graduate job and studying:	6%	Average starting non-graduate salary:	£16,623
Studying:	13%		
Employed in non-graduate job and studying:	2%	The letters that appear in the Research Quality column indicate the
Employed in non-graduate job:	20%	proportion of staff included in the assessment, A showing that
Unemployed:	8%	almost all staff were included and F showing that hardly any were.

Agriculture and Forestry

Newcastle is comfortably ahead of the pack in agriculture and forestry, with high entry standards and the most satisfied students. Only fourth-placed Harper Adams University College has a better employment score, while Reading and Bangor, in second and third respectively, have better research grades. Nottingham, the perennial leader in this table, has dropped out this year because there were not enough students to compile scores for some measures.

Edinburgh, in fifth place, had by far the highest entry grades in 2006–07. Aberdeen is the only other university in Scotland to offer agriculture or forestry, but the Royal Agricultural College, Sheffield Hallam and Lincoln have all joined the ranking since it was last published.

This is one of the few subject areas in which no university achieved full marks in the 1996–98 teaching assessment or in the 2001 research assessment. Scores in both were tightly bunched, covering only three grades in the case of research. However, students have appeared generally satisfied with their courses in the first three national surveys. There was a good response rate and above-average levels of approval.

A quarter of those enrolling for degrees in agriculture and more than a third in forestry do so without A levels, often coming with relevant work experience. Nearly one in seven arrives through the Clearing system. The 2,200 applications for degree places in agriculture at the start of 2008 showed a decline in comparison with the previous year, when there was a 12.5 per cent increase. A healthy rise in demand for Foundation degrees prevented a bigger overall decline. Forestry is a much smaller area, with only 75 degree applications by the official deadline for courses starting in 2008. As befits a firmly vocational area, employment rates are high, although almost as many graduates start in lower-level jobs as in graduate-level employment. The subjects are near the bottom of the earnings league, with even those in graduate jobs starting on little more than £17,000 on average.

Agriculture and Forestry cont.

- Institute of Chartered Foresters: **www.charteredforesters.org**
- Royal Agricultural Society of England: **www.rase.org.uk/**
- Royal Forestry Society: **www.rfs.org.uk**
- Royal Scottish Forestry Society: **www.rsfs.org/**
- Sector Skills Council for the Environmental and Land-Based Sector (LANTRA):
  www.lantra.co.uk

Agriculture and Forestry	Research quality/5	Entry standards	Student satisfaction %	Graduate prospects %	Overall rating
1 Newcastle	4B	289	86	70	100.0
2 Reading	5A	278	81	56	97.7
3 Bangor	5C			61	97.6
4 Harper Adams	3bE	296	86	83	96.0
5 Edinburgh		427		47	93.0
6 Imperial College		379	76	64	89.8
7 Queen's, Belfast	4C	281		59	89.0
8 Wolverhampton	3bA			45	82.0
9 Aberystwyth	3aC	256	81	41	81.1
10 Plymouth	3aE	288	65	59	78.5
11 Sheffield Hallam		261	74	60	77.1
12 Bath Spa		271		55	76.0
13 Aberdeen	3aC			35	73.6
14 Nottingham Trent		259	75	48	73.3
15 Royal Agricultural College	3aE	289	70	33	72.9
=16 Central Lancashire		281	66	46	70.5
=16 Greenwich	3aD			36	70.5
18 Bournemouth		281		38	69.5
19 West of England		276	57	48	66.3
20 Lincoln		231	72	36	66.0

Employed in graduate job:	39%	Average starting graduate salary:	£17,229
Employed in graduate job and studying:	7%	Average starting non-graduate salary:	£14,654
Studying:	8%		
Employed in non-graduate job and studying:	3%	The letters that appear in the Research Quality column indicate the	
Employed in non-graduate job:	37%	proportion of staff included in the assessment, A showing that	
Unemployed:	6%	almost all staff were included and F showing that hardly any were.	

American Studies

The American studies ranking has always been subject to big swings, largely because of variations in graduate employment scores. Now student satisfaction has added to the flux, but Warwick hangs on to first place with the highest entry standards and good scores on the other indicators. Leicester jumps from the bottom half of the table to second place with an 89 per cent satisfaction rating, added to a good employment record.

Hull and Sheffield were the two universities to see two thirds of its leavers go straight into graduate-level jobs or postgraduate study. Fewer than one in three were as fortunate at Derby, Liverpool John Moores or Winchester. Hull was also the closest challenger to Leicester in terms of student satisfaction, and had the university entered the 2001 Research Assessment Exercise in American studies, it would certainly have broken into the top ten.

Nottingham is the only university with a 5* research grade, but relatively low scores for graduate employment and student satisfaction have seen it slip from second to sixth. Satisfaction levels were generally high in the latest National Student Survey: only at Ulster did less than two thirds of undergraduates say they were satisfied or very satisfied with their course.

There is no Scottish representative in the ranking. Swansea just pips Aberystwyth to the leading place in Wales. Derby is the best-placed of six new universities.

There is a wide spread of entry qualifications, but only one university averages (just) less than 200 points. Nine out of ten students taking American studies have A levels or equivalent qualifications. There is an impressive level of firsts and 2:1s, and, although still uncomfortably close to the foot of the employment league, the subject is at least off the bottom this year. Half of all graduates went straight into graduate jobs or postgraduate training. Those who did find graduate-level work had average salaries of £18,296.

The number of places in American studies has been falling gradually, with the demand for places in more rapid decline over the past three years. Another above-average decline at the start of 2008 meant that there were barely 2,000 applications nationally.

- British Association for American Studies: **www.baas.ac.uk**

American Studies	Research quality/5	Entry standards	Student satisfaction %	Graduate prospects %	Overall rating
1 Warwick	5A	422	80	56	100.0
2 Leicester	5A	305	89	60	99.3
3 Sheffield	5B		81	68	98.4
4 Lancaster	4A	402	78	52	93.9
5 Liverpool	5A	308	81	54	93.3
6 Nottingham	5*B	365	77	49	92.7
7 Birmingham	4B	372	80	58	92.5
8 Sussex	5B	388	71	61	92.2
9 Keele	5B	315	77	50	87.7
10 Manchester	5B	377	69	49	86.5
11 East Anglia	4C	358	78	50	85.5
12 Swansea	3aA	283	79	50	83.8
13 Aberystwyth	4B	261	83	46	83.5
14 Hull		304	87	67	82.2
15 Goldsmiths College		363	75	55	75.6
16 King's College London		361	74	55	75.0

	Research quality/5	Entry standards	Student satisfaction %	Graduate prospects %	Overall rating
17 Portsmouth		276	76	64	74.5
18 Derby	3aB		81	26	73.3
19 Kent	4B	272	84	49	72.8
=20 Essex		259	80	51	71.3
=20 Winchester	3aD	290	80	29	71.3
22 Canterbury Christ Church		234	84	44	69.3
23 Plymouth		196	77	48	64.9
24 Liverpool John Moores		219	73	32	59.3
25 Ulster	4C		51	36	58.2

Employed in graduate job:	32%	Average starting graduate salary:	£18,296
Employed in graduate job and studying:	4%	Average starting non-graduate salary:	£14,025
Studying:	14%		
Employed in non-graduate job and studying:	5%	The letters that appear in the Research Quality column indicate the	
Employed in non-graduate job:	38%	proportion of staff included in the assessment, A showing that	
Unemployed:	6%	almost all staff were included and F showing that hardly any were.	

Anatomy and Physiology

Anatomy, physiology and pathology suffered the biggest drop in applications of any group of subjects when the official deadline passed for courses beginning in 2008. The switch from six choices per applicant to five appears to have hit the area particularly hard – perhaps because it is often the fall-back for those whose first four targets are medical degrees. There had been an 18 per cent drop in 2007, but the latest decline, of almost 30 per cent, left 18,000 candidates for about 3,000 places.

Edinburgh takes over from Cambridge at the top of the table, with the highest entry standards and the most satisfied students, while third-placed Bristol has one of the three 5* research grades in anatomy. The others, in a category entered by only eight of the 27 universities in the ranking, went to King's College London and Dundee. More universities – 14 in all – were assessed for physiology, but only Liverpool and Manchester reached the top grade.

Ulster again has the best employment record, despite missing a place in the top 20, followed by Leicester in 17th place. Scores in the National Student Survey were generally high, with only one university registering less than 70 per cent satisfaction among final-year undergraduates. However, a relatively low score almost cost Oxford a place in the top ten.

Several new universities have dropped out of the ranking in recent years. Only London South Bank, Northampton and Westminster remain and all three are rooted to the bottom of the table. Eighth-equal Cardiff is the only Welsh university in the ranking, while Edinburgh is the top Scottish institution.

The proportion of graduates going straight into work or further training ranges from under half to almost 90 per cent. Unemployment six months after graduation is around average nationally, while more than a third go straight onto another full-time course. Average earnings in graduate jobs are below average, at less than £18,500.

Despite awarding generally high marks for teaching, assessors in England found wide variations in some areas. The proportion of students awarded 2:1s, for example, ranged from 30 per cent in one unnamed university to 90 per cent in another. Some equipment was found to be outdated, but students acquired good knowledge of the subjects and skills that are in demand from employers.

- Anatomical Society of Great Britain and Ireland: **www.anatsoc.org.uk**
- British Association of Clinical Anatomists: **www.liv.ac.uk/HumanAnatomy/BACA.html**
- Physiological Society: **www.physoc.org**

Anatomy and Physiology	Research quality/5 Anatomy	Research quality/5 Physiology	Entry standards	Student satisfaction %	Graduate prospects %	Overall rating
1 Edinburgh		4A	504	91	71	100.0
2 Cambridge	5A	4B		86	85	99.1
3 Bristol	5*A	4A	403	84	82	98.8
4 Liverpool	4A	5*A	362	84	68	92.7
5 University College London	5A	4A	423	77	74	92.6
6 King's College London	5*B		380	80	71	92.2
7 Dundee	5*B		408	79	66	91.7
=8 Cardiff	5A			79	66	91.3
=8 Oxford	5B	5A	487	70	72	91.3
10 Aberdeen		5B	382		75	90.6
11 Leeds		5B	383	86	63	90.1
12 Loughborough		4A	352	87	64	89.8
13 Newcastle		5A	415	72	66	89.1
14 Nottingham		5A	392	71	70	88.9
=15 Salford		3aA		83	75	88.8
=15 Manchester		5*B	439	71	65	88.8
17 Leicester			387		87	81.5
18 Sheffield			391	78	69	72.9
19 St Andrews			397		63	72.0
20 Queen's, Belfast			326	79	66	70.2
=21 Bradford			266	81	69	69.1
=21 Ulster			311	65	89	69.1
=21 Sussex			366		61	69.1
24 Glasgow			385	80	51	68.7
=25 Westminster			210	72	45	55.8
=25 London South Bank		3aD			45	55.8
27 Northampton			216		51	55.0

Employed in graduate job:	25%	Average starting graduate salary:	£18,435
Employed in graduate job and studying:	4%	Average starting non-graduate salary:	£13,862
Studying:	36%		
Employed in non-graduate job and studying:	3%	The letters that appear in the Research Quality column indicate the	
Employed in non-graduate job:	25%	proportion of staff included in the assessment, A showing that	
Unemployed:	6%	almost all staff were included and F showing that hardly any were.	

Anthropology

Anthropology offers the best chance of a good degree in the social sciences, but the unemployment rate is among the highest for any subject, at 9 per cent. A quarter of all graduates go on to take a higher degree or some form of postgraduate training, but almost four in ten take non-graduate jobs.

Oxford has taken over at the top after a long period of Cambridge supremacy. Cambridge has dropped to third, with the London School of Economics retaining second place with the highest research grade and by far the best employment record. Nottingham Trent, which is second from bottom overall, is the only other university to have seen more than seven out of ten graduates go straight into graduate-level work or further study.

University College London, which ties with St Andrews for fourth place, has the other 5* research grade, but did not enter as high a proportion of academics for assessment as the LSE. St Andrews has by far the most satisfied students. Oxford has strong scores across the board, but only led the way on entry standards. It was one of 12 universities, including Roehampton, to be awarded grade 5 for research. However, East London emerges fractionally ahead of Roehampton as the leading new university of five in the ranking.

Average entry qualifications are down slightly in the latest table for anthropology, although only two universities averaged less than 270 points. Although applications were down by 10 per cent at the start of 2008, this was close to the average for degree courses and followed three years of rising demand for places. Nine per cent of the 619 students admitted in 2006 secured their place through Clearing.

• Royal Anthropological Institute: **www.therai.org.uk**

Anthropology	Research quality/5	Entry standards	Student satisfaction %	Graduate prospects %	Overall rating
1 Oxford	5A	493	82	69	100.0
2 London School of Economics	5*A	423	75	76	99.4
3 Cambridge	5A	484		67	98.8
=4 St Andrews	5A	454	87	51	94.9
=4 University College London	5*B	424	79	68	94.9
6 Sussex	5A	384	68	59	85.8
7 Durham	5B	366	74	59	84.8
8 Kent	5B	294	83	53	84.5
9 Lampeter	3aA			69	83.5
10 Brunel	4A	308	69	67	82.7
11 School of Oriental and African Studies	5B	358	73	55	82.5
12 Queen's, Belfast	5B	345	81	43	82.3
13 Aberdeen	4A	288		59	81.2
=14 Edinburgh	5B	410	69	47	80.5
=14 Swansea	3aA		81	50	80.5
16 Goldsmiths College	5A	303	70	48	80.4
17 Manchester	5B	388	74	41	79.7

	Research Quality				
18 Hull	3aB		79	55	78.2
19 East London	4B		71	57	77.4
20 Roehampton	5B	211	71	58	77.1
21 Oxford Brookes	4A	272	67	49	74.6
22 Nottingham Trent		284	72	72	67.5
23 Bath Spa		241	63	53	55.7

Employed in graduate job:	32%	Average starting graduate salary:	£18,694
Employed in graduate job and studying:	4%	Average starting non-graduate salary:	£14,407
Studying:	18%		
Employed in non-graduate job and studying:	4%	The letters that appear in the Research Quality column indicate the	
Employed in non-graduate job:	33%	proportion of staff included in the assessment, A showing that	
Unemployed:	9%	almost all staff were included and F showing that hardly any were.	

Archaeology

Cambridge holds on to first place in archaeology, with the highest entry standards and one of the three 5* research grades. Cambridge's response rate in the National Student Survey was too low to produce a score, so we have given it a substitute based on its other three measures in the table. The most satisfied students are at fifth-placed Reading, which also shares with Oxford and Cambridge the distinction of a 5* research grade. However, better employment prospects and higher entry grades leave Durham as the nearest challenger to Cambridge. By far the best employment score is at Strathclyde, which was the only university to see eight out of ten graduates go straight into graduate-level work or continue their studies.

Glasgow remains the top university in Scotland for archaeology, however, while Lampeter is the leader in Wales. Robert Gordon, which is second only to Strathclyde for student satisfaction, is the leading new university, followed by Central Lancashire and Bournemouth. The number of universities in the ranking has grown by leaps and bounds – the 2005 *Guide* contained only 25 institutions, compared with this year's 43. New universities are mainly responsible, their numbers growing from three to 17 over the same period. The change has had the effect of spreading out entry scores, which now range from less than 200 points to almost 500.

Archaeology, which was grouped together with history in the first three National Student Surveys, has produced some of the highest scores. Only two universities in the ranking saw less than two thirds of their students express satisfaction with their course in the results published in 2007.

Archaeology appears to have been one of the victims of top-up fees – perhaps because of the uncertain employment prospects and relatively low salaries for those who make a career in the subject. The number of applications for pure archaeology degrees was down by 22 per cent at the start of 2008, following a 10 per cent decline in the previous year, when most other subjects were up. The broader category of archaeological sciences, which is grouped together with forensic science, did better but was also down by more than the average for all subjects.

Assessments of teaching quality generally found high-quality teaching and a broad curriculum. Unemployment six months after graduation was relatively high, at 8 per cent, and archaeologists were among the lowest paid of all subjects, averaging little more than £17,000 in graduate jobs and less than £13,400 for non-graduate work.

Archaeology cont.
- Council for British Archaeology: **www.britarch.ac.uk/**
- TORC (Training Online Resource Centre for Archaeology): **www.torc.org.uk/**

Archaeology	Research quality/5	Entry standards	Student satisfaction %	Graduate prospects %	Overall rating
1 Cambridge	5*A	484		64	100.0
2 Durham	5A	419	84	73	95.7
=3 Oxford	5*A	475	79	64	95.6
=3 University College London	5A	385	86	74	95.6
5 Reading	5*A	314	89	62	92.2
6 Exeter	5A	360	87	59	90.1
7 Leicester	5A	347	86	56	87.8
8 Liverpool	5A	368	82	57	87.3
9 Southampton	5A	354	82	56	86.4
10 Glasgow	4A	352	85	56	84.8
11 Queen's, Belfast	5A	287	81	60	84.1
12 Sheffield	5A	357	78	54	84.0
13 York	3aA	376	81	60	83.1
14 Bristol	4B	382	74	67	83.0
15 Bradford	5B	268	77	70	82.6
16 Birmingham	4B	372	77	62	82.2
17 Nottingham	4A	344	75	59	81.0
=18 Strathclyde		401	77	82	79.8
=18 Edinburgh	3aA	430	74	52	79.8
=20 Lampeter	4A	267	70	70	79.3
=20 Manchester	5B	341	73	56	79.3
22 Robert Gordon		319		77	77.7
23 Cardiff	5A	300	73	46	76.4
24 Hull		303	85	73	76.2
25 Newcastle	3aB	326	70	60	74.2
26 Central Lancashire		289	81	68	71.6
27 Bournemouth	3aC	244	76	56	70.2
28 West of England		277	85	57	69.3
29 UWCN, Newport	3aA		67	54	69.1
30 Kent		269	76	67	68.2
31 Winchester	3aA	228	76	40	67.3
32 Chester		270	82	56	67.1
33 Staffordshire		252	85	53	66.5
34 De Montfort		195	86	55	65.1
35 Swansea		301	79	49	64.8
36 Nottingham Trent		273	65	69	64.5
37 Glasgow Caledonian		299	71	54	62.8
38 Glamorgan		264	72	53	61.6
39 Derby		250		54	61.3

40 Anglia Ruskin	241	72	53	60.6
41 Lincoln	266	68	49	58.5
42 Liverpool John Moores	242	62	57	57.8
43 Teesside	260	67	48	57.4

Employed in graduate job:	32%	Average starting graduate salary:	£17,226
Employed in graduate job and studying:	4%	Average starting non-graduate salary:	£13,376
Studying:	21%		
Employed in non-graduate job and studying:	5%	The letters that appear in the Research Quality column indicate the
Employed in non-graduate job:	31%	proportion of staff included in the assessment, A showing that
Unemployed:	8%	almost all staff were included and F showing that hardly any were.

Architecture

Cardiff has won back top place in architecture, having surrendered it to Cambridge by a narrow margin when this table was last published two years ago. Cardiff does not have a clear lead on any single indicator, although it was one of five universities to reach grade 5 in the last research assessments, when there were no 5* departments. The others were second-placed Bath, Sheffield, Brighton and Ulster. Bath, which is only a fraction of a point behind Cardiff in this year's table, also shares with Sheffield Hallam the distinction of having the most satisfied students.

Cambridge has by far the highest entry standards, but an uncharacteristically low research grade restricts it to third place. Employment prospects are good in architecture – at least 60 per cent of graduates had "positive prospects" at nearly every university – but only Ulster saw every leaver go straight into graduate work or further training. The rate was at least 90 per cent at all but two of the top 20.

Dundee just edges out Edinburgh as the top department in Scotland. Sheffield Hallam's high satisfaction rating helps it to become the top new university, just ahead of Oxford Brookes.

A third of all undergraduates enter architecture degrees with qualifications other than A level, Highers or equivalents. There is a wide spread of entrance scores, from more than 500 points at Cambridge to less than 180 at London South Bank.

Only five subjects have a better employment record, but the success rate is not reflected in starting salaries. Architecture is only just outside the bottom ten subjects, with those in non-graduate jobs or self-employment less than £3,000 a year behind those securing traditional graduate work. Nine out of ten graduates go on to complete their professional training, either with further study or within a job. The training is long, but the subject remains popular: four successive increases in applications ended in 2008, but the 3.5 per cent decline, brought about by the reduction in choices per applicant, was much lower than the average for all subjects. Three years into their careers, architects were among the least likely of all graduates to say that they wished they had taken a different degree or chosen a different profession.

- Commission for Architecture and the Built Environment: **www.cabe.org.uk/**
- Royal Institute of British Architects: **www.architecture.com/**

Architecture

	Research quality/5	Entry standards	Student satisfaction %	Graduate prospects %	Overall rating
1 Cardiff	5A	481		96	100.0
2 Bath	5B	489	84	95	99.6
3 Cambridge	4A	523		94	98.3
4 University College London	4C	460	83	99	95.8
=5 Nottingham	4A	432		93	93.4
=5 Sheffield	5B	449	75	92	93.4
7 Manchester	4C	410	79	97	91.3
8 Ulster	5A	319	71	100	91.0
9 Newcastle	4C	450	73	94	89.3
10 Dundee	4B	395	71	93	87.9
11 Edinburgh	3aB	439	72	88	86.3
12 Strathclyde	4C	378	70	98	86.1
13 Liverpool	4B	423	65	93	85.9
14 Sheffield Hallam	3aE	295	84	95	84.8
15 Oxford Brookes	4D	370	73	95	84.5
16 De Montfort	4A	267	67	92	82.5
17 Brighton	5B	345	60	90	81.5
18 Queen's, Belfast	2B	362	66	97	79.7
19 Portsmouth	3aD	313	77	82	79.3
20 Northumbria	3bD	298	73	94	79.1
=21 Lincoln	3aD	277	69	91	76.7
=21 Leeds Metropolitan	3bD	288	66	97	76.7
=23 East London	4D	254	62	98	75.9
=23 Nottingham Trent	3aB	288	64		75.9
25 Liverpool John Moores	3bC	312	69	83	75.8
26 Westminster	4D	309	69	79	75.1
27 Robert Gordon	3bD	333		83	74.0
28 West of England		291	71	90	73.6
29 Glamorgan	3bC	206	73		73.4
30 Kingston		298	74	83	72.9
31 Plymouth		331	68	87	72.6
32 Huddersfield		275		88	70.6
33 London South Bank	3bD	178		93	70.2
34 Coventry	3bC	232			68.9
35 UWIC, Cardiff		219	60	92	66.2
36 Birmingham City	2F	262		76	64.1
37 Greenwich	3bE	230	55	81	62.9
38 Southampton Solent		188	61	71	58.6
39 Wolverhampton	3aB	196	61	40	56.9

Employed in graduate job:	58%	Average starting graduate salary:	£17,778
Employed in graduate job and studying:	20%	Average starting non-graduate salary:	£15,073
Studying:	14%		
Employed in non-graduate job and studying:	1%	The letters that appear in the Research Quality column indicate the
Employed in non-graduate job:	5%	proportion of staff included in the assessment, A showing that
Unemployed:	3%	almost all staff were included and F showing that hardly any were.

Art and Design

Most courses in art and design are at new universities – often in former art colleges – but the top nine in this year's ranking are all older institutions. University College London remains the leader, despite not having the top score on any single indicator. Brunel is now the nearest challenger, moving up from fifth place with a consistent set of scores. At UCL, students attend the Slade School of Fine Art, while at Oxford the Fine Art degree is taught at the Ruskin School of Drawing. However, Oxford only just makes the top ten because little more than half the graduates in the latest statistics were in graduate-level work or further study six months after completing the course.

Edinburgh, in seventh place, boasts the highest entry qualifications and Salford, in 11th, is the only university rated internationally outstanding for research. Art and design was one of the few areas to record poorer research grades in 2001 than in previous assessments – fifth-placed Reading was the only one of eight departments awarded grade 5 to enter a full complement of academics. Teesside has the most satisfied students and is one of only three universities with a satisfaction level of 80 per cent or more.

Bangor is the leader in Wales, having achieved a rare 100 per cent graduate employment record in a group of subjects where immediate employment is hard to come by. However, the 22 per cent graduate employment rate at Oxford Brookes was one of the lowest scores in any subject. Brighton remains the best-placed new university, retaining its place in the top ten. Nottingham Trent, Kingston and University College Falmouth also made the top 20. Low entry grades and research scores count against many of the new universities and colleges, although most artists would argue that these are of less significance than in other subjects.

Graduate unemployment in art and design has improved since the last table was published, but is still well above average at 9 per cent. Artists and designers often have a period of self-employment early in their career while they find a way to pursue their vocation, but two thirds of those surveyed three years after graduation said they would make the same choice again. Average starting salaries for those who do find work within six months of graduating are in the bottom four of the 60 subject areas.

The acceptance rate for applicants in the various branches of art and design is among the highest in any subject area, despite rising applications in recent years. There was a big increase in 2007, while the large pool of applications for design courses held up better than other courses at the start of 2008. The much smaller Foundation degree route saw continued strong growth.

- Design Council: **www.designcouncil.org.uk/**
- National Society for Education in Art and Design: **www.nsead.org/**
- Sector Skills Council for the Audio Visual and Publishing Industries: **www.skillset.org/**
- Sector Skills Council for Fashion and Textiles: **www.skillfast-uk.org/**

Art and Design	Research quality/5	Entry standards	Student satisfaction %	Graduate prospects %	Overall rating
1 University College London	5B	386		68	100.0
2 Brunel	4A	360	77	68	97.2
3 Glasgow	4C	398	76	74	96.6
4 Loughborough	4C	363	80	58	91.7
5 Reading	5A	316	68	66	91.2
6 Goldsmiths College	5B	307	72	64	89.6
7 Edinburgh		437	75	68	89.0
8 Oxford	4A			53	88.3
9 Bangor		226	81	100	87.4
10 Brighton	5B	295	71	59	86.8
11 Salford	5*A	220	72	54	85.6
12 Leeds	3aA	383	63	56	85.4
13 Aberystwyth	3aA	297	79	44	84.4
14 Dundee	4B	328	69	52	84.1
15 Lancaster	3aC	345	74	52	83.8
16 Kent		305	79	71	83.0
17 Nottingham Trent	3aE	300	69	76	82.4
18 University College Falmouth	3aE	275	76	67	81.8
19 Kingston	4D	288	71	64	81.7
20 Newcastle	4B	359	56	61	81.6
21 Robert Gordon	3aD	313		59	80.3
22 Westminster	4D	321	75	42	79.8
23 Southampton	4C	359	61	52	79.6
24 Bournemouth	5D	270	64	67	79.1
25 Greenwich		244	76	75	78.4
26 Coventry	3aD	286	71	56	78.0
27 Heriot-Watt	3bB	312	59	66	77.9
28 Northumbria	4D	276	66	60	77.3
29 Ulster	5D	258	68	57	77.1
30 University of the Arts, London	5D	323	62	52	76.9
31 Napier	3aD	288		53	75.8
32 Staffordshire	4D	248	75	45	75.7
33 De Montfort	4C	255	67	50	75.4
=34 UWIC, Cardiff	4D	249	72	48	75.3
=34 Chichester	2A	321	73	36	75.3
36 Middlesex	3aC	225	71	55	75.1
37 Teesside		240	83	51	75.0
38 West of England	4D	250	74	44	74.8
39 Leeds Metropolitan	3aD	241	72	51	74.0
40 Sunderland	4C	247	63	53	73.8
41 Derby	3bD	281	69	49	73.7
42 Manchester Metropolitan	4E	266	69	51	73.6
43 Portsmouth	3aD	254	73	44	73.4

=44 Sheffield Hallam	5C	257	61	46	72.6
=44 Plymouth	3aC	260	66	47	72.6
=44 Central Lancashire	3bE	248	68	60	72.6
47 Birmingham City	4E	301	66	44	72.4
48 Gloucestershire	3aC	270	67	41	72.2
49 Glamorgan		234	71	63	71.8
50 Buckinghamshire New	3aD	240	68	48	71.2
=51 Lincoln	3aD	266	67	45	71.1
=51 Bath Spa	3aD	266	62	54	71.1
=51 Northampton	2E	263	69	53	71.1
=54 London South Bank		239	76	49	70.9
=54 Anglia Ruskin	3bA	251	62	47	70.9
=54 Huddersfield	3bF	247	73	49	70.9
57 UWCN, Newport	5E	247	63	54	70.7
=58 Bolton	2E	202	76	51	70.5
=58 Southampton Solent	3bB	239	63	50	70.5
60 Cumbria	3bE	249	68	51	70.2
61 University College for Creative Arts	3aD	238	65	50	69.9
62 Hertfordshire	3aD	248	63	50	69.7
63 Worcester		250	68	56	69.5
64 Thames Valley	1E		62	65	69.2
65 Glasgow Caledonian		301		44	68.7
66 Liverpool John Moores	3aC	216	62	50	68.5
67 Chester	3bD	277	69	32	68.2
=68 East London	4D	179	61	58	67.7
=68 Oxford Brookes	3bB	318	64	22	67.7
70 Canterbury Christ Church		275	62	51	66.2
71 Bedfordshire		232	68	45	64.9
72 Wolverhampton	3aF	216	67	40	63.1
73 York St John		251	59	44	60.9
74 Essex		211	51	51	56.3

Employed in graduate job:	44%	Average starting graduate salary:	£16,829
Employed in graduate job and studying:	3%	Average starting non-graduate salary:	£13,439
Studying:	7%		
Employed in non-graduate job and studying:	4%	The letters that appear in the Research Quality column indicate the	
Employed in non-graduate job:	33%	proportion of staff included in the assessment, A showing that	
Unemployed:	9%	almost all staff were included and F showing that hardly any were.	

Biological Sciences

Cambridge has maintained its lead over its rivals in the fourth year of the combined biological sciences table. The best possible research grade, the highest entry qualifications, the top employment score and the most satisfied students give the light blues a clean sweep. Only Oxford comes close, despite missing one of the ten 5* research grades. Bristol and Sheffield have overtaken Imperial College, London to finish third and fourth respectively. Both were among four English universities with maximum points for teaching and research, together with Cambridge, while Dundee managed the same feat under the separate Scottish system.

High entry standards and satisfied students help St Andrews to the leading position in Scotland, while Cardiff is well clear of the competition in Wales. Of 38 new universities in the ranking, only Portsmouth, which managed a grade 5 in the last Research Assessment Exercise despite entering a full complement of academics, features in the top 40.

Although entrants to both Cambridge and Oxford average around 500 points, entry standards elsewhere are more tightly bunched than in many other subjects. Ten other universities average over 400 points and only four dip below 200 points, despite the fact that a relatively high proportion of students (11 per cent) enter through Clearing. Graduate prospects nationally are slightly below average for all subjects, especially in terms of starting salaries.

Biology has not suffered the recruitment problems experienced by other sciences. Although applications fell by more than average at the start of 2008, when the number of choices per applicant was reduced from six to five, there had been a 6 per cent increase in the previous year. The total of 20,000 was still ahead of chemistry and physics. Two thirds of all entrants arrive with A levels or their equivalent, and more than half of the undergraduates are awarded firsts or 2:1s. More than a third go on to take postgraduate courses, either full or part-time.

- Biochemical Society: **www.biology4all.com**
- British Society for Cell Biology: **www.bscb.org/**
- Institute of Biology: **www.iob.org**
- Society for Experimental Biology: **www.sebiology.org/**

Biological Sciences	Research quality/5	Entry standards	Student satisfaction %	Graduate prospects %	Overall rating
1 Cambridge	5*A	537	86	85	100.0
2 Oxford	5A	497	85	80	95.1
3 Bristol	5*A	427	82	76	91.5
4 Sheffield	5*A	418	84	69	90.8
5 Imperial College	5*B	440	78	83	89.3
6 St Andrews	5B	406	84	68	86.8
7 Bath	5B	429	78	78	86.6
8 University College London	5B	438	78	75	86.2
9 Leicester	5*B	373	82	69	86.1
10 Surrey	5*A	318	75	84	85.8
11 Cardiff	5A	370	84	61	85.6
12 Ulster	5*A	276	77	83	85.0
13 York	5B	391	82	66	84.8
14 Manchester	5*B	418	78	66	84.7
15 Birmingham	5B	381	82	65	84.1
=16 Nottingham	5A	362	78	71	84.0
=16 Durham	5B	467	75	68	84.0
18 Edinburgh	5A	424	78	62	83.9

19 East Anglia	5B	348	85	59	83.7
20 Warwick	5B	409	78	66	83.2
21 Liverpool	5B	344	81	66	82.6
22 Newcastle	5*B	357	77	67	82.4
23 Kent	4A	271	79	78	82.3
24 Dundee	5*B	352	83	52	82.1
25 Glasgow	5B	364	83	53	81.2
26 Queen's, Belfast	4B	328	83	63	81.1
27 Keele	4C	289	83	73	81.0
28 Southampton	5B	395	78	58	80.7
=29 Lancaster	4B	342	79	65	80.2
=29 Sussex	5B	354	75	69	80.2
=29 Leeds	5B	349	79	61	80.2
32 Royal Holloway	5C	321	75	74	79.2
33 Exeter	4B	334	77	67	78.9
34 King's College London	3aC	361	76	69	77.8
35 Reading	4B	329	78	59	77.5
36 Portsmouth	5A	244	77	61	77.4
37 Essex	4B	261	80	62	77.1
38 Heriot-Watt	4A	289	78	57	77.0
39 Queen Mary, London	4B	337	75	63	76.9
40 Aston	3aC	292	77	74	76.8
41 Aberdeen	5C	294		62	75.9
=42 Aberystwyth	3aA	270	82	50	75.6
=42 Brunel	4C	307	74	69	75.6
44 Hull	4D	252	82	62	75.4
45 West of England		236	84	72	75.0
46 Stirling	4A	276		53	74.4
47 Bangor	4A	302	74	52	73.7
48 Brighton	5C	236	76	61	73.4
=49 Swansea	3aA	295	72	61	73.3
=49 Salford	3aA	233	78	55	73.3
51 Greenwich	3aA	181	78	59	72.2
52 Nottingham Trent	5D	206	70	79	72.0
53 West of Scotland	3bC			66	71.8
54 Central Lancashire	3bB	252	69	77	71.7
55 Oxford Brookes	3aA	246	72	60	71.3
56 Chester		265	77	69	71.0
57 Robert Gordon		232		71	70.1
58 Glasgow Caledonian		271	74	70	69.7
59 UWIC, Cardiff		249	74	73	69.4
60 Manchester Metropolitan	2D	235	77	59	69.0
61 Abertay		286		60	68.7
=62 Queen Margaret Edinburgh		293		59	68.6
=62 Teesside		257	82	49	68.6
64 Bradford		266	76	60	68.4
=65 Plymouth	3aE	289	76	50	68.2

		Research quality/5	Entry standards	Student satisfaction %	Graduate prospects %	Overall rating
=65	Sheffield Hallam		248	73	70	68.2
=65	Staffordshire		253	82	48	68.2
68	Napier	4D	211		58	67.9
69	Huddersfield		242	74	65	67.7
=70	Wolverhampton	3aC	183	70	66	67.6
=70	Leeds Metropolitan		248	68	78	67.6
72	Hertfordshire	3aC	258	67	64	67.4
73	Northumbria	2E	259	71	64	67.1
=74	Kingston	3aC	208	72	56	66.8
=74	Sunderland	3aB	214	75	44	66.8
76	Bournemouth		212	77	59	66.7
=77	Bath Spa	3bE	249	76	49	66.1
=77	Coventry	2C	253	76	47	66.1
79	Roehampton		216	73	66	66.0
80	Bolton		171	74	64	65.0
81	Glamorgan		218	74	55	64.2
82	Strathclyde		329	69	52	63.9
83	Anglia Ruskin		236	78	43	63.8
84	Westminster	3bC	214	69	53	63.7
85	East London	2D	175	71	57	63.0
86	Bedfordshire	2D		74	47	62.8
87	Liverpool John Moores		218	77	42	62.6
88	Derby		292	69	48	61.8
89	Worcester	2D		78	33	61.0

Employed in graduate job:	29%		Average starting graduate salary:	£17,902
Employed in graduate job and studying:	5%		Average starting non-graduate salary:	£13,664
Studying:	30%			
Employed in non-graduate job and studying:	3%		The letters that appear in the Research Quality column indicate the	
Employed in non-graduate job:	27%		proportion of staff included in the assessment, A showing that	
Unemployed:	7%		almost all staff were included and F showing that hardly any were.	

Building

Loughborough tops the building table after slipping to third the last time it was published, with by far the most satisfied students and one of only two 5* research grades. It also has one of the highest entry scores and almost all of the leavers went straight into graduate jobs or further training. Fourth-placed Reading and Anglia Ruskin, in ninth, did even better on employment, with 100 per cent "positive destinations".

Nottingham remains second, with the highest entry standards, although there were not enough students to compile scores for graduate destinations or student satisfaction. Salford, which has the other 5* research grade, is up to third, while Strathclyde, the previous leader, has dropped out of the ranking with too little data to be included this year. Heriot-Watt, in seventh place, takes over as the top university in Scotland.

The top seven are all pre-1992 universities, while the rest are former polytechnics or colleges. Northumbria is best-placed of the new universities, in eighth, but most are tightly bunched, with good graduate employment scores and student satisfaction ratings. Employment scores are good throughout the table, with no university dropping below a 75 per cent success rate. Indeed, building is in the top ten subjects for employment and only just outside it for starting salaries in graduate jobs, which average nearly £22,000.

Applications for building have held up well, even in the year when top-up fees were introduced, and the increase in 2007 was one of the largest for any subject. There was only a small decline at the start of 2008, when the switch from six choices per applicant to five caused a serious downturn in many subjects. Building is one of the best prospects for a place in Clearing: nearly 14 per cent of entrants found a place that way in 2006.

Universities admit 44 per cent of students with qualifications other than A level. Those who do take the A-level route tend not to require the highest grades – scores at the top of the table are actually lower than they were two years ago. Nottingham and University College London have reached 350 points in the latest table, but only one has dropped below 200.

- Chartered Institute of Building: **www.ciob.org.uk**

Building	Research quality/5	Entry standards	Student satisfaction %	Graduate prospects %	Overall rating
1 Loughborough	5*B	330	85	98	100.0
2 Nottingham	4A	350			99.2
3 Salford	5*A	304		95	97.0
4 Reading	5B	329	71	100	94.4
5 Ulster	5A	282	70	95	90.7
6 University College London	4C	350	75	89	90.2
7 Heriot-Watt	5B	274	76	80	84.9
8 Northumbria	3bD	277	75	92	84.1
9 Anglia Ruskin	2B	283	63	100	83.6
10 Oxford Brookes	4D	236	75	92	83.3
11 Robert Gordon	3bD	307		87	82.4
12 Plymouth	4E	292	76	83	82.1
13 Nottingham Trent	3aB	240	63	96	82.0
14 Glasgow Caledonian	3aD	268	71	89	81.8
15 Leeds Metropolitan	3bD	249	71	91	80.8
16 Liverpool John Moores	3bC	258	67	91	80.4
17 West of England		265	74	89	80.0
18 Glamorgan	3bC	212	73	90	79.5
19 Brighton	3bC	242	67	90	79.2
20 Central Lancashire	3aD	270	66	85	78.2
21 Coventry	3bC	276		80	77.2
22 Napier	3bD	256		85	77.1
23 Sheffield Hallam	3aE	248	69	84	76.6
24 Bolton		201	81	83	76.3
25 Greenwich	3bE	250		84	75.4

Building cont.

	Research quality/5	Entry standards	Student satisfaction %	Graduate prospects %	Overall rating
26 Kingston		237	68	88	75.3
27 Wolverhampton	3aB	201	61		73.6
28 London South Bank	3bD	176		86	71.1
29 Westminster	3aD	276	54	76	70.6
30 Birmingham City	2F	230		77	68.5

Employed in graduate job:	72%	Average starting graduate salary:	£21,914
Employed in graduate job and studying:	16%	Average starting non-graduate salary:	£15,638
Studying:	3%		
Employed in non-graduate job and studying:	1%	The letters that appear in the Research Quality column indicate the	
Employed in non-graduate job:	5%	proportion of staff included in the assessment, A showing that	
Unemployed:	3%	almost all staff were included and F showing that hardly any were.	

Business Studies

Taken together, the various branches of business and management represent by far the most popular area of higher education. Even without the many dual or combined honours degrees that are common for both of the main areas, there were nearly 95,000 applications by the official deadline for courses beginning in 2008. That represented a decline that was close to the average for all subjects, but it followed a boom year when management was up by 11 per cent and business combinations saw a 25 per cent increase, attracting more than 45,000 applications.

Cambridge takes over from Oxford, which has headed the table since teaching grades were dropped from the *Guide* two years ago. Cambridge moves up from third place with the best graduate employment record, but no data for entry standards or student satisfaction. The London School of Economics slips to third, with Bath less than a point behind.

Fifth-placed Warwick and Lancaster, in tenth, are the only universities rated internationally outstanding for research, while Newport boasts the most satisfied students, with Exeter close behind. St Andrews has resumed its position as the top university in Scotland, with Edinburgh dropping out of the top 30 because of low student satisfaction and employment scores. Cardiff remains the clear the leader in Wales.

Although Oxford's Said Business School is exclusively postgraduate, the colleges offer management in joint honours first-degree courses. Their entry standards are by far the highest in the table. London and Manchester business schools, like Cranfield and Cambridge's Judge School of Management, are also absent from the table because they do not offer first degrees.

More than 3,000 undergraduates – about 10 per cent of those securing places – entered through Clearing in 2006. Both entrance qualifications and employment rates vary widely in this, one of the largest tables in the *Guide*. There are more than 100 institutions in this latest edition, over half of them new universities or colleges, but only Portsmouth and Oxford Brookes feature in the top 40. Ten have average entry grades of less than 200 points, but those universities are well represented among the 23 where fewer than half the leavers were in graduate jobs or postgraduate training within six months.

Unemployment levels are no higher than average for all subjects, but a third of all leavers start off in a non-graduate job. The range of starting salaries is predictably wide, given the large number of graduates, but the average of more than £20,000 for graduate jobs is only just outside the top 20 for all subject areas. Satisfaction levels improved in the last National Student Survey.

- Chartered Management Institute: **www.managers.org.uk**
- Confederation of British Industry: **www.cbi.org.uk/**
- Institute of Management Consultancy: **www.imc.co.uk**

Business Studies	Research quality/5	Entry standards	Student satisfaction %	Graduate prospects %	Overall rating
1 Cambridge	5A			92.1	100.0
2 Oxford	5A	514	83.3	86.5	99.3
3 London School of Economics	5A	437	77.9	90.0	94.0
4 Bath	5A	428	79.6	86.8	93.8
5 Warwick	5*B	440	78.5	77.7	91.2
6 Loughborough	4C	405	87.4	81.3	91.0
7 Exeter	4C	378	88.1	81.5	90.3
8 King's College London	4B	408		83.1	89.9
9 St Andrews	4A	407	83.2	68.6	88.6
10 Lancaster	5*B	398	80.0	69.7	88.3
11 Aston	5B	386	80.3	75.7	87.9
12 Imperial College	5B	403	72.7	78.5	85.1
=13 City	5C	383	76.5	77.1	84.2
=13 Strathclyde	4C	380	82.6	68.4	84.2
15 Nottingham	5B	399	70.6	76.4	83.3
16 Manchester	5A	414	70.3	66.9	83.2
17 Glasgow	4C	382	79.5	63.9	81.5
18 Leicester	3aB	316	84.9	62.6	81.4
19 Reading	5C	330	77.8	71.1	81.3
20 Cardiff	5B	383	75.2	59.7	81.1
=21 Southampton	4B	377	74.1	65.6	80.1
21 East Anglia	3aC	341	81.5	65.5	80.1
23 Leeds	5C	395	69.2	72.0	79.4
24 Bangor	5B	245	74.9	74.0	78.7
=25 Newcastle	3aC	378	72.3	72.7	78.2
=25 Sheffield	4B	370	72.4	62.7	78.2
27 Hull	4C	269	80.8	65.6	77.9
28 Keele	4B	281	72.9	73.9	77.6
29 University College London		416	71.6	83.9	77.3
=30 Durham	3aD	340	76.8	68.8	77.0
=30 Stirling	4B	275		65.9	77.0

Business Studies cont.	Research quality/5	Entry standards	Student satisfaction %	Graduate prospects %	Overall rating
32 Edinburgh	4B	419	64.3	66.4	76.6
33 Kent	3aC	279	77.2	71.0	76.5
34 Birmingham	4D	402	70.2	64.8	75.8
35 Queen's, Belfast	4B	336	76.4	48.4	75.6
36 Aberdeen	3aB	307		61.5	75.4
37 Portsmouth	4C	269	75.0	67.5	75.2
38 Surrey	4C	354	67.7	69.7	75.1
39 Essex	5C	308	72.3	61.6	75.0
40 Oxford Brookes	2F	309	79.6	66.6	73.8
41 Salford	3aB	280	73.8	61.2	73.5
42 Sussex		361	71.9	75.0	73.1
43 Royal Holloway	4B	338	62.8	68.1	72.9
=44 Swansea	3aD	280	74.1	67.1	72.6
=44 Bournemouth	3aE	295	74.6	68.5	72.6
=46 Brighton	3aE	280	76.2	65.3	72.1
=46 Heriot-Watt	4D	305	71.7	62.5	72.1
48 Nottingham Trent	3bD	269	66.8	85.5	71.7
49 De Montfort	3aC	244	77.0	57.6	71.6
50 York		329	71.6	74.4	71.4
51 Bradford	4C	237	73.8	59.4	71.2
=52 West of England	3aD	244	75.2	64.2	71.0
=52 Harper Adams		269		73.0	71.0
54 Aberystwyth	3bC	279	77.7	50.4	70.5
55 Glamorgan	3bD	244	78.4	57.8	70.4
56 Lincoln	3bD	248	77.3	58.6	70.1
57 Robert Gordon	2F	285		70.1	69.7
58 Central Lancashire	3bE	259	74.6	64.5	69.6
59 Ulster	3aD	264	77.6	48.0	69.3
60 Gloucestershire	3aD	246	71.7	62.6	68.8
61 Queen Mary, London		315	72.6	63.1	68.6
62 Liverpool		365	68.8	62.3	68.4
63 Winchester		265	79.3	55.0	68.3
64 Napier	3bE	231		69.1	68.1
=65 Sheffield Hallam	3bF	261	74.8	59.1	67.6
=65 Northumbria	3bF	302	68.3	66.8	67.6
67 UWCN, Newport		201	89.2	39.5	67.4
68 Brunel	4C	299	63.9	55.1	67.2
69 Royal Agricultural College		311	73.5	55.3	67.1
70 Hertfordshire	3aC	257	69.7	52.6	66.9
71 Plymouth	3bE	264	72.0	57.8	66.7
72 Teesside		234	77.0	56.5	66.2
73 Manchester Metropolitan	3aE	274	68.3	58.2	65.8
74 Birmingham City	2F	234	77.6	50.6	65.7

Rank	University	Research Quality				
75	St Mary's College		214	79.6	51.3	65.5
76	Sunderland	2F	205	77.4	54.9	65.4
77	Northampton	2E	210	76.8	52.7	65.3
78	Worcester		222	74.9	59.1	65.2
=79	Canterbury Christ Church		223	79.8	47.6	65.1
=79	Leeds Metropolitan	2F	269	69.7	60.2	65.1
81	Bath Spa		237	76.8	51.3	64.9
82	Glasgow Caledonian	3aE	280	71.8	44.5	64.6
=83	Liverpool John Moores	3bE	233	71.2	55.5	64.5
=83	Chester		269	70.1	59.4	64.5
=85	Kingston	3aE	225	69.6	56.6	64.1
=85	Edge Hill		256	76.8	44.9	64.1
87	Coventry	2E	239	73.8	48.3	63.8
=88	Anglia Ruskin	2D	253	70.1	51.5	63.6
=88	York St John		324	66.9	53.8	63.6
90	Staffordshire	3bE	245	69.3	52.7	63.2
=91	Huddersfield	3bE	275	71.9	38.6	62.4
=91	Southampton Solent		213	71.4	57.3	62.4
93	London South Bank	3aE	161	78.7	39.5	62.3
94	Bedfordshire	3aE	175	74.2	44.6	61.6
95	Derby	2E	262	68.3	46.4	61.2
96	Cumbria		240	72.8	44.5	61.1
97	Westminster	3bE	239	68.4	45.6	60.7
98	Chichester		208		53.4	60.0
99	Wolverhampton	3bF	181	71.0	49.2	59.7
100	Queen Margaret Edinburgh	2C	223		41.5	59.5
101	Roehampton		186	65.9	59.4	58.7
102	Abertay	3bE	203		42.9	58.0
=103	Greenwich	3bF	180	66.3	52.3	57.8
=103	Thames Valley		172	71.5	45.3	57.8
105	West of Scotland	2E	224		39.8	57.3
106	Middlesex	3aE	163	64.8	46.6	56.5
107	Buckinghamshire	2E	209	64.3	42.8	55.9
108	East London	2E	149	69.6	38.4	55.4
109	Bolton	1D	172	63.9	41.0	53.4
110	UWIC, Cardiff		220	62.7	37.6	53.0
111	University of the Arts, London		184	61.0	37.4	50.5

Employed in graduate job:	47%	Average starting graduate salary:	£20,080
Employed in graduate job and studying:	7%	Average starting non-graduate salary:	£15,486
Studying:	7%		
Employed in non-graduate job and studying:	3%	The letters that appear in the Research Quality column indicate the	
Employed in non-graduate job:	31%	proportion of staff included in the assessment, A showing that	
Unemployed:	6%	almost all staff were included and F showing that hardly any were.	

Celtic Studies

Aberystwyth has regained the leadership of the Celtic studies table, which was among those not published last year. Cambridge, the previous leader and holder of one of the four 5* research grades in these subjects, has dropped out because there were not enough students to compile scores for the other indicators. Aberystwyth, which has another of the 5* research grades, just beats Cardiff to the top position.

The addition of student satisfaction scores has made a big difference to the order. Ulster repeats its outstanding performance in graduate employment, which saw it jump from seventh place to second in the last edition of the table, but by far the lowest satisfaction rating sends the university back down to sixth again. Even its 5* research grade cannot keep it ahead of Queen's, Belfast.

The final research star is third-placed Bangor, which had the most satisfied students. Glasgow, the last surviving Scottish representative, has also dropped out of the table for lack of data, while Liverpool – a long-established centre for Irish Studies – is the only English university left in the ranking.

The subjects have relatively small enrolments – little more than 500 had applied for places by the official deadline for entry in 2008, a drop of almost 25 per cent in the year when the number of choices per applicant was cut from six to five. About half of the graduates go on to further study – only law has a higher proportion in this category. Partly as a result, only three in ten go straight into a graduate-level job, but the 5 per cent unemployment rate is below the average for all subjects. However, Celtic Studies is rock bottom of the earnings league with average starting salaries of only £15,600 in graduate jobs.

- Intute Celtic Studies portal: **www.intute.ac.uk/artsandhumanities/celtic/**
- Kilmartin House museum: **www.kilmartin.org/**

Celtic Studies	Research quality/5	Entry standards	Student satisfaction %	Graduate prospects %	Overall rating
1 Aberystwyth	5*A	354	88	78	100.0
2 Cardiff	5A	370	80	86	99.2
3 Bangor	5*A	346	89	75	98.8
4 Swansea	5A	256	80	76	85.9
5 Queen's, Belfast	5A	328	78	56	85.4
6 Ulster	5*B	273	51	94	84.0
7 Lampeter	3bC		78	71	77.4
8 Liverpool		306	81	68	75.0

Employed in graduate job:	30%	Average starting graduate salary:	£15,652
Employed in graduate job and studying:	8%	Average starting non-graduate salary:	*
Studying:	37%		
Employed in non-graduate job and studying:	4%	The letters that appear in the Research Quality column indicate the
Employed in non-graduate job:	16%	proportion of staff included in the assessment, A showing that
Unemployed:	5%	almost all staff were included and F showing that hardly any were.

Chemical Engineering

Cambridge tops the chemical engineering table for the seventh year in a row, with much the highest entry standards and one of the best employment scores. However, second-placed Imperial College London has the better rating for research – 5*, like Birmingham and University College London, which have slipped down the table this year.

Seventh-placed Surrey was the only university to see all its chemical engineers go straight into graduate-level work or further study, although all but two universities in the table registered "positive destinations" for at least three quarters of those graduating. Student satisfaction is high, too. Only two universities had satisfaction levels below 70 per cent, while 85 per cent of undergraduates at Loughborough were satisfied, or very satisfied, with their course.

Heriot-Watt remains the best-placed Scottish institution, while Swansea is the only representative of Wales. London South Bank is the only new university left in the ranking.

Chemical engineering is one of the smaller branches of engineering, but a 17 per cent surge by the start of 2007 took the total number of applications over 7,000. The appeal of the subject has been growing for several years: there was an increase of nearly 9 per cent in 2006, against the national trend, and an even bigger rise in the previous year. Applications were still above 7,000 at the official deadline for courses beginning in 2008, in spite of the cut in choices per applicant. The fact that only medicine and dentistry enjoy higher average starting salaries may have something to do with it. Chemical engineers in graduate jobs six months into their career averaged more than £25,000, while even those in non-graduate work averaged over £20,000.

Four out of five students have A levels or equivalent qualifications, and average entry grades are the highest for any engineering subject. This helps produce engineering's largest proportion of firsts and 2:1s. Almost two thirds of students go straight into graduate jobs, although the 6 per cent unemployment rate is average for all subjects. Teaching quality assessors found the overall standard in English universities to be high in relation to international competition, with most courses offering industrial placements in the final year and leading to Chartered Engineer status.

- Institution of Chemical Engineers: **cms.icheme.org/**
- Royal Society of Chemistry: **www.rsc.org**

Chemical Engineering	Research quality/5	Entry standards	Student satisfaction %	Graduate prospects %	Overall rating
1 Cambridge	5A	531		94	100.0
2 Imperial College	5*A	469	83	87	97.5
3 Manchester	5A	412	76	86	89.9
4 Loughborough	4A	359	85	79	88.3
5 Heriot-Watt	4A	394	79	80	86.8
6 Queen's, Belfast	4A	346	76	89	86.2
7 Surrey	4B	281	78	100	86.1
=8 Sheffield	4B	352	76	92	85.7
=8 Newcastle	5B	361	71	95	85.7

	Research quality/5	Entry standards	Student satisfaction %	Graduate prospects %	Overall rating
10 Birmingham	5*A	394	69	78	85.3
11 Bath	4A	376	76	81	84.9
12 University College London	5*A	377	74	71	84.6
13 Swansea	4A	276	77	90	84.1
14 Nottingham	4B	369	72	84	81.9
15 Edinburgh	4C	449	73	75	81.6
16 Leeds	5C	310	71	89	80.4
17 Strathclyde		386	78	85	78.1
18 Aston	5C	293	71	63	72.0
19 London South Bank	3aE		62	76	64.9

Employed in graduate job:	59%	Average starting graduate salary:	£25,136
Employed in graduate job and studying:	6%	Average starting non-graduate salary:	£20,364
Studying:	18%		
Employed in non-graduate job and studying:	2%	The letters that appear in the Research Quality column indicate the
Employed in non-graduate job:	9%	proportion of staff included in the assessment, A showing that
Unemployed:	6%	almost all staff were included and F showing that hardly any were.

Chemistry

The number of universities in the chemistry ranking dipped below 50 for the first time, following a much-publicised series of closures, but the total is back up to the half-century this year. Last year saw the fourth successive increase in applications, a rise of 11 per cent, taking the total over 20,000 for the first time for many years. Although there was a decline at the start of 2008, it was only marginally more than the average for all subjects in a year when the number of choices per applicant had been cut from six to five. Forensic science has become an attractive alternative to the pure subject but, for many, chemistry remains the classic science.

A much-improved set of research assessments in 2001 produced challengers for Cambridge and Oxford for the first time, but the pair lead the ranking again. Both have the maximum research score and average entry grades of more than four As at A level. Durham, the other top research scorer, remains third, while Imperial College London, Bristol and University College London also boast 5* grades with a smaller proportion of academics entered for assessment.

Surrey has a 100 per cent record for graduate employment or further study among its chemists, while Loughborough has the highest level of satisfaction, at 90 per cent. Strathclyde takes over top place in Scotland, while Cardiff wins back the leadership in Wales from Bangor. Queen's, Belfast, is still in the top 20, but no longer the top university outside England.

Chemistry is old university territory, with Huddersfield the only former polytechnic in the top 40. Almost nine out of ten undergraduates have A levels or their equivalent, but entry requirements are not far above the average for all subjects. The unemployment rate, at 6 per cent, is average for higher education as a whole, but chemistry is only just outside the top ten subjects for "positive destinations" after graduation. Almost 80 per cent of leavers either undertake further study or go straight into graduate-level jobs, with only two universities in the table falling below 60 per cent on this measure. Starting salaries are no more than average for all subjects, however.

- European Association for Chemical and Molecular Sciences: **www.euchems.org/**
- Royal Society of Chemistry: **www.rsc.org**
- Society of Dyers and Colourists: **www.sdc.org.uk/**

Chemistry	Research quality/5	Entry standards	Student satisfaction %	Graduate prospects %	Overall rating
1 Cambridge	5*A	539	86	85	100.0
2 Oxford	5*A	513	86	85	98.7
3 Durham	5*A	483	84	84	96.5
4 Southampton	5A	410	86	84	93.1
5 York	5A	412	88	79	92.6
5 Imperial College	5*B	466	81	85	92.6
7 Warwick	5A	426	81	81	90.2
8 Sheffield	5B	390	84	86	90.1
9 Strathclyde	4A	368	83	87	89.2
10 Loughborough	4B	300	90	88	89.0
11 St Andrews	5C	451	83	83	88.9
12 Sussex	5A	391	78	85	88.8
13 Bath	4A	376	80	88	88.0
14 Bristol	5*B	385	82	76	87.7
15 Liverpool	5A	326	82	80	87.4
16 Reading	4A	320	83	83	86.4
=17 Queen's, Belfast	4A	337	82	82	86.1
=17 University College London	5*B	401	78	76	86.1
19 Surrey	3aA	301	77	100	85.9
20 Leicester	4A	339	85	75	85.3
21 Nottingham	5A	358	75	79	84.4
22 Aston	5C	293		91	83.8
=23 Edinburgh	5A	421	77	66	83.7
=23 Cardiff	4A	323	79	81	83.7
25 Glasgow	4C	379	81	82	83.4
26 Manchester	5B	409	77	72	83.0
27 Birmingham	5B	370	72	84	82.8
=28 Aberdeen	3aC	324		93	82.4
=28 Leeds	5B	358	74	80	82.4
=28 Hull	4C	287	84	83	82.4
31 Bradford	4B	267	77	89	81.8
32 East Anglia	5B	342	81	66	80.9
33 Newcastle	4C	336	76	82	79.9
=34 Heriot-Watt	4A	312	75	73	79.4
=34 Keele	3aA	287	78	78	79.4
36 Bangor	3aA	260	79	79	79.1

Chemistry cont.

	Research quality/5	Entry standards	Student satisfaction %	Graduate prospects %	Overall rating
37 Kent		281	75	93	74.3
38 Huddersfield	4C	219	77	71	73.3
39 Brighton	5C	249	71	74	73.2
=40 Plymouth	4C	289	77	62	73.0
=40 Kingston	3aC	225	67	91	73.0
42 Manchester Metropolitan	4A	227	76	57	72.2
43 Northumbria	3bC	275	74	74	71.5
44 Nottingham Trent	3aD	202	68	87	70.2
45 Coventry	4C			66	69.8
46 Queen Mary, London		284	72	76	67.6
47 Sheffield Hallam		252	71	78	66.7
48 West of Scotland	2C			70	64.4
49 Abertay		258		59	60.7
50 Liverpool John Moores		207	67	61	58.4

Employed in graduate job:	34%	Average starting graduate salary:	£19,904
Employed in graduate job and studying:	6%	Average starting non-graduate salary:	£13,886
Studying:	39%		
Employed in non-graduate job and studying:	1%	The letters that appear in the Research Quality column indicate the	
Employed in non-graduate job:	14%	proportion of staff included in the assessment, A showing that	
Unemployed:	6%	almost all staff were included and F showing that hardly any were.	

Civil Engineering

Cambridge continues to lead in civil engineering, having entered the ranking last year for the first time right at the top. The university has a predictably enormous lead over the rest on entry standards and one of the top research grades. Cardiff, which enjoyed an extended period of dominance in civil engineering, remains in second place. Cardiff was one of seven universities considered internationally outstanding in the 2001 Research Assessment Exercise, the others being Bristol, Cambridge, Imperial College, Salford, Southampton and Swansea.

Ulster saw all its civil engineers go straight into graduate-level employment or further training. Surrey almost repeated the feat and more than half of the universities in the table registered "positive destinations" for at least 90 per cent of their leavers. Nationally, civil engineering is among the top ten subjects for job prospects: the 3 per cent unemployment rate is well below average, and over 80 per cent of leavers go straight into graduate work. Average salaries in such jobs are over £22,000.

Loughborough has the most satisfied students, with Portsmouth not far behind. There is a wide spread of entry scores, from more than 500 points at Cambridge to barely 200 at Kingston. More than a quarter of the 40 institutions in the civil engineering table are new universities, but Plymouth is the only one outside the bottom ten.

Only four out of ten undergraduates are admitted with A levels or the equivalent, their grades close to the average for all subjects. The subject has been expanding: a 13 per cent increase in applications at the start of 2007 represented the fourth successive rise, and there was only a small decline in 2008, in spite of the cut in the number of choices per applicant, leaving the total close to 19,000.

- Engineering and Technology Board: **www.etechb.co.uk/**
- Institute of Civil Engineers: **www.ice.org.uk**
- Institution of Structural Engineers: **www.istructe.org/**

Civil Engineering	Research quality/5	Entry standards	Student satisfaction %	Graduate prospects %	Overall rating
1 Cambridge	5*A	536	84	96	100.0
2 Cardiff	5*A	404	82	93	93.6
3 Bristol	5*C	442	84	94	92.4
4 Southampton	5*B	426	82	90	91.4
5 Dundee	5A	385	78	95	90.7
6 Loughborough	4B	352	87	95	90.6
7 Edinburgh	5B	426	76	97	90.1
=8 Sheffield	5B	429	77	93	89.1
=8 Imperial College	5*B	464	72	92	89.1
10 Queen's, Belfast	5B	370	77	96	88.7
11 Nottingham	5A	390	81	86	88.5
12 Bath	5B	443	75	92	88.4
13 Heriot-Watt	4A	380	80	89	87.3
14 Ulster	5A	267	74	100	87.2
15 Swansea	5*B	305	78	91	86.3
16 Surrey	4C	344	76	99	85.5
17 Portsmouth	3aC	256	85	98	85.1
18 Salford	5*A	230	70	97	84.9
19 Liverpool	4A	319	75	93	84.6
20 Newcastle	5B	353	70	94	84.4
21 Bradford	4B	270	75	96	83.2
22 Manchester	5B	399	72	84	82.8
23 University College London	5A	395	71	80	82.5
24 Leeds	5D	352	75	90	81.6
25 City	4B	285	67	95	80.1
26 Birmingham	5C	376	69	86	80.0
27 Aberdeen	4C			89	79.1
28 Glasgow	4C	378	70	85	78.8
29 Plymouth	4E	261	76	92	77.3
30 Strathclyde	4C	361	58	94	77.1
31 Kingston	3aC	204	81	80	74.8
32 Leeds Metropolitan	3aB	215		87	74.3
33 Nottingham Trent	3aB	222	59	96	73.8
34 Northumbria		267	75	89	73.6
35 Coventry	3bC	259	76	79	73.0
36 Brighton	3bC	280	69		72.3

Civil Engineering cont.	Research quality/5	Entry standards	Student satisfaction %	Graduate prospects %	Overall rating
37 Napier	4C			79	71.6
38 West of Scotland	3aC	232		82	71.0
39 East London	2D		79	72	68.7
40 Teesside		218	76	79	68.4

Employed in graduate job:	72%	Average starting graduate salary:	£22,364
Employed in graduate job and studying:	11%	Average starting non-graduate salary:	£17,045
Studying:	7%		
Employed in non-graduate job and studying:	0%	The letters that appear in the Research Quality column indicate the	
Employed in non-graduate job:	7%	proportion of staff included in the assessment, A showing that	
Unemployed:	3%	almost all staff were included and F showing that hardly any were.	

Classics and Ancient History

Oxford and Cambridge have been locked together at the top of the classics table since it was first published five years ago, when their scores were identical. Cambridge maintains its lead in the latest ranking with the best scores in the table for both graduate prospects (shared with Bristol) and entry standards. Like fourth-placed King's College London, both universities took maximum points for teaching and research.

University College London matched the top three with a 5* research rating and nine of the remaining 18 universities reached grade 5. Bristol shares the top employment score for classics with Cambridge. Both saw 82 per cent of leavers go straight into graduate jobs or postgraduate study. However, third-placed Exeter was easily the top performer in the National Student Survey, with 93 per cent of final-year undergraduates satisfied or very satisfied with their course.

Several universities offer the subjects as part of a modular degree scheme. St Andrews remains the clear leader in Scotland, but there is no new university representation on either side of the border. A-level grades in classics are among the highest for any group of subjects, but most universities teach the subject from scratch, as well as to more practised students.

The subjects' reputation for attracting analytical high-fliers helps in the jobs market, but relatively few (33 per cent) go directly into graduate jobs. The 6 per cent unemployment rate six months after graduation is no more than average for all subjects, but the proportion going on to postgraduate courses is high. Average starting salaries of almost £20,000 in graduate jobs are just outside the top 20 subjects. There was a small rise in applications in 2007, but the nearly 18 per cent decline at the official deadline for courses beginning in 2008 was among the highest for any subject.

- Classical Association: **www.classicalassociation.org/**
- Society for the Promotion of Roman Studies: **www.romansociety.org/**

	Research quality/5	Entry standards	Student satisfaction %	Graduate prospects %	Overall rating
1 Cambridge	5*A	498		82	100.0
2 Oxford	5*A	486	89	74	97.7
3 Exeter	5A	395	93	76	93.0
4 King's College London	5*A	409	83	60	88.5
5 Durham	5B	450	80	77	86.9
6 Warwick	5A	431	80	64	86.5
7 St Andrews	5B	451	81	63	84.9
8 Bristol	5B	444	73	82	84.8
9 University College London	5*B	424	76	65	84.0
10 Birmingham	5A	373	84	45	81.3
11 Royal Holloway	5A	335	78	63	80.9
12 Glasgow	4B	361	85	57	78.7
13 Nottingham	4A	402	78	47	78.1
14 Liverpool	4A	331	82	56	77.9
15 Leeds	4B	371	78	63	77.4
16 Edinburgh	4B	439	67	63	75.8
17 Reading	5A	303	74	46	73.8
18 Swansea	4A	318	81	39	73.4
19 Manchester	5B	423	66	32	70.2
20 Newcastle	3aA	400	70	39	69.6
21 Lampeter	3aC	318	75		64.5
22 Kent		256	78	47	57.3

Employed in graduate job:	28%	Average starting graduate salary:	£19,938
Employed in graduate job and studying:	5%	Average starting non-graduate salary:	£14,263
Studying:	26%		
Employed in non-graduate job and studying:	4%	The letters that appear in the Research Quality column indicate the	
Employed in non-graduate job:	30%	proportion of staff included in the assessment, A showing that	
Unemployed:	6%	almost all staff were included and F showing that hardly any were.	

Communication and Media Studies

Communication and media studies are mainly the preserve of the new universities, but the top 13 places are all filled by older institutions. Sheffield has taken over from Loughborough at the head of the table, largely thanks to by far the best student satisfaction score. The 90 per cent satisfaction rating reflects well on Sheffield's journalism course because big city universities tend to lag behind campus institutions in the National Student Survey. Loughborough, which has one of the three 5* research ratings, only slips as far as second. The other research stars are East Anglia, in seventh place, and Goldsmiths, which entered fewer academics for assessment and does not make the top ten.

Queen Mary, University of London, a new entrant since the table was last published two years ago, has easily the best graduate employment score, with more than nine out of

Communication and Media Studies cont.

ten leavers going straight into graduate jobs or continuing with their studies. At three universities, only a quarter of those graduating were as lucky. Central Lancashire is the best-placed of five new universities in the top 20. The ranking contains no fewer than 20 more universities than the last edition.

Third-placed Cardiff remains the top university in Wales, while Stirling has extended its lead in Scotland. Only three universities average more than 400 points at entry, while three average less than 200. Warwick has the highest total, the equivalent of three As at A level and almost another at AS level.

Controversy has raged over the subjects' currency in the employment market, and the division of jobs into graduate and non-graduate hits communication and media studies harder than any other group of subjects. Only one set of subjects has a lower proportion of "positive destinations". Academics in the field argue that it is normal for students completing media courses to take "entry level" work that is not classified as a graduate job. Nevertheless, the subjects are in the bottom five for graduate starting salaries.

The demand for places remains strong. A 10 per cent decline in applications for media studies degrees at the start of 2008 was close to the average for all subjects, following the switch from six choices per applicant to five. Teaching quality assessors in 1996–98 found that courses varied from conventional academic degrees to advanced vocational training. Their main concern was a shortage of resources in a fast-changing area of study.

- Broadcast Journalism Training Council: **www.bjtc.org.uk/**
- Chartered Institute of Journalists: **www.cioj.co.uk/**
- National Union of Journalists: **www.nuj.org.uk/**
- Sector Skills Council for the Audio Visual and Publishing Industries: **www.skillset.org/**

Communication and Media Studies	Research quality/5	Entry standards	Student satisfaction %	Graduate prospects %	Overall rating
1 Sheffield	4C	412	90	73	100.0
2 Loughborough	5*A	358	78	53	93.0
3 Cardiff	5B	383	77	58	91.0
4 Leeds	4C	372	73	73	89.0
5 Warwick	5B	415		40	88.5
6 Leicester	3aB	375		57	86.5
7 East Anglia	5*A	311	78	39	86.3
8 Royal Holloway	5B	363	72	48	84.7
9 Queen Mary, London		336	73	91	83.9
10 Aberystwyth	5B		77	44	83.2
11 Goldsmiths College	5*C	331	69	56	82.2
12 Sussex	4A	380	64	50	82.1
13 Liverpool		389	80	57	81.8
14 Stirling	5C	302		55	81.6
15 Central Lancashire	3bC	304	69	79	81.1
16 Birmingham	3aC	384	68	56	80.5
17 Robert Gordon	3bD	333		63	79.8

18 Glasgow Caledonian	3aB	325	74	48	79.3
19 Nottingham Trent	5D	275	69	69	78.8
20 Bournemouth		347	72	69	77.9
21 King's College London		402		45	77.5
22 Keele		294	71	80	77.3
23 Brunel		294	73	73	76.4
24 Surrey		293	71	74	75.2
25 Napier	3aD	295		54	74.5
26 Westminster	5D	330	63	51	74.2
=27 West of England	4C	284	74	39	74.0
=27 City	3bD	336	62	64	74.0
29 Staffordshire	4D	259	77	43	73.5
30 Oxford Brookes		299	77	53	73.4
=31 Bangor		285		60	72.7
=31 Huddersfield		271	86	41	72.7
33 Leeds Metropolitan	3aD	277	70	52	72.4
34 Lancaster		325	77	45	72.3
=35 Bath Spa	3bC	272	75	43	72.1
=35 Birmingham City		284	72	62	72.1
37 De Montfort	3aB	243	72	42	71.4
38 Hull		306		50	70.6
39 Portsmouth		302	77	40	69.8
40 Ulster	4B	272	63	37	69.3
41 Lincoln		279	74	49	69.1
42 Sunderland	3aD	260	71	42	68.8
43 Greenwich	3bC	212	75	45	68.7
44 University College Falmouth		297	62	65	68.5
45 Canterbury Christ Church		226	77	53	68.4
46 Southampton		365		31	68.1
47 Salford		319	62	57	68.0
=48 Winchester	3aD	271	74	31	67.9
=48 Chichester		300	78	32	67.9
50 Brighton	3bD	284	67	44	67.7
=51 Southampton Solent		260	70	55	67.5
=51 Swansea		276	74	44	67.5
53 Middlesex	3aD	210	71	47	67.3
54 St Mary's College		246	78	42	67.2
55 Liverpool John Moores	3bE	261	70	45	67.0
56 Hertfordshire	1D	276	71		66.9
57 Queen's, Belfast		331	69	37	66.8
58 Northumbria	4D	273	63	41	66.7
59 East London	5D	193	72	39	66.5
=60 York St John		236	83	29	65.5
=60 Marjon, Plymouth		231	74	46	65.5
62 Essex		314	61	50	65.3
63 Sheffield Hallam	3aE	264	64	45	65.2
64 Queen Margaret Edinburgh	2D	229		50	64.7

Communication and Media Studies cont.	Research quality/5	Entry standards	Student satisfaction %	Graduate prospects %	Overall rating
65 Worcester		225	73	46	64.5
66 Coventry	3bE	230	67	46	64.1
67 Wolverhampton	2E	181	77	40	63.8
68 Gloucestershire		264	67	46	63.7
=69 Kingston		237	65	55	63.5
=69 London South Bank	3bD	216	67	44	63.5
71 Thames Valley	1A	206	62	53	61.6
72 Teesside	2A	207	72	25	61.4
73 Buckinghamshire New		217	69	43	61.1
74 Edge Hill		250	68	36	60.6
75 Derby		227		44	60.5
76 Roehampton		207		48	60.4
77 Manchester Metropolitan		241	68	35	60.0
78 Anglia Ruskin		236		40	59.8
=79 UWIC, Cardiff		247	72	25	59.5
=79 Chester		253	62	42	59.5
=81 Bedfordshire	3aE	169	77	21	59.2
=81 Northampton		219	71	33	59.2
83 Glamorgan		237	66	36	59.0
84 University of the Arts, London		255	55	47	57.6
85 West of Scotland		215		30	53.9
86 Cumbria		215	42	50	49.1

Employed in graduate job:	41%	Average starting graduate salary:	£16,947
Employed in graduate job and studying:	3%	Average starting non-graduate salary:	£13,972
Studying:	6%		
Employed in non-graduate job and studying:	3%	The letters that appear in the Research Quality column indicate the
Employed in non-graduate job:	39%	proportion of staff included in the assessment, A showing that
Unemployed:	8%	almost all staff were included and F showing that hardly any were.

Computer Science

There are still 100 institutions in the computing table, but uncertainty in the dotcom economy has had a damaging effect on what was once seen as a guaranteed career path. Applications had stabilised in 2007 and 2008, but only after a prolonged period of decline, in which universities reduced the number of full-time degree places on offer. Only one (much smaller) subject has a higher unemployment rate in the latest figures, which showed 10 per cent of graduates out of work six months after completing a course. The good news for computer scientists is that almost two thirds of leavers still go straight into graduate jobs or further training – about average for all subjects. The rewards are good for those who do find graduate-level work: average starting salaries of almost £21,000 are in the top 20 for all subjects and pay for non-graduate work is in the top ten.

Cambridge remains ahead of Oxford at the top of the table, with higher entry scores and a better employment record. Cambridge also has one of eight 5* research grades, although, at 5* only Edinburgh, Surrey and Salford entered a full complement of academics for the 2001 Research Assessment Exercise. Third-placed Imperial College, York, Manchester and Southampton were the other institutions to reach 5* with a more selective staff entry. Imperial also had the best employment record in the latest survey, a distinction it shared with Bangor.

Five universities – Heriot Watt, Loughborough, Newcastle, Southampton and Strathclyde – tied for the highest levels of satisfaction in the National Student Survey published in 2007. However, three years after graduation, more than a quarter of computing students said they would be "very likely" to choose a different course if they had their time again – the second-highest total among 19 groups of subjects.

Edinburgh has a slim lead over St Andrews as the top Scottish university, while Cardiff remains the top university in Wales. York St John is the best-placed new university, and one of only three in the top 50, the others being Gloucestershire and Central Lancashire. Entry standards for nine universities near the top average more than 400 points, while six of those towards the bottom average less than 180.

- British Computer Society: **www.bcs.org**

Computer Science	Research quality/5	Entry standards	Student satisfaction %	Graduate prospects %	Overall rating
1 Cambridge	5*B	519		92	100.0
2 Oxford	5A	511		86	98.0
3 Imperial College	5*B	475	78	93	95.2
4 Edinburgh	5*A	398	78	84	91.9
5 Southampton	5*B	388	83	83	91.6
6 Surrey	5*A	346	79	89	91.4
=7 St Andrews	5A	403		81	90.5
=7 York	5*B	421	76	88	90.5
9 Bristol	5A	432	78	80	90.3
10 Warwick	5B	436	82	74	89.2
11 Glasgow	5B	363	81	82	88.1
12 University College London	5A	403	75	81	87.7
13 Sheffield	5B	357	78	87	87.2
14 Newcastle	5B	313	83	75	85.1
=15 Cardiff	5A	324	78	72	84.1
=15 Bath	4A	418	72	78	84.1
17 Durham	4B	398	72	85	84.0
18 Loughborough	3aB	307	83	80	83.8
19 Dundee	4A	381	82	59	83.4
20 Manchester	5*B	375	73	73	83.3
21 Aberdeen	4C	336		87	83.0
22 Birmingham	5B	375	76	71	82.7
23 Lancaster	5A	350	76	67	82.6
24 Royal Holloway	5B	259		84	81.8

Computer Science cont.

		Research quality/5	Entry standards	Student satisfaction %	Graduate prospects %	Overall rating
=25	Strathclyde	3aD	363	83	72	81.5
=25	Aberystwyth	4A	252	81	74	81.5
27	Bangor	4B	223		93	81.4
28	Reading	4B	328	77	75	81.2
29	Nottingham	5B	327	72	79	80.9
=30	Sussex	5A	357	68	75	80.8
=30	Kent	4B	290	76	81	80.8
32	Leeds	5D	368	77	75	80.6
=33	King's College London	4B	348	74	76	80.5
=33	Swansea	5B	304	75	75	80.5
35	Heriot-Watt	4A	299	83	58	80.2
36	East Anglia	4B	301	79	67	79.2
37	Liverpool	5B	340		63	78.7
38	Essex	4B	298	76	69	78.0
39	Queen's, Belfast	4A	313	68	77	77.8
40	Exeter	4B	317	69	77	77.2
=41	Aston	5C	274	71	78	76.5
=41	Hull	3aC	237	78	79	76.5
43	Leicester	4B	296	68	79	76.4
44	Salford	5*A	262	71	59	76.2
45	York St John		245		93	75.7
46	Brunel	5B	295	69	60	72.9
47	Keele	3bC	284	72	75	72.8
48	City	4B	256	65	76	72.1
49	Gloucestershire	3aD	242	78	66	72.0
=50	Central Lancashire		246	80	73	71.9
=50	Queen Mary, London	4B	258	71	63	71.9
=52	Robert Gordon	3aD	212		81	71.4
=52	Northumbria	3bC	281	77	59	71.4
54	Plymouth	5E	259	75	66	71.2
55	Ulster	4E	261	75	67	71.0
56	Derby		275		74	69.9
57	West of England	3aC	219	71	70	69.8
=58	Glamorgan	4D	208	76	60	69.4
=58	Oxford Brookes	3bD	227	71	75	69.4
60	De Montfort	4C	190	71	67	69.1
61	Manchester Metropolitan	3aD	246	72	62	67.9
62	Nottingham Trent	3aE	225	64	84	67.7
63	Stirling	3bC	261		62	67.4
64	Brighton	4E	233	66	74	67.2
=65	Hertfordshire	4C	189	69	63	67.0
=65	Sunderland	3aC	245	71	56	67.0
67	Worcester		226	75	66	66.4

=68 Greenwich	4D	180	73	58	65.9
=68 Portsmouth		244	70	72	65.9
=68 Staffordshire		247	71	69	65.9
=68 London South Bank	4D		75	47	65.9
72 Anglia Ruskin		225	77	58	65.7
73 Chester		233	73	66	65.6
=74 Liverpool John Moores	3aB	196	63	68	65.5
=74 Bournemouth	2E	228	66	75	65.5
=76 Napier	3aD	215		63	65.3
=76 Sheffield Hallam	3bE	221	71	63	65.3
78 Bradford	4E	221	69	63	65.2
79 West of Scotland	3aC	273		49	64.9
80 Huddersfield	3aE	241	70	59	64.7
81 Goldsmiths College	3bB	211	67	60	64.6
82 Kingston	3bD	201	68	65	64.1
83 Teesside	2F	270	71	54	63.9
84 Abertay		319		51	63.4
=85 Cumbria		247	64	71	62.5
=85 Buckinghamshire New		224	75	52	62.5
87 East London	2E	176	71	60	62.0
88 Glasgow Caledonian	3bE	274		51	61.9
89 Southampton Solent		174	70	65	61.6
90 Coventry	2E	245		54	60.8
91 Canterbury Christ Church		185	72	54	60.3
92 Edge Hill		183	65	69	60.2
93 Roehampton		185	74	48	59.8
94 Leeds Metropolitan	3bC	221	61	56	59.6
95 Birmingham City		184	68	52	57.2
96 UWCN, Newport		164	67	55	56.9
97 Westminster	3aF	163	66	52	56.6
98 Wolverhampton	2F	163		49	54.0
99 Lincoln		244	56	46	51.9
100 Middlesex	3aE	156	57	48	51.5

Employed in graduate job:	52%	Average starting graduate salary:	£20,935
Employed in graduate job and studying:	4%	Average starting non-graduate salary:	£15,742
Studying:	9%		
Employed in non-graduate job and studying:	2%	The letters that appear in the Research Quality column indicate the	
Employed in non-graduate job:	22%	proportion of staff included in the assessment, A showing that	
Unemployed:	10%	almost all staff were included and F showing that hardly any were.	

Dentistry

Not even medicine can match dentistry's 100 per cent graduate employment rate.
In all but three of the 13 undergraduate dental schools, every leaver was in a graduate job or studying six months after finishing the course. Applications are correspondingly

Dentistry cont.

buoyant: there was a small decline at the start of 2008, but the cut in the number of choices per applicant had much less impact than in most subjects.

Dentistry is not a subject for academic slouches: entrants to every one of the schools averaged more than 400 points on the UCAS tariff. Most demand chemistry and may give preference to candidates who also have biology A level.

Queen's, Belfast, takes over the leadership from Sheffield this year, despite having the lowest research grade at any dental school. Sheffield could hardly be closer, but loses out on entry grades. The top two share the best student satisfaction score. King's College London and Bristol have the two 5* research ratings in dentistry, but relatively low student satisfaction scores keep them out of the top five.

Dundee has overtaken Glasgow to assume top place in Scotland, while Cardiff offers the only dentistry degree in Wales. There are no new universities in the ranking. However, that will change when there are data for Central Lancashire, which opened a purpose-built dental school in 2007. Another has opened at the Peninsula Medical School, in Plymouth and Exeter.

Most degrees last five years, although several universities offer a six-year option for those without the necessary scientific qualifications. Shortages of dentists are such that no university has less than 99 per cent of graduates going into employment or further training. The average starting salary of £28,000 is second only to that enjoyed by doctors. The number of places is growing to tackle shortages in the profession.

- British Dental Association: **www.bda.org.uk**
- Dental Practitioners Association: **www.uk-dentistry.org/**

Dentistry	Research quality/5	Entry standards	Student satisfaction %	Graduate prospects %	Overall rating
1 Queen's, Belfast	3aC	455	87	100	100.0
2 Sheffield	5C	448	87	100	99.8
3 Dundee	5D	454	83	100	99.7
4 Glasgow	3aD	455	80	100	99.5
=5 Leeds	4C	442	75	100	98.9
=5 Cardiff	4C	444	75	100	98.9
=5 Newcastle	5D	457	83	99	98.9
=5 King's College London	5*C	448	70	100	98.9
9 Bristol	5*D	448	70	100	98.8
10 Queen Mary, London	5B	410	73	100	97.9
=11 Liverpool	4C	421	69	100	97.8
=11 Birmingham	4D	442	80	99	97.8
13 Manchester	4B	446	62	99	97.3

Employed in graduate job:	84%	Average starting graduate salary:	£28,030
Employed in graduate job and studying:	16%	Average starting non-graduate salary:	*
Studying:	0%		
Employed in non-graduate job and studying:	0%	The letters that appear in the Research Quality column indicate the	
Employed in non-graduate job:	0%	proportion of staff included in the assessment, A showing that	
Unemployed:	0%	almost all staff were included and F showing that hardly any were.	

Drama, Dance and Cinematics

Warwick retains the leadership of a thriving group of subjects, with high entry standards and one of the two 5* research grades, even though fewer than half of its graduates found graduate-level jobs or started another course within six months. Employment levels are low throughout most of the table, although UWIC, Cardiff, which was the only university ever to register full employment or further training among graduates in these subjects, managed 91 per cent "positive destinations".

Bristol, which drops to third place from second last year, has the other 5* research grade, as well as sharing the highest entry standards with Warwick. Glasgow moves up to separate the two research stars with one of the best employment scores – albeit still only registering "positive destinations" for two thirds of its graduates. The most satisfied students are at Bishop Grosseteste University College, in Lincoln, with University College Falmouth the only institution to get within five points on this measure.

UWIC is the top post-1992 university and has been joined by Queen Margaret University in Edinburgh in the top 20. The leading group also includes the Central School of Speech and Drama, which is part of the University of London.

This is another table where the gulf in qualifications between entrants to new and old universities is evident, although for drama and dance in particular, this is unlikely to be the main criterion for selection. Entry standards have been rising: there are now only two out of nearly 80 institutions where the average is less than 200 points. But the average tariff score remains the lowest in any of the subject tables.

Drama, dance and cinematics also have the lowest proportion of "positive destinations" of any group of subjects, despite an unemployment rate that is on the average of 6 per cent, and the subjects are only one place off the bottom of the earnings league for new graduates. Freelancing and periods of temporary employment are common throughout the performing arts, but this does not seem to put off prospective students. Drama is one of the top 15 subjects in terms of applications, while dance and cinematics had both weathered the switch from six choices per applicant to five better than most subjects at the start of 2008.

- The Stage: **www.thestage.co.uk**
- UKP-Arts: **www.ukperformingarts.co.uk/**

Drama, Dance and Cinematics	Research quality/5	Entry standards	Student satisfaction %	Graduate prospects %	Overall rating
1 Warwick	5*B	420	84	49	100.0
2 Glasgow	4B	391	79	66	96.7
3 Bristol	5*A	420	65	57	96.4
4 Surrey	4A	352	72	76	96.1
5 East Anglia	4A	375	83	52	95.0
6 Royal Holloway	5B	406	76	53	94.7
7 Exeter	4B	389	84	50	93.8
8 Kent	5B	333	81	56	92.7
9 Lancaster	4A	390	73	53	91.6
10 Loughborough	5C	388	71	56	89.5

Drama, Dance and Cinematics cont.	Research quality/5	Entry standards	Student satisfaction %	Graduate prospects %	Overall rating
11 Birmingham	4C	413	72	52	88.4
12 Essex	4B	307	75	64	88.3
13 Goldsmiths College	4A	352	71	50	87.4
14 Manchester	5C	419	68	48	87.3
15 Central School of Speech and Drama	2D	328	75	80	87.2
16 Reading	5B	329	80	40	87.0
17 UWIC, Cardiff		266	81	91	86.9
18 Hull	4C	344	71	63	86.5
19 Aberystwyth	5B	287	78	46	84.8
20 Queen Margaret Edinburgh	3aD	276		75	84.1
21 Bishop Grosseteste University College		286	92	58	83.0
22 University College Falmouth		245	88	65	80.7
23 Middlesex	3aD	313	71	61	80.5
24 Brighton	5B	305	68	43	80.3
25 Queen Mary, London		373	82	47	80.2
26 Chichester	3aA	299	66	53	79.5
27 Aberdeen		318		62	79.4
28 Huddersfield	3aD	258	82	52	79.1
29 Queen's, Belfast	3bA	341	65	51	78.6
=30 Ulster	3aB	224	74	56	77.4
=30 Birmingham City		286	74	67	77.4
32 Brunel	3aB	290	70	45	76.9
33 Manchester Metropolitan	3aD	269	75	50	75.9
34 Nottingham Trent	5C	267	60	57	75.7
35 Roehampton	4B	250	71	43	75.6
36 Cumbria		303	82	45	75.2
37 Bournemouth	3bD		66	63	75.1
38 De Montfort	3aC	259	67	55	74.5
=39 Bangor		313	72	55	74.2
=39 Westminster		301	74	55	74.2
41 Worcester	3aC	228	77	40	72.5
42 Oxford Brookes		302	74	49	72.4
43 Liverpool John Moores	2E	275	71	54	72.2
44 University of the Arts, London		323	64	56	71.5
45 Sunderland	2D	257	71	51	71.1
46 Glamorgan	2C	272	70	46	71.0
47 Leeds		339	60	57	70.7
48 Northampton	3bA	216	73	40	70.6
49 Hertfordshire		240	77	52	70.3
50 Canterbury Christ Church		290	74	42	69.4
51 Salford		288	62	59	69.1
52 Leeds Metropolitan		266	70	50	68.5
=53 Plymouth		237	81	40	68.3

=53 St Mary's College		252	73	49	68.3
55 Winchester	3bD	264	71	36	68.2
56 Central Lancashire		269	66	53	67.7
57 West of England		266	75	40	67.6
58 Portsmouth		278	68	46	67.0
=59 Coventry		244	76	42	66.9
=59 Thames Valley		231	57	72	66.9
=61 Kingston		247	69	48	65.9
=61 Chester		284	70	39	65.9
63 York St John	3bE	282	61	44	65.5
64 Gloucestershire		277	69	37	64.6
65 Sheffield Hallam		302	69	30	63.7
66 London South Bank		232	71	41	63.6
67 Bath Spa		266	64	43	63.0
68 Derby		278	69	30	62.2
69 Anglia Ruskin		227	77	25	61.3
70 Southampton Solent		248	70	32	60.9
71 Wolverhampton		185	66	47	59.5
72 Staffordshire		221	76	23	59.4
73 Northumbria	2C	246	41	59	59.2
74 Edge Hill		246	61	36	58.4
75 Buckinghamshire New		182	71	35	58.2
76 Bedfordshire		213	64	37	57.6
77 East London		224		36	57.2
78 Lincoln		272	48	44	56.0

Employed in graduate job:	36%	Average starting graduate salary:	£16,563
Employed in graduate job and studying:	4%	Average starting non-graduate salary:	£13,874
Studying:	9%		
Employed in non-graduate job and studying:	4%	The letters that appear in the Research Quality column indicate the	
Employed in non-graduate job:	39%	proportion of staff included in the assessment, A showing that	
Unemployed:	8%	almost all staff were included and F showing that hardly any were.	

East and South Asian Studies

The select group of universities offering East and South Asian studies now has ten members, compared with seven when the table was last published two years ago. The number may well grow, with the clamour for more interaction with China and India. However, student numbers are small as yet – fewer than 4,000 students take the languages at any level of higher education. Yet more than half those completing degrees go straight into graduate jobs and starting salaries are in the top 20 for all subjects, at more than £21,000.

Japanese is still the biggest draw, with almost 1,000 applications by the official deadline for courses beginning in 2008, but burgeoning interest in all things Chinese can be expected to have an effect before long. Applications for Chinese studies grew in 2006 and 2007, but the latest UCAS statistics showed a surprising downturn, with only 636 applications.

East and South Asian Studies cont.

Cambridge is well clear at the top of the table, with the most satisfied students and easily the best employment record. Second-placed Oxford is, like Cambridge, rated internationally outstanding for research. Edinburgh is the only university outside England in the ranking, while Westminster is the only new university.

Four out of five students enter with tariff scores that are above average for all subjects, so degree classifications are also high. Most undergraduates learn their chosen language from scratch, although universities expect to see evidence of potential in other modern language qualifications.

- Association of South-East Asian Studies (UK): **mercury.soas.ac.uk/aseasuk**
- British Association for Chinese Studies: **www.bacsuk.org.uk/**
- British Association for Japanese Studies: **www.bajs.org.uk/**
- British Association for Korean Studies: **www.dur.ac.uk/BAKS/**
- British Association for South Asian Studies: **www.basas.ac.uk**
- Royal Asiatic Society: **http://royalasiaticsociety.org/**
- Royal Society for Asian Affairs: **www.rsaa.org.uk/**

East and South Asian Studies	Research quality/5	Entry standards	Student satisfaction %	Graduate prospects %	Overall rating
1 Cambridge	5*B	500	87	81	100.0
2 Oxford	5*B	498	82	68	92.0
3 School of Oriental and African Studies	5B	378	68	76	84.1
4 Edinburgh	5B	457	68	65	82.0
5 Nottingham	5B	387	76	63	81.9
6 Sheffield	4D	408	86	64	80.9
7 Leeds	5C	387	74	67	80.2
8 Durham	4C		74	67	78.3
9 Central Lancashire		236	77	55	61.8
10 Westminster	5E	270	61		61.4

Employed in graduate job:	47%	Average starting graduate salary:	£21,311
Employed in graduate job and studying:	5%	Average starting non-graduate salary:	£15,909
Studying:	15%		
Employed in non-graduate job and studying:	1%	The letters that appear in the Research Quality column indicate the	
Employed in non-graduate job:	23%	proportion of staff included in the assessment, A showing that	
Unemployed:	9%	almost all staff were included and F showing that hardly any were.	

Economics

Cambridge has won back the top place in economics that it lost to the London School of Economics two years ago. Although not one of the top scorers for research, Cambridge has the highest entry standards and the best employment record. Second-placed LSE has one of the five 5* research grades, the others having gone to Warwick, Essex, Lancaster and University College London. However, the most satisfied students are at the University of East Anglia, which does not make the top ten overall.

A total of 15 English universities offering economics achieved maximum points for teaching quality – among them the new universities of Leeds Metropolitan, Oxford Brookes and Staffordshire – but all teaching scores are no longer used in the table because of their age. Portsmouth, in 43rd place, is now the leading new university, with Coventry the only other representative of the sector in the top 50.

St Andrews is the leading university in Scotland, in twelfth place, while Cardiff is the leader in Wales. Birmingham has made the most progress in the upper reaches of the table, jumping 11 places to seventh with the second-best student satisfaction score, while Bath has moved in the opposite direction.

Economics remains a popular option for undergraduates, with more than 38,000 applications at the start of 2008, when it was one of the few subjects to register an increase in demand for places. Employers look favourably because they see it as combining the skills of the sciences and the arts. Indeed, many prospective students underestimate the mathematical skills required for an economics degree.

Starting salaries are in the top four for all subjects, averaging nearly £24,500 for graduate-level jobs and over £16,500 for other types of employment. But economics is not the sure-fire bet for a good job that many assume it to be: almost 30 per cent of leavers are in non-graduate jobs or unemployed after six months.

- Economics and Business Education Association: **www.ebea.org.uk/**
- Royal Economics Society: **www.res.org.uk/**
- Why Study? Economics: **www.whystudyeconomics.ac.uk**

Economics	Research quality/5	Entry standards	Student satisfaction %	Graduate prospects %	Overall rating
1 Cambridge	5B	528		93	100.0
2 London School of Economics	5*A	510	74	89	97.5
3 Oxford	5B	512	84	84	97.1
4 University College London	5*A	459	72	87	93.9
5 Warwick	5*B	473	73	90	93.2
6 Durham	4B	462	79	82	90.5
7 Birmingham	4B	410	85	77	90.4
8 Nottingham	5A	453	72	81	90.0
9 Bristol	4A	458	73	84	89.4
10 Exeter	5B	397	81	73	88.6
11 East Anglia	4B	327	89	72	88.1
12 St Andrews	4B	430	76	80	87.2
13 York	5A	448	71	71	86.6
14 Lancaster	5*B	394	75	69	85.9
15 Bath	5B	441	70	77	85.1
16 Loughborough	3aB	374	82	72	84.4
17 Southampton	5A	399	67	75	83.9
18 Glasgow	4B	413	76	71	83.8
19 Essex	5*B	337	76	65	83.0
20 Leicester	5B	325	81	62	82.9
21 Kent	4A	286	80	68	82.7

Economics cont.	Research quality/5	Entry standards	Student satisfaction %	Graduate prospects %	Overall rating
22 Edinburgh	4B	442	68	77	82.2
23 Royal Holloway	4B	348	73	78	82.1
24 Surrey	3aA	286	75	83	81.8
25 Cardiff	5B	394	73	65	81.6
25 Hull	4C	290	81	76	81.6
27 Sussex	4B	350	75	73	81.5
28 School of Oriental and African Studies	4B	360	69	79	80.8
=29 Strathclyde	4C	385	82	57	80.7
=29 Leeds	5C	413	70	72	80.7
31 Keele	3aA	276	73	83	80.1
32 Newcastle	4C	394	69	77	79.6
33 Aberdeen	3aA	292		71	77.9
34 Queen Mary, London	5B	351	66	66	77.0
=35 Swansea	4A	278	75	58	76.8
=35 Reading	5C	320	72	66	76.8
37 Stirling	4A	279		62	76.7
38 Sheffield	3aB	369	71	66	76.6
39 Manchester	4B	397	68	59	75.7
40 Ulster	4C	287	80	54	75.1
41 City	3aB	333	67	70	74.1
42 Liverpool	4B	361	64	65	74.0
43 Portsmouth	4C	240	78	56	73.2
44 Heriot-Watt	4D	298	72	67	73.0
45 Queen's, Belfast	4B	347	67	56	72.8
46 Dundee	3aA	300	73	49	72.3
47 Brunel	4A	304	63	60	72.1
48 Bradford	3bD	207	79	69	72.0
49 Salford	3aB		74	53	71.4
50 Coventry		228	84	65	70.9
51 Manchester Metropolitan	3aC	274	70	64	70.5
52 Nottingham Trent	3bD	229	72	71	69.5
53 Liverpool John Moores		251	77	68	68.7
54 East London	3aD	176	75	63	68.1
55 Aberystwyth	3bC	279	78	44	67.9
56 Northumbria	3bE	268	71	60	66.0
57 West of England		242	80	52	65.9
58 Hertfordshire	3aC	228	68	54	65.1
=59 Leeds Metropolitan		235	76	57	64.3
=59 Plymouth	3bE	231	75	50	64.3
61 Oxford Brookes		300	70	58	64.1
62 Greenwich	3bF	209	70	46	58.4
63 Kingston		183	65	56	56.7
64 Middlesex		175	61	64	56.3

Employed in graduate job:	42%	
Employed in graduate job and studying:	14%	
Studying:	15%	
Employed in non-graduate job and studying:	3%	
Employed in non-graduate job:	20%	
Unemployed:	6%	

Average starting graduate salary:	£24,466
Average starting non-graduate salary:	£16,587

The letters that appear in the Research Quality column indicate the proportion of staff included in the assessment, A showing that almost all staff were included and F showing that hardly any were.

Education

This is the only ranking that still contains teaching scores – because teacher training assessments by Ofsted remain current. Cambridge heads the table with the best performance in those assessments, as well as the highest entry standards in England. Second-placed Aberdeen, last year's leader, is the only university to register 100 per cent positive destinations, although a dozen others reached the 90 per cent mark.

Two of last year's top three – Oxford and Bristol – have dropped out of the table this year because, like several other universities, they offer only postgraduate courses in education. As such, they are not included in the National Student Survey for the subject and neither entry scores nor graduate destinations are comparable. Since Bristol has one of the two 5* research grades, that leaves Cardiff the clear leader for research. The most satisfied students are at Aberystwyth, while Brighton is the highest-placed new university and only just misses a place in the top ten.

Overall, education scores highly on employment and student satisfaction. Employment scores at different universities reflect to some extent the differences in demand for new staff in primary and secondary schools and in different parts of the UK. But even in the bottom ten, there are universities where at least eight out of ten leavers went straight into graduate jobs or further study. Low entry scores have been a concern in the past, but only one university averages less than 200 points in the latest table, while most score more than 250.

Satisfaction levels are high, not only among the final-year undergraduates who complete the National Student Survey, but also in the early stage of careers. Three years after graduation, those with education degrees were among the most satisfied at work and least inclined to wish they had taken a different subject.

The 3 per cent unemployment level is among the lowest for any subject, and eight out of ten of all those completing teacher training courses went into schools or postgraduate study. However, education has slipped down the earnings league. The average starting salary of £19,585 for those in graduate jobs is only just in the top 30 for all subjects, compared with 20th last year.

Education remains among the ten most popular subjects at undergraduate level, even though the postgraduate route into teaching has become the norm for secondary training and has been growing for primary. Numbers were down by marginally more than the average for all subjects at the start of 2008.

- Education Institute of Scotland: **www.eis.org.uk/**
- Graduate Teacher Training Registry (GTTR): **www.gttr.ac.uk/**
- NAS UWT: **www.nasuwt.org.uk/**
- National Union of Teachers: **www.teachers.org.uk/**
- TeacherNet: **www.teachernet.gov.uk/**
- Training and Development Agency for Schools: **www.tda.gov.uk**

Education

	Research quality/5	Teaching quality/5	Entry standards	Student satisfaction %	Graduate prospects %	Overall rating
1 Cambridge	5B	3.8	447	83	95	100.0
2 Aberdeen	5A		366		100	94.5
3 Exeter	5C	3.7	348	83	70	89.6
4 Dundee	3aA		329	78	91	88.2
5 Stirling	4C		297		97	86.7
6 Edinburgh	4D		368	71	93	85.3
7 Manchester	4C	3.7	359	78	53	84.7
8 Cardiff	5*A		354	68	65	84.5
9 Warwick	4B	3.3	340	73	77	84.0
10 Durham	5C	3.0	371	69	91	83.6
11 Aberystwyth	3aB		281	86	69	83.5
12 Brighton	3bD	3.3	303	77	95	83.2
13 Canterbury Christ Church	3aE	3.7	310	67	91	82.3
14 Glasgow	4F		328	72	98	81.9
15 Birmingham City	3bF	3.3	290	82	84	81.4
16 Sussex	5B	3.0			75	81.2
=17 Hull	3aD	3.2	260	78	90	80.9
=17 Birmingham	5B	3.2	344	73	56	80.9
19 Swansea	3aB			84	57	80.5
20 Strathclyde	4E		320	71	89	80.3
21 Oxford Brookes	3bE	3.2	289	82	77	80.1
22 Edge Hill	3bF	3.3	276	77	88	79.6
23 Reading	3aC	3.0	289	70	94	79.3
24 Northumbria	3bE	3.5	294	74	69	78.5
25 St Mary's College		3.0	289	79	89	78.4
=26 Brunel	3aC	3.0		70	92	78.3
=26 Leeds	4B	3.0	354	72	55	78.3
=28 Kingston		3.0	239	85	88	78.1
=28 UWIC, Cardiff			258	79	85	78.1
30 Sunderland	3aF	3.3	260	72	90	77.9
=31 Goldsmiths College	4C	2.8	239	74	95	77.8
=31 Winchester	3bE	3.3	272	74	80	77.8
33 Hertfordshire	3bE	3.0	265	82	78	77.7
34 York	4B	2.7	354	75	59	77.6
=35 Chichester	2D	3.0	254	81	82	77.4
=35 Nottingham Trent	3bD	3.0	287	77	78	77.4
37 Bishop Grosseteste UC		2.5	344	79	91	77.3
38 Newman		3.2	244	79	86	77.1
39 Manchester Metropolitan	4E	3.2	284	69	81	76.9
40 York St John		3.2	275	75	83	76.8
41 Keele	3aB	3.0	289	79	53	76.6
=42 Northampton	3bE	3.3	244	77	73	76.5
=42 Bangor	3aF		252	77	82	76.5

=42 Plymouth	3aE	3.3	246	78	69	76.5
45 Worcester	3bD	3.0	273	76	77	76.4
46 Marjon, Plymouth	2F	3.2	238	78	81	76.2
47 De Montfort			241	77	83	75.8
48 Bedfordshire		3.3	253	73	81	75.6
49 UWCN, Newport			243	76	82	75.3
=50 Cumbria	3bE		274	68	87	75.1
=50 Sheffield Hallam	3aE	3.2	285	68	75	75.1
=52 Wolverhampton	2F	3.3	216	76	79	74.9
=52 Roehampton	3aE	3.2	234	77	69	74.9
54 Chester		3.0	268	77	75	74.4
55 Liverpool John Moores	3bF	3.3	244	74	67	73.7
56 Derby	3bD	3.0	259	76	64	73.5
=57 Gloucestershire	3aE	2.8	258	71	84	73.4
=57 Anglia Ruskin	3bD	3.0	288	64	80	73.4
59 West of England	3aE	3.2	246	64	78	72.3
60 Central Lancashire	3bC		240	70	69	72.1
61 Middlesex	2D	3.0	205	67	91	71.8
62 Leeds Metropolitan	3aE	2.8	279	71	68	71.7
63 Bath Spa	2F	2.7	266	75	74	71.3
64 Greenwich	3aE	3.0	211	59	83	68.5
65 London South Bank	4B	2.5			50	66.3
66 Huddersfield	3bE	3.0			49	65.6
67 East London	3bD	3.0	153	64	61	64.1
68 Essex			268	53	63	61.5

Employed in graduate job:	64%		Average starting graduate salary:	£19,585
Employed in graduate job and studying:	4%		Average starting non-graduate salary:	£13,143
Studying:	10%			
Employed in non-graduate job and studying:	2%		The letters that appear in the Research Quality column indicate the	
Employed in non-graduate job:	16%		proportion of staff included in the assessment, A showing that	
Unemployed:	3%		almost all staff were included and F showing that hardly any were.	

Electrical and Electronic Engineering

Cambridge sweeps the board in electrical and electronic engineering, again extending
its lead over Southampton with by far the highest entry standards in the table, the best
destinations score and the most satisfied students. It also has one of the seven 5*
research grades awarded in 2001. Southampton has another of the 5* research grades,
but the rest are spread quite widely: Surrey, Sheffield and Edinburgh are in the top ten,
while Manchester is 12th and Leeds, which entered a relatively small proportion of its
academics, 16th.

Strathclyde has been overtaken by Edinburgh as the top university in Scotland,
while Cardiff again takes the honours in Wales. Robert Gordon is the leading new
university and the only one in the top 30 of a table where old universities predominate.

Both entry standards and employment rates vary considerably among the 67
universities in the table. While 20 institutions saw at least 80 per cent of leavers go
straight into graduate jobs or further training, the proportion dropped below half at

Electrical and Electronic Engineering cont.

eight others. Similarly, six universities average more than 400 points at entry, but four dip below 200.

Like computing, the subjects have suffered from troubles in high-tech industries: applications were down by more than 15 per cent at the start of 2008, when the number of choices per applicant dropped from six to five. Almost 600 entrants (12 per cent) secured a place in Clearing in 2006. About half of the students – more in electrical engineering – come with qualifications other than A levels. Yet it is electrical engineering which has the higher proportion of firsts and 2:1s.

Although more than half of the leavers nationally go straight into graduate jobs, the unemployment rate is high, at 10 per cent. For those who do find graduate work, the average starting salary of £21,655 is in the top 15 for all subjects.

- Institution of Electrical Engineers: **www.iee.org**
- Institution of Engineering and Technology: **www.theiet.org/**

Electrical and Electronic Engineering	Research quality/5	Entry standards	Student satisfaction %	Graduate prospects %	Overall rating
1 Cambridge	5*A	536	84	96	100.0
2 Southampton	5*A	404	82	84	90.6
3 Imperial College	5B	463	82	83	89.4
4 Surrey	5*A	340	83	81	87.8
5 Bristol	5A	417	78	83	86.8
6 Edinburgh	5*B	419	75	87	86.2
7 Loughborough	5B	339	83	89	85.9
=8 Sheffield	5*B	354	79	88	85.8
=8 Queen's, Belfast	5A	351	79	87	85.8
10 Strathclyde	5B	388	83	76	85.3
11 Newcastle	5A	354	75	86	83.5
12 Manchester	5*B	358		73	82.4
13 University College London	5A	391	70	83	81.9
14 Cardiff	5A	360	76	70	80.8
15 Essex	5B		75	82	80.6
16 Leeds	5*D	372	78	82	80.3
17 Nottingham	4A	331	74	84	80.0
18 Birmingham	5C	408	77	72	79.9
19 Bath	4C	331	81	81	79.6
20 Liverpool	5A	362	71	72	79.0
21 York	3aA	378	76	73	78.5
22 Heriot-Watt	4B	335	75	80	78.0
23 Reading	5B	326	74	74	77.5
24 Glasgow	5B	379	74	61	76.9
25 Kent	4C		80	68	76.3
26 Robert Gordon	3bD	353		85	75.0
=27 Hull	4C	243	76	87	74.8
=27 King's College London	5D	311	76	76	74.8

29 Brunel	5B	302	74	66	74.7
30 Sussex	5B		70	73	74.5
31 Aberdeen	4C			74	74.0
32 Warwick	5B	382	61	75	73.2
33 Ulster	3bA	232	81	72	73.1
34 Bangor	4B			62	71.6
35 Aston	5C	305	65	80	71.3
=36 Swansea	4C	253	71	79	70.9
=36 Plymouth	4E	259	83	64	70.9
38 Bradford	4E	252	79	74	70.7
39 Aberystwyth	2A		73	76	70.5
40 Queen Mary, London	3aB	242	78	63	70.4
41 Westminster	4D	234	84	47	68.3
42 Coventry	3aC	252	76	58	67.9
43 Central Lancashire	3aE	267	76		66.7
44 West of England		276	71	80	66.1
45 Northumbria	3bC	262	74	54	64.9
46 Portsmouth	2E	227	72	73	64.2
47 Hertfordshire	3aD	195	74	56	62.9
48 Liverpool John Moores	3aD		70	57	62.7
49 City	3aC	201	69	61	62.5
50 Greenwich	3aB		66	54	62.2
51 East London	2D		78	39	60.7
52 Bolton		209	71	67	60.2
53 Oxford Brookes		211	68	71	59.9
=54 Manchester Metropolitan		208	77	50	59.8
=54 Huddersfield	3bF	277	71	48	59.8
56 Teesside		225	76	46	59.1
57 Derby		290	64	60	58.5
58 De Montfort	3aC	161	61	67	57.8
59 Birmingham City		234		55	57.5
60 Nottingham Trent	3aE	251	59	63	57.4
61 West of Scotland	3aC			41	57.1
62 Glasgow Caledonian	2C			50	56.1
63 Sheffield Hallam		188	69	56	55.9
64 Anglia Ruskin	2C		62	53	54.2
65 UWIC, Cardiff		190	68	41	52.1
66 London South Bank	4D		63	32	51.8
67 Glamorgan		210	64	28	48.3

Employed in graduate job:	51%
Employed in graduate job and studying:	5%
Studying:	13%
Employed in non-graduate job and studying:	2%
Employed in non-graduate job:	19%
Unemployed:	10%

Average starting graduate salary:	£21,656
Average starting non-graduate salary:	£17,335

The letters that appear in the Research Quality column indicate the proportion of staff included in the assessment, A showing that almost all staff were included and F showing that hardly any were.

English

English is one of those rare tables in which Oxford and Cambridge do not have the highest entry standards. Durham is ahead of both and, with strong scores on the other measures as well, retains the leadership for the third year in a row. All the top six – and seven others – are rated internationally outstanding for research. Leicester, one of only two members of the top ten without a 5* rating, has the most satisfied students at any university, although even that score is eclipsed by Bishop Grosseteste University College, in Lincoln, where nine out of ten undergraduates were satisfied or very satisfied with their course. The college almost makes the top 30 as a result and is the highest-placed institution outside the old universities.

Employment levels are comparatively low at many institutions: English is one of the few tables in which no university registers 80 per cent "positive destinations" for its graduates. Second-placed University College London and Brighton, in 81st position, come closest with 77 per cent of leavers finding graduate-level work or continuing their studies within six months. Brighton has had the best destinations score for the last four years, but suffers in the table for not having entered the 2001 Research Assessment Exercise in English.

English commands notoriously high entry grades. No fewer than 20 universities average more than 400 points in this year's table, while only three have average scores below 200 points. The subject remains among the top four degree choices, with 50,000 applications by the official deadline for courses beginning in 2008.

The subject produced among the best results in the National Student Survey published in 2007, most universities finding that at least 70 per cent of students were satisfied or very satisfied. Cardiff is clearly the leading university in Wales, while St Andrews has widened its lead over Edinburgh in Scotland.

The proportion of English students gaining a first or 2:1, at seven out of ten, is among the highest in any subject. A third of all graduates go on to further study, either full or part-time, and the 6 per cent unemployment rate is average for all subjects. But more than a third of those completing English degrees in 2006 were in non-graduate jobs six months later. The table shows big variations, with a minority of students at 20 universities finding graduate jobs or study places within six months of graduation.

- Alliance of Literary Societies: **www.alllitsoc.org.uk/**
- Poetry Society: **www.poetrysociety.org.uk/**
- Royal Society of Literature: **www.rslit.org/**
- Society of Authors: **www.societyofauthors.org/**
- Society for Editors and Proofreaders: **www.sfep.org.uk/**
- Teaching English as a Foreign Language: **www.eflweb.com**

English	Research quality/5	Entry standards	Student satisfaction %	Graduate prospects %	Overall rating
1 Durham	5*A	499	85	76	100.0
2 University College London	5*A	478	83	77	98.7
3 Oxford	5*A	475	86	71	98.6

4 Cambridge	5*B	470		73	96.3
5 St Andrews	5*B	466	81	75	94.5
6 Leeds	5*A	440	82	64	92.8
7 Leicester	5A	375	89	62	92.4
8 York	5*A	472	75	67	91.2
9 Warwick	5*B	454	78	70	90.7
10 Exeter	5B	421	85	61	89.7
11 Edinburgh	5*A	423	77	63	89.6
12 Southampton	5A	382	84	59	89.0
=13 Glasgow	5*B	396	83	61	88.7
=13 Royal Holloway	5A	412	78	66	88.7
15 Nottingham	5A	439	77	65	88.5
16 Liverpool	5*B	416	82	58	88.3
17 Cardiff	5*B	397	83	56	87.9
18 Queen Mary, London	5A	366	81	64	87.7
19 Dundee	4A	342	85	62	87.3
=20 Loughborough	5C	361	88	59	86.9
=20 Hull	5B	323	81	72	86.9
=22 Newcastle	5A	418	75	65	86.4
=22 Lancaster	5A	400	80	56	86.4
=24 Aberdeen	4B	328		75	86.3
=24 Bristol	5C	458	76	68	86.3
26 Queen's, Belfast	5A	347	79	64	86.0
27 Kent	5B	332	83	64	85.9
28 East Anglia	5B	379	81	58	84.9
29 Goldsmiths College	5A	348	76	64	84.4
30 Stirling	5B	313		67	84.3
=31 Bishop Grosseteste University College		304	90	76	83.9
=31 Reading	5*B	354	83	48	83.9
33 King's College London	4B	420	78	58	83.5
34 Sheffield	5B	432	74	59	83.4
35 Keele	5B	322	76	67	82.4
=36 De Montfort	5A	266	80	58	82.2
=36 Oxford Brookes	5C	339	78	66	82.2
38 Newman	3bD	252	81	85	81.9
39 Essex	4B	312	81	59	81.1
40 Lampeter	5B	304	77	60	80.7
41 Aberystwyth	4B	324	84	48	80.4
42 Hertfordshire	3aB	278	77	70	79.8
43 Swansea	4A	323	78	48	78.9
44 Birmingham City	3aD	268	81	68	78.4
45 Manchester	5B	421	70	52	78.3
46 Sussex	5B	423	67	57	78.1
47 Gloucestershire	4A	276	82	41	77.4
48 Birmingham	5C	413	68	59	77.2
=49 Bolton	3aC	182	83	64	77.0
=49 Central Lancashire	3aC	260	80	62	77.0

English cont.

	Research quality/5	Entry standards	Student satisfaction %	Graduate prospects %	Overall rating
=51 Salford	5A	278	74	50	76.9
=51 Nottingham Trent	5C	254	74	66	76.9
=53 Strathclyde	5B	342	69	57	76.8
=53 West of England	4B	278	75	59	76.8
55 Portsmouth	4C	307	79	52	76.5
56 Edge Hill	3bD	265	83	56	75.4
57 Manchester Metropolitan	4C	318	75	53	75.2
=58 Roehampton	4B	240	73	61	74.9
=58 Chichester	3aA	291		50	74.9
60 Bangor	4B	322	73	50	74.8
61 Middlesex	4D	246	75	65	74.6
=62 Northumbria	3aC	304	77	52	74.3
=62 University college falmouth	3bB	271		61	74.3
64 Bath Spa	4B	299	74	49	74.2
65 Sunderland	4C	242	77	56	74.1
=66 Bedfordshire		242	80	70	74.0
=66 Chester	2C	304	82	50	74.0
68 London South Bank	4B			48	73.7
=69 Glamorgan	4B	245	78	45	73.2
=69 Anglia Ruskin	5C	272	69	59	73.2
=69 Winchester	3aD	275	81	49	73.2
72 St Mary's College	4D	238	80	51	73.1
73 Sheffield Hallam	4B	294	76	42	73.0
74 Brunel	3aB	305	73	51	72.9
75 Kingston	3aB	240	78	47	72.4
76 Plymouth	3aB	286	78	39	72.0
77 Ulster	4C	252	75	50	71.9
78 York St John	3bD	279	75	59	71.7
79 Marjon, Plymouth	3aE	220	83	48	71.2
80 Worcester	3bC	263	73	58	71.1
81 Brighton		292	68	77	70.9
=82 Liverpool John Moores	4C	247	77	43	70.8
=82 Huddersfield	3aC	293	76	42	70.8
=84 Teesside		269	80	50	69.7
=84 UWCN, Newport		232	78	60	69.7
86 Cumbria		276	69	73	69.6
87 Staffordshire	3aD	246	75	50	69.3
88 Northampton	4C	215	74	46	69.1
89 Westminster	3bD	239	73	53	68.1
90 Bradford		210	77	53	66.6
91 Derby		256	80	40	66.1
92 Leeds Metropolitan		273	71	54	65.3
93 Canterbury Christ Church		251	77	42	65.0

94 Greenwich	222	78	43	64.4
95 Lincoln	278	72	44	63.9
96 Buckinghamshire New	189	73	44	61.1
97 Wolverhampton	191	73	45	61.0

Employed in graduate job:	30%	Average starting graduate salary:	£17,803
Employed in graduate job and studying:	3%	Average starting non-graduate salary:	£13,794
Studying:	23%		
Employed in non-graduate job and studying:	5%	The letters that appear in the Research Quality column indicate the	
Employed in non-graduate job:	33%	proportion of staff included in the assessment, A showing that	
Unemployed:	6%	almost all staff were included and F showing that hardly any were.	

Food Science

Surrey stays on top of the food science table, with the best research score in the subject and the best employment record. Only Leeds, in eighth place, can match Surrey's 5* research grade and it entered a much smaller proportion of its academics in the last Research Assessment Exercise. King's College London has overtaken Nottingham to move into second place since the table was last published two years ago.

Robert Gordon, which has the highest entry score, remains the leading new university, in fourth place. Leeds Metropolitan is the next highest, at seventh. It has the most satisfied students at any of the 26 institutions – a notable feat for the department since overall Leeds Met is in the bottom five for student satisfaction. Around two thirds of the students were satisfied with their course at every university where the response to the National Student Survey was sufficient to compile a score.

Most of the institutions offering food science are new universities, but higher entry scores and research grades give their older counterparts an advantage in our table. Entry standards have been rising: no university with an entry score in this year's ranking averages less than 200 points, while 11 universities average more than 300. Almost a third of entrants to food science courses arrive with alternative qualifications to A levels. After four years of substantial increases in the number of applications for food science, the bubble appeared to have burst in 2007, with a decline of more than 50 per cent. But there was better news at the start of 2008, when the drop following the switch from six choices per applicant to five was lower than average for all subjects.

Teaching quality assessors in England were concerned at the high dropout rate on more than half of the courses: more than 20 per cent of students failed to progress to the next stage of their degree. Career prospects are good in food science, with two thirds of graduates going straight into graduate-level work or further study, although graduate unemployment had crept above the average for all subjects in the latest statistics.

- Institute of Food Science and Technology: **www.ifst.org**
- Society of Food Hygiene and technology: **www.sofht.co.uk/**

Food Science	Research quality/5	Entry standards	Student satisfaction %	Graduate prospects %	Overall rating
1 Surrey	5*A	384	77	90	100.0
2 King's College London	5B	383		85	99.1

	Research quality/5	Entry standards	Student satisfaction %	Graduate prospects %	Overall rating
3 Nottingham	5A	366	80	81	96.2
4 Robert Gordon	3bE	408		89	93.6
5 Reading	5A	317	80	81	93.0
6 Newcastle	4B	354	84	59	88.4
7 Leeds Metropolitan	3bC	280	88	79	87.4
8 Leeds	5*C	360	66	83	87.0
9 Queen's, Belfast	4C	319		72	85.1
10 Nottingham Trent	5D		75	79	84.2
11 Coventry		277		86	81.2
12 Plymouth	3aE	319	65	87	78.9
13 Oxford Brookes		297		74	78.1
=14 Ulster		272	81	69	77.5
=14 Greenwich	3aA			55	77.5
16 Glasgow Caledonian		320	75	64	75.7
17 Manchester Metropolitan		292		68	75.3
18 Westminster		233	80	72	75.2
19 Sheffield Hallam		287	79	61	75.1
20 Bath Spa		298		64	74.5
21 Teesside	2B		82	44	73.9
22 UWIC, Cardiff	3bC	231		69	73.2
23 Northumbria	2E		77	55	72.4
24 London South Bank	3aE			58	70.3
25 Liverpool John Moores		221	79	59	70.1
26 Chester		312	66	58	69.5

Employed in graduate job:	48%	Average starting graduate salary:	£18,781
Employed in graduate job and studying:	4%	Average starting non-graduate salary:	£14,507
Studying:	14%		
Employed in non-graduate job and studying:	2%	The letters that appear in the Research Quality column indicate the	
Employed in non-graduate job:	24%	proportion of staff included in the assessment, A showing that	
Unemployed:	8%	almost all staff were included and F showing that hardly any were.	

French

Cambridge remains the top university for French, with Oxford the only serious challenger. The ancient rivals were among seven universities awarded 5* research grades and have easily the highest entry standards. Strathclyde, in seventh place, has far and away the best employment record, with 95 per cent of leavers going straight into graduate-level jobs or further training, while the most satisfied students are to be found at Leicester.

Aberdeen, Royal Holloway, Southampton, Birmingham and Manchester are the other institutions rated internationally outstanding for research. They are spread about the table, with Birmingham, Aberdeen and Manchester outside the top 20. Strathclyde has overtaken St Andrews to become the top university in Scotland for French, while Cardiff remains the clear leader in Wales. Kingston is the leading new university and the only one in the top 40 apart from Portsmouth.

The subject commands high entry grades, with 15 universities averaging at least 400 points and none of the 53 in the table slipping below 230. French still attracts twice as many degree applications as any other language, although the total was down to 3,800 at the start of 2008, despite three successive increases before the cut in the number of choices allowed by each applicant. Nine out of ten undergraduates enter with A levels or their equivalents, almost 10 per cent securing their place in Clearing in 2006.

About two thirds go on to graduate jobs or further study within six months and the 4 per cent unemployment rate is comfortably better than average for all subjects. No university dipped below the 50 per cent success mark for graduate destinations – a significant improvement on last year, when four did.

Modern languages, as a group, have done well in the first three National Student Surveys. At least three quarters of final-year undergraduates were satisfied or very satisfied at most of the universities in the table. However, starting salaries are below average for all subjects, at £18,644 in graduate jobs.

- Alliance Française: **www.alliancefrancaise.org.uk/**
- Chartered Institute of Linguists: **www.iol.org.uk/**
- National Centre for Languages (CILT): **www.cilt.org.uk**
- Society for French Studies: **www.sfs.ac.uk/**

French	Research quality/5	Entry standards	Student satisfaction %	Graduate prospects %	Overall rating
1 Cambridge	5*A	500		81	100.0
2 Oxford	5*A	482	84	76	95.4
3 Durham	5B	470	86	76	92.5
4 University College London	5A	445	81	78	91.4
5 Warwick	5A	440	82	74	90.4
6 Royal Holloway	5*A	386	85	67	89.3
7 Strathclyde	4C	343	82	95	88.3
8 St Andrews	4B	431	81	79	88.1
9 Bath	5A	417	80	72	88.0
10 King's College London	5A	428	78	70	86.6
11 Bristol	5A	423	75	73	86.0
11 Southampton	5*A	383	80	64	86.0
11 Liverpool	5A	361	84	67	86.0
14 Leicester	3aB	346	89	76	85.8
15 Hull	4B	303	87	75	84.6
16 Queen Mary, London	5A	349	78	70	83.8
17 Sheffield	5B	392	81	64	83.1
17 Cardiff	5A	384	80	61	83.1
19 Queen's, Belfast	4A	380	78	70	83.0
19 Exeter	4B	412	78	71	83.0
21 Birmingham	5*C	384	87	58	82.9

	Research quality/5	Entry standards	Student satisfaction %	Graduate prospects %	Overall rating
22 Heriot-Watt	4B	376	86	60	82.4
23 Aberdeen	5*A	364		56	82.3
24 Glasgow	5B	410	78	63	82.2
25 Kent	4A	303	85	65	82.1
26 Nottingham	5A	384	76	63	82.0
26 Leeds	4B	396	83	62	82.0
28 Edinburgh	5C	440	69	78	81.6
28 Stirling	5B	311		73	81.6
30 Lancaster	5C	372	76	75	81.5
31 Reading	5B	329	79	70	81.3
32 Aberystwyth	3aA	315	84	69	81.0
33 Newcastle	4A	425	75	62	80.8
34 Salford	5A		82	51	80.0
35 Aston	5C	370	80	64	79.9
36 Swansea	4A	278	81	64	78.7
37 Kingston	4A		73	67	78.4
38 Bradford	4D		77	74	77.8
39 Manchester	5*C	415	72	58	77.5
40 Portsmouth	5C	254	84	64	77.3
41 Oxford Brookes	5B	296	73	67	76.1
42 East Anglia	3bB	325	76	68	74.9
43 Nottingham Trent	4B	242	73	71	74.2
44 Bangor	4D	300	85	55	74.1
44 Sussex	4A	398	67	57	74.1
46 York		407	72	70	72.3
47 Central Lancashire	3bA	253	80		72.1
48 Keele	2A	322	75	58	70.5
49 Leeds Metropolitan		294	72	76	69.6
50 Ulster	4C	270	66	58	66.5
51 Northumbria	3bE		74	59	65.9
52 Manchester Metropolitan		263	76	58	64.8
53 Westminster	3aD	236	72		63.8

Employed in graduate job:	40%	Average starting graduate salary:	£18,644
Employed in graduate job and studying:	5%	Average starting non-graduate salary:	£14,966
Studying:	21%		
Employed in non-graduate job and studying:	3%	The letters that appear in the Research Quality column indicate the	
Employed in non-graduate job:	26%	proportion of staff included in the assessment, A showing that	
Unemployed:	4%	almost all staff were included and F showing that hardly any were.	

General Engineering

There is no change at the top of the general engineering table, with Cambridge extending its lead over Oxford, thanks to the highest entry standards in the ranking and a graduate employment record that is bettered by only one university. The two ancient rivals are the only universities left in the ranking with 5* research grades, since neither Imperial College London nor Southampton appears in the table this year.

Fifth-placed Bristol is top of the pile for employment, all its leavers having gone straight into graduate jobs or further training. Leicester had the most satisfied engineers in the National Student Survey results published in 2007. Liverpool John Moores, which has an exceptional grade 5 for research, is the first new university to reach the top ten in this table. Aberdeen again pips Strathclyde to the accolade of top university in Scotland, while Glamorgan is the only representative of Wales this year.

As in the specialist branches of engineering, entry grades vary enormously, from well over 500 points at Oxford, Cambridge and Bristol to less than 200 at Oxford Brookes and some of the universities which have too few students to publish a reliable entry score. There were more than 8,000 applications for general engineering courses by the official deadline for entry in 2008, only a small decline in spite of the cut in choices per applicant. At the extremes, employment prospects also vary widely by institution, from Bristol's 100 per cent success rate to only 40 per cent of leavers at Birmingham City finding graduate work or starting postgraduate courses within six months of completing a course. Nationally, the subject is in the top 20 for employment, with three quarters of all graduates going straight into graduate jobs or further study, but the 7 per cent unemployment rate is slightly above average for all subjects. Nevertheless, the subject is among the ten most rewarding financially, with average starting salaries of £22,488 for graduate-level jobs and £17,120 in other types of employment. The assessors of teaching in England found that the courses nurtured the transferable skills required for later specialisation, but they worried about first-year dropout rates.

- Engineering Council: **www.engc.org.uk**
- Engineering and Technology Board: **www.etechb.co.uk/**
- Institution of Engineering and Technology: **www.theiet.org/**

General Engineering	Research quality/5	Entry standards	Student satisfaction %	Graduate prospects %	Overall rating
1 Cambridge	5*A	536	84	96	100.0
2 Oxford	5*A	521	82	86	95.9
3 Durham	5B	472	80	86	89.1
4 Leicester	5A	324	89	75	87.9
5 Bristol		521	84	100	87.4
6 Warwick	5B	421	73	80	82.1
7 Leeds	5C		71	88	80.3
8 Aberdeen	4C	402			77.6
9 Exeter	4C	318	78	74	76.9
10 Liverpool John Moores	5A		73	58	76.1
11 Lancaster	4B		70	73	74.6
12 Strathclyde	5A	349	67	63	74.2
13 Greenwich	3aB		71	70	72.4
14 Ulster	3bA	236	74	77	72.2
15 Brunel	5B		67	60	70.3

	Research quality/5	Entry standards	Student satisfaction %	Graduate prospects %	Overall rating
16 Northumbria	3bC		75	64	69.8
=17 Sheffield Hallam	3aF	250	72	77	67.3
=17 Bournemouth	3bF		79	61	67.3
19 Hertfordshire	3aD		71	62	66.2
20 Central Lancashire	3aE		67	71	64.9
21 Napier	4D			59	64.4
22 West of England	3bD	275	64	63	61.9
23 Wolverhampton	3aB	203	67	50	61.0
=24 Oxford Brookes	3bD	185	68		59.4
=24 Birmingham City	3bF	236	77	40	59.4
26 Anglia Ruskin	2C		64	59	58.8
27 Queen Mary, London		248	62	69	58.6
28 Glasgow Caledonian		312		50	58.2
29 De Montfort		207	61	65	55.6
30 Glamorgan		213	64	57	55.5

Employed in graduate job:	54%	Average starting graduate salary:	£22,488
Employed in graduate job and studying:	9%	Average starting non-graduate salary:	£17,120
Studying:	14%		
Employed in non-graduate job and studying:	1%	The letters that appear in the Research Quality column indicate the	
Employed in non-graduate job:	16%	proportion of staff included in the assessment, A showing that	
Unemployed:	7%	almost all staff were included and F showing that hardly any were.	

Geography and Environmental Sciences

The ranking for geography and environmental sciences is one of the most competitive in this year's *Guide*. Cambridge has regained top spot from the London School of Economics, with the highest entry standards and the second-best scores for employment and student satisfaction. The LSE is down to fifth, despite having an employment score that is 12 percentage points better than any other institution, 74 per cent satisfaction among its students and entry scores averaging more than three As at A level and one at AS level.

Oxford moves up to second place, in spite of an uncharacteristically low research grade, while third-placed Durham is one of the six universities rated internationally outstanding for research. The others are Bristol, University College London, Edinburgh, Royal Holloway and Cardiff. Staffordshire has the most satisfied students in a group of subjects that produced some of the best results in the National Student Survey.

St Andrews has overtaken Edinburgh to become the top university in Scotland, and Aberystwyth has overtaken Cardiff in Wales. While ten universities average more than 400 points at entry, even some old universities have averages of less than 300 and the figure dips below 200 at three institutions. Plymouth is the highest-placed new university, closely followed by Staffordshire, the other post-1992 institution in the top 40.

Geography and environmental sciences have been benefiting from rising interest in "green" issues among potential students. Physical geography and environmental sciences are slightly more popular than human and social geography, but both had around 15,000 applicants early in 2008. Neither area is a strong recruiter in Clearing.

In the latest survey, a third of graduates were in low-level jobs six months after completing their courses, but the unemployment rate was below average for all subjects. Universities are more tightly bunched in this table than many others in terms of their graduates' success in the jobs market, but still only around half of those leaving many institutions went straight into graduate work or higher-level courses.

- British Cartographic Society: **www.cartography.org.uk/**
- Royal Geographical Society (with the Institute of British Geographers): **www.rgs.org/**
- Royal Scottish Geographical Society: **www.geo.ed.ac.uk/rsgs/**

Geography and Environmental Sciences	Research quality/5	Entry standards	Student satisfaction %	Graduate prospects %	Overall rating
1 Cambridge	5A	503	89	79	100.0
2 Oxford	4A	484	84	78	95.1
3 Durham	5*A	451	80	77	94.8
4 University College London	5*A	428	82	74	93.5
5 London School of Economics	5A	429	74	91	92.8
6 Bristol	5*A	459	79	71	92.7
7 St Andrews	4B	424	88	67	90.0
8 Royal Holloway	5*A	353	84	67	89.7
9 Southampton	5A	384	81	68	88.2
10 Edinburgh	5*A	410	71	72	86.5
11 Reading	4A	351	84	65	86.1
12 Aberystwyth	4A	302	88	64	85.8
=13 Sheffield	5A	397	77	66	85.7
=13 Loughborough	5B	366	83	65	85.7
15 Cardiff	5*A	319	82	59	85.4
16 Nottingham	5B	425	76	66	84.7
17 Leicester	4B	328	87	59	83.7
18 Birmingham	4B	379	80	65	83.6
19 Glasgow	4C	361	87	60	83.5
20 Dundee	4A	336	78	69	83.4
21 Newcastle	5A	367	71	71	83.2
22 East Anglia	4A	382	79	59	82.7
23 Exeter	4B	368	81	61	82.3
24 Queen Mary, London	5A	295	78	64	81.9
25 Hull	5B	293	83	61	81.7
26 Leeds	5B	365	75	65	81.6
27 Manchester	4B	402	80	55	81.4
28 King's College London	4A	354	75	65	81.1
29 Aberdeen	4B	300		66	80.6
30 Lancaster	4A	369	77	58	80.5
31 Liverpool	4A	345	80	54	80.3

Geography and Environmental Sciences cont.	Research quality/5	Entry standards	Student satisfaction %	Graduate prospects %	Overall rating
32 Queen's, Belfast	4A	312	80	57	79.9
33 Strathclyde	3aC	328	82	63	79.6
34 Brunel	3aB			65	79.4
35 Keele	3aB	294	79	68	78.9
36 Swansea	4A	305	81	52	78.6
37 Hertfordshire	2B	272	85	64	77.4
38 Plymouth	4B	279	81	54	77.0
39 Staffordshire	3bC	244	92	49	76.3
40 Sussex	4B	379	70	56	75.3
41 Portsmouth	3aB	282	80	54	75.0
42 Bath Spa	2A	275		65	74.3
43 Stirling		270		70	74.0
=44 Coventry	3aB	261		57	73.5
=44 Anglia Ruskin	3bA		72	67	73.5
46 Northumbria	3bD	276	84	53	73.4
47 Huddersfield	2B		77	63	72.9
48 Edge Hill		211	86	64	72.8
49 Canterbury Christ Church		268	89	52	72.7
50 Brighton	3bB	265	82	49	72.6
51 Nottingham Trent	3aB	251	73	62	72.3
52 Kingston	3bB	224	77	61	72.1
53 Ulster	3bC	242	81	55	71.8
54 St Mary's College		238		68	71.3
55 Sunderland	3bC	249	80	53	71.1
=56 Salford	3aA	261		47	71.0
=56 Chester		276	82	58	71.0
=58 East London	2D			64	70.9
=58 Manchester Metropolitan	4C	263	76	50	70.9
60 Bradford	3bD	216	77	65	70.8
61 Northampton	2B	228	81	52	70.0
62 West of England	2D	263	81	50	69.6
63 Gloucestershire	3aC	254	76	50	69.5
64 Bangor		254	70	75	69.2
65 Central Lancashire		241	80	54	67.6
66 Oxford Brookes		282	76	51	66.5
67 Sheffield Hallam		269	86	32	65.9
68 Greenwich	3bE	181	74	58	65.0
69 Worcester	2C	215		51	64.2
70 Bournemouth	2D	237		42	61.1
71 Derby		231	74	42	60.9
72 Cumbria		238	61	65	60.8
73 Liverpool John Moores	3bC	197	68	44	60.4
74 Leeds Metropolitan		211		46	59.9

75 Southampton Solent	186	71	46	58.2
76 Glamorgan	217	73	30	56.2

Employed in graduate job:	34%	Average starting graduate salary:	£18,650
Employed in graduate job and studying:	5%	Average starting non-graduate salary:	£14,431
Studying:	22%		
Employed in non-graduate job and studying:	3%	The letters that appear in the Research Quality column indicate the	
Employed in non-graduate job:	30%	proportion of staff included in the assessment, A showing that	
Unemployed:	5%	almost all staff were included and F showing that hardly any were.	

Geology

The top three in the geology ranking remain the same as last year, although Cambridge's lead over Oxford is down to less than a point. Cambridge has the highest entry standards in the table, while Oxford graduates have the best employment record. They are both among four universities rated internationally outstanding for research, the others being third-placed Imperial College and Bristol, in sixth place.

Leicester has the most satisfied students and Aberdeen is only one percentage point behind Oxford's outstanding employment score. Three Scottish universities appear in the top dozen, with Glasgow still the leader. Cardiff remains well ahead of the competition in Wales.

Two new universities have dropped out of this year's table and the remaining four are all in the bottom six places, with Plymouth the best-placed. Oxbridge apart, there is less contrast in entry standards than in many other subjects. The average is above 200 points at every university in the ranking, and only eight average less than 300.

Three quarters of geology students go on to graduate jobs or further study within six months of graduation, and the unemployment level has come down, although it is slightly above the average for all subjects, at 7 per cent. Average salaries for graduate-level jobs are also around average, but those in non-graduate work are the lowest-paid in any subject, averaging less than £13,000 a year.

Applications to read geology fell below 6,000 at the start of 2008, with the switch from six choices per applicant to five. But the 10 per cent decline was close to the average for all subjects and followed an increase of similar proportions in 2007. Relatively few places are filled in Clearing.

- Geological Society of London: **www.geolsoc.org.uk/**

Geology	Research quality/5	Entry standards	Student satisfaction %	Graduate prospects %	Overall rating
1 Cambridge	5*A	539	86	85	100.0
2 Oxford	5*A	514	83	94	99.4
3 Imperial College	5*A	440	79	80	91.5
4 Liverpool	5A	332	84	82	88.8
5 Glasgow	4B	359	86	85	87.7
6 Bristol	5*A	416	76	69	86.4
7 St Andrews	4B	384	81	81	85.1
=8 University College London	5B	383	79	78	84.6

Geology cont.

	Research quality/5	Entry standards	Student satisfaction %	Graduate prospects %	Overall rating
=8 Southampton	5A	334	84	65	84.6
=8 Leeds	5A	362	74	83	84.6
=11 Edinburgh	5A	387	76	74	84.2
=11 Leicester	4A	351	88	61	84.2
13 Cardiff	5A	316	80	69	83.0
14 Durham	4B	404	80	71	82.6
15 Royal Holloway	5B	343	77	75	81.8
16 Aberdeen	4C	277		93	81.0
17 Manchester	5B	356	82	61	80.8
18 Exeter	4B	332	77	81	80.6
19 Keele	3aB	274	87	68	79.4
20 Birmingham	3aC	319	81	72	77.0
21 East Anglia		385	82	72	74.5
22 Plymouth	4C	242	81	57	71.8
23 Bangor		266	79	85	71.7
24 Aberystwyth		292	78	71	68.7
25 Portsmouth	3bA	222	71	59	65.7
26 Kingston	4B	207	67	42	61.5
27 Liverpool John Moores		208	67	63	58.1

Employed in graduate job:	41%	Average starting graduate salary:	£19,642
Employed in graduate job and studying:	4%	Average starting non-graduate salary:	£12,823
Studying:	28%		
Employed in non-graduate job and studying:	2%	The letters that appear in the Research Quality column indicate the	
Employed in non-graduate job:	19%	proportion of staff included in the assessment, A showing that	
Unemployed:	7%	almost all staff were included and F showing that hardly any were.	

German

Cambridge makes it four years in a row as the leader in German, but there is considerable movement in the rest of the ranking. Exeter leaps from 14th place last year to second, while University College London falls from third place to 21st. St Andrews goes from 23rd to 11th, while Nottingham is down from fifth to 13th. The inclusion of scores from the National Student Survey is largely responsible. Although Cambridge is not affected because its students did not respond in sufficient numbers for a score to be published, Exeter registered the highest level of satisfaction in the table, while UCL's score was almost the lowest.

Ten universities were awarded 5* research grades in the 2001 assessments, two of which (Royal Holloway and UCL) are not even in this year's top 20. The top two are among the other research stars, as are Birmingham, King's College London, Edinburgh, Nottingham, Southampton and Manchester. Cambridge boasts the highest entry standards, while Hull has the best employment score – an impressive 93 per cent finding graduate jobs or continuing their studies within six months of finishing courses. Of the seven new universities in the ranking, Portsmouth comes closest to making the top 30.

The number of universities in the German table is down again, this time by ten, following a drop of seven institutions two years ago. This reflects a worldwide decline in the language that has been worrying the German government, as well as academic linguists. The numbers taking A level have been dropping, although degree applications recovered in some style in 2007, with an increase of nearly 20 per cent. A 5 per cent decline at the start of 2008, following the cut in choices per applicant, was half the average for all subjects, but there were still fewer than 1,500 applications. Nine out of ten enter with A levels or equivalent qualifications, and entry standards are relatively high, especially at the leading universities. All the top ten universities with enough students to compile reliable entry scores average more than 400 points.

As in other modern languages, career prospects are reasonable: two thirds of leavers go straight into graduate jobs or further study, and the unemployment rate is below average. The subject has moved into the top 20 for starting salaries, with an average of nearly £21,000 in graduate-level jobs. Most universities in the table offer German *ab initio* as part of a languages package.

- Chartered Institute of Linguists: **www.iol.org.uk/**
- Goethe-Institut: **www.goethe.de/enindex.htm**
- National Centre for Languages (CILT): **www.cilt.org.uk**

German	Research quality/5	Entry standards	Student satisfaction %	Graduate prospects %	Overall rating
1 Cambridge	5*A	500		81	100.0
2 Exeter	5*A	427	92	67	94.8
3 Warwick	5A	430	91	74	94.4
4 Oxford	5A	494	84	72	93.3
5 Birmingham	5*B	424	88	76	93.0
6 Bath	5A	418	81	79	90.6
7 King's College London	5*A	403	79	76	90.0
8 Durham	4A	470	81	76	89.9
9 Edinburgh	5*B	437	76	84	89.7
10 Aberdeen	4A			78	88.9
11 St Andrews	4C	456	85	79	88.7
12 Bristol	5B	403	79	85	88.2
=13 Nottingham	5*A	382	79	70	87.4
=13 Sheffield	4A	419	79	78	87.4
15 Hull	3aC	330	87	93	87.0
16 Cardiff	5A	391	78	75	86.8
17 Aston	5C	351	86	72	84.2
18 Southampton	5*A		82	51	84.0
19 Swansea	5A	310	81	71	83.9
20 Manchester	5*B	428	82	50	83.4
21 University College London	5*A	445	69	64	83.3
22 Heriot-Watt	4B	376	86	60	82.9
23 Queen's, Belfast	4A	379	78		82.4

	Research quality/5	Entry standards	Student satisfaction %	Graduate prospects %	Overall rating
24 Leeds	4C	398	86	60	82.1
25 Liverpool	5A	324	83	56	81.2
26 Royal Holloway	5*C	336	78	70	80.5
27 Bangor	3aA	307	86	62	80.2
28 Lancaster	5C	356	76	69	78.8
29 Queen Mary, London	5A	334	78	55	78.7
30 Kent	4B		81	59	78.6
31 Portsmouth	5C	254	84		77.1
32 Reading	4B	355	79	55	76.9
33 East Anglia	3bB	370	76	68	76.4
34 Glasgow	4C	420	77	52	76.3
35 Oxford Brookes	4B		73	67	75.9
36 Nottingham Trent	3aB	242	73	71	72.0
=37 Newcastle	4A		71	50	71.3
=37 Central Lancashire	3bA	253	80		71.3
39 Northumbria	3bE		74	67	68.9
40 Leeds Metropolitan		294	72	76	68.5
41 Ulster	3aC		66	58	65.0
42 Manchester Metropolitan		263	76	58	64.6

Employed in graduate job:	40%	Average starting graduate salary:	£20,942
Employed in graduate job and studying:	5%	Average starting non-graduate salary:	£14,481
Studying:	20%		
Employed in non-graduate job and studying:	3%	The letters that appear in the Research Quality column indicate the	
Employed in non-graduate job:	26%	proportion of staff included in the assessment, A showing that	
Unemployed:	5%	almost all staff were included and F showing that hardly any were.	

History

The top five places in the history table are unchanged, with York has moving up from
eighth to join Warwick in a tie for sixth place. Cambridge leads again, with the highest
entry qualifications and one of the best employment records, as well as one of eight 5*
research ratings. Another of the research stars went to Oxford Brookes, the leading new
university and one of the few to achieve this level in any subject in the 2001 Research
Assessment Exercise.

Durham and King's College London, in second and third places respectively, are two
of the remaining universities with 5* research grades. The others are the London School
of Economics, the School of Oriental and African Studies, East Anglia and Bradford.

The most satisfied students are at Portsmouth, in 35th place, and Chichester, which
does not make the top 50. Satisfaction levels are high throughout the table, with nearly
all universities satisfying at least 70 per cent of its undergraduates. The LSE, in fifth
place, has the best employment record, as one of three universities where eight out of
ten historians went straight into graduate jobs or further study. The others were table-
topping Cambridge and Bolton, in 40th place.

St Andrews remains the top university in Scotland, while Cardiff does the same in Wales. History remains one of the most popular subjects at degree level: it was in the top ten again in terms of total applications at the beginning of 2008, when a 7 per cent decline following the switch from six choices per applicant to five was better than the average for all subjects. Entry standards are high, with almost 20 universities averaging over 400 points on the UCAS tariff and only one slipping (just) below 200.

Career prospects are mixed: surveys have shown a strong representation of historians among business leaders, celebrities and senior politicians, but more are in non-graduate jobs than those categorised as graduate occupations six months after completing courses. Some universities in the bottom half of the table, like Roehampton and Newport, do well on this measure, but a dozen others scored less than 40 per cent on the proportion of leavers going straight into graduate-level employment or further training. Only law and anatomy have lower proportions of leavers going straight into graduate jobs.

- Historical Association: **www.history.org.uk/**
- Institute of Historical Research: **www.history.ac.uk/**
- Royal Historical Society: **www.royalhistoricalsociety.org/**

History	Research quality/5	Entry standards	Student satisfaction %	Graduate prospects %	Overall rating
1 Cambridge	5*A	482		81	100.0
2 Durham	5*A	479	89	76	97.9
3 King's College London	5*A	447	84	77	94.4
4 Oxford	5A	479	85	78	94.2
5 London School of Economics	5*B	425	78	83	89.2
=6 York	5A	460	83	64	89.0
=6 Warwick	5A	460	81	69	89.0
8 Exeter	5A	409	86	65	88.6
9 University College London	5A	439	76	73	87.0
10 St Andrews	5B	456	80	67	86.1
11 Leeds	5B	422	83	67	85.9
12 Southampton	5A	381	85	56	84.9
13 Queen Mary, London	5B	364	83	70	84.6
14 Hull	5A	298	85	64	84.1
15 Leicester	5A	358	85	56	83.9
16 Royal Holloway	5A	381	78	64	83.2
17 Sheffield	5B	433	78	62	82.9
18 Glasgow	5B	412	85	51	82.8
19 East Anglia	5*B	377	85	49	82.7
20 Birmingham	5B	400	82	57	82.5
21 Cardiff	5A	395	82	48	82.0
22 Nottingham	4A	421	78	59	81.8
23 Bristol	4A	429	74	67	81.5
24 Dundee	5B	354	85	52	81.0
25 Essex	5A	328	83	51	80.7
26 Edinburgh	5B	432	72	64	80.3

	Research quality/5	Entry standards	Student satisfaction %	Graduate prospects %	Overall rating
27 Oxford Brookes	5*A	337	78	48	79.7
=28 Lancaster	4A	374	82	49	79.5
=28 Liverpool	5B	377	82	49	79.5
30 Keele	5A	316	78	58	79.4
31 Aberystwyth	4A	309	86	50	79.2
32 Huddersfield	5A	283	84	49	79.1
33 Central Lancashire	4A	273	82	60	78.4
34 Kent	4B	333	81	60	78.1
35 Portsmouth	4C	294	91	51	78.0
36 School of Oriental and African Studies	5*B	358	75	53	77.8
37 Stirling	5A	273		52	77.3
38 Aberdeen	4B	333		58	76.9
39 Sussex	4A	385	70	61	76.6
=40 Queen's, Belfast	5B	342	76	53	76.0
=40 Bolton	3bD			80	76.0
=42 Bangor	4B	270	81	60	75.9
=42 Lampeter	4A	262	77	62	75.9
=44 Hertfordshire	5B	269	83	49	75.7
=44 Reading	4B	328	79	54	75.7
46 Manchester	5B	426	72	48	75.6
=47 Swansea	4A	302	80	48	75.4
=47 De Montfort	4B	271	86	48	75.4
49 Newcastle	4A	406	66	60	75.3
50 Bradford	5*A	253	78	40	74.8
51 Bath Spa	3bA	277	81	60	73.7
52 Chichester	3aA	241	91	37	73.6
53 Nottingham Trent	3aB	270	79	60	73.1
54 Northampton	4B	245	88	38	73.0
55 Strathclyde	4B	345	77	45	72.9
56 Goldsmiths College	4B	296	77	52	72.6
57 Canterbury Christ Church	3aA	247	86	39	72.3
58 Teesside	5C	256	88	34	71.9
59 Sunderland	4C	250	80	55	71.2
60 Roehampton	5B	234	70	64	71.1
61 Salford	5A	256	68	52	70.7
62 Glamorgan	3aC	223	78	65	70.5
63 Brunel	3aB	306	76	50	70.4
64 Kingston	4B	220	72	64	70.3
=65 West of England	4B	264	79	41	70.0
=65 Chester	3bC	282	86	44	70.0
67 Sheffield Hallam	5B	285	74	39	69.2
=68 Edge Hill	3bC	218	87	45	68.6
=68 Ulster	4B	259		44	68.6

70 Winchester	4C	262	81	37	68.0
71 St Mary's College	3aC	238	74	60	67.9
72 Wolverhampton	4B	194	75	51	67.8
73 Northumbria	3aC	305	75	44	66.6
74 Plymouth	3aC	275	76	44	66.4
75 Gloucestershire	3aC	268	77	41	65.9
76 Staffordshire	3bC	278	81	36	65.7
77 Cumbria	3aD	261	74	54	65.6
78 Greenwich	3aA	219	74	40	65.0
79 Worcester	3aC	240	73	47	64.2
80 Liverpool John Moores	4B	232	73	33	63.7
81 Derby		302		47	62.9
82 Lincoln		268	75	51	61.4
83 Leeds Metropolitan	3aD	252		39	60.6
84 Westminster	3aB	221		31	60.2
85 Manchester Metropolitan	3aC	285	69	32	59.9
86 York St John	3aD	218	72	41	59.8
87 Anglia Ruskin	3aC	217	73	31	59.4
88 Coventry		243		46	59.3
89 Brighton		263	71	50	59.2
90 UWCN, Newport		206	67	68	59.0
91 Middlesex	3bC		70	35	56.4

Employed in graduate job:	27%	Average starting graduate salary:	£18,957
Employed in graduate job and studying:	4%	Average starting non-graduate salary:	£13,932
Studying:	24%		
Employed in non-graduate job and studying:	4%	The letters that appear in the Research Quality column indicate the	
Employed in non-graduate job:	34%	proportion of staff included in the assessment, A showing that	
Unemployed:	6%	almost all staff were included and F showing that hardly any were.	

History of Art, Architecture and Design

Cambridge has held onto the top position in art history that it took from London's Courtauld Institute two years ago. Second-placed Courtauld has the only 5* research rating and the best graduate employment record, but Cambridge's lead in entry standards is sufficiently wide to keep the university ahead. Birmingham has moved up to third since the table was last published, two years ago, while York has slipped from second to fourth.

The most intriguing entry is De Montfort's, which has the most satisfied students despite also recording by far the lowest employment score, with little more than a quarter of leavers finding graduate-level employment or starting a postgraduate course within six months. Employment scores are low at many of the universities. Only the Courtauld and London's School of Oriental and African Studies registered "positive destinations" for more than 70 per cent of graduates, and the rate was below 60 per cent at more than half of the institutions in the ranking, including one in the top five.

Glasgow has overtaken St Andrews to become the top university in Scotland but, with Aberystwyth dropping out of the table this year, there is no Welsh representative.

History of Art, Architecture and Design cont.

Only five new universities, led by Oxford Brookes, appear in the ranking for a subject that has traditionally been associated with the older institutions.

Nationally, the specialised nature of the jobs market makes for uncertain prospects immediately after graduation. History of art is in the bottom four subjects for positive destinations, although unemployment is no lower than average, with 43 per cent of leavers starting their careers in non-graduate jobs. Starting salaries are only slightly below the average for all subjects, however.

Fewer than 4,000 undergraduates take full-time degrees in the history of art, although another 1,000 are registered on part-time courses. The majority of students are female. Entry standards are high, with a third of the table averaging more than 400 points and only one university averaging less than 250 points. Teaching quality assessors in England found that most students were well supported, although about a third of libraries were under pressure.

- Association of Art Historians: **www.aah.org.uk/**
- Society of Architectural Historians of Great Britain: **www.sahgb.org.uk/**

History of Art, Architecture and Design	Research quality/5	Entry standards	Student satisfaction %	Graduate prospects %	Overall rating
1 Cambridge	5A	492		67	100.0
2 Courtauld	5*A	415	75	80	96.4
3 Birmingham	5A	433	82	62	95.1
4 York	5A	415	83	59	94.1
5 Warwick	5A	364	81	63	91.2
6 Glasgow	5B	388	85	53	90.7
7 St Andrews	5A	411	80	52	90.6
8 University College London	5B	422	76	62	89.0
9 East Anglia	5B	330	85	56	88.4
10 Sussex	5A	383	70	67	86.8
11 Bristol	3aB	433	74	69	86.4
12 School of Oriental and African Studies	3aA	341	75	77	85.9
13 Leeds	3aA	373	83	46	84.8
14 Reading	4A	333	79	53	84.7
15 Edinburgh	4B	410	72	62	84.4
16 Goldsmiths College	3bA	341	77	62	81.4
17 Nottingham	3bC	377	78	57	80.8
18 Oxford Brookes	3aA	342	78	41	79.3
19 Manchester	5B	343	72	44	78.5
20 Aberdeen	4C			50	77.6
21 De Montfort	3bC		86	27	75.5
22 Brighton	5B	223	71	54	75.1
23 Kingston	4D	268	72	48	71.2
24 Loughborough	3aC			38	69.4
25 Sheffield Hallam		258	74	36	63.9

Employed in graduate job:	28%	Average starting graduate salary:	£18,758
Employed in graduate job and studying:	4%	Average starting non-graduate salary:	£15,032
Studying:	19%		
Employed in non-graduate job and studying:	4%		
Employed in non-graduate job:	39%		
Unemployed:	6%		

The letters that appear in the Research Quality column indicate the proportion of staff included in the assessment, A showing that almost all staff were included and F showing that hardly any were.

Hospitality, Leisure, Sport, Recreation and Tourism

Another seven institutions have joined this wide-ranging ranking this year, which covers some of the biggest real growth areas in higher education. With eight more joining last year, the table has grown by a third in four years. Most are new universities, although all but two of the top ten are older establishments. The exceptions are Brighton and De Montfort, which is up to sixth in the latest table, and Brighton at tenth.

Loughborough remains the overall leader, with a consistent set of scores, including the highest entry standards and one of the five 5* research grades (albeit with a low proportion of academics assessed). Birmingham, Glasgow, Liverpool John Moores and Manchester Metropolitan are the other universities rated internationally outstanding for research. Birmingham moves up a place to second, while Exeter capitalises on one of the best student satisfaction ratings to rise three places to third.

Newman University College, in Birmingham, has the best employment record and almost makes the top 20, while Aberystwyth has the most satisfied students. In addition to De Montfort and Brighton, three new universities appear in the top 20: Liverpool John Moores, Nottingham Trent and Chichester. Glasgow is the top university in Scotland – and might have been even higher than fourth if more than half of its leavers had found graduate-level jobs or continued their studies within six months. Bangor, one place lower, is still the leader in Wales.

The category covers a variety of courses, most directed towards management in the leisure and tourism industries. Several, including Loughborough, Exeter and eighth-placed Bath, concentrate on sport. Only Loughborough and Bath average more than 400 points at entry, while 15 average less than 200 points.

Unemployment is below the average for all subjects, but the subjects are still in the bottom ten of the jobs table. More than 40 per cent of the 2006 leavers were in non-graduate jobs six months after completing their course. The subjects are also in the bottom ten for starting salaries in graduate-level jobs, averaging less than £17,500. Nevertheless, sports science, in particular, has been growing in popularity and is only just outside the top ten subjects for applications. Although there was a 10 per cent decline at the start of 2008, with the switch from six applications per applicant to five, there had been a corresponding increase in 2007, taking the total to 44,000. The smaller hospitality and tourism area did even better, with a 30 per cent increase in applications in 2007, and only a 4 per cent decline in 2008.

- Association for Tourism in Higher Education: **www.athe.org.uk/**
- British Association of Sport and Exercise Sciences: **www.bases.org.uk/**
- Council for Hospitality Management Education: **www.chme.org.uk/**
- English Institute of Sport: **www.eis2win.co.uk**
- Institute of Hospitality: **www.instituteofhospitality.org/**
- Leisure Studies Association: **www.leisure-studies-association.info/**

Hospitality, Leisure, Recreation, Sport and Tourism	Research quality/5	Entry standards	Student satisfaction %	Graduate prospects %	Overall rating
1 Loughborough	5*C	414	85	70	100.0
2 Birmingham	5*A	379	80	61	96.9
3 Exeter	5C	356	87	64	93.6
4 Glasgow	5*A	347	83	47	91.6
5 Bangor	5A	238	84	61	88.2
6 De Montfort	4B		77	69	88.0
7 Aberdeen	4B	264		69	87.8
8 Bath	3aC	401	71	69	87.7
9 Leeds	3aC	350	75	63	84.4
10 Brighton	4A	281	81	53	84.2
11 Liverpool John Moores	5*B	273	74	56	83.7
12 Stirling	4B	271		58	82.9
13 Brunel	4B	312	70	62	82.5
=14 Strathclyde	4C	275	82	55	81.7
=14 Essex		299	84	68	81.7
16 Nottingham Trent	3aC	260	77	66	81.0
17 Manchester	4C	321	72	57	80.4
18 Durham		364	69	71	79.8
19 Chichester	3aC	225	86	58	79.7
20 Surrey	4C	300	70	57	78.3
21 Newman		232	81	74	78.1
22 Ulster	4D	295	82	45	77.7
23 Manchester Metropolitan	5*C	243	72	52	76.4
24 Northumbria		283	84	55	75.9
=25 Bedfordshire	4C	211	74	58	75.0
=25 Portsmouth		244	86	56	75.0
27 Edinburgh	3aD	359	66	49	74.6
=28 Aberystwyth		254	92	45	74.5
=28 Sheffield Hallam	4E	270	77	52	74.5
30 Southampton		336	73	55	74.1
=31 Swansea		267	88	46	73.6
=31 Leeds Metropolitan	3aD	267	69	58	73.6
33 UWCN, Newport		171	89	60	73.2
34 Hertfordshire	3aC	264	73	48	73.0
=35 Robert Gordon		287		53	72.7
=35 Oxford Brookes		276	75	59	72.7
=35 Bournemouth		269	71	65	72.7
38 Canterbury Christ Church	3bC	200	80	52	72.3
39 Central Lancashire		253	81	53	71.9
=40 Worcester		235	78	59	71.4
=40 Hull		250	73	62	71.4
42 University of the Arts, London		294		49	71.1
43 Chester		255	78	53	70.8

44 Staffordshire	3aE	199	87	43	70.6
45 Teesside		248	83	46	70.3
46 Queen Margaret Edinburgh		257		53	69.9
47 Roehampton	3bD	193	74	56	69.5
48 York St John		232	78	53	69.3
=49 St Mary's College		207	78	56	68.9
=49 UWIC, Cardiff	3aF	248	74	50	68.9
51 Kent		178	86	50	68.7
52 London South Bank	3aD	177	79	48	68.6
53 Coventry		244	76	50	68.1
54 Gloucestershire	3bE	239	74	46	67.4
=55 Glamorgan	3bB	185	76	41	66.5
=55 Cumbria		255	60	65	66.5
57 Westminster	3aD		81	33	66.3
58 East London		150	68	71	66.0
59 Kingston		195	74	54	65.6
60 Glasgow Caledonian	3aE	261	74	34	64.8
61 Northampton		187	79	46	64.6
62 Abertay		237		46	64.4
63 Salford		215	77	43	64.1
64 Wolverhampton	3aE	181	74	45	64.0
=65 Winchester		218	73	45	63.6
=65 Edge Hill		232	74	42	63.6
67 Greenwich		212	62	60	63.4
68 Lincoln		215	72	46	63.1
69 Plymouth		251	73	38	62.9
70 Marjon, Plymouth		188	78	39	61.7
71 Anglia Ruskin	2B	208	70	34	61.0
72 West of Scotland		212		43	60.5
73 Southampton Solent		188	71	45	60.2
74 Huddersfield		229	64	44	59.5
75 Buckinghamshire New	3bE	199	66	40	59.4
76 Heriot-Watt		218	72	35	59.2
77 West of England		244	56	46	57.7
78 Derby		219	58	45	56.2
79 Middlesex		183	64	41	55.6
80 Thames Valley		153	59	44	52.5

Employed in graduate job:	34%	Average starting graduate salary:	£17,456
Employed in graduate job and studying:	4%	Average starting non-graduate salary:	£13,968
Studying:	13%		
Employed in non-graduate job and studying:	4%	The letters that appear in the Research Quality column indicate the
Employed in non-graduate job:	39%	proportion of staff included in the assessment, A showing that
Unemployed:	5%	almost all staff were included and F showing that hardly any were.

Iberian Languages

Cambridge remains well ahead of the field for Iberian languages, with the highest entry standards and one of six 5* ratings for research. The other research stars were King's College London, Manchester, Southampton, Nottingham and Queen Mary, London. All of them are headed by St Andrews and Bath, which move up to second and third respectively.

Oxford, in fourth place, has the best destinations score of 84 per cent of leavers going straight into graduate-level work or postgraduate study. Hull, in 15th, boasts the most satisfied students, narrowly ahead of Heriot-Watt, in 13th. Both have risen nine places up the table as a result.

Portsmouth is the only new university in the top 30, with a grade 5 for research and one of the best student satisfaction ratings. Oxford Brookes and Roehampton are its nearest challengers. Entry standards are high, with nine universities averaging over 400 points and none coming close to slipping below 200.

Spanish has been growing in popularity as an alternative to French in schools, and is a common choice as an element of a broader modern languages degree. There had been 1,800 applications by the official deadline for entry in 2008, in spite of a 7 per cent decline brought about by the cut in the number of choices per applicant. The table also includes Portuguese, which only had a handful of applicants at degree level.

The languages are a little below halfway in the employment table, with nearly a third of leavers in non-graduate jobs six months after completing courses. Average graduate starting salaries are lower than for other languages. However, employment prospects appear to be more evenly spread than in many subjects: only two of the 46 universities in the table (compared with ten last year) saw fewer than half of their leavers go into graduate jobs or further training in 2006.

- Association for Contemporary Iberian Studies: **www.iberianstudies.net/**
- Association of Hispanists of Great Britain and Ireland: **www.dur.ac.uk/hispanists/**
- Instituto Cervantes: **http://londres.cervantes.es/en/default.shtm**
- National Centre for Languages (CILT): **www.cilt.org.uk**

Iberian Languages	Research quality/5	Entry standards	Student satisfaction %	Graduate prospects %	Overall rating
1 Cambridge	5*A	500		81	100.0
2 St Andrews	5A	470	85	76	94.2
3 Bath	5A	398	85	82	93.7
4 Oxford	5B	481	80	84	93.0
5 King's College London	5*A	393	79	73	89.4
6 Durham	4B	470	81	76	89.2
7 Birmingham	5A	380	80	66	85.4
=8 Sheffield	5A	390	83	59	85.0
=8 Swansea	5B	295	84	75	85.0
10 Nottingham	5*A	374	72	70	84.5
11 Lancaster	5C	384	76	81	84.4
12 Southampton	5*A	392	77	57	83.9

=13	Heriot-Watt	4B	376	86	60	83.5
=13	Bristol	4B	413	79	68	83.5
15	Hull	4A	285	87	67	83.4
16	Liverpool	4A	333	83	66	83.3
17	Queen Mary, London	5*A	324	78	63	83.0
=18	Edinburgh	5A	429	66	73	82.9
=18	Kent	4B	295	81	79	82.9
20	University College London	4A	445	72	67	82.6
21	Manchester	5*A	410	68	63	81.7
22	Queen's, Belfast	4A	371	76	67	81.5
23	Leeds	4B	396	76	68	81.4
24	Cardiff	5A	372	75	56	80.0
25	Glasgow	3aB	379	77	65	79.0
26	Newcastle	5A	415	71	53	78.9
27	Aberystwyth	3aA		84	52	78.0
28	Exeter	4B	396	70	66	77.9
29	Salford	5A	346	77	48	77.6
30	Portsmouth	5C	254	84	61	77.5
=31	Strathclyde	4C	348	82	54	76.6
=31	Royal Holloway	4A	340	78	51	76.6
33	Oxford Brookes	3aC		73	67	72.9
34	Roehampton	3aA	236	68	75	72.7
35	East Anglia		370	76	68	72.6
36	Central Lancashire	3bA	253	80		72.4
37	Leeds Metropolitan		294	72	76	69.8
38	Westminster	3bD	242	72	67	67.8
39	Chester		264	81	56	67.6
40	Northumbria	3bE		74	60	67.2
41	Nottingham Trent		242	73	71	67.0
42	Aberdeen	4D	306		51	66.7
43	Manchester Metropolitan		263	76	58	65.5
44	Sussex		377	68	45	62.2
45	Ulster		275	66	58	61.1
46	Liverpool John Moores		223	67	52	57.3

Employed in graduate job:	43%		Average starting graduate salary:	£17,704
Employed in graduate job and studying:	4%		Average starting non-graduate salary:	£15,362
Studying:	17%			
Employed in non-graduate job and studying:	3%			

Employed in non-graduate job: 28%   The letters that appear in the Research Quality column indicate the

Unemployed: 6%   proportion of staff included in the assessment, A showing that

almost all staff were included and F showing that hardly any were.

Italian

Cambridge continues to lead a group of 24 universities offering Italian – ten fewer than two years ago, when this table was last published. It has the highest entry standards, the top employment score and is one of six universities rated internationally outstanding

Italian cont.

for research. Oxford is another research star, and it retains second place, sharing the best student satisfaction score with Warwick and Leeds.

High scores on at least one of the measures can be found throughout most of the ranking. Three of the bottom ten universities have satisfaction ratings of 80 per cent or more and four have grade 5 research ratings. The top research grades were widely spread in 2001, after a sharp improvement on the previous assessments. Birmingham, University College London, Leeds and Reading were the other universities awarded the 5* grade. Edinburgh is the top university in Scotland, while Swansea overtakes Cardiff to assume the leadership in Wales. Most of the table is made up of old universities, but Portsmouth leads a handful of former polytechnics at the foot of the table.

Fewer than 500 students take the language as a separate subject at degree level, although others include Italian in combined degree programmes. A high proportion secure places in Clearing – more than 15 per cent of entrants took that route in 2006. Most students have no previous knowledge of the language, but there is a high completion rate. The low numbers can make for big swings in the annual statistics: the unemployment rate, for example, was much better than average in last year's table, but has fallen back below average this year. By contrast, only six subjects had lower average starting salaries for graduate jobs in last year's survey, whereas Italian is in the middle of the earnings table this time.

- Chartered Institute of Linguists: **www.iol.org.uk/**
- National Centre for Languages (CILT): **www.cilt.org.uk**
- Society for Italian Studies: **www.sis.ac.uk/**

Italian	Research quality/5	Entry standards	Student satisfaction %	Graduate prospects %	Overall rating
1 Cambridge	5*A	500		81	100.0
2 Oxford	5*A	489	85	77	96.8
3 Bristol	5A	402	83	68	88.5
3 Birmingham	5*B	419	84	66	88.5
5 Bath	5A	389	79	70	86.8
6 Warwick	5A	417	85	56	86.2
7 Edinburgh	4A	426	71	77	83.9
8 Exeter	4B	358	77	78	83.0
9 Leicester	4A		84	57	82.1
10 Leeds	5*D	350	85	63	81.2
11 Reading	5*A	307	79	55	81.0
12 University College London	5*A	445	64	63	80.9
13 Swansea	4A	312	81	62	80.6
14 Durham		470	81	76	80.0
15 Royal Holloway	4A	345	78	59	79.1
16 Cardiff	5A	344	76	54	78.7
17 Kent	4B	305	81		78.3
18 Manchester	5B	393	73	56	77.3
19 Portsmouth	5C	254	84	58	77.1

	Research Quality	Entry Standards			Score
20 Glasgow	3bA		77	66	76.0
21 Lancaster	5C		76	59	74.7
22 Central Lancashire	3bA	253	80		72.2
23 Nottingham Trent		242	73	71	67.0
24 Manchester Metropolitan		263	76	58	65.2

Employed in graduate job:	42%	Average starting graduate salary:	£19,325
Employed in graduate job and studying:	5%	Average starting non-graduate salary:	£14,365
Studying:	15%		
Employed in non-graduate job and studying:	4%		
Employed in non-graduate job:	28%		
Unemployed:	7%		

The letters that appear in the Research Quality column indicate the proportion of staff included in the assessment, A showing that almost all staff were included and F showing that hardly any were.

Land and Property Management

This year's land and property management table contains less than a third of the universities listed in the 2005 edition of the *Guide*. The subject tends to have small intakes, often making it impossible to calculate reliable destinations scores, UCAS tariff averages or student satisfaction rates. Cambridge maintains the lead over Reading that it enjoyed when the table was last published, two years ago. Cambridge has the highest entry standards, while Reading has the best employment score and also shares the distinction of hosting the most satisfied students with third-placed Ulster and Birmingham City, which is fourth out of the eight institutions.

No university in the ranking is rated internationally outstanding for research. Salford managed the only 5* rating but is one of those to have dropped out of the table. The top three were awarded grade 5, but Ulster submitted a bigger proportion of its academics for assessment. Cambridge is nearly 150 points ahead of the next university (Reading) in terms of entry scores.

The Royal Agricultural College is fifth, in its first appearance in the ranking. It is third in the table for entry standards and employment, but did not enter the 2001 Research Assessment Exercise.

Land and property management has a healthy employment record, finishing in the top ten for graduates' "positive destinations" this year. At least 75 per cent of leavers at all eight institutions were in graduate-level jobs or continuing their studies within six months. Graduates' prospects inevitably depend to some extent on the state of the property market, which was still buoyant when these statistics were collected. Nearly 80 per cent went straight into graduate jobs at the time of the latest survey, almost half of them continuing to study at the same time. Starting salaries reflect this, averaging nearly £21,800 and almost making the top ten in the earnings table.

Completion rates tend to be higher at the universities with more demanding entrance requirements. Only about 2,000 students are taking the subject at degree or diploma level, although the subjects are often included in wider environmental programmes.

- Chartered Institute of Housing: **www.cih.org/**
- Institute of Residential Property Management: **www.irpm.org.uk/**
- Royal Institution of Chartered Surveyors: **www.rics.org/**

Land and Property Management	Research quality/5	Entry standards	Student satisfaction %	Graduate prospects %	Overall rating
1 Cambridge	5B	504		89	100.0
2 Reading	5B	366	78	92	96.9
3 Ulster	5A	313	78	83	92.9
4 Birmingham City	3bE	258	78	80	83.8
5 Royal Agricultural College		316	74	85	83.7
6 Portsmouth	3aB		75	75	79.7
7 Westminster	3aD	257	68	75	77.9
8 Greenwich	3bE	196	66	82	76.9

Employed in graduate job:	42%	Average starting graduate salary:	£21,769
Employed in graduate job and studying:	35%	Average starting non-graduate salary:	*
Studying:	4%		
Employed in non-graduate job and studying:	2%	The letters that appear in the Research Quality column indicate the	
Employed in non-graduate job:	13%	proportion of staff included in the assessment, A showing that	
Unemployed:	4%	almost all staff were included and F showing that hardly any were.	

Law

Law attracts more applications than any other single subject – nearly 80,000 at the start of 2007, despite a 9 per cent drop with the switch from six choices per applicant to five. And entry standards reflect its popularity: nine subjects have higher average entry scores, but only in medicine do so many universities make such testing demands. More than 25 of the 87 universities have average entry scores of more than 400 points. However, it is still possible to secure a place at a handful of new universities with less than 200 points.

Cambridge retains its position at the top, with Oxford rising to second followed by the London School of Economics and King's College London, all of whom overtook University College London and Aberdeen. Cambridge has the highest entry standards and the best employment record, with 95 per cent of leavers in graduate-level jobs or continuing their studies six months after finishing the course. It also has one of the eight 5* research grades, the others going to UCL, Oxford, LSE, Durham, Keele, Southampton and Queen Mary, University of London.

Oxford and Cambridge did not secure a sufficient response to the National Student Survey to compile a satisfaction score, but ratings elsewhere were high. Derby had the most satisfied students, with Sunderland close behind. Aberdeen remains the top university in Scotland, while Cardiff is just ahead of Aberystwyth in Wales. Buckingham holds the highest position outside the traditional universities, breaking into the top 40 despite not being eligible, as a private university, to enter the 2001 Research Assessment Exercise. Robert Gordon is the top new university, just ahead of Sunderland.

Destinations scores are generally high: no fewer than 29 universities saw at least 80 per cent of leavers go straight into graduate jobs or further study. The requirement for further professional training for solicitors and barristers means that more than half continue to study, either full or part-time. Many law graduates opt for careers in other areas, but the 4 per cent unemployment rate shows that they are still in demand. Average starting salaries are not as high as tales of riches in "magic circle" firms might suggest, however. The £18,592 average for graduate-level jobs is only just outside the bottom 20 for all subjects, while most of those in other types of employment earn only around £14,500.

- Law Society of England and Wales: **www.lawsociety.org.uk/**
- Law Society of Northern Ireland: **www.lawsoc-ni.org/**
- Law Society of Scotland: **www.lawscot.org.uk/**

Law	Research quality/5	Entry standards	Student satisfaction %	Graduate prospects %	Overall rating
1 Cambridge	5*A	524		95	100.0
2 Oxford	5*B	522		88	94.9
3 London School of Economics	5*A	500	79	92	94.0
4 King's College London	5A	449	89	84	93.2
5 University College London	5*A	467	75	90	90.4
6 Aberdeen	5B	412		94	89.6
7 Durham	5*A	485	74	86	89.3
8 Leicester	5A	396	86	80	88.3
9 Dundee	5B	400	82	88	87.1
=10 Southampton	5*B	412	84	75	86.4
=10 Nottingham	5A	477	74	83	86.4
=12 Bristol	5B	436	76	89	86.1
=12 Queen Mary, London	5*B	395	80	82	86.1
14 Newcastle	5C	435	84	78	85.5
15 Edinburgh	5B	448	74	87	84.9
=16 Strathclyde	5A	444	74	81	84.6
=16 Manchester	5A	452	76	75	84.6
18 Birmingham	5C	424		84	84.5
=19 Warwick	5B	469	76	77	84.0
=19 Glasgow	5B	460	74	82	84.0
21 East Anglia	5B	400	83	74	83.8
22 School of Oriental and African Studies	5A	431	69	84	82.7
23 Exeter	5C	425	79	78	82.2
24 Hull	5B	331	80	83	82.1
25 Keele	5*A	312	74	83	81.7
26 Kent	5B	352	80	78	81.5
27 Liverpool	4B	424	75	82	81.4
28 Queen's, Belfast	5B	411	72	82	81.1
29 Reading	5B	373	78	76	81.0
30 Leeds	5A	444	67	77	80.3
31 Essex	5B	330	77	75	78.7
32 Cardiff	5C	403	75	74	78.5
33 Lancaster	5B	398	75	67	78.2
34 Aberystwyth	4B	318	79	73	77.3
35 Sussex	4B	392	77	64	76.7

Law cont.

	Research quality/5	Entry standards	Student satisfaction %	Graduate prospects %	Overall rating
36 City	5B	350	62	89	75.9
37 Buckingham		251	87	87	75.6
38 Brunel	5A	350	63	81	75.5
39 Robert Gordon	3aD	295		89	75.2
40 Sheffield	5C	406	66	77	75.1
41 Sunderland		249	91	78	75.0
42 Derby		284	92	68	73.9
43 Nottingham Trent	4F	299	77	87	73.6
44 Surrey	5C	355	63	83	73.4
=45 Central Lancashire	4E	276	75	84	72.8
=45 Northumbria		362	79	76	72.8
47 Oxford Brookes	4D	346	74	71	72.6
48 Liverpool John Moores	3bC	267	81	73	72.5
49 Swansea	3aB	301	76	64	71.5
50 Ulster	5C	325	73	60	70.7
51 Napier	3aD	265		79	70.2
52 West of England	4F	294	78	71	69.8
53 Manchester Metropolitan		318		76	69.5
54 Teesside		266	88	61	69.4
55 De Montfort	4E	240	78	70	68.8
56 Hertfordshire	3aC	250	72	71	68.5
57 Kingston		268	77	76	68.2
58 Glamorgan		247	82	68	67.9
59 Staffordshire	3aF	266	81	64	67.8
60 Glasgow Caledonian	3bE	362		63	67.2
61 Portsmouth		300	74	73	67.0
62 Sheffield Hallam	3aF	283	74	68	66.4
63 Bournemouth	3aE	285	70	71	66.3
64 East London	3aE	177	79	66	65.6
65 Huddersfield	3bE	244	70	74	65.2
66 Brighton		284	72	72	65.1
67 Southampton Solent	3aD	172	78	62	64.7
68 Westminster	5F	286	67	72	64.6
69 Coventry		273	78	58	64.3
=70 Stirling		313		62	63.8
=70 Plymouth	3bE	280	75	56	63.8
72 Anglia Ruskin	2B	267	72	57	63.3
73 Birmingham City		268	74	61	62.8
74 Wolverhampton	3aE	196	74	61	62.3
75 Middlesex		220	63	82	61.4
76 Bedfordshire		165	81	55	60.9
77 Edge Hill		251	83	37	60.2
=78 Lincoln		252	76	49	59.9

=78 Bangor		294	73	49	59.9
80 Greenwich	3bF	244	69	57	59.1
=81 London South Bank		200	71	60	58.5
=81 Northampton		214	77	47	58.5
83 Buckinghamshire		174	69	66	58.1
84 Bradford		271	72	42	56.9
85 Leeds Metropolitan	3aE	289	49	62	53.6
86 Abertay		325		33	52.8
87 Thames Valley	2F	179	64		52.7

Employed in graduate job:	21%	Average starting graduate salary:	£18,592
Employed in graduate job and studying:	5%	Average starting non-graduate salary:	£14,499
Studying:	47%		
Employed in non-graduate job and studying:	5%	The letters that appear in the Research Quality column indicate the
Employed in non-graduate job:	19%	proportion of staff included in the assessment, A showing that
Unemployed:	4%	almost all staff were included and F showing that hardly any were.

Librarianship and Information Management

Loughborough has taken back the lead in librarianship and information management from Sheffield, which drops to second place despite having the only 5* research grade in the subjects. Loughborough has the most satisfied students and the best employment record. University College London has the highest entry qualifications in a table where almost half of the departments have too few students to calculate a reliable score on this measure.

Loughborough's record of four out five graduates in graduate-level work or further study six months after completing a course is the best in a table that is down to nine universities from 14 three years ago because of low student numbers at some of the smaller providers.

Fifth-placed Brighton is the leading new university in a ranking that has no Scottish representatives and only Aberystwyth from Wales. Students appear generally satisfied with their courses, but employment prospects vary widely for a ranking of only nine universities. Three universities registered "positive destinations" for less than 40 per cent of their graduates – lower scores than when the table was last published, two years ago.

As the small size of the table suggests, librarianship and information management are minority interests at degree level, and this makes the subjects vulnerable to swings in employment statistics. Graduate unemployment was below average in the last edition of the table, but it is up to 9 per cent this year. Librarianship and information management are not the poor payers that their reputation might suggest, but the subjects have also slipped down the earnings league a little. Average starting salaries in graduate-level jobs are close to £19,500 – mid-way in the listing of subject areas.

- Association for Information Management: **www.aslib.com/**
- Chartered Institute of Library and Information Professionals: **www.cilip.org.uk/**

Librarianship and Information Management	Research quality/5	Entry standards	Student satisfaction %	Graduate prospects %	Overall rating
1 Loughborough	5B	342	88	75	100.0
2 Sheffield	5*A	331	76	72	95.8
3 University College London	4A	382	72	66	92.5
4 Aberystwyth	3aB		77	63	87.7
5 Brighton	3bD	273	83	57	80.9
6 London South Bank	3bD		80	38	77.3
7 Northumbria	3bC	278	68	62	75.8
8 Leeds Metropolitan	4E		73	38	73.3
9 Manchester Metropolitan	4C		66	28	69.3

Employed in graduate job:	44%	Average starting graduate salary:	£19,469
Employed in graduate job and studying:	3%	Average starting non-graduate salary:	£13,614
Studying:	7%		
Employed in non-graduate job and studying:	2%	The letters that appear in the Research Quality column indicate the	
Employed in non-graduate job:	34%	proportion of staff included in the assessment, A showing that	
Unemployed:	9%	almost all staff were included and F showing that hardly any were.	

Linguistics

Cambridge has won back the lead it lost to Oxford when this table was last published two years ago. Oxford has the most satisfied students at any university in the ranking, but Cambridge leads on entry standards and graduate destinations. Both of the ancient universities have 5* research grades, as do Queen Mary, University of London and University College London, which entered a smaller proportion of its academics for the 2001 Research Assessment Exercise.

Edinburgh is Scotland's only representative in the table, while Cardiff is well ahead of Bangor in Wales. Portsmouth is the best-placed new university in a ranking that is dominated by the older foundations. Wolverhampton and Westminster are the only other post-1992 universities in the top 20.

The number of applications for degrees in linguistics had fallen below 2,500 at the start of 2008, after an 11 per cent fall, attributed mainly to the switch from six choices per applicant to five. Eight out of ten students arrive with A levels or their equivalent. Entry standards are relatively high: seven of the 27 universities averaged more than 400 points among students with A levels and Highers and only two fell marginally below 250 points. More than 10 per cent of the places were filled through Clearing in 2006.

Linguistics is close to the bottom ten subjects for immediate employment prospects in this year's *Guide*, although the 7 per cent unemployment rate is only just above average. In the latest statistics, almost four out of ten graduates were in lower-level jobs six months after completing their courses. Average starting salaries for graduate jobs are in the bottom ten, at less than £17,500.

- British Association for Applied Linguistics: **www.baal.org.uk/**
- Linguistics Association of Great Britain: **www.lagb.org.uk/**

Linguistics	Research quality/5	Entry standards	Student satisfaction %	Graduate prospects %	Overall rating
1 Cambridge	5*A	522		82	100.0
2 Oxford	5*A	487	86	77	96.4
3 Newcastle	5A	446	75	72	86.2
4 Queen Mary, London	5*A	340	81		84.8
5 University College London	5*C	399	82	67	83.1
6 Durham	5B		77	67	81.8
7 Lancaster	5B	375	78	64	80.3
8 Sussex	4A	416	67	75	79.8
9 York	5A	421	69	63	79.6
10 Edinburgh	5C	421	77	50	75.8
11 Essex	5B	288	75	63	74.6
12 Leeds	3aC	378	77	54	71.9
13 Manchester	5B	390	69	45	71.5
14 Reading	3aB		78	50	71.0
15 Portsmouth	5C	243	78		69.2
16 East Anglia	3bB		80	46	68.9
17 Wolverhampton	3aA		73	46	68.7
18 School of Oriental and African Studies	3aA	352	67		68.4
19 Sheffield		416	71	62	67.1
20 Westminster	5C	247	73	51	67.0
21 Hertfordshire	3aA	267	71	52	66.9
22 Cardiff		370	77	46	63.6
23 York St John		282	82	48	63.2
24 King's College London		371	73	49	62.6
25 West of England		287	75	55	61.5
26 Bangor	3bB	256	63	39	55.9
27 Ulster	3aE	292	51	35	48.5

Employed in graduate job:	27%	Average starting graduate salary:	£17,441
Employed in graduate job and studying:	5%	Average starting non-graduate salary:	£14,089
Studying:	21%		
Employed in non-graduate job and studying:	4%	The letters that appear in the Research Quality column indicate the	
Employed in non-graduate job:	35%	proportion of staff included in the assessment, A showing that	
Unemployed:	7%	almost all staff were included and F showing that hardly any were.	

Materials Technology

Cambridge and Oxford have swapped places at the head of the ranking for materials technology with the light blues now at number one, but beneath them the order is little changed since the last publication two years ago. The only movement in the rest of the top ten is an exchange of places between Swansea and Manchester, in eighth and tenth places respectively. Cambridge has by far the highest entry standards and is one of the five universities rated as internationally outstanding for research. The others are second-placed Oxford and Birmingham, in fourth, Sheffield and Manchester.

Materials Technology cont.

Loughborough has the most satisfied students, while Imperial College has the best employment record, with 92 per cent of leavers going straight into graduate jobs or further study. Exeter is only one percentage point behind on employment, after exceeding the 90 per cent mark for the second time in a row. Swansea is the only Welsh university in the table and there is no representative from Scotland. Four new universities remain in the ranking, of which Manchester Metropolitan has the best scores.

Outside Oxbridge, entry scores for materials technology are (mostly) tightly bunched. Only Imperial and Bath average more than 400 points, while only the bottom three slip below 250 points.

Student satisfaction and graduate destinations show rather more variation.

Courses cover three distinct areas: materials science, mining and engineering; textiles technology and printing; and marine technology. Employment prospects have improved slightly since the table last appeared: the unemployment rate is down from 11 per cent to 7 per cent. But average starting salaries of less than £18,700 are slightly below average for those who find graduate jobs.

- Institute of Materials, Minerals and Mining: **www.iom3.org/**
- UK Centre for Materials Education (materials science): **www.materials.ac.uk/**

Materials Technology	Research quality/5	Entry standards	Student satisfaction %	Graduate prospects %	Overall rating
1 Cambridge	5*A	539		85	100.0
2 Oxford	5*A		82	81	93.2
3 Imperial College	5A	424	75	92	89.9
4 Birmingham	5*A	384	81	71	88.2
5 Sheffield	5*A	341	76	68	83.8
6 Nottingham	5B		79	72	80.2
7 Loughborough	4B	275	84	78	78.9
8 Swansea	4A	295	71	76	75.9
9 Queen Mary, London	5B	302	70	70	74.3
10 Manchester	5*B	384	61	55	72.3
11 Bath		462	77	79	71.5
12 Exeter		328	78	91	69.6
13 Leeds	5C	326	70	58	69.2
14 Manchester Metropolitan	4A	262	59	68	67.2
15 De Montfort	4A	245	54	47	59.2
16 Buckinghamshire New	3bB	236	65	41	55.0
17 University of the Arts, London		183		48	44.5

Employed in graduate job:	43%	Average starting graduate salary:	£18,661
Employed in graduate job and studying:	5%	Average starting non-graduate salary:	£14,429
Studying:	16%		
Employed in non-graduate job and studying:	3%	The letters that appear in the Research Quality column indicate the	
Employed in non-graduate job:	26%	proportion of staff included in the assessment, A showing that	
Unemployed:	7%	almost all staff were included and F showing that hardly any were.	

Mathematics

The mathematics table again shows considerable movement, although the top two remain the same. St Andrews has shot eight places up the table to third, while Bristol, having gone up six places last year, is down eight to joint eleventh this time. The addition of student satisfaction scores is responsible for most of the volatility: Leicester, for example, where 88 per cent of final-year undergraduates were satisfied with their course, moves up 15 places to fifth as a result.

Oxford has cut Cambridge's lead at the top of the table, but still has marginally lower entry standards and employment prospects. Cambridge is also the only university with 5* research grades in pure and applied maths and statistics. The three different research categories meant that 5* grades were sprinkled liberally among the leading universities. Bristol, Oxford, Warwick and Imperial College each achieved two top grades. Even Kent, in 39th place, has one.

Greenwich, the only new university in the top 30, boasts the most satisfied students, while Edge Hill has the best destinations scores, with 95 per cent of leavers going straight into graduate-level employment or further study. Maths had among the most satisfied students in the NSS results published in 2007, only four universities satisfying less than 70 per cent of their undergraduates.

Maths is still among the top 20 subjects for applications, having seen four successive years of increases. The subject bucked the national trend with an 11 per cent increase in applications in 2006. A 7 per cent decline at the start of 2008, with the cut in choices per applicant, was still less than the average for all subjects. Only medicine, dentistry and veterinary medicine have higher entry standards. More than 20 universities average over 400 points at entry and none of those for which data are available drops below 200.

Often cited as one of the subjects most likely to lead to a high salary, maths is also in the top 20 subjects for "positive destinations". It does better still in the earnings league: although no longer in the top ten, starting salaries in graduate-level jobs average £21,760. Despite the large number of universities in the table, all but one had more than half of their leavers in graduate-level work or on postgraduate courses within six months of graduation.

- London Mathematical Society: **www.lms.ac.uk/**
- Maths Careers: **www.mathscareers.org.uk**
- Royal Statistical Society: **www.rss.org.uk**

Mathematics	Research quality/5 Pure	Research quality/5 Applied	Research quality/5 Statistics	Entry standards	Student satisfaction %	Graduate prospects %	Overall rating
1 Cambridge	5*A	5*A	5*B	548		89	100.0
2 Oxford	5*B	5A	5*C	528	87	88	96.0
3 St Andrews	5B	5B	5A	472	84	76	89.2
4 Imperial College	5*B	5*B	5B	499	78	81	88.6
5 Leicester	5B	5B		333	88	84	88.5
6 Durham	5B	5*B	4B	522	77	79	87.5
7 Warwick	5B	5*A	5*B	513	73	77	86.3

Mathematics cont.

	Research quality/5 Pure	Research quality/5 Applied	Research quality/5 Statistics	Entry standards	Student satisfaction %	Graduate prospects %	Overall rating
8 University College London	5B	5B	5B	470	78	79	85.8
9 Lancaster	4A		5*B	414	83	71	85.5
10 Birmingham	5C	5B	4B	428	82	78	85.4
=11 Nottingham	5B	5B	5A	442	78	74	84.9
=11 Bristol	5B	5*A	5*A	469	69	79	84.9
13 Surrey		5A	5A	398	71	85	84.4
14 Bath	5A	5*B	5B	473	69	82	84.2
15 Glasgow	5D	5A	5A	395	81	75	84.1
16 London School of Economics			4B	501	70	88	83.7
17 Edinburgh	5*A	5B	4C	445	79	70	83.4
=18 Heriot-Watt		5B	5C	418	79	74	82.6
=18 East Anglia	5A	4B		402	85	60	82.6
=20 Exeter	4A	5A	4A	376	82	64	82.3
=20 York	5B	5A		439	74	72	82.3
22 Keele	2C	5A	3aA	294	81	88	82.0
23 Loughborough		4B		364	81	76	81.9
24 Cardiff	5A			392	75	68	81.6
25 Sheffield	5B	4B	5C	395	81	69	81.3
26 Southampton	5C	5B	5A	412	73	76	81.1
27 Sussex	4A	5B	4A	393	79	67	81.0
28 Newcastle	5C	4B	5A	399	76	72	80.8
29 Hull	4B	4A			80	70	80.7
30 Greenwich			3aA	226	90	69	80.0
31 Manchester	5A	5A	4B	448		54	79.7
32 Oxford Brookes		3aB		274		91	79.6
33 Aston		5C		326		78	79.1
34 Strathclyde		5B	4C	393	77	71	79.0
35 Leeds	5B	5B	5B	412	72	69	78.9
36 Reading	3aA	5A	4B	345	78	68	78.8
37 Liverpool	5B	5B	4A	379	77	61	78.2
38 Queen's, Belfast	3aC			369	78	80	77.9
=39 Kent	3aC	5A	5*D	286	73	84	77.5
=39 Royal Holloway	5C			368	77	69	77.5
41 Stirling	3aA			293		77	77.4
42 Hertfordshire		4C		220	79	84	76.9
43 Portsmouth		5C		249	79	74	76.5
44 York St John				437		80	76.2
=45 Queen Mary, London	5A	4B	5A	286	72	69	76.0
=45 West of England		3aC		259	84	73	76.0
47 King's College London	5C	5B		417	69	67	75.5
48 Bangor	3aC					78	74.8
49 Dundee		5B		363		51	73.9

#	University							
50	Chester	3bA			320		72	73.6
51	Nottingham Trent	3aC	3aD		235		86	73.5
52	Edge Hill				231		95	73.1
=53	Sheffield Hallam				247	89	76	72.8
=53	Swansea	5C			334	72	64	72.8
55	Brunel	5A	4B		284	73	57	72.5
56	Essex	3aA	3aA		321	72	61	71.6
57	Aberystwyth	3bA	4A		324		57	71.5
58	Aberdeen	5C	4E	4A	310		62	71.4
59	Manchester Metropolitan				274	82	72	69.2
60	City	4A	3aC		307	68	60	68.5
61	Plymouth	3bA	3aC	3aE	272	79	54	68.0
62	Brighton	3aC			268		63	67.4
63	Coventry	3aC	3aE		226		70	66.3
64	Wolverhampton				201		79	65.2
65	Northumbria		3aD		254		62	64.4
66	Ulster	4E					66	63.9
67	Glamorgan				227	81	58	63.3
68	Liverpool John Moores				266		64	62.2
69	Kingston				205		69	61.3
=70	Glasgow Caledonian	3bD					60	59.9
=70	De Montfort	3bA					47	59.9

Employed in graduate job:	34%	Average starting graduate salary:	£21,760
Employed in graduate job and studying:	13%	Average starting non-graduate salary:	£15,081
Studying:	26%		
Employed in non-graduate job and studying:	3%	The letters that appear in the Research Quality column indicate the
Employed in non-graduate job:	18%	proportion of staff included in the assessment, A showing that
Unemployed:	5%	almost all staff were included and F showing that hardly any were.

Mechanical Engineering

Cambridge comfortably maintains the lead in mechanical engineering that the university established on its debut in the table last year. It has increased the gap at the top with the highest entry standards, the maximum research grade and a near-perfect destinations score. Only Robert Gordon, the one new university in the top 20, has a better employment record. All its mechanical engineers had graduate-level jobs or had started further training six months after completing a degree.

Bath, which shares second place with Bristol, is another of the seven holders of 5* research grades, the others being Liverpool, Imperial College, Southampton, Queen's, Belfast and Leeds. Loughborough, in sixth place, has the most satisfied students.

Cardiff remains the top university in Wales, while Strathclyde has stretched its lead over Aberdeen in Scotland. The number of institutions in the ranking has dropped by six this year, the majority of the survivors being old universities, which occupy all but two of the top 30 places. The open access policies pursued by many of the former polytechnics are reflected in the fact that more than a third of their entrants are admitted without A levels or equivalents. However, the number of universities with average entry scores of below 200 points is down to one this year.

Mechanical Engineering cont.

Mechanical engineering now attracts more applicants than any other branch of the wider discipline. The 22,000 applications at the start of 2008 represented a drop of less than 5 per cent – much better than most subjects at a time when the number of choices per applicant had been reduced. Nearly 10 per cent of places were filled in Clearing in 2006.

All but two of the 55 universities in the table registered "positive destinations" for more than half of their graduates in the latest statistics. Nationally, two-thirds go straight into graduate jobs, but the 7 per cent unemployment rate is slightly above average. Mechanical engineering is in the top ten subjects for starting salaries in graduate-level jobs, with an average approaching £22,500.

- Engineering and Technology Board: **www.etechb.co.uk/**
- Institution of Mechanical Engineers: **www.imeche.org/**

Mechanical Engineering	Research quality/5	Entry standards	Student satisfaction %	Graduate prospects %	Overall rating
1 Cambridge	5*A	536	84	96	100.0
=2 Bath	5*A	455	81	84	91.8
=2 Bristol	5A	466	83	83	91.8
4 Southampton	5*A	412	83	78	89.7
5 Imperial College	5*B	495	75	83	88.6
6 Loughborough	5B	375	86	84	88.1
7 Queen's, Belfast	5*B	362	80	81	85.0
=8 Cardiff	4A	367	80	80	83.8
=8 Sheffield	5A	387	74	82	83.8
10 Liverpool	5*A	356	70	85	82.9
=11 Strathclyde	5B	405	73	81	82.2
=11 Edinburgh	4C	422	77	82	82.2
=11 Nottingham	5B	370	75	83	82.2
14 Aberdeen	4C			93	81.8
15 Manchester	5A	405	69	74	79.9
16 Newcastle	4B	357	75	80	79.4
17 Hull	4C	300	76	90	78.7
18 Heriot-Watt	4A	370	69	79	77.9
19 Glasgow	5B	383	70	73	77.6
20 Robert Gordon	3bD	310		100	77.0
21 Surrey	4B	300	73	82	76.6
22 Leeds	5*B	328	69	72	76.1
23 Birmingham	4C	386	71	76	76.0
24 Sussex	5B	340	70	74	75.9
25 Ulster	4A	240	73	80	75.3
26 King's College London	5C	339	74	69	75.0
27 Brunel	5C	330	70	71	73.4
28 Aston	5C	284	67	83	73.1

29 Swansea	4A	251	67	81	72.8
30 Harper Adams		297	74	94	72.5
31 Coventry	3aC	266	75	76	72.3
32 University College London	5B	376	64	64	72.1
33 Liverpool John Moores	3aE	269	76	78	71.3
34 Lancaster		339	70	87	70.6
35 Manchester Metropolitan	3aA	235	80	54	70.5
36 West of England	3bD	262	74	79	70.3
37 Dundee		303	76	79	70.2
38 Greenwich	3aB		71	67	70.1
39 Queen Mary, London	5B	321	69	50	69.0
40 Portsmouth	4D	227	68	81	67.9
41 Plymouth	4E		77	58	67.6
42 Bradford	5B	271	72	45	67.4
43 Central Lancashire		228	76	79	67.2
=44 Glasgow Caledonian	3aD		67	73	66.4
=44 Northumbria	3bD	264	67	77	66.4
46 Huddersfield	4E	231	77	60	65.9
=47 Oxford Brookes		260	69	79	65.1
=47 Staffordshire	3bA	238	65	70	65.1
49 City	4D	223	67	69	64.2
=50 Brighton	3bC		69	61	63.5
=50 Hertfordshire	3aD	252	65	67	63.5
52 Nottingham Trent	3bD		55	91	62.7
53 Kingston	3aC	200	65	67	62.1
54 London South Bank	3aD		63	58	58.8
55 Sheffield Hallam	3aF	185	62	74	58.6

Employed in graduate job:	60%	Average starting graduate salary:	£22,378
Employed in graduate job and studying:	7%	Average starting non-graduate salary:	£15,721
Studying:	10%		
Employed in non-graduate job and studying:	1%		
Employed in non-graduate job:	15%		
Unemployed:	7%		

The letters that appear in the Research Quality column indicate the proportion of staff included in the assessment, A showing that almost all staff were included and F showing that hardly any were.

Medicine

Medicine is one of the most tightly-bunched tables, with four percentage points covering every school in the table. Cambridge remains top, by virtue of higher average entry grades than Oxford and a very small difference in employment scores. Cambridge is one of 17 universities (out of 27) registering full employment among their graduates. Oxford is among the remainder, on 99 per cent. Both have 5* research grades in three of the four research categories, although Oxford entered a higher proportion of academics for assessment in the community and hospital medicine categories.

Universally high entry standards and destinations scores, even in the recently established medical schools, make it hard for applicants to distinguish between the 27 universities in the ranking. But the research grades provide a pointer to the different areas of expertise: Edinburgh and Imperial College London are rated internationally

Medicine cont.

outstanding in hospital medicine, while Bristol has the only 5* outside Oxbridge for community medicine. The top grades are more widely spread in clinical and laboratory category, with Imperial College, Newcastle, Dundee and Birmingham joining Oxford and Cambridge on 5*.

Medical students have been generally satisfied with their teaching in the first three National Student Surveys, but are highly critical of standards of feedback and assessment. St Andrews and Southampton registered the best scores in 2007.

The subject is a notoriously difficult one in which to win a place: Government quotas mean that candidates with three or four As at A level are frequently turned away. The designation of the first new medical schools for more than 20 years was expected to ease this pressure, but the number of applicants also increased and some of the new courses cater for graduates and other mature students. As a result, entry standards have risen again this year, with only one medical school averaging less than 420 points.

Applications for courses beginning in 2007 fell by almost 4 per cent, the first drop for several years, and were down again, by 3 per cent, for 2008. The decline was less severe than in most subjects, although medicine should not have been affected by the reduction in choices per applicant because there already was a limit of four medical schools per candidate.

Undergraduates have to be prepared to work long hours, particularly towards the end of the course. The latest survey shows hardly any unemployment, and medicine is top of the earnings league, as the only subject with average starting salaries of more than £30,000.

- British Medical Association: **www.bma.org.uk**
- NHS Careers: **www.nhscareers.nhs.uk/**
- Student BMJ: **http://student.bmj.com/**

Medicine	Research quality/5 Clinical Laboratory	Research quality/5 Community	Research quality/5 Hospital	Research quality/5 Pre-Clinical	Entry standards	Student satisfaction %	Graduate prospects %	Overall rating
1 Cambridge	5*A	5*B	5*B		539		100	100.0
2 Oxford	5*A	5*A	5*A		524		99	99.8
3 Imperial College	5*B	5B	5*B	5B	500	71	100	98.7
=4 University College London		4B	5B		484	73	100	98.5
=4 Newcastle	5*D	5C	5C		487	78	100	98.5
=6 Aberdeen	4B	5C	4B		482		100	98.3
=6 Edinburgh		4B	5*C		497	77	99	98.3
=8 Glasgow	5B	4C	5C		471	71	100	98.0
=8 Bristol	5A	5*C	3aB		469	67	100	98.0
=8 Nottingham	3aB	3aC	4B	5A	484	69	100	98.0
=11 St Andrews				5B	483	84	99	97.9
=11 Southampton	5A	3aB	5B		442	83	99	97.9
=13 Liverpool	5B	4B	4B		463	67	100	97.8
=13 Birmingham	5*B	4D	5C	5C	492	67	100	97.8
=15 Keele		4A	3aA		426		100	97.7

=15 Hull-York		5A	3aB		453			97.7
17 Leeds	5C	4C	4C		455	76	100	97.6
=18 Dundee	5*B	4D	5E		468	80	99	97.5
=18 St George's	4A	4B	4A	5A	441	71	99	97.5
=18 King's College London	5C	4C	4B	5C	452	73	100	97.5
=21 Leicester	4B	3aB	4B		462	79	99	97.3
=21 Sheffield		4B	5C	5C	472	67	100	97.3
23 Cardiff	5C	4B	4B		466	58	100	97.2
24 Manchester	4B	5C	5C	5B	466	67	99	97.1
25 Queen's, Belfast	4C	5E	3aC		442	75	100	97.0
=26 Peninsula Medical School		3aC	5A		406	73		96.8
=26 Queen Mary, London	3aB	3aB	4B		427	70	100	96.8

Employed in graduate job:	88%	Average starting graduate salary:		£30,520
Employed in graduate job and studying:	6%	Average starting non-graduate salary:		*
Studying:	6%			
Employed in non-graduate job and studying:	0%	The letters that appear in the Research Quality column indicate the		
Employed in non-graduate job:	0%	proportion of staff included in the assessment, A showing that		
Unemployed:	0%	almost all staff were included and F showing that hardly any were.		

Middle Eastern and African Studies

Oxford maintains an impressive lead in Middle Eastern and African studies, with by far the highest entry standards and sharing the best satisfaction score with second-placed Exeter.

Edinburgh enters the ranking in third place, with one of the two 5* research grades. Birmingham, two places lower, has the other.

Destinations scores vary enormously, from the 30 per cent success rate at Birmingham to 77 per cent at Durham. Nationally, Middle Eastern and African studies are a little below average for "positive destinations", but the 13 per cent unemployment rate is by far the highest of any subject. The small numbers make for big swings even in the national statistics; the rate was 9 per cent when the table was last published, two years ago. The subjects are only just outside the top 20 for starting salaries in graduate jobs, with an average close to £20,000.

Edinburgh is the only university from outside England in the table and there are no new universities among the eight remaining. Of them, only Leeds and Durham fell below Grade 5 in the last Research Assessment Exercise and, Oxford apart, most of the average entry scores are tightly bunched.

Middle Eastern Studies is the larger of two small subjects, in terms of student numbers. There were fewer than 500 applications for Middle Eastern subjects at the official deadline for entry in 2008, nearly 20 per cent down on the previous year, and only 106 for African studies. The vast majority – all, in the case of African studies – come with A levels or their equivalent.

Completion rates are good, and a high proportion graduate with a first or 2:1.

- African Studies Association of the UK: **www.asauk.net/**
- British Society for Middle Eastern Studies: **www.dur.ac.uk/brismes**
- Egypt Exploration Society: **www.ees.ac.uk/**
- Society for the Promotion of Byzantine Studies: **www.byzantium.ac.uk/**

Middle Eastern and African Studies	Research quality/5	Entry standards	Student satisfaction %	Graduate prospects %	Overall rating
1 Oxford	5A	487	82		100.0
2 Exeter	5B	411	82	69	89.6
3 Edinburgh	5*A	418	68	68	88.1
4 Durham	4A		74	77	86.2
5 Birmingham	5*A	316	78	30	78.5
6 Leeds	4C	359	75	67	77.0
7 Manchester	5B	340	69	55	74.7
8 School of Oriental and African Studies	5B	339	65	71	73.7

Employed in graduate job:	37%	Average starting graduate salary:	£19,984
Employed in graduate job and studying:	9%	Average starting non-graduate salary:	*
Studying:	20%		
Employed in non-graduate job and studying:	1%	The letters that appear in the Research Quality column indicate the	
Employed in non-graduate job:	20%	proportion of staff included in the assessment, A showing that	
Unemployed:	13%	almost all staff were included and F showing that hardly any were.	

Music

Oxford has won back the leadership of the music ranking after a three-year gap, mainly on the basis of the top student satisfaction score – something the university shares with Bangor. Cambridge has the highest entry standards in the table and is ahead of Oxford on employment prospects, but neither is enough to compensate for the wide gap on student satisfaction. Both are among nine universities to boast 5* research grades. Third-placed Nottingham, Birmingham, Southampton, Manchester, Newcastle, Royal Holloway and City are the others.

The specialist institutions do best for graduate destinations. The Royal Academy of Music saw 97 per cent of leavers go straight into graduate jobs or further study, while the Royal College of Music, the Royal Scottish Academy of Music and the Royal Northern College of Music all have success rates of more than 90 per cent. Of the universities, only Ulster and Glamorgan come close.

Edinburgh has won back its position as the top university in Scotland while Bangor remains ahead of Cardiff in Wales. Oxford Brookes is the top new university, just ahead of Birmingham City and Huddersfield, but none of them make the top 30. As in most subjects, the new universities suffer for their lower entry grades, although selection is as much a matter of musical ability as academic achievement.

The 5 per cent unemployment rate in the latest survey was surprisingly low for a subject in which career prospects are notoriously uncertain. Indeed, music is in the top half of the employment table, although almost 30 per cent of leavers were in non-graduate jobs six months after graduation. Salaries are a different matter, however: the subject has dropped into the bottom three for average starting pay in graduate jobs and is lowest of all for other types of employment.

Nevertheless, music has been growing in popularity as a degree subject. There were 20,000 applications at the start of 2008, including a growing number seeking places on two-year Foundation degrees. Although this represented a 10 per cent decline on the previous year, the drop was mainly due to the cut in choices per applicant. There had been increases for most of the decade.

Nine out of ten applicants come with A levels. There can be considerable variation in the character of courses, from the practical and vocational programmes in conservatoires to the more theoretical. But entry standards tend to be high throughout: eight of the 65 universities in this year's ranking average at least 400 points, while only one slips (just) below 200.

- Incorporated Society of Musicians: **www.ism.org/**
- Royal Musical Association: **www.rma.ac.uk/**

Music	Research quality/5	Entry standards	Student satisfaction %	Graduate prospects %	Overall rating
1 Oxford	5*A	442	88	80	100.0
2 Cambridge	5*B	461	79	83	94.7
3 Nottingham	5*A	442	80	71	93.7
4 King's College London	5A	446	74	80	90.8
5 York	5A	389	78	81	90.5
6 Durham	4A	441	72	81	88.1
7 Southampton	5*A	339	81	67	88.0
8 Sheffield	5B	343	83	74	87.6
9 Manchester	5*B	428	72	74	87.4
10 Newcastle	5*A	335	76	68	85.5
11 Reading	3aB		80	82	85.2
12 Birmingham	5*B	430	74	60	85.1
13 Bristol	5A	383	70	76	84.6
14 Bangor	5C	287	88	70	84.5
15 Queen's, Belfast	5B	369	80	59	83.6
16 Edinburgh	4B	416	75	67	83.4
17 Cardiff	5C	334	80	69	82.2
18 Goldsmiths College	5A	329	71	72	81.8
19 Royal Academy of Music	4E	318	76	97	81.5
20 Royal Northern College of Music	4E		76	91	80.8
21 School of Oriental and African Studies	5B			67	80.7
22 Surrey	3aA	338	75	73	80.6
23 Glasgow	4A	361	73	63	80.3
24 Royal College of Music	4E	314	74	96	80.1
25 Keele	4A	301	73	70	79.4
26 East Anglia	4B	278	73	82	79.2
27 Liverpool	4A	361	73	56	78.6
28 Sussex	5A	373	67	59	78.4
29 Lancaster	4A	320	72	65	78.2
30 Hull	5B	284	76	61	78.0
31 Royal Holloway	5*B	351	67	63	77.9
=32 Royal Scottish Academy of Music and Drama	3bE			92	77.7
=32 Oxford Brookes	3aA	265	83	56	77.7

Music cont.

	Research quality/5	Entry standards	Student satisfaction %	Graduate prospects %	Overall rating
34 Ulster	3aD	282	74	89	77.4
35 Birmingham City	3aE	293	76	83	76.5
=36 Leeds	4C	365	71	60	76.0
=36 Huddersfield	5C	288	79	55	76.0
38 Glamorgan		305	74	88	74.7
39 City	5*C	295	64	74	74.1
40 Roehampton	3aA	245	75	62	73.7
41 Salford	4A	259	69	62	73.2
42 Aberdeen	3aA			57	72.5
43 De Montfort	4A	257	70	54	71.7
44 Bath Spa	3aC	277	73	60	71.2
45 Coventry		276	79	64	70.2
46 Canterbury Christ Church	3bA	234	75	57	70.1
47 Strathclyde		293	71	76	70.0
48 Napier	2C	339		60	69.9
49 Westminster	4D	275	71	60	69.8
50 Hertfordshire	3bB	248	72	59	68.9
=51 Liverpool John Moores	2D		71	63	67.0
=51 Anglia Ruskin	3bB	248	70	56	67.0
53 Kingston	3bC	234	69	65	66.9
54 Thames Valley	2A	243	65	67	65.8
55 York St John		245	70	70	65.3
56 Middlesex		232	67	69	63.0
57 Wolverhampton		184	71	66	61.9
58 Central Lancashire		294	70	44	61.7
59 Chichester	1A	223	70	47	61.1
60 Northampton	3bB		70	33	60.7
=61 Brighton		305	68	40	60.4
=61 Derby		269	69	46	60.4
63 Brunel		291	50	67	56.5
64 West of Scotland		253		35	54.2
65 Buckinghamshire New		219	59	37	50.6

Employed in graduate job:	35%	Average starting graduate salary:	£16,809
Employed in graduate job and studying:	6%	Average starting non-graduate salary:	£13,344
Studying:	26%		
Employed in non-graduate job and studying:	3%	The letters that appear in the Research Quality column indicate the	
Employed in non-graduate job:	25%	proportion of staff included in the assessment, A showing that	
Unemployed:	5%	almost all staff were included and F showing that hardly any were.	

Nursing

Nursing has been one of the main growth points of higher education since becoming a graduate profession, and a number of universities have taken in nursing and midwifery colleges. Indeed, the 47,000 applications placed nursing just outside the five most popular subjects at the start of 2008. This represented a fall of almost 10 per cent, but it followed three years of double-digit increases and was no more than average with the reduction in the number of choices allowed to each applicant.

Edinburgh has jumped from sixth place to first in this year's table, with the highest entry grades and the most satisfied students. York entered the table at the top last year, but has slipped back to fourth despite being one of eight universities with 100 per cent employment among the graduates of 2006. Only three of the 57 institutions in the ranking fell below 90 per cent graduate-level employment or further study six months after graduation. The unemployment rate nationally was only 2 per cent.

Portsmouth, a previous leader of this table and by far the best-placed new university, stays in second position, while Surrey, with the only 5* nursing grade, is third.

Thames Valley, Oxford Brookes, Teesside, Robert Gordon and Kington/St George's are the other new universities in the top 20. Entry scores have risen slightly since last year, but are still more closely bunched than in many tables. Only Edinburgh, Surrey, Southampton and Robert Gordon averaged more than 350 points for A levels and Highers, while Hull was the only university with an A-level entry score to dip fractionally below 200 points.

Almost two thirds of the students arrive without A levels, but there are five applications per place. A quarter of those who join pre-registration programmes drop out, but the wastage rate is nearer 10 per cent thereafter. There has been turbulence in the employment market since the figures used in this table were compiled, but only medicine, dentistry and veterinary medicine had more "positive destinations" in 2006. Nor are starting salaries for nursing as poor as its reputation suggests: the average of more than £20,700 is in the top 20 subjects in this year's *Guide* and even those in non-graduate jobs average more than £17,000.

- Just for Nurses: **www.justfornurses.co.uk/**
- The Royal British Nurses' Association: **www.r-bna.com/**
- Royal College of Nursing: **www.rcn.org.uk**

Nursing	Research quality/5	Entry standards	Student satisfaction %	Graduate prospects %	Overall rating
1 Edinburgh	3aB	403	91	96	100.0
2 Portsmouth	5A		83	98	98.7
3 Surrey	5*A	356	75	98	97.3
4 York	5B			100	96.8
5 King's College London	4A	302	77	100	93.5
6 Manchester	5B	333	76	94	92.1
=7 Sheffield	5D		78	100	91.5
=7 Southampton	3bA	357	74	98	91.5
9 Liverpool	3aB	331	81	92	91.3

Nursing cont.

	Research quality/5	Entry standards	Student satisfaction %	Graduate prospects %	Overall rating
10 Glasgow	3aD	313	79	100	90.9
11 Thames Valley	3bA		77	98	90.2
12 Cardiff	4D	305	75	99	89.6
13 Oxford Brookes	3bF	336	80	97	89.4
=14 Leeds	4A	325	66	97	89.0
=14 Nottingham	3aC	340	72	97	89.0
16 Stirling	3bB			98	88.5
17 City	4B	260	76	95	88.2
18 Teesside		293	82	98	87.9
=19 Robert Gordon	2F	373		95	87.8
=19 Kingston/St George's	3aA	243	76		87.8
21 Glamorgan	3bB	234	81	97	87.7
22 Glasgow Caledonian	3aE	306	75	98	87.1
23 Salford	3aA	296	72	92	86.6
24 Coventry		294		99	85.9
=25 Swansea	3bB	259	71	99	85.7
=25 Huddersfield		299	80	94	85.7
27 Birmingham	3bD	336	75	89	85.4
28 Abertay		272		100	85.2
29 Ulster	4D	231	76	97	85.1
30 De Montfort	3aD	314	70	95	85.0
31 Brighton	2F	317	70	99	84.9
32 Central Lancashire	3bE	309	73	95	84.8
33 Queen Margaret Edinburgh		264		100	84.7
34 Bangor		228	79	100	84.4
35 West of England	3bC	248	72	97	84.0
36 Canterbury Christ Church		245		100	83.3
37 Plymouth	3bC	304	68	93	83.2
=38 Chester		240	74	100	83.0
=38 Sheffield Hallam		261	73	99	83.0
=38 Anglia Ruskin	3aD	264	71	95	83.0
=41 Cumbria	2F			98	82.9
=41 Keele	2E	262		97	82.9
=41 Leeds Metropolitan	3bE	269	75	93	82.9
44 Hertfordshire	4D	238	70	96	82.8
45 Bradford	3bB		69	94	82.7
46 London South Bank	3aE	232		98	82.6
47 Hull	3aE	199	74	99	82.1
48 Birmingham City	2E	277		93	81.5
49 Dundee		231		98	81.0
50 Liverpool John Moores	3aC	223	65	98	80.8
51 Northampton		225		97	80.0
52 Edge Hill		250	83	83	79.8

53	Greenwich		225	74	93	79.1
54	Bournemouth	3bF	232	72	91	78.4
55	Staffordshire		242	64	97	77.8
56	Middlesex	3aF		68	90	76.6
57	Northumbria	3aC	298	77	66	76.3

Employed in graduate job:	87%	Average starting graduate salary:	£20,763
Employed in graduate job and studying:	7%	Average starting non-graduate salary:	£17,145
Studying:	1%		
Employed in non-graduate job and studying:	0%	The letters that appear in the Research Quality column indicate the
Employed in non-graduate job:	3%	proportion of staff included in the assessment, A showing that
Unemployed:	2%	almost all staff were included and F showing that hardly any were.

Other Subjects Allied to Medicine

The "allied to medicine" category covers audiology, complementary therapies, counselling, health services management, health sciences, nutrition, occupational therapy, optometry, ophthalmology, orthoptics, osteopathy, physiotherapy, podiatry, radiography and speech therapy. Traditional universities dominate the top ten, but big names such as Bristol and Durham find themselves outside the top 30.

Cardiff has stretched its lead since the last publication of the table two years ago, with one of the two 5* research grades and a high employment score. Manchester, in fifth place, is the other university rated internationally outstanding for research, but Cardiff entered more of its academics for assessment. Cambridge has moved up from 18th place to second, with the most satisfied students and by far the highest entry standards, and might have been higher still if it had entered the 2001 Research Assessment Exercise in this category.

Stiff competition for places in subjects such as optometry and physiotherapy has been pushing up entry grades, with six universities averaging more than 400 points on the UCAS tariff and only one dropping below 200. Nearly a dozen institutions recorded positive destinations for at least 90 per cent of their graduates, with Leeds recording 98 per cent going straight into graduate-level employment or continuing their studies.

Queen Margaret has the highest position in the table among the new universities and is joined by Glasgow Caledonian in the top ten. The table is more mixed than most in terms of the performance of new and old universities.

Across the whole range of subjects, almost half of the students arrive without A levels. Applications were down by more than 13 per cent at the start of 2008 to less than 24,000, compared with almost 32,000 two years ago. The subjects are now just outside the top 20 most popular degree choices. Seven out of ten leavers go straight into graduate jobs – also on the fringe of the top 20 – but average starting salaries are below average for all subjects, at just less than £19,000.

- Association of Health Professions in Ophthalmology: **www.ahpo.org/**
- British Association/College of Occupational Therapy: **www.cot.org.uk/**
- British Society of Audiology: **www.thebsa.org.uk/**
- Chartered Society of Physiotherapy: **www.csp.org.uk/**
- General Chiropractic Council: **www.gcc-uk.org**
- General Osteopathic Council: **www.osteopathy.org.uk**
- General Optical Council: **www.optical.org**

Other Subjects Allied to Medicine cont.

- Health Professions Council: **www.hpc-uk.org**
- NHS Careers: **www.nhscareers.nhs.uk**
- Royal College of Radiologists: **www.rcr.ac.uk/**
- Royal College of Speech and Language Therapists: **www.rcslt.org/**
- Society of Chiropodists and Podiatrists: **www.feetforlife.org/**
- Society of Radiographers: **www.sor.org/**

Other Subjects Allied to Medicine	Research quality/5	Entry standards	Student satisfaction %	Graduate prospects %	Overall rating
1 Cardiff	5*A	378	77	94	100.0
2 Cambridge		539	86	85	97.1
3 Strathclyde	5A	375	79	87	96.9
4 Aston	5C	372	83	95	96.8
5 Manchester	5*B	410	69	95	95.2
6 Bradford	5B	367	78	89	94.9
7 Leeds	5D	327	82	98	93.0
8 Newcastle	5A	405	75	72	92.8
9 Queen Margaret Edinburgh	4A	329		87	91.7
=10 Nottingham	3aC	392	82	81	91.2
=10 Glasgow Caledonian	4C	397	79	80	91.2
12 Southampton	3aA	387	77	79	90.6
13 Portsmouth	5A	269	75	92	90.5
14 City	5C	338	75	94	90.4
15 Sheffield	4B	375	78	74	89.6
16 King's College London	4B	385	77	73	89.1
17 Robert Gordon	3bC	363		87	85.9
18 Imperial College		465		70	85.4
19 Liverpool	3aB	327	68	95	85.2
20 Brighton	5C	358	70	78	85.1
21 St George's	3aE	310	78	91	84.7
22 University College London	5C	387	65	81	84.6
23 Teesside	3aC	296	81	77	84.4
=24 Oxford Brookes		348	83	80	83.9
=24 Sheffield Hallam	4D	318	75	83	83.9
26 Salford	3aA	300	73	80	83.6
27 East Anglia	3bA	372	70	78	83.4
28 Ulster	4F	340	76	87	83.2
=29 Hull	4D	304	73	87	82.7
=29 York	5A			52	82.7
31 West of England	3aB	294	73	81	82.6
32 Anglia Ruskin	3bA	304	71	86	82.3
33 Napier	4D			80	82.1
34 Durham		388	79	73	82.0
35 Greenwich	3aA	282	81	59	81.9

Rank	University	Research Quality				Score
=36	Keele		354		84	81.6
=36	Northumbria		364	76	83	81.6
=38	Northampton	2C	260	77	93	81.5
=38	Birmingham		401	75	76	81.5
40	Hertfordshire	3bB	290	70	87	80.5
41	Bristol		316	77	86	80.4
42	UWIC, Cardiff	3bD	292	75	84	80.2
43	Reading		405		68	80.0
44	Kent		264	84	78	79.7
45	East London	2C	302	76	75	79.1
46	Bedfordshire		314	71	93	78.8
47	Birmingham City		323		82	78.4
48	Cumbria		308		84	78.0
49	Central Lancashire	3bA	298	71	69	77.9
50	York St John	2E	296	77	74	77.6
51	Lancaster		331		78	77.5
52	Coventry	3aE	324		74	77.2
53	De Montfort	4C	261	72	68	76.9
54	Leeds Metropolitan	3aE	303	72	74	76.8
55	Liverpool John Moores	4A	206	72	63	76.6
56	Manchester Metropolitan	3bD	351	72	60	76.1
57	Westminster	3aC		70	64	75.4
58	Brunel	3aE	362	63	77	75.3
59	Kingston	3aC		71	61	74.7
60	St Mary's College		284	81	60	74.6
61	Plymouth	3bC	284	65	77	73.8
62	Glamorgan		319	61	93	73.5
63	Nottingham Trent	5D	217	65	81	73.3
64	Huddersfield		340	68	68	72.4
65	Derby		347	66	72	72.3
66	Chester	3aB	224	76	44	71.3
67	Wolverhampton	3aC	172	75	62	71.0
68	Canterbury Christ Church	2C	232	62	88	70.9
69	Middlesex		238	65	85	69.3
70	Swansea		302	72	45	66.7
71	Lincoln		233	71	61	66.4
72	Bath Spa	2E			61	65.6
73	Roehampton	2F			63	65.1
74	Marjon, Plymouth		315	60	60	64.8
75	West of Scotland	3bC			27	54.4

Employed in graduate job:	63%	Average starting graduate salary:	£18,937
Employed in graduate job and studying:	7%	Average starting non-graduate salary:	£13,868
Studying:	7%		
Employed in non-graduate job and studying:	1%		
Employed in non-graduate job:	16%		
Unemployed:	6%		

The letters that appear in the Research Quality column indicate the proportion of staff included in the assessment, A showing that almost all staff were included and F showing that hardly any were.

Pharmacology and Pharmacy

Edinburgh has come from outside the top 20 to lead the pharmacology and pharmacy ranking, with exceptionally high entry standards and the most satisfied students. It is not among the five universities with 5* research grades, which are spread widely through the table. Only Bath, in second place, and Manchester, sixth, are rated internationally outstanding in pharmacy. The three top grades in pharmacology went to University College London in 13th, Dundee, 14th place, and Newcastle, in 23rd.

Queen's, Belfast is the only university to see all leavers go straight into graduate jobs or continue their studies, but Nottingham, Aston, Robert Gordon, Brighton, Liverpool John Moores and the School of Pharmacy, in London, all registered 99 per cent "positive destinations". Another nine institutions reached the 90 per cent mark.

Portsmouth is the top new university and is joined by Sunderland and Robert Gordon in the top 20. Third-placed Cardiff is the only representative of Wales in a table that contains five more institutions than in its last edition. Entry scores are high, with five universities averaging more than 400 points and only two less than 250.

Departments in England are evenly split between those specialising in pharmacy and pharmacology. Only four cover both. Since 1997, pharmacy degrees have been converted to the four-year MPharm, whereas pharmacology is available either as a three-year BSc or as an extended course. Surprisingly, applications were down by more than 16 per cent at the start of 2008, after three successive large rises.

Career prospects are excellent, especially in pharmacy, with only 2 per cent unemployment across both subjects in the latest survey. Only medicine, dentistry, nursing and veterinary medicine had a higher proportion of "positive destinations". Only one university dropped below a success rate of 60 per cent, although surprisingly, the subjects come out below average for starting salaries in graduate jobs.

- Association of Pharmacy Technicians UK: **www.aptuk.org/**
- British Pharmacological Society: **www.bps.ac.uk/**
- National Pharmaceutical Association: **http://npa.co.uk**
- Royal Pharmaceutical Society of Great Britain: **www.rpsgb.org.uk/**

Pharmacology and Pharmacy	Reasrch quality/5 Pharmacology	Reasrch quality/5 Pharmacy	Entry standards	Student satisfaction %	Graduate prospects %	Overall rating
1 Edinburgh	4A		553	91	82	100
2 Bath		5*A	434	74	97	94.7
3 Cardiff		5A	397	82	97	94.4
=4 Cambridge	5A			86	85	93.8
=4 Queen's, Belfast		4B	394	88	100	93.8
6 Manchester		5*B	422	80	94	93.7
7 Strathclyde		5B	411	79	92	90.5
8 Bristol	4A		384	83	89	90.3
9 Nottingham		5A	399	71	99	90
10 School of Pharmacy		5A	383	70	99	89
11 Liverpool	5A		339	84	79	88.4

		Research Quality		Entry Standards	NSS	Destinations	Overall
12	Leeds	5B		379	87	72	87.9
13	University College London	5*A		430	79	60	87.6
14	Dundee	5*B		368	80	75	86.4
=15	Portsmouth	5A		273	76	94	85
=15	Aston		3aC	384	77	99	85
=17	Sunderland		3aB	310	83	96	84.8
=17	King's College London		5B	370	72	90	84.8
19	Robert Gordon	3bC		387		99	83.7
20	Bradford		4B	314	77	94	83.5
21	De Montfort		4C	283	82	93	82.5
22	Brighton	5C		342	70	99	82.4
23	Newcastle	5*D			75	85	79.8
24	Hertfordshire	3aC		288	87	65	76.6
=25	Glasgow			369	81	78	75
=25	Aberdeen			355		86	75
27	Liverpool John Moores			320	74	99	74.7
28	Greenwich	4A		249	74	67	74.1
29	Southampton			365	81	58	70
30	Nottingham Trent	5D			62	83	69.5
31	Kingston	3aC		246	69	74	68.5
32	Hull			272	74	83	68.3

Employed in graduate job:	68%	Average starting graduate salary:	£18,491
Employed in graduate job and studying:	17%	Average starting non-graduate salary:	£15,083
Studying:	8%		
Employed in non-graduate job and studying:	0%	The letters that appear in the Research Quality column indicate the	
Employed in non-graduate job:	4%	proportion of staff included in the assessment, A showing that	
Unemployed:	2%	almost all staff were included and F showing that hardly any were.	

Philosophy

Cambridge has retaken top place in philosophy after being runner-up to Oxford in the last two editions of the table. It has the highest entrance qualifications in the table and shares the best destinations score with the London School of Economics, in third place. Cambridge also leads Oxford on research, albeit only through a higher proportion of academics submitted for assessment. The LSE, King's College London and Edinburgh are the other universities rated internationally outstanding for research.

Entry standards are high, even outside Oxbridge. Another dozen universities average more than 400 points and only one of the 41 in the ranking dropped (just) below 200. The subject's popularity has been growing, but the 13 per cent decline in applications at the start of 2008 was more than average for all subjects, even allowing for the reduction in choices per applicant.

Scores in the National Student Survey have been high, at least 70 per cent of final-year undergraduates declaring themselves satisfied with their course at all but three universities. The most satisfied are at St Andrews, with Oxford, Dundee and Cardiff all close behind. Employment prospects are comparatively poor, however, with a minority of leavers at many of the universities in the bottom half of the table going straight into graduate jobs or continuing their studies.

Philosophy cont.

St Andrews, in fourth place, is the top university in Scotland, while Cardiff is top in Wales but does not reach the top 20. Central Lancashire is the only new university in the top 30 and one of only seven in the table.

Graduate unemployment is back down to the average for all subjects, but philosophy is still in the bottom 20 for "positive destinations". However, those who do find graduate-level work are in the top half of the earnings league, with average starting salaries in excess of £19,500.

- British Philosophical Association: **www.bpa.ac.uk/**
- Philosophical Society of England:
  http://atschool.eduweb.co.uk/cite/staff/philosopher/philsocindex.htm
- Royal Institute of Philosophy: **www.royalinstitutephilosophy.org/**

Philosophy	Research quality/5	Entry standards	Student satisfaction %	Graduate prospects %	Overall rating
1 Cambridge	5*A	516		85	100.0
2 Oxford	5*B	509	84	76	93.8
3 London School of Economics	5*A	452	76	85	91.8
4 St Andrews	5A	438	86	59	88.4
5 Durham	5B	477	78	76	87.2
6 Bristol	5A	455	77	66	86.1
7 King's College London	5*A	434	75	59	84.6
8 Warwick	5B	453	73	69	82.4
9 Sheffield	5A	430	77	54	82.2
10 York	5B	450	76	60	82.0
11 Hull	4B	302	82	67	79.9
12 Southampton	4A	372	77	59	79.2
13 Nottingham	5B	397	71	64	78.3
14 Aberdeen	3aB	315		78	78.1
15 University College London	5B	422	68	67	77.8
16 Edinburgh	5*C	422	65	77	77.6
17 Dundee	3aB	310	84	58	77.3
=18 Bradford	4B		78	55	77.0
=18 Reading	5B	349	79	48	77.0
20 Manchester	4B	418	78	46	76.9
21 Essex	5B	308	80	49	76.6
22 Stirling	5B	293		60	76.3
23 Cardiff	3aC	388	84	48	76.2
24 East Anglia	5B	337	79	45	76.1
25 Birmingham	4C	381	74	64	75.5
26 Leeds	5C	398	76	49	75.2
27 Glasgow	4C	413	78	45	74.8
=28 Kent	4C	293	77	63	73.8
=28 Central Lancashire	3bA		82	45	73.8
30 Liverpool	4A	359	71	50	73.2

31 Exeter		375	82	62	72.1
32 Lancaster	3aB	349	76	48	71.9
33 Sussex	5B	386	64	51	71.0
34 Keele	3aB	290	72	60	70.6
35 Hertfordshire	4B	247	78	41	69.5
36 Queen's, Belfast	3aD	325	80	39	68.5
37 Manchester Metropolitan	3aC	253	80	43	68.2
38 Greenwich	3bC	193	79	50	65.6
39 Oxford Brookes		292	79	47	64.2
40 Brighton		262	79	46	63.2
41 Roehampton		259	72	53	60.5

Employed in graduate job:	30%	Average starting graduate salary:	£19,611
Employed in graduate job and studying:	5%	Average starting non-graduate salary:	£14,149
Studying:	23%		
Employed in non-graduate job and studying:	4%	The letters that appear in the Research Quality column indicate the	
Employed in non-graduate job:	31%	proportion of staff included in the assessment, A showing that	
Unemployed:	6%	almost all staff were included and F showing that hardly any were.	

Physics and Astronomy

The top four in physics and astronomy remain unchanged. Cambridge has stretched is lead over Oxford with one of the five 5* research ratings and the most satisfied students, jointly with Keele. Satisfaction levels are high throughout the table, only the bottom university having fewer than 70 per cent of students declare themselves satisfied with their course. The other research stars are Oxford, third-placed Imperial College, Southampton and Lancaster.

The subjects command high entry grades: all the top four average at least 500 points for A levels and Highers. Just seven of the 44 universities in the table average less than 300 points, leaving the rest tightly bunched. At the very top, Oxford and Cambridge are within a single point of each other on this measure.

Durham, a previous leader, stays in fourth place. Glasgow has made the most progress in the upper reaches of the table, breaking into the top ten. But St Andrews, in sixth place, remains the top university in Scotland, while Swansea is the leader in Wales. Only three of the institutions in the table are new universities, of which Hertfordshire is clearly the best-placed.

Destinations scores are generally good, although Heriot-Watt is the only university to see more than nine out of ten leavers go straight into graduate jobs or further study. Two thirds of universities in the table register "positive destinations" for at least 70 per cent of their physicists.

The subjects had recovered from recruitment problems with three successive rises in applications. But a 14 per cent decline at the start of 2008 was worse than average for all subjects. Nevertheless, the 16,000 total underlined the subjects' steady popularity.

The profile of undergraduates is among the most traditional: only one in five is female and a similar proportion arrive without A levels or their equivalent. About 5 per cent transfer to other courses or drop out, usually at the end of the first year, but over half of those who remain get firsts or 2:1s. The 7 per cent unemployment rate is just above average for all subjects, but three-quarters find graduate jobs or go on to higher-

Physics and Astronomy cont.

level courses. The subjects are only just outside the top five for starting salaries, averaging over £22,500 in graduate-level jobs. However, there is a much bigger gap than in most subject between these salaries and those for other types of employment.

- British Astronomical Association: **http://britastro.org/**
- Institute of Physics: **www.iop.org/**

Physics and Astronomy	Research quality/5	Entry standards	Student satisfaction %	Graduate prospects %	Overall rating
1 Cambridge	5*A	539	86	85	100.0
2 Oxford	5*A	538	79	83	95.2
3 Imperial College	5*A	509	81	81	94.8
4 Durham	5A	512	85	76	94.0
5 Leeds	5A	406	83	79	90.6
6 St Andrews	5B	484	82	80	90.5
=7 Glasgow	5B	387	85	81	89.9
=7 Liverpool	5A	344	85	78	89.9
=7 Warwick	5A	488	81	72	89.9
10 Lancaster	5*A	389	80	68	87.8
11 Birmingham	5B	431	85	68	87.5
12 Exeter	5A	356	84	69	87.4
=13 Leicester	5A	348	81	75	86.7
=13 Nottingham	5A	422	77	74	86.7
=13 Bristol	5A	430	76	75	86.7
16 Sheffield	5B	383	83	73	86.2
17 Keele	3aB	300	86	86	85.8
18 Heriot-Watt	4A	356	74	91	85.7
19 King's College London	4B	372	77	88	85.6
20 Manchester	5A	445	76	69	85.4
=21 Southampton	5*B	418	79	62	84.1
=21 Sussex	5A	383	78	68	84.1
=23 Strathclyde	4A	351	81	72	83.9
=23 Royal Holloway	5B	336	80	73	83.9
25 Hull	4C	266	84	83	82.9
26 York	4B	393	83	65	82.8
27 Edinburgh	5B	443	76	67	82.7
=28 Swansea	5A	297	75	76	82.4
=28 University College London	5B	420	73	74	82.4
=28 Surrey	5A	355	74	73	82.4
31 Queen's, Belfast	5A	371	74	67	81.7
32 Newcastle	4B		81	68	81.4
33 Bath	4A	427	75	66	81.3
34 Aberystwyth	4A	265	78	74	80.8
35 Loughborough	4C	331	83	69	80.7
36 Queen Mary, London	5B	300	77	70	79.9

37 Hertfordshire	4B	230	82	71	79.8
38 Cardiff	5A	345	77	58	79.7
39 Kent	3aC	291	75	87	78.8
40 Dundee		311	82	86	77.4
41 Reading	4B	327	80	56	76.8
42 Salford	4A	216		69	76.7
43 Central Lancashire	4B		77	50	72.2
44 Nottingham Trent	3aD	219	68	75	68.2

Employed in graduate job:	30%	Average starting graduate salary:	£22,624
Employed in graduate job and studying:	8%	Average starting non-graduate salary:	£14,054
Studying:	36%		
Employed in non-graduate job and studying:	2%	The letters that appear in the Research Quality column indicate the
Employed in non-graduate job:	16%	proportion of staff included in the assessment, A showing that
Unemployed:	7%	almost all staff were included and F showing that hardly any were.

Politics

Politics has been enjoying a boom as a degree subject. After four consecutive years of substantial increases, applications held steady in 2006, when other social sciences were struggling to recruit students. A year later, the upward trend had resumed, with an 8 per cent increase bringing the total close to 24,000. Entry scores have been rising as a result, with this year's average up significantly on those in the last edition of the *Guide*. Fourteen universities (compared with 11 last year) average over 400 points and only one (just) less than 200 points.

Oxford holds onto top place with by far the highest entry scores and one of the five 5* research grades, although it entered a lower proportion of academics for assessment than Aberystwyth, Essex, King's College London or Sheffield. The fourth-placed London School of Economics has the best record for graduate destinations, just ahead of Durham, in tenth place.

St Andrews, in third place, remains well clear of its rivals in Scotland, while Aberystwyth pips Cardiff for that honour in Wales, reversing last year's positions. Portsmouth just misses a place in the top 20 and is the only new university in the top 40, having produced by far the best results in the National Student Survey published in 2007.

Employment prospects varied widely in this ranking. While a handful of universities saw three quarters of their graduates go straight into employment or further study, 17 were below the 50 per cent mark, and at three universities the success rate fell below a third. Nationally, the 7 per cent of leavers out of work after six months is just above the average for all subjects, but more than a third were in low-level employment. Politics is just outside the top 20 subjects for average starting salaries in graduate-level jobs.

- Political Studies Association of the UK: **www.psa.ac.uk/**
- Politics Association: **www.politicsassociation.com/**

Politics

	Research quality/5	Entry standards	Student satisfaction %	Graduate prospects %	Overall rating
1 Oxford	5*B	513	84	80	100.0
2 King's College London	5*A	440	80	70	95.5
3 St Andrews	5A	487	79	71	94.5
4 London School of Economics	5A	467	74	84	93.8
5 Cambridge	4A	490	76	82	93.1
6 Hull	5A	325	84	74	92.7
7 Sheffield	5*A	441	77	64	92.4
8 Essex	5*A	339	80	64	90.8
9 Warwick	5B	457	75	74	89.6
=10 Durham	4C	466	77	83	89.2
=10 Bath	5A	430	73	72	89.2
12 Aberystwyth	5*A	329	81	57	89.1
13 York	5A	451	72	66	88.2
14 Birmingham	5B	387	80	62	87.8
15 Exeter	5B	399	79	61	87.4
16 Bristol	5A	435	68	76	87.1
17 University College London	3aA	392	75	82	86.9
18 Glasgow	5B	392	79	59	86.2
19 Nottingham	4A	407	72	69	84.9
20 Cardiff	5A	381	74	55	84.5
21 Newcastle	5B	391	71	70	84.1
=22 Keele	5A	299	75	63	84.0
=22 Portsmouth	5C	266	90	48	84.0
24 Leeds	4B	386	74	68	83.5
=25 Strathclyde	5B	359	79	52	83.4
=25 Dundee	4B	349	83	50	83.4
27 East Anglia	4B	342	83	49	83.1
=28 Queen Mary, London	4A	356	72	69	82.9
=28 School of Oriental and African Studies	4B	392	75	63	82.9
=28 Lancaster	4B	362	79	56	82.9
31 Loughborough	5B	303	81	52	82.8
32 Leicester	3aB	314	83	58	82.2
33 Southampton	4B	367	77	57	81.7
34 Brunel	4B	307	73	74	81.1
35 Bradford	5B	265	74	70	81.0
36 Manchester	5B	422	71	51	80.9
37 Reading	5B	343	74	55	80.8
38 Sussex	4A	387	66	67	80.2
39 Aberdeen	4A	313		54	80.1
=40 Kent	3aB	280	79	66	79.9
=40 Queen's, Belfast	5A	350	70	50	79.9
42 De Montfort	5B	219	82	47	79.7
43 Edinburgh	4C	411	68	71	79.2

44 Swansea	3aB	296	76	65	78.8
45 Oxford Brookes	3aA	303	74	58	77.4
46 Royal Holloway	4B	333	67	66	76.9
47 Liverpool	4A	360	67	53	76.8
48 Robert Gordon	3aA			54	76.7
49 Stirling	3aB	269		65	76.3
50 Kingston	4A	205	74	55	75.9
51 Coventry	4C	226	79	54	75.8
52 Nottingham Trent	3aC	215	76	68	75.1
53 West of England	4C	255	79	47	74.8
54 Salford	5A	251	70	38	73.3
55 Ulster	3aB	267	76	46	73.2
56 Aston		333	78	54	71.1
57 Birmingham City	3aC	236	76	44	70.3
=58 Northumbria	3aD	266	75	45	69.5
=58 Wolverhampton	3aD		74	49	69.5
=58 Huddersfield	3aC	246	77	36	69.5
61 Plymouth	3aC	243	74	41	68.7
62 London South Bank	4B		68	39	68.4
63 Goldsmiths College		271	75	59	68.2
64 Leeds Metropolitan	3aA	238	71	31	67.9
65 Manchester Metropolitan	3aC	259	73	34	66.9
66 Liverpool John Moores	3aD	240	78	29	66.8
67 Westminster	4C	249	70	33	66.0
=68 Greenwich		197	69	53	60.9
=68 Lincoln		230	72	42	60.9

Employed in graduate job:	35%	Average starting graduate salary:	£20,423
Employed in graduate job and studying:	5%	Average starting non-graduate salary:	£14,863
Studying:	20%		
Employed in non-graduate job and studying:	4%	The letters that appear in the Research Quality column indicate the	
Employed in non-graduate job:	30%	proportion of staff included in the assessment, A showing that	
Unemployed:	7%	almost all staff were included and F showing that hardly any were.	

Psychology

Only law and medicine had attracted more applications than psychology at the start of 2008. Although the switch from six choices per applicant to five prompted a 10 per cent decline, the subject that was the phenomenon of the 1990s still attracted more than 70,000 applications. Most undergraduate programmes are accredited by the British Psychological Society, which ensures that key topics are covered, but the clinical and biological content of courses still varies considerably. Some universities require maths and/or biology A levels among an average of at least three Bs, but others are much less demanding. The contrast is obvious in the ranking, with nearly 20 universities averaging more than 400 points at entry and only two dipping below 200 points.

Cambridge still has a comfortable lead over Oxford at the top of the table, with by far the highest entrance and destinations scores, as well as a 5* research grade. York has jumped three places to third, while St Andrews has moved down one place to fourth.

Psychology cont.

All the top seven are considered internationally outstanding for research, as are Cardiff, Newcastle, Reading, Birmingham and Bangor. Oxford is the only university to approach Cambridge's average entry grades or graduate destinations.

Cardiff is the top university in Wales, and St Andrews is the leader in Scotland. Portsmouth and Northumbria are the only new universities to make the top 40, although Plymouth has a grade 5 research rating.

Employment scores are more bunched and much lower than in many other tables, with only the top two recording three quarters of their psychologists in graduate-level jobs or taking further courses within six months of graduation. Only one of the bottom 20 universities in the table had such "positive destinations" for more than half of their graduates. Nationally, psychology is in the bottom five subjects on this measure, although the unemployment rate is no higher than average at 6 per cent. Half of all leavers are either in low-level jobs or without work six months after graduation.

- British Psychological Society: **www.bps.org.uk/**

Psychology	Research quality/5	Entry standards	Student satisfaction %	Graduate prospects %	Overall rating
1 Cambridge	5*A	539	86	85	100.0
2 Oxford	5*A	490	82	79	94.3
3 York	5*A	459	84	66	90.7
4 St Andrews	5*A	428	82	67	88.6
5 University College London	5*B	466	80	65	87.0
=6 Glasgow	5*C	383	81	69	83.8
=6 Bristol	5*A	427	74	65	83.8
8 Exeter	5B	409	80	61	82.9
9 Cardiff	5*A	425	76	55	82.5
10 Surrey	5A	379	76	64	81.7
=11 Lancaster	5A	389	77	57	80.8
=11 Southampton	5A	410	79	51	80.8
=13 Bangor	5*A	311	77	61	80.1
=13 Loughborough	4B	394	81	56	80.1
15 Bath	5B	446	68	70	79.7
16 Hull	3aC	320	81	72	79.6
17 City	4A	342	77	64	79.4
=18 Sheffield	5A	429	74	52	79.0
=18 Birmingham	5*C	413	76	58	79.0
20 Reading	5*B	390	77	49	78.6
21 Sussex	5A	391	71	60	78.3
22 Nottingham	5A	426	70	57	78.0
23 Leeds	5C	421	76	56	77.9
24 Essex	5A	333	73	63	77.8
25 Durham	5A	415	70	55	77.0
=26 Aberdeen	4B	306		65	76.9
=26 Kent	4B	355	75	62	76.9

28 Warwick	5B	418	67	65	76.7
29 Brunel	4B	319	76	60	75.9
30 Royal Holloway	5A	377	73	49	75.8
=31 Leicester	4B	368	72	62	75.5
=31 Liverpool	4C	383	78	50	75.5
33 Edinburgh	5C	431	72	52	75.2
34 Goldsmiths College	4A	300	77	53	75.0
35 Stirling	5A	297		51	74.9
36 Dundee	4B	348	77	46	74.0
=37 Portsmouth	3aD	317	76	65	73.9
=37 Swansea	4A	340	75	48	73.9
=37 Queen's, Belfast	4A	364	77	41	73.9
40 Northumbria	4D	323	80	52	73.7
=41 Keele	4B	316	69	65	73.4
=41 East Anglia		337	87	45	73.4
43 Strathclyde	4B	349	71	56	73.2
44 Newcastle	5*C	406	65	59	73.1
45 Central Lancashire	3aE	298	78	61	72.3
=46 Nottingham Trent	3aC	294	72	64	71.5
=46 Aston	5C	363	67	57	71.5
48 Manchester	5B	408	67	46	71.4
49 Hertfordshire	4B	290	72	52	70.7
50 Newman		239	81	59	70.0
51 Oxford Brookes	3aC	361	71	48	69.6
52 Teesside		263	82	53	69.4
53 Thames Valley	1C	196	76	68	68.4
54 Coventry	2D	280	76	54	68.3
55 East London	3aC	189	74	59	68.0
=56 Westminster	3aD	318	72	48	67.4
=56 Gloucestershire		278	81	45	67.4
=56 Plymouth	5C	305	73	37	67.4
59 Middlesex	3aD	200	70	68	67.1
60 Staffordshire	3aD	264	77	43	66.9
61 Winchester	2B	275	78	40	66.5
62 Glasgow Caledonian	4E	300	75	41	66.4
63 Bradford		238	76	54	65.8
=64 Worcester	2D	243	77	45	65.6
=64 Derby	3aC	275	70	48	65.6
66 London South Bank	4B	227	68	49	65.3
=67 Canterbury Christ Church		239	74	57	65.2
=67 St Mary's College		234	75	54	65.2
69 De Montfort	3aD	250	72	48	65.1
70 York St John		258	73	56	65.0
71 Bath Spa		264	73	54	64.9
72 Southampton Solent	2D	249	75	46	64.5
73 Northampton		239	78	44	64.2
74 Chester		275	76	44	64.1

	Research quality/5	Entry standards	Student satisfaction %	Graduate prospects %	Overall rating
75 West of Scotland	3aC	238		46	64.0
76 West of England		280	78	37	63.8
77 Manchester Metropolitan	3aD	308	72	34	63.4
78 Bedfordshire	2E	228	72	51	63.1
79 Wolverhampton	3bD	249	68	51	63.0
=80 Abertay	3bB	233		44	62.9
=80 Lincoln	2D	301	71	40	62.9
=82 Sunderland	3bD	262	69	47	62.8
=82 Sheffield Hallam	3bC	309	69	39	62.8
=84 Ulster	3aD	275	74	31	62.6
=84 Greenwich	3bC	229	67	52	62.6
86 Huddersfield		271	76	36	62.4
87 Liverpool John Moores		275	72	45	62.3
88 Bournemouth		234	77	38	62.0
=89 UWIC, Cardiff		247	74	42	61.6
=89 Brighton		303	67	50	61.6
91 Glamorgan		224	72	47	61.3
92 Leeds Metropolitan		305	66	49	61.1
93 Salford		300	71	39	60.8
94 Edge Hill		263	74	34	60.4
95 Bolton	3bD	246	69	39	60.3
96 Anglia Ruskin		274	70	41	60.1
97 Kingston		252	66	49	59.3
98 Buckinghamshire New		207	70	46	58.8
99 Queen Margaret Edinburgh		252		39	58.5
100 Roehampton	3aE	217	65	46	58.3

Employed in graduate job:	29%	Average starting graduate salary:	£17,374
Employed in graduate job and studying:	5%	Average starting non-graduate salary:	£13,597
Studying:	17%		
Employed in non-graduate job and studying:	5%	The letters that appear in the Research Quality column indicate the
Employed in non-graduate job:	39%	proportion of staff included in the assessment, A showing that
Unemployed:	6%	almost all staff were included and F showing that hardly any were.

Russian and Eastern European Languages

Five universities have dropped out of the ranking for Russian and Eastern European languages since it was last published two years ago. Oxford and Cambridge tie for first place, the only table in which there is not a clear leader. Cambridge has much the highest entry standards, while Oxford leads on graduate destinations, as well as having one of the four 5* research grades.

St Andrews has dropped from second to equal fifth after a poor year for graduate employment, although it still boasts the most satisfied students. Oxford, Birmingham and Portsmouth are all close behind on that measure, while Cambridge students did not respond to the National Student Survey in sufficient numbers for a score to be published.

Sheffield, the clear leader of this ranking until teaching quality scores were removed because of their age, is back up to fourth place. It is one of four universities rated internationally outstanding for research, the others being Birmingham, Oxford and Bristol. St Andrews is the top university in Scotland, but there are no Welsh universities left in the table. Portsmouth, which has a grade 5 research rating, is the only new university this year.

Entry standards have declined since the last edition of the table, but five of those for which scores could be compiled average over 400 points and only two less than 350. Fewer than 700 students take Russian at degree level, and less than half of the universities assessed in England offer Russian as a single-honours degree. Most of the students were learning the language *ab initio*, and there was a high dropout rate from some universities, despite an "excellent rapport" between staff and students. The small numbers make for exaggerated swings in employment prospects: no subject had a higher unemployment rate when this table was last published, but the rate is below the average for all subjects this year. Russian is just outside the bottom 20 subjects for positive destinations, but it is in the top half of the earnings league, with average starting salaries of almost £20,000 in graduate-level jobs and a healthy £16,716 in other types of employment.

- British Association for Slavonic and East European Studies: **www.basees.org.uk/**
- National Centre for Languages (CILT): **www.cilt.org.uk**

Russian and East European Languages	Research quality/5	Entry standards	Student satisfaction %	Graduate prospects %	Overall rating
=1 Cambridge	5A	500		81	100.0
=1 Oxford	5*B	482	84	85	100.0
3 Birmingham	5*B		84	78	98.5
4 Sheffield	5*A	382	81	72	95.2
=5 Bristol	5*A	428	76	61	91.1
=5 St Andrews	4A		85	55	91.1
7 University College London	5A	445	77	66	91.0
8 Bath	5A		80	61	90.9
9 Leeds	4B	353	81	70	88.0
10 Manchester	4A	409	76		85.9
11 Nottingham	5A	335	77	52	85.4
12 Portsmouth	5D	254	84	58	82.4
13 Glasgow	4B		77	36	77.8

Employed in graduate job:	38%	Average starting graduate salary:	£19,934
Employed in graduate job and studying:	4%	Average starting non-graduate salary:	£16,716
Studying:	18%		
Employed in non-graduate job and studying:	5%	The letters that appear in the Research Quality column indicate the	
Employed in non-graduate job:	30%	proportion of staff included in the assessment, A showing that	
Unemployed:	5%	almost all staff were included and F showing that hardly any were.	

Social Policy

The London School of Economics has resumed its accustomed position at the head of the social policy ranking, having overtaken Manchester, which has plummeted down to 26th place with the least satisfied students in the table and almost the lowest employment score. The LSE has easily the highest entry standards, one of the three 5* research grades and a share in the best employment record, with second-placed Bristol. The top two were the only universities to see more than two thirds of leavers go straight into graduate jobs or continue their studies.

The other research stars are third-placed Loughborough and Kent, in 11th position. Hull and Glasgow have the most satisfied students, but Stirling remains just ahead of Glasgow as the top university in Scotland, while Cardiff remains the clear leader in Wales. There are a dozen new universities in the table, but only London South Bank, Portsmouth and Nottingham Trent make the top 25.

Entry standards at the top of the table are comparatively low, with just the LSE averaging over 400 points. Only one university has an average of less than 200 points, but a dozen others have too few students to compile reliable entry scores. Although two thirds of entrants come with A levels or their equivalent, some courses cater very largely for mature students. The proportion of students getting firsts or 2:1s is relatively low.

Demand for places in social policy has fluctuated in recent years. There was an 11 per cent increase in applications in 2007, but a decline of similar proportions a year later, when the number of choices per applicant had been cut to five. Over 13 per cent of places were filled in Clearing in 2006.

Social policy is in the bottom five subjects in the graduate destinations league, although unemployment is only just above average at 7 per cent. Average starting salaries in graduate jobs are higher in comparison to other subjects, at almost £18,000, but still in the bottom half of the table.

- National Institute for Economic and Social Research: **www.niesr.ac.uk/**
- UK Social Policy Association: **www.social-policy.com/**

Social Policy	Research quality/5	Entry standards	Student satisfaction %	Graduate prospects %	Overall rating
1 London School of Economics	5*A	414	74	73	100.0
2 Bristol	5A	336	75	73	94.9
3 Loughborough	5*A	342	77	58	93.9
4 York	5A	352	73	65	92.4
5 Nottingham	4A	364	74	64	91.4
6 Leeds	5A	316	76	61	91.2
7 Hull	4B		82	59	90.8
8 Stirling	5B			61	90.6
9 Glasgow	4B		82	57	90.3
10 Queen's, Belfast	5A		76	53	89.5
11 Kent	5*A	244	75	60	88.8
12 London South Bank	4B		76	61	87.4
13 Keele	5B	319	70	66	87.3

14 Cardiff	5A	344	69	55	87.1
15 Birmingham	4C	317	77	63	86.8
16 Bath	5B	370	68	55	85.9
17 Southampton	5A		76	42	85.7
18 Sheffield	5B	365	67	56	85.3
19 Swansea	3aB	272	80	60	85.0
20 Edinburgh	4B		73	58	84.2
21 Newcastle	4B	341	66	63	83.9
22 Portsmouth	3aB		79	48	82.4
23 Bangor	3aA		72	54	81.4
24 Nottingham Trent	3aB	245	72	61	80.3
25 Ulster	4C	239	81	43	79.2
26 Manchester	5B	366	59	37	75.6
=27 Brighton	3bC	270	72	43	73.6
=27 Plymouth	4D		72	44	73.6
29 Salford	3aA	214	71	35	71.9
30 Lincoln	3aD		68	48	71.7
31 Anglia Ruskin	3aD		73	30	68.2
32 Sheffield Hallam	3aC	263	67	30	68.1
33 Bolton	2B	155		46	63.8

Employed in graduate job:	30%	Average starting graduate salary:	£17,897
Employed in graduate job and studying:	4%	Average starting non-graduate salary:	£14,140
Studying:	15%		
Employed in non-graduate job and studying:	5%	The letters that appear in the Research Quality column indicate the	
Employed in non-graduate job:	38%	proportion of staff included in the assessment, A showing that	
Unemployed:	7%	almost all staff were included and F showing that hardly any were.	

Social Work

The social work ranking is unrecognisable from the last time it was published, two years ago. None of the top three was in the table then. York has the highest entry standards and one of the best research grades. Lancaster, the previous leader, is down to fourth because of a big fall in entry standards, while Bath, the runner-up two years ago, is down to eighth.

Bristol, another previous leader, has the only 5* research grade, but only just makes the top 30 because of low scores for employment and student satisfaction. Marjon University College, Plymouth, has the most satisfied students, just ahead of Southampton Solent but neither is in the top 20. Even the top scorers for employment – Middlesex, Oxford Brookes and Reading, all of whom saw all their social workers find graduate jobs or further courses within six months of graduation – are between 14th and 23rd in the table.

The ranking has been particularly volatile since student numbers began to mushroom with the switch to a graduate profession. Social work used to be unusual for having more students taking certificate or diploma courses than degrees, but the diploma has now been withdrawn. The new degree registered big increases in applications until the beginning of 2008, and even then an 8 per cent decline was below the average for all

Social Work cont.

subjects following the reduction in choices per applicant from six to five.

Extra places at undergraduate level have brought another 24 universities into the table this year. Third-placed Stirling (yet another former leader) is the top university in Scotland, but Queen's, Belfast, one place higher, is the leading university outside England. Robert Gordon remains the leading new university, although Middlesex, Huddersfield, Oxford Brookes, Nottingham Trent and De Montfort are also in the top 20. Entry requirements are the lowest of any of the tables in this year's *Guide*: only three universities average more than 350 points, while four average less than 200.

The vocational nature of the subject generally produces good employment figures, although ten universities had "positive destinations" below 60 per cent. The latest survey placed social work among the top 20 subjects for overall employment prospects. Perhaps surprisingly, it is in the top ten in the earnings league, with average starting salaries of more than £22,500 for graduate-level jobs.

- British Association of Social Workers: **www.basw.co.uk/**
- General Social Care Council: **www.gscc.org.uk**
- Social Care Association: **http://socialcareassociation.co.uk/**

Social Work	Research quality/5	Entry standards	Student satisfaction %	Graduate prospects %	Overall rating
1 York	5A	365	72		100.0
2 Queen's, Belfast	4B	360	74	98	94.1
3 Stirling	5B			94	93.5
4 Lancaster	5A	281	77	89	93.1
5 Durham	4A		77	91	92.3
6 Southampton	3aB	366	75	91	91.4
7 Dundee	4B		78	96	91.0
8 Bath	5B		70	93	87.6
9 Robert Gordon	3aA	277		90	86.5
10 Birmingham	4C	335	71	85	86.3
11 Kent	4C		79	85	86.1
12 Edinburgh	4B		69	96	84.8
13 Huddersfield	5C	228	77	81	82.6
14 Oxford Brookes		299	80	100	82.5
15 Middlesex	4C		67	100	82.0
16 Hull	3aB	228	72	94	81.0
17 Bradford	4D	283	70	86	79.6
18 Nottingham Trent	3aB	237	63	98	77.9
19 De Montfort	3aD	212	72	97	77.2
20 Strathclyde		303	74	84	76.6
=21 Coventry	3bE		76	87	76.4
=21 Anglia Ruskin	3aD	232	75	82	76.4
23 Reading	3bD	289	61	100	76.0
24 Northumbria	3aB	267	69	63	75.7

		Research Quality			
25	Southampton Solent		217	84	84	75.4
26	Central Lancashire	3aD	257	66	89	75.2
27	Bristol	5*C	303	57	57	74.5
28	Staffordshire	3bC	224	72	75	73.2
29	West of England		230	72	97	72.8
30	Salford	3aA	271	58	64	72.2
31	Birmingham City		230	71	95	72.0
32	Gloucestershire		223	76	85	71.9
33	Portsmouth		219	74	90	71.8
34	Ulster	3bD	270	71	62	71.7
35	East London	3bD		68	81	70.7
36	Marjon, Plymouth		163	85	76	70.5
=37	Plymouth	4D	208	64	78	69.7
=37	Bedfordshire	3aC	211	67	67	69.7
39	Brunel	3aD		65	76	69.2
=40	Leeds		306	72	54	69.1
=40	Manchester Metropolitan	3aE	242	67	69	69.1
42	Sunderland	3aB	202	69	53	68.7
43	Chichester		268	75	52	67.7
44	Hertfordshire	3bE		61	89	66.7
=45	Sheffield Hallam		212	62	95	66.2
=45	Lincoln		223	65	83	66.2
47	Cumbria		221	72	60	64.7
48	Wolverhampton		180	72	59	61.5
49	Greenwich		179	63	79	61.0
50	Canterbury Christ Church		222	69	50	60.9
51	Leeds Metropolitan		203	69	54	60.6
52	UWCN, Newport		174	74	51	60.1
53	Edge Hill		204	78	28	59.6
54	Bournemouth		209	55	70	57.5
55	Liverpool John Moores	3bC	210	47	56	55.8

Employed in graduate job:	66%	Average starting graduate salary:	£22,566
Employed in graduate job and studying:	6%	Average starting non-graduate salary:	£15,418
Studying:	5%		
Employed in non-graduate job and studying:	2%		
Employed in non-graduate job:	16%		
Unemployed:	6%		

The letters that appear in the Research Quality column indicate the proportion of staff included in the assessment, A showing that almost all staff were included and F showing that hardly any were.

Sociology

The popular image of sociology may still be stuck in the 1960s, but it remains one of the largest of the social sciences. Applications were down by 10 per cent at the start of 2008, with the switch from six choices per applicant to five, but this followed a series of increases and was little more than the average for all subjects. The 88 institutions in the latest table make it one of the largest in the *Guide*.

Cambridge remains at the head of the table, registering by far the highest entry standards and the best employment score. But it is not among the seven universities

Sociology cont.

rated internationally outstanding for research. They range from second-placed Surrey through Loughborough, Essex, Lancaster, Manchester and Kent, to Goldsmiths in 31st place. Ulster has the most satisfied students, but does not make the top 40 because of low scores on all the other measures.

Edinburgh has overtaken Aberdeen as the leading university in Scotland, while Cardiff is best-placed in Wales. Oxford Brookes is the only new university in the top 30, but Glasgow Caledonian, Portsmouth and Nottingham Trent are all the top 40.

The employment scores show wide variations, with 81 per cent of Cambridge graduates going straight into graduate jobs or higher-level courses, but less than 50 per cent doing the same in almost half of the institutions in the table. Entry qualifications are more consistent, with only four universities averaging more than 400 points and seven under 200 points.

Other subjects such as criminology, urban studies, women's studies and some communication studies were also covered in the assessments, which included a large number of institutions where sociology is taught as part of a combined studies or modular programme. Although the unemployment rate is no higher than average for all subjects, at 6 per cent, only two subject areas have a lower proportion of "positive destinations" in the latest table. Some 45 per cent of those completing courses were in low-level jobs six months after graduation.

• The British Sociological Association: **www.britsoc.co.uk/**

Sociology	Research quality/5	Entry standards	Student satisfaction %	Graduate prospects %	Overall rating
1 Cambridge	5A	490	76	81	100.0
2 Surrey	5*A	322	85	62	93.9
3 Warwick	5A	385	79	61	91.2
4 Loughborough	5*A	345	76	60	89.2
5 Leeds	5A	339	76	66	88.7
=6 Exeter	5B	363	80	58	88.0
=6 Essex	5*A	320	80	52	88.0
8 Durham	4A	364	75	67	87.9
9 Edinburgh	5A	413	76	52	87.7
=10 Aberdeen	5A	299		59	86.0
=10 London School of Economics	5A	427	70	55	86.0
12 Lancaster	5*B	345	76	56	85.7
13 Manchester	5*A	402	72	47	85.6
14 Glasgow	4A	369	77	52	84.9
=15 Kent	5*A	281	77	53	84.5
=15 York	5A	365	74	51	84.5
17 Southampton	5A	358	78	44	84.2
18 Bath	5B	346	68	70	83.7
19 Cardiff	5A	346	73	50	82.9
=20 Leicester	4B	316	75	62	82.6
=20 Bristol	5B	396	61	71	82.6

22 Birmingham	3aC	368	78	55	82.3
23 Nottingham	4A	328	75	53	82.1
24 Sheffield	5B	349	71	56	82.0
25 Aston	5B	307	74	55	81.3
26 Liverpool	4B	322	74	55	80.7
27 Queen's, Belfast	5A	311	73	48	80.5
28 Oxford Brookes	4A	297	74	53	80.3
29 Strathclyde	3aB	327	73	60	80.2
30 Stirling	5B	283		52	80.1
31 Goldsmiths College	5*A	254	73	47	79.9
32 Sussex	4A	364	66	57	79.4
33 Keele	5B	296	69	59	79.0
34 Newcastle	4B	345	65	63	78.5
35 Brunel	5A	297	69	50	78.4
=36 Nottingham Trent	3aB	239	75	62	77.8
=36 Glasgow Caledonian	3aC		81	47	77.8
=38 Hull	3aB	270	78	50	77.4
=38 Reading	3aB		76	51	77.4
40 Portsmouth	3aB	287	73	56	76.9
41 Teesside	3aC	221	78	56	75.9
42 Ulster	3bD	272	87	36	75.0
43 Northumbria	3aB	275	73	48	74.5
44 City	4A	280	61	59	73.8
45 Staffordshire	3aD	246	85	35	73.5
46 Brighton	3bC	272	76	49	73.4
=47 Bangor	3aA	240	71	50	73.1
=47 Worcester	2C	265	77	51	73.1
49 Robert Gordon		261		61	73.0
50 Central Lancashire	3bC	241	78	46	72.5
51 London South Bank	4B	184	77	41	72.1
52 Anglia Ruskin	3aD	258	76	45	72.0
=53 Bradford	4D	229	69	58	71.5
=53 Greenwich	3aB	208	73	48	71.5
55 Bedfordshire		197	78	58	70.9
56 Bath Spa		266	77	48	70.1
57 Salford	4A	251	70	33	70.0
=58 Kingston	4A	218	68	42	69.8
=58 Plymouth	4C	244	72	39	69.8
60 Napier		239		55	69.3
61 East London	4B	196	66	51	69.2
=62 Canterbury Christ Church		230	78	49	69.1
=62 West of England	3aB	249	71	39	69.1
64 Gloucestershire		234	81	41	68.9
65 Winchester		243	77	47	68.8
66 Middlesex	4C	198	66	53	68.7
67 Chester		284	76	42	68.6
=68 Northampton	3bD	208	79	39	68.4

Sociology cont.

	Research quality/5	Entry standards	Student satisfaction %	Graduate prospects %	Overall rating
=68 West of Scotland	3aC	224		46	68.4
70 Southampton Solent	2D	198	81	38	68.3
71 East Anglia		328	74	38	68.1
72 Huddersfield	2D		77	40	67.9
73 Manchester Metropolitan	3aC	252	71	35	67.2
74 Lincoln		251	74	47	67.1
75 Coventry		251	78	39	67.0
76 Abertay		211		54	66.9
77 Wolverhampton		181	75	53	66.7
78 Roehampton	3aC	207	68	42	65.6
79 Westminster	3aB	233	66	38	65.1
80 Derby	2B	235	70	38	64.7
81 Birmingham City		251	73	38	64.5
82 Leeds Metropolitan		244	70	43	63.4
83 Liverpool John Moores		214	74	34	62.2
84 Sheffield Hallam		242	72	33	61.4
85 UWIC, Cardiff		223	71	36	60.9
86 Buckinghamshire New		170	68	48	60.8
87 Glamorgan		208	72	32	60.2
88 Sunderland	3aB	226	58	33	59.1

Employed in graduate job:	30%	Average starting graduate salary:	£17,693
Employed in graduate job and studying:	4%	Average starting non-graduate salary:	£14,096
Studying:	14%		
Employed in non-graduate job and studying:	4%	The letters that appear in the Research Quality column indicate the	
Employed in non-graduate job:	41%	proportion of staff included in the assessment, A showing that	
Unemployed:	6%	almost all staff were included and F showing that hardly any were.	

Theology and Religious Studies

Cambridge holds on to the top place in theology and religious studies that it won two years ago, when the table was last published. As it did then, it does not lead on any of the measures used in the ranking, but still restricts Oxford to second place. Oxford has the highest entry standards and is one of four universities with 5* research grades. Nottingham, Cardiff and Manchester are the others rated internationally outstanding for research.

Hull has the best employment rate, and leaps up to 15th from one place off the bottom as a result. Oxford Brookes, which is in the bottom five, thanks partly to one of the lowest research scores in any table, has the most satisfied students. St Andrews has climbed from ninth place to fourth, overtaking both Glasgow and Edinburgh, to become the top university in Scotland. Cardiff has that honour in Wales.

Scores in the top half of the table are unusually close, with ten points covering eight universities. No new university makes the top 20, but St Mary's University College, Twickenham, is only one place away.

Entry qualifications are relatively high. The top five and one other university further down the table average more than 400 points, and only one of the 35 institutions in this year's table slip below 250 points.

Theology and religious studies have enjoyed substantial increases in popularity recently, with big rises in three of the four years up to 2007. There were still more than 5,000 applications early in 2008, despite a drop of nearly 13 per cent with the reduction in choices per applicant. By no means all graduates go into the church, but the vocation helps the subjects in the graduate employment table. The subjects are in the top 25, with an unemployment rate that is better than average. Even in the earnings table, theology and religious studies are only just in the bottom 20, with average starting salaries of virtually £18,500 in graduate jobs.

- British Association for the Study of Religions: **http://basr.open.ac.uk/**
- Society for the Study of Theology: **www.bris.ac.uk/thrs/sst/**

Theology and Religious Studies	Research quality/5	Entry standards	Student satisfaction %	Graduate prospects %	Overall rating
1 Cambridge	5A	460		78	100.0
2 Oxford	5*B	471	85	73	98.4
3 Durham	5B	437	86	82	98.3
4 St Andrews	5A	422	86	77	97.8
5 Edinburgh	5A	414	82	78	95.9
6 Sheffield	5A	376	84	71	93.0
7 Nottingham	5*A	382	82	65	92.4
8 Cardiff	5*A	340	84	63	91.0
9 Aberdeen	5B	310		80	89.4
10 Lancaster	5A	340	84	63	89.0
11 Leeds	4A	364	81	68	88.4
12 Exeter	5A	382	82	55	87.2
13 Manchester	5*B	393	81	52	86.2
14 School of Oriental and African Studies	5B	315	74	79	85.8
15 Hull	3aD	270	85	83	85.4
16 Glasgow	5B		78	67	85.1
17 King's College London	5A	379	70	67	84.7
18 Bristol	5B	406	69	69	84.5
=19 Bangor	4B	259	82	72	83.8
=19 Stirling	5C			69	83.8
21 St Mary's College	3bD	265	82	82	82.4
22 Gloucestershire	4B	278	77	70	81.4
23 Bath Spa	4A	285	81	55	80.7
24 Chester	3aD	280	82	71	80.4
25 York St John	1C	287	85	71	80.1
26 Lampeter	5C	306	75	66	80.0
27 Birmingham	5B	359	71	59	79.9
28 Kent	3aD	284	75	78	79.3
29 Queen's, Belfast		366	81	66	78.8

	Research quality/5	Entry standards	Student satisfaction %	Graduate prospects %	Overall rating
30 Winchester	4B	287	74	63	78.2
31 Oxford Brookes	1D	300	88	54	76.5
32 Roehampton	4A	263	72	58	76.0
33 Newcastle	5A		70	52	75.8
34 Canterbury Christ Church	3aA	241	76	49	72.7
35 Cumbria		257	72	72	71.2

Employed in graduate job:	31%	Average starting graduate salary:	£18,496
Employed in graduate job and studying:	5%	Average starting non-graduate salary:	£13,093
Studying:	29%		
Employed in non-graduate job and studying:	5%	The letters that appear in the Research Quality column indicate the	
Employed in non-graduate job:	24%	proportion of staff included in the assessment, A showing that	
Unemployed:	5%	almost all staff were included and F showing that hardly any were.	

Town and Country Planning and Landscape

Cambridge extends its lead slightly in the ranking for town and country planning and landscape studies, largely thanks to the university's usual high entry standards. Cardiff, which has the only 5* research grade, is back up to second place.

Three universities – including Kingston, which is only just outside the bottom five – have 100 per cent employment records. The others are third-placed Reading and University College London, in 14th. The most satisfied students are at Gloucestershire, which has moved up to eighth place, becoming the leading new university in the process. Oxford Brookes is also in the top ten.

Sixth-placed Aberdeen is the top university in Scotland, while Cardiff is the only representative of Wales. Five more universities have entered the ranking this year in a group of subjects that were once available only at postgraduate level. Entry standards are moderate: only Cambridge averages more than 400 points, although none is below 200 points.

More than 5,000 students now take first degree courses, with almost another 1,000 taking certificates, diplomas or Foundation degrees. The size of departments varies from more than 500 students to less than 150, with about a third of the total being post-graduates. Applications for planning courses were down by less than the average for all subjects at the start of 2008, but the smaller area of landscape design saw a more serious decline. About 12 per cent of places across the whole category were filled through Clearing in 2006.

Fewer than half of the students are awarded firsts or 2:1s, but jobs prospects are good, with unemployment well below average, at 4 per cent, and 80 per cent of leavers in graduate-level work or studying after six months. The subjects are just outside the top 20 in the earnings league, with average starting salaries of over £20,000 for graduate jobs.

- Royal Town Planning Institute: **www.rtpi.org.uk/**
- Planning Officers Society: **www.planningofficers.org.uk/**
- Landscape Institute: **www.landscapeinstitute.org/**

Town and Country Planning and Landscape	Research quality/5	Entry standards	Student satisfaction %	Graduate prospects %	Overall rating
1 Cambridge	5B	504		89	100.0
2 Cardiff	5*A	316	80	85	94.8
3 Reading	5B	394	71	100	92.1
4 Sheffield	5A	365	71	91	90.7
5 Manchester	4B	349	77	83	87.4
6 Aberdeen	5B	318		83	86.2
7 Liverpool	4A	336	67	93	85.3
8 Gloucestershire	4A	294	82	60	84.9
9 Newcastle	5B	312	69	89	84.8
10 Oxford Brookes	4C	323	76	87	84.7
11 Heriot-Watt	3aB	290	76	93	84.6
12 Loughborough	3aB	323	75	79	82.5
13 Sheffield Hallam	4D	274	79	83	81.3
14 University College London	4C	343	63	100	81.0
15 Queen's, Belfast	3bA	329	68	91	80.8
16 Nottingham Trent	3aB	289	68	92	79.9
17 Dundee	3bD	361	77	70	79.4
18 West of England	3aB	257	73	82	79.1
19 Strathclyde	3aC		70	86	77.8
20 Leeds Metropolitan	3aB	200	78	72	77.2
21 Birmingham		356		76	74.8
22 Liverpool John Moores	3aA	231	68		74.7
23 Kingston		203	70	100	71.2
24 Manchester Metropolitan		287	64	94	70.3
25 London South Bank	4D			63	67.9
26 Westminster	3aD	207	61	69	64.3
27 Ulster		253	70	35	59.7
28 Birmingham City	3bE			58	59.5

Employed in graduate job:	48%	Average starting graduate salary:	£20,124
Employed in graduate job and studying:	13%	Average starting non-graduate salary:	£15,705
Studying:	19%		
Employed in non-graduate job and studying:	2%	The letters that appear in the Research Quality column indicate the	
Employed in non-graduate job:	13%	proportion of staff included in the assessment, A showing that	
Unemployed:	4%	almost all staff were included and F showing that hardly any were.	

Veterinary Medicine

Only medicine itself compares with veterinary medicine for high entry standards. The deadline for entry in 2007 saw an emphatic end to a three-year decline in the number of applications, with a 22 per cent increase. A year later, veterinary medicine was one of the few subjects to attract more applications, a near 7 per cent increase bringing the total to more than 7,000. There are about 20 applications for each place. This, combined with the uncanny closeness of grades for research, plus the virtual guarantee

Veterinary Medicine cont.

of a job for graduates who choose to practise, make it difficult to separate the six schools in the table. Nottingham opened a new school in 2006, but does not yet have sufficient data to join the ranking.

The addition of student satisfaction scores has created a little movement, although Cambridge retains the leadership, with Liverpool still close behind. Cambridge students did not respond to the National Student Survey in sufficient numbers for a score to be published, but the university's commanding lead on entry standards was enough to outweigh Liverpool's top scores for satisfaction and graduate destinations. Every veterinary school registered "positive destinations" for at least 95 per cent of graduates, but at Liverpool the success rate was 99 per cent.

The only change is an exchange of positions between Glasgow and Edinburgh, which becomes the top school in Scotland. In research, all six schools were awarded grade 4 in 1996; in 2001 they had all moved up to grade 5, having entered similar numbers of academics. Bristol and the Royal Veterinary College entered a slightly lower proportion of staff than the rest in the last Research Assessment Exercise.

Cambridge and the Royal Veterinary College set applicants a specialist aptitude test also used by a number of medical schools. Vets' final qualifications are not classified, but between 5 and 15 per cent are awarded a commendation. The five-year courses have to meet the requirements of the Royal College of Veterinary Surgeons, and they vary in size from 65 to 155 students. Up to 10 per cent drop out, but those who complete the course are in high demand. Only medicine and dentistry have a lower unemployment rate. Starting salaries are high, at almost £23,500, but vets are also behind economists and chemical engineers on this measure.

- Royal College of Veterinary Surgeons: **www.rcvs.org.uk/**

Veterinary Medicine	Research quality/5	Entry standards	Student satisfaction %	Graduate prospects %	Overall rating
1 Cambridge	5B	532		98	100.0
2 Liverpool	5B	468	77	99	99.5
3 Edinburgh	5B	478	70	96	96.2
4 Glasgow	5B	454	73	95	95.5
5 Royal Veterinary College	5C	442	66	98	92.9
6 Bristol	5C	451	70	95	92.5

Employed in graduate job:	81%		Average starting graduate salary:	£23,437
Employed in graduate job and studying:	4%		Average starting non-graduate salary:	*
Studying:	13%			
Employed in non-graduate job and studying:	0%			
Employed in non-graduate job:	1%		The letters that appear in the Research Quality column indicate the	
Unemployed:	2%		proportion of staff included in the assessment, A showing that	
			almost all staff were included and F showing that hardly any were.	

Making Your Application

Once the nerve-wracking business of choosing courses is over, you may feel you can sit back and concentrate on getting the right results. Don't be fooled – there is another vital stage to go through if you are to attract the right offers and win that coveted place in higher education. Too many people take their eye off the ball in actually making the application. Surprising numbers of applicants each year spell their own name wrongly, or enter an inaccurate date of birth, or the wrong course code. And that is to say nothing of the damage that can be done in the personal statement and teachers' references.

In an era when there are relatively few interviews and more candidates each year achieve high A-level grades, what goes on your UCAS form is becoming more and more important – too important, many would say. The art of conveying knowledge of and enthusiasm for your chosen subject – preferably with supporting evidence from your school or college – can make all the difference. And, while UCAS will decode misspelt names, other errors in grammar or spelling present admissions officers with an easy starting point in cutting applications down to a more manageable number.

The application process

Most applications for full-time higher education courses go through UCAS, although specialist admissions bodies still handle applications to the music conservatoires (Conservatoires UK Admissions Service: www.cukas.ac.uk) and some postgraduate courses, including teacher training (Graduate Teacher Training Registry: www.gttr.ac.uk). Universities that have not filled all their places, even during Clearing, will accept direct applications up to and after the start of the academic year, but UCAS is both the official route and the only way into the most popular courses.

Since 2006, all UCAS applications have been made online. The *Apply* electronic system is accessed via the UCAS website and is straightforward to use. For those who do not have the internet at home and prefer not to use school or college computers, the UCAS website lists 900 libraries, all over the UK, where you can make your application. *Apply* is available 24 hours a day, and, when the time comes, information on the progress of your application may arrive at any time.

Registering with *Apply*

The first step in the process is to register. If you are at a school or college, you will need to obtain a "buzzword" from your tutor or careers adviser – it is used when you log on to register. It links your application to the school or college so that the application can be sent electronically to your referee (usually one of your teachers) for your reference to be attached. If you are no longer at a school or college, you do not need a "buzzword", but you will need details of your referee. More information is given on the UCAS website.

To register go to the UCAS website and click on "Apply". The system will guide you through the business of providing your personal details and generating a username and password, as well as reminding you of basic points, such as amending your details in case of a change of address. You can register separate term-time and holiday addresses – a useful option for boarders, who could find offers and, particularly, the confirmation of a place, going to their school when they are miles away at home. Remember to keep a note of your username and password in a safe place.

Throughout the process, you will be in sole control of communications with UCAS and your chosen universities. Only if you nominate a representative and give them your unique nine-digit application number (sent automatically by UCAS when your application is submitted), can a parent or anyone else give or receive information on your behalf, perhaps because you are ill or out of the country.

Once you are registered, you can start to complete the Apply screens. The details required cover the following areas:

- Personal details and some addition non-educational details for UK applicants.
- Your university choices.
- Details of your education so far including examination results and examinations still to be taken.
- Details of any jobs you have done.
- Your personal statement.
- A reference from one of your teachers.
- A declaration that you confirm that the information is correct and that you will be bound by the UCAS rules.
- Payment details (applications cost £15, or £5 if you apply to just one course).

The sections that follow cover the most important sections.

Personal details

This information is taken from your initial registration, and you will be asked for additional information, for example, on ethnic origin and national identity, used to monitor equal opportunities in the application process.

Choices

Since 2007–08, you have been restricted to a maximum of five, rather than six, courses on your UCAS form. The switch met remarkably little resistance – perhaps because most applicants, having set their heart on one or two courses with genuine appeal, were going through the motions by the time it came to choosing a sixth. Applicants in medicine, dentistry and veterinary science were already restricted to four choices, so they now have the option of only one additional choice in another subject.

The other restrictions are for art and design applicants following Route B (mainly for those taking Foundation courses; see UCAS website for details), where only three choices are allowed, and for those seeking places at Oxford or Cambridge, who cannot apply to

---

What matters most?

UCAS and the environmental group, Friends for the Future asked 25,000 applicants in 2007–08 what had been "very important" to them in choosing a course:

- 54% said the quality of teaching
- 44% said the reputation of the course
- 44% said the reputation of the institution
- 35% said the teaching methods on the course

Only 8% gave the same priority to nightlife, while 22% considered the distance from home "very important".

both. Oxford and Cambridge also have additional application procedures. For Oxford you will need to submit an Oxford application form directly (a revised form will be available from the Oxford website). For Cambridge, you will be asked to complete a Supplementary Application Questionnaire once Cambridge has received your application from UCAS. The deadline for Oxbridge applications – and for all medicine, dentistry and veterinary science courses – is 15 October, while Route B applicants have until the following March. For all other applications the deadline is 15 January.

Other applicants do not have to use up all five choices, although obviously you may reduce your chances of success by narrowing your options. If you do choose fewer than five courses, you can still add another to your form up to June 30, as long as you have not accepted or declined any offers. Nor do you have to choose five different universities if more than one course at the same institution attracts you – perhaps because the institution itself is the real draw and one course has lower entrance requirements than the other. Universities are not allowed to see where else you have applied, or whether you have chosen the same subject elsewhere. But they will be aware of multiple applications within their own institution. It is, in any case, more difficult to write a convincing personal statement if it has to cover more than one subject.

For each course you select, you will need to put the UCAS code on the form – and you should check carefully that you have the correct code and understand any special requirements that may be detailed on the UCAS description of the course. You will also need to indicate whether you are applying for a deferred entry (for example, if you are taking a gap year – see page 180).

Education

In this section you will need to give details of the schools and colleges you have attended, and the qualifications you have obtained or are preparing for. The UCAS website gives plenty of advice on the ways in which you should enter this information, to ensure that all your relevant qualifications are included with their grades. While UCAS does not need to see qualification certificates, it can double-check results with the examination boards to ensure that no-one is tempted to modify their results,

Personal statements

As the competition for places on popular courses has become more intense, so the value attached to the personal statement has increased. Admissions officers look for a sign of potential beyond the high grades that growing numbers of applicants offer. Many (but not all) value success in extracurricular activities such as drama, sport or the Duke of Edinburgh award scheme. But your first priority should be to demonstrate an interest in and understanding of your chosen subject beyond the confines of the exam syllabus.

This is not easy in a relatively short statement that can easily sound trite or pretentious. You should resist the temptation to lie, particularly if there is any chance of an interview. A claim to have been inspired by a book that you have not read will backfire instantly under questioning and, even without an interview, experienced academics are likely to see through grandiose statements that appear at odds with a teacher's reference. Genuine experiences of after-hours clubs, lectures or visits – better still, work experience or actual reading around the syllabus – are much more likely to strike the right note. Take advice from teachers and, if there is still time before you make your application, look for some subject-related activities that will help fill out your statement.

Admissions officers are also looking for evidence of character that will make you a productive member of their university and, eventually, a successful graduate. Taking responsibility in any area of school or college life suggests this, while evidence of initiative and self-discipline is also valuable, since higher education involves much more independent study than sixth-formers are used to.

Your overall aim in writing your personal statement is to persuade the admissions officer to pick you out of the piles of applications on his or her desk. That means trying to stand out from an often rather dull and uniform set of statements based around the curriculum and the more predictable sixth-form activities. Everyone is going to say they love reading, for example; narrow your interest down to an area of (real) interest. Don't be afraid to include the unusual, but bear in mind that an academic's sense of humour may not be the same as yours.

Give particular thought to why you want to study your chosen subject – especially if it is not one you have taken at school or college. You need to show that your interests and skills are well-suited to the course and, if it is a vocational degree, that you know how you envisage using the qualification. Admissions officers want to feel that you will be committed to their subject for the length of the course, which could be three, four or even five years, and capable of achieving good results.

Your school or college should be the best source of advice, since they see personal statements every year, but there are others. The UCAS website has a useful checklist of themes that you may wish to address, while sites such as www.studential.com also provide tips. But do not fall into the trap of cutting and pasting from the model statements included on such sites – both UCAS and individual universities have software that will spot plagiarism immediately. No fewer than one in twenty applicants came to grief in this way last year, with more than 200 claiming to trace a passion for science back to setting their pyjamas on fire when experimenting with a chemistry set that they received as a birthday present. Plagiarists of this type are unlikely to be disqualified, but they destroy the credibility of their application.

Try not to cram in more than the limited space will allow – admissions officers will have many statements to go through, and judicious editing may be rewarded. As long as you write clearly – preferably in paragraphs and possibly with sub-headings – it will be up to you what to include. It is a *personal* statement. But consider these points:

- What attracts you to this subject (or subjects, in the case of dual or combined honours)?
- Have you undertaken relevant work experience or voluntary activities, either through school or elsewhere?
- Have you taken part in other extra-curricular activities that demonstrate character – perhaps as a prefect, on the sports field or in the arts?
- Have you been involved in other academic pursuits, such as Gifted and Talented programmes, widening participation schemes, or courses in other subjects?
- Which aspects of your current courses have you found particularly stimulating?
- Are you planning a gap year? If so, explain what you intend to do and how it will affect your studies. Some subjects – notably maths – actively discourage a break in studies.
- What other outside interests might you include that show that you are a rounded individual?

The *Apply* system allows 4,000 characters, or 47 lines for your statement. While there is no requirement to fill all the space, it should not look embarrassingly short. UCAS recommends using a word-processing package to compile the statement before pasting it into the application system. This is because *Apply* will time-out after 35 minutes of inactivity, so there is a danger of losing valuable material. Working offline also has the advantage of leaving you with a copy and making it easier to show it to others.

References

Hand in hand with your personal statement goes the reference from your school, college or, in the case of mature students, someone who knows you well but is not a friend or family member. The reference has to be independent – you are specifically forbidden to change any part of it if you send off your own application – but that does not mean you should not try to influence what it contains. Most schools and colleges conduct informal interviews before compiling a reference, but it does no harm to draw up a list of the achievements that you would like to see included. Referees cannot know every detail of a candidate's interests and most welcome an aide memoire.

The UCAS guidelines skirt around the candidate's right to see his or her reference, but it does exist. Schools' practices vary, but most now show the applicant the completed reference. Where this is not the case, the candidate can pay UCAS £10 for a copy, although at this stage it is obviously too late to influence the contents. Better, if you can, to see it before it goes off, in case there are factual inaccuracies that can be corrected.

Timing

The general deadline for applications through UCAS is 15 January and even those received up to 30 June will be considered if the relevant courses still have vacancies. After that, you will be limited to Clearing, or an application for the following year. In theory –

Timetable for Applications

May onwards	Find out about courses and universities. Attend open days.
September	Registration starts for UCAS *Apply*.
15 October	Final day for applications to Oxford and Cambridge and for all courses in medicine, dentistry and veterinary science.
15 January	Final day for all other applications from UK and EU students to ensure that your application is given equal consideration with all other applicants.
16 January – 30 June	New applications still accepted by UCAS, but only considered by universities if the relevant courses have vacancies.
26 February	Start of applications through UCAS Extra.
24 March	Final day for applications for art and design Route B (for full details of important dates for Route B, see the UCAS website).
31 March	Universities should have sent decisions on all applications received by 15 January.
6 May	Final day by which applicants have to decide on their choices if application submitted by 15 January (exact date for each applicant will be confirmed by UCAS when final university decision confirmed).
1 July	Any application received from this date held until Clearing starts.
7 July	Final day for applications through UCAS Extra.
mid August	Clearing starts after publication of exam results.

and usually in practice – all applications submitted by the January deadline are given equal consideration. But the best advice is to get your application in early: before Christmas, or earlier if possible. Applications are accepted from September onwards, so the autumn half-term is a sensible target date for completing the process.

While no offers are made before the deadline, many admissions officers look through applications as they come in and may make a mental note of promising candidates. If your form arrives with the deadline looming, you may appear less organised than those who submitted in good time; and your application may be one of a large batch that receives a more cursory first reading than the early arrivals. Under UCAS rules, last-minute applicants should not be at a disadvantage, but why take the risk?

Next steps

Once your application has been processed by UCAS, you will receive a welcome letter confirming your choices and summarising what will happen next. The letter will contain a reminder of your identification number and the username and password that you used to apply. These will also give you access to *Track*, the online system that allows you to follow the progress of your application. Check all the details carefully: you have 14 days to contact UCAS to correct any errors.

After that, it is just a matter of waiting for universities to make their decisions, which can take days, weeks or even months, depending on the university and the course. Some obviously see an advantage in being the first to make an offer – it is a memorable moment to be reassured that at least one of your chosen institutions wants you – and may send their response almost immediately. Others take much longer, perhaps because they have so many good applications to consider, or maybe because they are waiting to see which of their applicants withdraw when Oxford and Cambridge make their offers. Universities are asked to make all their decisions by the end of March, and most have done so long before that.

Interviews

Unless you are applying for a course in health or education that brings you into direct contact with the public, the chances are you will not have a selection interview. For prospective medics, vets, dentists or teachers, a face-to-face assessment of your suitability will be crucial to your chances of success. Likewise in the performing arts, the interview may be as important as your exam grades. Oxford and Cambridge still interview applicants in all subjects, and a few of the top universities see a significant proportion. But the expansion of higher education has made it impractical to interview everyone, and many admissions experts are sceptical about interviews anyway.

What has become more common, however, is the "sales" interview, where the university is really selling itself to the candidate. There may still be testing questions, but the admissions staff have already made their minds up and are actually trying to persuade you to accept an offer. Indeed, you will probably be given a clear indication at the end of the interview that one is on its way. The technique seems to work, perhaps because you have invested time and nervous energy in a sometimes lengthy trip, as well as acquiring a more detailed impression of both the department and the university.

The difficulty can come in spotting which type of interview is which. The "real" ones require lengthy preparation, revisiting your personal statement and reading beyond the exam syllabus. Dress smartly and make sure that you are on time. Impressions count for a lot at interviews, so have a question of your own ready, as well as being prepared to give answers.

While you would not want to appear ignorant at a "sales" interview, lengthy preparation might be a waste of valuable time during a period of revision. Naturally, you should err on the side of caution, but if your predicted grades are well above the standard offer and the subject is not one that normally requires an interview, it is likely that the invitation is a sales pitch. It is still worth going, unless you have changed your mind about the application.

Offers

When your chosen universities respond to your application, there will be one of three answers:

- Unconditional Offer (U): This is a possibility only if you applied after satisfying the entrance requirements – usually if you are applying as a mature student, while on a gap year, after resitting exams or, in Scotland, after completing Highers.
- Conditional Offer (C): The university offers a place subject to you achieving set grades or points on the UCAS tariff.
- Rejection (R): You do not have the right qualifications, or have lost out to stronger competition.

If you have chosen wisely, you should have more than one offer to choose from, so you will be required to pick your favourite as your firm acceptance – known as UF if it was an unconditional offer and CF if it was conditional. Candidates with conditional offers can also accept a second offer, with lower grades, as an Insurance choice (CI). You must then decline any other offers that you have.

You do not have to make an Insurance choice – indeed, you may decline all your offers if you have changed your mind about your career path or regret your course decisions. But most people prefer the security of a back-up route into higher education if their grades fall short. You must be sure that your firm acceptance is definitely your first choice because you will be allocated a place automatically if you meet the university's conditions. It is no good at this stage deciding that you prefer your Insurance choice because UCAS rules will not allow a switch.

The only way round those rules – if your personal circumstances have changed, or you do much better than expected and are determined to "trade up" to another university – is through direct contact with the universities concerned. Your firm acceptance institution has to be prepared to release you so that your new choice can award you a place in Clearing. Neither is under any obligation to do so but, in practice, it is rare for a university to insist that a student joins against his or her wishes. Admissions staff will do all they can to persuade you that your original choice was the right one – as it may well have been, if your research was thorough – but it will almost certainly be your decision in the end.

UCAS Extra

If things do go wrong and you receive five rejections, that need not be the end of your higher education ambitions. From the end of February until the end of June, you have another chance through UCAS Extra, a listing of courses that still have vacancies after the initial round of offers. You will be notified if you are eligible for Extra and can then select courses marked as available on the UCAS website. Applications are made, one at a time, through UCAS *Track*. If you do not receive an offer, or you choose to decline one, you can continue applying for other courses until you are successful. About half of those applying through Extra normally find a place.

Results Day

Rule Number One on results day is to be at home, or at least in communication. Places are filled extremely rapidly with the newest electronic admissions systems, and you cannot afford to be on some remote beach if there are complications. If you get the grades stipulated in your conditional offer, the process should work smoothly and you can begin celebrating. You don't need to do anything – *Track* will let you know as soon as your place is confirmed and the paperwork will arrive in a day or two. You can phone the university to make quite sure, but it should not be necessary and you will be joining a long queue of people doing the same thing.

If the results are not what you hoped – and particularly if you just miss your grades – you need to be on the phone and taking advice from your school or college. In a year when results are better than expected, some universities will stick to the letter of their offers, perhaps refusing to accept your AAC grades when they had demanded ABB. Others will forgive a dropped grade to take a candidate who is regarded as promising, rather than go into Clearing to recruit an unknown quantity. Admissions staff may be persuadable – particularly if there are extenuating personal circumstances, or the dropped grade is in a subject that is not relevant to your chosen course. Try to get a teacher to support your case, and be persistent if you detect that there is any prospect of flexibility.

One option, if your results are lower than predicted, is to ask for papers to be re-marked, as growing numbers do each year. The school may ask for a whole batch to be re-marked, and you should ensure that your chosen universities know this if it may make the difference to whether or not you satisfy your offer. If your grades improve, the university will review its decision, but if by then it has filled all its places, you may have to wait until next year to start the course.

Results Day is bound to be stressful, unless you are absolutely confident that you achieved the required grades – more of a possibility in an era of modular courses with marks along the way. But for thousands of students *Track* has removed the agony of opening the envelope or scanning a results noticeboard. From midnight on the eve of A-level results day, the system informs those who have already won a place on their chosen course. You will not learn your grades until later, but at least your immediate future is clear.

If you took Scottish Highers, you will have had your results for more than a week by the time the A-level grades are published. If you missed your grades, there is no need to wait for A levels before you begin approaching universities. Admissions staff at English universities may not wish to commit themselves before they see results from south of the border, but Scottish universities will be filling places immediately and all should be prepared to give you an idea of your prospects.

Clearing

If the worst comes to the worst and you do not have a place on Results Day, there will still be plenty of options through the UCAS Clearing scheme. Almost 40,000 people –

approaching 10 per cent of all applicants – found a place through this route in 2007. Although the most popular courses fill up quickly, many remain open up to and beyond the start of the academic year. And, at least at the start of the process, the range of courses with vacancies is much wider than in Extra. You will not find Oxford or Cambridge, but most universities will list some courses, and most subjects will be available somewhere.

Clearing runs from Results Day until late September, matching students without places to full-time courses with vacancies. As long as you are not holding any offers and you have not withdrawn your application, you are eligible automatically. Indeed, you will go straight into Clearing if you apply after 30 June. You will be sent a Clearing Passport and *Track* will show your Clearing number to quote to universities.

After that, it is just a matter of trawling through the lists on the UCAS website, and elsewhere, before making a direct approach to the university offering the course that appeals most, and where you have a realistic chance of a place. Tens of thousands of hopefuls will be doing the same thing, so do not waste time on courses where the standard offer is far above your grades. Universities run Clearing hotlines and have become adept at dealing with a large number of calls in a short period, but you can still spend a long time on the phone at a time when the most desirable places are beginning to disappear. If you can't get through – or even if you can – send an email setting out your grades and detailing the course that interests you.

The best advice is to plan ahead and not to wait for Results Day to draw up a list of possible Clearing targets. Many universities publish lists of courses that are likely to be in Clearing on their websites from the start of August. Think again about some of the courses that you considered when making your original application, or others at your chosen universities that had lower entrance requirements – perhaps dual honours, rather than single honours. But beware of switching to another subject simply because you have the right grades – you still have to sustain your interest and be capable of succeeding over three or more years. Many of the students who drop out of degrees are those who chose the wrong course in a rush during Clearing.

In short, you should start your search straight away if you do find yourself in Clearing, and act decisively, but do not panic. Apply the same criteria that you used in choosing courses initially: look at the syllabus and satisfy yourself that you will enjoy the course, that the university is one which you are happy to attend, and that the qualification will take you where you want to go in your career. You can make as many approaches as you like, until you are accepted on the course of your choice.

Most of the available vacancies will appear in Clearing lists, but some of the universities towards the top of the league tables may have a limited number of openings that they choose not to advertise – either for reasons of status or because they do not want the administrative burden of fielding large numbers of calls to fill a handful of courses. If there is a course that you find particularly attractive – especially if you have good grades and are applying late – it may be worth making a speculative call. Sometimes a number of candidates holding offers drop grades and you may be on the spot at the right moment.

What are the alternatives?

If your results are lower than expected and there is nothing you want in Clearing, there are several things you can do. The first is to resit one or more subjects. The modular nature of most courses means that you will have a clear idea of what you need to do to get better grades. You can go back to school or college, try a "crammer" or take a job and revise in the evenings. Although some colleges have a good success rate with re-takes, you have to be highly focused and realistic about the likely improvements. Some of the most competitive courses, such as medicine, may demand higher grades for a second application, so be sure you know the details before you commit yourself to a year's delay.

Other options are toget a job and study part-time, or to take a break from studying and return later in your career. The part-time route can be arduous – many young people find a job enough to handle without the extra burden of academic work. But others find it just the combination they need for a fulfilling life. It all depends on your job, your social life and your commitment to the subject you will study. It may be that a relatively short break is all that you need to rekindle your enthusiasm for studying. Many universities now have a majority of mature students, so you need not be out of place if this is your chosen route.

Taking a gap year

The other increasingly popular option is to take a gap year – about 8 per cent of applicants now defer their entry until the following year while they travel, or do voluntary or paid work. A whole industry has grown up around tailor-made activities, many of them in Asia, Africa or Latin America. Some have been criticised for doing more for the organisers than the underprivileged communities that they purport to assist, but there are programmes that are useful and character-building, as well as safe. Most of the overseas programmes are not cheap, but raising the money can be part of the experience. The alternative is to stay closer to home and make your contribution through organisations like Community Service Volunteers (www.csv.org.uk) or to take a job that will make higher education more affordable when the time comes.

Many admissions staff are happy to facilitate gap years because they think it makes for more mature, rounded students than those who come straight from school. The right programme may even increase your chances of winning a place, if it is relevant to your course. But there are subjects – maths in particular – that discourage a break because it takes too long to pick up study skills where you left off. From the student's point of view, you should also bear in mind that a gap year postpones the moment at which you embark on a career. This may be important if your course is a long one, such as medicine or architecture.

If you are considering a gap year, it makes sense to apply for a deferred place, rather than waiting for your results before applying. The application form has a section for deferments. That allows you to sort out your immediate future before you start travelling or working, and leaves you the option of changing your mind if circumstances change. Dealing with universities from the other side of the world is not ideal.

Useful websites

The following websites will help you find out more about the topics discussed in this chapter. For specific information on universities, visit their websites and for general information, consult the websites listed at the end of chapter 1.

Applications

The essential website for making an application is, of course, that of UCAS:
www.ucas.com
Within the UCAS site, there is much practical advice on how to apply:
www.ucas.com/students/startapplication/apply
For applications to music conservatoires, visit Conservatoires UK Admission service:
www.cukas.ac.uk
For applications for graduate teacher training, visit the Graduate Teacher Training Registry: **www.gttr.ac.uk**
For advice on your personal statement, visit
www.ucas.com/students/startapplication/apply/personalstatement
www.studential.com

Gap years

To help you consider options and start planning, visit:
www.gapadvice.org
For links to volunteering organisations in the UK, visit:
www.dfes.gov.uk/volunteering
For links to many not-for-profit gap year organisations:
www.yearoutgroup.org
For work placements relevant to university courses, visit Year in Industry:
www.yini.org.uk

Also worth consulting

Community Service Volunteers: **www.csv.org.uk**
(formerly Millennium Volunteers): **www.wearev.com**
Worldwide Volunteering: **http://wwv.org.uk**
Latitude Global Volunteering: **www.latitude.org.uk**
Volunteer Africa: **www.volunteerafrica.org**

5 Finding Somewhere to Live

Going to university will be the first time most students have thought about living away from home. This makes the decision about where to live – both in terms of location and the type of accommodation – so important. It may even influence your choice of university, since big differences can be found across the sector in the cost and standard of accommodation – and your choice can have a significant impact on the quality of your life as a student.

The choices you have

The options that you can select from are increasing – no longer are you just faced with the choice between a university hall of residence and a poor quality rented house. A report from the National Union of Students puts accommodation into sixteen categories, ranging from luxurious university halls to a bedsit in a shared house. The major choices include:

- University hall of residence, with individual study bedrooms and with a full catering service; some will have en-suite accommodation.
- University accommodation where you have to provide your own food.
- Private, purpose-built student accommodation.
- Rented houses or flats, shared with fellow students.
- Living at home.
- Living as a lodger in a private house.

This chapter will provide you with more information to help you decide where you would like to live and whether you can afford it.

Making your choice

Financial considerations are not the only factor you should consider when deciding where to live. Feeling comfortable and happy in your student home is of crucial importance to your success at university and to the quality of your experience. It is therefore worth investing some time to find the right place to live, and to avoid the false economy of choosing somewhere cheap where you may end up feeling depressed and isolated. Most students who drop out of university do so in the first few months, when homesickness and loneliness can be felt most acutely. Being warm and well fed is likely to have a positive effect on your studies.

UNITE Student Experience Report 2007

- 40% of students live in private rented accommodation.
- 17% of students live at home.
- 75% of students say their accommodation is good value for money.

- Compared with 2006, the cost of university accommodation increased by 7% while private rented accommodation fell by 11%.

Perhaps for these reasons, most undergraduates in their first year plump for living in university halls, which offer a convenient, safe, and reliable standard of accommodation, along with a supportive community environment. If meals are included, then this adds further peace of mind both for students and their parents.

Wherever you chose to live, there are some general points you will need to consider, such as how safe the neighbourhood seems to be, and how long it might take you to travel to and from the university – especially during rush hour. A recent survey of travel time between term-time accommodation and the university found that most students in London can expect a commute of 30 minutes minimum and often over an hour, while those living in Wales are usually much less than 30 minutes away from their university. Be sure to make use of any local or national Student Travel Card and any university or students' union transport system that may be provided to help you get back to your accommodation cheaply and safely.

Information to help you

In the university profiles (which are in the second half of this book), we provide details of what accommodation each university offers. You will be able to find the following:

- The number of university-provided places. A quick check against the number of undergraduates will show you how well provided for the university is.
- The percentage of places that are catered.
- The percentage of places that are self-catered.
- The weekly cost of catered and self-catered accommodation.
- A summary of the offer of accommodation that can be made to first years.
- A summary of the offer of accommodation that can be made to international students.
- The web address for details of the university's accommodation provision.

How much will it cost?

Inevitably, you will have to consider what you can afford. Students in the UK are estimated to spend a total of nearly £4 billion a year on rent – almost twice as much as their combined spending on food, going out, books and music. A recent survey suggested that the average student is paying a weekly rent of £73, with those living in London paying around £102 a week and those at the cheapest end of the spectrum in Sheffield and Leicester paying more like £59 per week. Generally speaking, the cost of student accommodation is highest in London and the southeast of England and lowest in the Midlands, Wales, Scotland and Northern Ireland.

Working out your finances first ought to help you sift through what could be a bewildering array of options – especially if your university is located in or near a large city. It is important to remember that both your living costs and your potential earnings in a particular location should be factored into your calculations when deciding where to live. While living costs in London are, unsurprisingly, the highest – an estimated average of £159 a week excluding rent – your earnings potential is double what it might be in other parts of the country. Students in London can earn around £146 a week, compared with those in Lancaster, who can expect to earn not much more than £70 a week, according to the Royal Bank of Scotland.

What universities offer

You might think that opting to live in university accommodation is the most straight-forward choice, especially since places in halls of residence are usually guaranteed for first-year students. Certainly if you go for university residences you benefit from being able to make arrangements in advance and at a distance, rather than having to be in the right place at the right time, as is often the way when searching for private housing.

However, you may still need to select from a range of options, even if you decide to start off in university living quarters. Some universities will have a variety of accommodation on offer, and you will need to consider which best suits your pocket and your preferred lifestyle.

New university accommodation

At the top end of the market, partnerships between universities and private firms have recently begun to lead the way. Private organisations such as UNITE plc (www.unite-students.com) have been paid by universities to build and manage some of the most luxurious student accommodation the UK sector has ever seen. Rooms in these complexes are typically en suite and include facilities such as your own phone line, satellite TV, and internet access. Shared kitchens are also top quality and fitted out with all the latest equipment. This kind of accommodation naturally comes at a higher price, but offers the advantages of flexibility both in living arrangements and through a range of payment options.

Halls of residence

Many new or recently refurbished university-owned halls offer a standard of accommodation that is not far short of the privately built residences. One of the reasons for this is that rooms in these halls can be offered to conference delegates during vacations. Even though these halls are also at the pricier end of the spectrum, you will probably find that they are in great demand, and you may have to get your name down for one quickly to secure one of the fancier rooms. That said, you can often get a guarantee of some kind of university accommodation if you give a firm acceptance of an offered place by a certain date in the summer. This may not be the case, however, if you have gained your place through Clearing – although rooms in private halls might still be on offer at this stage.

Royal Bank of Scotland Student Living Index 2007

The RBS Student Living Index was calculated as follows: for each town listed, average local weekly student expenditure on living and accommodation costs was divided by average local weekly income for working students. This provided a relative value, by which the 27 university towns were ranked. At the top is Leeds, where an average student spends £186 a week but earns £128 from part-time work. At the bottom was Nottingham, where an average student spends £211 a week but earns only £78.40 from part-time work.

1. Leeds	10. Newcastle	19. Belfast
2. Brighton	11. Sheffield	20. Canterbury
3. Dundee	12. Coventry	21. York
4. London	13. Cambridge	22. Bath
5. Liverpool	14. St Andrews	23. Edinburgh
6. Leicester	15. Manchester	24. Oxford
7. Birmingham	16. Cardiff	25. Lancaster
8. Glasgow	17. Durham	26. Southampton
9. Bristol	18. Aberdeen	27. Nottingham

While a few halls are single sex, most are mixed, and typically can house over 500 students. They are therefore great places for making friends and becoming part of the social scene. One possible downside is that they can also be noisy places where it can be difficult at times to get down to some work. The more successful students learn, before too many essay deadlines and exams start to loom, to get the balance right between all-night partying and escaping to the library for some undisturbed study time. On the upside, if you feel in need of either personal or study support, this is often at hand either through a counselling service or from fellow students.

University self-catering accommodation
An alternative to halls, offered particularly by some older universities, are smaller, self-catering properties fitted out with a shared kitchen and other living areas. Students looking for a more independent and flexible lifestyle may prefer this option. Remember that if you choose this kind of university housing, you will be responsible for feeding yourself, and you may also have heating and lighting bills to pay. University properties are often on campus or nearby, and so travel costs should not pose a problem.

Catering in university accommodation
Many universities have responded to a general increase in demand from students for a more independent lifestyle, by providing more flexible catering facilities. A range of eateries, from fast food outlets to more traditional refectories, can usually be found on campus. Students in university accommodation may now be offered pay-as-you-eat deals as an alternative to full-board packages.

What after the first year?
After your first year of living in university residences you may well wish to, and will probably be expected to, move out to other accommodation. The only exceptions are in collegiate universities – particularly Oxford and Cambridge – which may allow you to stay on in college halls for another year or two, and particularly for your final year. Students from outside the EU are also sometimes guaranteed accommodation.

Practical details
If you have decided to start out in university accommodation, then you will probably be expected to sign an agreement to cover rent. These contracts can be for around 40 weeks, which includes the Christmas and Easter holiday periods or for just the length of the three university terms. These term-time contracts are common when a university uses its rooms for conferences during vacations. You will be required to leave your room empty during vacations. It is therefore advisable to check whether the university has storage space for you to leave your belongings – otherwise you will have to make arrangements to take all your belongings home between terms. International students may be offered special arrangements, in which they can stay in halls during the short vacation periods. Organisations like www.hostuk.org can also arrange for overseas students to stay in a UK family home at holiday times such as the Christmas break.

Continuing to live at home
A report published by the Sutton Trust in 2008 suggests that a growing number of students are choosing to live at home. The potential financial benefits of this are

obvious, and the rise in the average level of student debt is probably the cause. The obvious downside is that you may miss out on a lot of the student experience, especially the social scene and the opportunity to make new friends. However, there is no evidence that students living at home do any worse academically. The quality of your home environment should influence your decision when weighing up whether or not to take this option. If it is stressful or not conducive to studying then you are probably better off moving out, even if it means having to take a job to make ends meet. On the other hand, there is a lot to be said for making use of supportive and flexible home conditions where these exist. If you are studying at a "new" university, you are more likely to have fellow students who also live at home.

UNITE Student Experience Report 2006	
Reasons for Living at Home	(%)
To save money or cut costs	38
Just want to	20
Cannot afford to live away	16
Near to university of choice	8
To concentrate on my studies	6
For an easy life; to be looked after	3
Parents wanted me to	2
Other reasons	7

Being a lodger or staying in a hostel
A small number of students live as a lodger in a family home, an option most frequently taken up by international students. The usual arrangement is for a study bedroom and some meals to be provided, while other facilities such as a washing machine are shared. Students with particular religious affiliations or those from certain countries may wish to consider living in one of a number of hostels run by charities catering for certain groups. Most of these can be found in London. More details are available from the British Council's publication *Studying and Living in the United Kingdom* (www.educationuk.org/downloads/study_live_uk.pdf).

Renting from the private sector
Recent growth in the number of private sector complexes and residences, often created in partnership with universities, means that students who prefer to go private have plenty of choice. As well as apartments that are rented out and managed by companies like UNITE, every university city or town is awash with privately owned accommodation available via agencies or offered by individual landlords. A much more professional attitude and approach to managing rental accommodation has emerged among smaller providers, thanks to a combination of greater regulation and increasing competition. Nevertheless, it is wise to take certain precautions when seeking out private residences.

How to start looking for rented property
Contact your university's accommodation service and ask for their list of approved rented properties. Some may have a Student Accommodation Accreditation Scheme, run in collaboration with the local council. To get onto an approved list under such schemes, landlords must show they are adhering to basic standards of safety and security, such as having an up-to-date gas and electric safety certificate. University accommodation officers should also be able to advise you on any hidden charges. For instance, you may be asked to pay a booking or reservation fee to secure a place in a particular property, and fees for references or drawing up a tenancy agreement are also sometimes charged. The practice of charging a "joining fee", however, has been outlawed.

Making a choice

Once you have made an initial choice on the area you would like to live in and the size of property you are looking for, the next stage is to look at possible places. If you plan to share, it is important that you all have a look at the property. If you will be living by yourself, take a friend with you when you go to view a property, since he or she can help you assess what you see objectively, and avoid any irrational or rushed on-the spot decisions. Don't let yourself be pushed into signing on the dotted line there and then. Take time to visit and consider a number of options. It is often helpful to spend some time in the area in which you may be living, to check out the local facilities, transport, and the general environment at various times of the day and different days of the week. If you can stay in the area for a few days, this will help you get a more accurate idea of what living in the district will be like.

If you are living in private rented accommodation, it is likely that at least some of your neighbours will not be students. Local people often welcome students, but resentment sometimes builds up, particularly in areas of towns and cities that are dominated by student housing. It is important to respect your neighbours' rights, and not to behave in an anti-social manner.

Preparing for sharing

The people you are planning to share a house with may not be as unsavoury as the characters in the TV comedy The Young Ones, but you can be sure they will have some habits that you find at least mildly irritating. How well you cope with some of the downsides of co-habiting will be partly down to the kind of person you are – where you are on the spectrum between laid back and highly strung – but it will help a lot if you are sharing with people whose outlook on day-to-day living is not too far out of line with your own. If you have not already selected your own group of friends, universities and landlords can help by taking personal preferences and lifestyle into account when grouping tenants together. You can make this task easier if you give full details about yourself when filling in accommodation applications forms.

Potential issues to consider when deciding whether to move into a shared house include whether any of the housemates smoke, own a loud musical instrument that they may decide to play at any time of the day or night, or have a habit of spending hours on the telephone. With most students owning a mobile phone, the latter should not be a problem unless someone decides to save on their mobile bills by using a landline phone in your shared house instead. If this is the case, then you should arrange for individual billing, provided by a number of phone companies such as The Phone Co-op (www.thephone.coop). It will also be important to sort out broadband arrangements that will work for everyone in the house, and that you will be able to arrange access to the university system. It may seem like a drag, but it is usually a good idea to agree from the outset a rota for everyone to share in the household cleaning chores. Otherwise it is almost certain that you will live in a state of permanent unhygienic squalor or that one or two individuals will be left to clear up everyone else's mess.

The practical details about renting

It is a good idea to ask whether your house is covered by an accreditation scheme or code of standards. Such codes provide a clear outline of what constitutes good practice and the responsibilities of both landlords and tenants. Adhering to schemes like the

National Code of Standards for Larger Student Developments compiled by Accreditation Network UK (www.anuk.org.uk) may well become a requirement for larger properties, including those managed by universities, now that the Housing Act is in force.

HMOs

If you are renting a private house it may be is subject to the rules and regulations of the 2004 Housing Act in England and Wales (similar legislation applies in Scotland and Northern Ireland). Licenses are compulsory for all private Houses in Multiple Occupation (HMOs) with three or more stories that house five or more unrelated residents. The provisions of the Act also allow local authorities to designate whole areas in which HMOs of all sizes must be licensed. The good news is that these regulations are likely to be applied in sections of university towns and cities where most students live. This means that a house must be licensed, well-managed and must meet various health and safety standards, and its owner subject to various financial regulations. The bad news is that this could lead to a reduction in the number and range of privately rented properties on the market, or an increase in rental prices.

Tenancy agreements

Whatever kind of accommodation you go for, you must be sure to have all the paperwork in order and be clear about what you are signing up to before you move in. If you are taking up residence in a shared house, flat or bedsit, the first document you will have to grapple with is a tenancy agreement or lease offering you an "assured shorthold tenancy". Since this is a binding legal document you should be prepared to go through every clause with a fine-tooth comb. Remember that it is much more difficult to make changes or overcome problems arising from unfair agreements once you are a tenant than before you become one.

You would be well advised to seek help, in the likely event of your not fully understanding some of the clauses. Your university accommodation office or students' union are a good place to start, since they should know all the ins and outs, and have model tenancy agreements to refer to. A Citizens Advice Bureau or Law Advice Centre should also be able to offer you free advice. Watch out in particular for clauses that may make you jointly responsible for the actions of others with whom you are sharing the property. If you name your parent as a guarantor to cover any costs not covered by you, then they may also be liable for charges levied on all tenants for any damage that might not be your fault. A rent review clause could allow your landlord to increase the rent at will, whereas without such a clause, they are restricted to one rent rise a year. Make sure you keep a copy of all documents, and get a receipt (and keep it somewhere safe) for anything you have to pay for.

Contracts tend to be longer than for university accommodation – they will frequently commit you to paying rent for 52 weeks of the year. There are probably more advantages than disadvantages to this kind of arrangement. It means you don't have to move out in vacation periods, which you might have to in university halls to make way for conference delegates. You can store your belongings in your room when you go away (but don't leave anything really valuable behind if you can help it). You may be able to negotiate a rent discount for those periods when you are not staying in the property. The other advantage, particularly important for cash-strapped students, is that you have a base from which to find work and hold down a job during the vacations.

Deposits

On top of the agreed rent, You will need to provide a deposit or bond to cover any possible breakages or damage. This will probably set you back the equivalent of another month's rent. The deposit should be returned, less any deductions, at the end of the contract. However, be warned that disputes over the return of deposits are quite common, with the question of what constitutes reasonable wear and tear often the subject of disagreements between landlords and tenants. To protect students from unscrupulous landlords who withhold deposits without good reason, the 2004 Housing Act has introduced a National Tenancy Deposit Scheme under which deposits are held by an independent body rather than by the landlord. This is designed to ensure that deposits are fairly returned, and that any disputes are resolved swiftly and cheaply.

Inventories and other paperwork

You should get an inventory and schedule of condition of everything in the property. This is another document that you should check very carefully – and make sure that everything listed is as described. Write on the document anything that is different. The National Union of Students even suggests taking photographs of rooms and equipment when you first move in (putting the date on the pictures if you are using a digital camera), to provide you with additional proof should any dispute arise when your contract ends and you want to get your deposit back. If you are not offered an inventory, then make one of your own. You should have someone else witness and sign this, send it to your landlord, and keep your own copy.

You should ask your landlord for a recent gas safety certificate issued by a qualified CORGI engineer, a fire safety certificate covering the furnishings, and a record of current gas and electricity meter readings. Take your own readings of meters when you move in to make sure these match up with what you have been given, or make your own records if the landlord doesn't supply this information. This also applied to water meters if you are expected to pay water rates (although this isn't usually the case).

If you are sharing a house with other full-time students only, then you will not have to pay Council Tax. However, you may be liable to pay a proportion of the Council Tax bill if you are sharing with anyone who is not a full-time student. You may need to get a Council Tax exemption certificate from your university as evidence that you do not need to pay Council Tax or should pay only a proportion, depending on the circumstances.

Security in rented accommodation

As students living in private housing are twice as likely to be burgled as those in university halls, it is worth running through this security checklist provided by the NUS:

- Check that the front and back doors are fitted with five-lever mortise locks in addition to standard catch locks.
- Make sure the door to your room has a lock, and always lock up when you leave it –especially for long periods such as during vacations.
- Check the locks and catches on accessible windows, especially those at ground-floor level.
- Before you move in, try to talk to neighbours about how safe the area is and whether there have been many instances of burglary or car crime.
- Ask your landlord to ensure that all previous tenants and holders of keys no longer have copies.

- If you find a property that you are keen to rent, but you are unsure about some of the security aspects, speak to the letting agency or landlord to discuss your concerns. They may be able to make the necessary changes to make the property more secure before you move in.

Safety and security

Once you have arrived and settled in, remember to take care of your own safety and the security of your possessions. You are particularly vulnerable as a fresher, when you are still getting used to your new-found independence. This may help explain why a fifth of students are robbed in the first six weeks of the academic year. Take care with valuable portable items such as mobile phones, iPods and laptops, all of which are tempting for criminals. Ensure you don't use them or have them obviously on display when you are out and about. If your mobile phone is stolen, call your network or 08701 123 123 to immobilise it.

Students' unions, universities and the police will provide plenty of practical guidance when you arrive. Following their advice will reduce the chance of you becoming a victim of crime, and so able to enjoy living in the new surroundings of your chosen university town.

Insurance

It is a false economy not to have adequate insurance to cover you for the loss or theft of valuable items. Your students' union will probably be able to advise you on where to go for the best deals. It may be that your parents' insurance will cover you when you are a student, and you should certainly check this. You should also keep a record somewhere safe of the serial and model numbers of expensive electrical equipment. If you have to claim on your insurance for these items you will need these details. Remember that whether you say it out loud or subconsciously think it, courting the notion that "it won't happen to me" is one of the best ways to ensure that it probably will.

Useful websites

The following websites will help you find out more about the topics discussed in this chapter. In the university profiles later in this book, we give an indication of costs for university-provided accommodation and details of university accommodation websites.

For advice on a range of housing issues, visit:
www.nusonline.co.uk/info/housing

The Shelter website has separate sections covering different housing regulations in England, Wales, Scotland and Northern Ireland:
www.shelter.org.uk

Private accommodation

As an example of a provider of private hall accommodation, visit:
www.unite-students.com

There are a number of sites that will help you find accommodation, among which are:

www.accommodationforstudents.com
www.homesforstudents.co.uk
www.studentaccommodation.org
www.studentpad.co.uk

For guidance on private accommodation:
Accreditation Network UK runs an accreditation scheme for larger schemes (with Unipol):
www.anuk.org.uk
www.unipol.org.uk/national

To find your nearest Citizen's Advice Bureau, visit:
www.nacab.org.uk

To find your nearest Law Centre, visit:
www.lawcentres.org.uk/lawcentres

For security advice on renting, visit the NUS security checklist:
www.nusonline.co.uk/info/housing/270520.aspx

For telephone sharing, visit the Phone Co-op:
www.thephone.coop

For general advice on safety, this Home Office site gives practical advice:
www.homeoffice.gov.uk/crime-victims/how-you-can-prevent-crime/student-safety/

6 Finding Out About University Sport

Sport used to be low down most applicants' list of priorities when choosing a university – it was a minority pursuit, mainly for dedicated hearties playing in competitive teams. Not any more. A growing proportion of students want to keep fit, even if they don't play competitive sport, and universities have joined a race of their own to provide the best facilities. Sport may still be a secondary consideration for most applicants, but particularly good (or particularly poor) facilities can sometimes swing the balance.

Where universities have been able to attract Lottery funding or have made a major investment in sport, the standard of facilities can be breath-taking. Several campuses will host teams competing at the 2012 Olympics, and a number of universities already contain national centres of excellence in major sports. Naturally, not all can aspire to those standards, but most now offer facilities to compare with the best available commercially – and usually at a fraction of the price.

Being a full-time student offers unrivalled opportunities to discover and play a vast range of sports. Many universities still encourage departments not to schedule lectures and seminars on Wednesday afternoons, to give students free time for sport. Even those who spend long hours in the laboratory have more time for leisure activities now than they will be able to spare later in life. There are student-run clubs for all the major sports and – particularly at the larger universities – a host of minor ones. Or you can content yourself with high-quality gyms, with staff on hand to devise personalised training regimes. The cost varies widely between universities, and membership fees can represent a large amount to lay out at the start of the year, but most provide good value if you are going to be a regular.

All universities are conscious of the need to provide for a spread of ability. Sports scholarships for elite performers are now commonplace, but there will be plenty of opportunities, too, for beginners. University teams demand a hefty commitment in terms of training and practice sessions – often several a week – and in many sports standards are high. University teams often compete in local and national leagues. The University of London women's volleyball team recently won the English Volleyball Championships, for example, and Bath University's "Team Bath" have tasted success in the FA Cup.

For those who don't aspire to such heights, or whose interests are primarily social, there are thriving internal, or intramural, leagues. These provide opportunities for teams from halls of residence or faculties, or even a group of friends, to form a team and participate on a regular basis. Nor is university sport a male preserve – student teams were among the pioneers in mixed sport and are still strong in areas such as women's cricket, football and rugby.

British university sport has not become big business, as it is in the United States, but competitive standards have been rising. The British Universities Sports Association (BUSA) runs competitions in almost 50 sports, and ranks participating institutions. There is also international competition in a number of sports, and numerous examples of students being selected for Olympic and professional teams. The World Student Games have become one of the biggest occasions in the international sporting calendar.

From the summer of 2008, a new organisation will bring together the administration of university sport and the job of lobbying for the best possible facilities. British University College Sport will have a student membership, but will also play a role in the wider sporting community, as well as negotiating with the Government and other national and international bodies to promote, develop and enable participation in sport and active recreation.

A few universities are known particularly for sport, and are benefiting from its increasing popularity as a degree subject, as well as an extra-curricular activity. Several of this elite group had a head start as former physical education colleges. Loughborough is probably the best-known of them, but Leeds Metropolitan and Brunel are others with a similar pedigree. Other universities with different traditions, such as Bath and the University of East Anglia, also have a variety of outstanding facilities, while the likes of Stirling and UWIC have the same in a narrower range of sports.

As in so much else, Oxford and Cambridge are in a category of their own. The Boat Race and the Varsity Match (in rugby union) are the only UK university sporting events with a regular popular following, and there is a high standard of competition in other sports, but there is an ambivalent attitude to them in many colleges. While star rowers and rugby players do turn up on postgraduate diploma courses, the days of special consideration for sporty undergraduates appear to be over, and there are few of the sports scholarships offered at other universities.

For most universities, it is in the area of "sport for all" that most attention has been focused. Beginners are welcomed and coaching provided in a range of sports, from ultimate Frisbee to tai-chi, that would be difficult to match outside the higher education system. Check on university websites to see whether your usual sport is available, but don't be surprised if you come across a new favourite when you have the opportunity to try out some new sports as a student. Many universities have programmes designed to encourage students to take up a new sport, with expert coaching provided.

You may even end up wanting to coach, umpire or referee – and this is another area in which higher education has much to offer. Many university clubs and sports unions provide subsidised courses for students to gain qualifications that may be of use to the individual in later life, as well as benefiting university teams in the short term. Or you might want to try your hand at some sports administration, with an eye to your career. In most universities there is a sports (or athletic) union, with autonomy from the main students' union, which organises matches and looks after the wider interests of those who play. There are plenty of opportunities for those seeking an apprenticeship in the art of running a club, or larger organisation.

University sports facilities

Even the smallest university should provide reasonable indoor and outdoor sports facilities – a sports hall, modern gym equipment and outdoor pitches (usually including an all-weather surface and floodlights). Most will also have a swimming pool and extras such as climbing walls, but the smaller universities tend to make arrangements for students to use local sports centres and clubs when it is not feasible to provide for minority sports. The same goes for the really expensive ones, like golf, which is usually the subject of an arrangement with one or more local clubs that give students a discount. Specialist facilities, like boat houses and climbing huts, obviously depend on location, but the most landlocked university is likely to have a sailing club that organises regular activities away from campus, and a skiing club that runs at least annual trips to the mountains.

Many of the larger universities have spent millions of pounds improving their sports facilities, sometimes in partnership with local authorities, national sporting bodies or the Lottery. University campuses are ideal locations for national coaching centres, and many have been established in recent years. While some of the facilities are naturally reserved for elite performers, opportunities always exist for ordinary students to make use of them at reasonable rates, as well as occasionally rubbing shoulders with star players.

Overall, close to £400 million has been spent on new or upgraded sports facilities at UK universities over the past five years. Universities now boast a significant proportion of the UK's 50-metre pools, for example, and more are planned. Other innovative schemes include Leeds Metropolitan's development of the Headingley cricket and rugby league grounds, providing teaching space for students during the week and improved facilities for players and spectators on match days.

Both the scale of investment and the emphasis on sport can be expected to increase in the run-up to the 2012 Olympic Games, in London. Universities all over the country have been drawing up plans associated with the games, from research programmes to new capital projects designed to lure teams to training camps. The legacy for students should be considerable, as it was at the Commonwealth Games in Manchester and the World Student Games in Sheffield.

Beyond scrutinising the prospectus for the extent of university facilities, there are two important questions to ask: where are they and how much do they cost? Neither is easy to track down on the average university website.

How much?

Students who are used to free (if inferior) facilities at school often get a nasty surprise when they find that they are expected to pay to join the Athletic Union and then pay again to use the gym or play football. Because most university sport is subsidised, the charges are reasonable compared to commercial facilities, but the best deal may require a considerable outlay at the start. Some campus gyms and swimming pools now charge more than £300 a year, for example, which is still considerably cheaper than paying per visit if you intend to use the facilities regularly (and provides an incentive to carry on doing so). Most universities offer a variety of peak and off-peak membership packages – some for the entire length of your course.

Outdoor sports are usually charged by the hour, although clubs will also charge a membership fee. You may be required to pay up to £25 for membership of the Athletic Union (although not all universities require this). Fees for intra-mural sport are seldom substantial; teams will usually pay a fee for the season, while courts for racket sports tend to be marginally cheaper per session than in other clubs.

How far away?

University prospectuses tend to major on the quality of the five-a-side pitches without being as forthcoming about the prices. The other common complaint by students is that the playing fields are too far from the campus – understandable in the case of city centre universities, but still aggravating if you are having to arrange your own transport. This is where campus universities have a clear advantage.

For the rest, there has to be some trade-off between the quality of outdoor facilities and the distance you have to travel to use them. But universities are beginning to realise that long journeys depress usage of important (and expensive) facilities, and some have tried to find suitable land closer to lectures and halls of residence. Indoor sports centres should all be within easy reach.

Sport as a degree subject

Sports science and other courses associated with sport have seen big increases in recent years – so much so that the subject is close to the top ten in terms of popularity, with more than 50,000 applications in 2006–7. Specialist courses are available in everything from sport psychology to sport journalism and even sport history. As those who have taken sports science at A level will know, an interest in sport is invaluable but far from sufficient. The same goes for sporting excellence. If you are hoping to be rewarded with an academic qualification for three years on the sports field, you will be disappointed because there is serious science involved.

However, sport is a growing employment field and one that demands qualifications like any other. The way in which higher education statistics are collected makes it hard to separate sport from other subjects in the same category, such as tourism and hotel management, but the universities that specialise in sport tend to have good employment records in this area. Entrance requirements vary widely, with some of the top courses asking for 360 points on the UCAS tariff, while others ask half this number or less.

Some, but not all, sports science degrees expect candidates to have studied the subject at A or AS level. Other degrees in the sports area are more closely focused on management, with careers in the leisure industry in mind – golf course management, for example, has proved popular with students despite being a target of those who see anything beyond the traditional academic portfolio as "dumbing down". Such courses are usually no less rigorous than general management degrees. The question is not whether the courses are up to standard, but whether a less specialised one will offer more career flexibility if a decline in popularity for the particular sport limits future opportunities. The chance to combine work and play for three years holds obvious attractions, but there will be opportunities to pursue your chosen sport in any case.

Sports scholarships

The number and range of sports scholarships have expanded just as rapidly as courses in the subject, but the two are usually not connected. Sports scholarships are for elite performers, regardless of what they are studying – indeed, they exist at universities with barely any degrees in the field. Imported from the United States, scholarships now exist in an array of sports. At Birmingham University, for example, there are specialist golf awards (as there are at ten other universities) and a scholarship for triathletes, as well as others open to any sport.

The value of scholarships varies considerably – sometimes according to individual prowess. The Royal and Ancient scholarships for golfers, for example, range from £1,500 for promising handicap golfers to £10,000 for full internationals. All of them demand that you meet the normal entrance requirements for your course and maintain the necessary academic standards, as well as progressing in your sport. In practice, most departments will be flexible about attendance and deadlines, as long as you make your requests well in advance.

Many sports scholarships offer benefits in-kind, in the form of coaching, equipment or access to facilities. The Government-funded Talented Athletes Scholarship Scheme, which is restricted to students at English universities who have achieved national recognition at under-18 level and are eligible to represent England, is one such example. The scholarships are worth £3,000 a year and can be put towards costs such as competition and training costs, equipment or mentoring. Further details are available at www.tass.gov.uk.

Part-time work

University sports centres are an excellent source of term-time (and out-of-term) employment. They beat other campus jobs, such as bar work, in terms of enjoyment and healthiness. Depending on your qualifications, you could earn up to £17 an hour for coaching, or more like £7 an hour as a receptionist or for other forms of assistance. You may also be trained in first aid, fire safety, customer care and risk assessment – all useful skills for future employment. The experience will help you secure employment in commercial or local authority facilities – and even for jobs such as stewarding at football grounds and music venues.

Administrative work within the Athletic Union of university sports organisation, is more likely to be unpaid, but may still provide useful experience that will add to your CV. So, indeed, does a position of responsibility in a club, or even captaining a team. Many employers value sport as an indication of self-confidence and teamworking qualities. Most universities also have a sabbatical post in the Athletic Union or similar body, a paid position with responsibility for organising university sport and representing the sporting community within the university.

Useful websites

The following websites will help you find out more about the topics discussed in this chapter.

BUSA British Universities Sports Association
www.busa.org.uk
UCS University and College Sport
www.ucsport.net
UK Sport
www.uksport.gov.uk
London 2012
www.london2012.com
Talented Athlete Scholarship Scheme
www.tass.gov.uk

Table of university sporting facilities

The following six pages outline the sporting facilities available at each of the universities covered in this book. The information has been compiled from a survey undertaken by University and College Sport in 2007. The information only covers the facilities that universities provide centrally for all their students, and ignores any facilities there may be in halls of residence or colleges. At Oxford and Cambridge, for example, many colleges have facilities that are not reflected in the tables. The table provides the following information:

- British Universities Sports Association (BUSA) League Rankings 2006–07, based on all sports.
  Teams get points each year for their success in inter-university competitions and BUSA uses them
  to compile an annual league table. The universities with the highest rankings (eg, Loughborough,
  Bath and Birmingham) are therefore overall the most successful competitively. A number of
  institutions with teams in BUSA are not universities and so do not appear in the following table.
  The BUSA rankings are based on all teams in the leagues.
- An indication of whether the university has (Y for "yes") or does not have (N for "no") the following
  facilities:
  - Sports hall
  - Swimming pool
  - Squash courts
  - Climbing wall
  - Indoor tennis courts
  - Fitness facilities
  - Winter grass pitches (eg, for football, rugby, etc.)
  - Cricket pitches
  - Artificial turf pitches
- The number of different sports with student clubs.
- The number of indoor sports with intramural competitions.
- The number of outdoor sports with intramural competitions.
- Whether instruction classes are available to encourage new participants (Y = yes; N = no).
- Whether sports scholarships or bursaries are available. Full details will need to be checked on
  university websites.
- Details of university websites devoted to sports. Students' unions websites usually have sports
  information as well. Where the main university website is given, visit that site and search for sports.
  The full web address is too long to give in this table.

Grey boxes show where information is not available.

University Sporting Facilities

Universities	BUSA ranking 2006–07	Sports hall?	Swimming pool?	Squash courts?	Climbing wall?	Indoor tennis court(s)?	Fitness facilities?
Aberdeen	28	Y	Y	Y	N	N	Y
Abertay	99	N	N	N	N	N	Y
Aberystwyth	68	Y	Y	Y	Y	Y	Y
Anglia Ruskin	112	Y	Y	Y	Y	Y	Y
Aston	76	Y	Y	Y	Y	N	Y
Bangor	81	Y	N	Y	Y	N	Y
Bath	2	Y	Y	Y	Y	Y	Y
Bath Spa	140	No further information reported					
Bedfordshire	84	No further information reported					
Birmingham	3	Y	Y	Y	Y	N	Y
Birmingham City	103	N	N	N	N	N	N
Bolton	107	Y	N	N	Y	N	Y
Bournemouth	38	Y	Y	Y	Y	N	Y
Bradford	94	Y	Y	Y	Y	Y	Y
Brighton	31	Y	N	N	Y	N	Y
Bristol	13	Y	Y	Y	N	Y	Y
Brunel	23	Y	N	Y	Y	N	Y
Cambridge	12	N	Y	Y	N	N	Y
Canterbury Christ Church	89	Y	N	N	N	N	Y
Cardiff	16	Y	N	Y	N	N	Y
Cardiff, University of Wales Institute	7	Y	Y	Y	N	Y	Y
Central Lancashire	56	Y	N	N	N	Y	Y
Chester	83	Y	Y	Y	N	N	Y
Chichester	58	Y	N	N	Y	Y	Y
City	115	Y	N	Y	N	N	Y
Coventry	57	Y	N	N	N	N	Y
Cumbria		Y	N	N	N	N	Y
De Montfort	102	Y	N	Y	N	N	Y
Derby	112						
Dundee	34	No further information reported					
Durham	6	Y	N	Y	Y	N	Y
East Anglia	64	Y	Y	Y	Y	N	Y
East London	138						
Edge Hill	85	No further information reported					
Edinburgh	4	Y	Y	Y	Y	N	Y
Essex	42	Y	N	Y	Y	N	Y
Exeter	10	Y	Y	Y	Y	Y	Y
Glamorgan	61	Y	N	Y	Y	N	Y
Glasgow	26	Y	Y	Y	N	N	Y
Glasgow Caledonian	78	Y	N	N	N	N	Y

Winter grass pitch(es)?	Cricket pitch(es)?	Artificial turf pitch(es)?	Number of different sports with student clubs	Number of indoor sports with intra-mural competitions	Number of outdoor sports with intra-mural competitions	Instruction classes available?	Sports scholarships or bursaries available?	Sport website
Y	Y	Y	53	0	2	Y	Y	www.abdn.ac.uk/sportandrec
N	N	N	16	3	3	Y	Y	www.sport.abertay.ac.uk/
Y	Y	Y	50	0	1	Y	N	www.aber.ac.uk/sportscentre/
Y	N	N	60	5	5	Y	Y	www.anglia.ac.uk
Y	Y	Y	37	0	0	Y	Y	www.aston.ac.uk/sport
Y	N	Y	39	3	3	Y	Y	www.maesglas.co.uk
Y	Y	Y	47	8	6	Y	Y	www.teambath.com
								www.bathspa.ac.uk/bath/
								www.beds.ac.uk/studentlife/campus
Y	Y	Y	43	3	4	Y	Y	www.sport.bham.ac.uk
Y	N	Y	20	1	1	Y	N	www.birminghamcitysu.com
N	N	N	9	3	0	Y	N	www.bolton.ac.uk/sport/
Y	Y	N	15	7	3	Y	Y	www.bournemouth.ac.uk/sport
Y	Y	Y	34	13	14	Y	N	www.brad.ac.uk/sports/
Y	Y	N	24	0	4	Y	Y	www.brighton.ac.uk/sport
Y	Y	Y	56	7	4	Y	Y	www.bris.ac.uk/sport
Y	N	Y	39	3	2	Y	Y	www.brunel.ac.uk/sport
Y	Y	Y	53	12	7	Y	Y	www.sport.cam.ac.uk
Y	N	N	15	0	4	Y	Y	www.canterbury.ac.uk/sport
Y	Y	Y	59	0	3	Y	Y	www.cardiff.ac.uk/sport
Y	Y	Y	19	0	0	Y	Y	www2.uwic.ac.uk/UWIC/schools/sport/
Y	Y	Y	35	0	1	Y	Y	www.uclan.ac.uk/sport
Y	N	Y	33	3	3	Y	Y	www.chester.ac.uk/sportandrecreation/
Y	N	Y	17	0	1	Y	Y	www.chisu.org & www.chiuni.ac.uk
N	N	N	16	5	0	Y	N	www.city.ac.uk/sportscentre/
Y	Y	Y	34	4	2	Y	Y	www.coventry.ac.uk/sportandrecreation
N	N	N	12	8	2	Y	Y	www.ucsm.ac.uk/sportsrec
N	N	N	26	0	0	Y	N	www.dmu.ac.uk
								www.derby.ac.uk
								www.dundee.ac.uk/ise
Y	Y	Y	51	8	9	Y	Y	www.teamdurham.com
Y	Y	Y	46	18	8	Y	Y	www.sportspark.co.uk
								www.uel.ac.uk
								www.edgehill.ac.uk/sportingedge
Y	Y	Y	59	3	5	Y	Y	www.sport.ed.ac.uk
Y	Y	Y	45	15	7	Y	Y	www.essex.ac.uk/sport
Y	Y	Y	47	6	6	Y	Y	www.sport.ex.ac.uk
Y	N	Y	25	6	1	Y	Y	www.glam.ac.uk/sports
Y	Y	Y	46	2	2	Y	Y	www.gla.ac.uk/services/sport
N	N	N	24	0	0	Y	Y	www.gcal.ac.uk/arc/

University Sporting Facilities cont.

Universities	BUSA ranking 2006–07	Sports hall?	Swimming pool?	Squash courts?	Climbing wall?	Indoor tennis court(s)?	Fitness facilities?
Gloucestershire	36	No further information reported					
Goldsmiths College	128	Y	N	N	N	N	Y
Greenwich	92	Y	N	N	N	Y	Y
Heriot-Watt	46	Y	N	Y	Y	N	Y
Hertfordshire	50	Y	Y	Y	Y	N	Y
Huddersfield	110	Y	N	Y	N	N	Y
Hull	66	Y	N	Y	Y	N	Y
Imperial	29	Y	Y	Y	Y	N	Y
Keele	72	Y	Y	Y	Y	N	Y
Kent	41	Y	N	Y	Y	Y	Y
King's College	52	N	N	Y	N	N	Y
Kingston	79	N	N	N	N	N	Y
Lampeter		No further information reported					
Lancaster	44	Y	Y	Y	Y	N	Y
Leeds	15	Y	N	Y	Y	N	Y
Leeds Met	14	Y	Y	Y	Y	Y	Y
Leicester	80	Y	N	Y	N	Y	Y
Lincoln	74	Y	N	Y	N	N	Y
Liverpool	32	Y	Y	Y	Y	N	Y
Liverpool Hope	107	No further information reported					
Liverpool John Moores	54	Y	Y	N	Y	N	Y
London School of Economics	62	No further information reported					
London South Bank	92	Y	N	N	N	N	Y
Loughborough	1	Y	Y	Y	Y	Y	Y
Manchester	11	Y	Y	Y	N	N	Y
Manchester Metropolitan	55	Y	N	Y	N	N	Y
Middlesex	60	Y	N	N	N	N	Y
Napier	69	No further information reported					
Newcastle	9	Y	N	Y	N	N	Y
Northampton	86	Y	N	N	N	N	Y
Northumbria	18	Y	N	Y	N	N	Y
Nottingham	5	Y	Y	Y	Y	Y	Y
Nottingham Trent	43	Y	N	Y	Y	N	Y
Oxford	8	Y	Y	Y	Y	N	Y
Oxford Brookes	37	Y	N	Y	Y	N	Y
Plymouth	45	N	N	Y	N	N	Y
Portsmouth	47	Y	N	Y	N	N	Y
Queen Margaret	119	Y	N	N	N	N	Y
Queen Mary, London	82	Y	N	Y	N	N	Y

Winter grass pitch(es)?	Cricket pitch(es)?	Artificial turf pitch(es)?	Number of different sports with student clubs	Number of indoor sports with intra-mural competitions	Number of outdoor sports with intra-mural competitions	Instruction classes available?	Sports scholarships or bursaries available?	Sport website
								www.yourstudentunion.com
Y	Y	N	17	1	1	Y	N	www.gold.ac.uk/sports
Y	N	N	7	0	0	N	Y	www.gre.ac.uk/about/sports
Y	N	Y	32	3	2	Y	Y	www.hw.ac.uk/sports
Y	N	Y	24	1	2	Y	Y	www.student.hertssportsvillage.co.uk
N	N	N	28	0	0	Y	N	www.hud.ac.uk/stu_svc/sports.htm
Y	Y	Y	38	1	1	Y	N	www.hullstudent.com
Y	Y	Y	73	5	4	Y	Y	www.imperial.ac.uk/sports
Y	Y	Y	32	2	1	Y	N	www.keelefm.co.uk
Y	Y	Y	40	5	4	Y	Y	www.kent.ac.uk/sports
Y	Y	N	51	0	0	Y	N	www.kclsu.org/clubs.php
Y	Y	N	27	0	1	Y	Y	www.kingston.ac.uk/sport
								www.lamp.ac.uk
Y	Y	Y	30	7	7	Y	N	www.lancs.ac.uk/lancuni/sports
Y	Y	Y	63	9	6	Y	Y	www.leeds.ac.uk/sport
Y	N	Y	40	1	2	Y	Y	www.leedsmet.ac.uk/sport
Y	Y	Y	32	8	4	Y	Y	www.le.ac.uk/sports
Y	N	Y	40	2	1	Y	Y	www.lincoln.ac.uk
Y	Y	Y	43	3	3	Y	Y	www.liv.ac.uk/sports
								www.hope.ac.uk/
Y	N	Y	30	0	3	Y	Y	www.ljmu.ac.uk/StudyLJMU/Sport/
								www.lsesu.com
Y	Y	N	13	1	0	Y	Y	www.lsbu.ac.uk/sports
Y	Y	Y	53	28	14	Y	Y	www.loughboroughsport.com
Y	Y	Y	44	5	7	Y	Y	www.manchester.ac.uk/sport
N	N	N	35	2	2	Y	N	www.mmu.ac.uk/sport
Y	Y	N	12	2	2	Y	Y	www.mdx.ac.uk/sport
								www.napier.ac.uk/napierlife/
Y	Y	Y	65	2	4	Y	Y	www.ncl.ac.uk/cprs
Y	N	N	15	0	1	Y	Y	www.northamptonunion.com
Y	Y	Y	27	4	2	Y	Y	www.teamnorthumbria.com
Y	Y	Y	73	4	6	Y	Y	www.nottingham.ac.uk/sport
Y	Y	Y	38	3	1	Y	Y	www.ntu.ac.uk/sport
Y	Y	Y	81	28	18	Y	Y	www.sport.ox.ac.uk
Y	Y	Y	30	1	1	Y	Y	www.brookes.ac.uk/sport
N	N	N	57	2	3	Y	Y	www.plymouth.ac.uk/recreation
Y	N	Y	49	6	3	Y	Y	www.port.ac.uk/sport
N	N	Y	12	0	0	Y	N	www.qmu.ac.uk/sports
N	N	N	30	4	7	Y	N	www.qmsu.org

University Sporting Facilities cont.

Universities	BUSA ranking 2006–07	Sports hall?	Swimming pool?	Squash courts?	Climbing wall?	Indoor tennis court(s)?	Fitness facilities?
Queen's, Belfast	109	Y	Y	Y	Y	N	Y
Reading	27	Y	N	Y	N	N	Y
Robert Gordon	71	Y	Y	Y	Y	Y	Y
Roehampton	98	Y	N	N	N	N	Y
Royal Holloway	63	Y	Y	Y	N	N	Y
Salford	91	No further information reported					
Sheffield	21	No further information reported					
Sheffield Hallam	20	Y	N	N	N	N	Y
SOAS	131	No further information reported					
Southampton	19	Y	Y	Y	Y	N	Y
Southampton Solent	70	Y	N	N	N	N	Y
St Andrews	25	Y	N	Y	Y	N	Y
Staffordshire	75	Y	N	N	Y	Y	Y
Stirling	17	Y	Y	Y	N	Y	Y
Strathclyde	49	Y	Y	Y	N	N	Y
Sunderland	77	Y	Y	N	N	N	Y
Surrey	73	Y	N	Y	Y	N	Y
Sussex	53	Y	N	Y	N	N	Y
Swansea	24	Y	Y	Y	Y	N	Y
Teesside	90	Y	N	Y	Y	N	Y
Thames Valley	124	No further information reported					
Ulster	116	Y	N	Y	N	Y	Y
University of the Arts London	131	N	N	N	N	N	N
University College London	39	Y	N	Y	N	N	Y
UWE, Bristol	35	Y	N	N	N	N	N
Wales, Newport	117	Y	N	N	N	N	N
Warwick	22	Y	Y	Y	Y	Y	Y
Westminster	123	No further information reported					
West of Scotland	127	No further information reported					
Winchester	105	Y	N	Y	N	N	Y
Wolverhampton	96	Y	N	Y	N	N	Y
Worcester	51	Y	Y	N	N	N	Y
York	48	Y	N	Y	N	N	Y
York St John	87	Y	N	N	Y	N	Y

Grey boxes mean information is not available.

A number of institutions with teams in the British Universities Sports Association League are not universities and so do not appear in the above table. The BUSA rankings above are based on all teams in the leagues.

Winter grass pitch(es)?	Cricket pitch(es)?	Artificial turf pitch(es)?	Number of different sports with student clubs	Number of indoor sports with intra-mural competitions	Number of outdoor sports with intra-mural competitions	Instruction classes available?	Sports scholarships or bursaries available?	Sport website
Y	Y	Y	53	6	5	Y	Y	www.qub.ac.uk/sport
Y	Y	Y	50	5	2	Y	Y	www.sport.reading.ac
N	N	N	30	0	0	Y	Y	www.rgu.ac.uk/rgusport
Y	N	N	20	0	3	Y	N	www.roehamptonstudent.ac.uk
Y	Y	N	36	0	0	Y	Y	www.rhul.ac.uk/sports
								www.salfordstudents.com
								www.usport.co.uk
Y	Y	Y	38	3	2	Y	Y	www.shu.ac.uk/sporthallam
								www.soasunion.org/pages/activities/
Y	Y	Y	70	7	9	Y	Y	www.sportrec.soton.ac.uk
Y	Y	N	27	16	5	Y	Y	www.solent.ac.uk/sport
Y	Y	Y	46	7	7	Y	Y	www.st-andrews.ac.uk/sport
Y	N	Y	35	0	0	Y	N	www.staffs.ac.uk/recservices
Y	Y	Y	38	0	7	Y	Y	www.stir.ac.uk/sport
Y	Y	Y	36	3	0	Y	Y	www.strath.ac.uk/sport
N	N	N	33	3	0	Y	N	www.unisportsunderland.com
Y	Y	Y	35	7	1	Y	Y	www.unisport.co.uk
Y	Y	Y	20	5	1	Y	Y	www.sussexsport.com
Y	Y	Y	50	6	1	Y	Y	www.swan.ac.uk/sport
Y	N	Y	40	0	1	Y	Y	www.tees.ac.uk/sections/studentlife/
								www.tvu.ac.uk/students/
Y	Y	Y	42	2	0	Y	Y	www.uusport.com
N	N	N	17	0	0	N	N	www.suarts.org
Y	Y	N	33	3	0	Y	Y	www.uclunion.org/sport
Y	Y	N	40	2	0	Y	Y	www.uwe.ac.uk/sport
N	N	N	0	2	1	Y	N	www.sports-centre.newport.ac.uk
Y	Y	Y	75	2	5	Y	Y	www.warwick.ac.uk
								www.wmin.ac.uk/page-403
								www.uws.ac.uk
Y	Y	N	27	3	2	Y	N	www.winchesterstudents.co.uk
N	N	N	28	7	0	Y	Y	www.wlv.ac.uk/sport
Y	Y	Y	42	0	0	Y	Y	www.worc.ac.uk
Y	Y	Y	58	5	9	Y	N	www.york.ac.uk/univ/sports
Y	N	Y	23	1	0	Y	Y	www.ysjactive.yorksj.ac.uk

The Cost of Studying

Getting a place at university is one thing, but these days perhaps an equally big challenge is navigating the maze of student finance and working out how you are going to make ends meet during and after your time in higher education.

Students have always been relatively poor, but studying for a degree today is a major financial undertaking that requires careful planning not just on the part of the would-be student but in most cases their family too. Whether you are studying full- or part-time, living at home or away, studying botany or philosophy, and almost whatever your background, the question of how to manage your money will loom large even before you have set foot on campus.

Getting into debt is now a fact of life for almost all students. Estimates of average levels of debt after graduation range from £12,363 (NatWest Student Money Matters Survey 2007) to £27,615 for students in London (National Union of Students). The Skipton Building Society and Barclays Bank agree that average graduate debt will reach £20,000 by 2010. The greatest proportion of debt is in the form of student loans, available to cover the cost of tuition fees and everyday expenses, but many students also have bank overdrafts and owe money on credit cards.

Having said all of that, the Government and some independent researchers are adamant that it is still worth investing in a degree course – providing you pick the right course and you work hard enough to ensure you at least gain your qualification. The extra amount you earn during a lifetime, over and above what you would have got without a degree, still outweighs the cost of your higher education, they say.

Forewarned is forearmed, and a little bit of careful financial planning and research into help that is available can go a long way to helping you emerge from your university education with a level of debt that is not going to become a millstone for life. As well as student loans, which are still provided at very generous rates and under very favourable terms and conditions, you can shop around for university bursaries and scholarships and other sponsorship packages, and seek out any supplementary support to which you may be entitled. The latter may include a maintenance grant: recent changes to the means-testing for these have made them available to a much larger slice of the population.

But even with a grant, you will need to gather together all the resources you can to survive. Analysis by the NUS suggests that it is not possible to get by on student loans and grants alone. Savings, earnings, and help from family and friends generally have to be added to the pot. The information provided below should at least help you understand how big your pot needs to be, and what you can expect to be added and taken away from it.

University tuition fees

A new student funding system was introduced in England and Northern Ireland in 2006, and this has had a major impact on the systems in Scotland and Wales. The sands are still shifting, for instance at the time of this *Guide* going to press, the Scottish Parliament was conducting a fresh review of student finance which could in effect restore the principle of "free" higher education in Scotland for Scottish students. The main effect of these changes is the abolition of the Scottish graduate endowment (see below). Across the UK, changes, whether large or small, have become almost an annual occurrence, and so it is best to always consult the latest information provided by Government agencies. What follows is a summary of the position as at March 2008.

Tuition fees have been introduced in all four countries of the UK, but there are differences in the rules and regulations governing them, and they do not apply to all students. Up-front payment of fees is no longer compulsory, as students can take out a fee loan (see below) to cover them. This is only repayable at a certain point after graduation, when your earnings reach a certain level.

In England and Northern Ireland the maximum tuition fee for 2008–09 will rise in line with inflation to £3,145. For the rest of the decade, only inflation-linked increases on these fees are allowed, subject to any further legislation. A review of tuition fees is due to take place in 2009, after which it is possible that new laws will be proposed to allow universities to charge significantly more. However, such a decision will be a political hot potato, and the outcome of the review is far from certain. Individual universities can, theoretically, vary tuition fees, including charging different amounts for different courses. But in reality so far almost every institution has been charging the top rate, and trying to lure students instead with a range of bursaries, scholarships, and other offers such as free laptops. Only two universities, Leeds Metropolitan University (£2,000) and the University of Greenwich (£2,835), charge less than the maximum tuition fee, and some that used to charge less have now increased their fees to the maximum allowable and are offering scholarships or bursaries to compensate.

In Scotland, the fee is £1,775 (£2,825 for medical students), but only students coming to study in Scotland from other UK countries have to pay it. These students can also avoid having to pay up front by applying for a student loan administered by their local education authority or devolved Government. Students whose home is in Scotland and are studying at a Scottish university apply to the Student Awards Agency for Scotland (SAAS) to have their fees paid for them. Scottish students no longer have to contribute to a graduate endowment to cover this cost, following a decision by the Scottish Parliament to abolish graduate endowments.

The Welsh Assembly Government has agreed a similar fee policy to England, with universities allowed to charge variable fees of up to £3,145. However, students who normally live in Wales and choose to study in Wales may be eligible for a tuition fee grant of up to £1,890 a year to offset this cost.

Tuition fees in the UK by country

Country	Level
England	£3,145
Northern Ireland	£3,145
Wales	£3,145 (with grants up to £1,890 to students whose homes are in Wales)
Scotland	£1,775 (no fees paid by students whose homes are in Scotland)
Scotland (medicine)	£2,825 (no fees paid by students whose homes are in Scotland)

- Universities in England, Northern Ireland and Wales can charge reduced fees.
- The Scottish fees are fixed.

Student loans

Around 80 per cent of students take out a student loan, and it is not difficult to work out why. First of all, as noted earlier, it is very difficult to get by financially without one. If you don't take out a loan to cover your fees, then you will have to pay for them up front, and with living costs estimated to average more than £9,000 a year (over £11,000 in London), most students find it impossible to cover everything on savings and earnings alone. The only reason to consider paying your fees up front might be if your university is offering a discount if you do so. The University of Gloucestershire, for instance, offers a 10 per cent discount to those who pay the full fee in advance.

The second reason is perhaps even more compelling for the financially astute. Any money you borrow via the Student Loans Company that administers the scheme, is lent at a "nominal" interest rate. This doubled in 2007–08 to 4.8 per cent, but despite the recent increase, this is still very attractive compared with any loans you might be offered by high-street banks or credit card companies (apart from limited period 0 per cent offers). Some students try to make their loan money for living costs go further by putting it into a high interest bank account or an ISA. Whatever you do with it, you won't have to start making repayments until you graduate and begin earning at least £15,000 a year. Even then, under new rules from 2008–09, you will be able to take a "repayment holiday" of up to five years after graduation, so you don't have to repay a penny in that time.

Remember, however, that interest on your loan continues to accrue from the time you take it out to until you have paid it off. The good news is that the amount you repay each month is linked to your income, rather than the amount you owe. Repayments are deducted through the tax system at a rate of 9 per cent on anything you are earning above £15,000 a year: for example monthly repayments for a graduate earning £20,000 a year would work out at £37.50 per month. If your income falls below the £15,000 threshold, then your repayments stop until you start earning more again.

There are two types of student loan – one to cover the cost of tuition fees (a fees loan) and another to help you cover the cost of living (a maintenance loan). In the case of fees

Maintenance Grant and Loan Amounts for a New First-year English Student 2008

Household income	Maintenance grant	Maintenance loan living away from home but not in London	Maintenance loan living away from home in London	Maintenance loan living at parents' home
£25,000	£2,835	£3,365	£5,215	£2,320
£30,000	£2,002	£3,365	£5,215	£2,320
£40,000	£998	£3,627	£5,477	£2,582
£50,000	£524	£4,101	£5,951	£3,056
£60,006	£0	£4,625	£6,475	£3,580

Source: Department for Innovation, Universities and Skills

- Above £60,006, the size of the maintenance loan is reduced on a sliding scale to £2,685 (living at parents' home), £3,470 (living away from home but not London) and £4,855 (living away from home in London).
- Total funding available is the maintenance grant plus the relevant maintenance loan.
- Schemes are different in Northern Ireland, Wales and Scotland, and the relevant funding organisations should be consulted.

loans, everyone can borrow up to the full amount needed to cover the cost of their tuition fees. For Welsh students studying in Wales this can mean only having to borrow £1,255 a year, as the rest can be covered by a non-repayable fee grant. Scots studying in Scotland are even better off, as there are no tuition fees to pay and so no need to take out a fees loan.

The second type of student loan, a maintenance loan, is means-tested. The amount you can borrow therefore depends on a number of factors, including your family income, where you intend to study, and whether you expect to be living at home. Final-year students also receive less than those in earlier years. The maximum maintenance loan available in 2008–09 is £6,475 for a full academic year. Three quarters of the maintenance loan is available to you regardless of your family circumstances, while the remaining quarter is means-tested. If your parents are separated, divorced or widowed, then only the parent with whom you normally live will be assessed. However, if that parent has married again, entered into a civil partnership, or has a partner of the opposite sex, then both their incomes will be taken into account.

In Scotland, the rules and regulations for maintenance loans are different. The loans available are lower than the rest of the UK, particularly in the case of students going to study in London. In 2007–08 the maximum loan available was £5,565. All the latest details can be found at www.saas.gov.uk.

Mature students (those who are over the age of 25, married, or have supported themselves for at least three years before entering university) are assessed for loan and grant entitlements on their own income plus that of their spouse or partner. Grants are also available for those with children, for single parents, and for students with adult dependents. Further support is available for students with children through the Parents' Learning Allowance and Child Tax Credit system.

Maintenance loans are usually paid in three instalments into your bank or building society account. English and Welsh students must apply for both loans and grants (see below) through their Local Education Authority, Scottish students through the Student Awards Agency for Scotland, and those in Northern Ireland through their Education and Library Board. You should make your application as soon as you have received an offer of a place at university. European Union students from outside the UK will usually be sent an application form by the university that has offered them a place.

Grants

In the good old days, most students didn't have to pay fees and many received relatively generous maintenance grants to help them cover day-to-day costs. After a brief disappearance, these non-repayable grants have made a comeback, and are particularly significant if you come from a low-income family. The size and type of grants available, and the rules and regulations governing their distribution, are different for each country of the UK. To receive a grant, students whose home is in England or Wales must apply to their local education authority, those from Scotland must apply to the Student Awards Agency for Scotland, and those from Northern Ireland to their Education and Library Board. In addition, there are various types of bursaries and scholarships you can apply for, and other types of grants or support in each country to help students in particular circumstances, such as those that have a disability. What follows is a description of the maintenance grant arrangements country-by-country.

England

Students from England can apply for a maintenance grant from the Government and a bursary from their university. Maintenance grants in England are worth up to £2,835 in 2008–09, but the amount you actually get (paid in three instalments) depends on your family or "household residual" income. If you come from a household with an income of £25,000 a year or less, then you can get a full grant. A partial grant is available for all of those from households earning between £25,000 and £60,005 a year. The actual amount you will get in this case is subject to a fairly complicated calculation to work out how much your family should theoretically contribute to your upkeep. There is no obligation on your family to provide their share, but you will certainly receive some kind of grant from the state. However, those whose family income is calculated to be higher than £60,005 will not receive a grant. Another important rule is that for every £1 you receive in maintenance grant, the amount you can borrow in student loans falls by £1. Thus, it is not possible to have both a full grant and a maximum student loan.

The almost bewildering array of bursaries and scholarships on offer from universities is discussed in a separate section below.

Northern Ireland

Arrangements for applying for and receiving means-tested maintenance grants and university bursaries and scholarships are very similar in Northern Ireland to those in England. The main difference is that there is a more generous upper limit (£3,335 for 2008–09) on grants in Northern Ireland. There is also a Special Support Grant of the same value for full-time students who may be eligible to receive benefits such as Income Support or Housing Benefit while they are studying. However, you cannot receive both the maintenance grant and the Special Support Grant.

Wales

Students from Wales can apply for a means-tested Assembly Learning Grant of up to £2,835. In addition, every full-time higher education student, regardless of where they come from in the UK, will be considered for a means-tested Welsh Bursary worth a maximum of £310 a year. This comes on top of whatever scholarships and bursaries Welsh institutions may offer.

Scotland

In Scotland, the maintenance grant is known as a Young Student's Bursary, and is also means-tested and does not have to be repaid. For 2008–09, the maximum bursary is £2,575 if you come from a family with an annual income of £18,820 or less. If your family income is between this amount and £33,330 you will be entitled to a partial bursary, but if it is higher than £33,330 you will receive nothing. You can get an additional student loan if your family income is £21,210 or less.

Bursaries and scholarships

Bursaries and scholarships offered by universities and colleges are an important part of the student financial support system ushered in by the Government to try to ensure people could still afford to go to university. All English universities and colleges charging more than £2,835 a year for a course are required to provide a non-repayable bursary or scholarship to students on these courses from low-income families who are receiving the full maintenance grant. What this means is that students who receive a full grant and are being charged the maximum tuition fee of £3,145 are entitled to a bursary or scholarship of at least £310. However, most universities are offering far more than this – and have also extended the principle to cover students in receipt of a partial grant. University College Falmouth, for instance, offers means-tested bursaries of up to £850 a year for students from households with an annual income of up to £40,000.

There is now such a variety of bursaries and scholarships on offer that while, on the one hand, it is worth shopping around to see what you can get, on the other, you could well feel bewildered by the experience of doing so. The Universities and Colleges Admissions Service (UCAS) has done its best to help by getting institutions to provide information about what's on offer to students applying for particular courses on its course search pages at www.ucas.com. Another handy tool for students considering studying in England is an online "bursary map" where you can explore what is available from each English institution (http://bursarymap.direct.gov/). The websites of individual institutions also carry details of scholarships, bursaries and other financial support available. Details are given in the table at the end of this chapter.

The whole system of bursaries and scholarships is overseen for England and Wales by the Office for Fair Access. It requires all universities to submit what are called "Access Agreements" that contain details of what fees they intend to charge and what scholarships and bursaries they are offering. Access Agreements also describe other

Funding timetable

It is vital that you sort out your funding arrangements before you start at university. Note that each funding agency has its own arrangements, and it is very important that you find out the exact details from them. The dates below give general indications of key dates.

March/April

Online and paper application forms become available from funding agencies.
You must contact the appropriate funding agency to make an application. For admission in 2009 in England you can contact www.studentfinanceengland.co.uk as well as your LEA.
Complete application form as soon as possible. At this stage select the university offer that will be your first choice.
Check details of bursaries and scholarships available from your selected universities.

May/June

Funding agencies will give you details of the financial support they can offer.
Last date for making an application to ensure funding is ready for you at the start of term (exact date varies significantly between agencies).

August

Tell your funding agency if the university or course you have been accepted for is different from that originally given them.

September

Take letter confirming funding to your university for registration.
After registration, the first part of funds will be released to you.

kinds of financial support, such as "hardship funds". Some awards are guaranteed depending on your personal circumstances, while others are available through open competition. St Mary's University College, Twickenham, for instance, has 75 "entry scholarships" worth up to £1,000 each for students who can demonstrate a high level of commitment and ability in sport, creativity, or work for the community. Copies of access agreements can be found at www.offa.org.uk.

Do take note of the application procedures for scholarships and bursaries, as these vary from institution to institution, and even from course to course within individual institutions. There may be a particular deadline you have to meet to apply for an award, or in some cases the university will work out for you whether you are entitled to an award by referring to your LEA financial assessment. Remember, too, that if your personal circumstances change part way through a course then your entitlement to a scholarship or bursary may be reviewed.

If you feel you still need more help or advice on scholarships or bursaries, you can get this in most cases by referring to a university's website or prospectus. Some institutions also maintain a helpline.

Some questions you will need to know the answer to include whether the bursary or scholarship is automatic or conditional and, if the latter, when you will find out whether your application has been successful. For some awards, you won't know whether you have qualified until you get your exam results.

Another obvious question is how the scholarship or bursary on offer compares with awards made by another university you might consider applying to. Watch out for institutions that list entitlements that others don't mention but you would get anyway.

Some institutions offer "fee remission" (a lower tuition fee) rather than scholarships or bursaries, which means you may have less cash in hand during your course, but will owe less after you have graduated.

Living in one country, studying in another

As each of the countries of the UK develop their own distinctive systems of student finance, they have been keen to address the question of how students leaving home in one country to go and study in another are affected. For instance, both the Scottish Parliament and the Welsh Assembly have put arrangements in place to try to ensure that Scottish and Welsh students accepting places at English universities are not financially disadvantaged.

UK students who cross borders to study pay the tuition fees of their chosen university and are eligible for a fees loan to cover these. They are also entitled to apply for the scholarships or bursaries on offer from that institution. Any maintenance loan or grant will still come from the awarding bodies of their home country.

The fees loan for Scottish students going to study in Northern Ireland, England or Wales is not dependent on family income, but students from low-income families can get relief from a means-tested non-repayable Students Outside Scotland Bursary. The income thresholds used to decide who qualifies for this are the same as those for the Young Students' Bursary (for Scottish students studying in Scotland, see above) but the maximum award is lower, at £2,095 (cf. £2,575) for 2008–09.

For students studying in Wales from September 2008, every eligible full-time higher education student, regardless of where they come from in the UK, will be considered for a means-tested Welsh Bursary of a maximum of £310 a year.

European Union laws stipulate that EU students from outside the UK must be charged the same tuition fees as those paid by UK students who are studying in their home country, rather than the higher fees paid by students from outside the EU. They can also apply for a fee loan and may be considered for some of the scholarships and bursaries offered by individual institutions. Only students who have been living and studying in the UK for at least three years can apply for a maintenance loan or grant. If you haven't, then you will need to apply for such assistance from the authorities in your own country. Tuition fee rules for non UK European Union students are the same in Scotland as for Scottish students – that is, you do not have to pay a tuition fee. There are also no fees to pay for exchange students coming to the UK, including those on the Socrates Programme.

As noted earlier, the rules and regulations governing student finance seem to change on an annual basis in each individual country, so it is worth checking the following websites for the latest information:

- England: **www.dius.gov.uk/policy/highereducation.html** and, from September 2008, **www.studentfinanceengland.co.uk**
- Wales: **www.studentfinancewales.co.uk**
- Scotland: **www.saas.gov.uk**
- Northern Ireland: **www.studentfinanceni.co.uk**

Further sources of income
If you are feeling daunted by the potential costs, you can take some comfort from this section outlining just some of the ways you can raise additional money to help you cover your expenses.

Taking a gap year
You can begin the process of earning money to help pay for your higher education even before you enter university, by taking a gap year. Many students are attracted to the idea of taking a year out because it offers them a chance to travel, gain new experiences, grow up a little – and maybe earn some money. Indeed, necessity seems to have recently shifted the reasons for taking a gap year from an emphasis on personal development to one more focused on boosting the bank balance in preparation for beginning life as a student. Of course, there is still potentially much more to taking a gap year than financial gain, and while short-term considerations may be focusing your mind in that direction, the longer-term benefits of taking part in cultural exchanges and courses, expeditions, volunteering, or structured work placements are considerable for most people. Such benefits include gaining a place at university and embarking on a worthwhile career after graduation. Both university admissions officers and employers look for evidence in candidates that they have more about them than academic ability. The experience you gain on a gap year can help you develop many of the attributes they are looking for, such as interpersonal, organisational and teamwork skills, leadership, creativity, experience of new cultures or work environments, and enterprise.

Various organisations can help you find voluntary work, if this is the way you prefer to spend at least some of your year out. Some examples include v (www.wearev.com), Lattitude Global Volunteering (www.lattitude.org.uk) and Volunteer Africa (www.volunteerafrica.org).

Work placements can be structured or casual. An example of the structured variety is the Year in Industry Scheme (www.yini.org.uk). Sponsorship is available mainly to those wishing to study engineering or business. To find out more, visit www.everythingyouwantedtoknow.com.

Further Government support

There are various types of support available from Government sources for students in particular circumstances, other than the main loans, grants and bursaries.

Undergraduates in financial difficulties can apply for help from the Access to Learning Fund (Financial Contingency Fund in Wales, Hardship Fund in Scotland, Support Funds in Northern Ireland). These are allocated by universities to provide support for anything from day-to-day study and living costs to unexpected or exceptional expense. The university decides which students need help and how much money to award them. These funds are often targeted at older or disadvantaged students and finalists.

Students with children can apply for a childcare grant, worth up to £225 a week if you have two or more children; and a parents' learning allowance, for help with course-related costs of between £50 and £1,470.

Students with disabilities can apply for a disabled students' allowance, worth up to £20,000 for full-time students.

Any students with a partner, or another adult such as a family member who is financially dependent on them, can apply for an adult dependants' grant of up to £2,575.

If you do not qualify for any of this kind of financial support you may still be able to apply for a Career Development Loan available from Barclays, the Cooperative Bank, and the Royal Bank of Scotland, in partnership with the Learning and Skills Council. Students on a wide range of vocational courses can borrow from £300 to £8,000 at a fixed rate of interest to fund up to two years of learning.

Part-time work

The need to hold down a part-time job during term time is now a fact of life for more than half of students. Unsurpris-ingly, students from a working-class background are more likely to need to earn while they learn. A recent UNITE report showed that 51 per cent of students from low-income families worked during term time, compared with just over a third of those from higher-income families. If you need or want to earn during term time, it is important to try to ensure that you do not work so many hours that it starts to affect your studies. A survey by the NUS found that 59 per cent of students who worked felt it had an impact on their studies, with 38 per cent missing lectures and over a fifth failing to submit coursework because of their part-time jobs.

UNITE Student Experience Report 2007
- 40 per cent of students work whilst studying.
- They work an average of 14 hours per week, getting paid an average of £7.61 per hour.
- The pay gap starts early, as males earn £1 an hour more than females.
- Computer and maths students are paid the most, architecture students the least.

Student employment agencies, which can now be found on many university campuses, can help you get the balance right. These introduce employers with work to students seeking work, sometimes even offering jobs within the university itself. But they also abide by codes of practice that regulate both minimum wages and the maximum number of hours worked in term-time (typically 15 hours a week). According to the Halifax Building Society, the average working student puts in about 18 hours a week, and makes around £6,000 a year out of this.

Some firms, such as the big supermarkets, offer continuing part-time employment to their school part-time employees when they go to university. Some students show some enterprise by making use of their expertise in areas like web design to earn some extra money. But most take on casual work in retail stores, restaurants, bars and call centres.

Most students, including those who don't work during term time, get a job during vacations. A Government survey found that 86 per cent of students in their second year of study or above worked during their summer vacation. Most of this kind of work is casual, but some is formalised in a scheme like the Shell Technology Enterprise Programme (www.shell.org.uk) or may be part of a sponsorship programme. Many vacation jobs are fairly mundane, but with a bit of imagination and get-up-and-go, it is possible to find more interesting work. Some students broaden their experience by working abroad, others work as film extras earning up to £140 a day, or do a variety of jobs at big events such as the Farnborough Air Show. It is also a good idea to try to use the summer holidays to get some work experience in a field that has some relevance to your career aspirations. Even if you don't get paid, this can significantly enhance your chances of finding employment after graduation.

Banks

You can be certain that once you become a student you will be inundated with special offers from banks, all keen to win you as a customer in the hope that you will remain so after graduation and well into your life as a highly paid professional. Make sure you shop around and try to think beyond the introductory offers of cash, discounted driving lessons, railcards, etc., and consider which account has the best long-term benefits. Banks are sympathetic to your financial situation as a student, and will generally be ready to offer modest free overdraft facilities.

What you will need to spend money on
Living costs

The National Union of Students estimated that in 2007–08 the average student living outside London would spend £9,176 a year on regular living costs, including rent, food, personal items, travel and leisure. For those living in the capital, the estimated average expenditure was £11,142. Little surprise, then, that a growing number of students are choosing to live at home and study at a local university. However, even this option is not necessarily low cost, once travel to and from the university is taken into account.

Certain costs are unavoidable. You have to have a roof over your head, eat enough, clothe yourself, and probably do a certain amount of travelling. But the cost of even these essential items can be cut down significantly through a mixture of shopping around and careful budgeting. If you set aside a certain amount of money a week for food, you will find it goes much further if you keep takeaways and ready-meals to a minimum, and stick to a shopping list when you go to a supermarket (shop at one of the cheaper supermarkets if possible). Some catering outlets at your university or in the students' union may well offer good value meals. If so, making use of these facilities can be a good way to ensure you eat reasonably healthily without blowing your budget. But probably the most economical way to eat is to cook and share meals with fellow students with whom you may be living in a shared house. Charity shops and markets are good places to hunt out bargain clothes, especially basic items such as jeans and tee shirts. Make sure you make full use of student travel cards and other offers and facilities available locally to help you cut the cost of travel. In certain locations, a bicycle is a very worthwhile investment (though not buying a lock for it may well prove a false economy).

If you can keep your essential costs down without starving yourself, then this will leave more money for what you would probably prefer to spend your money on – going out, and personal items. Most students spend a good proportion of their budget on socialising, and this is certainly an important part of the university experience. You can have plenty of fun and keep your leisure costs down by making the most of the facilities, clubs and events provided by your students' union.

Studying costs

The NUS estimates that the average student spends £471 a year on costs associated with course work and studying, but the amount you spend will be determined largely by the nature of your course and what you study. For some, the costs could amount to significantly more than £471. Additional financial support may be available for certain expenditure, but this is unlikely to cover you fully for spending on books, stationery, equipment, fieldwork or electives. A long reading list could prove very expensive if you tried to buy all of the required books brand new. Find out as soon as possible which books are available either in your university library or local libraries (you may need to be quick off the mark to get your hands on any books that are the first ones to be covered on your course). Another standard approach is to buy books second hand from students who no longer need them. Your students' union or your university may run second-hand book sales or offer a service helping students to buy and sell books. Another possible tactic is to share books with a fellow student: the only drawback being that you may both need to be working from a particular book at the same time!

Other costs

The first thing to say about any other costs you may incur is that you should do everything you can to keep them as low as possible. This may sound trite, but it is easy to let "other costs" get out of hand to the extent that they start to eat into your budget for

UNITE Student Experience Report 2007
Average student expenditure, based on a survey of 1,600 students

Per term week

Accommodation	£62.80
All food	£25.00
Going out/entertainment	£18.90
Alcoholic drinks	£16.20
Clothes	£12.40
Travel & transport	£11.70
Mobile phones	£9.60
Non-alcoholic drinks	£7.00
Toiletries	£5.50
Films	£2.90
Internet access	£2.90
Music	£2.40

Per term

Course books	£63.70
Course related equipment	£34.40
Course related trips	£12.80
Stationery	£11.70
Other course-related expenses	£8.90
Printing	£8.00
Photocopying	£5.70

day-to-day living. Mobile phone bills are a case in point. Look at your previous bills, or think carefully about your usage, and then shop around for the best deal to cover this. Remember that extras like downloading games or music, or sending pictures, can add significantly to your bill. Most of all, try to avoid getting tied up with an expensive and inflexible contract.

Another cost it is best to avoid is the cost of debt. Many banks offer free overdraft facilities for students, but if you go over that limit without prior arrangement, you can end up paying over the odds for your borrowing. Credits cards can be useful if managed properly. The best deals offer zero per cent interest on both balance transfers and purchases for a limited period – but if you don't pay off your debt before the offer period expires, you will start to incur hefty interest charges. Aside from these offers, the best way to manage a credit card is to set up a direct debit to pay off your balance in full every month, which means you will avoid paying any interest. One of the worst ways is just paying the minimum charge each month, which can cost you a small fortune over a long period. If you are the kind of person that spends impulsively and doesn't keep track of that spending, then you are probably better off without a credit card.

One kind of additional spending that can actually end up saving you money is getting insurance cover for your possessions. Most students arrive at university with a number of items, such as digital cameras, mobile phones, laptops, CD players, MP3 players, and portable TVs, that are tempting and offer all-too-easy pickings for petty thieves. It is estimated that around a third of students fall victim to crime at some point during their time at university. If you shop around, you should be able to get a reasonable amount of cover for these kinds of items without it costing you an arm and a leg. It may be possible to add cover cheaply to your parents' policy.

Planning your budget

University websites and many other sites offer guidance on preparing a budget, usually with the basic headings provided for you to complete. First list out your likely income (grants, bursaries, loans, part-time work, savings, parental support) and then see how this compares with what you will spend. Try to be realistic and not too optimistic about both sides of the equation. Hopefully, you will end up either only slightly in the red, or preferably far enough in the black for you to be able to afford things you would really like to spend your money on.

Above all, remember to keep track of your finances so that your university experience isn't ruined by money worries or finding you can't go to the ball because the cash machine has eaten your card.

Useful websites

The following websites will help you find out more about the topics discussed in this chapter.

As a starting point, the Student Finance section within the direct.gov website covers the basics:
www.direct.gov.uk/en/EducationAndLearning/UniversityAndHigherEducation/StudentFinance
UCAS also provides helpful advice:
www.ucas.com/students/studentfinance

For England, visit Student Finance England, a new service that starts in September 2008:
www.studentfinanceengland.co.uk
Before then, visit Student Finance Direct:
www.studentfinancedirect.co.uk
The Student Finance Direct site has a financial support calculator. From the Home page, click on "I am planning to go into higher education" and then on "Calculate my entitlement".
Office for Fair Access:
www.offa.org.uk

For Wales, visit Student Finance Wales:
www.studentfinancewales.co.uk

For Scotland, visit the Student Awards Agency for Scotland:
www.saas.gov.uk

For Northern Ireland, visit the Department for Employment and Learning:
www.delni.gov.uk/index.cfm/area/information/page/StudentFinance
Online applications are made through Student Finance Northern Ireland:
www.studentfinanceni.co.uk

All UK student loans are administered by the Student Loan Company:
www.slc.co.uk

Bursaries

Each university in England, Wales an Northern Ireland has its own bursary scheme. Website details are given in the University Profiles in this book (chapter 11). You can also find out about bursaries using this online map:
http://bursarymap.direct.gov.uk/

Scholarships

Each university in the United Kingdom has its own selection of scholarships. Consult university websites. Course-related scholarships are included on the UCAS site in the description of a course.

Further help can be obtained from the following sites

Career Development Loans (CDL):

www.lifelonglearning.co.uk/cdl

Educational Grants Advisory Service (EGAS):

www.egas-online.org.uk

HM Revenue and Customs:

www.hmrc.gov.uk/students

Need 2 Know, a student advice site:

www.need2know.co.uk/money/students

NHS Student Bursaries for students on pre-registration health professional training courses:

www.nhsstudentgrants.co.uk

Support 4 Learning:

www.support4learning.org.uk/money

Gap Year ideas

To help you consider options and start planning, visit:

www.gapadvice.org

For links to volunteering organisations in the UK, visit:

www.dfes.gov.uk/volunteering

For links to many not-for-profit gap year organisations;

www.yearoutgroup.org

For work placements relevant to university courses, visit Year in Industry:

www.yini.org.uk

Also worth consulting:

(formerly Millennium Volunteers):

www.wearev.com

Worldwide Volunteering:

http://wwv.org.uk

Fees and bursaries at universities in England, Northern Ireland, Scotland and Wales

The table on the next eight pages provides information on the fees charged to UK, EU and other international (non-EU) students. It also gives information on the bursary schemes offered by each university to UK students.

- Wherever possible the information relates to 2008–09.
- In the headings, "those on full grant" refers to those receiving a full maintenance grant from their funding body; "those on partial grant" refers to those receiving any grant other than a full grant.
- HI refers to "Household Income". For young students this is usually the income of their parents. In England in 2008–09, a household income of £25,000 or less qualifies a student for a full grant. See page 208 for further details.

Note that Scotland has no bursary system and Wales has its own system of fees and bursaries.

ENGLAND	Undergraduate fees UK / EU students	Undergraduate fees International students	University bursary for those on full grant (HI = Household Income)	University bursary for those on partial grant (HI = Household Income)
Anglia Ruskin	£3,145	£9,300–£10,925	£310	n/a
Aston	£3,145	£9,500–£11,570	£800	HI up to £38K: sliding scale £640–£160
Bath	£3,145	£10,300–£13,150	£1,200	HI up to £50K: sliding scale £900–£300
Bath Spa	£3,145	£9,000–£9,580	£1,128	HI up to £38.3K: sliding scale £1,128–£100
Bedfordshire	£3,145	£8,000–£8,200	HI up to £18.3K: £820 then £625	HI up to £39.3K: sliding scale £625–£460. Above £39.3K, fixed bursary of £310
Birmingham	£3,145	£9,450–£12,250 £22,350 (clinical)	£840	HI up to £34.6K: £840
Birmingham City	£3,145	£8,880–£13,500	£525	HI up to £60K: sliding scale £525–£245
Bolton	£3,145	£7,800	£320	HI up to £60K: sliding scale £270–£70
Bournemouth	£3,145	£7,500–£8,500	£1,310	HI up to £37.5K: sliding scale up to £1,000
Bradford	£3,145	£7,980–£10,310 [1]	Year 1 £500 Year 2 £700 Year 3 £900	HI up to £40K: Year 1 £500 Year 2 £700 Year 3 £900 HI up to £60K: Year 1 £400 Year 2 £500 Year 3 £600
Brighton	£3,145	£9,000–£10,500	£1,050	HI up to £39.3K: sliding scale £840–£520
Bristol	£3,145	£10,800–£13,900 £25,100 (clinical)	£1,160 + £1,050 (local students)	HI £25K–£40K: £740 HI £40K–£50K: £300 All plus £1,050 (local students)
Brunel	£3,145	£8,300–£10,200	£1,000	HI up to £60K: £500
Buckingham	£8,000 [2]	£13,500 [2]	n/a	n/a
Buckinghamshire New	£3,145	£7,150–£7,750	£500	£500

Cambridge	£3,145 [3]	£9,327–£12,219 [4] £22,614 (clinical) [4]	£3,145	HI up to £70K: sliding scale £1,900–£50

Canterbury Christ Church	£3,145	£7,650–£8,130	Sliding scale: £820–£510	HI up to £49K: sliding scale £510–£0
Central Lancashire (UCLan)	£3,145	£8,950–£9,450	£1,000	HI up to £60K: £1,000
Chester	£3,145	£6,894–£7,506	£1,000	n/a
Chichester	£3,145	£7,400–£7,880	£1,050	HI up to £50K: sliding scale £1,000–£250
City	£3,145	£7,750–£9,850 [1]	Sliding scale: £750–£350	HI up to £30K: sliding scale £750–£350
Coventry	£3,145	£7,900	£310	HI up to £60K: £310
Cumbria	£3,145	Contact university	£1,260	HI up to £60K: sliding scale £1,045–£210
De Montfort	£3,145	£7,990–£8,955	£400 + £250 (local students)	£400 + £250 (local students)
Derby	£3,145	£7,600–£8,200	£800 + £300 (local address) or £400 (local school)	HI £25K–£35K: £500 HI £35K–£50K: £200 All + £300 or £400 local bursary
Durham	£3,145	£10,050–£13,110	HI up to £18.5K: £1,285 (£2,570 if local) then: £525 (£750 if local)	HI up to £28.7K: £525 (£750 if local)
East Anglia	£3,145	£9,300–£11,500 £18,000 (clinical)	£600	£300
East London	£3,145	£9,000–£12,500	£310	n/a
Edge Hill	£3,145	Contact university	£500 + £200 Learning support bursary	£200 learning support bursary
Essex	£3,145	£9,250–£11,990	£310	HI at £25K £310, increasing to max. £1,574 at £33K decreasing to £0 at £60K
Exeter	£3,145	£9,150–£11,100 [1]	£1,500	HI £25K–£30K: £1,000 HI £30K–£35K: £500 HI £35K–£45K: £250
Gloucestershire	£3,145	£8,000	£310	n/a
Goldsmiths	£3,145	£9,580–£13,290	HI up to £19K: £1,000 then £500	HI up to £40K: up to £500
Greenwich	£2,835	£8,650	n/a	n/a

ENGLAND	Undergraduate fees UK / EU students	Undergraduate fees International students	University bursary for those on full grant (HI = Household Income)	University bursary for those on partial grant (HI = Household Income)
Hertfordshire	£3,145	£8,500	50% of maintenance grant	HI up to £40K, 50% of maintenance grant
Huddersfield	£3,145	£8,000–£9,000	£500	n/a
Hull	£3,145	£8,500–£10,500	£1,000	HI up to £40K: £500
Imperial	£3,145	£17,350–£19,450 £23,800–£35,500 (medicine)	£3,000	HI up to £60K sliding scale £2,000–£50
Keele	£3,145	£8,500–£11,300 £17,000–£20,700 (medicine)	£310	n/a (various schemes for HI up to £39K)
Kent	£3,145	£9,400–£10,500	£1,000	HI up to £40K sliding scale: £750–£250
King's College London	£3,145	£10,980–£13,800 £25,600 (clinical)	50% of maintenance grant	50% of maintenance grant
Kingston	£3,145	£9,000–£10,050	HI up to £1K: £1,000 then £600	HI up to £39.3K: £310
Lancaster	£3,145	£8,750–£10,600	HI up to £18,360: £1,315 then £500	HI up to £27.8K: £500
Leeds	£3,145	£9,700–£12,600 £23,500 (clinical)	£1,500	HI up to £36K: sliding scale £1,300–£325
Leeds Metropolitan	£2,000	£7,500–£8,300	n/a	n/a
Leicester	£3,145	£9,050–£21,995	£1,310	HI up to £39.3K: sliding scale £1,010–£100
Lincoln	£3,145	£8,524–£9,038	£600	Up to £599 based on size of maintenance grant
Liverpool	£3,145	£9,100–£11,650 £18,000 (medicine)	HI up to £17,910: £1,330 [1]	HI £17,911–£38,330: £1,025 [1]
Liverpool Hope	£3,145	£6,600	HI up to £17.5K Year 1 £530 Year 2 £800 Year 3 £1,070	HI £25K–£38K: £400 (same value for all three years)

			HI £17.5K–£25K Year 1 £400 Year 2 £600 Year 3 £1,100	
Liverpool John Moores	£3,145	£13,190–£14,167	£1,050	HI £25–£50K: £420
London Metropolitan	£3,145	£8,200	HI up to £18K: £1,000 then sliding scale £975–£775[1]	HI £25.2K–£40K: sliding scale £750–£300 [1]
London School of Economics	£3,145	£12,360–£13,872	£2,500 (England and Wales)	HI up to £38.3K payments on sliding scale
London South Bank	£3,145	£8,120–£8,360 [1]	Year 1 £500 Year 2 £750 Year 3 £750 (+ £250 graduation bonus for Hons graduates) [1]	Year 1 £500 Year 2 £750 Year 3 £750 (+ £250 graduation bonus for Hons graduates) [1]
Loughborough	£3,145	£9,850–£12,800	£1,360	HI up to £34,750: £630
Manchester	£3,145	£10,500–£12,900 £23,500(clinical)	£1,000	HI up to £27.8K: £1,000
Manchester Metropolitan	£3,145	£7,595–£12,150 [1]	HI up to £20,460: £1,000; then sliding scale £900–£800	HI £39.3K: sliding scale £700–£10
Middlesex	£3,145	£9,200	£310	n/a
Newcastle	£3,145	£9,915–£12,970 £24,015 (clinical)	HI up to £18,360: £1,240 then £930	HI £25K–£26,222: £930 HI £26,223–£31,466: £620
Northampton	£3,145	£7,450–£8,250	£1,000	HI up to £30K: £700. HI up to £40K: £500
Northumbria	£3,145	£8,300–£8,700	£310	n/a
Nottingham	£3,145	£10,200–£14,230 £24,500 (clinical)	£1,050	HI up to £33.5K: £1,050 HI £33.5K–£34.6K: £790 HI £34.6K–£42.5K: £525
Nottingham Trent	£3,145	£7,550–£10,800	£1,050	HI up to £40K: sliding scale £650–£350

ENGLAND	Undergraduate fees UK / EU students	Undergraduate fees International students	University bursary for those on full grant (HI = Household Income)	University bursary for those on partial grant (HI = Household Income)
Oxford	£3,145 [3]	£9,605–£12,810 [4] £23,475 (clinical) [4]	£3,150	HI up to £50K: sliding scale £3,150–£200
Oxford Brookes	£3,145	£9,400–£10,900	HI £0–£5K: £1,800 HI £5K–£21K: £1,560 HI £21K–£25K: £1,050	HI up to £36K: sliding scale £1,050–£150
Plymouth	£3,145	£8,250–£8,750	£1,015	HI £25K–£40K: £300
Portsmouth	£3,145	£7,100–£9,650	£900	HI up to £32K: £600
Queen Mary	£3,145	£8,850–£14,250 £23,350 (clinical)*	£1,050	HI up to £34.6K: £839
Reading	£3,145	£9,350–£11,300	£1,350	HI up to £35K: £900 HI up to £45K: £450
Roehampton	£3,145	£8,875	£500	£500
Royal Holloway	£3,145	£11,555–£12,785	£750	HI up to £39.3K: £750
Salford	£3,145	£8,400–£10,500	£310	(subject and academic bursaries available)
Sheffield	£3,145	£9,920–£13,050 £23,580 clinical)	HI up to £16,784: £680 HI up to £25K: £420	HI up to £34.6K: £420 (subject and academic bursaries available)
Sheffield Hallam	£3,145	£7,500–£9,345*	£700	£700 payable to students receiving at least £1K in maintenance grant
SOAS	£3,145	£11,460	£740	HI £25K–£39.3K: £420
Southampton	£3,145	£9,380–£12,000 £21,800 (clinical)	£1,000	HI up to £32K: £500
Southampton Solent	£1,995–£3,145	£6,100–£7,990	HI up to £18.3K: £1,050 HI up to £23K: £750 HI up to £25K: £500	HI up to £39.3K: sliding scale £500–£250

Staffordshire	£3,145	£5,375–£8,650	HI up to £20.8K: £1,000 HI up to £25K: £850	HI up to £30.8K: £500
Sunderland	£3,145	£8,150	£525	HI up to £39,305: £525
Surrey	£3,145	£8,300–£10,700	HI up to £10K £2000, then sliding scale to £750	HI up to £35K: sliding scale £600–£500
Sussex	£3,145	£9,500–£12,150	£1,000 [1]	n/a
Teesside	£3,145	£8,000–£8,500	£1,000	n/a
Thames Valley	£3,145	£7,600–£8,900	£1,030	HI £25K–£40K: £515
Univ of the Arts London	£3,145	£10,400	£310	Considered for £1,000 University Access Bursary
University College London	£3,145	£11,810–£15,460 £23,060 (clinical)	For HI up to £15.8K: sliding scale £2,700–£1,600 then at least 50% of maintenance grant	At least 50% of maintenance grant
Warwick	£3,145	£10,250–£13,350	£1,800	HI up to £36K: £1,800
West of England	£3,145	£8,250–£8,700	HI up to £18,360: £1,250 then £750	HI £25K–£27K: £750
Westminster	£3,145	£9,450	£310	£310
Winchester	£3,145	£7,549	£820	HI up to £39.3K: £410
Wolverhampton	£3,145	£8,200 or £8,350	£500	HI up to £35K: £300
Worcester	£3,145	£8,000	£750	£750; if not eligible for maintenance grant: £500
York	£3,145	£9,510–£12,555	£1,400	HI up to £35K: £700; HI up to £40K: £350
York St John	£3,145	£7,800–£10,800	HI up to £18,360: £1,570 HI up to £20,970: £1,050 HI up to £25K: £525.	n/a

[1] Figures for 2007–08

[2] Duration of degree course is two years

[3] UK & EU students eligible for tuition fee support not liable for College fees

[4] Plus College fees (£3,300–£4,900)

	Undergraduate fees UK / EU students	Undergraduate fees International students	University bursary for those on full grant (HI = Household Income)	University bursary for those on partial grant (HI = Household Income)
NORTHERN IRELAND				
Queen's, Belfast	£3,145	£8,550–£11,576 / £21,830 (clinical)	£1,125	HI up to £22.9K: £600 / HI up to £32K: £100 for sports or books
Ulster	£3,145	£8,540	HI up to £18,360: £1,040 / HI up to £21K: £620 / HI up to £25K:£310	HI up to £39.3K: £310
SCOTLAND	Fees for Scottish students and eligible non-UK EU students	Fees for students from elsewhere in the UK	International fees	
Aberdeen	Tuition fee paid by SAAS	£1,775	£9,000–£11,250 / £21,500 (clinical)	
Abertay	Tuition fee paid by SAAS	£1,775	£8,150	
Dundee	Tuition fee paid by SAAS	£1,775 / £2,825 (medicine)	£8,500–10,500 / £13,100 (preclinical medicine) / £20,800 (clinical medicine)	
Edinburgh	Tuition fee paid by SAAS	£1,775 / £2,825 (medicine)	£10,500–£13,800 / £17,100 (preclinical medicine) / £28,950 (clinical medicine)	
Glasgow	Tuition fee paid by SAAS	£1,775 / £2,825 (medicine)	£9,400–12,350 / £17,500 (veterinary medicine) / £21,600 (medicine)	
Glasgow Caledonian	Tuition fee paid by SAAS	£1,775	£8,500–£9,000	
Heriot-Watt	Tuition fee paid by SAAS	£1,775	£8,380–£10,920	
Napier	Tuition fee paid by SAAS	£1,775	£8,350–£9,690	
Queen Margaret	Tuition fee paid by SAAS	£1,775	£8,800–£9,700	

Robert Gordon	Tuition fee paid by SAAS			Contact university
St Andrews	Tuition fee paid by SAAS		£1,775 / £2,825 (medicine)	£10,950 / £17,300 (medicine)
Stirling	Tuition fee paid by SAAS		£1,775	£9,100–£11,200
Strathclyde	Tuition fee paid by SAAS		£1,775	£8,695–£11,025 [1]
West of Scotland	Tuition fee paid by SAAS		£1,775	£7,500–£8,300
WALES	Undergraduate fees for UK and EU students. Welsh students eligible for fee grant up to £1,890.	Undergraduate fees International students	University bursary for those on full grant with HI up to £18,370 All UK nationals eligible for Welsh National Bursary of £310 in addition to figures below	University bursary for those on partial grant (HI = Household Income) Not eligible for Welsh National Bursary
Aberystwyth	£3,145	£8,475–£10,750	HI up to £25K: sliding scale £690–£290	HI from £25K to £39.3K: sliding scale £600–£200
Bangor	£3,145	£8,500–£9,500	£1,000	HI up to £39.3K: either £500 or £1,000
Cardiff	£3,145	£9,100–£11,700 £21,000 (clinical)	£740	HI up to £25K: £1,050 HI up to £39.3K: £500
Cardiff (UWIC)	£3,145	£7,500–£8,500 £11,000 (podiatry)	£750	HI up to £27K: £500 HI £27K–£38.3K: £300
Glamorgan	£3,145	£9,000	£500 residential allowance for non-local UK & EU students	£500 residential allowance for non-local UK & EU students
Lampeter	£3,145	£8,988	No additional bursary	n/a
Newport	£3,145	£7,250–£8,250	HI up to £20K: £1,000	HI up to £30K: £600 HI up to £40K: £300
Swansea	£3,145	£9,010–£11,460	No additional bursary	n/a
Swansea Metropolitan	£3,145	£6,950[1]	£500 if living more than 45 miles from University	£500 if living more than 45 miles from University (UK & EU students)

8 What Parents Should Do

One of the ironies of the botched introduction of top-up fees is that a measure removing any need for parents to pay for their children's tuition has encouraged many of them to demand a much closer involvement in the process of higher education. Many parents took responsibility for the original £1,000 fees introduced when Labour came to power because they had to be paid up-front, but the new, more costly variety will only be payable after graduation, when the graduate's salary reaches £15,000. Parents will not even know when repayments begin, let alone be required to make a contribution.

Yet universities have found that, in the controversy over the scale of top-up fees, the fact that mum and dad are no longer involved has passed many parents by. Anxious mothers and fathers are more inclined than ever to question what their children are getting for their £3,145 a year. There have been stories of parents challenging not just the amount and quality of tuition, but even the marking of essays and exams. The phenomenon, first reported in the United States, has given rise to the phrase "helicopter parents" – so called because they hover over their children's education when they should be letting go.

No one wants to think of themselves in that category, but it is not surprising – or reprehensible – that parents are taking more of an interest. Many more of today's parents have been to university themselves, so have the knowledge and confidence to offer advice, both in choosing where and what to study, and in the decisions facing students at university. One of the reasons that some then overstep the mark is that they are shocked that the amount of teaching and size of seminar groups are not what they recall from their own "free" higher education.

An associated reason is that family relationships have changed. Many teenage applicants are happy to accept a lift to an open day to get a second opinion on a university and their prospective course.

Undoubtedly the main spur for heightened parental interest, however, is that, regardless of who pays the fees, higher education is taking a bigger share of more family budgets. Hundreds of thousands of students – particularly mature students – pay their own way through university. But every survey shows that families play an important (and growing) role where students move straight from school to higher education. Even at today's rates, fees remain a much less significant burden than living costs.

This chapter looks at where to draw the line between constructive involvement and unwelcome interference. Nearly all students are adults, and university offers an environment where they can begin to make their own decisions and develop as

UNITE Student Experience Report 2007

Students are mostly responsible for choosing their accommodation themselves. There are some notable exceptions:

• 40 per cent of current residents of university halls claimed that parents did have some influence in their decision to stay there.

• 93 per cent of parents make some kind of financial contribution towards student costs.

• 60 per cent of parents contribute towards the cost of the accommodation and now more parents than before are paying 100 per cent of the costs of accommodation.

individuals. A good starting point is to offer advice only when it is sought, and to leave direct contact with university administrators and academics to the student.

It should go without saying that, throughout the *Guide*, all references to parents apply equally to guardians and step-parents.

Laying the ground

The first thing any parent can do to smooth the path to university is to be encouraging about the value of higher education. Ideally, this should have started long before the application process, but it is especially important at this point. Particularly now that student debt has become a frequent media topic, it is only natural for sixth-formers and others thinking of higher education to have second thoughts.

The lure of a regular wage packet will be tempting, and there are plenty of young people who are not suited to full-time higher education – even after the years of rapid university expansion, most people still do not go to university. But those who are capable of going generally do not regret the decision. Many people look back on their student days as the best period of their life, as well as the one that shaped their personality and their career.

It may involve financial sacrifice in the family budget – how much will be up to you – but three or four years as a student should pay off for the individual in terms of lifetime earnings, as well as personal development. A little reassurance at this stage may make all the difference.

Making the choice

Any parent wants to help a son or daughter through the difficult business of choosing where and what to study. How big a role you play will depend on a number of factors, not the least of which is the extent to which your advice is wanted. In the end, it is the student's decision, and you can do no more than offer relevant information.

One important factor is the quality of advice available at school or college. If this is good, parental involvement should be marginal. But sometimes that is not the case, and you may have to call on other resources, including your own research. A second factor is your own level of expertise: you may have opinions about particular universities or subjects, but are they up-to-date and based on evidence?

Try not to give advice that is coloured

UNITE Student Experience Report 2007
- 51 per cent of students said that parents were instrumental in motivating them to follow a higher education course.
- 27 per cent of students said that parents influenced the decision on which course to follow.
- 31 per cent of students said that parents influenced which university they chose.

by memories of your own student days. That was probably a quarter of a century ago, and higher education has changed out of all recognition in the intervening years.

Avoid second-hand opinions gleaned through the media or dinner party gossip. You may think that some subjects are a sure-fire route to lucrative employment, while others are shunned by employers, but are you right? And do you really know the strengths and weaknesses of more than 100 universities? The tables in chapter 1 offer a reality check, but even they cannot take account of institutional differences. The subject tables in chapter 3 show that the best graduate employment rates are often not at the obvious universities.

Above all, do not try to rewind your own career decisions through your children. The fact that you enjoyed – or hated – a subject or a university does not mean that they will. You may have always regretted missing out on the chance to go to Oxbridge, or to become a brain surgeon, but they have their own lives to lead. Students who switch courses or drop out of university frequently complain that they were pressured into their original choice by their parents.

Check that choices are being made for sensible reasons, not on the basis of questionable gossip or trivial criteria. But beyond that, you should stay in the background unless there is a very good reason to play a more substantive role. Make a point of looking for important aspects of university life that the applicant might miss. Security, for example, usually does not feature near the top of a teenager's list of priorities, and likewise other practical issues, such as the proximity of student accommodation to lectures, the library and the students' union.

Many universities now publish guides specifically for parents and put on programmes for them at Open Days. The latter may be a way of separating prospective applicants from their more demanding "minders", but the programmes themselves can be interesting and informative. Do not worry that you will be an embarrassment by attending Open Days – thousands of parents do so, and you may add a critical edge to the proceedings. Like prospectuses, Open Days are part of the sales process, and it is easy for a sixth former to be carried away by the excitement surrounding a lively university. You are much more likely to spot the defects – even if they are ignored in the final decision.

Finding a place

Once the choices have been made, get to know the UCAS system and quietly ensure that deadlines are being met. The school should be doing this, but there is no harm in providing a little back-up, especially on parts of the process that take time and thought, such as writing the personal statement.

There is little a parent can do as the offers and/or rejections come rolling in, other than to be supportive. If the worst happens and there are five rejections, you may have to start the advice process all over again for a new round of applications through UCAS Extra. If so, a cool head is even more necessary, but the same principles apply.

Then, before you know it, results day is upon you. Make sure you are at home, rather than in some isolated holiday retreat. Your son or daughter needs to have access to instant advice at school or college, and to be able to contact universities straight away if Clearing is required. And your moral support will be much more effective face to face, rather than down a telephone line.

Whatever happens, try not to transmit the anxiety that you will inevitably be feeling to your son or daughter, especially if the results are not what was wanted. It is easy to make rash decisions about re-sitting exams or rejecting an insurance offer in the heat of the moment. Try to slow the process down and encourage clear and realistic thinking.

As at other stages in the application, make sure you know in advance what might be required, such as where to access Clearing lists. After that, if it is Clearing, you will need to be on hand to offer advice and again provide a taxi service for visits to possible universities. Nowadays, Clearing is all but over in a week, so the agony should be short-lived.

Before they go

Little more than a month after the tension of results day, everything should be ready for the start of term. Unless your son or daughter is one of the growing band choosing to stay at home to study, there will be forms to fill in to secure university accommodation, as well as student loans to sort out and registration to complete. You can perform useful services, like supplying recipe books if the first year is to be spent in self-catering accommodation, but now is the time for independence to become reality. Make sure that important details like insurance are not forgotten, but otherwise stand clear.

The one thing parents must do before the fledgling student flies the nest, however, is to agree a budget – and make clear that it is a real one. How large that budget is will depend on family circumstances and your attitude to independent living. Some parents want to ensure that their children leave university debt-free; others could never afford to do that, while yet others believe that paying your own way is part of the learning experience. The important thing is that student and parents know where they stand.

After they've left

Any new student is going to be nervous if they are leaving home for the first time and having to settle into a strange environment. But in most cases it isn't going to last long because everyone is in the same boat and freshers' weeks hardly leave time for homesickness. In any case, they won't want to let their apprehension show. The people who are likely to be emotional are the parents – especially if they are left with an empty nest for the first time. It can take a while to get used to an orderly, quiet house after all those years of mayhem.

Resist any temptation to decorate their bedroom and turn it into an office – it is more common than you might think, and psychologists say it can do lasting damage to family relationships. Keep in touch by phone, text or email, but try not to pry. You're not going to be told everything anyway – which is probably just as well. They will be back soon enough: many more students go home at weekends than used to be the case and, just as you were getting used to having the place to yourself, the Christmas vacation will remind you of how things used to be.

Lastly, do not become a helicopter parent. Your son or daughter may well seek your advice if they are dissatisfied with the course, their accommodation, or some other aspect of university life. By all means, give advice, but leave them to sort the problem out. Universities will cite the Data Protection Act, or some other piece of legislation, as a reason that they can only deal with students, not their parents. What they really mean is that students are adults and should look after themselves.

Useful websites

Many universities now have special sections on their websites for parents of prospective students.

UCAS has a Parents section on its website:
www.ucas.com/parents
To find out more about open days, visit:
www.opendays.com

International Students

If you come from abroad to study in the United Kingdom (UK), you will be in good company. Britain is the world's second most popular study destination, and a recent survey suggests that, in the eyes of international students, it is now considered to be almost as attractive as the market leader, the United States. The number of international students starting degree courses in the UK rose by 7.9 per cent in 2007–08, and international students now make up around 15 per cent of all higher education students in the UK and almost a third of all postgraduates.

Large numbers of students continue to come from China, Hong Kong, India, Malaysia, Pakistan, the USA, France, Germany and Greece. There has also recently been a significant influx of students from many of the new European Union (EU) member states, particularly Cyprus, Poland and Lithuania. In many UK universities you can expect to have fellow students from over 100 countries from around the world.

The results of a study by the International Graduate Insight Group (i-graduate), published this year, suggest that international students are attracted to the UK chiefly because of the worldwide reputation of its universities and qualifications, high standards of teaching and research, and a perception that it is a safe place to live. Despite these attractions, the relatively high cost of studying and living in the UK is naturally a concern for many, and should be among your chief considerations when weighing up where to study. Within the UK itself, the cost of living varies by geographical area. Although London is the most expensive, accommodation costs in particular can also be high in many other major cities. You will want to factor into your decision:

- the availability, type and cost of accommodation;
- what financial and personal support is available;
- how easy it will be to find work if you need to supplement your income or broaden your experience;
- the location of your university, both within the UK and in relation to local facilities.

This chapter alone cannot provide all the answers, but it aims to be a good place to start and to point you in the direction of other useful sources of information. You should certainly find out as much as you can about what living in Britain will be like. Further advice and information is available through the British Council at its offices worldwide, at more than 60 university exhibitions that it holds around the world every year, or at its Education UK website (www.educationuk.org). Another useful website for international students is provided by the UK Council for International Student Affairs (UKCISA) at www.ukcisa.org.uk. We recommend some further websites at the end of the chapter.

Where to study in the UK

The UK is made up of three countries: England, Scotland and Wales – which collectively may be referred to as Great Britain – plus the province of Northern Ireland. The vast majority of the UK's universities and other higher education institutions are in England. Of the 116 universities covered in this *Guide*, there are 91 in England, 14 in Scotland, nine in Wales and two in Northern Ireland. It is now over a decade since Scotland gained its own parliament and Wales formed a National Assembly Government. Each has devolved powers and has developed its own rules and regulations for higher education, which in some cases has brought benefits for European Union students. For example, EU students from outside the UK are able to receive a tuition fee grant of £1,890 a year plus a tuition fee loan of £1,255 when studying at a university in Wales. Latest applications figures show that Wales is currently enjoying the greatest growth in popularity among overseas applicants, while Scottish universities are seeing the fastest increase in applications from EU students from outside the UK, who now do not have to pay any tuition fees.

The origins of UK universities can be traced back to the ancient seats of learning at Oxford (1096) and Cambridge (1209) – known collectively as "Oxbridge" – and St Andrews (1411) in Scotland. Although many people from outside Britain associate British universities with the Oxbridge image, in reality most higher education institutions in the UK are nothing like this. Some universities do still maintain a traditional culture, but most are modern institutions that place at least as much emphasis on teaching as research and offer many vocational programmes, often with close links with business,

Table 1 The Top Countries for Sending International Students to the UK

EU Countries		%	Non-EU Countries (Top 25)		%
Republic of Ireland	7,093	14.0	China	17,905	22.4
France	6,223	12.3	Malaysia	7,686	9.6
Germany	6,198	12.2	Hong Kong	6,438	8.0
Cyprus	5,500	10.8	India	3,980	5.0
Greece	4,733	9.3	Nigeria	3,338	4.2
Poland	3,766	7.4	United States	3,024	3.8
Spain	2,324	4.6	Pakistan	2,571	3.2
Sweden	2,028	4.0	Singapore	1,976	2.5
Italy	1,694	3.3	Japan	1,883	2.4
Belgium	1,494	2.9	South Korea	1,693	2.1
Portugal	1,268	2.5	Norway	1,545	1.9
Finland	1,116	2.2	Kenya	1,506	1.9
Lithuania	1,062	2.1	Sri Lanka	1,500	1.9
The Netherlands	1,017	2.0	Canada	1,295	1.6
Austria	654	1.3	Russia	1,078	1.3
Czech Republic	653	1.3	Mauritius	1,069	1.3
Denmark	604	1.2	United Arab Emirates	1,053	1.3
Luxembourg	577	1.1	Bangladesh	1,026	1.3
Slovakia	574	1.1	Zimbabwe	985	1.2
Latvia	562	1.1	Brunei	853	1.1
Hungary	514	1.0	Saudi Arabia	853	1.1
Gibraltar	470	0.9	Vietnam	826	1.0
Estonia	323	0.6	Switzerland	760	1.0
Malta	181	0.4	Thailand	740	0.9
Slovenia	72	0.1	Taiwan	732	0.9
All EU students	**50,700**		**All non-EU students**	**79,994**	

Conversion rate – £1.00 : EUR 1,09
Sale order paid by Mastercard: £18.98 (EUR 20,61)
Balance due: £0.00 (EUR 0,00)

This shipment completes your order.

You can always check the status of your orders or change your account details from the "Your Account" link at the top of each page on our site.

Thinking of returning an item?

PLEASE USE OUR ON-LINE RETURNS SUPPORT CENTRE

Our Returns Support Centre (www.amazon.co.uk/returns-support) will guide you through our Returns Policy and provide you with a printable personalised return label. Please have your order number ready (you can find it next to your order summary, above). Our Returns Policy does not affect your statutory rights.

Thank you for shopping at Amazon.co.uk!

Amazon EU S.à r.l; 5, Rue Plaetis. L – 2338 Luxembourg
VAT number : GB727255821

Please note – this is not a returns address – for returns – please see above for details of our online returns centre

26/DN36jtmnR/-2 of 2-//M/econ-jersey/2679574/0202-15:45/0130-07:54/dc-owl   Pack Type: CWF60

Invoice for DN36jtnnR 29 January, 2009

amazon.co.uk®
and you're done.™

www.amazon.co.uk

Paid by:
Kwok Tong Soo
6 Redwing Close
Heysham
Morecambe, Lancashire LA3 2BH
United Kingdom, GB

Delivered to:
Kwok Tong Soo
Department of Economics, Management School
Lancaster University
Lancaster, Lancashire LA1 4YX
United Kingdom, GB

Invoice number DN36jtnnR
29 January, 2009

Invoice/Receipt for

Your order of 21 January, 2009

Order ID 026–8131745–2973105

Qty	Item	Bin	Description	Our Price (excl. VAT)	VAT Rate	Total Price (excl. VAT)	Total Price (excl. VAT)
1	The "Times" Good University Guide 2009 O'Leary, John 0007273533	(** A–6 **)	Paperback	£11.19	0.00%	£11.19	EUR 12,15
1	ITV Sport Guide Grand Prix 2009 Jones, Bruce 18473262X	(** A–6 **)	Paperback	£7.79	0.00%	£7.79	EUR 8,46

Shipping Subtotal (excl. VAT) £0.00	Order Total	£18.98

industry and the professions. Table 2 shows the universities that are most popular with international students.

UK universities have a worldwide reputation for high quality teaching and research. They maintain this position by investing heavily in the best academic staff, buildings and equipment, and by taking part in rigorous quality assurance monitoring. The main regulatory bodies include the Quality Assurance Agency for higher education (QAA), higher education funding councils for each country of the UK, and the Office for Standards in Education. Professional bodies also play an important role, and there is an Independent Adjudicator for Higher Education that handles student complaints that have not been resolved by universities' own internal complaints procedures.

What subjects to study?

You will find that strongly vocational courses are favoured by international students. Many of these in professional areas such as architecture, dentistry or medicine take one or two years longer to complete than most other degree courses. Traditional first degrees are mostly awarded at Bachelor level (BA, BEng, BSc, etc.) and last three to four years.

Table 2 The Universities Most Favoured by EU and Non-EU Students

Institution (Top 25)	EU Students	Institution (Top 25)	Non-EU Students
Ulster	1,255	Manchester	2,753
Napier	1,199	Nottingham	2,482
Bedfordshire	1,168	University of the Arts, London	2,256
University of the Arts, London	1,093	Imperial College	2,158
Westminster	1,012	Northumbria	1,793
Coventry	969	University College London	1,724
Kingston	949	Warwick	1,637
Brighton	890	London School of Economics	1,483
Manchester	885	Middlesex	1,474
Kent	865	Greenwich	1,405
Middlesex	836	Hertfordshire	1,321
Wolverhampton	834	Edinburgh	1,187
Edinburgh	816	Bath	1,183
University College London	799	Birmingham	1,150
Portsmouth	742	Wolverhampton	1,132
King's College London	716	Leeds	1,127
Imperial College	709	Sheffield	1,099
Anglia Ruskin	691	Kingston	1,086
Aberdeen	666	Cardiff	1,084
Warwick	650	Manchester Metropolitan	1,082
Manchester Metropolitan	645	City	1,062
Robert Gordon	636	Sunderland	1,055
Greenwich	632	Cambridge	1,009
Heriot-Watt	591	King's College London	1,003
Nottingham	584	Oxford Brookes	1,002

There are also some "enhanced" first degrees (MEng, MChem, etc.) that take four years to complete. The relatively new Foundation Degree programmes are mostly vocational and take two years to complete, with an option to study for a further year to gain a full degree.

The tables at the end of this chapter select the 24 most popular subjects and show which universities for each subject have the greatest numbers of students. Remember, though, that you need also to consider the details of any course that you wish to study and to look at the overall ranking of that university as given in our main league table in chapter 2 and in the subject tables in chapter 3.

English language proficiency

The universities maintain high standards by generally setting high entry requirements, including proficiency in English. For international students, this usually includes a score of 6 or 7 in the International English Language Testing System (IELTS), which assesses English language ability through listening, speaking, reading and writing tests.

There are many private and publicly funded colleges throughout the UK that run courses designed to bring the English language skills of prospective higher education students up to the required standard. However, not all of these are Government approved. Visit www.dcsf.gov.uk/providersregister/faq-students.cfm for a list of

Table 3 The Most Popular Subjects for International Students

Subject Group	EU Students	Non-EU Students	Total
Business and administrative studies	11,158	22,401	33,559
Engineering and technology	5,436	12,707	18,143
Social studies	4,657	7,151	11,808
Creative arts and design	4,477	4,842	9,319
Subjects allied to medicine*	3,489	4,288	7,777
Law	2,375	5,344	7,719
Biological sciences	3,997	3,445	7,442
Computer science	2,400	4,627	7,027
Languages	3,717	1,792	5,509
Medicine and dentistry	933	2,914	3,847
Architecture, building and planning	1,669	2,045	3,714
Physical sciences	1,504	1,838	3,342
Mathematical sciences	778	2,440	3,218
Mass communications and documentation	1,582	1,471	3,053
Historical and philosophical studies	1,360	1,229	2,589
Education	551	468	1,019
Combined	284	346	630
Agriculture and related subjects	251	300	551
Veterinary science	83	347	430
Total	**50,701**	**79,995**	**130,696**

*Subjects allied to medicine include Pharmacy and Nursing.

Government approved education and training centres in the UK. Some private organisations such as INTO (www.into.uk.com) have joined with universities to create centres running programmes preparing international students for degree-level study. The British Council also runs English language courses at its centres around the world.

How to apply

You should read the information below in conjunction with that provided in chapter 4, which deals with the application process in some detail.

Some international students apply directly to a UK university for a place on a course, and others make their applications via an agent in their home country. But most applying for a full-time first degree course do so through the Universities and Colleges Admissions Service (UCAS). If you take this route, you will need to fill in an online UCAS application form at home, at school or perhaps at your nearest British Council office. There is lots of advice on the UCAS website about the process of finding a course and the details of the application system (www.ucas.ac.uk/students/nonukstudents).

Whichever way you apply, the deadlines for getting your application in are the same. For those applying from within an EU country, application forms must be received at UCAS by 15 January for most courses. Note that applications for Oxford and Cambridge and for all courses in medicine, dentistry and veterinary science have to be received at UCAS by 15 October. Some art and design courses also have different deadlines (see chapter 4 for more details).

If you are applying from a non-EU country, you can submit your application to UCAS at any time between 1 September and 30 June preceding the academic year in which you plan to begin your studies. Most people apply well before the 30 June deadline to make sure that places are still available and to allow plenty of time for immigration regulations, and to make arrangements for travel and accommodation.

Entry and employment regulations

Since various high profile terrorists attacks in the UK and USA, visa regulations have been tightened. However, the main countries that welcome international students – including the UK, the USA, Australia and Canada – have made serious efforts to streamline visa processes and entry requirements to make them appear more welcoming. Students in some countries can also study for a degree qualification provided by a British university by enrolling at a university in their home country.

A global drive to promote the UK's universities was introduced in June 1999 and was later expanded, setting the target of recruiting an additional 100,000 international students to the UK's universities by 2011. Streamlining visa and entry procedures has been a key part of the initiative. However, many of the new rules and regulations are very new, and so it remains to be seen how effective they will prove to be. The British Government has been criticised for increasing visa fees, doubling fees for visa extensions, and ending the right to appeal against refusal of a visa. The most recent development is the introduction of a points system for entry. Under this scheme, prospective students will be able to check whether they are eligible for entry against published criteria, and so assess their point score. Universities are also required to provide a Certificate of Acceptance for Study to their international student entrants.

Since September 2007, all students wishing to enter the UK to study have been required to obtain entry clearance before arrival. The only exceptions are British nationals living overseas, British overseas territories citizens, British Protected persons, British subjects, and non-visa national short-term students who may enter under a new Student Visitor route. You can find more about all the latest rules and regulations for entry and visa requirements at www.bia.homeoffice.gov.uk/studyingintheuk/.

Changes are also being made to make it easier for international student to work in the UK during and after their studies. The rules and regulations governing permission to work vary according to your country of origin. If you are from a European Economic Area (EEA) country (the EU plus Iceland, Liechtenstein and Norway), you don't need permission to work in the UK, although you will need to be ready to show an employer your passport or identity card to prove you are a national of an EEA country. Students from outside the EEA are allowed to work part-time for up to 20 hours a week during term time and to work full-time during vacations. From August 2008, a new International Graduate Scheme will be introduced in England, Wales and Northern Ireland that will allow all international graduates to work for up to two years after completing their course. In many ways this is similar to the existing Fresh Talent initiative in Scotland, set up to attract inward migration to counter a declining population. Under the scheme, international students can apply for an initial two-year extension to stay on after graduation, to live and work in Scotland. So far over 8,000 graduates have taken up this chance, and the scheme will continue to run under the new UK-wide points based migration system.

Bringing your family

In the UK, most universities can help to arrange facilities and accommodation for families as well as for single students. The family members you are allowed to bring with you are your husband or wife, civil partner (a same-sex relationship that has been formally registered in the UK or your home country) and dependant children.

If you are a national of any country from outside the EEA, your family will be subject to immigration policy. You will need to show that you can support them financially, that you can arrange appropriate accommodation, and that they will leave the UK when you have finished your studies. Your family members will usually be able to study (children under 16 are required to attend full-time education), and any over the age of 16 should be able to work as long as you have permission to stay for over 12 months. You can find out more about getting entry clearance for your family at www.ukcisa.org.uk/student/info_sheets/your_family.php.

Support from British universities

Support for international students is more comprehensive than in many countries and begins long before you arrive in the UK. Many universities have advisers – and sometimes offices or even whole campuses – in other countries. Some will arrange to put you in touch with current students or graduates who can give you a first-hand account of what life is like at a particular university. Pre-departure receptions for students and their families, as well as meet-and-greet arrangements for newly arrived students, are common. You can also expect an orientation and induction programme in your first week, and many universities now have "buddying" systems where current students are assigned to new arrivals to help them find their way around, adjust to their new surroundings, and make new friends. Each university also has a students' union that organises social, cultural and sporting events and clubs, including many specifically for international students. Both the university and the students' union are likely to have full-time staff whose job it is to look after the welfare of students from overseas.

International students also benefit from free medical and subsidised dental and optical care and treatment under the UK National Health Service, plus access to a professional counselling service and a university careers service.

At university, you will naturally encounter people from a wide range of cultures and walks of life. Getting involved in student societies, sport, voluntary work, and any of the wide range of social activities on offer will help you gain first-hand experience of British culture, and, if you need it, will help improve your command of the English language.

Useful websites

For information about studying in Britain, visit:
The British Council, with its dedicated Education UK site
www.educationuk.org
Within the Education UK site, you can download a copy of their guide *Studying and living in the United Kingdom*.

The UK Council for International Student Affairs (UKCISA). UKISA produce a wide range of factsheets on all aspects of studying in the UK:
www.ukcisa.org.uk

UCAS, for full details of courses available and an explanation of the application process:
www.ucas.com/students/nonukstudents

UK Student Life, a guide designed to explain British daily life and culture to international students:
www.ukstudentlife.com

For a general guide to Britain, available in many languages:
www.visitbritain.com

For the latest information on entry and visa requirements, visit:
www.bia.homeoffice.gov.uk/studyingintheuk

Table 4 The Most Popular Subjects and Universities For International Students

Business Studies

	EU	Non-EU
Bedfordshire	348	388
Middlesex	183	491
Westminster	350	305
Northumbria	270	358
Royal Holloway	140	452
Anglia Ruskin	415	126
Aston	93	423
Hertfordshire	139	364
Sunderland	114	385
Oxford Brookes	115	368
All overseas students	**8,550**	**13,751**

Computer Science

	EU	Non-EU
Middlesex	52	357
Greenwich	27	256
Northumbria	36	189
Bedfordshire	117	97
East London	26	168
Manchester	43	147
Imperial College	66	110
Napier	108	65
Teesside	120	52
Sunderland	28	139
All overseas students	**2,400**	**4,627**

Accounting and Finance

	EU	Non-EU
Manchester	71	353
City	90	321
London School of Economics	32	370
Essex	49	234
West of England	13	235
Warwick	49	192
London South Bank	44	180
Lancaster	47	170
Kent	19	192
Middlesex	44	140
All overseas students	**1,199**	**6,526**

Art and Design

	EU	Non-EU
University of the Arts, London	729	1,694
University College for Creative Arts	231	209
Nottingham Trent	41	185
Middlesex	103	78
Birmingham City	48	130
Kingston	64	110
Wolverhampton	109	53
Goldsmiths	55	73
Coventry	51	72
Brighton	56	58
All overseas students	**2,506**	**3,511**

Law

	EU	Non-EU
Northumbria	18	567
Wolverhampton	43	387
King's College London	147	168
Kent	116	187
London School of Economics	36	227
Leicester	132	115
Warwick	49	176
Nottingham	21	193
Essex	143	58
Manchester	25	176
All overseas students	**2,375**	**5,344**

Economics

	EU	Non-EU
London School of Economics	73	314
University College London	60	316
Warwick	79	289
Manchester	59	206
Essex	72	183
Royal Holloway	63	180
Portsmouth	41	153
Bath	28	164
Nottingham	65	120
Cambridge	41	132
All overseas students	**1,549**	**4,369**

Electrical and Electronic Engineering

	EU	Non-EU
Imperial College	76	277
Birmingham City	21	177
Manchester	26	167
Liverpool John Moores	38	149
Sheffield	10	177
Birmingham	9	166
Nottingham	10	163
Southampton	21	133
Northumbria	11	131
Liverpool	31	103
All overseas students	1,000	4,423

Mechanical Engineering

	EU	Non-EU
Imperial College	73	197
Nottingham	21	175
Bradford	40	111
Liverpool John Moores	25	113
Sheffield	10	118
Kingston	42	73
Hertfordshire	24	84
Coventry	44	63
Manchester	11	96
Southampton	38	66
All overseas students	1,024	2,622

Hospitality, Leisure, Recreation, Sport and Tourism

	EU	Non-EU
Thames Valley	148	283
Queen Margaret, Edinburgh	9	269
Brighton	157	44
University of the Arts, London	38	153
Leeds Metropolitan	81	85
Napier	57	86
Bournemouth	72	69
Oxford Brookes	58	80
Strathclyde	17	115
Bedfordshire	114	16
All overseas students	1,834	2,143

Medicine

	EU	Non-EU
King's College London	104	183
Manchester	47	167
Leicester	32	151
University College London	55	114
Nottingham	28	139
Imperial College	41	122
Edinburgh	39	123
Southampton	24	133
Cambridge	43	108
Queen Mary, London	24	124
All overseas students	860	2,665

Biological Sciences

	EU	Non-EU
Imperial College	69	200
Edinburgh	152	86
University College London	63	71
Manchester	46	78
Wolverhampton	46	72
Cambridge	40	53
Aberdeen	53	40
Nottingham	29	65
Leeds	24	67
Oxford	36	52
All overseas students	1,741	2,079

Civil Engineering

	EU	Non-EU
Napier	263	5
Imperial College	32	121
Nottingham	27	115
Queen's, Belfast	48	92
East London	62	72
Bradford	68	62
Liverpool	40	80
Portsmouth	85	28
Cardiff	19	83
Leeds	23	78
All overseas students	1,541	1,702

Mathematics

	EU	Non-EU
Imperial College	76	235
Warwick	46	187
University College London	33	184
Oxford	36	169
Cambridge	55	120
Manchester	42	116
London School of Economics	23	112
Bath	43	85
Heriot-Watt	25	84
Loughborough	5	88
All overseas students	**778**	**2,440**

Other Subjects Allied to Medicine

	EU	Non-EU
Bournemouth	92	103
Queen Margaret, Edinburgh	105	42
Dundee	13	110
Imperial College	34	79
Cambridge	40	53
Cardiff	27	66
Greenwich	35	45
Robert Gordon	70	7
University College London	23	50
Manchester Metropolitan	41	30
All overseas students	**1,467**	**1,282**

Politics

	EU	Non-EU
St Andrews	98	169
London School of Economics	56	186
Kent	192	50
Warwick	68	84
Sussex	68	29
Aberdeen	68	26
Edinburgh	27	68
Aberystwyth	52	39
Birmingham	54	36
SOAS	50	38
All overseas studentsts	**1,684**	**1,461**

Communication and Media Studies

	EU	Non-EU
Westminster	99	78
Goldsmiths	60	107
University of the Arts, London	67	84
Liverpool John Moores	17	134
Thames Valley	88	46
Middlesex	86	46
Wolverhampton	98	8
Bournemouth	43	44
Bedfordshire	68	12
Royal Holloway	25	39
All overseas students	**1,454**	**1,275**

Psychology

	EU	Non-EU
Nottingham	23	97
East London	50	50
Ulster	96	1
Middlesex	63	33
University College London	27	68
Aberdeen	61	28
Bedfordshire	70	15
York	5	79
St Andrews	38	31
Roehampton	33	35
All overseas students	**1,737**	**1,17**

Pharmacology and Pharmacy

	EU	Non-EU
Sunderland	117	193
Robert Gordon	235	29
Brighton	162	62
Nottingham	10	153
Bath	18	138
Manchester	26	129
Liverpool John Moores	51	100
Strathclyde	6	122
School of Pharmacy	11	107
Bradford	35	75
All overseas students	**892**	**1,630**

Architecture

	EU	Non-EU
Nottingham	28	187
Robert Gordon	68	79
Greenwich	81	35
Manchester Metropolitan	36	65
Oxford Brookes	53	47
East London	38	46
Dundee	63	18
London South Bank	46	34
Kingston	28	44
Cardiff	23	48
All overseas students	1,123	1,154

General Engineering

	EU	Non-EU
Coventry	338	20
Cambridge	61	190
Napier	113	41
Oxford	19	108
Wolverhampton	10	99
Warwick	15	52
Ulster	57	1
Manchester	9	47
Nottingham	3	47
Southampton	19	23
All overseas students	803	966

English

	EU	Non-EU
Portsmouth	79	163
Central Lancashire	77	60
Wolverhampton	82	25
Bedfordshire	69	9
Salford	48	27
St Andrews	12	49
Edinburgh	18	42
Ulster	52	0
Kent	36	16
Anglia Ruskin	26	20
All overseas students	1,227	878

Nursing

	EU	Non-EU
Dundee	32	251
Ulster	116	6
Bedfordshire	78	32
Napier	54	47
City	15	81
Queen Margaret, Edinburgh	15	59
Thames Valley	24	44
Glasgow Caledonian	30	25
De Montfort	4	42
Buckinghamshire New	5	35
All overseas students	683	1,001

Drama, Dance and Cinematics

	EU	Non-EU
University of the Arts, London	146	221
UC Creative Arts	84	57
Bedfordshire	66	50
UWCN, Newport	53	10
Kingston	47	16
Westminster	32	21
Kent	32	17
Aberystwyth	33	8
Roehampton	22	19
Central School of Speech	21	17
Thames Valley	27	11
All overseas students	1,103	740

Aeronautical and Manufacturing Engineering

	EU	Non-EU
Kingston	28	104
Imperial College	45	81
Nottingham	9	103
Sheffield Hallam	0	98
Sheffield	8	66
Bath	21	47
Manchester	11	56
Hertfordshire	20	44
Glamorgan	11	50
City	11	40
All overseas students	387	1,123

10 Oxbridge

Oxbridge (as Oxford and Cambridge are called collectively) is another world when it comes to university admissions. Although part of the UCAS network, the two universities have different deadlines from the rest of the system, and applications are made through UCAS direct to a specific college of one of the universities. There is little to choose between the two in terms of entrance requirements, but a formidable number of successful applicants have the maximum possible UCAS tariff.

However, that does not mean that the talented student should be shy about applying: both have fewer applicants per place than many less prestigious universities, and admissions tutors are always looking to extend the range of schools and colleges from which they recruit. For those with a realistic chance of success, there is little to lose except the possibility of a wasted space on the UCAS application. Now that UCAS no longer shows a chosen university the applicant's other choices, there is no risk that one institution might take offence at being thought second best to another on the list.

Overall, there are about three applicants to every place at Oxford and Cambridge, but there are big differences between subjects and colleges. As the tables in this chapter show, competition is particularly fierce in subjects such as medicine and English, but those qualified to read metallurgy or classics have a high chance of success. The pattern is similar to that in other universities, although the high degree of selection (and self-selection) that precedes an Oxbridge application means that even in the less popular subjects the field of candidates is likely to be strong.

These two universities' power to intimidate prospective applicants is based partly on myth. Both have done their best to live down the Brideshead Revisited image, but many sixth-formers still fear that they would be out of their depth there, academically and socially. In fact, the state sector produces about half the entrants to Oxford and Cambridge, and the dropout rate is lower than at many other universities. The "champagne set" is still present and its activities are well publicised, but most students are hard-working high achievers with the same concerns as their counterparts on other campuses. A joint poll by the two universities' student newspapers showed that undergraduates were spending much of their time in the library or worrying about their employment prospects, and relatively little time on the river or in the college bar.

State school applicants
Student organisations at both universities have put in a great deal of effort trying to encourage applications from state schools, and some colleges have launched their own campaigns. Such has been the determination to convince state school pupils that they will get a fair crack of the whip that a new concern has grown up of possible bias against independent school pupils. In reality, however, the dispersed nature of Oxbridge admissions discounts any conspiracy. Some colleges set relatively low standard offers to encourage applicants from the state sector, who may reveal their potential at interview. Some admissions tutors may give the edge to candidates from comprehensive schools over those from highly academic independent schools because they consider theirs the greater achievement in the circumstances. Others stick with tried and trusted sources of

good students. The independent sector still enjoys a degree of success out of proportion to its share of the school population.

Choosing the right college

Thorough research to find the right college is very important. Even within colleges, different admissions tutors may have different approaches, so personal contact is essential. The college is likely to be the centre of your social life, as well as your home and study centre for at least a year, so you need to be sure not only that you have a chance of a place, but that you want one at that college. Famously sporty colleges, for example, can be trying for those in search of peace and quiet.

The tables in this chapter give an idea of the relative academic strengths of the colleges, as well as the varying levels of competition for a place in different subjects. But only individual research will suggest which is the right place for you. For example, women may favour one of the few remaining single-sex colleges (New Hall, Newnham and Lucy Cavendish at Cambridge). Men have no such option.

The findings in the Tompkins Table (below) are not officially endorsed by Cambridge University itself. However, since 2007 we have been able to publish the "official" Norrington Table from Oxford. Sanctioned or not, both tables give an indication of where the academic powerhouses lie – information which can be as useful to those trying to avoid them as to those seeking the ultimate challenge. Although there can be a great deal of movement year by year, both tables tend to be dominated by the rich, old foundations. Both tables are compiled from the degree results of final-year undergrad-uates. A first is worth five points, a 2:1 four, a 2:2 three, a third one point. The total is divided by the number of candidates to produce each college's average.

In both universities, teaching for most students is based in the colleges. In practice, however, this arrangement holds good in the sciences only for the first year. One-to-one tutorials, which are Oxbridge's traditional strength for undergraduates, are by no means

Cambridge The Tompkins Table 2007

College	2007	2006	College	2007	2006
Emmanuel	1	1	Trinity Hall	16	16
Christ's	2	6	Clare	17	12
Downing	3	11	King's	18	17
Selwyn	4	7	St John's	19	15
St Catharine's	5	3	Robinson	20	18
Trinity	6	5	Girton	21	22
Pembroke	7	4	Newnham	22	23
Corpus Christi	8	8	New Hall	23	24
Jesus	9	10	Lucy Cavendish	24	26
Gonville and Caius	10	2	Peterhouse	25	21
Queens'	11	14	Homerton	26	25
Sidney Sussex	12	9	Wolfson	27	27
Magdalene	13	20	St Edmund's	28	28
Fitzwilliam	14	19	Hughes Hall	29	29
Churchill	15	13			

universal. However, teaching groups remain much smaller than in most universities, and the tutor remains an inspiration for many students.

Both Oxford and Cambridge give applicants the option of leaving the choice of college to the university. For those with no ready source of advice on the colleges, this would seem an attractive solution to an intractable problem, but it is also a risky one: a lower proportion succeeds in this way than by applying to a particular college and, inevitably, you may end up somewhere that you hate.

The applications procedure

Both universities have set a UCAS deadline of 15 October 2008 for entry in 2009. For Oxford you will need to submit an Oxford Application Form at the same time. The form will be available to download for 2009 applicants. For Cambridge you now only need to submit an application to UCAS. Once Cambridge receives this from UCAS, you will be asked to complete a Supplementary Application Questionnaire. You may apply to only one of Oxford or Cambridge in the same admissions year, unless you are seeking an Organ award at both universities. Interviews take place in September for those who have left school or applied early, but in December for the majority. By the end of October, the first group can expect an offer, a rejection or deferral of a decision until January. The main group of applicants to Oxford will receive either a conditional offer or a rejection by Christmas, while in Cambridge the news arrives early in the new year. There are other differences between the two universities, however. There are application tests for more subjects than at other universities (see details on page 19). Oxford is more likely than Cambridge to make an offer as low as two E grades if it is sure that it wants the applicant, but the practice is no longer common.

For general information about Oxford and Cambridge universities, see each institution's profile in chapter 11.

Oxford The Norrington Table 2007

College	2007	2006	College	2007	2006
Merton	1	1	Queen's	16	11
Magdalen	2	3	Keble	17	26
Christ Church	3	6	Wadham	18	7
Balliol	4	2	St Peter's	19	27
New College	5	4	Somerville	20	16
St John's	6	5	Brasenose	21	15
Trinity	7	12	Lady Margaret Hall	22	19
Lincoln	8	8	St Catherine's	23	20
Hertford	9	17	Corpus Christi	24	9
Pembroke	10	23	Exeter	25	25
Worcester	11	14	St Hugh's	26	24
University	12	10	St Hilda's	27	22
Jesus	=13	18	Mansfield	28	29
St Edmund Hall	=13	13	Oriel	29	28
St Anne's	15	21	Harris Manchester	30	30

Cambridge Applications and Acceptances by Course

Arts	Applications		Acceptances		Acceptances to Applications (%)	
	2007	2006	2007	2006	2007	2006
Anglo-Saxon, Norse and Celtic	66	58	27	25	40.9	43.1
Archaeology and Anthropology	144	159	54	65	37.5	40.9
Architecture	429	435	51	36	11.9	8.3
Classics	158	159	81	80	51.3	50.3
Classics (4 years)	37	35	8	7	21.6	20.0
English	895	906	208	207	23.2	22.8
Geography	312	335	97	94	31.1	28.1
History	744	752	201	215	27.0	28.6
History of Art	119	121	28	36	23.5	29.8
Modern and Medieval Languages	603	646	197	181	32.7	28.0
Music	176	155	76	70	43.2	45.2
Oriental Studies	171	148	38	30	22.2	20.3
Oriental Studies (combined)	n/a	44	n/a	14	n/a	31.8
Philosophy	258	311	54	46	20.9	14.8
Theology and Religious Studies	134	123	53	53	39.6	43.1
Total Arts	*4,246*	*4,387*	*1,173*	*1,159*	*27.6*	*26.4*

Social Science	2007	2006	2007	2006	2007	2006
Economics	1,160	1,080	177	161	15.3	14.9
Land Economy	235	190	57	44	24.3	23.2
Law	1,123	1,185	206	212	18.3	17.9
Social and Political Sciences	673	675	113	107	16.8	15.8
Total Social Sciences	*3,191*	*3,130*	*553*	*524*	*17.3*	*16.7*

Science and Technology	2007	2006	2007	2006	2007	2006
Computer Science	227	230	71	62	31.3	26.9
Engineering	1,224	1,223	297	286	24.3	23.4
Mathematics	1,116	1,118	231	243	20.7	21.7
Medical Sciences	1,395	1,607	268	311	19.2	19.4
Natural Sciences	2,013	1,848	641	597	31.8	32.3
Veterinary Medicine	351	351	66	78	18.8	22.2
Total Science and Technology	*6,326*	*6,377*	*1,574*	*1,577*	*24.9*	*24.7*

	2007	2006	2007	2006	2007	2006
Education	130	200	62	79	47.7	39.5
Total	**13,763**	**14,094**	**3,300**	**3,339**	**23.9**	**23.7**

Note: the dates refer to the year in which the acceptances were made.
Mathematics includes those applying for mathematics, mathematics with computer science, and mathematics with physics.
The tripos course at Cambridge in chemical engineering, linguistics, management studies and manufacturing engineering can only be
taken after Part 1 of another tripos. The entries for these courses are recorded under the first-year subjects taken by the student involved.

Oxford Applications and Acceptances by Course

Arts	Applications 2007	Applications 2006	Acceptances 2007	Acceptances 2006	Acceptances to Applications % 2007	Acceptances to Applications % 2006
Ancient and Modern History	82	83	16	16	19.5	19.3
Archaeology and Anthropology	72	62	21	23	29.2	37.1
Classical Archaeology and Ancient History	91	85	21	21	23.1	24.7
Classics	255	256	118	119	46.3	46.5
Classics and English	39	38	9	8	23.1	21.1
Classics and Modern Languages	31	30	9	7	29.0	23.3
Economics and Management	843	704	96	82	11.4	11.6
English	1,171	1,103	239	251	20.4	22.8
English and Modern Languages	143	135	23	26	16.1	19.3
European and Middle Eastern Languages	39	34	13	10	33.3	29.4
Fine Art	160	152	21	16	13.1	10.5
Geography	299	251	85	86	28.4	34.3
Modern History	780	756	236	232	30.3	30.7
Modern History and Economics	39	48	12	13	30.8	27.1
Modern History and English	84	87	9	16	10.7	18.4
Modern History and Modern Languages	102	98	19	18	18.6	18.4
Modern History and Politics	237	278	44	42	18.6	15.1
History of Art	73	57	9	10	12.3	17.5
Law	959	933	186	205	19.4	22.0
Law with Law Studies in Europe	277	269	29	21	10.5	10.4
Mathematics and Philosophy	81	102	19	28	23.5	27.5
Modern Languages	506	494	171	175	33.8	35.4
Modern Languages and Linguistics	76	54	20	20	26.3	37.0
Music	188	147	54	64	28.7	43.5
Oriental Studies	156	155	40	47	25.6	30.3
Philosophy and Modern Languages	55	63	13	23	23.6	36.5
Philosophy and Theology	102	108	19	23	18.6	21.3
Physics and Philosophy	86	69	13	12	15.1	17.4
PPE	1,291	1,157	238	235	18.4	20.3
Theology	114	131	50	47	43.9	35.9
Total Arts	*8,431*	*7,939*	*1,852*	*1,903*	*22.0*	*24.0*

Oxford Applications and Acceptances by Course cont

Sciences	Applications		Acceptances		Acceptances to Applications %	
	2007	2006	2007	2006	2007	2006
Biochemistry	238	220	99	93	41.6	42.3
Biological Sciences	280	206	105	94	37.5	45.6
Chemistry	507	408	190	176	37.5	43.1
Computer Science	82	75	24	33	29.3	44.0
Earth Sciences (Geology)	67	72	32	27	47.8	37.5
Engineering Science	462	419	136	148	29.4	35.3
Engineering, Economics and Management	120	71	15	12	12.5	16.9
Experimental Psychology	242	209	51	49	21.1	23.4
Human Sciences	100	106	31	37	31.0	34.9
Materials Science; Materials, Economics and Management	59	64	28	27	47.5	42.2
Mathematics	828	746	173	185	20.9	24.8
Mathematics and Computer Science	52	56	16	17	30.8	30.4
Mathematics and Statistics	143	120	29	26	20.3	21.7
Medicine	1,085	1,054	149	151	13.7	14.3
Physics	695	663	170	180	24.5	27.1
Physiological Sciences	61	45	24	19	39.3	42.2
PPP	187	153	36	26	19.3	17.0
Engineering and Computer Science	n/a	24	n/a	5	n/a	20.8
Total Sciences	*5,208*	*4,711*	*1,308*	*1,305*	*25.1*	*28*
Total Arts and Sciences	**13,639**	**12,650**	**3,160**	**3,208**	**23.0**	**25.0**

Note: the dates refer to the year in which the acceptances were made.

Useful websites

For further information about the application process and preparation for interviews, visit:

www.cam.ac.uk/admissions/
www.ox.ac.uk/admissions/

Oxford College Profiles

Balliol

Balliol College, Oxford OX1 3BJ
01865 277777   admissions@balliol.ox.ac.uk   www.balliol.ox.ac.uk
Undergraduates: 382

Famous as the alma mater of many prominent postwar politicians, including Harold
Macmillan, Denis Healey and Roy Jenkins, the university's last Chancellor, Balliol has
maintained a strong presence in university life and is usually well represented in the
Union and most other societies. Academic standards are formidably high, as might be
expected in the college of Wycliffe and Adam Smith, notably in the classics and social
sciences. PPE is notoriously oversubscribed. Library facilities are good and include the
Tylor law library. Balliol began admitting overseas students in the 19th century and has
cultivated an attractively cosmopolitan atmosphere. It is one of only two colleges to have
an entirely student-run bar, the focal point for evening socialising. Most undergraduates
are offered accommodation in college for three years, although there has been a trend in
recent years for second-year students to live out, mainly in east Oxford. Graduate
students are usually lodged in the Graduate Centre at Holywell Manor. Centrally located,
with a JCR pantry that is open all day, Balliol is convenient as well as prestigious.

Brasenose

Brasenose College, Oxford OX1 4AJ
01865 277510 (admissions)   admissions@bnc.ox.ac.uk   www.bnc.ox.ac.uk
Undergraduates: 345

Brasenose may not be the most famous Oxford college, but it makes up for its discreet
image with a consistent academic performance and an advantageous city-centre position.
The *alma mater* of David Cameron, Brasenose was one of the first colleges to admit
women in the 1970s, and now usually has a 50:50 split within each year, so that, for
example, the major undergraduate office, President of the JCR, has been filled as often
by a woman as a man. But BNC, as the college is often known, still has the image of a
rugby haven, and has the third-lowest proportion of students from state schools in the
university. Named after the door knocker on the 13th-century Brasenose Hall, the college
has a pleasant, intimate ambience which most find conducive to study. Law, PPE,
medicine and modern history are traditional strengths, and competition for places in
these subjects is intense. However, the college is a consistently poor performer in the
Norrington Table. Its library is open 24 hours a day and there is a separate law library.
All undergraduate rooms have internet connections. Sporting standards are as high as
at many much larger colleges and the college's rowing club is one of the oldest in the
university. Two annexes, the St Cross Building and Frewin Court, mean nearly all
undergraduates can live in.

Christ Church

Christ Church College, Oxford OX1 1DP
01865 276150   admissions@chch.ox.ac.uk   www.chch.ox.ac.uk
Undergraduates: 391

The college founded by Cardinal Wolsey in 1525 and affectionately known as The House has come a long way since Evelyn Waugh mythologised its aristocratic excesses in *Brideshead Revisited*. The social mix is much more varied than most applicants suspect, although it is still heavily dominated by students from private schools. Academic pressure at Christ Church is reasonably relaxed, although natural high-achievers prosper and the college's history and law teaching is highly regarded. The college has recently risen to third in the Norrington Table, and was the overall winner of this year's *University Challenge*. The magnificent 18th-century library is one of the best in Oxford. It is supplemented by a separate law library. Christ Church has its own art gallery, which holds over 2,000 works of mainly Italian Renaissance art. Sport, especially rugby, is an important part of college life. The river is close by for the aspiring oarsman, and the college has good squash courts. Accommodation for all three years is rated by Christ Church students as excellent and includes flats off Iffley Road as well as a number of beautifully panelled shared sets (double rooms) in college. The modern bar adds to the lustre of a college justly famous for its imposing architecture. Its chapel is also the cathedral of the Diocese of Oxford – England's smallest medieval cathedral. The college will remain at the centre of media attention over the next few years due to the presence of Bilawal Bhutto Zardari, son of the late Benazir Bhutto, who is studying history.

Corpus Christi

Corpus Christi College, Oxford OX1 4JF
01865 276693 (admissions tutor)   admissions.office@ccc.ox.ac.uk   www.ccc.ox.ac.uk
Undergraduates: 230

Corpus, until recently Oxford's smallest college, is naturally overshadowed by its Goliath-like neighbour, Christ Church, but makes the most of its intimate, friendly atmosphere and exquisite beauty. Like The House it has an exceptional view across the Meadows. Although the college has only around 340 students including postgraduates, it has an admirable library open 24 hours a day. Academic expectations are high and English, Classics, PPE and medicine are especially well-established. Corpus is able to offer accommodation to all its undergraduates, one of its many attractions to those seeking a smaller community in Oxford. The college is also one of the most generous with bursaries, giving travel, book and vacation grants at an almost unparalleled level across the university. Scholars are particularly well rewarded.

Exeter

Exeter College, Oxford OX1 3DP
01865 279648 (academic secretary)   admissions@exeter.ox.ac.uk   www.exeter.ox.ac.uk
Undergraduates: 329

Exeter is the fourth oldest college in the university and was founded in 1314 by Walter de Stapeldon, Bishop of Exeter. Nestling between the High Street and Broad Street, site of most of the city's bookshops, it could hardly be more central. The college boasts handsome buildings, the exceptional Fellows' garden and attractive accommodation for most undergraduates for all three years of their university careers, with plans afoot to refurbish the college's accommodation in the east of the city. Exeter does have academic pedigree, but has slipped down the Norrington Table in recent times. It is, however, often accused of being rather dull. Given its glittering roll-call of alumni, which includes Martin Amis, J.R.R. Tolkien, Alan Bennett, Richard Burton, Imogen Stubbs and Tariq Ali, this seems an accusation that, on the face of it at least, is hard to sustain. The arrival of a new rector, Frances Cairncross, has created a new dynamic at the college, with regular, high-profile, speaker events and the incorporation of a college careers service. College food is not rated highly by students although the bar is popular with students from other colleges. The social scene is lively.

Harris Manchester

Harris Manchester College, Oxford OX1 3TF
01865 271009 (admissions)   college.office@hmc.ox.ac.uk   www.hmc.ox.ac.uk
Undergraduates: 79

Founded in Manchester in 1786 to provide education for non-Anglican students, Harris Manchester finally settled in Oxford in 1889 after spells in both York and London. A full university college since 1996, the newest and smallest college, its central location with fine buildings and grounds in Holywell Street is very convenient for the Bodleian, although the college itself does have an excellent library. Harris Manchester admits only mature students of mostly 25 years and above to read for both undergraduate and graduate degrees, predominantly in the arts. All students must be 21 or older. There are also groups of visiting students from American universities and some men and women training for the ministry. Most of its members live in and all meals are provided, indeed the college encourages its members to dine regularly in hall. The college has few sporting facilities (a croquet lawn and a college punt), but members can use two central Oxford gyms without charge and can play football, cricket, swimming and chess as well as playing on other college or university teams. Other outlets include the college Drama Society and also the chapel, a focal point to many there.

Hertford

Hertford College, Oxford OX1 3BW
01865 279404   admissions@hertford.ox.ac.uk   www.hertford.ox.ac.uk
Undergraduates: 371

Though tracing its roots to the 12th century, Hertford is determinedly modern. It was one of the first colleges to admit women (in 1976). Hertford also helped set the trend towards offers of places conditional on A levels, which paved the way for the abolition of the entrance examination. It is still popular with state school applicants, and is one of the least stuffy colleges, with a reputation for attracting students from a broad range of backgrounds. The college lacks the grandeur of Magdalen, of which it was once an annex, but has its own architectural trademark in the Bridge of Sighs. It is also close to the History Faculty library (Hertford's neighbour), the Bodleian and the King's Arms, perhaps Oxford's most popular pub. Academic pressure at Hertford is relaxed, but the quality of teaching, especially in English, is generally thought admirable. Accommodation has improved, thanks in part to the Abingdon House and Warnock House complex close to the Thames near Folly Bridge, and the college can now lodge all of its undergraduates at any one time, albeit in disparate parts of the city. Like most congenial colleges, Hertford is often accused of being claustrophobic and inward-looking – a charge most Hertfordians would ascribe simply to jealousy.

Jesus

Jesus College, Oxford OX1 3DW
01865 279720   undergraduate.admissions@jesus.ox.ac.uk www.jesus.ox.ac.uk
Undergraduates: 330

Jesus, the only Oxford college to be founded in the reign of Elizabeth I, suffers from something of an unfair reputation for insularity. Its students, whose predecessors include T.E. Lawrence and Harold Wilson, describe it as "friendly but gossipy" and shrug off the legend that all its undergraduates are Welsh. Close to most of Oxford's main facilities, Jesus has three compact quads, the second of which is especially enticing in the summer. The college's JCR is well-equipped, with a pool table, large projector screen television, and a hatch serving tea and toast throughout the day. Academic standards are high and most subjects are taught in college. Physics, chemistry and engineering are especially strong. Rugby and rowing also tend to be taken seriously. Accommodation is almost universally regarded as excellent and relatively inexpensive. Self-catering flats in north and east Oxford have enabled every graduate to live in throughout his or her Oxford career. The range of accommodation available to undergraduates is similarly good and is available for the full length of any course. The college's Cowley Road development, also the site of the college's sports ground, has been described by the students' union as "some of the plushest student housing in Oxford".

Keble

Keble College, Oxford OX1 3PG
01865 272711   admissions@keb.ox.ac.uk   www.keble.ox.ac.uk
Undergraduates: 379

Keble, named after John Keble, the leader of the Oxford Movement, was founded in 1870 with the intention of making Oxford education more accessible and the college remains proud of "the legacy of a social conscience". With around 400 undergraduates, Keble is one of the biggest colleges in Oxford, while its uncompromising Victorian Gothic architecture also makes it one of the most distinctive. Once famous for the special privileges it extended to rowers, the college's academic performance varies year-on-year. It is strong in the sciences, where it benefits from easy access to the Science Area, the Radcliffe Science Library and the Mathematical Institute. The college's sporting record remains exemplary, with the rugby team regularly dominating university competitions, although some students find the overflow of the sporting ethos into the college's social life overbearing. Undergraduates are guaranteed accommodation in their first two years and the college can also accommodate most undergraduates in their final year. Its library is open 24 hours a day and all rooms have internet connections. The college hall, where students wishing to dine must wear gowns six nights a week, has recently been intensively cleaned to restore it to its former glory and is one of the most impressive in the university. The refurbished "spaceship" and Café Keble are particular attractions. The college also has a well-equipped gym and a modern theatre, the acoustics of which are rated the best in the university.

Lady Margaret Hall

Lady Margaret Hall, Oxford OX2 6QA
01865 274310/1 admissions@lmh.ox.ac.uk www.lmh.ox.ac.uk
Undergraduates: 393

Lady Margaret Hall, Oxford's first college for women, has been co-educational since 1978 and now enjoys an equal gender balance, but is in the bottom half of colleges for attracting students from state schools. For many students, LMH's comparative isolation – the college is three quarters of a mile north of the city centre – is a real advantage, ensuring a clear distinction between college life and university activities, and a refuge from tourists. For others it means a long journey to the Law, English and Social Sciences faculties. Although the neo-Georgian architecture is not to everyone's taste, the college's beautiful gardens back onto the Cherwell river, which allows LMH to have its own punt house and 12 acres of land. The students' union describes life at the college as "relaxed". Accommodation is guaranteed for first and third years, and for the great majority of second years. The college's two recent accommodation buildings have the remarkable attraction of private bathrooms in all their rooms. LMH shares most of its sports facilities with Trinity College, though it has squash and tennis courts on site and has become a leading rowing college. Recently, it has become one of Oxford's dramatic centres.

Lincoln

Lincoln College, Oxford OX1 3DR
01865 279836 admissions@lincoln.ox.ac.uk www.lincoln.ox.ac.uk
Undergraduates: 285

Small, central Lincoln cultivates a lower profile than many other colleges with comparable assets. The college's 15th-century buildings and beautiful library – a converted Queen Anne church – combine to produce a delightful environment in which to spend three years. Academic standards are high, particularly in arts subjects, although the college's relaxed atmosphere is justly celebrated. Accommodation is provided by the college for all undergraduates throughout their careers and includes rooms above The Mitre, a medieval inn. Students parade around Oxford in sub fusc (formal wear) on Ascension Day while choristers from the University Church beat the parish bounds. The college has a healthy rivalry with neighbouring Brasenose. Historically, Lincoln students must invite their Brasenose counterparts into the bar for free drinks every Ascension

Day, in recognition of a time when a Lincoln man was saved from a town mob by the college's neighbours. Graduate students have their own centre a few minutes' walk away in Bear Lane and at the EPA Science Centre close to the university science area. Finalists live in a recently refurbished complex on Museum Road, by Keble and the University Parks. Lincoln's small size and self-sufficiency have led to the college being accused of insularity. Lincoln's food is outstanding, among the best in the university. Sporting achievement is impressive for a college of this size, in part a reflection of its good facilities. One annoyance is the constant stream of American Methodists visiting the college to look at the John Wesley room.

Magdalen

Magdalen College, Oxford OX1 4AU
01865 276063   admissions@magd.ox.ac.uk   www.magd.ox.ac.uk
Undergraduates: 377

Perhaps the most beautiful college in Oxford or Cambridge, Magdalen is known around the world for its tower, its deer park and its May morning celebrations – when students threw themselves off Magdalen Bridge into the river Cherwell,. This practice has now been banned after shallow water resulted in a large number of injuries. The college has shaken off its public school image to become a truly cosmopolitan place, with a large intake from overseas and an increasing proportion of state school pupils. Magdalen's record in English, history and law is second to none, while its science park at Sandford is bound to bolster its reputation in the sciences. The college is academically very strong and has recently risen to second in the Norrington Table. Library facilities are excellent, especially in history and law. First-year students are accommodated in the Waynflete Building and allocated rooms in subsequent years by ballot. Undergraduates can be housed in college for the full length of their course. Rents are not cheap compared to other colleges, but as the college is very wealthy there is always financial help on offer. Sets in cloisters and in the palatial New Buildings are particularly sought after. Magdalen is also conveniently placed for the wealth of pubs and places to eat in east Oxford. The college bar is one of the best in Oxford and the college is a pluralistic place, proud of its drama society and choir. In recent years the college has become particularly strong at rowing. Elsewhere, enthusiasm on the sports field makes up for a traditional lack of athletic prowess.

Mansfield

Mansfield College, Oxford OX1 3TF
01865 270982   admissions@mansfield.ox.ac.uk   www.mansfield.ox.ac.uk
Undergraduates: 214

Mansfield's graduation to full Oxford college status in 1995 marked the culmination of a long history of development since 1886. Its spacious, attractive site is fairly central, close to the libraries, the shops, the University Parks and the river Cherwell. With just over 200 undergraduates, the community is close-knit, although this can verge on the claustrophobic. Recent moves to increase intake numbers may change that. The less intimidating atmosphere of Mansfield is, perhaps, helped by its strong representation of state-school students. First and third years live in college accommodation. Mansfield students share Merton's excellent sports ground and have numerous college teams. The college has recently become a hotbed of student journalism, providing numerous editors of university publications over the past few years. Despite its former theological background, students are not admitted on the basis of religion and can read a wide variety of subjects. Mansfield is home to the Oxford Centre for the Environment, Ethics and Society (OCEES) and also the American Studies Institute, evidence of the strong links between Mansfield and the United States, which is reflected by some 35 visiting students annually. It also spearheads the Oxford FE Initiative, which encourages applications to the university from further education colleges.

Merton

Merton College, Oxford OX1 4JD
01865 276329   undergraduateadmissions@admin.merton.ox.ac.uk   www.merton.ox.ac.uk
Undergraduates: 298

Founded in 1264 by Walter de Merton, Bishop of Rochester and Chancellor of England, Merton is one of Oxford's oldest colleges and one of its most prestigious. Quiet and beautiful, with the oldest quad in the university, Merton has high academic expectations of its undergraduates, consistently reflected in a position at the top of the Norrington Table, as in 2007. History, English, physics, PPE and chemistry all enjoy a formidable track record. The medieval library is the envy of many other colleges. Accommodation is some of the cheapest in the university, of a good standard and offered to students for all three years. Merton's food is well-priced and among the best in the university; formal Hall is served six times a week. Kitchens are provided for the first and third years who live in college. Merton's many diversions include the Merton Floats, its dramatic society, the Neave (Politics) Society, an excellent Christmas Ball and the peculiar Time Ceremony, which celebrates the return of GMT. Sports facilities are excellent, although participation tends to be more important than the final score.

New College

New College, Oxford OX1 3BN
01865 279551   admissions@new.ox.ac.uk   www.new.ox.ac.uk
Undergraduates: 391

New College is large, old (founded in 1379 by William of Wykeham) and much more relaxed than most expect when first confronting its daunting facade. It is a bustling place, as proud of its excellent music and its bar as of its strength in law, history and PPE. In the past two years the college has moved into the top five of the Norrington Table. The college has been making particular efforts to increase the proportion of state school students, inviting applications from schools that have never sent candidates to Oxford. The Target Schools Scheme, designed to increase applications from state schools, is well established. Nevertheless, it remains in the bottom ten colleges for proportion of students from state schools. Almost all undergraduates will be able to have college accommodation for three years. The college's library facilities are impressive, especially in law, classics and PPE. The sports ground is nearby and includes good tennis courts. Women's sport is particularly strong, especially on the river. A sports complex, named after Brian Johnston, opened in 1997, at St Cross Road. The sheer beauty of New College remains one of its principal assets and the college gardens are a memorable sight in the summer. In spite of these traditional charms, the college has strong claims to be considered admirably innovative. Music is a feature of college life, and the college has some of the best practice facilities in the university. The Commemoration Ball, held every three years, is a highlight of Oxford's social calendar.

Oriel

Oriel College, Oxford OX1 4EW
01865 276522   admissions@oriel.ox.ac.uk   www.oriel.ox.ac.uk
Undergraduates: 288

In spite of its reputation as a bastion of muscular privilege, Oriel is a friendly college with a strong sense of identity and has adjusted to co-educational admissions of women in 1985. In recent years the college has succeeded in ridding itself of its image of being home to the archetypal "Tory boy" characters. The college is sometimes described as having "a strong crew spirit" reflecting its traditions on the river. Academic standards are relatively low by Oxford standards, with the college hovering around the bottom of the Norrington Table. The well-stocked library is open 24 hours a day. Oriel's sporting reputation is certainly deserved and its rowing eight is rarely far from the head of the river. Other sports are well catered for, even if their facilities are considerably farther away than the boathouse, which is only a short jog away. Accommodation is of variable quality, but Oriel can provide rooms for all three years for those students who require them. Scholars and Exhibitioners chasing firsts in their final year are given priority in the ballot for college rooms. Extensive new accommodation has been completed one mile away off the Cowley Road and at the Island Site on Oriel Street. Oriel also offers a lively drama society, a Shakespearian production taking place each summer in the front quad. College meals are cheap, with students charged little more than £5 for three meals a day in hall.

Pembroke

Pembroke College, Oxford OX1 1DW
01865 276412   admissions@pembroke.ox.ac.uk   www.pembroke.ox.ac.uk
Undergraduates: 370

Although its alumni include such extrovert characters as Dr Johnson and Michael Heseltine, Pembroke is one of Oxford's least dynamic colleges. The college is historically poor financially, but academic results are solid, and have improved significantly in recent years. The college has Fellows and lecturers in almost all the major university subjects. Pembroke expects to accommodate all first years and most final-year undergraduates. The Sir Geoffrey Arthur building on the river, ten minutes' walk from the college, offers excellent facilities; in addition to 100 student rooms there is a concert room, computer room and a multigym. College food is reasonable, though some find formal Hall every evening rather too rich a diet. Rugby and rowing are strong, with Pembroke usually behind only Oriel and Magdalen on the river, and squash and tennis courts are available at the nearby sports ground. Over the past few years Pembroke's intake has had the lowest proportion of state-school students in the university.

Queen's

Queen's College, Oxford OX1 4AW
01865 279167   admissions@queens.ox.ac.uk   www.queens.ox.ac.uk
Undergraduates: 308

One of the most striking sights of the High Street, Queen's has now shed its exclusive "northern" image to become one of Oxford's liveliest and most attractive colleges. The college's academic record is mediocre, although results have improved recently. Modern languages, chemistry and mathematics are reckoned among the strongest subjects. Queen's does not normally admit undergraduates for the honours school of English language and literature, theology, computer science or geography, and is seen as strong in history and politics. The library is as beautiful as it is well stocked. All students are offered accommodation, first years being housed in modernist annexes in east Oxford, and the college is in the process of converting all rooms into en-suite facilities. The college's beer cellar is one of the most popular in the university and the JCR facilities are also better than average. An annual dinner commemorates a student who is said to have fended off a bear by thrusting a volume of Aristotle into its mouth. Postgraduates are accommodated in St Aldate's House, a modern building close to the centre of town.

St Anne's

St Anne's College, Oxford OX2 6HS
01865 274825   enquiries@st-annes.ox.ac.uk   www.st-annes.ox.ac.uk
Undergraduates: 419

Architecturally uninspiring (a Victorian row with concrete "stack-a-studies" dropped into their back gardens), St Anne's makes up in community spirit what it lacks in awesome grandeur. One of the largest colleges, it has a high proportion of state-school students. A women's college until 1979, its academic standing has fluctuated, having been in last place in the Norrington Table in the middle of the last decade, but now scoring around mid-table. PPE is particularly strong. The library is very well-stocked and is rich in law, Chinese and medieval history texts. Opening hours are long. Accommodation is guaranteed to almost all undergraduates and the college is to the north of the city centre, although not as far out as St Hugh's. Three new accommodation blocks contain 150 student rooms, including four for disabled students, while the older rooms have been refurbished. Half of all rooms are en suite.

St Catherine's

St Catherine's College, Oxford OX13UJ
01865 271703   admissions@stcatz.ox.ac.uk   www.stcatz.ox.ac.uk
Undergraduates: 437

Arne Jacobsen's modernist design for "Catz", one of Oxford's youngest and largest under-graduate colleges, has attracted much attention as the most striking contrast in the university to the lofty spires of Magdalen and New College. Close to the Law, English and Social Science faculties, the university science area and the pleasantly rural Holywell Great Meadow, St Catherine's is nevertheless only a few minutes' walk from the city centre. Academic standards are especially high in mathematics and physics though the college has recently plumbed the depths of the Norrington Table. The well-liked Wolfson library is open till midnight on most days. Rooms are small but tend to be warmer than in other, more venerable colleges, and are now available on site for first, second and third years. Squash, tennis and netball courts are all on the main college site. There is an excellent theatre, as well as an on-site punt house, gym and squash courts. The college is host to the Cameron Mackintosh Chair of Contemporary Theatre. Recent incumbents have included Sir Ian McKellen, Alan Ayckbourn and Lord Attenborough. St Catherine's has one of the best JCR facilities in Oxford.

St Edmund Hall

St Edmund Hall College, Oxford OX1 4AR
01865 279008   admissions@seh.ox.ac.uk   www.seh.ox.ac.uk
Undergraduates: 371

St Edmund Hall – "Teddy Hall" – has one of Oxford's smallest college sites but also one of its most populous. The college offers students the chance to live in its medieval quads right in the heart of the city. With the male/female ratio nearly equal, the college is shedding its image as a home for "hearties", and the authorities have gone out of their way to tone down younger members' rowdier excesses. Nonetheless, the sporting culture is still vigorous and the college usually does well in rugby, football and hockey. The college is also known across the university for its "bops" – the name given to student discos. Academically, the college has put recent poor performances behind it and is now found in the middle of the Norrington table, and has some impressive names among its fellowship as well as a marvellous library, originally a Norman church. College accommodation is reasonable and can be offered for three years, either on the main site or in North or East Oxford. The college has three annexes, one near the University Parks, and two on Iffley Road, where many of the rooms have private bathrooms. Hall food is better than average.

St Hilda's

St Hilda's College, Oxford OX4 1DY
01865 286620   college.office@st-hildas.ox.ac.uk   www.sthildas.ox.ac.uk
Undergraduates: 377

October 2008 marks a milestone for St Hilda's and the university as a whole, as the college will welcome its first mixed sex intake. Although the college, founded in 1893, lasted more than 100 years as an all-female institution, the governing body voted in 2006 to admit men. The college has long languished at the bottom end of the Norrington Table, but is a distinctive part of the Oxford landscape and is usually well represented in university life. The 65,000-volume library is growing fast and accommodation for readers was extended in 2005. St Hilda's also boasts one of the largest ratios of state school to independent undergraduates in Oxford. Accommodation is guaranteed to first years and finalists. The JCR has its own punts, which are available free for college members and their guests. Many of the rooms offer some of the best river views in Oxford. Social facilities are limited, but this is expected to change with the influx of men. The standard of food is high.

St Hugh's

St Hugh's College, Oxford OX2 6LE
01865 274910   admissions@st-hughs.ox.ac.uk   www.st-hughs.ox.ac.uk
Undergraduates: 367

One of the lesser-known colleges, St Hugh's was criticised by students in 1987 when it began admitting men. There is now an equal male/female ratio, a better balance than at most Oxford colleges. Like Lady Margaret Hall, St Hugh's picturesque setting is a bicycle ride from the city centre. It is an ideal college for those seeking a place to live and study away from the madding crowd, and is well liked for its pleasantly bohemian atmosphere and beautiful gardens. Academic pressure remains comparatively low, with the college rarely out of the lower regions of the Norrington Table. St Hugh's guarantees accommodation to undergraduates for all three years, although the standard of rooms is variable. Sport, particularly football, is taken quite seriously. As the college enjoys extensive grounds compared to most colleges, there is space for a croquet lawn and tennis courts.

St John's

St John's College, Oxford OX1 3JP
01865 277317   admissions@sjc.ox.ac.uk   www.sjc.ox.ac.uk
Undergraduates: 357

St John's is one of Oxford's powerhouses, excelling in almost every field and boasting arguably the most beautiful gardens in the university. Founded in 1555 by a London merchant, it is richly endowed and makes the most of its resources to provide undergraduates with an agreeable and challenging three years. The work ethic is very much part of the St John's ethos, and academic standards are high, with English, chemistry and history among the traditional strengths, though all students benefit from the impressive library. The college has, however, recently dropped out of the top two of the Norrington Table, but only as far as sixth. Discounting Harris Manchester, it has the highest proportion of state-school students in Oxford. As might be expected of a wealthy college, the accommodation is excellent and guaranteed for three or four years. The college's riches allow it to subsidise accommodation costs to a large degree, as well as providing generous book grants. St John's has a strong sporting tradition and offers good facilities, but the social scene is limited. As befits such an all-round strong college, entry is fiercely competitive. The college is very close to two of Oxford's landmark pubs: the Eagle and Child and the Lamb and Flag.

St Peter's

St Peter's College, Oxford OX1 2DL
01865 278863   admissions@spc.ox.ac.uk   www.spc.ox.ac.uk
Undergraduates: 341

Opened as St Peter's Hall in 1929, St Peter's has been an Oxford college since 1961. Its medieval, Georgian and 19th-century buildings are in the city centre and close to most of Oxford's main facilities. Though still young, St Peter's is well represented in university life and has pockets of academic excellence, rising to tenth in the Norrington Table in 2004, although it has since fallen far back into the bottom half. History tutoring is particularly good. There are no Fellows in classics at the college. Accommodation is offered to students for first and third years and about 60 per cent of second years. Students are prohibited from cooking on the main site. Student rooms vary from traditional rooms in college to new purpose-built rooms a few minutes' walk away. The college's facilities are impressive, including one of the university's best JCRs. The college has a proud sporting heritage, being particularly strong at rugby and rowing. St Peter's is known as one of Oxford's most vibrant colleges socially. It is strong in acting and journalism, and has a recently refurbished bar. It has recently suffered from a severe shortage in funding, and made its chaplain redundant.

Somerville

Somerville College, Oxford OX2 6HD
01865 270629   secretariat@somerville.ox.ac.uk   www.somerville.ox.ac.uk
Undergraduates: 342

The announcement, early in 1992, that Somerville was to go co-educational sparked an unusually acrimonious and persistent dispute within this most tranquil of colleges. Protests were doomed to failure, however; the first male undergraduates arrived in 1994 and now account for half the students. Lady Thatcher was one of those who flocked to their old college's defence, illustrating the fierce loyalty Somerville inspires. The college's atmosphere appears to have survived the momentous change, although the culture of protest reappeared when a number of students refused to pay the Government's tuition fees in 1998. The college has strong state-school representation. Accommodation, including 30 small flats for students, is of a reasonable standard, and is guaranteed for first years and students sitting university examinations, as well as roughly a third of all other students. The JCR operates a rent equalisation scheme for those who live out in their second year. There are kitchens in all college buildings, but hall food is towards the cheaper end of the university. Sport is strong at Somerville and the women's rowing eight usually finishes near the head of the river. The college's hockey pitches and tennis courts are nearby. The 100,000-volume library is open 24 hours a day and is one of the most beautiful in Oxford. Students at the college have a strong track record of involvement in the university's student union.

Trinity

Trinity College, Oxford OX1 3BH

01865 279910   admissions@trinity.ox.ac.uk   www.trinity.ox.ac.uk

Undergraduates: 281

Architecturally impressive and boasting beautiful lawns (which you can walk on), Trinity is one of Oxford's least populous colleges, admitting some eighty undergraduates each year. It is ideally located, beside the Bodleian, Blackwell's book shop and the White Horse pub. Cardinal Newman, an alumnus of Trinity, is said to have regarded Trinity's motto as "Drink, drink, drink". Academic pressure varies, but the college has recently made impressive steps up the ranks of the Norrington Table of academic performance and the college produces its fair share of Firsts, especially in arts subjects. Trinity has shaken off its reputation for apathy, and whilst members are active in all walks of university life, the college has its own debating and drama societies, as well as sharing a fierce rivalry with neighbouring Balliol. The proportion of state-school entrants has been rising, but is still poor. Accommodation is of a reasonable standard and undergraduates can live in for three years. All undergraduates are given a room on the main site in their first and second year, with the great majority of third and fourth-year students living in a purpose built block 1.5 miles north of the college.

University

University College, Oxford OX1 4BH

01865 276601   admissions@univ.ox.ac.uk   www.univ.ox.ac.uk

Undergraduates: 365

University is the first Oxford college to be able to boast a former student in the Oval Office. Indeed, the college seems certain to benefit from its unique links with former President Clinton, a Rhodes Scholar at University in the late 1960s. The college is probably Oxford's oldest, though highly unlikely to have been founded by King Alfred, as legend claims. Academic expectations are high and the college prospers in most subjects, although it maintains a relatively modest standing in the Norrington Table. Physics, PPE and maths are particularly strong. That said, University has fewer claims to be thought a powerhouse in the manner of St John's, arguably its greatest rival. Students who are accepted to read courses with a mathematical element are invited to a free week-long maths course just before the beginning of their first term, providing a head-start in their studies. Accommodation is guaranteed to undergraduates for all three years, with third years lodged in an annexe in north Oxford about a mile and a half from the college site on the High Street. Sport is strong and University is usually successful on the river, but the college has a reputation for being quiet socially. Students from the state sector are poorly represented, with the college offering the second-lowest proportion of places to state-school students.

Wadham

Wadham College, Oxford OX1 3PN
01865 277947   admissions@wadham.ox.ac.uk   www.wadham.ox.ac.uk
Undergraduates: 427

Founded by Dorothy Wadham in 1609, Wadham is known in about equal measure for its academic track record – the college generally ranks in the top third in examination performance – and its leftist politics. The JCR – or student union as it has rebranded itself – is famously dynamic and politically active, although the breadth of political opinion is greater than its left-wing stereotype suggests. Wadham students are notoriously trendy, although some in the university find the atmosphere at the college slightly forced. That said, the college is very strong in admitting students from state schools. And for somewhere supposedly unconcerned with such fripperies, its gardens are surprisingly beautiful. The somewhat rough-hewn chapel is similarly memorable. The college has a good 24-hour library. Accommodation is guaranteed for at least two years and there are many large, shared rooms on offer. Journalism and drama play an important part. Highlights in the social calendar are Queerbop, a celebration of all things gay, and Wadstock, the college's open-air music festival. Tickets to both are always sold out.

Worcester

Worcester College, Oxford OX1 2HB
01865 278391   admissions@worc.ox.ac.uk   www.worc.ox.ac.uk
Undergraduates: 379

Worcester is to the west of Oxford what Magdalen is to the east: an open, rural contrast to the urban rush of the city centre. The college's rather mediocre exterior conceals a delightful environment, including some characteristically muscular Baroque Hawskmoor architecture, a garden and a lake. The college has been rising up the Norrington Table and was only just outside the top ten in 2007 – its best result of the decade. The 24-hour library is strongest in the arts. Accommodation, guaranteed for two years and provided for the majority of third years, varies in quality from ordinary to conference standard in the Canal Building. More en-suite accommodation, next to the new gym, will be available in 2008–9. Sport plays an important part in college life, as befits the only college with playing fields on site. Worcester has had recent successes in football, hockey and cricket. Formal halls are available six nights a week and a bargain at less than £2. More than half of the 2007 intake was from the state system, but the average over the last three years (which the university considers more representative) is still less than 50 per cent.

Cambridge College Profiles

Christ's

Christ's College, Cambridge CB2 3BU
01223 334953   admissions@christs.cam.ac.uk   www.christs.cam.ac.uk
Undergraduates: 395

Christ's prides itself on its academic strength, but offers one third of places on "easy offers", anything as low as two E grades at A levels. This means the college is confident of its ability to identify potential high-flyers at interview and, in effect, prepared to circumvent A-levels as the principal criteria for entry. However, to receive an "easy offer", applicants need to have a strong academic record and "be making outstanding progress in their current studies." The college has a 53:47 state-to-independent ratio and women make up 38 per cent of the students. Christ's has a reputation for being dominated by hard-working natural scientists and mathematicians. Students have described the atmosphere at the college as intimate and cosy, but some complain of short bar opening hours and a poor relationship between undergraduates and Fellows. Accommodation is guaranteed to all undergraduates in college, with many, particularly first years, housed in the infamous New Court "Typewriter", which is set for refurbishment over the next year. Also to be redeveloped is the excellent New Court theatre, home to Christ's Amateur Dramatics Society and Christ's Films – widely considered to be one of the best film societies in the university. College sport has flourished in recent years, with teams competing to a good standard. The playing fields (shared with Sidney Sussex) are just over a mile away.

Churchill

Churchill College, Cambridge CB3 0DS
01223 336202   admissions@chu.cam.ac.uk   www.chu.cam.ac.uk
Undergraduates: 440

Students at Churchill claim they are the most unpretentious of Cambridge colleges – and proud of the fact the college allows its students to walk on the grass. This informality stems from the youth of the college, as well as its high state-school intake, 70 per cent. Founded in 1960 to help meet "the national need for scientists and engineers and to forge links with industry", Churchill's recent rise in the Tompkins Table seems to have halted in recent years. Deferred entry is encouraged in all subjects. The college has a noticeably high proportion of scientists and men: only one in three students is female. Compared to the breathtaking architecture of other Cambridge colleges, Churchill's modern and functional architecture strikes many as ugly, with some students saying the "1960s brutalism is something you get used to." Another perceived flaw is its distance from the city centre. Others argue that the distance offers much-needed breathing space. One undeniable advantage is Churchill's ability to provide every undergraduate with a room in college for all three years. Also, the college's weekly "pav" dances have become popular amongst Cambridge students in recent years. There are extensive on-site playing fields, and the college does well in rugby, hockey and rowing. The university's only student radio station (broadcasting to Churchill and New Hall) is based here.

Clare

Clare College, Cambridge cB2 1TL

01223 333246   admissions@clare.cam.ac.uk   www.clare.cam.ac.uk

Undergraduates: 440

Though for many Clare's outstanding features are its gardens and harmonious buildings, hard-pressed undergraduates are just as likely to praise the rent and food charges, which are among the lowest in the university. Accommodation is guaranteed for all three years, either in college or nearby hostels. The 49:51 ratio of male to female students is better than many colleges, while systematic attempts to raise the proportion of state-educated students has left those from independent schools in a minority (56:44). Clare's extracurricular life is a big attraction. Music thrives. The choir records and tours regularly. Clare Cellars (comprising the bar and JCR) has fast become one of the best run student venues in the university – providing everything from jazz to hip hop to comedy. One gripe amongst students is that its playing fields are well away from its location in the centre of the city.

Corpus Christi

Corpus Christi College, Cambridge CB2 1RH

01223 338056   admissions@corpus.cam.ac.uk   www.corpus.cam.ac.uk

Undergraduates: 250

Corpus Christi's small size inevitably makes it one of the more intimate colleges in Cambridge, with the fewest undergraduates in the university. Some argue that allows for a cohesive community, others feel it can become a goldfish bowl. Although small, it is traditionally broad-based academically. The new Taylor Library, which was opened to students in January 2008, has improved study facilities in the college. The kitchen fixed charge is above average but the college is known for a good formal hall. Almost all undergraduates are allocated a room in college or neighbouring hostels. The library is open 24 hours a day. There is a fairly even social balance: the independent-to-state ratio is about 40:60. The college bar has an enviable atmosphere. The sporting facilities, at Leckhampton (just over a mile away), are among the best in the university and include an outdoor swimming pool. The size of the college means that its sporting reputation owes more to enthusiasm than success, however. Drama is also well catered for, and the college owns The Playroom, the university's best small theatre.

Downing

Downing College, Cambridge CB2 1DQ

01223 334826   admissions@dow.cam.ac.uk   www.dow.cam.ac.uk

Undergraduates: 405

Hidden away behind the bustle of Regents Street, close to the city centre yet off the tourist trail, lies Downing College. As a result, its neo-Classical quadrangle and beautiful architecture is easily missed by anyone not looking for it. Founded in 1800 for the study of law, medicine and natural sciences, these are still thought to be the college's strong subjects. Indeed Downing is often called "the law college". A reputation for hard-playing, hard-drinking rugby players and oarsmen is proving hard to shake off. The college has many successful sports teams – with its own on-site tennis, netball and squash courts, a gym and plenty of open space (The Paddock). The college also claims the best Cambridge boat club. Downing currently guarantees a place in college accommodation for three years; the completion of a new accommodation block in 2000 allowed students to be housed throughout a first degree. The library, opened in 1993, has won an award for its architecture. There is close to a balance between students with state and independent school backgrounds (57:43). The student-run bar/party room has improved college social life, particularly after the three candlelit formal dinners a week.

Emmanuel

Emmanuel College, Cambridge CB2 3AP
01223 334290   admissions@emma.cam.ac.uk   www.emma.cam.ac.uk
Undergraduates: 454

Emmanuel is currently the top academic college according to the unofficial Tompkins Table. It has topped the rankings for four of the last five years. It is also one of the wealthier colleges at Cambridge. Thanks in no small part to its huge and stylish, strikingly modern bar, Emmanuel has something of an insular reputation. An almost even state–independent ratio contributes to the college's unpretentious atmosphere, however, and just over half the undergraduates are women. All students are guaranteed accommodation. Second years are housed in college hostels. With self-catering facilities limited, most students eat in Hall. The college offers expedition grants to undergraduates every year, and has a large hardship fund. In the summer, the college tennis courts and open-air swimming pool offer a welcome haven from exam pressures. The duck pond is one of the most picturesque spots in Cambridge. The sports grounds are excellent, if some distance away.

Fitzwilliam

Fitzwilliam College, Cambridge CB3 0DG
01223 332030   admissions@fitz.cam.ac.uk   www.fitz.cam.ac.uk
Undergraduates: 475

Based in the city centre until 1963, Fitzwilliam now occupies a large, modern site on the Huntingdon Road. What it may lack in architectural splendour, "Fitz" makes up in friendly informality. Nearly two-thirds of its undergraduates come from the state sector, and about 40 per cent are women, though the college hopes "significantly to raise this proportion in the coming years". College accommodation is now available for all undergraduates with the completion of the Wilson Building. Fitzwilliam's academic record has been improving. Applications to heavily academic subjects like natural sciences and law are encouraged. But so are those interested in studying archaeology and anthropology, classics, social and political sciences and music. On the extracurricular front, in recent years Fitz has been amongst the best sporting colleges in the university.

The football and rugby teams have enjoyed great success, and there are extensive and well-kept sports facilities close by, including gym, football, rugby, cricket, hockey and tennis grounds – as well as squash courts on site. Music also thrives at the college. Fitz is the only college in Cambridge to have access to a professional string quartet and its Ents (college entertainments) are exceptionally popular.

Girton

Girton College, Cambridge CB3 0JG
01223 338972   admissions@girton.cam.ac.uk   www.girton.cam.ac.uk
Undergraduates: 503

As students at Girton readily admit, "you've probably never heard of Girton, half of Cambridge students haven't." Its anonymity is due to its distance from the city centre. Admittedly, the centre is only a 15-minute bike ride away, but in Cambridge terms that is as long a commute as you can get. However, its comparative isolation inevitably encourages a strong community spirit, and students do get to enjoy its beautiful grounds away from the tourists and the relative bustle of the city. Girton stands on a 50-acre site and there is no question of overcrowding: rooms are available for the entire course. The majority of second-year students live in Wolfson Court (near the University Library). Some find that the long corridors remind them of boarding school. Since becoming coeducational in 1979, the college has maintained a balanced admissions policy. Just over half of the undergraduates are from state schools. Girton also has the highest proportion of women Fellows in any mixed college. The on-site sporting facilities, which include a swimming pool, are excellent. The college is active in most sports and particularly strong in football. The formal Hall, though excellent and popular, is held only once a week.

Gonville and Caius

Gonville and Caius College, Cambridge CB2 1TA
01223 332447   admissions@cai.cam.ac.uk   www.cai.cam.ac.uk
Undergraduates: 475

Gonville and Caius College – to confuse the outsider, the college is usually known as Caius (pronounced "keys") – is among the most beautiful of Cambridge's colleges, as well as one of the most central. It has an excellent academic reputation, especially in medicine and history, though maths and law are also highly rated. Caius also has one of the largest and most architecturally impressive student libraries in Cambridge, housed in the Cockerell Building next door to the college. Accommodation, though guaranteed for three years, varies in quality depending on how lucky you are. Most first years are housed in Harvey Court, a five-minute walk away across the river. Adjacent to Harvey Court is the £13-million Stephen Hawking Building, which opened its doors to first-year undergraduates in October 2006. Providing en-suite accommodation for 75 students and eight fellows, the building boasts some of the highest-standard student accommodation in Cambridge. Third years live in the idyllic surroundings of the old courts. Those unlucky in the room ballot though, especially second years, live in college hostels over a mile away. An ongoing gripe is that undergraduates are obliged to eat in Hall at least 45 times a term. Self catering facilities are often poor. Some argue that enforced Halls ensure that students meet regularly though – and they tend to be louder and more informal than at other colleges. The college's public school reputation comes from its low ratio of state to independent schoolers – only 42 per cent come from state schools. However, Caius is "eager to extend the range of its intake". Caius has one of the best and most competitive boat clubs in the university, but most sports are fairly relaxed. A lively social scene is helped by the fortnightly "bops".

Homerton

Homerton College, Cambridge CB2 2PH
01223 507114   admissions@homerton.cam.ac.uk   www.homerton.cam.ac.uk
Undergraduates: 564 and 553 PGCE

Homerton's origins were in 18th-century London, and it moved to Cambridge in 1894. Although still formally an "Approved Society", its students had been university members for a quarter of a century. The college will continue to specialise in education, including teacher training – through the BA degree and the postgraduate certificate in education (PGCE) courses offered by the Faculty of Education – but has started to offer places for many of the other courses offered by the university at both undergraduate and postgraduate level. All first years have rooms in college in new accommodation blocks. In the second year, accommodation may be in college or in private rented houses, but final-year students can live in if they wish. Due to its history as an institution for Education Studies, the student body is predominantly female and from a state-school background. The college's position, a mile from the city centre in its own large grounds, means that the onus is on Homerton students to take the initiative and get involved in university activities. Many do. Homerton is like the other undergraduate colleges in what it offers, and students can take advantage of Formal Hall, sport (there are on-site playing fields), music and drama.

Hughes Hall

Hughes Hall, Mortimer Road, Cambridge CB1 2EW
01223 334898   admissions@hughes.cam.ac.uk   www.hughes.cam.ac.uk
Undergraduates: 70

Hughes Hall admits mature undergraduates over the age of 21 and affiliated students (who already have a good honours degree from another university). The College is the oldest graduate College in the University, founded in 1885 for the training of graduate women teachers. Since then it has become a lively and cosmopolitan community of 500 mature undergraduate and graduate students studying for nearly all the degrees offered by the University. Accommodation within the College is available for all single undergraduates and affiliated students throughout their course. The college is centrally located, with a new accommodation block and attractive gardens.

Jesus

Jesus College, Cambridge CB5 8BL

01223 339495 undergraduate-admissions@jesus.cam.ac.uk www.jesus.cam.ac.uk

Undergraduates: 489

For those of a sporting inclination Jesus is perhaps the ideal college. Within its spacious grounds there are football, rugby and cricket pitches, as well as three squash courts and no less than ten tennis courts, while the Cam is just a few hundred yards away. With these facilities, it is hardly surprising that sports, in particular rowing, rugby and hockey, rate high on many students' agenda. That said, sporting prowess is far from the whole story. The music society thrives, and has extensive practice facilities. Although Jesus lacks a theatre of its own, the college is active in university drama. On the academic front, the Fellows-to-undergraduates ratio is generous. There is an excellent and stylish new library which, unlike many college libraries, is open 24 hours. Accommodation is another plus. Rooms in college are guaranteed for all first and half of third-year students. All other students live in college houses directly opposite the college. Regardless of where you are placed though, you are likely to have good lodgings, though first years have complained that their cooking facilities are poor. Over half the undergraduates are state educated and the college is keen to encourage more applications from the state sector. The college grounds – particularly The Chimney walkway to the porter's lodge – are attractive. The '60s-built North Court is not, though it is undergoing a multi-million pound refit.

King's

King's College, Cambridge CB2 1ST

01223 331417 undergraduate.admissions@kings.cam.ac.uk www.kings.cam.ac.uk

Undergraduates: 400

The reputation of King's as the most right-on place in the university has become something of an in-joke. Despite its grand surroundings, it has done away with many Cambridge traditions. Gone are gowns, a Fellows' "High Table" at dinner, and superior rooms to reward good results. Formal Halls are banned, and May Balls replaced in favour of politically correct June Events. The college has a 70/30 state-to-independent ratio and is actively involved in an initiative to increase the number of candidates from socially and educationally disadvantaged backgrounds. It is also keen to encourage applications from ethnic minorities and from women. The students' union is active politically. The famous King's Bar is painted a socialist red, with some students insisting on painting on a yellow hammer and sickle for the full effect. The college has fewer undergraduates than the grandeur of its buildings might suggest, one result being that accommodation is guaranteed, either in college or in hostels a few hundred yards away. With the highest ratio of Fellows to undergraduates in Cambridge, it is not surprising that King's has been one of the most academically successful colleges, although it has been in the middle of the Tompkins Table recently. Sport at King's is anything but competitive. The world-famous chapel and choir form the heart of an outstanding music scene.

Lucy Cavendish

Lucy Cavendish College, Cambridge CB3 0BU

01223 330280   lcc-admissions@lists.cam.ac.uk   www.lucy-cav.cam.ac.uk

Undergraduates: 127 (women only)

Lucy Cavendish pitches itself as the college for "smart, inspirational women". Since its creation in 1965, Lucy Cavendish has given hundreds of women over the age of 21 the opportunity to read for Tripos subjects. A number of its students had already started careers and/or families when they decided to enter higher education. The college seeks to offer financial support to those with family responsibilities, though as yet it has no childcare facilities. Accommodation is provided for all who request it, either in the college's three Victorian houses or in its three modern residential blocks. The college's small size enables all students to get to know one another. Plans to increase the intake are unlikely to alter the intimate and informal atmosphere. All the Fellows are women. For subjects not covered by the Fellowship, there is a well-established network of university teachers. One concern amongst students is the lack of a vibrant social atmosphere, meaning student have to venture elsewhere for fun, though the college does have close ties with other mature colleges.

Magdalene

Magdalene College, Cambridge CB3 0AG

01223 332135   admissions@magd.cam.ac.uk   www.magd.cam.ac.uk

Undergraduates: 346

As the last college to admit women (1988), Magdalene has still to throw off a lingering image as home to hordes of public school hearties: 55 per cent of its undergraduates come from the independent sector. However, about half of those undergraduates are now women. That said, the sporty emphasis, on rugby and rowing in particular, is undeniable. The nearby playing fields are shared with St John's and the college has its own Eton fives court. Magdalene's poor academic standing has improved of late. Students are heavily involved in university-wide activities from drama to journalism, as well as sport. Accommodation is provided for all undergraduates, either in college or in one of 21 houses and hostels, "mostly on our doorstep". Magdalene is proud of its river frontage, the longest in the university, which is especially memorable in the summer. One attractive prospect for undergraduates is that they may also be eligible for travel grants from the college, ranging from £50 to £2,000.

New Hall

New Hall, Huntingdon Road, Cambridge CB3 0DF

01223 762229   admissions@newhall.cam.ac.uk   www.newhall.cam.ac.uk

Undergraduates: 360 (women only)

One of three remaining all-women colleges, New Hall enjoys a largely erroneous reputation for feminism and academic underachievement, not helped by a much-publicised whitewash on University Challenge. Founded in 1954 to increase the number

of women in the university, it occupies a modern grey-brick site next door to
Fitzwilliam. Students are split 60:40 between state and independent schools.
The college lays claim to certain paradoxes. While a rent strike early in the 1990s is still
remembered, tradition is far from rejected. The following year saw New Hall's first-ever
May Ball, an event hosted jointly with Sidney Sussex. Its results regularly place the
college near the bottom of the academic league. The college is known for its unusual
split-level bar, but many students choose to socialise elsewhere. Accommodation has
improved in recent years, with new rooms, many en suite, now on offer. Sport is a good
mixture of high-fliers and enthusiasts, with grounds, shared with Fitzwilliam, half a mile
away. The college is particularly proud of its collection of contemporary women's art –
the second largest in the world.

Newnham

Newnham College, Cambridge CB3 9DF
01223 335783   adm@newn.cam.ac.uk   www.newn.cam.ac.uk
Undergraduates: 381 (women only)

Newnham has long had to battle with a blue-stocking image. Its entry in the university
prospectus used to insist that it "is not a nunnery" and that the atmosphere in this all-
women college is no stricter than elsewhere. It even has a "Newnham Nuns" drinking
club to make the point. With about a 50:50 state–independent ratio, the college has also
cast off a reputation for public-school dominance. Newnham is in the perfect location
for humanities students, with the lecture halls and libraries of the Sidgwick Site just
across the road. All of the Fellows are women. Around 95 per cent of students live in for
all three years. This is not to say that ventures into the social, sporting and artistic life of
the university are the exception rather than the rule. Newnham students are anything
but insular. As well as being blessed with the largest and most beautiful lawns in
Cambridge, Newnham has its playing fields on site. The boat club has been notably
successful, while the college competes to a high standard in tennis, cricket and a number
of minority sports.

Pembroke

Pembroke College, Cambridge CB2 1RF
01223 338154   admissions@pem.cam.ac.uk   www.pem.cam.ac.uk
Undergraduates: 400

Another college with a reputation for public school dominance, Pembroke's image is
changing. Today, 54 per cent of its intake come from state schools. Rowing and rugby
still feature prominently however, but with a female population of about 48 per cent,
the heartiness is giving way to a more relaxed atmosphere. Around two thirds of all
undergraduates live in college, including all first years. The rest are housed in fairly
central college hostels, though the standards of these are variable. Academically,
Pembroke is towards the top of the Tompkins Table. Engineering and natural sciences
are thought to have the largest number of undergraduates. The bar is inevitably the
social focal point, but a restriction on advertising means that Pembroke "bops" attract

few students from other colleges. The Pembroke Players generally stage one play a term in the Old Reader, which also doubles as the college cinema, and many Pembroke students are involved in university dramatics. The Old Library is a popular venue for classical concerts. Indeed music is a Pembroke strength. In a city of memorable college gardens, Pembroke's are among the best.

Peterhouse

Peterhouse, Cambridge CB2 1RD
01223 338223   admissions@pet.cam.ac.uk   www.pet.cam.ac.uk
Undergraduates: 251

The oldest and among the smallest of the colleges, Peterhouse has also had to contend with an image problem. But while by no means as reactionary as its critics would have it, Peterhouse is certainly not overly progressive. There is a 2:1 male-female split, while the state–independent ratio is around 56:44. The college's diminutive size inevitably makes for an intimate atmosphere, but this does not mean that its undergraduates never venture beyond the college bar. Peterhouse is known above all as "the history college", and while history is indeed seen as a traditional strength, there are thought to be no more historians than physicists or engineers. Academically, the college is generally a mid-table performer, but has recently fallen down the Tompkins Table. Relations between students and fellows broke down after the cancellation in November 2007 of the 2008 May Ball. Student protests and boycotts of Hall and the college bar followed. The 13th-century candle-lit dining hall provides what by common consent is the best food in the university. Rents are below average, and undergraduates live in for at least two years, the remainder choosing rooms in college hostels, most within ten minutes' walk. The sports grounds are shared with Clare and are about a mile away. The college teams have a less than glittering reputation, not surprisingly, given its size.

Queens'

Queens' College, Cambridge CB3 9ET
01223 335540   admissions@quns.cam.ac.uk   www.quns.cam.ac.uk
Undergraduates: 490

There is a strong case for claiming that Queens' is the most tightly knit college in the university. With all undergraduates housed in college for the full three years, a large and popular bar (open all day) and outstanding facilities, including Cambridge's first college nursery, it is easy to see why. Queens' also has the distinction of attracting an above-average number of applicants. The state–independent ratio is around 53:47, but only 42 per cent of students are female. Though not to all tastes, the mix of architectural styles, ranging from the medieval Old Court to the 1980s Cripps Complex, is as great as any in the university. In addition to three excellent squash courts, the Cripps Complex is also home to Fitzpatrick Hall, a multipurpose venue containing Cambridge's best-equipped college theatre and the hub of Queens' renowned social scene. Friday and Saturday night "bops" are extremely popular. The college has an excellent academic record. Apart from squash, Queens' is not especially sporty. The playing fields (one mile away) are shared with Robinson.

Robinson

Robinson College, Cambridge CB3 9AN

01223 339143   undergraduateadmissions@robinson.cam.ac.uk   www.robinson.cam.ac.uk

Undergraduates: 397

Robinson is the youngest college in Cambridge and admitted its first students in 1979. Its unspectacular architecture has earned it the nickname "the car park". On the other hand, having been built with one eye on the conference trade, rooms are more comfortable than most, and the majority have their own bathrooms and online links to the university computer network. Almost all students live in college or in houses in the attractive gardens. The college is one of the few with rooms adapted for disabled students. Robinson has sometimes been close to the bottom of the academic tables. After a brief surge up the academic tables a couple of years ago, it has fallen back once more. One in four Fellows are women, the second highest proportion in any mixed college. Its youth and admissions policy (36 per cent are from independent schools) ensure that Robinson has one of the more unpretentious atmospheres. The auditorium is the largest of any college and is a popular venue for films, plays and concerts. The college fields (shared with Queens') are home to excellent rugby and hockey sides, and the boat club is also successful. Graduate students will also be well catered for, as the college has started construction work on two new graduate buildings providing state-of-the-art facilities as well as 48 new graduate rooms.

St Catharine's

St Catharine's College, Cambridge CB2 1RL

01223 338319   undergraduate.admissions@caths.cam.ac.uk   www.caths.cam.ac.uk

Undergraduates: 436

Known to everyone as "Catz", this is a medium-sized, 17th-century college standing opposite Corpus Christi on King's Parade. The principal college site, with its distinctive three-sided main court, though small, provides accommodation for all its first and third years. The majority of second years live in flats at St Chad's Court, a ten-minute walk away. Catz was once not considered one of the leading colleges academically. However, its status is much changed. Having been top of the Tompkins Table in 2005, the college has hovered around top spot ever since. It has a reputation as a friendly place. About half of the students are women, and the split between independent and state school pupils is around 47:53. A new library and JCR have improved the facilities considerably, and there is a strong musical tradition. College social life centres on the large bar, which has been likened, among other things, to a ski chalet or sauna. With a reputation for being sporting rather than sporty, Catz is one of the few colleges that regularly puts out three rugby XVs, and also has a good record in football and hockey. The playing fields are a ten-minute walk away and the college boasts its own Astroturf pitch.

St Edmund's College

St Edmund's College, Mount Pleasant, Cambridge CB3 0BN
01223 336250   admissions@st-edmunds.cam.ac.uk   www.st-edmunds.cam.ac.uk
Undergraduates: 100

St Edmund's is primarily a graduate college, with over half its students coming from overseas. Of 350 members, there are 100 mature undergraduates (at least 21 years of age) including affiliated students, who have a prior degree from another university. The College is set in quiet grounds and is conveniently placed to the northwest of the city centre. The College buildings currently house 130 single students, and some of the accommodation has been constructed specifically for students with physical disabilities. In addition there are six maisonettes that are suitable for students with children, and three flats for married couples. A new building with an additional 70 student rooms opened in October 2006. It also includes additional teaching, computing and library facilities. In recent times, St Edmund's students have become regulars in the university sports team, earning an impressive number of "blues" (awarded for competing in a varsity match against Oxford).

St John's

St John's College, Cambridge CB2 1TP
01223 338685   admissions@joh.cam.ac.uk   www.joh.cam.ac.uk
Undergraduates: 550

Second only to Trinity in size and wealth, St John's has an enviable reputation in most fields and is sometimes resented for it. The wealth translates into excellent accommodation in college for almost all undergraduates throughout their three years, as well as book grants and a new 24-hour library. St John's riches ensure the best possible facilities, both academic and social. Its May Ball, a bi-annual end-of-year party was voted the "seventh-best party in the world". First years are housed together, which can hinder integration. St John's has a formidable academic record. English and natural sciences have been recent strengths. A reputation for heartiness persists and the female intake is around 40 per cent, slightly below average. The state–independent split is about 44:56. The boat club has a powerful reputation, but rugby, hockey and cricket are all traditionally strong. In such a large community, however, all should be able to find their own level. Extensive playing fields shared with Magdalene are a few hundred yards away, and the boathouse is extremely good. The college film society organises popular screenings in the Fisher Building, which also contains an art studio and drawing office for architecture and engineering students. Music is dominated by the world-famous choir. Excellent as the facilities are, some students find that the sheer size of St John's can be daunting, and this makes it hard to settle into. Others argue that such a large college provides a diverse atmosphere where "everybody can find their niche".

Selwyn

Selwyn College, Cambridge CB3 9DQ
01223 335896   admissions@sel.cam.ac.uk   www.sel.cam.ac.uk
Undergraduates: 350

Described by one undergraduate as "the least overtly intellectual college", Selwyn has a down-to-earth and relatively unpressured atmosphere. Usually a mid-table performer in the Tompkins Table, its standing has regularly improved in recent years and was placed fourth in 2007. Located behind the Sidgwick Site, it is in an ideal position for humanities students, though engineering is a perceived strength. One of the first colleges to go mixed (1976) now approaching half of Selwyn's undergraduates are female. Its state–independent ratio stands at about 52:48. Accommodation is provided for all students, either in the college itself or in hostels, all of which are close by. Students also claim that the food at hall has improved dramatically following a joint effort with the head chef. The college was a leader in IT provision, being one of the first to provide all college rooms with online connections, and there are two well-stocked computer rooms. As well as the usual college groups, the Music Society is especially well supported. The bar is popular if a little "hotel-like". In sport, the novice boat crews have done well in recent years, as have the hockey and badminton sides, but the emphasis is as much on enjoyment as achievement. The grounds are shared with King's and are three quarters of a mile away.

Sidney Sussex

Sidney Sussex College, Cambridge CB2 3HU
01223 338872   admissions@sid.cam.ac.uk   www.sid.cam.ac.uk
Undergraduates: 340

Students at this small, central college are forever the butt of jokes about Sidney being mistaken for the branch of Sainsbury's over the road. Two other, more serious, aspects of life at Sidney stand out: almost every year its undergraduates raise more for the Rag Appeal than any others, while rents are comfortably the lowest in the university (all students are housed either in college or one of 11 nearby hostels). Exam results have improved in recent years, with Sidney around the top 10 Cambridge colleges for the last two years. The college has recently updated its IT facilities with new computers, and providing every room with internet access. The unpretentious atmosphere is cultivated by the students, 63 per cent of whom are from state schools, and half are women. Despite its size, Sidney has an active social life, boasting one of the few student run bars in the university and maintaining fortnightly "bop" dances like many of the larger colleges. Sports are taken less seriously, with enthusiasm and enjoyment the focus of the students' sporting endeavours. The sports grounds are shared with Christ's and are a 10-minute cycle ride away. Sidney's size means that the college is a tight-knit community. Some students find such insularity suffocating rather than supportive.

Trinity

Trinity College, Cambridge CB2 1TQ
01223 338422   admissions@trin.cam.ac.uk   www.trin.cam.ac.uk
Undergraduates: 657

The legend that you can walk from Oxford to Cambridge without ever leaving Trinity land typifies Cambridge undergraduates' views about the college, even if it is not true. Indeed, the college is almost synonymous with size and wealth – it is the largest and wealthiest of all Cambridge colleges. Founded by Henry VIII, its endowment is almost as big as the other colleges' put together. However, the view that every Trinity student is an arrogant public schoolboy is less easily sustained. That said, it is true that only about 44 per cent of undergraduates come from state schools and around 41 per cent of them are women, one of the lowest proportions in any college. On the other hand, there is little obvious bias in the admissions policy. Being rich, Trinity offers book grants to every student as well as generous travel grants and spacious, reasonably priced rooms in college for all first and third-year students as well as many second years. The accommodation is set to get better for first years with the renovation of the Wolfson building, and the rooms are amongst the cheapest at the university as they are subsidised by the college. The college generally features in the top ten academically. Trinity rarely fails to do well in most sports, with cricket in the forefront. The playing fields are half a mile away.

Trinity Hall

Trinity Hall, Cambridge CB2 1TJ
01223 332535   admissions@trinhall.cam.ac.uk   www.trinhall.cam.ac.uk
Undergraduates: 359

Trinity Hall or "Tit Hall" is one of the oldest and smallest colleges in Cambridge, resulting in a remarkably close community of students. The outstanding performance of its oarsmen has ensured the prevailing view of Trinity Hall as a "boaty" college, but it is also known for its drama, music and bar. The Preston Society is one of the better college drama groups, and stages regular productions. Weekly recitals keep the Music Society busy. The small bar is invariably packed. Not surprisingly, many undergraduates rarely feel the need to go elsewhere for their entertainment, although there has been considerable involvement in the students' union recently. The college is strong academically, despite an unusually low position in the recent tables. Almost half of the undergraduates are women, and in recent years the college has dramatically increased the number of state school students at the college, who now make up 55 per cent of the student body. All first years and approximately half the third years live in college, which is situated on the Backs behind Caius. The remainder take rooms either in two large hostels close to the sports ground, or in college accommodation about five minutes' walk away.

Wolfson

Wolfson College, Barton Road, Cambridge CB3 9BB

01223 335900) ug-admissions@wolfson.cam.ac.uk www.wolfson.cam.ac.uk

Undergraduates: 90

Wolfson, although primarily a graduate college, has about 90 mature or affiliated undergraduates, about 15 per cent of the total college student population. Wolfson is one of three colleges that admit students for the Graduate Course in Medicine. Its life is enriched by the high proportion (about 50 per cent) of overseas students. The relationship between senior and junior members is informal; common rooms, facilities and social activities are equally open to both. The College is situated in west Cambridge, close to the University Library and the arts faculties – or as the students say, nearer to the M11 than the Cam. The main buildings of Wolfson College were built in the 1970s around attractive garden courts. The College has accommodation for most students who want to live in College. There is also some accommodation for couples.

11 University Profiles

The following profiles contain valuable information about each university. Each profile includes some standard information, which is described below:

- the postal address.
- the telephone number for admission enquiries.
- the e-mail or web address for admissions and prospectus enquiries.
- the address of the main university website.
- the address of the students' union website.

The Times **rankings** These figures are taken from the main League Table. See pages 40–45 for this table and the sources of the data. The headings follow those in the main League Table. Please refer to page 36 for a full explanation of this measure.

Undergraduates The first figure is for full-time undergraduates. The second figure (in brackets) gives the number of part-time undergraduates. The figures are for 2006–07, and are the most recent provided by HESA.

Postgraduates The first figure is for full-time postgraduates. The second figure (in brackets) gives the number of part-time postgraduates. The figures are for 2006–07, and are the most recent provided by HESA.

Mature students The percentage of first degree entrants who were 21 or over at the start of their studies. The figures are from 2005–06, and are from HESA.

Overseas students The number of undergraduate overseas students (both EU and non-EU) as a percentage of full-time undergraduates. All figures relate to 2006–07, and are based on HESA data.

Applications per place The number of applicants per place for 2007 as calculated by UCAS.

From state-school sector The number of young full-time undergraduate entrants from state schools or colleges in 2005–06 as a percentage of total young entrants. The figures are published by HESA.

From working-class homes The number of young full-time undergraduate entrants in 2005–06 whose parental occupation is skilled, manual, semi-skilled or unskilled (Social Classes IIIM–V) as a percentage of total young entrants. The figures are published by HESA.

Accommodation The information was obtained through a survey made of all university accommodation services, and their help in compiling this information is gratefully acknowledged.

Undergraduate fees and bursaries A summary of the fees and bursaries being offered in 2008 unless otherwise indicated. This is not comprehensive, so check the details with the individual universities and see chapter 7, *The Cost of Studying*. The information was obtained with the assistance of the individual universities and their help is gratefully acknowledged. Bursary schemes can change every year and must be checked with universities. Universities also have many scholarship schemes, for example, to encourage applicants for particular subjects or from particular areas. Again, it is essential to check university websites for further information. Wherever possible, a specific website address is given.

Comments on campus facilities apply to the universities' own sites only. New universities, in particular, operate "franchised" courses at further education colleges, which are likely to have lower levels of provision. Prospective applicants should check out the library and social facilities before accepting a place away from the parent institution.

Some famous names are missing from our university listings: the Open University, the separate business and medical schools, Birkbeck College and Cranfield University among them. Their omission is no reflection on their quality, simply a function of their particular roles. The *Guide* is based on provision for full-time undergraduates and the factors judged to influence this. The Open University (www.open.ac.uk), though Britain's biggest university, with 75,000 students, is not included because most of the measures used in our listing do not apply to it. As a non-residential, largely part-time institution, Birkbeck College, London (www.bbk.ac.uk), could also not be compared in many key areas. Although Cranfield (www.cranfield.ac.uk) offers undergraduate degrees on two of its campuses, it is primarily for graduate students. Manchester Business School (www.mbs.ac.uk) and London Business School (www.lbs.ac.uk) were excluded for the same reason. Specialist institutions such as the Royal College of Art (www.rca.ac.uk) and St George's Hospital Medical School (sgul.ac.uk) could not fairly be compared with generalist universities. A number of colleges with degree-awarding powers also do not appear because they have yet to be granted university status. However, at the end of the book, we list higher education colleges with their addresses and websites.

The University of London is a federal university composed of a number of institutions. In this profile section, the pages on the University of London (pages 406–7) outline the colleges of the university that are not listed separately in this guide. There are separate entries on the leading undergraduate colleges.

Founded in 1893, the University of Wales is also a federal university. Separate profiles can be found for the leading institutions. Other members are North East Wales Institute; Trinity College, Carmarthen; and the Royal Welsh College of Music and Drama. The University of Cardiff is no longer a member of the University of Wales. See www.wales.ac.uk.

University of Aberdeen

Aberdeen has been marking the early years of its sixth century with a series of ambitious projects. Aided by one the most successful fundraising schemes at any UK university, it has been recruiting high-calibre academics and has transformed the student services. Next on the list is a £23-million sports centre, due to open in 2009, and a futuristic new library planned for the following year.

The university built on a sharply improved performance in the last Research Assessment Exercise, when the number of internationally rated departments shot up from two to ten. The relatively small French department achieved the only 5* rating, but other top grades were divided among the university's three colleges. These successes, which have been accompanied by con-sistently good teaching grades, have brought record applications, although the demand for places has dipped slightly in the last two years.

The university has boosted its external research funds so successfully that it is now in the top 20 in the UK on this measure. Only three subjects were rated less than Highly Satisfactory in the initial round of teaching inspections, and the pattern continued in the audits carried out in the early years of this decade. French, biology, sociology and community-based medicine

have top ratings for both teaching and research.

Female students now outnumber the men, but Aberdeen still considers itself a "balanced" university because roughly half of its students study medicine, science or engineering, half the arts or social sciences. Most are not even admitted to a particular department, allowing them to try out three or four subjects before committing themselves at the end of their first or even second year. The modular system, covering almost 600 first-degree programmes, is so flexible that the majority of students change their intended degree before graduation.

Medicine, law and divinity head Aberdeen's traditional strengths – the university established the English-speaking world's first chair in medicine and has produced its share of advances since. The Institute of Medical Sciences, which has brought together all Aberdeen's work in this area, boasts state-of-the-art laboratory facilities. Another £16.5 million is being invested on the same site in a teaching and learning centre for anatomy and clinical skills.

Biological sciences have developed considerably in recent years, becoming second only to the social sciences in terms of size. Biomedicine is particularly strong, and the university's links with the oil industry show in geology's high reputation.

King's College
Aberdeen AB24 3FX
01224 272090/91 (admissions)
sras@abdn.ac.uk
www.abdn.ac.uk
www.ausa.org.uk

The Times Rankings
Overall Ranking: 26

Student satisfaction:	=8	(80%)
Research quality:	=43	(4.0)
Entry standards:	36	(350)
Student–staff ratio:	16	(13.5)
Services & facilities/student:	36	(£1,168)
Expected completion rate:	79	(78.8%)
Good honours:	25	(69.7%)
Graduate prospects:	16	(76.2%)

The university is also the main centre for agriculture in Scotland and part of a new European network for the subject.

Today's university is a fusion of two ancient institutions which came together in 1860. With King's College dating back to 1495 and Marischal College following almost a century later, Aberdeen likes to boast that for 250 years it had as many universities as the whole of England. The original King's College buildings are the focal point of an appealing campus, complete with cobbled main street and some sturdily handsome Georgian buildings, about a mile from the city centre. Medicine is at Foresterhill, a 20-minute walk away, adjoining the Aberdeen Royal Infirmary. Buses link the two sites with the Hillhead residential complex, and there is a free late-night service. The Aberdeen arm of Northern College has now joined the fold and moved to the main campus, restoring the university's original involvement in teacher training, and forming its fifth faculty. More than a third of all students come from the north of Scotland, but taking one in ten from outside Britain ensures a cosmopolitan atmosphere. Students from England and the 120 nationalities from further afield are generally prepared for Aberdeen's remote location and, although the winters are long, the climate is warmer than the uninitiated might expect. As the energy capital of Europe, transport links are good. Students find the city lively and welcoming but expensive, although its prosperity does provide a good selection of part-time jobs from the JobLink service.

Student facilities are good: there an NHS medical practice on campus and the new students' centre – The Hub – brings together dining and retail outlets with support services, including the Students' Association and Accommodation Office. There is also a city centre bar and first-class sports facilities, which will be improved still further with the opening of the new sports centre, part-funded by Aberdeen City Council and Sports Scotland. The ICT network has over 1,000 computers for student use. The university's residential stock has been growing and all new undergraduates are guaranteed a place.

Undergraduate Fees and Bursaries
- Scottish-domiciled and EU students: no fees payable.
- Non-Scottish UK-domiciled student fees: £1,775 a year (£2,825 medicine).
- International student fees: £9,000–£11,250; £21,500 (clinical medicine)
- Scholarships based on circumstances or by competition. For full details see the university's website: www.abdn.ac.uk/sras/undergraduate/ bursaries_scholarships.shtml

Students

Undergraduates:	8,865	(1,290)
Postgraduates:	2,100	(1,770)
Mature students:	15.6%	
Overseas students:	12.9%	
Applications per place:	5.8	
From state-sector schools:	84.0%	
From working-class homes:	25.7%	

For detailed information about fees, grants and bursaries and how they work, see chapter 7.

Accommodation

Number of places and costs refer to 2008–09
University-provided places: about 2,544
Percentage catered: 30%
Catered costs: £116–£137 a week (38 weeks).
Self-catered costs: £72–£113 a week (38–40 weeks).
First-year students are guaranteed accommodation.
International students: as above.
Contact: studentaccomm@abdn.ac.uk

University of Abertay

Abertay doubled in size during the 1990s and has grown further since up-front tuition fees were abolished for Scottish students. There are now more than 5,500 students, mainly in Dundee but with several hundred in locations as far afield as Malaysia, Singapore and India. The former central institution has enjoyed a series of good teaching scores, but a projected dropout rate of 22 per cent is higher than the UK average for the courses on offer, taking into account students' entry qualifications. Almost a quarter of the undergraduates come from socially deprived areas and practically all attended state schools. More than a third come from working-class homes.

The former Dundee Institute of Technology had already established its academic credentials when university status arrived in 1994, with teaching in economics rated more highly than in some of Scotland's elite universities. Subsequent assessments were solid, without living up to that early promise, but economics, engineering and environmental sciences were given the highest possible rating in later inspections. More recently, two of the first four degree accreditations awarded by Skillset, the Government-sponsored training council for the creative industries, went to Abertay courses.

Research is not being ignored. Abertay is proud of its record in establishing a series of specialist centres, in areas as diverse as wood technology, urban water systems and bioinformatics. The university opened Europe's first research centre dedicated to computer games and digital entertainment and a major environmental science centre. The last research assessments showed a big improvement on 1996, doubling the average score, although only environmental sciences (with the best rating in Scotland) reached any of the top three grades.

Abertay plays to its strengths with a limited range of courses, and is not shy about its achievements. Among them is a high-tech approach that permeates all four of the university's schools, while spending on libraries and computers is among the highest per student in Britain, providing one computer for every four students.

Based mainly in the centre of Dundee, all the university's buildings are within 15 minutes' walk of each other. The imposing Dudhope Castle is a conference and events venue, but the other buildings are more modern and functional. New facilities are gradually being added: the £8-million library is also the university's largest IT resource, and was opened by the Queen. A further £6 million was spent on the student centre, which opened in 2005. A 500-bed student village is next on the list.

Entrance requirements have been rising,

Bell Street
Dundee DD1 1HG
01382 308080
sro@abertay.ac.uk
www.abertay.ac.uk
www.abertaystudents.com

The Times Rankings
Overall Ranking: 100

Student satisfaction:	–	(–)
Research quality:	=99	(0.7)
Entry standards:	=77	(264)
Student–staff ratio:	96	(20.3
Services & facilities/student:	9	(£1,671)
Expected completion rate:	112	(64.0%)
Good honours:	99	(47.6%)
Graduate prospects:	108	(51.4%)

although for most courses they are still modest. Degrees are predominantly vocational, with more subjects being added every year. Forensic science, forensic psychobiology, computer arts and sports coaching and development have been followed recently by the likes of food and consumer sciences, creative sound production, and ethical hacking and countermeasures. All courses can be taken on a part-time basis, and the aim is for new programmes to offer students the chance to spend at least 30 per cent of their time in industry.

The university's revamped modular degree scheme means that undergraduates take a maximum of eight modules a year. First-year students are assessed by coursework alone in the first semester, with examinations at the end of the year. Students can complete a Certificate of Higher Education after one year, a diploma after two, an ordinary degree after three, or honours in four years. Abertay is piloting a new problem-based learning approach among first-year students focusing on real-world issues and learning by doing rather than sitting in lectures.

Dundee has a large student population and is improving as a youth centre where the cost of living is modest. Relatively low student numbers translate into a moderate social scene, particularly at weekends. More than 30 per cent of the undergraduates are over 21 on entry, many living locally. This lifts the pressure on university-owned beds sufficiently to allow all first years to be guaranteed accommodation.

Undergraduate Fees and Bursaries

Scottish-domiciled and EU students: no fees payable.
- Non-Scottish UK-domiciled student fees: £1,775 a year.
- International student fees: £5,750–£7,750
- Scholarships based on circumstances or by competition. For full details see the university's website: www.abertay.ac.uk

Students

Undergraduates:	3,185	(315)
Postgraduates:	360	(320)
Mature students:	31.0%	
Overseas students:	17.4%	
Applications per place:	4.6	
From state-sector schools:	97.2%	
From working-class homes:	37.2%	

For detailed information about fees, grants and bursaries and how they work, see chapter 7.

Accommodation

Number of places and costs refer to 2008–09
University-provided places: 650
Percentage catered: 0%
Self-catered costs: £52.00–£100.66 a week (36 or 38 weeks).
New first years are given priority provided conditions are met. Some residential restrictions.
International students: prioritised by distance from Dundee.
Contact: accommo@abertay.ac.uk

Aberystwyth University

The oldest of the Welsh universities, Aberystwyth has changed its title to emphasise its independence. Although its degrees will still come from the University of Wales, the title of Aberystwyth University will make its status clear, especially for overseas applicants. Aber has long prided itself on a modern outlook: the modular degree system has been running since 1993, covering academic and vocational courses, and the principle of flexibility was established long before that. Uniquely in the UK, every student is offered the opportunity of a year's work experience in commerce, industry or the public sector, either at home or abroad. Students who have taken advantage of the scheme have achieved better than average degrees and enhanced their employment prospects. The mix served Aberystwyth well in the national student satisfaction survey, winning it a place in the top ten and making it the clear leader in Wales. Geography and environmental science, history and archaeology, modern languages and biology all produced outstanding results.

Aber is always heavily oversubscribed even though the number of places has increased. Almost a third of the students are from Wales. An agreement to collaborate with Bangor University in a range of subjects, from business to science,

emphasises teaching in Welsh. An attractive seaside location does the university no harm when the applications season comes around, although the demand for places was down at the start of 2008, in common with other Welsh universities.

The college has expanded significantly in recent years, with a new School of Management and Business as well as a department of Sports and Exercise Science among the additions. A £3.6-million centre for theatre, film and television studies, and a purpose-built sports and exercise science centre are among the latest developments on the Penglais campus, which overlooks the town. A new building for the highly rated International Politics Department opened in 2006 and a £10-million Visualisation Centre followed in 2007, providing virtual reality facilities for academic and industrial partnerships.

More than 90 per cent of the undergraduates come from state schools or colleges – a far higher proportion than the mix of subjects would imply – but less than 30 per cent come from working-class homes and only about half that number hail from areas that send few students to higher education. However, the dropout rate of around 10 per cent is the lowest at any university in Wales.

The Institute of Rural Sciences allows Aber to claim the widest range of land-related courses in the UK. The institute shares the Llanbadarn campus with

---

Old College
King Street,
Aberystwyth, Ceredigion SY23 2AX
01970 622021 (admissions)
ug-admissions@
  aber.ac.uk
www.aber.ac.uk
www.aberguild.co.uk

The Times Rankings
Overall Ranking: 43

Student satisfaction:	=6	(81%)
Research quality:	=43	(4.0)
Entry standards:	52	(296)
Student–staff ratio:	=75	(19.0)
Services & facilities/student:	66	(£997)
Expected completion rate:	30	(89.8%)
Good honours:	46	(61.8%)
Graduate prospects:	97	(56.2%)

information and library studies and a further education college. Teaching ratings were impressive, especially in the arts and social sciences. Offers of places are made on the basis of the UCAS tariff, which not only recognises general studies as full A or AS levels, but also gives credit for Key Skills qualifications. Celtic studies and politics were rated internationally outstanding in the latest research assessments, while theatre, film and television studies reached the next rung of the ladder. Criminology was added to the degree portfolio in 2006 and psychology has followed.

Entrance scholarships and bursaries are available in a range of subjects, even though Welsh students have been spared the full impact of top-up fees. Aber boasts one of higher education's most informative websites and also publishes a 12-page guide for parents. There is 24-hour access to the computer network, and the four university libraries are complemented by the National Library of Wales.

The town of Aberystwyth is compact and travel to other parts of the UK slow, so applicants should be sure that they will be happy to spend three years or more in a tight-knit community. The students' guild is the largest entertainment venue in the region and the arts centre has been extended at a cost of £3.5 million. The highly professional Alternative Prospectus, produced by students, has stopped

describing the seaside town of 25,000 people as the "Welsh California", but a recent survey rated it students' favourite university town in the UK. There is plenty of out-of-season accommodation to supplement the university's 3,700 places, all of which are now online. Sports facilities are good for the size of institution, with 50 acres of pitches, a newly refurbished swimming pool, a climbing wall and specialist outdoor facilities for water sports.

Undergraduate Fees and Bursaries

- Welsh-domiciled student fees: £3,145, with grant of up to £1,890
- Non-Welsh UK domiciled and EU student fees: £3,145
- International student fees: £8,100–£10,275
- Welsh National Bursary for all UK students, means-tested with maximum of £310.
- Scholarships based on circumstances or by competition. For full details see the university's website: www.aber.ac.uk/en/scholarships/

Students

Undergraduates:	6,155	(2,105)
Postgraduates:	830	(1,670)
Mature students:	8.5%	
Overseas students:	8.0%	
Applications per place:	4.3	
From state-sector schools:	92.6%	
From working-class homes:	27.6%	

For detailed information about fees, grants and bursaries and how they work, see chapter 7.

Accommodation

Number of places and costs refer to 2007–08
University-provided places: more than 3,800
Percentage catered: 27%
Catered costs: £80.75–£92.50 a week (30 weeks).
Self-catered costs: £62.00–£85.25 a week (36 weeks).
First years are guaranteed accommodation if they fulfill requirements.
International students: housing guaranteed.
Contact: www.aber.ac.uk/residential
accommodation@aber.ac.uk

Anglia Ruskin University

The last university to retain the polytechnic title discarded it in 2005 to avoid confusion among employers and overseas applicants. The former APU took the name of John Ruskin, who founded the Cambridge art school that evolved into the university. Campus developments have continued apace since the change. A new student centre on the larger of the university's two main sites, in Chelmsford, houses support services as well as the normal union facilities, while the music and arts faculty building in Cambridge has new and enhanced teaching and practice facilities.

The university has also acquired the former Homerton College School of Health Studies in Cambridge, after a long period of partnership. A new Institute of Health and Social Care, in Chelmsford, opened in 2007 with bespoke counselling rooms, simulated hospital wards, operating theatres, and a complementary medicine suite. A £15-million faculty building, which will include a mock courtroom for law students, follows in September 2008. The 22-acre Rivermead campus also boasts an impressive business school and a new sports hall. The total construction bill is expected to reach £55 million.

The region's first polytechnic was an amalgamation of two well-established higher education colleges, but the twin bases in Chelmsford and Cambridge remain distinct. The two very different locations are far enough apart to limit contact, although electronic networking and a central administration mean that key academic facilities are available throughout the university.

The university has more than 20,000 full and part-time students who are taught primarily on the two main campuses, but also through a network of ten regional partners. Anglia Ruskin has recently signed up to deliver higher-education courses in Peterborough, Harlow and King's Lynn in partnership with local further education colleges.

East Anglia has always lagged behind other parts of England for participation in higher education and, although the university has continued to grow, it has sometimes struggled to fill its places. Applications were down for the first year of top-up fees, but bounced back spectacularly in 2007, with a 23 per cent increase, and remained healthy in 2008. Nearly all the students attended state schools or colleges and more than a third are from working-class homes.

Most teaching ratings were solid, rather than spectacular, although there was an improvement in the latter years of assessment. There were good reports, under the new healthcare assessments, for nursing and midwifery and allied health

---

Rivermead Campus: Bishop Hall Lane, Chelmsford, Essex CM1 1SQ
Cambridge Campus: East Road, Cambridge CB1 1PT
0845 271 3333 (enquiries)
answers@anglia.ac.uk
www.anglia.ac.uk
www.angliastudent. com

The Times Rankings
Overall Ranking: 106

Student satisfaction:	=93	(70%)
Research quality:	=107	(0.5)
Entry standards:	=85	(256)
Student–staff ratio:	=53	(17.1)
Services & facilities/student:	108	(£647)
Expected completion rate:	111	(64.8%)
Good honours:	79	(52.3%)
Graduate prospects:	=77	(60.6%)

professions. The last research grades also showed improvement, but only English made the top three categories, and only one university submitted a lower proportion of academics for assessment. Management, biological sciences and social work were the best performers in the latest national student satisfaction survey. The introduction of a benchmarking system to take account of the mix of subjects at each university saw Anglia Ruskin tumble down *The Times* League Table and it has made only a marginal recovery.

The university has a strongly international outlook, providing a large number of exchange opportunities in Malaysia and China, as well as Europe and the United States. Each undergraduate has an adviser to help compile a degree package which looks at the chosen subject from different points of view to maximise future job prospects. Employers play a part in planning courses which are integrated into a modular system which extends from degree level to professional programmes, including a modest selection of vocational two-year Foundation degrees. The Business School, for example, has developed a work-based course with Barclays Bank, where the students are sponsored and salaried for all three years.

The social scene varies between the two campuses. Cambridge students have to shrug off the tag of attending the lesser institution. There is limited collaboration with Cambridge University, for example on a new cricket academy and a base for Anglia Ruskin's rowing club. Some students find Chelmsford dull, but the social scene is said to be improving. Neither base is far from London by train.

Undergraduate Fees and Bursaries

- Fees for UK/EU students: £3,145
- International student fees: £9,300–£10,925
- Bursary on full grant: £310
- The university does not award bursaries for students on partial maintenance grants.
- Scholarships based on circumstances or by competition. For full details see the university's website: www.anglia.ac.uk/ruskin/en/home/study/ukstudents/fees/fees_2008/undergraduate_ft/scholarships.html

Students		
Undergraduates:	9,265	(7,590)
Postgraduates:	765	(2,680)
Mature students:	44.8%	
Overseas students:	7.9%	
Applications per place:	4.2	
From state-sector schools:	98.1%	
From working-class homes:	34.5%	

For detailed information about fees, grants and bursaries and how they work, see chapter 7.

Accommodation

Number of places and costs refer to 2008–09
University-provided places: Cambridge, 794 plus 182 nomination rooms; Chelmsford, 511
Percentage catered: 0%
Self-catered costs: Cambridge: £62.10–£120.00; Chelmsford: £76.59–£83.46 a week.
Most first years are accommodated (residential restriction at Cambridge campus only).
International students: conditions apply.
Contact : cambaccom@anglia.ac.uk
essexaccom@anglia.ac.uk

Aston University

Aston has always gloried in its role as a tight-knit, vocational, urban university, which has swum against the tide of British higher education over the past decade. Small and lively, set in the heart of Birmingham, it has remained resolutely specialist in science and technology, business and languages, concentrating on the sandwich degrees which have served its graduates so well in the employment market. The mix helped Aston break into the top 20 in *The Times* table over the last three years, although it has slipped back this year, mainly due to less favourable staffing levels and lower spending on student facilities.

Despite some modest growth recently, the university still has little more than 7,000 undergraduates. This used to make for a bumpy ride financially, with the funding council having to provide special help several times to avoid damaging budget cuts. But now, with healthy funding from industry and commerce, Aston is able to invest in its future, boosting staffing in business, engineering and languages, and developing the campus. Applications were near the national average at the start of 2007, following strong growth in the previous year. Even though entry grades have been rising, the general trend has been upwards for most of the decade.

There were much-improved research grades in the last assessment exercise, with four of the five subject areas judged to be producing work of international quality. Business and management, languages and European studies, general engineering and neurosciences all achieved top scores. Academic restructuring, designed mainly to break down barriers between departments, has since reduced the number of schools to four.

As befits a one-time college of advanced technology, Aston's strengths are on the science side, although the business school is highly rated and accounts for almost half of the students. A £20-million extension to the business school has seen an increase in staff from 80 to over 120. After a bruising introduction to the teaching quality assessments, ratings improved considerably, with maximum points for pharmacy, business and management and good scores for optometry and biological sciences.

There is a wide range of combined honours programmes for those who prefer not to specialise. Four out of five Aston graduates go straight into jobs, spurning the postgraduate courses and training programmes which have become the first port of call for many of their counterparts in the old universities. Often they are returning to the scene of work placements, which have become the norm for 70 per cent of Aston's undergraduates.

Aston Triangle
Birmingham B4 7ET
0121 204 4674 (general
  admissions)
admissions@aston.ac.uk
www.aston.ac.uk
www.astonguild.org.uk

The Times Rankings
Overall Ranking: 28

Student satisfaction:	=26	(76%)
Research quality:	=47	(3.9)
Entry standards:	35	(351)
Student–staff ratio:	=56	(17.4)
Services & facilities/student:	10	(£1,607)
Expected completion rate:	33	(88.4%)
Good honours:	38	(65.8%)
Graduate prospects:	=14	(76.4%)

The university is flexible about entry requirements for mature students, but average entry grades for school-leavers have now reached 350 points and the rising demand for places is likely to prolong the trend. The dropout rate has been improving and is now well below the 12 per cent national average for Aston's subjects. Socially, the intake is diverse, with more than a third of the undergraduates coming from working-class homes.

The 40-acre campus, a ten-minute walk from the centre of Birmingham, is barely recognisable from the university's early days. Carefully landscaped, it has benefited from a £16-million building programme, which has brought all Aston's residential and academic accommodation onto the same site. Almost half of the undergraduates live there, with places guaranteed for first years. New developments in sporting facilities have included the addition of a new gymnasium, while an £8-million Academy of Life Sciences merges research with private practice in eye care and brain imaging. Another £4 million has been spent upgrading the IT and computing network.

Aston was among the pioneers of "smart cards", giving students access to university facilities and enabling them to make purchases on campus, once they have money in their accounts. There is plenty of opportunity to use them in a buzzing social scene, which most students find to their taste. The guild of students has always been very active, both socially and politically.

Undergraduate Fees and Bursaries

- Fees for UK/EU students: £3,145
- International student fees: £9,500–£11,570
- Bursary on full grant: £800
- Bursaries on partial grant: household income up to £38K: sliding scale £640–£160.
- Scholarships based on circumstances or by competition. For full details see the university's website: www.aston.ac.uk/fees

Students

Undergraduates:	6,700	(330)
Postgraduates:	1,315	(1,215)
Mature students:	7.6%	
Overseas students:	13.8%	
Applications per place:	6.4	
From state-sector schools:	89.0%	
From working-class homes:	35.2%	

For detailed information about fees, grants and bursaries and how they work, see chapter 7.

Accommodation

Number of places and costs refer to 2008–09

University-provided places: 2,117

Percentage catered: 0%

Self-catered accommodation: £65.00 (standard) – £101.11 (en suite) a week.

First years are guaranteed accommodation if they fulfil requirements and apply by the deadline.

International fee-paying students: as above.

Contact: accom@aston.ac.uk;

www.aston.ac.uk/accommodation

Bangor University

Bangor is another part of the University of Wales to assert its independence, taking the title of Bangor University while continuing to award the federal university's degrees. It has recorded strong performances in the first three National Student Satisfaction surveys. While Bangor slipped slightly in 2007, it still finished only just outside the top 30 universities in the UK.

Students in sports science, performing arts, modern languages and finance and accounting were the most satisfied. The "small and friendly" nature of the university and the city no doubt helped. Bangor's community focus dates back to a 19th-century campaign which saw local quarrymen putting part of their weekly wages towards the establishment of a college. The School of Lifelong Learning continues the tradition with courses across North Wales, but the university has also built a worldwide reputation in areas such as environmental studies and ocean sciences.

The last research assessments were an improvement on 1996, although only psychology and Welsh were rated internationally outstanding. Three quarters of the researchers were placed in the top three categories of seven. Teaching assessments were more impressive, with half of the subjects rated as excellent. As well as traditional strengths, such as biology and forestry, the list includes social policy, placing Bangor at 23 in *The Times* ranking for the subject. There is a high proportion of small-group teaching and tutorials, as well as one of Britain's largest peer guiding schemes, which sees senior students mentoring new arrivals.

Bangor merged with a nearby teacher training college, Colleg Normal, in 1996, and that site is now part of the university. All schools are within walking distance of each other, apart from ocean sciences, which is two miles away in Menai Bridge. The university estate is being redeveloped, with the addition of a £5-million environmental sciences building, while a £3.5-million Cancer Research Institute is attracting specialists of international repute.

An academic reorganisation has grouped the 26 academic schools into 6 colleges: arts and humanities; business, social sciences and law; education and lifelong learning; natural sciences; health and behavioural sciences; and physical and applied sciences. A combination of private funds and a £5-million European grant has been used to establish a new Management Development Centre on a waterfront site. A new National Institute for Excellence in the Creative Industries has been established, offering a variety of new

Bangor
Gwynedd LL57 2DG
01248 382018
admissions@bangor.ac.uk
www.bangor.ac.uk
www.undeb.bangor.ac.uk

The Times Rankings
Overall Ranking: 51

Student satisfaction:	=18	(77%)
Research quality:	=47	(3.9)
Entry standards:	61	(279)
Student–staff ratio:	=69	(18.4)
Services & facilities/student:	56	(£1,023)
Expected completion rate:	=86	(77.0%)
Good honours:	68	(55.6%)
Graduate prospects:	=51	(65.9%)

courses including film studies, creative studies with law, media studies, English with publishing, and creative technologies. Other developments include new courses in cancer biology, electronics, information and communications technology, law with media studies, English with songwriting, and 4-year Masters degrees in marine science and environmental science.

Based little more than a stone's throw from Snowdonia with its attractions for sports enthusiasts, Bangor is an expanding centre for Welsh-medium teaching. As well as a single honours degree in Welsh, some courses are only available in Welsh while others are offered in either English or Welsh. Although a majority of students come from outside Wales – there is a strong link with Ireland, for example – more than 10 per cent of the students speak the language and one of the seven halls of residence is Welsh-speaking. The university also has a flourishing international exchange programme, with some unusual partner institutions: Poland and Italy are favourite destinations for linguistics students, while biologists tend to head for Sweden or Norway.

Bangor does better than most traditional universities when judged against access benchmarks. More than nine out of ten students come from state schools or colleges, and one in three come from working-class homes. Over £2.5 million has gone into a new bursary scheme, offering students from low-income families up to £1,000 a year on some courses, as well as 40 merit scholarships of £3,000 for high-fliers. Applications have been increasing each year but, as in the rest of Wales, there was a dip at the official deadline for courses beginning in 2008.

There is a strong focus on student support – the pioneering dyslexia unit, for example, offering individual and group support throughout students' courses. New investment in residential accommodation means that all first-year students can be offered places. Bangor is also one of the most cost-effective places in which to study – one survey made it the fourth-cheapest university in the UK.

Undergraduate Fees and Bursaries

- Welsh-domiciled student fees: £3,145, with grant of up to £1,890
- Non-Welsh UK domiciled and EU student fees: £3,145
- International student fees: £8,500–£9,500
- Welsh National Bursary for all UK students, means-tested with maximum of £310.
- Bursary scheme available.
- Scholarships based on circumstances or by competition.For full details see the university's website: www.bangor.ac.uk/studyatbangor/bursary

Students

Undergraduates:	6,100	(2,400)
Postgraduates:	1,205	(825)
Mature students:	22.6%	
Overseas students:	6.0%	
Applications per place:	4.5	
From state-sector schools:	93.9%	
From working-class homes:	32.7%	

For detailed information about fees, grants and bursaries and how they work, see chapter 7.

Accommodation

Number of places and costs refer to 2007–08
University-provided places: 1,913
Percentage catered: 16%
Catered costs: £86.87–£90.37 a week (31 weeks).
Self-catered costs:£53.62–£79.80 a week (31–39-weeks).
All first-year students are guaranteed places.
International students: as above.
Contact: halls@bangor.ac.uk

University of Bath

Bath is in the throes of a £70-million "campus enhancement plan" and the next few years will see the addition of further facilities for science, extra student accommodation and more teaching space. But, for the moment, it remains a relatively small university with 9,000 undergraduates. The additional places will cater to some degree for the burgeoning demand at an institution that enjoys both an attractive location and a high academic reputation. Although applications were down by more than the national average in 2008, they had shot up by almost 16 per cent a year earlier, continuing a trend that lasted throughout a period of rising entrance requirements. Bath's healthy showing in league tables may be one reason for its popularity – it has never been out of the top 20 in *The Times* League Table.

Students like the "small and friendly" image the university projects, and one of the lowest dropout rates in Britain suggests that they are well supported. The library is open 24 hours a day, seven days a week. Few can fail to be impressed by the magnificence of the city's architecture. The modern campus on the edge of Bath, with some undistinguished buildings dating from its origins as a technological university in the 1960s, offers an unfortunate contrast. But the 200-acre site has pleasant grounds and is functional, with academic, recreational and residential facilities in close proximity. New teaching facilities for chemistry were added in 2003, followed by a £2.8-million physics facility, and 468 new study bedrooms have also been added recently. More lecture theatres and computer laboratories have eased the pressure on teaching space.

The university has abandoned plans for a campus in Swindon and has withdrawn from a small site there, which catered for 300 full and part-time students, bringing higher education to one of the few remaining counties without a university. Research is Bath's greatest strength, with applied mathematics, mechanical engineering and pharmacy all rated internationally outstanding in the last assessments. Teaching assessments confirmed the university's excellence in science and technology, with biosciences, physics, mathematics and statistics all achieving maximum points. Arts and social science ratings were mixed, but there were successes in management economics and politics, while European languages and architecture scored well in the 2007 national student satisfaction survey.

The latest academic developments have seen the establishment of a School for Health and an Institute for Contemporary

Claverton Down
Bath BA2 7AY
01225 386959 (admissions)
admissions@bath.ac.uk
www.bath.ac.uk
www.bathstudent.com

Edinburgh
Belfast
London
Cardiff BATH

The Times Rankings
Overall Ranking: 15

Student satisfaction:	=39	(75%)
Research quality:	=12	(5.2)
Entry standards:	11	(428)
Student–staff ratio:	=49	(16.6)
Services & facilities/student:	28	(£1,291)
Expected completion rate:	9	(95.3%)
Good honours:	10	(77.3%)
Graduate prospects:	7	(81.0%)

Interdisciplinary Arts, both engaged in teaching as well as research. Most courses throughout the university have a practical element, and assessors have praised the university for the work placements it offers. The majority of students take sandwich courses or include a period of study abroad, which helps to produce consistently outstanding graduate employment figures.

The university's other great claim to fame lies in its sports facilities, which were already among the best in Britain before the addition of a £30-million training village, funded with Lottery money. The campus acquired a 50-metre swimming pool by this route, to which it has added an indoor running track, a new multipurpose sports hall, eight indoor tennis courts, an indoor jumps and throws hall, air pistol and fencing sale, a judo dojo and even a simulated bobsleigh and skeleton start area. There is a strong tradition in competitive sports: the university pioneered sports scholarships more than 20 years ago, and they are now worth up to £12,000 a year for performers of international calibre. There are also courses to do the facilities justice, as recognised in a near-perfect score for teaching quality in sport and leisure. Bath claims that its students have access to more free sports facilities than any other university in Britain, from the swimming pools to badminton, squash and tennis courts to grass and astroturf pitches.

Students – nearly a quarter of whom were educated at independent schools – may find the campus quiet at weekends and struggle to afford some of Bath's attractions, but they value its location. When they tire of the beauty of Bath, the nightlife of Bristol is only a few minutes away. The two cities have a combined student population of more than 50,000. The students' union is active and the university has been upgrading its student support services, for example through the introduction of a new virtual learning environment and the provision of laptops adapted for use by students with disabilities. More than nine out of ten students surveyed say they would recommend the university to family and friends.

Undergraduate Fees and Bursaries

- Fees for UK/EU students: £3,145
- International student fees: £10,300–£13,150
- Bursary on full grant: £1,200
- Bursaries on partial grant: household income up to £50K: sliding scale £900–£300.
- Scholarships based on circumstances or by competition. For full details see the university's website: www.bath.ac.uk/students/scholarships

Students

Undergraduates:	8,470	(560)
Postgraduates:	1,550	(3,675)
Mature students:	7.7%	
Overseas students:	19.7%	
Applications per place:	7.3	
From state-sector schools:	75.9%	
From working-class homes:	18.7%	

For detailed information about fees, grants and bursaries and how they work, see chapter 7.

Accommodation

Number of places and costs refer to 2008–09
University-provided places: 3,302
Percentage catered: 0%
Self-catered cost:£77.50–£115.50 a week.
First years guaranteed accommodation if conditions are met, and applications received by 3 September.
International students: as above. Exchange students are housed on a reciprocal basis.
Contact:
www.bath.ac.uk/accommodation/enquiry/

Bath Spa University

Bath Spa is one of the growing number of new "teaching-led" universities created under Government reforms. But it is far from new in other respects and not without research strengths. Its Newton Park headquarters, four miles outside the World Heritage city of Bath, is in grounds landscaped by Capability Brown in the 18th century, with a handsome Georgian manor house as its centrepiece and owned by the Prince of Wales. A second campus, housing the Bath School of Art and Design, boasts one of the city's famous Georgian crescents, although this is being sold to finance a purpose-built site. The history of the predecessor colleges goes back 150 years, with some famous alumni, including Body Shop founder Anita Roddick and Turner Prize winner Sir Howard Hodgkin.

The new university has been undertaking its biggest-ever building programme to take advantage of a doubling in the number of applications over the past five years. Although applications were down by marginally more than the national average at the start of 2008, the 26 per cent increase a year earlier was one of the biggest rises at any UK university. With around 7,000 students, it is still comparatively small, but the range of courses and the number of places have been growing steadily. At Newton Park, the base for all students except those taking art and design subjects, the students' union has practically doubled in size, a new library has added about 120 workstations and £4.8 million has been spent on an impressive university theatre with a 200-seat auditorium. A new creative writing centre is housed in the 14th-century gatehouse, bringing it into student use for the first time.

Bath Spa has been awarding its own degrees since 1992 – much longer than some of the other new arrivals on the university scene. Subjects assessed for teaching quality averaged 22 points out of 24 and results in the first three National Student Surveys have been good. The university has been designated a national centre for excellence in teaching and learning in the creative industries, bringing significant investment in the Schools of Music and Performing Arts, English and Creative Studies, and Art and Design. English and Study of Religions did well in the last research assessments, when the 43 per cent of academics entered for the exercise represented a much larger proportion than at many of the former polytechnics. About a third of the students are postgraduates. The university has now applied for the power to award its own research degrees.

Newton Park
Newton St Loe
Bath BA2 9BN
01225 875875
enquiries@bathspa.ac.uk
www.bathspa.ac.uk/
   prospectus/order
www.bathspasu.co.uk

The Times Rankings		
Overall Ranking: 72		
Student satisfaction:	=73	(72%)
Research quality:	=66	(1.5)
Entry standards:	=64	(274)
Student–staff ratio:	=79	(19.5)
Services & facilities/student:	111	(£563)
Expected completion rate:	42	(85.7%)
Good honours:	41	(64.7%)
Graduate prospects:	=102	(55.2%)

Despite a setting that would seem to be a magnet for applicants from independent schools, 95 per cent of the home intake is state-educated and more than a quarter are from working-class homes. Two thirds of the students are female, reflecting the arts and social science bias in the curriculum, and 25 per cent are over 25. The latest projected dropout rate, of less than 12 per cent, is significantly better than the national average for the university's courses and entry grades. There are about 500 overseas students from a variety of countries.

The university has a number of partner further education colleges in the region, where a range of two-year Foundation degrees are delivered, the latest of which include heritage management, arts management, theatre production, counselling and international marketing and management. Many students then progress to the university campuses to complete an honours degree. About 85 per cent of first years attending Bath Spa itself are offered hall places. Students like the "small and friendly" atmosphere, which the university is anxious to retain in spite of the temptation to go for more substantial growth. Sports facilities are not extensive, but the countryside – on and off campus – is a major draw.

Undergraduate Fees and Bursaries

- Fees for UK/EU students: £3,145
- International student fees: £9,000–£9,580
- Bursary on full grant: £1,128
- Bursaries on partial grant: household income up to £38.3K: sliding scale £1,128–£100.
- Scholarships based on circumstances or by competition. For full details see the university's website: www.bathspa.ac.uk/prospectus/money-matters/getting-money/scholarships.asp

Students

Undergraduates:	4,105	(400)
Postgraduates:	615	(1,990)
Mature students:	24.9%	
Overseas students:	3.7%	
Applications per place:	6.1	
From state-sector schools:	95.4%	
From working-class homes:	26.5%	

For detailed information about fees, grants and bursaries and how they work, see chapter 7.

Accommodation

Number of places and costs refer to 2007–08
University provided places: 891
Percentage catered: 0%
Self catered: £84–£99 a week
First years are housed in university-managed or accredited accommodation provided requirements are met. Residential restrictions apply.
International students: as above.
Contact: accommodation@bathspa.ac.uk

University of Bedfordshire

The former Luton University took most of the higher education world by surprise in 2006 by taking over De Montfort University's Bedford campus and establishing the University of Bedfordshire. The move made the new university the main provider of higher education in a relatively prosperous county and allowed it to shed a name that – however unfairly – had become a liability. In fact, Luton's teaching ratings were described by no less an authority than Charles Clarke, as Education Secretary, as "bloody brilliant" and one survey showed it winning more research contracts per pound of state funding than any other university. But there was no escaping the unglamorous image.

With two quite different sites to its name, the new university is expanding and developing, with an £80-million investment programme. The Luton campus had already seen the addition of a well-equipped media arts centre and an impressive learning resources centre. A new student centre is in the pipeline. A redevelopment programme for the Bedford campus involves a new campus centre with a students' union and a 280-seat auditorium, as well as a £20-million accommodation block for 500 students. Two new gyms and a series of sports science laboratories opened in 2006. A free shuttle bus service operates between the two sites.

The Bedford campus, once a teacher training college, is a 20-minute walk from the town centre in a "self-contained leafy setting". It houses the Faculty of Education and Contemporary Studies, with 3,000 students and plans for more. Although there are partner colleges in Bedford, Dunstable and Milton Keynes, the bulk of the students will remain in Luton. The borough council has considered making the Park Square campus the centre of a refurbished "cultural quarter". The centrepiece of the campus, in the midst of the shopping area, is the striking atrium which leads into the learning resources centre. Luton has also added extensive residential accommodation in recent years.

There is also an attractive management centre and conference venue at Putteridge Bury, a neo-Elizabethan mansion three miles outside Luton. Nursing and midwifery students in the growing Faculty of Health and Social Sciences, are scattered more widely, with Stoke Mandeville Hospital and Wycombe General Hospital the centres in Buckinghamshire, while Bedford, and Luton and Dunstable hospitals provide the equivalent for Bedfordshire. A postgraduate medical school is run in partnership

---

Park Square
Luton
Bedfordshire LU1 3JU
01582 489286
admissions@beds.ac.uk
www.beds.ac.uk
www.ubsu.co.uk

The Times Rankings
Overall Ranking: 89

Student satisfaction:	=64	(73%)
Research quality:	=104	(0.6)
Entry standards:	104	(220)
Student–staff ratio:	105	(21.2)
Services & facilities/student:	8	(£1,685)
Expected completion rate:	95	(75.4%)
Good honours:	=102	(47.0%)
Graduate prospects:	83	(59.6%)

with Hertfordshire and Cranfield universities, as part of the Government's £1-billion investment in healthcare across Bedfordshire and Hertfordshire.

Courses in the new university will maintain the vocational character that Luton pursued after dropping a number of traditional academic subjects. The portfolio of 44 two-year Foundation degrees, for example, is among the largest in the country, stretching from football studies and international tennis management to youth justice and nutritional therapy. Bedfordshire students will also benefit from a national centre of excellence in personal development planning and employability, awarded to Luton in 2005. The first official measure of graduate prospects showed the university to have the lowest unemployment rate of any university. Luton also pioneered electronic assessment, with more than 10,000 students in disciplines from accountancy to biology tested by computer.

Applications for courses beginning in 2007 showed a big increase on the previous year's figures for Luton and the Bedford campus of De Montfort, but the 9 per cent increase at the start of 2008 was even more impressive since most universities saw a decline with the switch from six choices per applicant to five. Luton claimed to have the second most

diverse intake in Britain, with almost one student in three coming from an ethnic minority and a similar proportion arriving without traditional academic qualifications. Almost all of Bedfordshire's entrants are from state schools and 43 per cent come from working-class backgrounds. A high proportion are mature students, many taking access courses to bring them up to degree or diploma standard, with about a third of the school-leavers arriving through Clearing.

Neither Luton nor Bedford is particularly famous for its social scene, but both have their share of pubs, clubs and restaurants. London is only half an hour away by train for those seeking something livelier. There is enough accommodation to guarantee a place for all first years, and the sports facilities are improving, albeit from a low base in Luton.

Undergraduate Fees and Bursaries

- Fees for UK/EU students: £3,145
- International student fees: £8,000–£8,200
- Bursary on full grant: household income up to £18.3K: £820; then £625.
- Bursaries on partial grant: household income up to £39.3K: sliding scale £625–£460. Above £39.3K, fixed bursary of £310.
- Scholarships based on circumstances or by competition. For full details see the university's website: www.beds.ac.uk/howtoapply/money

---

Students

Undergraduates:	8,270	(4,050)
Postgraduates:	1,020	(1,210)
Mature students:	54.3%	
Overseas students:	21.1%	
Applications per place:	3.5	
From state-sector schools:	99.6%	
From working-class homes:	43.0%	

For detailed information about fees, grants and bursaries and how they work, see chapter 7.

Accommodation

Number of places and costs refer to 2007–08
University-provided places: about 1,617
Percentage catered: 0%
Self-catered costs: £71.50–£100 a week.
Policy for first-year students: all first years are guaranteed a place provided conditions are met.
International students: as above.
Contact: www.beds.ac.uk/studentlife/accommodation
studentservices.bedford@beds.ac.uk
accommodation@beds.ac.uk uk

University of Birmingham

Birmingham set itself the target of becoming the "Oxbridge of the Midlands", which may have been ambitious, but its position in *The Times* ranking is a good starting point. A consultants' report in 2004 found the university had a boring image, but that is being addressed. And, despite offering an unusually wide range of subjects, its teaching and research ratings seldom slip.

Students come to Birmingham from more than 150 countries, but the university enjoys particularly high prestige in its own region. From October 2008 it will be made up of five colleges. Entry standards are high, averaging the equivalent of more than ABB at A level. With nearly eight applicants for each place, they are likely to remain so, but aspiring students still flock to the largest open days in Britain each June. There is also an additional open day for upper sixth-formers in September. Applications were down at the start of 2008, although only by about the national average with the decline in the number of choices available to each applicant.

The university's enduring reputation is based on its research, with two thirds of its departments considered nationally or internationally outstanding in the last assessments. A dozen 5* ratings tripled the number awarded in 1996, with languages doing particularly well: French, German, Italian and Russian all reached the top level, as did chemical engineering and metallurgy and materials.

Many of the teaching scores were impressive, too, with mathematics, biological sciences, physiotherapy, sociology, and electrical and electronic engineering all recording maximum points. Birmingham also did well in the 2007 National Student Survey, finishing ahead of most of the big city universities. Economics, maths, geography and European languages produced the best results.

In recent years, Birmingham has added an £11.8-million student facilities building at the Medical School, a new £16.4-million home for Sport and Exercise Sciences and a £10-million learning centre, and spent £47.5 million on refurbishing student accommodation as part of an investment programme in staff, buildings and equipment that is costing a total of £225 million. Engineering has been reorganised, following a year-long review, to promote an interdisciplinary approach, responding to employers' wish for more flexibility. Students can enter either a BA or BSc degree programme, combining technology with subjects ranging from Latin or modern Greek to the management of floods and other natural disasters.

Edgbaston
Birmingham B15 2TT
0121 415 8900 (admissions)
admissions@bham.ac.uk
www.bham.ac.uk
www.guildofstudents.com

The Times Rankings
Overall Ranking: 25

Student satisfaction:	=18	(77%)
Research quality:	=37	(4.3)
Entry standards:	17	(402)
Student–staff ratio:	=31	(15.3)
Services & facilities/student:	22	(£1,342)
Expected completion rate:	=18	(92.4%)
Good honours:	=29	(68.4%)
Graduate prospects:	42	(70.4%)

The 230-acre campus in leafy Edgbaston is dominated by a 300-foot clocktower, which is one of the city's best-known landmarks, and boasts its own station. Dentistry is located in the city, while the Department of Theology and part of the School of Education are in Selly Oak, a mile from the Edgbaston campus. Drama is also located there, along with the BBC Drama Village, which is part of a strategic alliance between the university and the corporation.

Most of the halls and university flats are conveniently located in an attractive parkland setting near the main campus. There are around 5,000 university-owned beds, following a ten-year programme of expansion, and private sector accommodation is also plentiful.

The campus is less than three miles from the centre of Birmingham, but the area has plenty of shops, pubs and restaurants of its own. With its own nightclub among the facilities on campus, some students do not even stray that far, but the city is acquiring a growing reputation among the young, which is helping to make the university even more popular. Some 40 per cent of Birmingham graduates choose to make the city their home.

Student facilities are on a par with the best in the country, with many restaurants and bars, a live music venue, an art gallery, a medical practice on campus, and an outdoor pursuits centre on Coniston Water, in the Lake District. Birmingham has always been concerned with the body as well as the mind; compulsory exercise was only abandoned in 1968. The Active Lifestyles Programme, the voluntary modern-day equivalent, attracts 4,000 students to 150 different courses. Tutors with national qualifications run classes from beginner to advanced level. In addition, Birmingham has ranked in the top three in British Universities competitions for the past 15 years.

Undergraduate Fees and Bursaries
- Fees for UK/EU students: £3,145
- International student fees: £9,450–£12,250 (£22,350 clinical)
- Bursary on full grant: £840
- Bursaries on partial grant: household income up to £34.6K: £840.
- Scholarships based on circumstances or by competition. For full details see the university's website: www.as.bham.ac.uk/study/support/finance/

Students		
Undergraduates:	16,285	(2,200)
Postgraduates:	5,340	(6,595)
Mature students:	8.1%	
Overseas students:	8.5%	
Applications per place:	7.7	
From state-sector schools:	76.5%	
From working-class homes:	19.9%	

For detailed information about fees, grants and bursaries and how they work, see chapter 7.

Accommodation
Number of places and costs refer to 2008–09
University-provided places: 4,924
Percentage catered: 53%
Catered costs: £114.69–£142.26 a week.
Self-catered costs: £77.88–£115.10 a week.
All first years are guaranteed housing (subject to conditions).
International students: as above
Contact: ugradaccomm@bham.ac.uk
www.birminghamstudentpad.co.uk

Birmingham City University

The former UCE Birmingham (originally the University of Central England) has been rechristened Birmingham City University to emphasise its location, reinforce its close links with the city and give the university a stronger identity. The latest name change is part of the new Vice-Chancellor's strategy to build on the university's traditionally close links with business and the professions. An emphasis on employability is underlined by a £300,000 project to create "future-proof" graduates with training and education resources to help develop skills and knowledge for the workplace.

The annual satisfaction survey goes to half of the student body, in a model that helped inform the new national equivalent. The results are taken seriously: a recent exercise has led to the introduction of internet tutorials in engineering, and new help with research for undergraduates in law and social science. The long-standing initiative is just one of the activities of the influential Centre for Research into Quality, headed by one of the university's most senior academics.

The university has a proud record of extending access to higher education: more than 40 per cent of its students come from working-class homes and 97 per cent attended state schools. Some 17 per cent drop out, but this is less than the national average for the university's courses and entry grades. About half of the full-time students come from the West Midlands, many from ethnic minorities. BCU also has one of the largest programmes of part-time courses in Britain, making it the biggest provider of higher education in the region. Students also enter through the network of associated further education colleges, which run foundation and access programmes. Demand for places was holding up well at the start of 2008, when most universities saw a much bigger decline in applications.

Eight campuses straggle across the city, but about half of students are concentrated on the modern City North campus at Perry Barr, three miles from the city centre. A new city-centre campus in the Eastside district, near Millennium Point, will open in 2008, as part of a £250-million investment in new and improved facilities. It will cater for about 10,000 students in creative and performing arts, media, technology and design. The 2001 relocation of engineering and computing to Millennium Point provided a new focus for the university. Facilities in the £114-million Lottery-funded centre are open to the public. The Birmingham School of Acting also moved into £4-million purpose-built facilities at Millennium Point in 2007.

Perry Barr
Birmingham B42 2SU
0121 331 5595 (enquiries)
choices@bcu.ac.uk
www.bcu.ac.uk
www.birminghamcitysu.com

The Times Rankings
Overall Ranking: 71

Student satisfaction:	=84	(71%)
Research quality:	=92	(0.8)
Entry standards:	73	(268)
Student–staff ratio:	38	(15.8)
Services & facilities/student:	43	(£1,138)
Expected completion rate:	84	(77.3%)
Good honours:	63	(56.6%)
Graduate prospects:	57	(63.8%)

The Edgbaston campus has been refurbished for the Faculty of Health, with a prize-winning library, IT suites, teaching facilities and recreational space. The Birmingham Institute of Art and Design (BIAD) spreads over four campuses from Gosta Green and the impressive listed Venetian Gothic Fine Art campus at Margaret Street, both in the city centre, to Bournville. This facility was refurbished at a cost of £20 million and occupies part of the Cadbury village. The largest Institute of its kind outside London, it also includes the world famous and newly refurbished School of Jewellery in the city's famous Jewellery Quarter.

One of the university's best-known features is its Conservatoire, housed in part of Birmingham's smart convention centre. Courses from opera to world music have given it a reputation for innovation, which was recognised in an excellent rating for teaching. Most other teaching ratings were mediocre, although art and design, education and health subjects scored well and the teacher education courses consistently produce among the best scores in Ofsted inspections. The university was awarded a national Centre for Excellence in Teaching and Learning health and social care.

The university has been increasing its portfolio of high-tech degree courses like electronic commerce, communications and network engineering, electronic systems and mechanical engineering systems. The last research assessments showed improvement on 1996, but only art and design reached any of the top three grades. However, income from research contracts has always been healthy.

University-owned accommodation is guaranteed for first years, and there is a relatively cheap and plentiful private sector housing sector. The Pavilion, adjacent to the City North Campus, has added £4.5 million of conference and sports facilities, comprising 43 acres – giving 12 outdoor pitches for field sports. Further new sports facilities are planned for City North Campus by 2009–10. A new students' union complex opened on the Westbourne campus in the summer of 2006, and the city's youth scene is highly rated.

Undergraduate Fees and Bursaries

- Fees for UK/EU students: £3,145
- International student fees: £8,880–£13,500
- Bursary on full grant: £525
- Bursaries on partial grant: household income up to £60K: sliding scale £525–£245.
- Scholarships based on circumstances or by competition. For full details see the university's website:
www.bcu.ac.uk/become_a_student/index.html

Students

Undergraduates:	13,105	(6,365)
Postgraduates:	1,565	(2,825)
Mature students:	32.6%	
Overseas students:	4.8%	
Applications per place:	5.5	
From state-sector schools:	97.0%	
From working-class homes:	42.8%	

For detailed information about fees, grants and bursaries and how they work, see chapter 7.

Accommodation

Number of places and costs refer to 2007–08
University-provided places: 2,146
Percentage catered: 0%
Self-catered costs: £58.50–£93.50 a week.
Accommodation guaranteed for first years if conditions are met. Residential restrictions apply.
International students are guaranteed a room in Halls for the duration of their course.
Contact: accommodation@bcu.ac.uk

University of Bolton

The largest town in England finally got a university in 2005, after eight years of trying. From 2008, it will have a single site in the town centre with additional and enhanced teaching space, facilities to interact with industry and a new students' union. University status had an instant impact: Bolton recorded the biggest increases in applications in the UK for two successive years. Although there had been a big fall at the start of 2008, the demand for places was still well above pre-university days.

The university traces its roots back as far as 1824 to one of the country's first three mechanics institutes. There are already more than 8,000 students and there are no plans for dramatic growth, despite the new-found popularity. The university sees itself as a regional institution, with three quarters of the students coming from the North West, many through partner colleges. But there is also an international dimension, with long-established links in Malaysia and a regular contingent of overseas students from 70 different countries.

Bolton has set itself the ambitious target of climbing into the top half of the university system within 15 years. Judged on our criteria, it has some way to go, but it is not unusual for brand-new universities to make their debut near the foot of the table. Even in its days as an institute of higher education, it was competitive in categories such as spending per student on the library and other facilities, but it is dragged down by other indicators. Student satisfaction is not one of these: the university almost made the top ten in rankings of the first National Student Satisfaction Survey and, although ratings slipped a little in 2007, Bolton remains in the top half of that table.

Teaching assessments were variable, but education, nursing and psychology all achieved maximum points and the last seven assessments all produced more than 20 points out of 24. The university is not research-driven, so not surprisingly, research grades were less impressive, but metallurgy and materials reached grade 4 in the last assessments. A centre for research and innovation in materials which opened in 2003 is to be the first of a series of "knowledge exchange zones". Bolton is not one of the new breed of "teaching-only" universities; it has been accredited for research degrees for more than ten years and acquired its new status under the old rules. About 1,700 of the students are postgraduates, taking qualifications up to and including PhDs.

The £11.3-million building programme at the Deane campus has included a design studio and three floors of teaching

---

Deane Road
Bolton BL3 5AB
01204 903903 (general enquiries)
enquiries@bolton.ac.uk
www.bolton.ac.uk
www.bisu.co.uk

The Times Rankings
Overall Ranking: 111

Student satisfaction:	=55	(74%)
Research quality:	=92	(0.8)
Entry standards:	=109	(203)
Student–staff ratio:	=102	(21.0)
Services & facilities/student:	100	(£772)
Expected completion rate:	113	(63.3%)
Good honours:	77	(52.6%)
Graduate prospects:	106	(51.8%)

and learning space where students work on live briefs for companies seeking design solutions; an Innovation Factory housing, among others, special effects laboratories, a product design studio and a student services centre with floor space the size of a football pitch. A swimming pool and sports complex will be next, if plans for a joint development with the local authority are approved. The 700 reasonably priced residential places go a long way in an institution with a high proportion of home-based students. More than half of the students are over 20 at entry.

The university exceeds all the access measures designed to widen participation in higher education: nearly all the students are state-educated, four in ten are from working-class homes and the proportion from areas without a tradition of higher education is almost twice the national average for Bolton's subjects and entry qualifications. The downside – and it's an important one – is that almost a third of the students are projected to leave without a qualification: by far the highest proportion in England. The university has an action plan to bring the rate down to the national average for its courses and qualifications by 2012.

Undergraduate Fees and Bursaries

- Fees for UK/EU students: £3,145
- International student fees: £7,800
- Bursary on full grant: £320
- Bursaries on partial grant: household income up to £60K: sliding scale £270–£70 .
- Scholarships based on circumstances or by competition. For full details see the university's website: www.bolton.ac.uk/ProspectiveStudents/ Undergraduate/Finance/UgFtFinance/ Home.aspx

Students

Undergraduates:	3,740	(2,635)
Postgraduates:	790	(950)
Mature students:	47.8%	
Overseas students:	7.7%	
Applications per place:	8.8	
From state-sector schools:	99.2%	
From working-class homes:	42.7%	

For detailed information about fees, grants and bursaries and how they work, see chapter 7.

Accommodation

Number of places and costs refer to 2007–08
University-provided places: 700
Percentage catered: 0%
Self-catered costs: £2,400 anually; £60 a week (40 weeks).
All first years are generally accommodated.
International students: accommodation is secured for these students.
Contact: accomm@bolton.ac.uk

Bournemouth University

Once a university that gloried in the absence of traditional academic disciplines, Bournemouth is subtly changing its image. Its latest corporate plan speaks of a university "geared to the professions with passionate commitment to academic excellence". Research has moved up the agenda with a £1-million investment in 80 PhD studentships, and the aim is to increase undergraduates' entry qualifications year on year.

Bournemouth's forte has always been in identifying gaps in the higher education market and then filling them with innovative programmes. Degrees in public relations, retail management, scriptwriting and tax law are among the examples. The university also boasts the National Centre of Computer Animation. The mix has been popular with students – applications held up well in 2008, when the cut in the number of choices for each student prompted a decline elsewhere. This followed a 10 per cent rise in applications in the previous year, when design, engineering and computing all registered increases of more than 50 per cent.

The university claims a number of firsts in its growing portfolio of courses, notably in the area of tourism, media-related programmes and conservation. It was no surprise to find the university among the pioneers of Foundation Degrees – two-year highly vocational courses, which remain at the heart of the Government's expansion plans for higher education. Now much expanded, the courses are being delivered in further education colleges from Cornwall to Wiltshire, supporting the needs of business in the creative arts, media and tourism.

Many of Bournemouth's courses have an international focus and all students are encouraged to improve their linguistic ability. A majority of undergraduates take sandwich courses, and 70 per cent do work placements. The result is an employment rate which is the university's proudest achievement: four out of five graduates go straight into jobs. The Retail Management degree notched up eight successive years of full employment and is still running at over 90 per cent. Students are offered personal development planning, both online and with trained staff, while 1,400 first-years also take advantage of peer-assisted learning, receiving advice from more experienced undergraduates.

Archaeology, television and video production, media studies and nursing achieved the best teaching grades, while psychology was the star performer in the first national student satisfaction survey. Media courses are a particular strength, with entry requirements well above the

---

Talbot Campus
Fern Barrow
Poole
Dorset BH12 5BB
01202 524111
enquiries@
  bournemouth.ac.uk
www.bournemouth.
  ac.uk
www.subu.org.uk

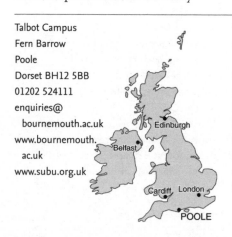

POOLE

The Times Rankings
Overall Ranking: 57

Student satisfaction:	=73	(72%)
Research quality:	=99	(0.7)
Entry standards:	57	(287)
Student–staff ratio:	=79	(19.5)
Services & facilities/student:	72	(£967)
Expected completion rate:	46	(85.2%)
Good honours:	62	(57.0%)
Graduate prospects:	38	(70.8%)

university's modest average. State-of-the-art equipment includes a motion capture facility for real-time animation, which is used in teaching and available for use by outside companies, and a £3.5-million Centre for Excellence in Media Practice is on the way. Computer animation was the star performer in the 2001 research assessments, which saw much-needed improvement on 1996.

Among the new developments planned is the world's first fully commercial teaching hotel, a four-star establishment with public- and private-sector backing, which is due to open in 2009. New teaching and residential accommodation has been added in recent years, with more to come. A multimillion-pound library opened in 2003. There are now two campuses – the original Talbot site in Poole and a dedicated campus in Bournemouth town centre – with associate colleges in Yeovil, Bournemouth and Poole, Cannington, Salisbury and Weymouth.

The southern seaside location and the subject mix attract more middle-class students than most new universities, although over 90 per cent attended state schools and colleges. Students are discouraged from bringing cars (which are banned within a mile of the town-centre campus), but many still do. The area has plenty to offer students during the summer season. Although it naturally becomes less lively in the winter months, Bournemouth no longer shuts up when the tourists go home. The students' union's Old Fire Station bar is the favourite among many nightlife options. Bournemouth offers a wide range of accommodation, from 1,700 places in university halls to bed-and-breakfast lets and shared houses.

Undergraduate Fees and Bursaries

- Fees for UK/EU students: £3,145
- International student fees: £7,500–£8,500
- Bursary on full grant: £1,310
- Bursaries on partial grant: household income up to £37.5K: sliding scale up to £1,000.
- Scholarships based on circumstances or by competition. For full details see the university's website: www.bournemouth.ac.uk/ futurestudents/undergraduate/funding/ index.html

Students

Undergraduates:	10,845	(4,580)
Postgraduates:	1,615	(835)
Mature students:	24.3%	
Overseas students:	5.7%	
Applications per place:	5.1	
From state-sector schools:	93.5%	
From working-class homes:	25.6%	

For detailed information about fees, grants and bursaries and how they work, see chapter 7.

Accommodation

Number of places and costs refer to 2007–08
University-provided places: about 2,450 (1,775 in halls; 675 head tenancy)
Percentage catered: 0%
Self-catered costs: £65–£84 a week.
The university expects to offer all first years a place to live. Residential restrictions apply.
International students: guaranteed if conditions are met.
Contact: accommodation@bournemouth.ac.uk

University of Bradford

The university celebrated its fortieth anniversary in 2006 with the opening of a distinctive atrium designed to provide a focal point for the campus and kickstart Bradford's innovative "Ecoversity" project. The four-storey Atrium has brought together all student support services in a single, open plan social space, while the main element of the Ecoversity will be to complete a sustainable student village for first-year and international students on the city-centre campus. The two developments are part of a £70-million modernisation plan that includes a £7-million investment in new and upgraded teaching facilities.

Still a relatively small university of 13,000 students, Bradford has carved out a niche for itself with mature students, who now make up over a quarter of all undergraduates. They relish the vocational slant and the accent on sandwich courses, which regularly place Bradford near the top of the graduate employment tables – it was second on this measure in last year's *Times* table. Demand for places recovered after a difficult period, although applications were down by more than the national average this year and last. Admission requirements have been rising, although they are modest compared with many old universities.

Nearly than one in five of the university's students are from overseas, many of them taught in partner institutions in locations as diverse as Warsaw, Delhi and Hong Kong. Nearer home, there are alliances with a number of further education colleges to help boost participation in a region where it is among the lowest in Europe. The colleges offer 10 Foundation degrees in areas such as public sector administration, community justice, engineering technology and enterprise in IT. Perhaps the best known is in health and social care, where the university was already expanding opportunities locally, bringing about a fourfold increase in enrolments by young women from South Asian families.

The relatively small, lively campus is close to the city centre. Health students have their own building a few minutes' walk away, while a shuttle bus service runs to the highly rated management school is two miles away in a 14-acre parkland setting. The eventual aim is to develop a health and science quarter, with the School of Health Studies housed in its own building on campus. Other projects will enhance the academic facilities and create more social space for students, beginning with improved laboratories for chemical and forensic science, more teaching accommodation and new sports facilities including a gym and climbing wall and an improved sports hall

Nursing, pharmacy and other health studies all did well in teaching quality

---

Bradford
West Yorkshire BD7 1DP
0800 073 1225 (freephone)
course-enquiries@
  bradford.ac.uk
www.bradford.ac.uk
www.ubuonline.co.uk

The Times Rankings
Overall Ranking: 49

Student satisfaction:	=26	(76%)
Research quality:	52	(3.4)
Entry standards:	60	(280)
Student–staff ratio:	=28	(15.0)
Services & facilities/student:	37	(£1,167)
Expected completion rate:	=61	(82.2%)
Good honours:	49	(60.5%)
Graduate prospects:	=26	(73.9%)

assessments, while politics and the inter-disciplinary human studies programme, which combines psychology, literature and sociology with the study of philosophy, was awarded full marks. The university also did well in the first national student satisfaction survey, although it was down to halfway in 2007, with finance and accounting the top scorer.

Research grades improved in the last assessment exercise, with European studies achieving the coveted 5* and archaeology, biomedical sciences, mechanical engineering and politics on the next rung of the ladder. Politics includes the university's best-known offering of peace studies, which has acquired an international reputation. A £6-million Institute of Pharmaceutical Innovation opened in 2003.

Bradford has launched suites of ICT and media studies courses to add to those in e-commerce and internet computing, computer animation and special effects, interactive systems and video games design. Computer-assisted learning is increasing in many subjects, making use of unusually extensive IT provision and a new wireless network. Some courses feature online assessment and the use of laptops in lectures.

More southerners are being attracted to Bradford's status as Britain's cheapest student city. The 1,700 places in self-catering halls are reasonably priced and all have internet connections. Many have been refurbished and more are promised in 2009. There is particularly good provision for disabled students, who account for 6 per cent of the university population. The university's senior management group includes a Director of Student Engagement to ensure that the student voice is heard in future developments. The students' union operates a free late-night "safety bus" for those living within two miles of the campus.

Undergraduate Fees and Bursaries

- Fees for UK/EU students: £3,145
- International student fees: £7,980–£10,310*
- Bursary of £900–£500 for those on a full grant, depending on year in course.
- Bursaries for those on partial grant based on household income up to £40K, depending on year in course £900–£500; up to £60K, £600–£400.
- Scholarships based on circumstances or by competition. For full details see the university's website: www.bradford.ac.uk/external/tuitionfees/support/bursaries.php

* Figures for 2007–08

Students		
Undergraduates:	7,645	(1,465)
Postgraduates:	1,480	(3,010)
Mature students:	25.8%	
Overseas students:	17.2%	
Applications per place:	4.9	
From state-sector schools:	93.8%	
From working-class homes:	43.7%	

For detailed information about fees, grants and bursaries and how they work, see chapter 7.

Accommodation

Number of places and costs refer to 2007–08
University-provided places: 1,681
Percentage catered: 0%
Self-catered costs: £61.50–£85.95 (en suite) a week (39, 42 or 51 weeks).
All first years are guaranteed accommodation (terms and conditions apply).
International students: all first-year students are guaranteed accommodation.
Contact: halls-of-residence@bradford.ac.uk
www.brad.ac.uk/accommodation

University of Brighton

Brighton came of age as one of the first new universities to be awarded a medical school, but is equally well known for imaginative initiatives in its region. It has set up a centre in Hastings and runs a number of schemes, both to draw people from the region into higher education and to help them with practical problems. The £28.5-million medical school, which is run jointly with neighbouring Sussex University, is training 128 doctors a year and has now proved its popularity with applicants. Brighton was already heavily engaged in other health subjects, such as nursing and midwifery. The medical school's head-quarters, on Brighton's Falmer campus, has also provided a new base for applied social sciences, such as criminology and applied psychology, which are among the university's most sought-after degrees.

The two universities have been collaborating since Brighton was a polytechnic. There is a joint research building for science policy and manage-ment studies, and a joint accord guarantees the offer of a place to all suitably qualified applicants from the Channel Island of Jersey. Brighton does the same for applicants from Sussex and is leading a new Learning Network for the county. Almost a third of undergraduates now come through the accords.

Only two new universities did as well as Brighton in the last Research Assessment Exercise, and only one entered such a high a proportion of its academics. Art and design, biological sciences and European studies were all rated nationally excellent, with some work of top international quality. Teaching ratings were also consistently good, never dropping below 20 points out of 24, with philosophy registering a maximum score. Education, physical geography and environmental science achieved the best scores in the latest National Student Survey. The plaudits have not gone unnoticed: a 20 per cent increase in applications at the start of 2007 was one of the biggest at any university, while a 4 per cent decline a year later, with the switch from six choices per applicant to five, was less than the national average.

Brighton's strengths in art and design – recognised in the award of national teaching centres in design and creativity – have been at the forefront of the university's rise. But the university also has a growing reputation in areas such as sport and hospitality, as well as scoring well in teacher education rankings. The Design Council's national archive is lodged on campus, and the four-year fashion textiles degree offers work placements in the United States, France and Italy, as well as Britain. The Faculty of Management and Information Sciences is now the largest in the university.

Mithras House
Lewes Road
Brighton BN2 4AT
01273 600900
enquiries@brighton.
  ac.uk
www.brighton.ac.uk
www.ubsu.net

The Times Rankings
Overall Ranking: 60

Student satisfaction:	=64	(73%)
Research quality:	=58	(1.7)
Entry standards:	=55	(288)
Student–staff ratio:	=83	(19.6)
Services & facilities/student:	96	(£806)
Expected completion rate:	58	(83.0%)
Good honours:	=56	(58.8%)
Graduate prospects:	46	(67.7%)

Four sites house the five faculties. Art and Design has the prime location opposite the Royal Pavilion, with sports science, service management and the health professions at Eastbourne and the other subjects on the outskirts of Brighton, at Falmer and Moulsecoomb, the university's headquarters.

Over £100 million has been spent on new facilities and refurbishment since university status arrived in 1992 and another £100 million has been committed for the next four years, half of it on student accommodation and learning facilities. Existing facilities include a flight simulator, a fully functional news room for the university's sports journalists, modern clinical skills laboratories for pharmacy, and a custom-designed culinary arts studio. At Eastbourne there is a new library and extensive sports and leisure facilities, including a sports centre with three gymnasia and a dance studio, a refurbished swimming pool and fitness facilities. Sport-science laboratories and 354 en-suite residential places have been added and improvements made to the learning resources centre, lecture theatres and refectory. The extensive modernisation of the Falmer campus continues, with extra accommodation, a library and a nursing and midwifery centre already added.

The university has a cosmopolitan air, with more overseas students and a more middle-class UK intake than most of the former polytechnics. Around a quarter of the full-time undergraduates are over 21 on entry, often attracted by strongly vocational courses and the prospect of three years at "London by the sea". Most undergraduates have a personal tutor who will advise on combinations within the modular degree scheme.

Students have taken to the "managed learning environment", known as Studentcentral, an interactive service providing online access to teaching materials and other information. Most also like Brighton, although the cost of living is high for those not in hall. There is a lively social scene and part-time work is plentiful. Eastbourne is also surprisingly popular, and both towns offer plentiful accommodation to supplement the university's stock.

Undergraduate Fees and Bursaries

- Fees for UK/EU students: £3,145
- International student fees: £9,000–£10,500
- Bursary on full grant: £1,050
- Bursaries on partial grant: household income up to £39.3K: sliding scale £840–£520.
- Scholarships based on circumstances or by competition. For full details see the university's website: www.brighton.ac.uk/studentlife/money/

Students

Undergraduates:	12,795	(4,290)
Postgraduates:	1,440	(2,610)
Mature students:	25.1%	
Overseas students:	10.4%	
Applications per place:	5.7	
From state-sector schools:	92.7%	
From working-class homes:	27.4%	

For detailed information about fees, grants and bursaries and how they work, see chapter 7.

Accommodation

Number of places and costs refer to 2006–07
University-provided places: 1,950; 300 in private sector university-managed houses or flats.
Percentage catered: 0%
Self-catered costs: £60–£87 a week.
First years guaranteed accommodation if conditions are met. Residential restrictions apply.
International students: as above.
Contact: accommodation@brighton.ac.uk
a.eastbourne@brighton.ac.uk

University of Bristol

Bristol has long been a natural alternative to Oxbridge, favoured particularly by independent schools, whose pupils take at least three in ten places. Departments are encouraged to make slightly lower offers to promising applicants from schools with poor records at A level, and some top schools have blamed the policy for the rejection of highly qualified applicants. As the most popular university in Britain in terms of applications per place, however, Bristol has always had to turn away excellent candidates. This strong demand saw a 16 per cent increase in applications by the official deadline for courses beginning in 2007 and a much smaller decline than the national average twelve months later, with the switch from six choices per applicant to five.

The university's academic credentials are not in doubt – it broke into the top 50 in *The Times Higher Education*/QS world rankings for 2007. But it has found it difficult to attract working-class teenagers, who fear that they would be out of place socially, if not academically. In 2005–06 only about one in six came from a working-class home – the lowest propor-tion outside Oxbridge. Tiny numbers are recruited from the schools in the bottom half of the A-level league tables and few come from Scotland or the north of England, but £1 million a year is being spent on efforts to recruit more widely.

Overall entry standards remain among the highest at any university. A modular course system is now well established, although the majority of students still take single or dual honours degrees. Bristol has no intention of aping the growth plans of some of its rivals, but there has been modest expansion to 12,000 full-time undergraduates and the university has continued to live up to expectations in assessments of teaching and research. A third of the staff assessed for research are in departments considered internationally excellent and three quarters saw their departments reach one of the top two grades. There are 31 Fellows of the Royal Society and similar numbers in other learned societies.

Research is Bristol's traditional strength. The 2001 assessments saw the university's tally of 5* subjects shoot up from one to 15, with another 21 subjects on the next of the seven grades. Only Cambridge, Oxford and University College London had more maximum scores. The 33 excellent teaching ratings also represent one of the largest totals in the university system, with veterinary medicine, anatomy, molecular biosciences, electronic engin-eering and, most recently, education all achieving perfect scores.

Bristol was given the best rating among

Senate House
Tyndall Avenue
Bristol BS8 1TH
0117 928 9000 (admissions)
ug-admissions@
bristol.ac.uk
www.bristol.ac.uk
www.ubu.org.uk

Edinburgh
Belfast
Cardiff   London
BRISTOL

The Times Rankings
Overall Ranking: 10

Student satisfaction:	=39	(75%)
Research quality:	=12	(5.2)
Entry standards:	=9	(430)
Student–staff ratio:	=25	(14.7)
Services & facilities/student:	12	(£1,535)
Expected completion rate:	8	(95.8%)
Good honours:	9	(78.4%)
Graduate prospects:	=5	(81.5%)

the small group of universities seeking to demonstrate their creditworthiness to the money markets. A funding appeal which has raised more than £100 million has helped the university to create new chairs and embark on a number of building projects. The highly rated chemistry department, for example, moved into a well-appointed new centre in 2000, allowing new medical science laboratories to be constructed in the department's former premises. Both chemistry and medical sciences now have national teaching and learning centres.

An impressive sports centre at the heart of the university precinct opened in 2004 and there are plans for a new boathouse and a health and fitness centre. Neurology and dynamics engineering opened new buildings in 2004 and a new students' union is among the projects included in investment plans totalling £300 million over the next six years. Life sciences, nanoscience, physics and mathematics are all scheduled to benefit from well-equipped new buildings between 2007 and 2010. The £11-million Centre for Nanoscience and Quantum Information, which opened in 2008, contains some of the "quietest" labs in the world, with extremely low levels of vibrational and acoustic noise and tight controls on temperature and air movement.

The city is one of the most attractive in Britain, as well as possessing a vibrant youth culture. It is also prosperous, offering job opportunities to students and graduates alike. The university merges into the centre, its famous Gothic tower dominating the skyline from the junction of two of the main shopping streets. Departments dot the hillside close to the picturesque harbour area.

The current students' union is less of a social centre than in some universities, partly because of the intense competition from nightclubs. Most students enjoy life in Bristol – a *New Musical Express* poll rated the social life the best at any university in 2004 – although some find the high cost of living a serious drawback, while parts of the city suffer from the same security concerns as any big urban conurbation. The dropout rate is among the lowest in Britain.

Undergraduate Fees and Bursaries

- Fees for UK/EU students: £3,145
- International student fees:£10,800–£13,900 (£25,100 clinical)
- Bursary on full grant:£1,160 + £1,050 (local students)
- Bursaries on partial grant: household income £25K–£40K: £740; £40K–£50K: £300. All plus £1,050 (local students).
- Scholarships based on circumstances or by competition. For full details see the university's website: www.bris.ac.uk/studentfunding

Students		
Undergraduates:	11,810	(3,515)
Postgraduates:	2,820	(4,630)
Mature students:	7.1%	
Overseas students:	8.3%	
Applications per place:	10.3	
From state-sector schools:	65.1%	
From working-class homes:	16.4%	

For detailed information about fees, grants and bursaries and how they work, see chapter 7.

Accommodation

Number of places and costs refer to 2008–09
University-provided places: about 4,500
Percentage catered: 37%
Catered costs: £116–£146 a week.
Self-catered costs: £68–£112 a week.
First years are guaranteed one offer of accommodation provided conditions are met.
International students: accommodation is guaranteed provided conditions are met.
Contact: Accom-office@bris.ac.uk

Brunel University

Brunel celebrated 40 years as a university in 2006 and is nearing the end of £250-million programme to upgrade and centralise its teaching, research and sporting facilities. For the first time since its early years, the whole university will be located on the main Uxbridge campus. The building programme already includes a £6.5-million outdoor sports complex and a £7-million indoor athletics and netball centre, which will be a fitting home for the former Borough Road College and its illustrious sporting traditions. There is also a hugely extended university library, increased residential accommodation, more catering and social amenities and enhanced teaching and research facilities.

There is still plenty of scope for development. The university has quadrupled in size, with almost 13,000 students sharing a spacious, but hitherto uninspiring, main campus that had an isolated feel despite affording easy access to central London.

In recent years, Brunel has introduced more variety into a portfolio of degrees that was once given over almost entirely to sandwich courses. About half of all undergraduates still take four-year degrees that incorporate work placements, but new developments have tended to be conventional three-year arts, social science or sports programmes. There has also been significant growth in courses specialising in new technologies, such as multimedia design, interactive computing and broadcast media. Other innovations include creative writing, journalism, sonic arts, aviation engineering and pilot studies, motorsport engineering and space engineering.

Work placements and the inclusion of skills modules, such as oral and written communication, business and computer literacy, in degree courses have helped maintain a consistently good record in the graduate employment market. Many courses are validated by professional institutions.

Teaching assessments were consistently good, with drama, education, sport science and politics producing the best scores. In 2006, all aspects of the learning opportunities in NHS-funded health programmes were reviewed and rated commendable, and Brunel also scored well in an institutional audit. The last research assessments showed further improvement, although only 61 per cent of the academics were entered and design lost its 5* rating. Law, general and mechanical engineering, library and information studies and sociology all reached grade 5. Substantial investment in research centres and academic recruitment should produce further progress in 2008, when a much

---

Uxbridge
Middlesex UB8 3PH
01895 265265 (admissions)
admissions@brunel.ac.uk
www.brunel.ac.uk
www.brunelstudents.com

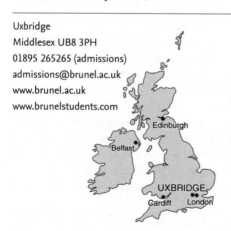

The Times Rankings
Overall Ranking: 52

Student satisfaction:	=97	(69%)
Research quality:	54	(3.1)
Entry standards:	=43	(313)
Student–staff ratio:	=42	(16.3)
Services & facilities/student:	15	(£1,475)
Expected completion rate:	=44	(85.4%)
Good honours:	=43	(63.7%)
Graduate prospects:	=58	(63.6%)

higher proportion of staff will be assessed. Sporting excellence is also being maintained, with Olympic gold-medal-winning rower James Cracknell and heavyweight boxer Audley Harrison the best-known alumni of recent times.

More than a third of the undergraduates are from working-class homes – significantly more than the national average for the subjects on offer – and almost 40 per cent come from ethnic minorities. The level of applications to the university has been rising, despite increased entry scores, which now average 320 points, but the decline in 2008 was greater than the national average. The projected total of 13 per cent leaving without a qualification is better than the UK average for Brunel's subjects and entry grades.

Student union facilities are good and students like Brunel's intimacy, although the university has not done well in the National Student Surveys, almost slipping out of the top 100 in 2007. The residential stock has been increased in recent years and new undergraduates will be guaranteed accommodation on campus in 2009.

Undergraduate Fees and Bursaries

- Fees for UK/EU students: £3,145
- International student fees: £8,300–£10,200
- Bursary on full grant: £1,000
- Bursaries on partial grant: household income up to £60K: £500.
- Scholarships based on circumstances or by competition. For full details see the university's website: www.brunel.ac.uk/ugfunding

Students

Undergraduates:	9,485	(870)
Postgraduates:	2,230	(2,935)
Mature students:	20.2%	
Overseas students:	10.6%	
Applications per place:	7.0	
From state-sector schools:	93.3%	
From working-class homes:	37.0%	

For detailed information about fees, grants and bursaries and how they work, see chapter 7.

Accommodation

Number of places and costs refer to 2007–08
University-provided places: 3,229
Percentage catered: 0%
Self-catered costs: £75.04–£92.05 a week.
All new full-time main-scheme first-year students are eligible for on-campus accommodation.
All new full-time international students are eligible for on-campus accommodation.
Contact: www.brunel.ac.uk/life/accommodation
accom-uxb@brunel.ac.uk

University of Buckingham

Britain's only private university describes itself as the country's smallest and friendliest – a claim borne out by the second National Student Survey, in which Buckingham students emerged as the most satisfied in England. The university was almost as successful in the latest survey, achieving unusually high scores in both business and law . Even before the advent of top-up fees elsewhere, Buckingham claimed to be no more expensive than other universities because its intensive two-year degrees cut maintenance costs and accelerate entry into employment. Now fees for UK undergraduates have been cut to £15,000, regardless of the length of course, and there are further discounts for payment in advance. Foreign students pay £26,500 and there is a range of scholarships for both home and overseas candidates.

The university, which celebrated its 30th anniversary in 2006, has no ambitions to follow its peers into the mass higher education market: it values the personal approach that comes with having fewer than 10 students to each member of staff, when the UK average is 17. One-to-one tutorials, which have all but disappeared outside Oxbridge and are by no means universal there, are common at Buckingham. The average teaching group contains about six students.

A Conservative-backed experiment of the 1970s, Buckingham had to wait almost ten years for its royal charter, but is now an accepted part of the university system. Although in 1992 it installed Baroness Thatcher as Chancellor, the university has no party political ties. Dr Terence Kealey, a biochemist from Cambridge University, became the latest Vice-Chancellor in April 2001, declaring an ambition for Buckingham to "one day" challenge the cream of American higher education. He has recruited a number of high-profile libertarians, including Chris Woodhead, the former Chief Inspector of Schools.

Buckingham's private status excludes it from the funding council's assessment of teaching and research, making it impossible to place in our league table. However, the university commissioned its own audit of teaching standards from the Quality Assurance Agency, which gave it a clean bill of health in 2004. The university's degrees carry full currency in the academic world and teaching standards are high. Education courses now have accreditation from the Teacher Training Agency, and law and business remain popular, but a 25 per cent drop in applications at the beginning of 2008 was considerably more than the national average.

The university runs on calendar years, rather than the traditional academic variety, although some courses give the option of

---

Hunter Street
Buckingham MK18 1EG
01280 820155 (enquiries)
admissions@
  buckingham.ac.uk
www.buckingham.ac.uk
student.union@
  buckingham.ac.uk

The Times Rankings
not applicable

entering in July or September. Most degree courses run for two 40-week years, minimising disruptive career breaks for the many mature students. About three quarters of the students are from overseas, but the proportion from Britain has been growing. Students have the option of a three-year degree in the humanities, and the university is still hoping to open the UK's first private medical school, despite the withdrawal of Brunel University from the scheme.

Even before the QAA audit, the two-year degree had been fully assessed by Professor John Clarke, a founder member of the university staff. Although hardly neutral, he concluded that the individual tuition given to Buckingham students, made possible by unusually generous staffing levels, allowed the system to succeed. He acknowledged that "undercapitalisation" has prevented the university achieving as much as it hoped, although only four universities spend as much per student on information technology.

Recent additions to the subjects on offer include multimedia journalism and media communications, both paired with English. A BSc has been added in business enterprise, complementing a new business advice hub for the locality. The most striking development, however, is the postgraduate medical school launched in 2008 with a two-year MD in clinical medicine. The course is expected to attract overseas medical graduates who find it difficult to secure junior doctor posts as a result of recent Government restrictions.

Campus facilities have improved considerably in recent years, although they cannot compare with those available at traditional universities. Buckingham operates on three sites, all within easy walking distance of each other, including a business school which opened in 1996. An academic centre containing computer suites, lecture theatres and student facilities provides a focal point that was missing previously.

The social scene is predictably quiet, given the size of the university and the workload, especially at weekends. A university cinema opened recently and the town is pretty with a good selection of pubs and restaurants. Milton Keynes or Oxford are near, except that Buckingham has no station, although a good bus service operates throughout the week with extra buses at weekends.

Undergraduate Fees and Bursaries

• Fees for UK/EU students:	£8,000*
• International student fees:	£13,500*[2]
• Bursary on full grant:	n/a
• Bursaries on partial grant:	n/a

* Duration of degree course is two years.

Students

Undergraduates:	575	(40)
Postgraduates:	200	(25)
Mature students:	n/a	
Overseas students:	68.0%	
Applications per place:	16.8	
From state-sector schools:	n/a	
From working-class homes:	n/a	

For detailed information about fees, grants and bursaries and how they work, see chapter 7.

Accommodation

Number of places and costs refer to 2008–09
University-provided places: 446
Percentage catered: 0%
Self-catered accommodation: £850–£1,300 a term.
First years are guaranteed accommodation.
International students: same as above.
Contact: accommodation@buckingham.ac.uk

Buckinghamshire New University

The youngest university in England had to wait a couple of years longer for its change of status than the group of higher education colleges promoted in 2005. But Buckinghamshire New University is making up for lost time with a £200-million campus redevelopment, a portfolio of innovative courses, and an attractive package of financial support and extra-curricular benefits for students. At the same time, collaboration with two of the world's biggest IT companies is developing one of the most advanced student networks in UK higher education.

Facilities on the three existing sites in and around High Wycombe should have been concentrated onto one by the time the academic year begins in 2009. The new Gateway Building will transform the town-centre campus with improved teaching, social and administrative space. The complex will include a new sports hall, gym, treatment rooms and sports laboratory, which will be available to the public as well as to students. An outdoor sports village is in the next phase of the university's ten-year development plan.

Sport is an important part of life at the new university, which sponsors the London Wasps rugby union team in a partnership which trades coaching for Bucks students for courses for Wasps players. But the university's main aim is contribute to the social and economic life of the region, embracing workplace learning and close ties with local businesses. Employees of the bed company, Dreams, which is based in High Wycombe, will take a new Foundation degree in retail management while at work, for example. Bucks has also won awards for its training of commercial pilots and its courses for music industry management. Other Foundation degrees include one for the motorsport industry and another in "protective security management".

There are almost 9,000 full and part-time students, more than 90 per cent of whom are taking first degrees and a third of whom are over 25. Nearly 60 per cent of the students are female. Academic departments are divided into three faculties: Creativity and Culture, Society and Health, and Enterprise and Innovation. Most of the teaching quality scores and all of the results in the 2001 Research Assessment Exercise were mediocre, but those were long before university status arrived. A more recent institutional audit expressed "broad confidence" in academic standards.

As Buckinghamshire Chilterns University College, the last projected

---

Queen Alexandra Road
High Wycombe
Buckinghamshire HP11 2JZ
0800 0565 660 (enquiries)
advice@bucks.ac.uk
www.bucks.ac.uk
www.bucksstudent.com

The Times Rankings
Overall Ranking: 108

Student satisfaction:	=99	(68%)
Research quality:	=92	(0.8)
Entry standards:	=109	(203)
Student–staff ratio:	73	(18.7)
Services & facilities/student:	65	(£999)
Expected completion rate:	63	(82.0%)
Good honours:	108	(44.7%)
Graduate prospects:	113	(45.2%)

dropout rate was a creditable 12 per cent – much lower than at most comparable institutions and nearly five percentage points better than the national average for its subjects and entry qualifications. Nor was this achieved by neglecting the Government's widening participation agenda: almost all the entrants are from state schools or colleges, and more than a third are from working-class homes.

The university has a particular focus on student support, devoting more than a third of its fee income to bursaries – one of the biggest proportions in England. All full-time UK undergraduates (apart from nursing students, who are eligible for Government bursaries) receive an annual, non means-tested £500 cash award. In addition, the Big Deal scheme offers free entry to all entertainment events, free use of all sports facilities and a programme of extra-curricular activities such as lessons in cookery and motor mechanics. The university also pays student representatives.

One disappointment has been a decline in scores in the National Student Survey, which has left Bucks in the bottom five. The extensive building work on the main campus may have been a factor. Its own annual survey, carried out by independent academics, has been more complimentary. Beyond the campus, High Wycombe has the usual range of pubs and clubs for a medium-sized town, but will not be a magnet for students. The university has opened an art gallery in the main shopping centre to showcase students' work, as part of its efforts to maintain a strong relationship with the town.

Undergraduate Fees and Bursaries

- Fees for UK/EU students: £3,145
- International student fees: £7,150–£7,750
- Bursary on full grant: £500
- Bursaries on partial grant: £500
- Scholarships based on circumstances or by competition. For full details see the university's website: www.bucks.ac.uk/courses/ undergraduate/fees_bursaries.aspx

Students

Undergraduates:	5,290	(3,010)
Postgraduates:	140	(480)
Mature students:	33.3%	
Overseas students:	12%	
Applications per place:	5.2	
From state-sector schools:	97.1%	
From working-class homes:	39.2%	

For detailed information about fees, grants and bursaries and how they work, see chapter 7.

Accommodation

Number of places and costs refer to 2008–09
University-provided places: 1,100
Percentage catered: 0%
Self-catered costs: a week: £68.60–£87.85 a week (44 weeks)
First-year students are guaranteed accommodation. Residential restrictions apply.
International students: same as above.
Contact: accom@bucks.ac.uk

University of Cambridge

Until 2001, Cambridge had enjoyed an unbroken run at the top of *The Times* League Table, and even now it is practically inseparable from first-placed Oxford. The university has the best record in the teaching and research assessments, topping far more of our subject tables than any of its rivals. Traditionally supreme in the sciences, where it was ranked best in the world by *The Times Higher Education*/QS in 2006, the university has also strengthened the arts and social sciences. Only Harvard University has finished ahead of Cambridge in the past two years of the world rankings.

All but one of the subjects assessed in the first rounds of teaching quality assessment were considered excellent and none dropped more than 2 points out of 24 under the later system. Cambridge students have not responded in sufficient numbers, however, for the university to be included in the first three National Student Surveys. Almost three quarters of the academics entered for research assessment were in subjects rated internationally outstanding, and only three subjects failed to reach the next-highest grade. The tripos system was a forerunner of the currently fashionable modular degree, allowing students to change subjects (within limits) midway through their courses. Students receive a classification for each of the two parts of their tripos degree.

More students now come from state schools than the independent sector – a trend the university is keen to continue – but the proportion of working-class undergraduates remains low, at only 12 per cent. Summer schools, student visits and, in some colleges, sympathetic selection procedures, are helping to attract more applications from comprehensive schools and further education colleges.

The application system has been simplified slightly for 2009, with candidates no longer required to complete an initial Cambridge form, as well as their UCAS form. However, they will still be sent the Supplementary Application Questionnaire, covering the applicant's academic experience in more detail.

A lively alternative prospectus, available from the students' union, used to say there was no such thing as Cambridge University, just a collection of colleges. Where applications are concerned, this is still true, as it is to some extent socially. Making the right choice of college is crucial, both to maximise the chances of winning a place and to ensure an enjoyable three years if you are successful. Applicants can take pot luck with an open application if they prefer not to opt for a particular college. But, though the

---

Kellet Lodge
Tennis Court Road
Cambridge CB2 1QJ
01223 333308
admissions@cam.ac.uk
www.cam.ac.uk
www.cusu.cam.ac.uk

Edinburgh
Belfast
CAMBRIDGE
Cardiff
London

The Times Rankings
Overall Ranking: 2

Student satisfaction:	–	–
Research quality:	1	(6.5)
Entry standards:	1	(518)
Student–staff ratio:	6	(12.2)
Services & facilities/student:	3	(£2,299)
Expected completion rate:	2	(97.9%)
Good honours:	2	(85.4%)
Graduate prospects:	2	(88.4%)

statistics show that this route is equally successful, only a minority take it. Most teaching is now university-based, especially in the sciences, and a shift of emphasis towards the centre has been taking place more generally. The trend may accelerate if a £1-billion funding appeal to mark the university's 800th anniversary is successful. It was two-thirds of the way there at the start of 2008, having raised £155 million in a year with 10,000 individual gifts.

The university's leading place in British higher education was underlined by its success in attracting Microsoft's first research base outside the United States. This is one of a series of technological partnerships with the private sector, several of which benefit undergraduates as well as researchers. Cambridge was also chosen for a Government-sponsored partnership with the Massachusetts Institute of Technology to promote entrepreneurship.

Such is the scale of development that almost £500-million worth of building is either planned or under construction. Although the medical school's facilities are being upgraded at Addenbrooke's Hospital, the university is looking to the outskirts to expand. The West Cambridge site will take a mixture of teaching and research buildings, and there are plans for more on green-belt land further north. In the long term, up to three new colleges could be built, but there will be few extra places for undergraduates in the foreseeable future.

For the moment, therefore, entrance requirements will remain the toughest in Britain. With around four applicants for each place – fewer still if you choose your subject carefully – the competition for places appears less intense than at the popular civic universities, but the real difference is that nine out of ten entrants have at least three A grades at A level. The pressure does not end there: the amount of high-quality work to be crammed into eight-week terms can prove a strain, although the dropout rate of less than 2 per cent is bettered only by Oxford.

Undergraduate Fees and Bursaries

- Fees for UK/EU students: £3,145*
- International student fees: £9,327–£12,219†
  (£22,614 clinical)†
- Bursary on full grant: £3,145
- Bursaries on partial grant: household income up to £70K: sliding scale £1,900–£50.
- Scholarships based on circumstances or by competition. For full details see the university's website: www.cam.ac.uk/admissions/undergraduate/finance/support.html www.admin.cam.ac.uk/univ/funds

* UK & EU students eligible for tuition fee support not liable for College fees.

† Plus College fees (£3,300–£4,900)

Students

Undergraduates:	11,765	(6,415)
Postgraduates:	5,395	(5,195)
Mature students:	4.5%*	
Overseas students:	10.7%	
Applications per place:	4.3	
From state-sector schools:	56.8%*	
From working-class homes:	12.4%*	

* Figures from 2006

For detailed information about fees, grants and bursaries and how they work, see chapter 7.

Accommodation

See chapter 10 for information about individual colleges.

Canterbury Christ Church University

This former Church of England college started branching out well before university status arrived in 2005. There is a network of campuses right across Kent, the most populous county in England but, until recently, one of the most sparsely provided with higher education. At the purpose-built campus at Broadstairs, for example, where applications were up by 28 per cent at the start of 2006, the university offers subjects as diverse as commercial music, digital media, business, police studies, computing, nursing, and child and youth studies. There is also an imposing country house and one-time convalescent home outside Tunbridge Wells, mainly for postgraduates, as well as a new Medway site at Chatham, operated partly in conjunction with Greenwich and Kent universities, and a new University Centre at Folkestone, offering performing and visual arts, also developed in partnership with Greenwich.

The majority of the 14,000 students, however, are at the new university's Canterbury headquarters. The main campus, which dates from 1962, is a few minutes walk from the city centre, but the university has several off-site buildings in other parts of Canterbury. One is being developed as a learning resource centre, with specialist teaching and IT facilities, to open in 2009.

The Church of England link was underlined with the installation of the Archbishop of Canterbury as the university's Chancellor in 2005. Religious studies is available as a single-honours degree or as part of the modular scheme, which cover the arts and humanities, business and science, education, and health and social care. The large health and teacher training programmes make the university the largest provider of higher education to the public services in Kent. Canterbury is one of the few Grade 1 providers of teacher training offering the full range of courses from early years to primary, secondary, further and higher education. Policing studies is another big recruiter.

Religious studies registered the best teaching quality grades, but all the assessments were good, as were the results from the first two national student satisfaction surveys. The university slipped down the table in 2007, but geography and history did well. Canterbury Christ Church entered an ambitious 34 per cent of academics for the last Research Assessment Exercise, but none of the subject areas reached the top three of the seven grades. This was not an issue when the institution sought to shed its college

---

North Holmes Road
Canterbury CT1 1QU
01227 782900 (prospectus)
admissions
 @canterbury.ac.uk
www.canterbury.ac.uk
www.ccsu.co.uk

Edinburgh
Belfast
Cardiff   London
CANTERBURY

The Times Rankings
Overall Ranking: 80

Student satisfaction:	=55	(74%)
Research quality:	=82	(1.1)
Entry standards:	96	(247)
Student–staff ratio:	60	(17.8)
Services & facilities/student:	112	(£559)
Expected completion rate:	56	(83.5%)
Good honours:	=102	(47.0%)
Graduate prospects:	62	(63.2%)

title because it has become one of the new "teaching-led" universities.

More than 95 per cent of the undergraduates are state-educated and about a third come from working-class homes. The dropout rate of around 14 per cent is better than the national average for the university's courses and entry qualifications. Overall, the university's applications were up by nearly 20 per cent at the start of 2007 and had increased again 12 months later, when most universities were suffering a decline because of the switch from six choices per applicant to five.

Recent capital development has been concentrated on the Medway campus, where 250 computers have been installed in the Rowan Williams Court building. All the campuses are connected by a microwave link, which provides fast access to teaching and learning materials, as well as email. The new Drill Hall Library at Medway provides 147,000 items, 370 computers and 250 study spaces for Canterbury, Greenwich and Kent students. Another £30 million is being spent on a library and learning resource centre, with integrated student services, at Canterbury. Due to open in 2009, it will have a café, two garden terraces, an atrium and multipurpose floor space for public events, conferences, exams, teaching and exhibitions.

Social and sports facilities naturally vary between the campuses, although the students' union is present on all of them. Residential accommodation is not plentiful, but first years are given priority.

Undergraduate Fees and Bursaries

- Fees for UK/EU students: £3,145
- International student fees: £7,650–£8,130
- Bursary on full grant: sliding scale: £820–£510.
- Bursaries on partial grant: household income up to £49K: sliding scale £510–£0.
- Scholarships based on circumstances or by competition. For full details see the university's website: www.canterbury.ac.uk/support/student-support-services/students/finance/finance-info-0809/flb0809.asp

Students

Undergraduates:	6,780	(4,580)
Postgraduates:	1,075	(2,510)
Mature students:	27.2%	
Overseas students:	4.3%	
Applications per place:	4.6	
From state-sector schools:	96.3%	
From working-class homes:	35.7%	

For detailed information about fees, grants and bursaries and how they work, see chapter 7.

Accommodation

Number of places and costs refer to 2008–09
University-provided places: 1,314
Percentage catered: 11%
Catered costs: £112.40–£117.40 a week. Food is purchased on Smart card basis.
Self-catered costs: £80–£96 a week.
Accommodation guaranteed for first years if conditions are met.
International students: as above.
Contact: accommodation@canterbury.ac.uk
www.canterbury.ac.uk/support/accommodation

Cardiff University

Cardiff has established itself as the front-runner in Welsh higher education and a leading player in the UK and beyond. During 2007, the university celebrated a second Nobel laureate on its staff, as Professor Sir Martin Evans won the prize for medicine, and it broke into the top 100 in *The Times Higher Education*/QS world rankings. A member of the Russell Group of 20 research-led universities, Cardiff had already left the University of Wales, believing that only full independence would enable it to compete with other top universities.

With more than 25,000 students and 5,500 staff, the university is a match for most rivals in teaching and research. A third of the students come from Wales, but the 3,000 from overseas testify to Cardiff's international reputation. Seven subjects – city and regional planning, civil engineering, education, English, optometry, psychology and theology – were rated internationally outstanding in the latest research assessments. Almost nine out of ten researchers reached the top two of the seven categories, one of the best ratios in Britain.

Teaching quality is also highly rated: the 21 subjects graded as excellent represent more than half of the university. An overall audit by the Quality Assurance Agency complimented the university on its "powerful academic vision and well-developed and effectively articulated mission to achieve excellence in teaching and research". Student support services, including counselling facilities and the help offered to dyslexics, were among the features singled out for praise.

Cardiff has done well in the first three National Student Surveys, only just missing a place in the top 20 in 2007. Philosophy, theology and religious studies, English, history and biology achieved the highest satisfaction levels. Many full-time degrees share a common first year, and the modular system of courses makes undergraduate study flexible thereafter. New courses include electronic and communication engineering and medical pharmacology.

The university enjoys a central location in Wales' capital, occupying a significant part of the civic complex around Cathays Park. In recent years, there has been major investment in new buildings and equipment, and extensive refurbishment. Recent projects include a £14-million student residence and almost £30 million invested in brain and body imaging facilities at the former University of Wales College of Medicine, which became part of the university with the backing of £60 million from the Welsh Assembly and other sources. Library services are being transformed in order to boost access to

P.O. Box 921
Cardiff CF10 3XQ
029 2087 4455 (enquiries)
enquiry@cardiff.ac.uk
www.cardiff.ac.uk
www.cardiffstudents.com

The Times Rankings
Overall Ranking: 29

Student satisfaction:	=18	(77%)
Research quality:	=29	(4.5)
Entry standards:	=23	(381)
Student–staff ratio:	21	(14.3)
Services & facilities/student:	51	(£1,085)
Expected completion rate:	27	(90.1%)
Good honours:	=32	(67.6%)
Graduate prospects:	30	(73.5%)

resources and improve the environment for the study of rare collections. The School of Optometry and Vision Sciences moved into a £21-million building in 2007 and a new Medical School building will open in 2008, making room for more students. The school is a mile away from the main campus at Heath Park, where the five healthcare schools share a 53-acre site with the University Hospital of Wales.

A new IT working environment will give students online access to information about their studies and social life, including reading lists and timetables to social events and networking groups. Other recent developments include the establishment of the Cardiff International Academy of Voice, providing individual training for opera stars of the future, while the School of Earth, Ocean and Planetary Sciences has invested in its own research vessel for a programme of research and teaching voyages.

With more than 5,000 rooms, the university can accommodate all first years and a considerable number of returning students. Rents are among the lowest in the UK, according to a National Union of Students survey.

Entry requirements have been rising, despite recent expansion, and the graduate employment record is good. Only eight universities had more applications than Cardiff at the start of 2008, although the 15

per cent decline with the switch from six choices per applicant to five was steeper than at most leading institutions. The University has been bucking the national trend with increases in applications in science, technology, engineering and maths. One undergraduate in six comes from an independent school, but still almost a quarter have a working-class background. The projected dropout rate increased in the latest figures to almost 10 per cent, but is still close to the UK average for the university's subjects and entry qualifications.

The city of Cardiff is popular with students. The main residential site at Talybont boasts a "sports village", and there is also a city-centre fitness suite and a sports ground available to students.

Undergraduate Fees and Bursaries

- Welsh-domiciled student fees: £3,145, with grant of up to £1,890
- Non-Welsh UK domiciled and EU student fees: £3,145
- International student fees: £9,100–£11,700; £21,000 (clinical)
- Welsh National Bursary for all UK students, means-tested with maximum of £310. University bursaries also available.
- Scholarships based on circumstances or by competition. For full details see the university's website: www.cardiff.ac.uk/for/prospective/ug/scholarships/index.html

Students		
Undergraduates:	16,390	(5,410)
Postgraduates:	3,705	(4,140)
Mature students:	13.7%	
Overseas students:	7.3%	
Applications per place:	7.5	
From state-sector schools:	83.9%	
From working-class homes:	21.1%	

For detailed information about fees, grants and bursaries and how they work, see chapter 7.

Accommodation

Number of places and costs refer to 2008–09
University-provided places: 5,164
Percentage catered: 5.2%
Catered costs: £70–£80 a week.
Self-catered costs: £56–£84 a week.
All first years are guaranteed accommodation if conditions are met.
Policy for international students: as above
Contact: residences@cardiff.ac.uk

Cardiff, University of Wales Institute (UWIC)

The University of Wales Institute in Cardiff has an international reputation for sport, but is no slouch in some academic fields either. The combination has been attracting record numbers of applicants: like the other universities in Wales, UWIC saw a decline in the demand for places at the start of 2008, but there has been a succession of large rises earlier in the decade. Students have a formal entitlement to individual tuition.

Extra places have been added, but plans for UWIC to become part of a much larger university through a merger with neighbouring Glamorgan or the University of Wales, Newport are on the back burner, despite enthusiasm from the Welsh Assembly. Two thirds of UWIC's 10,000 students are Welsh, half of them from Cardiff or the Vale of Glamorgan. More than 90 per cent attended state schools and, although little more than a quarter come from working-class homes, the 15 per cent who come from areas sending few students to higher education is close to the "benchmark" set according to the mix of courses. The dropout rate is lower than the average for new universities.

UWIC is one of Britain's leading centres for university sport, with team performances to match some excellent facilities. In recent years, the Institute has had British university champions in gymnastics, trampolining, athletics, rugby union, rugby league, boxing, squash, archery, weightlifting and judo. More than 240 past or present students are internationals in 28 sports, world and Olympic champions among them. The £7-million National Indoor Athletics Centre is UWIC's pride and joy, but other facilities are also of high quality.

Academically, art and design is the star performer, with teaching in ceramics, fine art and interior architecture rated excellent, and the whole area considered nationally excellent for research. All six teacher training courses are rated as excellent, but UWIC has slipped down the table in the latest National Student Survey. There were top scores for teaching quality in several sciences, but less than one academic in five was entered for the last Research Assess-ment Exercise, leaving UWIC near the bottom of the research table in terms of average grades per member of staff.

Entrance requirements are generally modest, but the menu of largely vocational courses means that many students come with qualifications other than A levels. About a fifth are mature students and there is a relatively high proportion from overseas. Many are among the 23 per cent

---

Cardiff Institute
Western Avenue
Cardiff CF5 2YB
029 2041 6070 (enquiries)
admissions@uwic.ac.uk
www.uwic.ac.uk
www.uwicsu.co.uk

The Times Rankings
Overall Ranking: 85

Student satisfaction:	=73	(72%)
Research quality:	=92	(0.8)
Entry standards:	97	(246)
Student–staff ratio:	=90	(19.9)
Services & facilities/student:	48	(£1,112)
Expected completion rate:	47	(85.1%)
Good honours:	93	(48.6%)
Graduate prospects:	=100	(55.3%)

postgraduates – the largest proportion in Wales.

UWIC is spending more than £50 million on its four sites, all within three miles of the centre of Cardiff. The Cyncoed campus, which houses education and sport, is the centre of activity, particularly for first-year students. The athletics centre is there, together with a multitude of outdoor facilities and also the Welsh Sports Centre for the Disabled. Student facilities, including the Institute's largest bar, have been upgraded recently. A £2-million learning centre opened in 2005; the IT suite has 250 computers available 24 hours a day.

Howard Gardens is the home of fine art, while the Llandaff campus hosts design, engineering, food science and health courses. A new £3-million student centre is at Llandaff, which includes a dyslexia support unit among a number of advice and representation services, and a learning centre with more than 300 computers opened in 2003. Business, hospitality and tourism are taught at the Colchester Avenue campus.

Students tend to like Cardiff as a city, and UWIC's enterprising union does its best to make their time there as lively as possible. It owns a nightclub and bar in the city centre to add to the campus choices. Before the recent expansion, it was possible to guarantee accommodation to all first years, and 90 per cent still live in halls. UWIC is the only university to have been awarded the Government's Charter Mark four times, the judges commenting particularly on the level of satisfaction among students. This was not especially evident in the national surveys, and the improvement noted in 2006 did not continue in 2007.

Undergraduate Fees and Bursaries
- Welsh-domiciled student fees: £3,145, with grant of up to £1,890
- Non-Welsh UK domiciled and EU student fees: £3,145
- International student fees: £7,500–£8,500; £11,000 (podiatry)
- Welsh National Bursary for all UK students, means-tested with maximum of £310. University bursaries also available.
- Scholarships based on circumstances or by competition. For full details see the university's website: www2.uwic.ac.uk/Advice4App/UG/finance/Bursaries/

Students

Undergraduates:	6,700	(905)
Postgraduates:	1,130	(2,030)
Mature students:	23.4%	
Overseas students:	8.5%	
Applications per place:	4.4	
From state-sector schools:	93.8%	
From working-class homes:	25.7%	

For detailed information about fees, grants and bursaries and how they work, see chapter 7.

Accommodation
Number of places and costs refer to 2007–08
University-provided places: 1,183
Percentage catered: 33%
Catered cost: £103.50–£114.00 a week.
Self-catered costs: £72.50–£90.00 a week.
First-year students have no guarantee, terms and conditons apply.
International students: accommodation is reserved, subject to availability and if conditions are met.
Contact: accomm@uwic.ac.uk

University of Central Lancashire (UCLan)

A big university at the heart of England's newest city, UClan does not dominate Preston to the extent that Cambridge or Durham do their cities, but students account for a sixth of the population during term time. The modern, town-centre campus has seen considerable development, as the university has doubled in size, and still the building continues. The new £5-million dental school was one of the first to open in over a century, while the £15-million Media Factory, with its facilities for music, theatre, dance, film, photography and media studies, has prompted a surge in applications for arts and fashion courses.

An extended and refurbished students' union boasts one of the largest student venues in the country, and well-equipped new buildings have opened recently for science, health and business subjects. The Centre for Employability through the Humanities follows a major theme for the whole university, which encourages all students to develop their CVs, engage in course-related employment during vacations and to draw on the experience of local employers and alumni.

Amid the expansion, the university has revamped its pioneering credit accumulation and transfer system, allowing undergraduates to mix and match from a menu of more than 3,000 courses. Electives are used to broaden the curriculum, so that up to 11 per cent of students' time is spent on subjects outside their normal range. There is particular encouragement to include a language as part of the package, and more than 2,000 students do so. UCLan won *The Times Higher Education Supplement*'s 2006 award for the best support for overseas students for its language programme for Chinese students.

The former polytechnic has acquired a high reputation in some apparently unlikely fields. American studies, psychology, education and nursing all achieved perfect scores for teaching quality. Journalism, which also scored well, is sufficiently popular to be able to demand the equivalent of three Bs at A level. Astrophysics, which benefits from two observatories in Britain and a share in the Southern African Large Telescope, saw applications increase by a third by the official deadline for courses beginning in 2008. The subject was one of the successes of the last research assessments, which were a definite improvement on 1996, although only history and law joined physics and astronomy in the top three categories. The university has since invested £10 million in ten research centres in areas as diverse as philosophy and nuclear science. Scores improved in the

---

Preston PR1 2HE
01772 201201
cenquiries@uclan.ac.uk
www.uclan.ac.uk
www.yourunion.co.uk

Edinburgh
Belfast
PRESTON
London
Cardiff

The Times Rankings
Overall Ranking: 63

Student satisfaction:	=39	(75%)
Research quality:	=88	(0.9)
Entry standards:	69	(271)
Student–staff ratio:	58	(17.5)
Services & facilities/student:	=68	(£984)
Expected completion rate:	=90	(76.9%)
Good honours:	83	(50.9%)
Graduate prospects:	=55	(64.4%)

latest National Student Survey, when UCLan was joint top for sociology.

The Cumbrian campus has been transferred to that county's new university, but UCLan is developing a £10-million campus in Burnley, which will open in 2009. A partnership with Burnley College already offers a number of the university's degree and Foundation degree courses. A new Centre for Outdoor Education being developed at Llangollen, in north Wales, which will be fully operational by September 2008, when the university is launching a degree in the subject.

More than a third of Central Lancashire's students come from working-class homes. A high proportion are local people in their twenties or thirties, many of whom come through the well-established lifelong learning networks run in colleges throughout the North West. No fewer than 14 per cent of the university's students are taught in colleges but, unlike some institutions involved in "franchising", Central Lancashire has won official praise for the quality of its external programmes. Applications were down only marginally at the start of 2008, when other universities suffered much more from the switch from six choices per applicant to five. UCLan actually increased its share of north-west England's total applications significantly.

The social scene in Preston may not compare with Manchester or Liverpool, but neither do the security risks, and the cost of living is low. Both cities are within easy reach, and the student union's "Feel" club nights have won national recognition. Although still not the most fashionable university, UCLan commands great loyalty among its students.

Rents for the nearly 1,500 places in university accommodation are among the lowest in Britain and the 60-acre Preston Sports Arena is among the best in any higher education institution. Three miles from the main campus, the centre is available to clubs throughout the region but there are reserved periods for students, who can also book at peak times.

Undergraduate Fees and Bursaries

- Fees for UK/EU students: £3,145
- International student fees: £8,950–£9,450
- Bursary on full grant: £1,000
- Bursaries on partial grant: household income up to £60K: £1,000.
- Scholarships based on circumstances or by competition. For full details see the university's website: www.uclan.ac.uk/fees/index.htm

---

Students

Undergraduates:	15,495	(9,920)
Postgraduates:	1,615	(2,815)
Mature students:	27.7%	
Overseas students:	5.4%	
Applications per place:	4.0	
From state-sector schools:	97.6%	
From working-class homes:	37.1%	

For detailed information about fees, grants and bursaries and how they work, see chapter 7.

Accommodation

Number of places and costs refer to 2008–09
University-provided places: around 2,000
Percentage catered: 0%
Self-cateredcosts: £69.93–£81.00 a week.
The Student Accommodation Service will assist all first years find suitable accommodation either in University owned/leased halls of residence, private sector registered halls, or shared houses.
International students: as above.
Contact: saccommodation@uclan.ac.uk

Chester University

The picturesque Roman city of Chester is one of those places that outsiders probably always expected to have its own university. Indeed, William Gladstone was among the founders of the first Church of England teacher training college there in 1839. Although it took until 2005 for that college to achieve university status, it had been building up a solid reputation recently in a number of subjects beyond education alone. Although applications were down by almost 20 per cent at the start of 2008, as the switch from six choices to five per applicant took its toll, this followed three years of substantial increases, leaving the demand for places far more buoyant than in pre-university days.

The main campus is only a short walk from the centre of Chester, a 32-acre site boasting manicured gardens and a number of new developments. A new sports hall is just one of a stream of improvements, which have included a new library and media centre, a large auditorium, a science building, an art and technology centre, and a swimming pool. The Faculty of Health and Social Care and the Faculty of Arts and Media both acquired new headquarters in 2007, when a new students' union building also opened. The Warrington campus, which has seven halls of residence, focuses on media courses and has seen the addition of state-of-the-art production facilities in collaboration with Granada Television and a new students' union. The library has been extended to three times its original size and a business centre opened for students and local firms. The campus is expected to be the focus of future development to accommodate modest increases in student numbers.

Chester was among the top 10 universities in the first National Student Survey. Although it has slipped out of the top 50 since then, it was the highest-scoring university for fine art, and boasted the only maximum score for teaching in geography and development studies. Sport was one of the top performers in the later rounds of teaching assessment, with maths also scoring 23 points out of 24. Although research activity has been growing, it has been from a low base: the average grades in the 2001 assessments were in the bottom ten of the universities in this year's *Guide*. Nevertheless, Chester was the first of the universities created in 2005 to be granted the power to award research degrees.

With 14,500 students, including part-timers, Chester is among the biggest of the new universities established that year. More than half of the undergraduates are mature students and three quarters are female. Nearly all are state-educated, and

---

Parkgate Road
Chester CH1 4BJ
01244 511000
enquiries@chester.ac.uk
www.chester.ac.uk
www.chestersu.com

The Times Rankings
Overall Ranking: =86

Student satisfaction:	=55	(74%)
Research quality:	=107	(0.5)
Entry standards:	=64	(274)
Student–staff ratio:	=61	(17.9)
Services & facilities/student:	105	(£734)
Expected completion rate:	93	(76.1%)
Good honours:	72	(54.3%)
Graduate prospects:	90	(57.6%)

more than a third have working-class roots. The projected dropout rate had crept above 20 per cent in the latest statistics – significantly worse than the national average for the university's courses and entry standards. About a third of the undergraduates take combined honours degrees and many courses of all types include a period of extended work experience. There is also a limited range of Foundation degrees, mainly in health subjects but now including courses in business or leadership and management for RAF personnel. The Foundation degree in Muslim youth work is the first of its kind.

A student contract of the type that is likely to become commonplace elsewhere in the higher education sector sets out clear conditions on the offer of a place, as well as detailing the university's responsibilities. Students promise to "study diligently, and to attend promptly and participate appropriately at lectures, courses, classes, seminars, tutorials, work placements and other activities which form part of the programme." The university undertakes to deliver the student's programme but leaves itself considerable leeway beyond that.

However, Chester offers considerable support and facilities for its students. There are libraries on both sites and extensive sports facilities, especially on the main campus, catering partly for the large physical education programme. Most first years are offered one of the growing number of hall places, although there is not yet enough university accommodation to make this a guarantee. Student union facilities form the basis of the social scene on both campuses, but Chester has more to offer for those looking further afield.

Undergraduate Fees and Bursaries

- Fees for UK/EU students: £3,145
- International student fees: £6,894–£7,506
- Bursary on full grant: £1,000
- Bursaries on partial grant: n/a
- Scholarships based on circumstances or by competition. For full details see the university's website: www.chester.ac.uk/undergraduate/moneymatters.html

Students		
Undergraduates:	7,290	(4,365)
Postgraduates:	620	(2,825)
Mature students:	19.4%	
Overseas students:	1.5%	
Applications per place:	6.8	
From state-sector schools:	97.4%	
From working-class homes:	34.4%	

For detailed information about fees, grants and bursaries and how they work, see chapter 7.

Accommodation

Number of places and costs refer to 2007–08
University-provided places: 1,050
Percentage catered: 46%
Catered costs: £63.00–£120.65 a week.
Self-catered costs: £52.85–£83.30 a week.
First years cannot be guaranteed accommodation.
International students: guaranteed accommodation if they apply by advertised date.
Contact: www.chester.ac.uk/accommodation

University of Chichester

Chichester is the smallest of the nine universities created in 2005, despite being an amalgamation of two former teacher training colleges. But it featured in the top ten in the first National Student Survey and was back there in 2007, when history, the creative arts and sports science all showed very high levels of satisfaction. Indeed, the university has had an extremely creditable debut overall in *The Times* League Table, finishing ahead of most of the former polytechnics, as well as all the remaining newcomers. These achievements came too late to influence applications in the first year of top-up fees, but there was a spectacular increase of 22 per cent for courses beginning in 2007. The 10 per cent decline a year later was mainly due to the switch from six choices per applicant to five.

The university traces its history back to 1839, when the college that subsequently bore his name was founded in memory of William Otter, the education-minded Bishop of Chichester. It became a teacher training college for women, who still account for two-thirds of the places. Two further stages preceded university status – twenty years as the West Sussex Institute of Higher Education, following an amalgamation with the nearby Bognor Regis College of Education, and then seven as University College Chichester. The Chichester campus – now the larger of two – continues to carry the Bishop Otter name, signifying a continuing link with the Church of England.

There are six schools divided between the two sites, all of them in the arts, social sciences or education. Degree subjects range from adventure education to humanistic counselling, fine art and theology. The PE teacher training course is the largest in the country – the university now trains one in five PE teachers in England – and highly rated by Ofsted. Media studies achieved full marks in the best of Chichester's teaching assessments and, while the university was less successful in the Research Assessment Exercise, it entered a larger proportion of its academics than any of its peer group. The Mathematics Centre, at Bognor, has an international reputation, working with over thirty countries as well as teaching the university's own students. It has become a focal point for curriculum development in Britain and elsewhere.

Almost all the students are state-educated and, while the proportions from working-class homes and areas of low participation in higher education are both below the national average for the university's courses and entry grades, this is attributed to its location. The projected dropout rate, at only 8.5 per cent, is barely

---

Bishop Otter Campus
College Lane
Chichester
W. Sussex PO19 6PE
01243 816002
admissions@chi.ac.uk
www.chi.ac.uk
www.chisu.org

The Times Rankings
Overall Ranking: 59

Student satisfaction:	=12	(78%)
Research quality:	=58	(1.7)
Entry standards:	=89	(253)
Student–staff ratio:	=83	(19.6)
Services & facilities/student:	106	(£733)
Expected completion rate:	37	(88.0%)
Good honours:	104	(46.7%)
Graduate prospects:	99	(55.5%)

more than half the benchmark figure. Two out of ten students are 21 or older on entry. The university runs summer taster sessions and has a series of partnerships with schools in the Channel Islands and Sussex to encourage a broader intake. Courses are also run in collaboration with Isle of Wight College, where fees are pegged at £1,200, and with the Academy of Play and Child Psychotherapy, in Uckfield, East Sussex.

Both of the university's campuses are within ten minutes' walk of the sea and the 520 residential places are roughly equally divided between them. There is a university bus service linking the two and student union bars at each. Sports facilities are good and competitive teams surprisingly successful for such a small university. The university has been chosen to provide training facilities for competitors in athletics, boxing, road cycling and table tennis before the 2012 Olympic Games. The bid was based on Chichester's expertise in sports science, as well as its facilities.

The small cathedral city of Chichester is best known as a yachting venue, while Bognor's days as a leading holiday resort are well in the past, but both offer a good supply of private housing and some student-oriented bars. Much of the surrounding countryside has been designated an area of outstanding natural beauty.

Undergraduate Fees and Bursaries

- Fees for UK/EU students: £3,145
- International student fees: £7,400–£7,880
- Bursary on full grant: £1,050
- Bursaries on partial grant: household income up to £50K: sliding scale £1,000–£250.
- Scholarships based on circumstances or by competition. For full details see the university's website: http://chi.ac.uk/applying/ChichesterBursaries.cfm

Students

Undergraduates:	3,060	(655)
Postgraduates:	340	(875)
Mature students:	22.1%	
Overseas students:	4.6%	
Applications per place:	5.4	
From state-sector schools:	97.8%	
From working-class homes:	29.6%	

For detailed information about fees, grants and bursaries and how they work, see chapter 7.

Accommodation

Number of places and costs refer to 2008–09
University-provided places: 647
Percentage catered: 66.5%
Catered costs: £94.45 (shared) – £126.30 (en suite) a week.
Self-catered costs: £73.50 (shared) – £104.30 (en suite) a week.
First years are accommodated on a first come–first served basis.
International students: as above.
Contact: accommodation@chi.ac.uk

City University

Once a college of advanced technology, a third of City students now study business, a third health subjects and the remaining third law, computing, engineering, journalism, and the arts. But the university has maintained its links with business, industry and the professions, reaping the benefits with consistently good graduate employment figures. The university's graduates play their part, with more than 4,000 of them offering practical help to current students through an online careers network. Courses have a practical edge, and many of the staff hold professional, as well as academic, qualifications.

The university is still comparatively small despite steady growth in the last five years, which has seen student numbers reach almost 23,000, including large contingents of postgraduates and part-timers. Numbers doubled during the 1990s, partly due to the incorporation of a nursing and midwifery college at nearby St Bartholomew's Hospital and the Charterhouse College of Radiography. Applications have increased steadily over the last four years, when other universities have experienced big swings in the demand for places. The 7.6 per cent increase at the start of 2008 was particularly impressive since it coincided with the reduction in choices per applicant from six to five.

Development has taken place at the university's headquarters, on the borders of the City of London, but the most ambitious project has been the £42-million home for the business school, in the financial district of the City of London. Opened in 2002, the new building, spread over eight floors, doubled the school's usable space, enabling it to expand its academic activity and executive programmes. Another £20 million has gone into an impressive new building for the School of Social Sciences.

The Cass Business School is one of City's great strengths. It was the first Western university to forge links with the Bank of China, running an Executive MBA programme in Shanghai as the first step to a wider role in business education throughout east and southeast Asia. City has links with 50 European universities and many more further afield, and many students spend a year of their course abroad.

The university had already boosted its legal provision by incorporating the Inns of Court School of Law in 2001. The City Law School, which includes the university's original department, offers London's only "one-stop shop" for legal training, from undergraduate to professional courses. City is also working with Queen Mary, University of London, in a range of subjects, starting with medicine and other health subjects, journalism and engineering. The two universities jointly host a

---

Northampton Square
London EC1V 0HB
020 7040 5060
ugadmissions@city.ac.uk
www.city.ac.uk
www.cusuonline.org

Edinburgh
Belfast
Cardiff
LONDON

The Times Rankings
Overall Ranking: 50

Student satisfaction:	=73	(72%)
Research quality:	50	(3.7)
Entry standards:	=41	(321)
Student–staff ratio:	67	(18.1)
Services & facilities/student:	86	(£878)
Expected completion rate:	=48	(85.0%)
Good honours:	=43	(63.7%)
Graduate prospects:	13	(77.1%)

national centre for teaching and learning in nursing and midwifery.

City has a particularly high reputation in music, where it is associated with the Guildhall School of Music and Drama, with its teaching rated as excellent and research internationally outstanding. The subject achieved the university's only 5* rating in the 2001 Research Assessment Exercise, but arts policy, business, information science, law and optometry all reached the next grade.

Early teaching assessments were disappointing. The university's response was to establish an educational development unit to enhance the quality of teaching and launch a review of the effectiveness of personal tutoring. Scores improved dramatically, with business and management, maths and statistics, and health leading the way. Finance and accounting produced the best scores in a relatively disappointing set of results from the latest National Student Survey.

Recent additions to the portfolio of degrees include environmental engineering and Anglo-American law, while the journalism department is highly regarded. There is also a flourishing sub-degree programme for adults, which ranges from sitcom writing to e-business. The changes have maintained City's position among the most popular universities in London, with eight applications per undergraduate place.

Official performance indicators for higher education have brought mixed news: the dropout rate has been falling but 14 per cent is still high for a traditional university. City has a good record among its peers for widening participation in higher education, with more than a third of its undergraduates from working-class homes. Students tend to be more concerned about their inability to afford the attractions of a trendy part of London. Most fall back on the extended students' union, but this is usually shut at weekends for lack of demand. Sports facilities are poor by current university standards, although the indoor sports centre is conveniently located.

Undergraduate Fees and Bursaries

- Fees for UK/EU students: £3,145
- International student fees: £7,750–£9,850*
- Bursary on full grant: sliding scale: £750–£350.
- Bursaries on partial grant: household income up to £30K: sliding scale £750–£350.
- Scholarships based on circumstances or by competition. For full details see the university's website: www.city.ac.uk/study/money/undergraduate/index.html

* Figures for 2007–08

Students

Undergraduates:	7,590	(7,065)
Postgraduates:	3,815	(5,365)
Mature students:	24.8%	
Overseas students:	15%	
Applications per place:	7.9	
From state-sector schools:	85.9%	
From working-class homes:	36.1%	

For detailed information about fees, grants and bursaries and how they work, see chapter 7.

Accommodation

Number of places and costs refer to 2008–09
University-provided places: 1,344
Percentage catered: 0%
Self-catered costs: £97–£180 a week.
Accommodation is guaranteed for first years if conditions are met. Residential restrictions apply.
International students: preference is given to new overseas students.
Contact: accomm@city.ac.uk
www.city.ac.uk/studentcentre/housing

Coventry University

Coventry is investing £160 million in its 33-acre campus close to the city centre, much of it going on student facilities. The showpiece library cost £20 million and is almost entirely naturally ventilated and lit. The £5-million student centre, opened in 2006, contains everything from the accommodation and careers services to the Finance and Academic Registry, as well as lounge space. The Centre for Academic Writing offers advice on essays and theses, with group sessions and one-to-one appointments, while the Maths Support Centre includes a statistics advisory service and specialist support service for students with dyslexia.

Among the next projects will be a student enterprise centre and a new engineering and computing building. Another initiative launched this year will be a Health and Wellbeing Centre for students and staff, covering sport, counselling, mental health, disability, the GP practice and spirituality and health. The university has already added other facilities, including more residential accommodation, a second students' union and a sports centre, during a decade in which student numbers doubled to more than 20,000. There is a £7-million arts centre and the students' union has dedicated facilities for mature and international students.

Coventry traces its origins back to 1843 with the foundation of the College of Design and its links with the motor industry of the Midlands were reflected in its earlier title of Lanchester Polytechnic, named after a leading engineering figure. It has adopted an innovative approach to computer-assisted learning, supported by an expanded computer network. The university was chosen to house national centres of excellence in teaching for e-learning in health and social care, as well as in maths, and transport and product design. Degrees in automotive engineering and design courses have been developed in collaboration with the motor industry, both in Coventry and further afield.

The university has a focus on employment, which is reflected in a predominantly vocational curriculum. The Start-Up Café encourages business networking and local employers are engaging with the programme of work-based learning. A rough balance is maintained between arts, technology, business and health studies in order to preserve an all-round educational environment. The majority of students exercise their right to take "free-choice modules" that cover the full range of university provision, with IT skills and languages particularly popular. Coventry has been building up its portfolio of courses, introducing eye-catching degrees in subjects such as disaster management,

---

Priory Street
Coventry CV1 5FB
024 7615 2222 (admissions)
studentenquiries
 @coventry.ac.uk
www.coventry.ac.uk
www.cusu.org

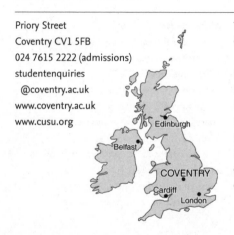

Edinburgh
Belfast
COVENTRY
Cardiff
London

forensic chemistry, criminology and boat design.

Teaching ratings were good, with history and politics, economics, health subjects and mathematics achieving near-perfect scores, following early successes for geography and mechanical engineering. Economics was the biggest success in the latest National Student Survey. Research grades improved considerably in the 2001 assessment exercise, but only design, materials and politics reached any of the top three categories. Design benefits from a revolutionary £1.6-million digital modelling workshop, sponsored by the Bugatti Trust, which provides full-scale vehicle modelling facilities for undergraduates as well as researchers.

Among the initiatives to improve the student experience has been the introduction of tangible rewards for excellent teaching and further development of electronic learning. Almost 40 per cent of the undergraduates have working-class backgrounds, many from areas of low participation in higher education. Applications have been healthy and were down by less than the national average at the start of 2008, following the switch from six to five choices per candidate. However, the projected dropout rate of almost 23 per cent is worse than the national average for the university's subjects and entry qualifications.

More than most universities, Coventry is a creature of its city, and the civic-minded approach of the university has created many town–gown links. The main buildings open out from the ruins of the bombed cathedral, as university and public facilities mingle in the city. Student residences are within easy walking distance of the campus and city centre. Students welcome the relatively low cost of living in Coventry, and, as at most new universities, the student body encompasses a wide range of ages.

Undergraduate Fees and Bursaries

- Fees for UK/EU students: £3,145
- International student fees: £7,900
- Bursary on full grant: £310
- Bursaries on partial grant: household income up to £60K: £310.
- Scholarships based on circumstances or by competition. For full details see the university's website: www.coventry.ac.uk/cu/studentfunding

---

Students

Undergraduates:	10,935	(5,490)
Postgraduates:	1,395	(1,480)
Mature students:	24%	
Overseas students:	10.4%	
Applications per place:	5.1	
From state-sector schools:	97.1%	
From working-class homes:	40.1%	

For detailed information about fees, grants and bursaries and how they work, see chapter 7.

Accommodation

Number of places and costs refer to 2008–09
University-provided places: 2,464
Percentage catered: 26.7%
Catered costs: £94 a week (10 meals).
Self-catered costs: £60–£128 (40–50 weeks).
First-year students are guaranteed housing provided conditons are met.
International students: given priority.
Contact: accomm.ss@coventry.ac.uk;
www.coventry.ac.uk/undergraduate-study/accommodation

Cumbria University

One of the largest counties without a university of its own has put that right through the amalgamation of a former teacher training college and an arts institute, with the addition of the two Cumbrian campuses of the University of Central Lancashire. The new University of Cumbria is divided between Carlisle, Penrith, Ambleside and Lancaster, as well as running a specialist teacher education centre in east London. There are also partnerships with the four further education colleges in the county to provide higher education locally.

The new university, which will have more than 14,000 students, was eight years in gestation and saw false starts in the expansion of provision, especially in Carlisle, where there are three separate sites. Finally established in August 2007, the university has four faculties: arts, design and media; business, social sciences and sport; health, medical science and social care; and science and natural resources.

The biggest of the component parts is the former St Martin's College, which was founded in Lancaster by the Church of England in 1964 to train teachers. It took in a nursing college and another teacher training college, in Ambleside, during the 1990s. There were more than 12,000 students by the time university status arrived, making the college the largest provider of higher education in Cumbria by a considerable margin. The main base remains in Lancaster, a ten-minute walk from the town centre, with a modern library and excellent sports facilities, including a £2.5-million sports complex, gymnastics centre and fitness centre. The Ambleside campus has an outdoor studies centre and a new learning resources centre. There are plans for more residences and improved sports facilities. The nearest railway station is a 20-minute drive away at Windermere.

Cumbria Institute of the Arts can trace its history in Carlisle back to 1822, eventually becoming the only specialist institute of the arts in the north west of England and one of only a small number of such institutions in the country. Its campus boasts a new Learning Gateway, an innovative multimedia learning resource centre, and a sports centre with a four-court sports hall and well-equipped fitness room. The creative arts are one of the main areas for development in the university's initial planning.

The main Cumbrian campus acquired from the University of Central Lancashire is a mile outside Penrith, in landscaped gardens overlooking the fells, and caters mainly for agriculture and forestry. A former agricultural college, it has

Fusehill Street
Carlisle
Cumbria CA1 2HH
01228 616234
info@cumbria.ac.uk
www.cumbria.ac.uk
www.thestudentsunion.org

Edinburgh
CARLISLE
Belfast
LANCASTER
London
Cardiff

The Times Rankings
Overall Ranking: 99

Student satisfaction:	=99	(68%)
Research quality:	=104	(0.6)
Entry standards:	=74	(267)
Student–staff ratio:	97	(20.4)
Services & facilities/student:	107	(£685)
Expected completion rate:	92	(76.6%)
Good honours:	100	(47.5%)
Graduate prospects:	32	(72.8%)

broadened into related areas such as environmental management and other subjects not directly related to land-based industries. Courses include outdoor education and leadership, geography, business, tourism, sport and computing. Library and learning resource facilities have been improved and residential accommodation expanded. There are also two farms, one adjacent to the campus and a working hill farm 15 miles away within the national park.

In the longer term, the university is planning a £160 million transformation of its estate, almost half of which will go on a new campus in Carlisle. The proposals include plans for further development at all the existing centres to maintain a "Cumbria-wide presence".

Combined scores from the Cumbria Institute and St Martin's College were used to produce Cumbria's first League Table entry, in the lower reaches but by no means at the bottom. Its position improved in this year's table. The early focus of the university is on attracting more students from a region of low participa-tion in higher education, as well as on serving the social and economic needs of the county. Applications were up by more than 10 per cent at the start of 2008, when there was a decline at most universities.

Undergraduate Fees and Bursaries

- Fees for UK/EU students: £3,145
- International student fees: contact the university
- Bursary on full grant: £1,260
- Bursaries on partial grant: household income up to £60K: sliding scale £1,045–£210.
- Scholarships based on circumstances or by competition. For full details see the university's website: www.cumbria.ac.uk/FutureStudents/ FeesFinance/MoneyMatters.aspx

Students

Undergraduates:	5,575	(4,795)
Postgraduates:	1,135	(1,785)
Mature students:	17.8%	
Overseas students:	2.1%	
Applications per place:	4.1	
From state-sector schools:	99.2%	
From working-class homes:	38.9%	

For detailed information about fees, grants and bursaries and how they work, see chapter 7.

Accommodation

Number of places and costs refer to 2008–09
University-provided places: 809
Percentage catered: 65%
Catered costs: £87.95–£99.95 (41 weeks).
Self-catered costs: £44–£78 a week.
First years are guaranteed halls accommodation if Cumbria is first choice.
International students: guaranteed halls if staying for full academic year.
Contact: www.cumbria.ac.uk/FutureStudents/ Accommodation/Accommodation.aspx

De Montfort University

Like the 13th-century Earl of Leicester after whom the university is named, De Montfort has a fiefdom of sorts: in this case a network of campuses in a 50-mile radius. Based on what was Leicester Polytechnic, the new university spread ever outwards, making it the biggest in the region. But DMU is now putting more than £100 million into consolidating a more manageable estate, some of it provided by the city council and local businesses. The Milton Keynes outpost closed in 2003, following the transfer of campuses in Lincolnshire to Lincoln University, and the Bedford campus has been sold to form half of the new Bedfordshire University.

There are now only two campuses, both in Leicester, following the relocation of health and life sciences to the university's headquarters. Another 12 colleges are associates, linked into the university's network and offering its courses. A formal agreement commits the colleges, which stretch from north Oxfordshire to Grantham, to work with each other as well as with De Montfort.

The investment includes a £9-million campus centre, incorporating a new students' union, music venue and other facilities, which opened in September 2003. Part of the ring road is being diverted to allow the university to open up the 15th-century Magazine Gateway building, which will become the focal point of a university quarter with public open spaces and new links to the city centre. A £35-million building for business and law, due to open in September 2009, will be at its heart.

The £3.7-million creative technology studios feature video, audio and radio production suites, recording studios and laboratories with the latest broadcast and audio analysis technology. A Performance Arts Centre for Excellence (PACE) has already opened, allowing the university deliver innovative teaching for students of dance, drama and music technology. The 24-hour library has been remodelled with wireless networks and rooms equipped with audio visual and IT facilities for preparing presentations.

The university has an uncompromisingly vocational emphasis in its courses, but has also invested in research. Probably the most innovative example is the Institute of Creative Technologies, which will act as a catalyst for research that defies the traditional boundaries of computer science, the digital arts and humanities, and is already exciting the interest of the business world. There were successes in the 2001 Research Assessment Exercise, when DMU registered the highest proportion of subjects of any new

The Gateway
Leicester LE1 9BH
08459 454647 (enquiries)
enquiry@dmu.ac.uk
www.dmu.ac.uk
www.mydsu.com

The Times Rankings
Overall Ranking: =77

Student satisfaction:	=73	(72%)
Research quality:	=69	(1.4)
Entry standards:	=92	(250)
Student–staff ratio:	=56	(17.4)
Services & facilities/student:	=91	(£831)
Expected completion rate:	=69	(80.6%)
Good honours:	92	(49.0%)
Graduate prospects:	54	(64.8%)

university in the top three categories. Politics and English were only one grade off the top of the seven-point scale, while the total of eleven subjects on the next grade was easily the highest among the former polytechnics.

Teaching ratings improved after a patchy start, with politics and international studies achieving full marks and the sport and leisure courses only one mark short of the maximum. The professional accounting courses were awarded "premier" status in a worldwide accreditation scheme, and the university houses a national teaching centre for drama, dance and theatre studies. The latest National Student Survey saw a big improvement on some poor results in the first two rounds, with history and archaeology, politics, and finance and accounting producing particularly high levels of satisfaction.

De Montfort's range of programmes has been expanding and student enrolments are healthy. Among the recent additions is a BSc in Public and Community health, tackling issues such as increases in sexually transmitted infections and obesity. The dropout rate has improved considerably: at less than 16 per cent, it is now exactly the national average for the university's courses and entry grades. The university is abandoning semesters and going back to a three-term year, partly because it believes the prospect of imminent assessment encouraged some students to give up at Christmas in their first year. De Montfort has a proud record for widening access to higher education with 41 per cent of students coming from working-class homes. It was one of the first to set up an employment agency to help students find part-time work during their course of study as well as find careers upon graduation. Strong links with local business and industry manifest themselves in courses such as the BSc in media production, run in conjunction with the BBC, and in the provision of facilities such as the telematics laboratory sponsored by Orange, the mobile telephone company.

Accommodation difficulties have been addressed – five new halls of residence opened in 2003. All first years, apart from locals, are now guaranteed a place in halls.

Undergraduate Fees and Bursaries

- Fees for UK/EU students: £3,145
- International student fees: £7,990–£8,955
- Bursary on full grant: £400 + £250 (local students).
- Bursaries on partial grant: £400 + £250 (local students).
- Scholarships based on circumstances or by competition. For full details see the university's website: www.dmu.ac.uk/funding

Students

Undergraduates:	13,960	(3,165)
Postgraduates:	750	(2,540)
Mature students:	22.8%	
Overseas students:	4.8%	
Applications per place:	5.5	
From state-sector schools:	96.6%	
From working-class homes:	41%	

For detailed information about fees, grants and bursaries and how they work, see chapter 7.

Accommodation

Number of places and costs refer to 2007–08
University-provided places: 2,499
Percentage catered: 0%
Self-catered costs: £69–£83 a week.
First years are guaranteed accommodation.
Residential and age restrictions apply.
International students: guaranteed accommodation.
Contact: housing@dmu.ac.uk

University of Derby

Derby sees itself as a prototype for the modern university, providing courses at all levels from the age of 16 into retirement. Although not as extensive as the original plans for spanning further and higher education in the same institution, a merger with High Peak College and the subsequent creation of the University of Derby College Buxton have stayed true to the model. While accepting that Derby will never scale the heights in league tables such as ours, the university set itself the target of becoming the pre-eminent university of its type by 2020. Its yardsticks are student satisfaction, employability and cost-effectiveness.

As the only higher education college promoted to university status with the polytechnics, Derby had to run to keep up with its peers in its early days. Student numbers doubled in four years, the residential stock increased fivefold and extra teaching space was built. The pace of expansion inevitably imposed strains, and at one time Derby was the only university with two Unsatisfactory verdicts in the teaching assessments, but scores improved subsequently. Indeed, after provision was rationalised, a failure in pharmacy turned into maximum points on re-inspection. Business and theology also scored well, as did biosciences and other health subjects.

The university takes pride in its record for widening access: it had the highest proportion state-educated undergraduates in 2005–06 in England – only 20 out of 2,795 entrants came from independent schools – and more than 4 in 10 are from working-class homes. But the projected dropout rate was almost 23 per cent in the latest statistics, having recently dropped below the national average for the subjects and entry qualifications found at Derby.

Development is still continuing, with a £21-million art and design campus bringing together courses previously spread around three different sites. The new site forms one part of a £55-million estates strategy that is creating a University Quarter for Derby. The college already has a new home in the centre of Buxton, where the purchase of the Devonshire Royal Hospital for a nominal fee has provided an ideal centre for courses in tourism and hospitality management, as well as further education programmes. The landmark building, which has a bigger dome than St Paul's Cathedral, will house a 4-star training hotel and health spa, in addition to academic facilities.

There are three main sites in and around Derby. The Kedleston Road campus, two miles north of the city centre, is the largest, catering for most of the main subjects as well as the students'

Kedleston Road
Derby DE22 1GB
08701 202330 (enquiries)
askadmissions@
 derby.ac.uk
www.derby.ac.uk
www.udsu.co.uk

The Times Rankings
Overall Ranking: 95

Student satisfaction:	=64	(73%)
Research quality:	=88	(0.9)
Entry standards:	=74	(267)
Student–staff ratio:	=86	(19.8)
Services & facilities/student:	54	(£1,054)
Expected completion rate:	=86	(77.0%)
Good honours:	96	(47.8%)
Graduate prospects:	112	(49.5%)

union headquarters and multifaith centre. The £1.5-million Clinical Skills Suite was built to NHS "Red Book" standards, featuring hospital wards, counselling rooms and diagnostic radiography facilities. The Mickleover campus, which specialises in education and health, is also in a suburban location. The university has also opened a new £400,000 centre in Chesterfield.

Courses are modular and a foundation programme allows students to begin work at a partner college before transferring to the university. Derby has also awarded more work-based qualifications than any other UK university. Distance learning is a growth area, either online or through Derby's nine regional centres. Prospective students can even sample a virtual open evening. Business and management is by far the biggest academic area, but work placements are encouraged in all subjects. The accent on employability continues with an eight-week course on key skills, such as CV preparation and interview technique. Derby has also been in the forefront of the adoption of new teaching methods, pioneering the use of interactive video for a national scheme. A variety of courses, from Foundation degrees to postgraduate qualifications, are available online. The School of Flexible and Partnership Learning, which spans the entire university, won an award for the imaginative use of distance learning.

The university has spent £30 million in five years to maintain its guarantee of accommodation for all first years. Students seem to appreciate the university's efforts because Derby comes out well in its own satisfaction surveys, although this was not reflected in the latest national equivalent. Law fared particularly well in the last two national surveys, with the most satisfied students in the country in the results published in 2007. The 3 per cent decline in applications at the start of 2008 was less than half the national average.

Undergraduate Fees and Bursaries

- Fees for UK/EU students: £3,145
- International student fees: £7,600–£8,200
- Bursary on full grant: £800 + £300 (local address) or £400 (local school).
- Bursaries on partial grant: household income £25K–£35K: £500; £35K–£50K: £200; All + £300 or £400 local bursary.
- Scholarships based on circumstances or by competition. For full details see the university's website: www.derby.ac.uk/fees

---

Students

Undergraduates:	9,130	(3,145)
Postgraduates:	490	(1,945)
Mature students:	38.0%	
Overseas students:	7.0%	
Applications per place:	6.0	
From state-sector schools:	99.4%	
From working-class homes:	40.9%	

For detailed information about fees, grants and bursaries and how they work, see chapter 7.

Accommodation

Number of places and costs refer to 2008–09
University-provided places: 2,336
Percentage catered: 0%
Self-catered costs: £67.97–£87.01.
First-year students are guaranteed accommodation if they aply before 31 August.
Policy for international students: as above.
Contact: www.derby.ac.uk/accommodation
Student Living – tel: 01332 594180
(126 Nuns St, Derby, DE1 3LQ)

University of Dundee

Dundee describes itself as "Scotland's most enterprising university" and, while there would be other claimants to that title, it has certainly been among the liveliest in recent years. A long series of good quality ratings and the acquisition of education, nursing and art colleges, which doubled its size and greatly increased its scope, have been complemented by high-profile research successes, especially in medicine and the life sciences. The message appears to be getting through to prospective students: applications shot up by 88 per cent in five years, although they were down by more than the Scottish and UK averages at the start of 2008.

The university now has more than 18,000 students, including a healthy number from overseas, and is looking outwards to achieve the "critical mass" which experts regard as essential to break into the higher education elite. Dundee has been appointing professors at the rate of one a month for the last four years and has embarked on a £200-million campus redevelopment designed by the leading architect, Sir Terry Farrell. Almost £40 million of this is being spent on wireless-networked student residences.

Best-known for the life sciences, where research into cancer and diabetes is recognised as world-class, the university has already opened new buildings for interdisciplinary research, applied computing and clinical research. The main library is being extended and the Faculty of Education and Social Work acquired new premises in 2007.

Set in 20 acres of parkland, the medical school is the one of the few components of the university outside the compact city-centre campus – some of the nursing and midwifery students are 35 miles away in Kirkcaldy, while education and social work are waiting to move from the former Northern College campus, two miles outside the centre.

Biochemistry is the flagship department, housed in the £13-million Wellcome Trust Building. Its academics were the first in Britain to be invited to take part in Japan's Human Frontier science programme and are now the most-quoted researchers in their field. Medicine and the biological sciences won Dundee's other 5* research ratings, while six more subjects were on the next rung of the research assessment ladder, leaving half of the university's researchers in departments rated in the top two categories.

The latest Scottish university to join the National Student Survey, Dundee makes its debut in the top 20, with high levels of satisfaction in history and archaeology, English, politics and

Nethergate
Dundee DD1 4HN
01382 384160
srs@dundee.ac.uk
www.dundee.ac.uk
www.dusa.co.uk

The Times Rankings
Overall Ranking: 44

Student satisfaction:	=12	(78%)
Research quality:	=41	(4.2)
Entry standards:	27	(373)
Student–staff ratio:	18	(13.7)
Services & facilities/student:	71	(£971)
Expected completion rate:	=108	(68.7%)
Good honours:	37	(66.3%)
Graduate prospects:	=26	(73.9%)

computer science. Teaching ratings were almost uniformly impressive, with only philosophy judged less than Highly Satisfactory. Vocational degrees predominate, helping to produce the university's consistently good graduate employment record. The university sends more graduates into the professions than any other institution in Scotland and only Oxbridge graduates came out ahead of Dundee's in a national survey of starting salaries. All degrees include a career planning module and an internship option, and students are now provided with their own personal development website. Among the new courses introduced recently are forensic anthropology, sports biomedicine and innovative product design. The highly rated design courses are taught at the former Duncan of Jordanstone College of Art.

There has been an emphasis on opportunities for women ever since Dundee's separation from St Andrews University in 1967, and the addition of teacher training has increased the female majority. Two thirds of Dundee's students are from Scotland and nearly one in ten from Northern Ireland. One in five come from areas with little tradition of higher education and more than a quarter are from working-class homes. They enjoy a welcoming atmosphere and a cost of living which is lower than in most university cities. Private accommodation is plentiful for those who are not housed by the university. New students even have their own website. The city is profiting from recent regeneration programmes and becoming more fashionable. Spectacular mountain and coastal scenery are close at hand, but social life tends to be concentrated on the students' union, which is one of the largest and most active in Scotland.

Undergraduate Fees and Bursaries

- Scottish-domiciled and EU students: no fees payable.
- Non-Scottish UK-domiciled student fees: £1,775 a year (£2,825 medicine).
- International student fees:£8,500–£10,500 £13,100 (preclinical medicine); £20,800 (clinical medicine).
- Scholarships based on circumstances or by competition. For full details see the university's website: www.dundee.ac.uk/admissions/ undergraduate/fees_funding/index.htm

Students

Undergraduates:	9,015	(3,235)
Postgraduates:	1,475	(4,500)
Mature students:	29.4%	
Overseas students:	9.1%	
Applications per place:	6.7	
From state-sector schools:	92.2%	
From working-class homes:	26.6%	

For detailed information about fees, grants and bursaries and how they work, see chapter 7.

Accommodation

Number of places and costs refer to 2008–09
University-provided places: 1,809
Percentage catered: 0%
Self-catered costs: £67.13–£105.00 a week.
Entrant students guaranteed accommodation if conditions are met. No residential restrictions.
International students are guaranteed accommodation if conditions are met.
Contact: residences@dundee.ac.uk
www.dundee.ac.uk/residences

Durham University

Long established as a leading alternative to Oxford and Cambridge, Durham has a collegiate structure and picturesque setting that attracts a largely middle-class student body. However, although more than a third of undergraduates come from independent schools, the university is recruiting more applicants from non-traditional backgrounds. Those who receive offers without interview are invited to a special open day to see if Durham is the university for them. Since around 80 per cent come from outside the northeast of England, most are seeing the small cathedral city for the first time. The proportion of regional students is much higher at the Stockton campus.

Applications are made to one of the 15 colleges, all of which are mixed since the decision of St Mary's to abandon its women-only tradition from 2004. The newest, Josephine Butler College – a self-catering college with around 400 bedrooms – accepted its first intake of students in 2006. Colleges range in size from 300 to 1,100 students and are the focal point of social life, although all teaching is done in central departments. There are significant differences in atmosphere and student profile, ranging from the historic University College, in Durham Castle, to modern buildings on the city's outskirts.

Although not quite as outstanding as the results published in 2006, the latest National Student Survey scores still placed Durham among the top 20 universities for student satisfaction. History, archaeology and English produced particularly good results. Winning a place is far from easy – entrance requirements are among the highest in Britain – but the dropout rate of less than 3 per cent is also among the lowest in any university. Six subjects (chemistry, applied mathematics, geography, law, English and history) reached the pinnacle of the last Research Assessment Exercise, and 14 others were considered nationally outstanding. Most of the teaching ratings also produced high scores. Biological sciences, physics and chemistry are particularly strong on the science side; history, philosophy, economics and theology among the stars of the arts. A £3-million grant to establish a centre for fundamental physics should place Durham at the forefront of world research on the structure of the universe. The Calman Learning Centre, on the science site, incorporates lecture theatres, seminar and conference facilities and a "techno café".

Durham is generally quite traditional. Wherever possible, teaching takes place in small groups and most assessment is by written examination. However, the establishment of the Queen's Campus, in Stockton-on-Tees, broke the mould of

University Office
Old Elvet, Durham DH1 3HP
0191 334 6123 (admissions office)
admissions@durham.ac.uk
www.durham.ac.uk
www.dsu.org.uk

Edinburgh
Belfast
DURHAM
London
Cardiff

The Times Rankings
Overall Ranking: 8

Student satisfaction:	=12	(78%)
Research quality:	=12	(5.2)
Entry standards:	6	(447)
Student–staff ratio:	=34	(15.4)
Services & facilities/student:	20	(£1,375)
Expected completion rate:	5	(96.4%)
Good honours:	8	(78.8%)
Graduate prospects:	19	(75.9%)

tradition. Initially a joint venture with Teeside University, Stockton is now Durham's own venture into community education. Entry standards are 360 points at A level, compared with an average of 479 for the main university, and subjects such as business, primary education and psychology have helped broaden the university's intake. The university has spent £500,000 improving social facilities for the 2,000 students there.

The Stockton campus has also seen the fulfilment of Durham's long-held ambition to restore the medical education it lost when Newcastle University went its own way almost 45 years ago. In another joint project, this time with Newcastle, 95 students do the first two years of their training on Teeside, concentrating on community medicine, before transferring to Newcastle to complete their training. Medicine has added to the 200-plus undergraduate study programmes. Undergraduates are also offered a variety of generalist "free elective" modules, such as environmental economics and personal language learning. The aim is to make Durham graduates even more employable.

The university dominates the city of Durham to an extent which sometimes causes resentment, but adds considerably to the local economy. For those looking for nightlife, or just a change of scene, Newcastle is a short train journey away.

Sports facilities are excellent, and Durham is among the premier universities in national competitions: it came sixth in the national student championships in 2007. Among the alumni are former England cricket captain, Nasser Hussain, current opener Andrew Strauss and rugby World Cup winner, Will Greenwood. The university runs Centres of Excellence in cricket and fencing, and has plans to build on its existing strengths in rowing, rugby and hockey.

Undergraduate Fees and Bursaries

- Fees for UK/EU students: £3,145
- International student fees: £10,050–£13,110
- Bursary on full grant: household income up to £18.5K: £1,285 (£2,570 if local); then: £525 (£750 if local).
- Bursaries on partial grant: household income up to £28.7K: £525 (£750 if local).
- Scholarships based on circumstances or by competition. For full details see the university's website: www.dur.ac.uk/undergraduate/finance/dgs

Students

Undergraduates:	11,565	(430)
Postgraduates:	2,935	(2,480)
Mature students:	5.9%	
Overseas students:	7.5%	
Applications per place:	7.9	
From state-sector schools:	61.8%	
From working-class homes:	16.4%	

For detailed information about fees, grants and bursaries and how they work, see chapter 7.

Accommodation

Number of places and costs refer to 2008–09
University-provided places: 6,373
Percentage catered: 70%
Catered costs: £4,347–£4,872 (3 terms, Durham)
Self-catered costs: £3,936 (3 terms, Durham)
£3,489 (38-week contract, Stockton campus).
All full-time students become a member of one of the university's colleges or societies.
International students: all first years and final years are offered accommodation.
Contact: admissions@durham.ac.uk

University of East Anglia

UEA was one of the big winners in the first three national student satisfaction surveys, finishing in the top ten every year, with psychology, economics, and history and archaeology producing outstanding results in 2007. Most subjects showed high levels of satisfaction: students appear to like the scale of this relatively small campus university, as well as the quality of its courses, but the news is only beginning to get through to sixth-formers. Applications were down by 9 per cent when top-up fees were introduced and the following year's increase was lower than the national average, but demand had barely dropped at the start of 2008 when most universities saw a sharp drop with the switch from six choices per candidate to five.

The university has been engaged in an ambitious building and refurbishment programme on the 320-acre site on the outskirts of Norwich. It has included 560 more en-suite student bedrooms, a new health centre, the extension and refurbishment of the central library, catering facilities and students' union, as well as a new building for the schools of Nursing and Midwifery and Medicine. The work has allowed the expansion of specialist provision for students with disabilities and other learning and health difficulties. Health studies have been among UEA's fastest-developing areas. The university was awarded one of the first new medical schools for 20 years, graduating its first doctors in 2007, and has since added pharmacy and speech and language therapy degree courses.

Some of the broad subject combinations that the university pioneered from its origins in the 1960s – such as development studies and environmental sciences – are highly regarded in the academic world. With successive 5* ratings for research and an excellent teaching grade, environmental sciences is the flagship school. The Climatic Research Unit and the Government-funded Tyndall Centre for Climate Change Research are among the leaders in the investigation of global warming – UEA contributed more than any other university in the world to the 2007 Nobel Prize-winning Intergovernmental Panel on Climate Change. History and film studies added to the 5* research grades in 2001.

Philosophy and politics joined American studies as the top performers in the teaching assessments. Like the English degrees, one of which includes star-studded creative writing, American studies is heavily oversubscribed. With authors Michèle Roberts and Andrew Cowan taking up where Andrew Motion, the Poet

---

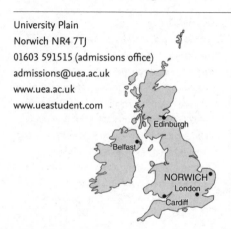

University Plain
Norwich NR4 7TJ
01603 591515 (admissions office)
admissions@uea.ac.uk
www.uea.ac.uk
www.ueastudent.com

The Times Rankings
Overall Ranking: 23

Student satisfaction:	=4	(82%)
Research quality:	=18	(5.0)
Entry standards:	34	(359)
Student–staff ratio:	=61	(17.9)
Services & facilities/student:	45	(£1,127)
Expected completion rate:	25	(91.2%)
Good honours:	34	(67.5%)
Graduate prospects:	=63	(63.0%)

Laureate, and the late Malcolm Bradbury left off, the attraction of creative writing for both undergraduates and postgraduates remains undimmed. Art history is another strong subject, aided by the presence of the Sainsbury Centre for the Visual Arts, perhaps the greatest resource of its type on any British campus. The centre, which has been refurbished and extended, houses a priceless collection of modern and tribal art, in a building designed by Lord (Norman) Foster.

Almost nine out of ten undergraduates come from state schools or colleges, but less than a quarter have a working-class background. Since 1999, most have had the opportunity of work experience as part of their course. An academic adviser guides all students on their options under the modular course system and monitors their progress right through to graduation.

Dropout rates have fluctuated, but the latest projected figure of 8 per cent is below the national average for UEA's courses and entry qualifications. Most students come from outside the region, although there is an unusually large contingent of mature students for a traditional university, who tend to be more local. The university also runs a programme of over 200 evening and day courses across Norfolk and Suffolk.

The number of university-owned beds has increased considerably, ensuring that first years can be guaranteed accommodation unless they live locally. The excellent sporting facilities are based around the £17.5-million Sports Park, which boasts an Olympic-sized swimming pool, fitness and aerobics centres, athletics track, climbing wall, courts and pitches. Student membership is only £17.50 a year, with discounted rates for all facilities. The university was chosen as the base for the English Institute of Sport in the East, developing a sports science network for the region.

The university is situated in parkland, with easy access to the medieval city of Norwich, which can boast a pub for every day of the year and was voted one of the best small cities in the world in the 2007 Liveable Communities awards. Rail links to London now take less than two hours, while Norwich airport offers flights through Amsterdam and Paris worldwide.

Undergraduate Fees and Bursaries

- Fees for UK/EU students: £3,145
- International student fees: £9,300–£11,500
  £18,000 (clinical)
- Bursary on full grant: £600
- Bursaries on partial grant: £300
- Scholarships based on circumstances or by competition.For full details see the university's website: www1.uea.ac.uk/cm/home/services/units/mac/aao/courses/UG/Fees

Students

Undergraduates:	10,090	(5,100)
Postgraduates:	2,880	(1,515)
Mature students:	14.9%	
Overseas students:	8.7%	
Applications per place:	5.1	
From state-sector schools:	86.5%	
From working-class homes:	22.9%	

For detailed information about fees, grants and bursaries and how they work, see chapter 7.

Accommodation

Number of places and costs refer to 2007–08
University-provided places: 3,400
Percentage catered: 0%
Self-catered costs: £1,893.92–£3,428 (38 weeks)
First years guaranteed accommodation provided conditions are met. Residential restrictions.
International students paying overseas fees are guaranteed accommodation if conditions are met.
Contact: accom@uea.ac.uk
www.uea.ac.uk/accom

University of East London

UEL has spent more than £190 million on its Docklands campus, which opened in 1999, and is now unrecognisable from its early days as a pioneering polytechnic. Student residences and recreational facilities sit side by side with academic buildings in a prize-winning waterside development for more than 7,000 students. The latest developments saw the opening of the business school and Knowledge Dock, a support centre for local companies, in September 2006. A £40-million student village lining the Royal Albert Dock added another 800 beds in 2007. The campus has helped to attract big increases in applications to UEL: the university bucked the national trend with a third successive substantial rise when top-up fees were introduced and applications were up by another 8 per cent at the start of 2007. Student numbers have shot up from 12,000 to 20,000 since 2001.

The capital's first new campus for 50 years, within sight of London City Airport, has given the university a new focal point, with its modern version of traditional university features like cloisters and squares. Students of fashion, fine art, graphic design, product design, media and cultural studies were first into new premises, followed by UEL's highly rated School of Architecture and the Visual Arts

and electrical and manufacturing engineering in 2005. Business, computing and technology have now completed the academic set.

The university's original campus in Stratford is also being redeveloped, with a new library and learning centre, student residences and facilities for part-time and evening courses. The Centre for Clinical Education in Podiatry, Physiotherapy and Sports Sciences, incorporating the new London Foot Hospital, opened there in April 2006. New buildings for education and law are next on the development plan. The Barking campus closed in 2005, replaced by a lifelong learning centre run in partnership with the neighbouring further education college and the local council.

With research in media studies judged to be nationally outstanding and sociology and art and design on the next grade, UEL was among the leading new universities in the last research assessments. Psychology, English and architecture did well in teaching quality assessments, but communication and media studies, and electrical and electronic engineering both registered unusually low scores. Engineering did better in a more recent assessment, when environmental sciences and law were also highly rated. Teacher training courses, too, were given good marks by the Office for Standards in

University House
Romford Road
London E15 4LZ
020 8223 3333 (admissions)
admiss@uel.ac.uk
www.uel.ac.uk
www.uelsu.net

Edinburgh
Belfast
Cardiff
LONDON

The Times Rankings
Overall Ranking: 109

Student satisfaction:	=93	(70%)
Research quality:	=69	(1.4)
Entry standards:	113	(187)
Student–staff ratio:	=99	(20.6)
Services & facilities/student:	33	(£1,218)
Expected completion rate:	110	(68.5%)
Good honours:	113	(40.6%)
Graduate prospects:	=84	(59.4%)

Education, while finance and accounting achieved the best results in the university's debut in the National Student Survey.

UEL's focus is more concerned with extending access to higher education than competing with the elite universities. Barely more than half of the new first year intake now arrive with A levels and a majority are over 21 on entry – many choosing to start courses in February, as 1,000 students did in 2006. Many degrees are vocational and employers are closely involved in course planning. The university has pioneered a work-based learning initiative, offering accredited placements with local employers.

Almost half of UEL's students come from working-class homes, many from the area's large ethnic minority population. A successful mentoring scheme for black and Asian students has become a model for other institutions. A guidance unit advises local people who are considering returning to education. The university is also strong on provision for disabled students and houses the new Rix Centre for Innovation and Learning Disability. The projected dropout rate has been improving considerably – the latest figure of almost 23 per cent is better than the national average for UEL's courses and entry qualifications. Graduate employment rates have also been improving, with the university working on both retention and

employability through mentoring and placement programmes that involve almost 1,000 businesses, including many in the City or Canary Wharf.

University-owned accommodation is still not plentiful for the number of students, although there are now more than 1,100 flats and studios on the Docklands campus and the rents are good value for London. Because many choose to live at home, all first years who request accommodation are housed. The social mix means that UEL has not been the place to look for the archetypal partying student lifestyle, although the new campus is beginning to change this. New students' union premises have been added on both the Stratford and Docklands campuses, each of which also has some sports facilities.

Undergraduate Fees and Bursaries

- Fees for UK/EU students: £3,145
- International student fees: £9,000–£12,500
- Bursary on full grant: £310
- Bursaries on partial grant: n/a
- Scholarships based on circumstances or by competition. For full details see the university's website: www.uel.ac.uk/students/being_student/money.htm

---

Students

Undergraduates:	9,365	(4,860)
Postgraduates:	2,265	(2,810)
Mature students:	56.2%	
Overseas students:	11.5%	
Applications per place:	4.1	
From state-sector schools:	98.7%	
From working-class homes:	48.8%	

For detailed information about fees, grants and bursaries and how they work, see chapter 7.

Accommodation

Number of places and costs refer to 2008–09
University-provided places: 1,100
Percentage catered: 0%
Self-catered costs: £92–£124 a week (39 weeks)
First-year students are guaranteed accommodation if conditions are met.
International students: same as above.
Docklands Campus 020 8223 5093/4
dlres@uel.ac.uk

Edge Hill University

Edge Hill has moved up our League Table, having corrected data that underestimated its performance in its first appearance in *The Times Guide*. University status brought the biggest rise in applications at any institution – more than 40 per cent – and there was another big rise in the number of people seeking places in 2008. Results have been good in the first three National Student Surveys. Edge Hill was in England's top 20 for student satisfaction in 2007 and it was among the leaders for nursing, management and physics. There were high levels of satisfaction, too, in education, history and English.

Although one of the universities to gain the title most recently, Edge Hill has been training teachers since the 19th century. Having moved to its 75-acre landscaped campus in Ormskirk, near Liverpool, in the 1930s, it has long since expanded into other subjects and has seen rapid growth in recent years. Student numbers have increased by more than 150 per cent in the current decade to more than 18,000. Over £60 million has been spent on the main campus and more is on the way. A new £14-million home to house the SOLSTICE e-learning centre and a 900-seat theatre is due to be completed in 2008.

There are also seven satellite campuses in Liverpool and the North West to facilitate local learning. The largest is based in the grounds of University Hospital Aintree, where students in the Faculty of Health can see at first-hand how a busy hospital runs. In addition, a range of further education colleges in the North West teach the university's Foundation degrees.

Edge Hill is determinedly vocational – 85 per cent of graduates leave with professional accreditation. The university is the largest provider of secondary teacher training and courses for classroom assistants. It has also won the lion's share of funding to deliver further training for qualified secondary school teachers. Other big recruiters are health subjects, business and media courses. A £5-million expansion of resources for the performing arts opened in 2005 and there are industry-standard facilities for animation, TV and other media areas.

Scores in the early years of teaching quality assessment were patchy, but the last six subject reviews have produced commendations. All students have a personal tutor, as well as access to counsellors and financial advice. There is a high proportion of working class students and more than a quarter come from areas without a tradition of higher education. Almost two thirds of the university's fee income goes on bursaries and outreach activities. Edge Hill won an award for a

St Helens Road
Ormskirk,
Lancs. L39 4QP
01695 575171
enquiries@edgehill.ac.uk
www.edgehill.ac.uk
www.edgehillsu.com

The Times Rankings
Overall Ranking: 98

Student satisfaction:	=26	(76%)
Research quality:	=111	(0.4)
Entry standards:	=92	(250)
Student–staff ratio:	=106	(22.1)
Services & facilities/student:	110	(£597)
Expected completion rate:	81	(78.3%)
Good honours:	109	(44.4%)
Graduate prospects:	92	(57.0%)

student finance support package that rewards achievement, as well as encouraging students to complete their studies, rather than simply offering incentives for enrolling. However, while the dropout rate has been falling, the latest projection of one in five is still marginally worse than the national average for the university's courses and entry qualifications.

There are almost 700 hall places on the Ormskirk campus, and 25 acres of sporting facilities. The £3.9-million Sporting Edge complex, which was part funded by a Lottery grant, is open to staff, students and the local community. The university has been chosen as a pre-Olympic training centre for athletics, road cycling and archery.

Undergraduate Fees and Bursaries

- Fees for UK/EU students £3,145
- International student fees contact university
- Bursary on full grant: £500 + £200 Learning support bursary.
- Bursaries on partial grant: £200 learning support bursary.
- Scholarships based on circumstances or by competition. For full details see the university's website: www.edgehill.ac.uk/ProspectiveStudents/Finance/index.htm

Students

Undergraduates:	6,120	(6,250)
Postgraduates:	675	(5,695)
Mature students:	24.4%	
Overseas students:	1.5%	
Applications per place:	4.7	
From state-sector schools:	98%	
From working-class homes:	38.5%	

For detailed information about fees, grants and bursaries and how they work, see chapter 7.

Accommodation

Number of places and costs refer to 2007–08
University-provided places: 678
Percentage catered: 45%
Catered costs: £79 a week (38–40 weeks)
Self-catered costs: £49–£63 a week (40 weeks).
First years cannot be guaranteed housing.
Priority to students living furthest away.
International students: guaranteed housing if conditions are met.
Contact: www.edgehill.ac.uk/study/accommodation

University of Edinburgh

Edinburgh retains a special status in Scotland, where the university is regarded as the nearest thing to Oxbridge north of the border. Although having to play second fiddle to St Andrews in our League Table recently, it is seldom far from the top ten in the UK and was in the top 25 universities in the world in the last *Times Higher Education*/QS global rankings.

Like Oxbridge, Edinburgh has been trying to widen its intake, especially since the arrival of Professor Tim O'Shea as Principal – the first non-Scot to hold the ancient office in modern times. More than £10 million has been raised for access bursaries of £1,000 a year, with the university steadily increasing number of awards, which now stand at 150. Other measures include an eight-week summer school for teenagers from local schools and support for students in the transition to higher education and later in their courses. The university has always attracted a high proportion of middle-class candidates – many from England – and is a favourite in independent schools, whose students take about a third of the places. Selection guidelines aim to look more broadly at candidates' potential, reducing minimum entry requirements and placing more weight on references and personal statements.

The measures appeared to have an instant impact, with a succession of big increases continuing in the last two years, when several Scottish universities experienced a decline. The 8 per cent increase in 2007 included healthy rises in generally problematic areas such as engineering and modern languages. There are plans for further increases in overseas students, who already number more than 6,000, testifying to Edinburgh's worldwide reputation.

The university, which is a member of the Russell Group of 20 UK research universities, has stepped up its fund-raising activities. They have already produced a new Medical Research Centre, alongside the recently relocated medical school. A new Informatics building is also nearing completion.

The incorporation of Moray House, whose Holyrood site houses education, made Edinburgh the largest university in Scotland, now with more than 24,000 students. Yet, despite the new approach to selection, entry standards for the 500 undergraduate degree programmes remain high, whether in A levels or Highers. The university's buildings are scattered around the city, but most border the historic Old Town. The science and engineering campus is two miles to the south.

The last research assessments showed a

Old College
South Bridge
Edinburgh EH8 9YL
0131 650 4360
sra.enquiries@ed.ac.uk
www.ed.ac.uk
www.eusa.ed.ac.uk

The Times Rankings
Overall Ranking: 18

Student satisfaction:	=64	(73%)
Research quality:	=18	(5.0)
Entry standards:	=9	(430)
Student–staff ratio:	=13	(13.3)
Services & facilities/student:	26	(£1,294)
Expected completion rate:	22	(92.2%)
Good honours:	4	(79.9%)
Graduate prospects:	=23	(74.9%)

big improvement on a disappointing outcome in 1996, when only two subjects reached the top grade. In the last Research Assessment Exercise, in 2001, nine were awarded the coveted 5* and another 19 achieved grade 5, accounting for three quarters of those entered for assessment. The 15 subjects rated as Excellent for teaching already amounted to the biggest haul in Scotland. Medicine is a traditional strength and the law faculty is the largest north of the border. The university enjoys a reputation for high quality across the board.

Departments organise visiting days in October for those thinking of applying and in the spring for those holding offers. There is also an annual open day in June and regular student-led guided tours. New students join one of three Colleges, which are divided into 21 Schools, and generally take three subjects in both their first and second years. Every student has a Director of Studies to help them narrow down the selection of a final degree and give personal advice when necessary.

Considerable sums have been spent making the university more accessible to the 1,600 disabled students, who can also call on the services of a disability office. All students are issued with a smart card for access to university facilities, which can be loaded with money to pay for a variety of goods and services. The students' union operates on several sites and sports facilities are excellent.

The city is a treasure-trove of cultural and recreational opportunities, even away from the Festival period. Most students thrive on Edinburgh life, even though the cost of living can make it difficult to do it justice. Some scientists complain of isolation, although there is a regular bus link with the main university area around George Square. The plentiful stock of residential accommodation was increased recently. The newest rooms are not only en suite, but come with their own television.

Undergraduate Fees and Bursaries

- Scottish-domiciled and EU students: no fees payable.
- Non-Scottish UK-domiciled student fees: £1,775 a year (£2,825 medicine).
- International student fees: £10,500–£13,800, £17,100 (preclinical medicine), £28,950 (clinical medicine)
- Scholarships based on circumstances or by competition. For full details see the university's website: www.scholarships.ed.ac.uk www.scholarships.ed.ac.uk/bursaries

---

Students

Undergraduates:	16,285	(695)
Postgraduates:	4,845	(2,395)
Mature students:	10.8%	
Overseas students:	11.8%	
Applications per place:	10.8	
From state-sector schools:	65.5%	
From working-class homes:	17.7%	

For detailed information about fees, grants and bursaries and how they work, see chapter 7.

Accommodation

Number of places and costs refer to 2008–09
University-provided places: about 6,100
Percentage catered: about 30%
Catered costs: £139–£173 a week
Self-catered costs: £81–£103 a week.
First years are guaranteed an offer of accommodation providing they fulfill requirements. Residential restrictions apply.
International students: accommodation guaranteed if conditions are met.
Contact: www.accom.ed.ac.uk

University of Essex

Essex has long since moved out of the shadow of its radical past, acquiring a reputation for high-quality research, especially in the social sciences. It did well in the last research assessments and was in the top 10 in our last League Table for teaching. There were some good results, too, in the first three national student satisfaction surveys – notably in sports science and politics in 2007 – although Essex did not do quite as well as some universities of similar size. There are still fewer than 9,000 full-time students, a quarter of whom are postgraduates.

Law was top-rated in the early teaching quality assessments and sociology is among the leading departments in Britain, attracting a series of prestigious research projects as well as a high score for teaching. Both sociology and government achieved their second successive 5* grades in the latest research assessments, with economics joining them on the top grade. With eight subjects on grade 5, three quarters of the researchers are in departments where most work is judged to be of international quality.

The social sciences are Essex's main strength, but the university has been building up its science departments – the biological sciences department is one of its largest. Electronic engineering recorded a perfect score for teaching quality to add to an improved research rating, and biosciences almost repeated the feat. Computer science is also strong and a BSc in computer games and internet technology shows Essex keeping pace with changing demands in graduate employment. The last four teaching assessments – for sports science, economics, philosophy and politics – all produced full marks.

But improvements in the university's academic performance could not disguise the fact that the glass and concrete campus, set in 200 acres of parkland on the outskirts of Colchester, was showing distinct signs of a quarter of a century's wear and tear. The university has been carrying out a programme of refurbishment at the same time as expanding student facilities. Teaching and administration blocks, which cluster around a network of squares, are gradually being transformed and extra catering and residential facilities added.

First-years and all overseas students are guaranteed university accommodation, all of which is now networked to the university IT system and equipped with telephones giving free access to the internal phone system. Some ground-floor flats on campus have been adapted for disabled students. The library has been extended to provide 1,100 reader spaces and is open for over 84 hours a week, with the Large Reading Room open 24 hours a day Monday to Thursday.

Wivenhoe Park
Colchester
Essex CO4 3SQ
01206 872002
admit@essex.ac.uk
www.essex.ac.uk
www.essexstudent.com

Edinburgh
Belfast
COLCHESTER
Cardiff
London

The Times Rankings
Overall Ranking: 42

Student satisfaction:	=39	(75%)
Research quality:	23	(4.8)
Entry standards:	46	(309)
Student–staff ratio:	20	(14.1)
Services & facilities/student:	40	(£1,149)
Expected completion rate:	57	(83.4%)
Good honours:	=50	(60.4%)
Graduate prospects:	65	(62.8%)

A new Networks Centre for computer science and electronic systems engineering features a powered floor system for robotics and an iDorm laboratory. Another £6 million has been spent on two 500-seat lecture theatres which can be combined for exhibitions, conferences or graduation ceremonies. And work has started on a new social sciences building.

The incorporation of the East 15 acting school, in Loughton, has enhanced the university's provision in theatre studies, and was the university's first venture beyond Colchester. However, a £75-million campus offering courses in business, health, education and the arts opened in Southend in 2007, in partnership with South East Essex College. And Essex is collaborating with the University of East Anglia on University Campus Suffolk, which will be based in Ipswich and have smaller centres in Bury St Edmunds, Great Yarmouth, Lowestoft and Otley. The first building should be ready in September 2008 and students will be awarded degrees jointly by the two universities. Essex degrees are also on offer at Writtle College, near Chelmsford, which specialises in agriculture, horticulture and related subjects.

Essex champions academic breadth, and in each of the four faculties, students follow a common first year before specialising. They may take four or five different subjects before committing themselves to a particular degree. The student population is unusually diverse for a traditional university, with high proportions of mature and overseas students. Nearly a third of the undergraduates are from working-class homes and over 90 per cent went to state schools or colleges – a significantly higher proportion than the subject mix would suggest.

Social and sporting facilities are good, the more so following an extension of the Sports Centre and the refurbishment of the students' union bars. There are now four bars, an enlarged and refurbished nightclub and numerous cafés on campus. Some 40 acres of land are devoted to sports facilities, used extensively by individual students and over 40 university sports clubs.

Undergraduate Fees and Bursaries
- Fees for UK/EU students: £3,145
- International student fees: £9,250–£11,990
- Bursary on full grant: £310
- Bursaries on partial grant: household income up to £25K £310, increasing to max. £1,574 at £33K decreasing to £0 at £60K.
- Scholarships based on circumstances or by competition. For full details see the university's website: www.essex.ac.uk/ newfundingarrangements

Students

Undergraduates:	7,170	(1,190)
Postgraduates:	1,715	(1,590)
Mature students:	16%	
Overseas students:	19.9%	
Applications per place:	6.2	
From state-sector schools:	94.3%	
From working-class homes:	32.3%	

For detailed information about fees, grants and bursaries and how they work, see chapter 7.

Accommodation

Number of places and costs refer to 2008–09
University-provided places: 3,384
Percentage catered: 0%
Self-catered costs: £61.46–£95.13 a week.
New first years living outside the borough of Colchester are guaranteed accommodation if conditions are met.
International students: new students are guaranteed accommodation if conditions are met; priority given to students in final year.
Contact: admit@essex.ac.uk

University of Exeter

Exeter is one of Britain's most popular universities in terms of first-choice applications, not only in its traditional strong suit of the arts, but increasingly in the sciences and social sciences as well. More than a quarter of the undergraduates come from independent schools – a much higher proportion than the national average for the subjects Exeter offers, although this figure has been dropping. Professor Steve Smith, the Vice-Chancellor, has put broadening the social mix at the top of his agenda, particularly targeting schools and colleges in the rural South West.

Location is partly responsible for the relatively rarified social mix. There is no large industrialised centre of population and despite sophisticated shopping and a lively entertainment scene, South West cathedral cities are not what every teenager is looking for. A dip in applications in the first year of top-up fees was reversed in 2007, with a 24 per cent increase, and the university outperformed most others at the official deadline for courses beginning in 2008. The biggest boom has been at the £100-million campus at Penryn, in Cornwall, where new degrees in law, history and politics and a range of combined honours degrees not available in Exeter have seen applications more than double.

The Camborne School of Mines, which has been a department of the university since 1993, is also based on the Cornwall campus, on a site shared with University College Falmouth.

The other big development of recent years was the opening of Peninsula Medical School, in association with Plymouth University, in 2002. Recruitment has been strong and Peninsula was the only successful bidder for a new dental school in 2006. The four-year Bachelor of Dental Surgery has an annual intake of 64 science graduates or health service professionals.

The last research assessments were an improvement on 1996: only German was considered internationally outstanding, but another 18 areas reached the next highest grade. Physics and the biosciences are among the beneficiaries in the first phase of a £140-million investment programme to accompany the restructuring which saw the controversial closure of chemistry and music in 2004. The University made 182 new academic appointments in 12 months, including some 30 professors in a range of disciplines. Exeter is also leading a £14-million partnership of southwest universities, including Bristol and Bath, to boost research in areas of economic importance.

Arabic and Islamic studies have benefited from support from the Middle East and in 2006 Exeter opened an office in Dubai as its Middle East base. A longstand-

---

Northcote House
The Queen's Drive
Exeter, Devon EX4 4QJ
01392 263855 (admissions)
ug-ad@exeter.ac.uk
www.exeter.ac.uk
www.exeterguild.org/
www.fxu.org.uk/

Student satisfaction:	=6	(81%)
Research quality:	=24	(4.7)
Entry standards:	=23	(381)
Student–staff ratio:	=51	(16.8)
Services & facilities/student:	34	(£1,183)
Expected completion rate:	=11	(94.8%)
Good honours:	5	(79.8%)
Graduate prospects:	44	(68.5%)

ing international focus is exemplified by the popular European law degree. All students are offered tuition in foreign languages in the recently refurbished Foreign Language Centre and even some three-year degrees include the option of a year abroad. Language degrees scored well in the teaching assessments, with German achieving a perfect score, as did education and archaeology.

English literature, drama, law, history and psychology are among the most heavily subscribed courses in their fields, and successful applicants appear not to be disappointed. The 5 per cent dropout rate is among the lowest in Britain, and Exeter was among the leading universities in the first three national student satisfaction surveys, finishing in the top five in 2007. There were particularly good scores in sports science, finance and accounting, management, business and maths. Flexible combined honours, previously available only from the second year, is now available to first-year students. Career management skills are built into degree programmes and students can gain work experience through the university's employability and business project programmes. The Careers and Employment Service has been expanded to increase the work experience and placement opportunities available to students, 7,000 of whom undertook employability training in 2007.

The main Streatham Campus, close to the centre of Exeter, is one of the most attractive in the country, with a lively campus social scene. The highly rated schools of education, sport and health studies are a mile away in the former St Luke's College. Some £38 million has been invested in new residential accommodation. The Students' Guild had a £2-million revamp, and there has been a substantial investment in sports facilities. A new £2-million cricket centre will open in autumn 2008. Exeter is one of the UK's top sporting universities and was placed 10th in the 2006–07 national rankings. The university's students devote around 100,000 volunteering hours per year, the most in Britain, while participation in student societies and union activities is unusually high.

Undergraduate Bursaries and Scholarships

- Fees for UK/EU students: £3,145
- International student fees: £9,150–£11,100*
- Bursary on full grant: £1,500
- Bursaries on partial grant: household income £25K–£30K: £1,000; £30K–£35K: £500; £35K–£45K: £250.
- Scholarships based on circumstances or by competition. For full details see the university's website: www.admin.ex.ac.uk/academic/scholarships/

* Figures for 2007–08

Students

Undergraduates:	9,155	(1,665)
Postgraduates:	2,350	(2,550)
Mature students:	9.3%	
Overseas students:	8.6%	
Applications per place:	6.0	
From state-sector schools:	72.5%	
From working-class homes:	18.2%	

For detailed information about fees, grants and bursaries and how they work, see chapter 7.

Accommodation

Number of places and costs refer to 2007–08
University-provided places: 4,083
Percentage catered: 47%
Catered costs: £93.59–£147.21 a week (31 weeks)
Self-catered costs: £62.51–£99.12 a week (40, 44 or 51 weeks).
Unaccompanied first years are guaranteed accommodation provided conditions are met.
International students: as above.
Contact: accommodation@exeter.ac.uk

University of Glamorgan

Glamorgan's plans to establish one of the largest universities in Britain, by merging with nearby UWIC, are on the back burner. But the desire for a foothold in the Welsh capital was fulfilled in September 2007 with the opening of a striking new campus in Cardiff. The university's new School of Creative and Cultural Industries offers an "eclectic mix of teaching and research in the theory and practice of media, design and the arts". Students work in an ultra-modern new building and have access to 1,350 rooms in privately run halls of residence.

Most of Glamorgan's 21,000 students will remain on the Treforest campus, 20 minutes by train from Cardiff, overlooking the market town of Pontypridd. Collaborative linking programmes operate in five overseas centres, while in Wales a growing number of further education colleges offer the university's courses. Four have become associate colleges, guaranteeing places on degree courses if students meet set conditions.

Originally based in a large country house, Glamorgan now has purpose-built premises for the science and technology departments. Teaching accommodation for mathematics and computing has also had a £5-million refurbishment. The law school and Faculty of Health Sport and Science are on the Glyntaff site, a short walk from the main campus. They are housed in new buildings and specially restored tramsheds, a reminder of the industrial past of the area. The Institute of Chiropractic was the first university-based centre for training chiropractors in the UK, while the Film Academy for Wales is another unique development, built on a successful range of film-related courses.

Glamorgan is committed to retaining its vocational slant, tailoring a diploma in management to the needs of the Driver and Vehicle Licensing Agency, for example. The business school is the largest in Wales, and the university was among the first providers of the two-year Foundation degree, focusing on human resources management and marketing, business and accounting. The range of courses has since expanded rapidly, covering subjects as diverse as nursing and product design, with a strong representation of Foundation degrees.

The vocational approach pays dividends for graduate employment, which is consistently good, although the dropout rate has been the highest among the university institutions in Wales. Almost three in ten students starting degree courses in 2004 were not expected to complete their course in the normal period, although the university has launched initiatives to improve retention. The intake

Llantwit Road
Treforest
Pontypridd
Mid Glamorgan CF37 1DL
0800 716925 (admissions)
enquiries@glam.ac.uk
www.glam.ac.uk
www.glamsu.com

PONTYPRIDD Cardiff

The Times Rankings
Overall Ranking: =77

Student satisfaction:	=39	(75%)
Research quality:	=73	(1.3)
Entry standards:	99	(237)
Student–staff ratio:	39	(15.9)
Services & facilities/student:	46	(£1,123)
Expected completion rate:	107	(69.3%)
Good honours:	81	(51.8%)
Graduate prospects:	89	(58.4%)

is more socially diverse than elsewhere in Wales. Over 40 per cent of undergraduates come from working-class homes and 30 per cent are from areas with no tradition of higher education – one of the highest figures at any UK university. The 13 per cent increase in applications by the official deadline for courses starting in 2006 was the biggest in Wales and the following two years have also been healthy.

Glamorgan was one of the top scorers among the former polytechnics in teaching quality assessments: 12 subjects were rated as Excellent at degree level, and there have also been awards for the remaining further education course provision. The university also did well in the first national student satisfaction survey, especially in health subjects and the creative arts. The success of the English and creative writing programmes is reflected in the establishment at the university of the National Centre for Writing, which opened in 2002. The Faculty of Advanced Technology has been designated a centre of excellence for Wales, while three National Partnership awards testify to high standards in course design and delivery. Degrees in computer forensics, computer games development, lighting and design technology and aerospace courses are all designed with employers' needs in mind.

Many of the 9,000 full-time undergraduates live around Pontypridd, while others choose Cardiff, which is both livelier and a better source of accommodation. However, the Pontypridd campus has been under development, with the addition of a recreation centre and an extension to the students' union, which is the focus of social life. Its bars are the only part of the university where smoking is allowed.

The sports facilities are good enough for Glamorgan to have been awarded the 2001 British University Games and to become one of six centres of excellence in cricket. The university is successful in student competitions, especially in rugby, and offers a number of sports bursaries for students with international potential. But there is also a wide range of health and fitness classes for those with lower aspirations.

Undergraduate Fees and Bursaries

- Welsh-domiciled student fees: £3,145, with grant of up to £1,890
- Non-Welsh UK domiciled and EU student fees: £3,145
- International student fees: £9,000
- Welsh National Bursary for all UK students, means-tested with maximum of £310.
- Bursary on full grant: £500 residential allowance for non-local UK & EU students.
- Bursaries on partial grant: £500 residential allowance for non-local UK & EU students.
- Scholarships based on circumstances or by competition. For full details see the university's website: www.glam.ac.uk/money

Students		
Undergraduates:	10,745	(8,050)
Postgraduates:	1,445	(1,955)
Mature students:	37.3%	
Overseas students:	12.6%	
Applications per place:	3.9	
From state-sector schools:	98.2%	
From working-class homes:	41.4%	

For detailed information about fees, grants and bursaries and how they work, see chapter 7.

Accommodation

Number of places and costs refer to 2008–09
University-provided places: 1,108
Percentage catered: 0%
Self-catered costs: £64 (standard) –£78 (en suite) a week (39 weeks).
First-year students are offered accommodation.
Local restrictions apply.
International students are guaranteed housing.
Contact: accom@glam.ac.uk

University of Glasgow

Glasgow enjoys the rare distinction of having been established by Papal Bull, and began its existence in the Chapter House of Glasgow Cathedral in 1451. Since 1871 it has been based next to Kelvingrove Park in the city's fashionable west end on the Gilmorehill campus, with its 104 listed buildings – more than any other British university. A major addition, opened in 2002, houses the prestigious medical school, while a £15-million cancer research centre followed in late 2006.

The university took in St Andrew's College to form a new faculty of education, which has been based on the Park campus, between Gilmorehill and the city centre, since summer 2002. The campus, formerly the Queen's College, was acquired from Glasgow Caledonian University, and provides the extra teaching accommodation needed to locate the education faculty close to the main campus. The Vet School and outdoor sports facilities are located at Garscube, four miles away, while the innovative Crichton College campus in Dumfries is taking higher education to southwest Scotland with three-year degrees.

A new student centre is under construction on the Gilmorehill site, while a £15-million small animal hospital for the Vet School is due to open early in 2009.

The new environmental research building has won awards as one of the "greenest" in Scotland. The university is proud of its green credentials, having been named the second most environmentally friendly university in Europe by Grist magazine.

More distinctively Scottish than its rivals in Edinburgh or St Andrews, almost half of the students come from within 30 miles of Glasgow and three quarters are from north of the border. There was a high proportion of home-based students long before the city became fashionable, but the university also attracts students from some 120 countries. The university finished in the top 20 in the latest National Student Survey, claiming the most satisfied undergraduates in Britain in business, computing and physical geography and environmental science.

Glasgow has adopted an increasingly outward-looking style in recent years, marked by two Queen's Anniversary prizes for opening up artistic, scientific and cultural resources and taking computing to local communities. A "synergy" agreement with neighbouring Strathclyde University has led to the development of teaching and research partnerships, the latest establishing a single department of naval architecture and marine engineering. Not that Glasgow is a stranger to innovation: it was the first university in Britain to have a school of engineering, for

University Avenue
Glasgow G12 8QQ
0141 330 4440 (prospectus hotline)
prospectus@gla.ac.uk
www.gla.ac.uk
www.theguu.com
www.qmu.org.uk

GLASGOW
Edinburgh
Belfast
London
Cardiff

The Times Rankings
Overall Ranking: =20

Student satisfaction:	=12	(78%)
Research quality:	=37	(4.3)
Entry standards:	18	(396)
Student–staff ratio:	15	(13.4)
Services & facilities/student:	21	(£1,373)
Expected completion rate:	43	(85.5%)
Good honours:	=29	(68.4%)
Graduate prospects:	22	(75.0%)

example, and the first in Scotland to have a computer. The huge science faculty is strong, having received top ratings for teaching in six subjects. Applications for science degrees reflect this quality, having risen by 25 per cent since the mid 1990s. Among other sources, the university has seen a steady flow of applicants from schools taking part in the university's access scheme. However, two years of healthy increases in applications came to an end in 2007 and continued downwards at the start of 2008.

The last research assessments were an improvement on a disappointing set of results in 1996, with arts and social sciences leading the way. Four subjects were rated internationally outstanding – English, European studies, psychology and sports science – a further 19 achieving grade 5 and 96 per cent of researchers were in the top three categories.

Overseas recruitment has remained strong, especially in engineering. Glasgow is also taking an active role in Universitas 21, the worldwide group of universities, involving partnerships on five continents. But the home market has not been overlooked. The Club 21 programme, which provides students with paid work experience placements, involves more than 50 employers from Abbey to T-Mobile, some of whom sponsor undergraduates at £1,000 a year, as part of an arrangement to forge closer links with local business. Another ten scholarships for students from poor backgrounds commemorate the life of Donald Dewar, Scotland's first First Minister and a well-respected Glasgow graduate.

Over a fifth of the students are from working-class homes, one in six from an area without a tradition of higher education. Most like the combination of campus and city life, with the relatively low cost of living an added attraction – the city has been rated among the most cost-effective in which to study. But the dropout rate of more than 14 per cent is above the average for the subjects on offer and entry qualifications. Undergraduates have the choice of two students' unions, plus a sports union supporting 46 different clubs and activities.

Undergraduate Fees and Bursaries
- Scottish-domiciled and EU students: no fees payable.
- Non-Scottish UK-domiciled student fees: £1,775 a year (£2,825 medicine).
- International student fees:£9,400–12,350; £17,500 (veterinary medicine); £21,600 (medicine)
- Scholarships based on circumstances or by competition. For full details see the university's website: www.gla.ac.uk/bursaries www.gla.ac.uk/studying/scholarships/

Students		
Undergraduates:	14,790	(4,170)
Postgraduates:	3,855	(2,485)
Mature students:	13.5%	
Overseas students:	6.1%	
Applications per place:	6.5	
From state-sector schools:	85.7%	
From working-class homes:	23.7%	

For detailed information about fees, grants and bursaries and how they work, see chapter 7.

Accommodation
Number of places and costs refer to 2008–09
University-provided places: 3,155
Percentage catered: 7%
Catered costs: £106.75–£118.44 a week.
Self-catered costs: £65.59–£81.69 (en suite)
First years are guaranteed accommodation if conditions are met. Local restrictions apply.
International students: first years are guaranteed accommodation if conditions are met. 20% of returners are also housed.
Contact: accom@gla.ac.uk

Glasgow Caledonian University

Glasgow Caledonian has spent more than £70 million transforming previously mediocre facilities into a single campus that does justice to a modern university of more than 17,000 students. Only Edinburgh, Glasgow and West of Scotland universities are bigger north of the border. Over 80 per cent of the buildings are new or have been upgraded, and improvements are still being made. The health building brings together teaching and research facilities and includes a virtual hospital, where students can hone their clinical and interpersonal skills. The Saltire Centre, which has brought all library and student services together for the first time, opened in 2006 with study spaces for 1,800 students.

With the accent firmly on widening participation in higher education, the university will always struggle in league tables such as ours, but it is well-regarded by employers, and applications have been healthy until a small decline set in at the start of 2007 that continued 12 months later. Caledonian is among the top UK universities for attracting students from areas without a tradition of higher education, and more than a third of its undergraduates come from working-class homes. The university has argued forcefully that extending access should be

rewarded more generously if such students are to receive the support they need to make a success of higher education.

Previous performance indicators suggested that one undergraduate in six would fail to complete the degree they embarked upon. Although the latest projection is closer to one in five, that is still significantly more than the UK average for Caledonian's courses and entry qualifications. The university has introduced a series of measures designed to improve retention. Telltale signs are monitored, such as non-attendance at lectures, and better academic, social and financial support offered to those at risk of dropping out.

Consolidated on its city-centre campus, Caledonian's original two sites have now been reduced to one with the sale of the Park Campus, in the west end of the city, to Glasgow University. Leisure facilities have been improved with a new building for the health faculty, opened by Thabo Mbeki, who named it in honour of his father. Physiotherapy was the only subject since chemistry's success in 1993 to be rated Excellent for teaching, and Caledonian now boasts among the most extensive health programmes in Britain.

A string of other subjects (mainly on the science side) were considered Highly Satisfactory. Business is the other big area,

70 Cowcaddens Road
Glasgow G4 0BA
0141 331 8681 (enquiries)
helpline@gcal.ac.uk
www.gcal.ac.uk
www.caledonianstudent.
com

GLASGOW
Edinburgh
Belfast
London
Cardiff

The Times Rankings
Overall Ranking: =68

Student satisfaction:	=55	(74%)
Research quality:	=76	(1.2)
Entry standards:	45	(311)
Student–staff ratio:	=86	(19.8)
Services & facilities/student:	88	(£850)
Expected completion rate:	98	(74.8%)
Good honours:	39	(65.7%)
Graduate prospects:	79	(60.5%)

the Caledonian Business School boasting more undergraduates than any other institution in Scotland, with over 1,000 in each year group. The university pioneered subjects such as entrepreneurial studies and risk management – the only university in the country to do so – and offers highly specialist degrees, such as tourism management, fashion marketing, leisure management and consumer protection.

Degrees in all areas are strongly vocational, and are complemented by a wide portfolio of professional courses. A high proportion of students choose sandwich courses, and the university operates on a modular system. The REAL@Caledonian online student facility combines enhanced learning technology with a informal cyber-café atmosphere.

The legacy of Queen's College, which catered mainly for women, has ensured that the proportion of female students is the highest of any university in Britain. Sports and social facilities have been among the priorities in the building programme. Some students find that the high proportion of their peers living at home detracts from the social scene, but Glasgow is a very lively city with a large student population.

Undergraduate Fees and Bursaries

- Scottish-domiciled and EU students: no fees payable.
- Non-Scottish UK-domiciled student fees: £1,775 a year.
- International student fees: £8,500–£9,000
- Scholarships based on circumstances or by competition.For full details see the university's website: www.gcal.ac.uk/student/money/index.html

Students

Undergraduates:	10,690	(3,230)
Postgraduates:	1,525	(2,005)
Mature students:	34.8%	
Overseas students:	4.6%	
Applications per place:	5.7	
From state-sector schools:	96.6%	
From working-class homes:	37.1%	

For detailed information about fees, grants and bursaries and how they work, see chapter 7.

Accommodation

Number of places and costs refer to 2008–09
University-provided places: 660
Percentage catered: 0%
Self-catered costs: £73–£84 a week.
Students under 19 living outside the Glasgow area have priority for accommodation.
International students: non-EU students given priority if conditions are met.
Contact: accommodation@gcal.ac.uk;
www.caledonian.ac.uk/study/studentlife/accommodation/index.html

University of Gloucestershire

Gloucestershire, one of the more recent additions to the list of UK universities, was also the first for more than a century to have formal links with the Church of England. Although its religious origins have been played down in recent years and students of all faiths are welcomed, the university will maintain an association that includes church appointees on its governing body and Lord Carey, the former Archbishop of Canterbury, as the first Chancellor. This did not prevent it dropping theology, its top-rated subject with good scores for both teaching and research, at undergraduate level, although a degree in religion, philosophy and ethics was introduced in 2006 and theology itself can now be studied part-time. The subject had been one of 14 degrees to go in a curriculum review that expanded leisure and tourism, social work and journalism.

Before university status in 2001, Cheltenham and Gloucester College of Higher Education had been the product of a merger between a church college and the higher education wing of a college of arts and technology. Teaching ratings were good enough to satisfy the assessors, without being spectacular, and the last research grades showed that Gloucestershire would not be out of place in the university system. More than 40 per cent of academics were entered for the 2001 Research Assessment Exercise – a figure exceeded by only four former polytechnics – and the average score per member of staff placed the new university seventh among that group for research. English and theology both achieved grade 4, denoting national excellence in virtually all of the work submitted.

After considerable expansion during the 1990s, there are now almost 9,000 students, including 3,200 part-timers, and 1,000 academic and support staff. The main subject areas are law and IT, business management, the arts, media and design, humanities, the environment, teacher education, leisure and tourism, social sciences and sport. The university prides itself on a good range of work placements, which include British Aerospace and Disneyworld.

The main campus is on the attractive site of the former College of St Paul and St Mary, a one-time botanical garden a mile outside Cheltenham. There has also been considerable development of the Gloucester campus, on the site of a former domestic science college which became part of the university in 2002. Although middle-class Cheltenham is a world away from more working-class Gloucester socially, the two centres are only seven miles apart and students are not as isolated as they are in some split-site institutions.

The Park Campus
The Park
Cheltenham GL50 2RH
08707 201100 (prospectus)
admissions@glos.ac.uk
www.glos.ac.uk
www.yourstudentsunion
.com

The Times Rankings
Overall Ranking: 58

Student satisfaction:	=64	(73%)
Research quality:	=58	(1.7)
Entry standards:	83	(258)
Student–staff ratio:	55	(17.2)
Services & facilities/student:	52	(£1,074)
Expected completion rate:	=71	(80.5%)
Good honours:	71	(54.9%)
Graduate prospects:	=81	(60.2%)

There are also two smaller sites in Cheltenham: Pittville for art and design, and Francis Close Hall for a range of subjects, including tourism. The latter also houses a national centre of excellence in the teaching of geography, environment and related disciplines. A free bus service links all four sites and also serves Cheltenham railway station. In addition, the Urban Learning Foundation, in London, became part of the university in 2003, providing a very different setting for teacher training courses.

Gloucestershire's intake is as diverse as its locations, with 94 per cent of under-graduates from state schools and nearly a third from working-class homes. The projected dropout rate has been improving, but the latest projection of 16 per cent, is still worse than the national average for the subjects offered and the students' entry qualifications. The new and well-equipped sport-oriented Oxstalls campus, in Gloucester, where participation in higher education has always been low, will focus particularly on access initiatives.

The university's sports facilities include a swimming pool, sports hall and tennis courts, but are not extensive for a university of 9,000 students. Likewise accommoda-tion, with around 1,300 beds, although the university assures its students that it has access to enough private sector places to meet all their needs. First years are given

priority in the allocation of hall places and "enhancement of the student experience" is one of the priorities in the university's strategic plan. Cheltenham is the livelier of the two bases in terms of nightlife, but neither is dull and facilities are improving.

Undergraduate Fees and Bursaries
- Fees for UK/EU students: £3,145
- International student fees: £8,000
- Bursary on full grant: £310
- Bursaries on partial grant: n/a
- Scholarships based on circumstances or by competition. For full details see the university's website: www.glos.ac.uk/fees/index.cfm

Students

Undergraduates:	5,405	(1,325)
Postgraduates:	495	(1,170)
Mature students:	23.7%	
Overseas students:	4.5%	
Applications per place:	5.1	
From state-sector schools:	94.3%	
From working-class homes:	32.7%	

For detailed information about fees, grants and bursaries and how they work, see chapter 7.

Accommodation
Number of places and costs refer to 2007–08
University-provided places: about 1,300
Percentage catered: 0%
Self-catered costs: £80–£92 a week.
First-year undergraduates have priority for halls.
International students: first years are guaranteed accommodation if conditions are met.
Contact: accommodation@glos.ac.uk

Goldsmiths, University of London

Dubbed the "campus of cool", Goldsmiths is best known for excellence in the arts, but it stresses that it brings the same creative approach to a wider range of subjects. The nickname, which does no harm in recruiting students, comes from the inclusion of Goldsmiths alongside MTV, Apple and the Tate among 50 "cool brandleaders" identified by the Brand Council. Alumni include Mary Quant and Damien Hirst among many other famous names, such as Malcolm McLaren and Linton Kwesi Johnson. Graduates of the college have won the Turner Prize no fewer than six times.

There is another side to Goldsmiths, however, in its tradition of community-based courses, which predates member-ship of the University of London. Evening and other part-time classes are still as popular as conventional degree courses and many subjects can be studied from basic to postgraduate levels. A history of providing educational opportunities for women is reflected in one of the largest proportions of female students in the British university system – nearly two thirds at the last count.

Determinedly integrated into their southeast London locality, the campus has a cosmopolitan atmosphere. Over a quarter of all undergraduates are over 21 on entry (a large proportion of these over 30), many coming from the area's ethnic minorities, and there is a growing proportion of overseas students. The age profile helped Goldsmiths to the biggest rise in applications in 2007, although the figure at the start of 2008 was close to the national average.

The older premises have been likened to a grammar school, with their long corridors of classrooms. But the Rutherford Building, containing library and IT services, won an award from the Royal Institute of British Architects, and a Grade II listed former baths building has been converted to provide more space for research and art studios. The new Ben Pimlott Building, which features a dramatic metal "scribble" by the acclaimed architect Will Alsop, contains state-of-the-art studio facilities and two multi-disciplinary centres for interaction between the arts and social sciences.

Although dominated by the arts, Goldsmiths' portfolio of subjects stretches through the social sciences as far as computing and psychology. Both media and communications and sociology were rated internationally outstanding in the last research rankings, which were a spectacular success for the college. Anthropology, art and design, music and

Lewisham Way
New Cross
London SE14 6NW
020 7919 7766 (admissions)
admissions@gold.ac.uk
www.goldsmiths.ac.uk
www.gcsu.org.uk

The Times Rankings
Overall Ranking: 46

Student satisfaction:	=64	(73%)
Research quality:	=21	(4.9)
Entry standards:	=47	(307)
Student–staff ratio:	36	(15.5)
Services & facilities/student:	98	(£793)
Expected completion rate:	=61	(82.2%)
Good honours:	40	(64.8%)
Graduate prospects:	=58	(63.6%)

English and comparative literature were close behind, leaving more than a third of the academics entered for assessment in the top two of seven categories. The research grades helped transform Goldsmiths' financial position, allowing more investment in teaching. Teaching quality scores were generally good though not spectacular, but psychology and history produced outstanding results in the first national student satisfaction survey. Employment prospects are good, especially for an institution with such a high proportion of students taking performing arts subjects, where a period of unemployment after graduation is commonplace. Indeed, on postgraduate courses, recent success rates have been among the best in Britain.

Student politics has survived at Goldsmiths to an extent not seen at many universities – the union building was given the name Tiananmen – while a college in which Alex James and Graham Coxon, from Blur, are just two of a number of successful rock alumni cannot fail to have a thriving music scene. The union has a strong tradition in volunteering and an award-winning newspaper, and recently won a gold Sound Impact Award recognising work on ethical and environmental issues.

The surrounding area has enjoyed a mini-boom as a prime location for loft apartments. Although sky-high prices put them way beyond the reach of the student housing market, there are plenty of more reasonably priced options in the vicinity. Most first years are allocated one of the 971 residential places within walking distance of the campus and overseas students can be housed throughout their course. Sports enthusiasts have been less well provided for, although a well-equipped and affordable gym opened on campus in 2006. There is a swimming pool and indoor complex in Deptford, but the main pitches are eight miles away.

Undergraduate Fees and Bursaries

- Fees for UK/EU students: £3,145
- International student fees: £9,580–£13,290
- Bursary on full grant: household income up to £19K: £1,000 then £500.
- Bursaries on partial grant: household income up to £40K: up to £500.
- Scholarships based on circumstances or by competition. For full details see the university's website: www.goldsmiths.ac.uk/costs/

Students

Undergraduates:	4,015	(760)
Postgraduates:	1,685	(985)
Mature students:	26.4%	
Overseas students:	14.0%	
Applications per place:	5.9	
From state-sector schools:	88.0%	
From working-class homes:	29.9%	

For detailed information about fees, grants and bursaries and how they work, see chapter 7.

Accommodation

Number of places and costs refer to 2007–08
University-provided places: 971 (college halls)
Percentage catered: 0%
Self-catered costs: £85–£109 a week.
First years are likely to receive an offer of accommodation (see website for further details).
Policy for international students: same as above.
Contact: accommodation@gold.ac.uk
www.goldsmiths.ac.uk/accommodation
020 7919 7130

University of Greenwich

Becoming one of three universities charging British and EU undergraduates less than £3,000 a year was a gamble that appeared not to pay off in the first year of top-up fees. Applications dropped by more than the national average, but the strategy looked more hopeful by 2007, when an increase of 15 per cent saw Greenwich outperform most of its peer group. The university was still performing better than the national average when the official deadline passed for courses beginning in 2008, when fees for degree courses will reach £2,835. The aim is to strike a balance between affordability for the maximum number of students and the need to invest in the university.

The university's move, completed in 2002, into the former Royal Naval College buildings designed by Sir Christopher Wren provided a campus worthy of one of the most desirable titles in the higher education world. Its name has always conjured up images of history and science in equal measure, and the main campus is now part of a World Heritage site.

Wren's baroque masterpiece is being used, with the former Dreadnought Hospital, to teach over half the university's students in humanities, business, law, maths, computing, and maritime studies. Four halls provide more than 1,300 places.

Under the leadership of Baroness Blackstone, the former Higher Education Minister, Greenwich has dropped the soubriquet of "regional university" but still draws primarily from southeast London and Kent, a populous county that until recently had only a single university. The Medway campus, centred on the former naval base at Chatham, has been developed in partnership with Kent and Canterbury Christ Church universities. Some £20 million has gone into one of the first new schools of pharmacy for 20 years, as well as the schools of science and engineering, the Natural Resources Institute, nursing and some business courses. A joint learning resources centre serves Chatham Maritime and the University of Kent's neighbouring premises. Another shared facility has improved teaching facilities and expanded student services, the campus having already exceeded the original target of 6,000 students.

Other departments are situated at Avery Hill, a Victorian mansion on the outskirts of southeast London, where a £14-million sports and teaching centre opened at the end of 2006 and a new gym is under construction. As well as a sports hall and 220-seat lecture theatre, there are laboratories for health courses that replicate NHS wards. A neighbouring building will be the main base for the School of Health and Social Care. The

---

Old Royal Naval College
Park Row,
Greenwich
London SE10 9LS
0800 005 006 (course
  enquiries)
courseinfo@greenwich.
  ac.uk
www.gre.ac.uk
www.suug.co.uk

The Times Rankings
Overall Ranking: 110

Student satisfaction:	=99	(68%)
Research quality:	=76	(1.2)
Entry standards:	=107	(212)
Student–staff ratio:	109	(23.4)
Services & facilities/student:	93	(£824)
Expected completion rate:	76	(79.7%)
Good honours:	111	(42.4%)
Graduate prospects:	=63	(63.0%)

campus also contains a student village of 1,300 rooms, as well as teaching accommodation for the social sciences, architecture, landscape and construction and the large education faculty, which is one of the few to offer both primary and secondary teacher training courses.

Most teaching assessments were favourable, with pharmacy and pharmacology, town planning, sociology and nursing the star performers. However, Greenwich was near the bottom of rankings from the first two national student satisfaction surveys, although maths produced an outstanding result in 2007. The university achieved some respectable grades in the last Research Assessment Exercise, with computing, German and materials leading the way, although less than a third of the academic staff entered. A fifth of its income is from research and consultancy – the largest proportion at any former polytechnic Strong links with institutions in Europe and further afield provide a steady flow of overseas students – mainly from China, India and Greece – as well as exchange opportunities for those at Greenwich. Eleven associated colleges in Kent and London teach the university's courses.

A commitment to extending access to higher education has led to low entrance requirements in many subjects and a relatively high proportion of mature students. More than 97 per cent of undergraduates are state-educated, almost half coming from working-class homes. Both figures are significantly higher than the national average for Greenwich's courses and entrance qualifications. The downside is a projected dropout rate of almost 18 per cent, although this is an improvement on previous figures and close to the university's benchmark.

Undergraduate Fees and Bursaries

- Fees for UK/EU students   £2,835
- International student fees   £8,650
- Bursary on full grant: n/a
- Bursaries on partial grant: n/a
- Scholarships based on circumstances or by competition. For full details see the university's website: www.gre.ac.uk/students/finance

Students

Undergraduates:	12,735	(5,255)
Postgraduates:	2,490	(4,435)
Mature students:	43.2%	
Overseas students:	14.0%	
Applications per place:	6.6	
From state-sector schools:	97.2%	
From working-class homes:	47.1%	

For detailed information about fees, grants and bursaries and how they work, see chapter 7.

Accommodation

Number of places and costs refer to 2008–09
University-provided places: 2,400
Percentage catered: 0%
Self-catered costs: £76.93–£157.71 a week.
First years are guaranteed a place.
International students: new students get priority.
Contact: www.gre.ac.uk/about/accommodation;
accommodation-AH@gre.ac.uk (Avery Hill)
accommodation-GM@gre.ac.uk (Greenwich)
accommodation-ME@gre.ac.uk (Medway)

Heriot-Watt University

Concentration on technology, languages and business is fitting for a university which commemorates James Watt, the pioneer of steam power, and George Heriot, financier to King James VI. Still evolving more than 40 years after attaining university status, in many ways Heriot-Watt is Scotland's most unconventional university. The main campus, on the outskirts of Edinburgh is among the most modern in Britain.

Still small in terms of full-time students – there are under 7,000 on campus – the university has a further 10,500 students in supported learning centres overseas and on distance learning courses. A new campus opened in Dubai in 2005 offering management, business, IT and a range of engineering subjects. With overseas students filling nearly a quarter of its places in Scotland, Heriot-Watt is one of the UK's most international universities. The university won the Scottish Council of Development and Industry's 2007 award for Outstanding International Achieve-ment in Scotland's Universities, partly for its support for international students.

For many years, Heriot-Watt's main claim to fame outside the academic community lay in its degree in brewing and distilling. But the university has a wide variety of vocational programmes, as well as more conventional degrees. Research in petroleum engineering is rated internationally outstanding, while modern languages are a more unexpected strength. Actuarial mathematics and statistics is one of only two centres in the UK, and photonics and optoelectronics, building and food science are all highly regarded.

Both teaching and research are heavily multidisciplinary with a focus on applying knowledge to real-world challenges. Computer sciences and chemical, electrical and electronic, mechanical and petroleum engineering all achieved the top Commendable grades used in teaching assessments. An institutional review in 2006 produced the top grade of "broad confidence". Languages produced the best results in the university's debut in the National Student Survey, in 2007.

Science, engineering, management and languages are located on the main campus at Riccarton. There is a postgraduate campus in Orkney, specialising in renewable energy, and a Scottish Borders Campus in Galashiels, 35 miles south of Edinburgh, where the university took over and upgraded the Scottish College of Textiles. Heriot-Watt and Borders College have signed a partnership agreement for a long-term collaboration to deliver higher and further education in the historically

Riccarton
Edinburgh EH14 4AS
0131 449 5111
enquiries@hw.ac.uk
www.hw.ac.uk
www.hwusa.org

The Times Rankings
Overall Ranking: 47

Student satisfaction:	=39	(75%)
Research quality:	=41	(4.2)
Entry standards:	37	(343)
Student–staff ratio:	=49	(16.6)
Services & facilities/student:	47	(£1,115)
Expected completion rate:	60	(82.3%)
Good honours:	70	(55.0%)
Graduate prospects:	34	(72.1%)

underprovided region. Both institutions will share the site, with the university concentrating on textiles, fashion design and management.

Heriot-Watt is also one of the most commercially diversified universities in Britain, with the share of private research funding consistently among the highest in the UK per member of academic staff. About half of the university's income, around £60 million, comes from research, training and commercial services.

The subject mix also serves graduates well: Heriot-Watt is seldom far from the top of the employment league tables. The latest projected dropout rate of 15 per cent is an improvement on previous figures, although still higher than the UK average for the university's subjects and entrance qualifications. More than half of the undergraduates are from Scotland, and 15 per cent from other parts of Britain, over 90 per cent of them from state schools and colleges.

The Edinburgh campus has an attractive parkland setting, with the students' union at its heart and halls of residence conveniently placed. Students have complained that the six-mile journey to the city centre leaves them isolated, but there are now frequent bus services. Sports enthusiasts are well provided for, and representative teams do well. Hearts, one of Edinburgh's two SPL clubs, have their

sports academy on campus, which is used by students and local people as well as the young professionals. Music also thrives: there is a professional musician-in-residence and a number of scholarships, as well as a varied programme of events.

Undergraduate Fees and Bursaries
- Scottish-domiciled and EU students: no fees payable.
- Non-Scottish UK-domiciled student fees: £1,775 a year.
- International student fees: £8,380–£10,920
- Scholarships based on circumstances or by competition. For full details see the university's website: www.undergraduate.hw.ac.uk/scholarships/

Students

Undergraduates:	4,775	(540)
Postgraduates:	1,535	(3,710)
Mature students:	14.4%	
Overseas students:	22.9%	
Applications per place:	4.4	
From state-sector schools:	92.1%	
From working-class homes:	30.7%	

For detailed information about fees, grants and bursaries and how they work, see chapter 7.

Accommodation

Number of places and costs refer to 2008–09
University places provided: 1,619
Percentage catered: 19%
Catered costs: £94.50–£103.00 a week.
Self-catered costs: £57–£82 a week.
All new first years are guaranteed accommodation provided conditions are met and applications in place by 22 August.
International students: as above.
Contact : SWS@hw.ac.uk

University of Hertfordshire

Hertfordshire has become a model for the "business-facing" university, serving the needs of local employers and improving the job prospects of its students in the process. The university even runs the local bus service and plays an important role in steering the local economy. A purpose-built £120-million campus, close to the existing Hatfield headquarters, opened in 2003, bringing the university together for the first time and providing outstanding facilities. The de Havilland campus, named after the aircraft manufacturer which once occupied the site, houses business, education and the humanities. It has a 24-hour resources centre, £15-million sports complex and 1,600 networked, en-suite residential places. The two sites are linked by cycleways, footpaths and shuttle buses. The blaze of publicity that accompanied the opening contributed to the biggest rise in applications at any UK university. The demand for places has remained healthy, although there was an above-average decline in applications at the start of 2008, when the number of choices per applicant was cut from six to five.

As Hatfield Polytechnic, the university's reputation was built on engineering and computer science, but health subjects now account for by far the largest share of places. An innovative degree in paramedic

science was Britain's first, and the university is still hoping for a medical school, although its last bid was not successful. The announcement of a £500-million hospital and cancer centre in Hatfield should strengthen the university's case, as should the launches of a new School of Pharmacy and a postgraduate medical school. The latter is a collaboration with Cranfield and Bedfordshire universities and the local health authority.

Art and design is also growing, particularly the multimedia courses. In 2005, the university launched a new School of Film, Music and New Media. The College Lane campus includes the largest art gallery in the eastern region, which mounts regular public exhibitions. A new 460-seat auditorium will enhance the cultural programme. An Automotive Centre has upgraded teaching facilities for that branch of engineering, as well as boosting interaction with industry.

Average grades for A-level entrants rose under the previous Vice-Chancellor, who called for a "tougher and more rigorous" academic style and declared a desire to propel Hertfordshire up the league tables. Professor Tim Wilson, the present incumbent, retains this ambition but is also trying to widen the university's base through collaboration with local further education colleges. The intake is more diverse than expected, given the location

---

College Lane
Hatfield
Herts AL10 9AB
01707 284800 (admissions)
admissions@herts.ac.uk
www.herts.ac.uk
www.uhsu.herts.ac.uk

The Times Rankings
Overall Ranking: 79

Student satisfaction:	=73	(72%)
Research quality:	=69	(1.4)
Entry standards:	=85	(256)
Student–staff ratio:	37	(15.6)
Services & facilities/student:	50	(£1,087)
Expected completion rate:	94	(75.9%)
Good honours:	=97	(47.7%)
Graduate prospects:	=69	(62.1%)

and subject mix: 97 per cent of undergraduates are state-educated and 40 per cent come from working-class homes. However, the projected dropout rate hit 20 per cent dropout rate in the last national survey, taking Hertfordshire beyond the national average for the subject mix and entry grades.

Many students include work placements in their degrees, the close links with employers sometimes bringing in valuable research and consultancy contracts, and contributing to a consistently good graduate employment record.

Environmental studies and philosophy achieved the best scores for teaching quality, with business and management, psychology and nursing close behind. Grades in the last Research Assessment Exercise showed considerable improvement on 1996, with history rated nationally outstanding and computing, nursing, physics and psychology all in the next category.

Even before the opening of the new campus, students were well served in terms of information technology. The award-winning library and resource centre on the main campus is Britain's biggest, offering 24-hour access to hundreds of computer workstations. A second centre on the de Havilland campus provides another 1,100 workstations. The StudyNet information system has been a leader in its field, giving all staff and students their own storage space. Students can use it for study, revision or communication, as well as to access university information.

The Hertfordshire Sports Village boasts some of the best university-based facilities in Britain. Although principally for student use, it is also open to local residents. The university claims to be one of the safest in the country.

Undergraduate Fees and Bursaries

- Fees for UK/EU students: £3,145
- International student fees: £8,500
- Bursary on full grant: 50% of maintenance grant.
- Bursaries on partial grant: household income up to £40K, 50% of maintenance grant.
- Scholarships based on circumstances or by competition. For full details see the university's website: http://perseus.herts.ac.uk/uhinfo/fees_new/fees2008/fees-and-funding-home.cfm

Students

Undergraduates:	16,095	(3,080)
Postgraduates:	2,050	(1,990)
Mature students:	24.2%	
Overseas students:	10.8%	
Applications per place:	4.9	
From state-sector schools:	97.4%	
From working-class homes:	39.7%	

For detailed information about fees, grants and bursaries and how they work, see chapter 7.

Accommodation

Number of places and costs refer to 2008–09
University-provided places: 3,300
Percentage catered: 0%
Self-catered costs: £60.62–£96.67 a week.
First years are guaranteed accommodation if conditions are met.
International students: as above.
Contact: accommodation@herts.ac.uk

University of Huddersfield

Official performance indicators for higher education have shown Huddersfield living up to its mission to help produce a more diverse student population, and it has opened satellite centres in Barnsley and Oldham to widen participation further. Almost four out of ten full-time students are from working-class homes and about a quarter are from areas without a strong tradition of higher education. Although 18 per cent are not expected to complete their degrees, this is no more than the national average for the university's courses and entry qualifications. Huddersfield achieved the highest possible score in an audit by the Quality Assurance Agency in 2004.

Imaginative conversions and new buildings have finally allowed the university to come together on one town-centre campus. The university capitalised on Huddersfield's industrial past to ease the strain on facilities that were struggling to cope with expansion which reached 13 per cent a year at its peak. Canalside, a refurbished mill complex, has provided new space for mathematics and computing, and education occupies another mill site – this time a £4-million recreation of the original. The university is even creating "pocket parks" and a landscaped area along the reopened

Narrow Canal to provide additional green space. Human and health sciences have also acquired new premises, and an additional £4 million has been spent on a new students' union, allowing drama courses to take over the existing union complex. The new union, opened by Huddersfield's Chancellor, *Star Trek* actor Patrick Stewart, includes alcohol-free social areas to encourage participation by those overseas students and ethnic minorities who would otherwise avoid the facilities.

A tradition of vocational education dates back to 1841, and the university has a long-established reputation in areas such as textile design and engineering. But there are less obvious gems such as music and social work, both of which were rated excellent for teaching and nationally outstanding for research. Electrical and electronic engineering achieved the best score in assessments of teaching quality. The university's own satisfaction surveys suggest that students value the friendliness and helpfulness of staff, and Huddersfield did reasonably well in the last national survey, which showed particularly high levels of satisfaction in health sciences.

The university adopted a much more selective approach to the last research assessments, entering half the number of academics it did in 1996. History matched

Queensgate
Huddersfield
West Yorkshire HD1 3DH
0870 901 5555 (prospectus)
admissions@hud.ac.uk
www.hud.ac.uk
www.huddersfield
student.com

The Times Rankings
Overall Ranking: 90

Student satisfaction:	=39	(75%)
Research quality:	=88	(0.9)
Entry standards:	79	(262)
Student–staff ratio:	=86	(19.8)
Services & facilities/student:	109	(£616)
Expected completion rate:	78	(78.9%)
Good honours:	75	(53.3%)
Graduate prospects:	105	(53.2%)

social work and music's grade 5, with mechanical engineering in the next category. A flourishing relationship with industry produces more private income than is achieved in many larger institutions, as well as influencing courses.

The most popular courses are in human and health sciences. Many arts and social science courses have a vocational slant. Politics, for example, includes a six-week work placement, which often takes students to the House of Commons. A third of the students in all subjects take sandwich courses, one of the highest proportions in Britain, and more than 4,000 have some element of work experience. The approach has been paying off with consistently good graduate employment figures and applications.

Most residential accommodation is now concentrated in the Storthes Hall Park student village, but additional accommodation is available at Ashenhurst, just over a mile from the campus. Recent developments mean the 1,712 residential places are enough to guarantee accommodation to first years, and private housing is cheap and plentiful in Huddersfield. Students are also encouraged to follow a structured fitness programme at the upgraded campus sports centre. Town–gown relations are good and the cost of living low. Most students like the town's friendly atmosphere, although they tend to base their social life on the students' union. It is not far to Leeds for those in search of serious clubbing.

Undergraduate Fees and Bursaries
- Fees for UK/EU students: £3,145
- International student fees: £8,000–£9,000
- Bursary on full grant: £500
- Bursaries on partial grant: n/a
- Scholarships based on circumstances or by competition. For full details see the university's website: www.hud.ac.uk/student_finance/

Students

Undergraduates:	11,120	(5,055)
Postgraduates:	1,100	(2,470)
Mature students:	27.2%	
Overseas students:	5.3%	
Applications per place:	5.1	
From state-sector schools:	97.0%	
From working-class homes:	38.6%	

For detailed information about fees, grants and bursaries and how they work, see chapter 7.

Accommodation

Number of places and costs refer to 2007–08
University-provided places: 1,712 in privately owned halls
Percentage catered: 0%
Self-catered costs: £59.95–£91.95 a week.
First years are guaranteed accommodation provided conditions are met.
International students: as above.
Contact: info@campusdigs.com;
www.campusdigs.com

University of Hull

Students at Hull are among the most satisfied in the country – the university has never been out of the top ten in the first three national surveys of their views. Languages, history and archaeology, business, physics and politics did particularly well, but most departments produced creditable scores. The university and the city have always commanded loyalty among students, who appreciate the modest cost of living and ready availability of accommodation. But the quality of courses is also high: drama and electronic engineering achieved perfect scores in teaching assessments, with politics and theology close behind.

A long-standing focus on Europe shows in the wide range of languages available at degree level, with the purpose-built Language Institute heavily used by students of all subjects. Strength in politics – confirmed by one of three grade 5 assessments for research, as well as the teaching quality success – is reflected in a steady flow of graduates into the House of Commons. The Westminster Hull Internship Programme (WHIP) offers a year-long placement and month-long internships for British politics and legislative studies students.

However, the university was criticised for deciding to close mathematics following poor recruitment to the honours degree.

No subject was rated internationally outstanding in the last research assessments, but law and geography joined politics in the next category. Social work collected a Queen's Anniversary Prize and was also rated excellent for teaching. An Institute for Learning tries to put research findings into practice, developing training courses for lecturers and encouraging the university's interest in lifelong learning.

After years of relative stability, Hull expanded rapidly, both on its spacious home campus and through mergers. First it added nursing to its portfolio of courses with the acquisition of the former Humberside College of Health, then it took in University College Scarborough in 2000 and finally the university bought the adjacent campus of the former Humberside University. There are now 19,000 undergraduates, including part-timers, but applications have been subject to big swings. There was a rise of almost 10 per cent in 2007, but the switch from six choices per applicant to five brought a 15 per cent drop.

The main academic development has been the establishment of a medical school in conjunction with York University, where demand for places continued to rise strongly in 2008. Hull's patient development, in collaboration with

---

Cottingham Road
Hull HU6 7RX
01482 466100
admissions@hull.ac.uk
www.hull.ac.uk
www.hullstudent.com

Edinburgh
Belfast
HULL
London
Cardiff

The Times Rankings
Overall Ranking: 45

Student satisfaction:	=8	(80%)
Research quality:	53	(3.2)
Entry standards:	51	(297)
Student–staff ratio:	=71	(18.6)
Services & facilities/student:	79	(£934)
Expected completion rate:	=54	(83.9%)
Good honours:	=64	(56.4%)
Graduate prospects:	37	(71.0%)

the local health authority, of a postgraduate medical school was rewarded with the award of a traditional school housed in a landmark building on the former Humberside (West) campus. The West Campus also contains a Business Quarter, incorporating the new-look Business School, which was refurbished in 2005, and the Logistics Institute and Enterprise Centre.

The original 94-acre main campus has also seen considerable development, with improvements to social facilities, new buildings for languages and chemistry, a Graduate Research Institute and a state-of-the-art sport, health and exercise science laboratory. The campus, with its art gallery and highly automated library, is less than three miles from the centre of Hull.

The Scarborough campus has also seen investment, with new laboratories for music technology and digital arts, and a renovated café bar. Hull has always maintained a roughly equal balance between science and technology and the arts and social sciences, believing that this promotes a harmonious atmosphere, but the Scarborough campus has tipped the scales towards the arts.

Only one traditional university in England has a higher proportion of state-educated students than Hull's 92 per cent. Three in ten are from working-class homes, but the projected dropout rate of

13 per cent has slipped above the funding council's benchmark for the subjects offered. Attempts to broaden the intake further in an area where participation in higher education has always been low, drew praise from Tony Blair.

Student leisure facilities, which were always good but becoming crowded, have been upgraded as part of the campus building programme. The students' union, which was rated the best in Britain in one survey, has been refurbished and has opened the popular "Asylum" nightclub. New football pitches have been added recently on campus and the Sports and Fitness Centre has been attracting praise.

Undergraduate Fees and Bursaries
- Fees for UK/EU students: £3,145
- International student fees: £8,500–£10,500
- Bursary on full grant: £1,000
- Bursaries on partial grant: household income up to £40K: £500.
- Scholarships based on circumstances or by competition. For full details see the university's website: www.hull.ac.uk/money

Students

Undergraduates:	10,525	(8,190)
Postgraduates:	1,485	(2,075)
Mature students:	20.1%	
Overseas students:	8.6%	
Applications per place:	3.8	
From state-sector schools:	92.5%	
From working-class homes:	30.1%	

For detailed information about fees, grants and bursaries and how they work, see chapter 7.

Accommodation
Number of places and costs refer to 2008–09
University-provided places: 2,601 (owned stock); 200 (leased/associated stock)
Percentage catered: 49%
Catered costs: £82.81–£122.99 (31 weeks).
Self-catered costs: £62.15–£83.02 a week (31–50 weeks).
Unaccompanied first years are guaranteed accommodation if conditions are met.
International students: as above.
Contact: rooms@hull.ac.uk

Imperial College of Science, Technology and Medicine

Regularly in the top three in *The Times* League Table, London's specialist college of science, engineering and medicine is also in the top five in the world rankings published by *The Times Higher Education* and QS. Over 6,000 academic staff include Nobel prizewinners, 66 Fellows of the Royal Society and 71 Fellows of the Royal Academy of Engineering. Three quarters of the academics entered in the latest Research Assessment Exercise were in departments considered internationally outstanding – the highest proportion in any university – and almost all were in one of the top two categories.

Teaching scores were up to the same high standard, with electrical and electronic engineering and materials science achieving maximum points. Physics, mathematics and medicine also did well. Imperial is not recommended for academic slouches, but tough entrance requirements ensure that they are a rare breed in any case. The projected dropout rate of 4 per cent is among the lowest in the country. Such is the level of competition that applications had been dropping, although there was a modest increase when the official deadline passed for courses beginning in 2007. Even though many of the subjects struggle for candidates elsewhere, entrants average better than an A and two Bs at A level. Nearly 40 per cent of the undergraduates are from independent schools – one of the highest proportions at any university and considerably more than the national average for Imperial's courses.

Engineering degrees last four years and lead to an MEng. Almost all branches of engineering achieved the coveted 5* rating for research. The college has been expanding its range of European exchanges, with a variety of prestigious technological institutions available for courses such as the MSc in physics.

Medicine was the main area of development in the 1990s: mergers with the St Mary's, Charing Cross and Westminster, and Royal Postgraduate teaching hospitals producing one of the biggest faculties of medicine in the UK. Top ratings for research in clinical medicine are a source of pride. Further mergers in 2000 brought in the Kennedy Institute of Rheumatology and Wye College, in Ashford, Kent, which has become a research centre and its courses transferred to the University of Kent. In 2007, Imperial formed the UK's first Academic Health Science Centre through the merger of St Mary's and Hammersmith Hospitals NHS Trusts and their integration with the college.

Exhibition Road
South Kensington
London SW7 2AZ
020 7594 8014
www3.imperial.ac.uk/
 registry/enquiries
www.imperial.ac.uk
www.imperialcollege
 union.org

The Times Rankings
Overall Ranking: 3

Student satisfaction:	=26	(76%)
Research quality:	4	(5.8)
Entry standards:	3	(473)
Student–staff ratio:	2	(10.4)
Services & facilities/student:	1	(£3,218)
Expected completion rate:	7	(96.0%)
Good honours:	26	(69.1%)
Graduate prospects:	1	(89.3%)

Imperial celebrated its centenary in 2007 and has left the University of London to trade on its global reputation. It has been redeveloping and expanding facilities on its main campus, in the heart of South Kensington's museum district, most recently with the construction of a new sports centre and halls of residence complex. The growing Tanaka Business School, rated excellent for teaching, is Imperial's main concession to the academic world beyond science, technology and medicine.

The Undergraduate Research Opportunities Programme provides opportunities for "hands-on" experience of the research activities of college staff and postgraduates. A voluntary scheme open to all undergraduates, it is especially popular in the summer vacation, when students can be paid bursaries and international undergraduates can participate without needing a work permit. There is also a vacation placement scheme during the summer for undergraduates to acquire work experience.

Imperial's specialisms have the effect of making it the most male-dominated university institution in Britain, although the number of female students doubled during the 1990s and now stands at more than a third. The imbalance shows in a social scene which many students find limited, despite the largest selection of clubs and societies in the country. Outdoor sports facilities are remote, but Wednesday afternoons are left free to encourage students to make the effort to exercise.

Undergraduate Fees and Bursaries

- Fees for UK/EU students: £3,145
- International student fees: £17,350–£19,450 £23,800–£35,500 (medicine)
- Bursary on full grant: £3,000
- Bursaries on partial grant: household income up to £60K sliding scale £2,000–£50.
- Scholarships based on circumstances or by competition. For full details see the university's website: www.imperial.ac.uk/bursaries www3.imperial.ac.uk/ugprospectus/moneyzone

Students		
Undergraduates:	8,350	(0)
Postgraduates:	3,880	(1,180)
Mature students:	5.6%	
Overseas students:	34.4%	
Applications per place:	6.3	
From state-sector schools:	61.3%	
From working-class homes:	17.3%	

For detailed information about fees, grants and bursaries and how they work, see chapter 7.

Accommodation

Number of places and costs refer to 2008–09
University-provided places: 2,613
Percentage catered: 0%
Self-catered costs: £55–£180 a week.
First years are guaranteed accommodation provided conditions are met.
International students: undergraduates, as above.
Contact:accommodation@imperial.ac.uk

University of Keele

Keele has set itself the goal of becoming the "ultimate 21st-century campus university" and is investing £73 million to provide the necessary facilities. The broad Foundation course and four-year degree that made the university's name is a fading memory, but it remains committed to breadth of study in order also to be the leading interdisciplinary institution in Britain. Eight out of ten students take more than one subject for their degree, usually drawing part of their programme from the other side of the arts–science divide in the first year, and the range of options is still widening. Among the more outlandish combinations are astrophysics and criminology, or music technology and medicinal chemistry. Most courses provide the opportunity of a semester abroad, which the university would like a quarter of all undergraduates to take.

American studies, education, politics and philosophy all produced perfect scores in teaching assessments, but the many dual honours programmes – especially those featuring politics or music – and international relations are the university's traditional strengths. Law is the only subject to be rated internationally outstanding for research, but seven more reached grade 5 in the last assessments. The improvement on the exercise in 1996 helped propel Keele up our League Table, although it has slipped back a little subsequently.

Science subjects have been gaining ground: biosciences and physics both scored well for teaching quality. However, it is in health subjects that the main development has been focused. First degrees in physiotherapy and nursing and midwifery were added to the well-established postgraduate medical school. Keele has also been teaching a five-year undergraduate medical course, from which students graduate with a Manchester degree. Some 130 students each year are taught in new facilities on the Keele campus and three miles away at the University Hospital of North Staffordshire NHS Trust. Students admitted from September 2007 onwards study the new Keele undergraduate degree programme (MB ChB), which is in the process of validation by the GMC. A part-time BSc in osteopathy has been introduced in collaboration with the College of Osteopaths and a well-equipped School of Pharmacy opened in 2006, building on a long-established track record in the subject at postgraduate level.

All Keele's courses are modular, with the academic year divided into two 15-week semesters, with breaks at Christmas and Easter. The university remains small by modern standards – around 7,600 full-time

---

Keele
Staffordshire ST5 5BG
01782 584005 (admissions)
undergraduate@
  keele.ac.uk
www.keele.ac.uk
www.kusu.net

Edinburgh
Belfast
KEELE
London
Cardiff

students – despite 75 per cent growth during the 1990s. The proportion of postgraduates has also been growing, with a quarter of the students now taking higher degrees. However, there was a 9 per cent drop in applications in 2007 – one of the biggest at any university – when most were enjoying increases. And the 15 per cent decline at the start of 2008, when the number of choices per applicant had been cut from six to five, was well above average.

Keele has had a good record for retaining students, although the projected dropout rate increased dramatically to 15 per cent in the latest statistics – significantly above the benchmark set according to the university's subjects and entry qualifications. Nine out of ten undergraduates are state-educated, a figure exceeded by only two traditional universities in England, and more than a quarter come from working-class homes. Keele has been proactive in trying to broaden its intake, targeting 12- and 13-year-olds with a special website, as well as running masterclasses in local schools and hosting a summer school at the university.

The attractive 617-acre campus near the M6 outside Stoke-on-Trent is the largest in England. Nearly 70 per cent of all undergraduates live on campus, which inevitably dominates the social scene as well as providing part-time employment for hundreds of students. The students'

union has been refurbished recently, and further improvements are planned under a five-year restructuring. Sports facilities are good, with £100,000 invested recently in refurbished synthetic pitches. The cost of living is also relatively low in the Potteries and the surrounding area.

Undergraduate Fees and Bursaries

- Fees for UK/EU students: £3,145
- International student fees: £8,500–£11,300 £17,000–£20,700 (medicine)
- Bursary on full grant: £310
- Bursaries on partial grant: household income up to £39K various schemes available.
- Scholarships based on circumstances or by competition. For full details see the university's website: www.keele.ac.uk/undergraduate/bursaries/index.htm

---

Students

Undergraduates:	6,330	(2,620)
Postgraduates:	1,320	(2,080)
Mature students:	11.9%	
Overseas students:	6.8%	
Applications per place:	7.1	
From state-sector schools:	92.1%	
From working-class homes:	26.9%	

For detailed information about fees, grants and bursaries and how they work, see chapter 7.

Accommodation

Number of places and costs refer to 2007–08
University-provided places: 3,200
Percentage catered: 0%
Self-catered costs: £58–£90 a week.
First years are guaranteed accommodation on campus if conditions are met.
International students are guaranteed accommodation for the duration of their course.
Contact: sas@keele.ac.uk

University of Kent

Kent has capitalised sensibly on its position near the Channel ports, specialising in international programmes, as well as the flexible degree structures that have been the hallmark of most 1960s universities. Styling itself "the UK's European university", Kent now has a postgraduate site in Brussels, as well as giving many undergraduates the option of a year spent elsewhere in Europe or in the United States. This process should accelerate with the establishment of the Transmanche University with four counterparts in northern France, which took its first students in 2006. The project, backed by both Governments, will involve joint courses at a variety of levels and research collaboration. Almost a quarter of Kent's undergraduates take a language for at least part of their degree, and European studies are among the most popular subject combinations.

The university is broadening its horizons at home as well, however, assuming a regional role. Access courses throughout the county allow students to upgrade their qualifications to university standard, but the main focus is on the Medway towns, where Kent is involved in ambitious projects with Greenwich and Canterbury Christ Church universities and Mid-Kent College. The Medway campus, based in the old dockyard has already exceeded its target of 6,000 students by 2010, with a new School of Pharmacy among the main features of a £50-million development. The first intake of pharmacists was 50 per cent larger than planned and the school is eventually expected to take 430 students.

The original low-rise campus, set in 300 acres of parkland overlooking Canterbury, is tidy rather than architecturally distinguished. The student centre has a nightclub big enough to attract big-name bands, as well as a theatre, cinema and bars. A university centre serves 1,400 part-time students in Tonbridge, and Kent has gone into partnership with Imperial College London to deliver business degrees at the former Wye College campus. In addition, a series of associate colleges offer university courses. Entry grades are variable, with offers pitched according to the UCAS points tariff, although those taking A levels are expected to pass at least three subjects (one of which may be general studies).

Applications have been increasing, partly thanks to the Medway development, and 2007 saw another 10 per cent rise in the demand for places. Medway's applications were up by 40 per cent. Kent is strongest in the social sciences, although biosciences, philosophy and drama, dance and theatre studies took

---

Canterbury
Kent CT2 7NZ
01227 827272 (all enquiries)
recruitment@kent.ac.uk
www.kent.ac.uk
www.kentunion.co.uk

Edinburgh
Belfast
Cardiff London
CANTERBURY

The Times Rankings
Overall Ranking: 36

Student satisfaction:	=10	(79%)
Research quality:	=43	(4.0)
Entry standards:	=47	(307)
Student–staff ratio:	=42	(16.3)
Services & facilities/student:	41	(£1,143)
Expected completion rate:	39	(87.0%)
Good honours:	54	(59.7%)
Graduate prospects:	=40	(70.5%)

pride of place in the teaching assessments, each registering a maximum score. The university takes teaching standards seriously, encouraging all academics to take a Postgraduate Certificate in Higher Education. Kent academics have been awarded National Teaching Fellowships in each of the last three years. Social policy and statistics were rated internationally outstanding in the last research assessments, which showed marked improvement on the disappointing grades in 1996.

Kent has been building up its science departments, among which computing is particularly well regarded, but still two thirds of the students take arts or social sciences. Graduates of all disciplines fare well in the employment market – the university regularly features among the top 20 for graduate starting salaries. It is also on the fringes of the top ten for student satisfaction, with the best record in the country for sports studies and excellent results in pharmacy and architecture.

The university has a more mixed intake than many in the south of England: nine out of ten undergraduates are from state schools and more than a quarter come from working-class homes. Significant numbers of American and European students give the university a cosmopolitan feel and campus security is good, but some complain that Canterbury itself is expensive and limited socially.

Students on the main campus are attached to one of four colleges, although they do not select it themselves. The colleges act as the focus of social life, and include academic as well as residential facilities. They provide accommodation for all first years. Among £100 million of completed or planned capital developments has been an expansion of sports facilities and the addition of 500 rooms at the Parkwood student village, bringing the total number of residential places to 4,300.

Undergraduate Fees and Bursaries

- Fees for UK/EU students: £3,145
- International student fees: £9,400–£10,500
- Bursary on full grant: £1,000
- Bursaries on partial grant: household income up to 40K sliding scale: £750–£250.
- Scholarships based on circumstances or by competition. For full details see the university's website: www.kent.ac.uk/studying/funding/

Students

Undergraduates:	11,075	(3,535)
Postgraduates:	1,130	(2,645)
Mature students:	17.7%	
Overseas students:	13.9%	
Applications per place:	4.8	
From state-sector schools:	90.9%	
From working-class homes:	25.7%	

For detailed information about fees, grants and bursaries and how they work, see chapter 7.

Accommodation

Number of places and costs refer to 2007–08
University-provided places: 4,300
Percentage catered: 18%
Catered costs: £97.58–£117.81 a week.
Self-catered costs: £79.03–£115.93 a week.
First years are guaranteed accommodation provided applications received before 31 July.
International students: as above
Contact: hospitality-enquiry@kent.ac.uk
www.kent.ac.uk/hospitality

King's College London

One of the oldest and largest of London University's colleges, King's is now concentrated on four main campuses close to the Thames. Most departments are within walking distance of each other, on the original Strand site or the Waterloo campus, with medicine and dentistry based not far away at Guy's Hospital, near London Bridge, and in the St Thomas' Hospital campus, across the river from the Houses of Parliament. A fifth site, at Denmark Hill, in south London, houses the Institute of Psychiatry and more medicine and dentistry.

Students seem to like the outcome: King's was the leading institution in London and in the top ten universities overall in the National Student Survey (NSS) published in 2007. An institutional audit by the Quality Assurance Agency gave King's the highest mark, stressing the excellence of the student support services. Applications have been steady, with 5 per cent growth in 2007, when King's broke into the top 25 universities in the world rankings published by *Times Higher Education* and QS. There are now 13,000 undergraduates and 6,200 graduate students in nine schools of study.

Medical subjects have been the main growth point, with King's boasting five Medical Research Council centres – more than any other university. Among almost 600 students training to become doctors or dentists are mature students on a new course designed to provide more variety in the medical profession.

A £500-million transformation of the college estate is still in progress. Biomedical and health sciences students occupy the largest university building in London, near Waterloo Station, and share purpose-built facilities on the Guy's Campus with medicine and dentistry. There is to be further development of the St Thomas' site for medical education and hospital use following the opening of the new and ground-breaking Evelina Children's Hospital.

Another property deal has created the largest new university library in Britain since World War II at the former Public Record Office in Chancery Lane. A donation of £4 million by a graduate has underwritten the spectacular new Maughan Library with 1,400 networked reader places. The first phase of restoration at the Strand was completed in 2006. A £40-million redevelopment of the Grade 1 listed King's Building has provided new teaching facilities, wireless internet access, social and catering facilities.

Once known primarily for science, King's now excels in a wide range of subjects in nine schools of study, including such unusual features as

Strand
London WC2R 2LS
020 7836 5454
ceu@kcl.ac.uk
www.kcl.ac.uk
www.kclsu.org

The Times Rankings
Overall Ranking: 11

Student satisfaction:	=18	(77%)
Research quality:	=24	(4.7)
Entry standards:	14	(406)
Student–staff ratio:	5	(11.9)
Services & facilities/student:	7	(£1,696)
Expected completion rate:	15	(93.2%)
Good honours:	18	(72.1%)
Graduate prospects:	8	(80.4%)

Britain's only department devoted entirely to Portuguese – one of four language departments rated internationally outstanding in the latest research assessments. War studies, developmental biology, dentistry, history, philosophy and psychiatry completed King's impressive haul of 5* grades. Almost one in three of those entered for the exercise were in starred departments. A further 14 departments achieved a 5 grade.

Classics, dentistry, war studies and philosophy are all top-rated for teaching. Clinical psychology, nursing, midwifery, health visiting and physiotherapy did well in a major review in 2005, while King's had the most satisfied law students in the country in the latest NSS. Medical science and pharmacy and the highly regarded war studies department also did well in the survey. Throughout the college, scientists remain in a majority.

King's was one of the two founding colleges of London University, and the full extent of the college's ambitions is clear from its mission statement, which includes having all its departments rated excellent for both teaching and research. The college was among the first to follow the example of American universities by submitting to a credit rating, which took account of its academic and financial standing. The "AA minus" result was better than many big cities have achieved.

King's is also a solid bet for a good degree for those who satisfy its demanding entry requirements, with over 70 per cent reaching the first or 2:1 classification. Nearly three undergraduates in ten come from independent schools. Every student is allocated a personal tutor, and much of the teaching is in small groups. Student facilities on the Strand and Guy's campuses have been upgraded recently. There are 2,654 residential places, and the college also has access to 511 places in the intercollegiate halls of London University. Some of the outdoor sports facilities are rather dispersed, but are accessible by train.

Undergraduate Fees and Bursaries

- Fees for UK/EU students: £3,145
- International student fees: £10,980–£13,800
  £25,600 (clinical)
- Bursary on full grant: 50% of maintenance grant.
- Bursaries on partial grant: 50% of maintenance grant.
- Scholarships based on circumstances or by competition. For full details see the university's website: www.kcl.ac.uk/funding

---

Students

Undergraduates:	11,545	(2,465)
Postgraduates:	3,770	(3,455)
Mature students:	18.4%	
Overseas students:	12.9%	
Applications per place:	9.6	
From state-sector schools:	70.3%	
From working-class homes:	21.3%	

For detailed information about fees, grants and bursaries and how they work, see chapter 7.

Accommodation

Number of places and costs refer to 2007–08
University-provided places: 2,654; 511 intercollegiate
Percentage catered: 17.7%; 100% intercollegiate
Catered costs: £107.66–£175.00 a week
Self-catered costs: £66.92–£119.21 (40 weeks).
New full-time students are guaranteed one year in accommodation if conditions are met.
International students: priority for those who have not previously lived or studied in the UK.
Contact: 020 7848 2759; www.kcl.ac.uk/accomm

Kingston University

Having established itself as one of the fastest-growing new universities, with over 22,000 students, Kingston is developing a learning environment to match. The university has set about revitalising its four sites, spending more than £65 million in a decade on capital projects. Three new buildings opened in 2007 alone. One provides six floors of teaching and study space and a new central courtyard on the main Penrhyn Road campus; another is a three-storey teaching extension at the Faculty of Engineering's Roehampton Vale site; while the Kingston Hill campus has acquired more computer study space in the learning resources centre and a Learning Café with computer facilities.

Applications have been buoyant, bucking the trend among former polytechnics and enabling the university to reduce the numbers recruited through Clearing. Results in the National Student Survey have been improving, after disruptive building work depressed initial satisfaction levels and contributed to a fall in our league table. The university hopes for further progress in the next survey, now that students are enjoying the use of new facilities which have won plaudits from staff and students alike.

The university markets itself as in "lively, leafy London", making a virtue of its suburban location as well as its proximity to the bright lights. It has four campuses in the southwest of the capital: two, close to Kingston town centre; another, two miles away at Kingston Hill, and the fourth in Roehampton Vale, where a site once used as an aerospace factory now contains a new technology block. A flight simulator and the university's own Learjet continue the tradition and a Foundation degree in aeronautical engineering is ministers' favourite example of the two-year course. Kingston boasts the third largest engineering faculty in London, behind Imperial College and Brunel.

The four campuses are linked by an extensive network of 2,000 computers. Among the facilities in the new buildings are multiple projection systems, video conferencing, interactive displays and built-in voting systems. Students can take advantage of 24-hour opening in some of the main learning resources centres and a high-tech self-issue system for borrowing books and other resources.

Research grades in the last assessment exercise showed improvement, with European studies, history and history of art scoring well, but teaching scores have shown Kingston's real strength. No department scored less than 20 points out of 24 in the final rounds of teaching assessment. The School of Life Sciences

River House
53–57 High Street
Kingston upon Thames
Surrey KT1 1LQ
020 8547 7053
admissions-info@
  kingston.ac.uk
www.kingston.ac.uk
www.kusu.co.uk

The Times Rankings
Overall Ranking: 93

Student satisfaction:	=84	(71%)
Research quality:	=76	(1.2)
Entry standards:	100	(236)
Student–staff ratio:	=86	(19.8)
Services & facilities/student:	73	(£966)
Expected completion rate:	80	(78.6%)
Good honours:	87	(50.0%)
Graduate prospects:	=81	(60.2%)

joined building and mechanical, aeronautical and manufacturing engineering in recording perfect scores, following on from some good performances under the original quality system. Politics and nursing also produced good results. Nursing is part of the Faculty of Health and Social Care Sciences, a successful collaboration with St George's Hospital Medical School, which recently added pharmacy to its portfolio of courses. The faculty came through a major review of its courses with flying colours in 2004. Creative writing is another innovation, with Hanif Kureishi, whose screenplay for the film *My Beautiful Launderette* was nominated for an Oscar, delivering masterclasses and supervising MA dissertations. Rachel Cusk, whose *Arlington Park* was shortlisted for the Orange Prize in 2007, teaches both undergraduates and MA students.

Around a quarter of Kingston's places go to mature students and more than a third to those from working-class families – both groups with low completion rates nationally. The latest projected dropout rate is 17 per cent, an improvement on the previous year and less than the national average for the subjects on offer. Students get extra support in their first, most difficult, year. The university's attempts to widen access to higher education have been particularly successful among ethnic minorities, who account for more than half of the undergraduates.

To make the university more responsive to its students, it provides a "one-stop shop", which deals with student issues ranging from careers and accommodation to complaints and financial advice. The university's responsiveness and the accessibility of staff were singled out for praise in a quality audit. Over £20 million has been spent on halls of residence, most recently with extensions and refurbishment of the two largest halls, which now have 2,360 rooms. Students like the location, on the fringe of London, although complaints about the high cost of living are common.

Undergraduate Fees and Bursaries

- Fees for UK/EU students: £3,145
- International student fees: £9,000–£10,050
- Bursary on full grant: household income up to £1K: £1,000 then £600.
- Bursaries on partial grant: household income up to £39.3K: £310.
- Scholarships based on circumstances or by competition. For full details see the university's website: www.kingston.ac.uk/undergraduate/money-matters/

Students

Undergraduates:	16,265	(1,935)
Postgraduates:	1,790	(3,015)
Mature students:	23.2%	
Overseas students:	13.5%	
Applications per place:	5.5	
From state-sector schools:	95.0%	
From working-class homes:	36.4%	

For detailed information about fees, grants and bursaries and how they work, see chapter 7.

Accommodation

Number of places and costs refer to 2008–09
University-provided places: 2,360
Percentage catered: 0%
Self-catered costs: £87.50–£109.75 a week.
First years are offered places provided requirements are met and subject to availability.
International students: offered places if application is made in good time and subject to availability.
Contact: accommodation@kingston.ac.uk

Lampeter, University of Wales

In the whole of England and Wales, only Oxford and Cambridge were awarding degrees before Lampeter. Yet only Buckingham University is smaller today. In fact, Lampeter claims to be the smallest publicly funded university in Europe, making a virtue of its size by stressing its friendly atmosphere and intimate teaching style. There has been pressure from the Welsh Assembly for closer collaboration between the Principality's small higher education institutions, but there is no prospect of a merger. Applications were down by more than a quarter, to less than 600, at the start of 2008, following a 15 per cent decline in the previous year. But those who go are enthusiastic about Lampeter: it has been among the leading institutions in all three National Student Surveys.

Based on an ancient castle and modelled on an Oxbridge college, St David's College (as it was originally known) was established to train young men for the Anglican ministry. That title receded into the small print, as the University of Wales allowed its member institutions to drop their college titles. But the original quadrangle remains and the chapel is in daily use. There have been significant changes in the last few years – notably a big expansion in distance learning and the introduction of such subjects as Chinese studies, anthropology, IT, management, and film and media studies. There are now 300 course combinations available in the joint honours programme. Medieval studies is an unusual construct, while creative writing and media production are among the new arrivals. A degree in Voluntary Sector Studies, which won a Queen's Anniversary Prize, is offered part-time and by distance learning so that students can combine study with volunteering and personal commitments. However, there is no immediate aim to go beyond 1,500 students.

Lampeter remains arts-dominated: even IT leads to a BA, and the Bachelor of Divinity is the only other undergraduate degree. Lampeter is best known for theology, one of the two top-rated research departments, the other being English. The small campus includes a mosque for the growing number of Muslim students attracted by a well-endowed programme of Islamic studies. But students are opting increasingly for broad courses such as medieval studies, which includes archaeology, classics and theology, as well as history, English and Welsh. Media studies, which benefits from a well-equipped media centre for film and television students, is also growing in popularity. A new research centre opened

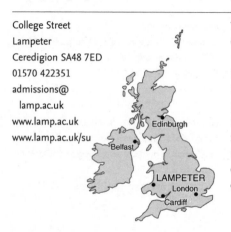

College Street
Lampeter
Ceredigion SA48 7ED
01570 422351
admissions@
 lamp.ac.uk
www.lamp.ac.uk
www.lamp.ac.uk/su

Edinburgh

Belfast

LAMPETER
London
Cardiff

The Times Rankings
Overall Ranking: 70

Student satisfaction:	=55	(74%)
Research quality:	=33	(4.4)
Entry standards:	=64	(274)
Student–staff ratio:	112	(25.0)
Services & facilities/student:	113	(£480)
Expected completion rate:	=90	(76.9%)
Good honours:	66	(56.1%)
Graduate prospects:	88	(58.8%)

in January 2008, housing the Founders' Library collections and the historical archives, bringing the university's library resources together on one site for the first time since 1966. Climate-controlled conditions will ensure the long-term conservation of a collection of pre-1800 books and manuscripts that includes a Bible dating from 1279.

Modular courses have been introduced, but degrees are still divided into two parts, with the first year designed to ensure breadth of study. Most courses now include the option of a January start and undergraduates can try a new language, such as Arabic, Greek or Welsh. Part two normally takes a further two years, although philosophy takes three. Lampeter is deep in Welsh-speaking rural West Wales, and both the university and the students' union have strong bilingual policies. The university is also taking Welsh to a wider audience, with the only university course teaching the language over the internet.

Although only four hours from London and two from Cardiff, Lampeter's geographical position could be a problem for the unprepared. The town has only 4,000 inhabitants, with among the lowest crime rates in Britain, and the nearest station is more than 20 miles away at Carmarthen. A high proportion of the students run cars. The students' union is the centre of social life – not surprising when the university's guide to the town lists its attractions as "cafés, pubs, a curry house and a French patisserie". Most students have made a deliberate choice to avoid the bright lights, and many would like to remain in the area after graduation, although jobs are scarce. The location helps to produce a relatively high proportion of students from areas with little tradition of higher education and almost 30 per cent from working-class homes. The college's size can make for big fluctuations in the various published indicators. The projected dropout rate, for example, had dipped below 10 per cent in the official statistics earlier in the decade, but have hovered around 20 per cent recently.

Undergraduate Fees and Bursaries

- Welsh-domiciled student fees: £3,145, with grant of up to £1,890
- Non-Welsh UK domiciled and EU student fees: £3,145
- International student fees: £8,988
- Welsh National Bursary for all UK students, means-tested with maximum of £310.
- Bursaries on full grant: no additional bursary.
- Bursaries on partial grant: n/a.
- Scholarships based on circumstances or by competition. For full details see the university's website: www.lamp.ac.uk/scholarships

Students

Undergraduates:	1,140	(5,950)
Postgraduates:	325	(1,515)
Mature students:	38.8%	
Overseas students:	11.4%	
Applications per place:	3.8	
From state-sector schools:	92.7%	
From working-class homes:	27.5%	

For detailed information about fees, grants and bursaries and how they work, see chapter 7.

Accommodation

Number of places and costs refer to 2008–09
University-provided places: around 500
Percentage catered: 0%
Self-catered costs: £58.69–£74.76 a week (30, 33 or 36 weeks).
First years can normally be placed in university accommodation.
International students: guaranteed housing for first year.
Contact: www.lamp.ac.uk/accommodation/index.htm

Lancaster University

Having celebrated its 40th birthday, Lancaster has almost completed a £200-million makeover for its campus to give it a more modern feel and increase its capacity by up to 50 per cent. Still a relatively small institution, the aim is to establish itself in the leading group of research universities and help improve the local economy. An assessment by investment analysts, who examined educational and financial issues, gave Lancaster a good rating, pronouncing it financially sound and capable of competing for students and research funds nationally and internationally. The process placed Lancaster among the top dozen universities for research – it is a member of the N8 Group of northern research universities – and in the top 20 for teaching. Official assessments place the university higher still: its last research grades were in the top ten and teaching ratings were consistently excellent. Lancaster has also done well in all three National Student Surveys, finishing just outside the top ten in the results published in 2007. The best results came in history and archaeology, physics and finance and accounting.

Results from the 2001 Research Assessment Exercise were an improvement on an already strong performance five years earlier. Business and management, physics, sociology and statistics were all rated internationally outstanding and, with another ten subjects achieving grade 5, more than 70 per cent of the academics were in departments placed in the top two categories. The university has also won eight National Teaching Fellowships since the scheme was launched in 2000.

A £25-million environment centre shared with the Natural Environment Research Council opened in 2003, reinforcing the university's strength in this area. A £15-million centre of excellence in information communication technology, Infolab 21, was launched in 2005, providing a new research, computing and communications centre on campus. It acts as a technology transfer and incubation facility and houses a training facility for high-tech businesses. The highly rated Management School has since added a £9.5-million leadership centre and the Lancaster Institute for the Contemporary Arts has brought together art, music and theatre studies with the university's public art gallery, concerts and theatre.

Social work, which has a dozen applications for every place, attracted one of a number of glowing reports for teaching. Education, philosophy and religious studies, psychology and music, art and theatre studies all achieved

Bailrigg
Lancaster LA1 4YW
01524 592028 (admissions)
ugadmissions@
 lancaster.ac.uk
www.lancaster.ac.uk
www.lusu.co.uk

The Times Rankings
Overall Ranking: 19

Student satisfaction:	=12	(78%)
Research quality:	=8	(5.4)
Entry standards:	26	(375)
Student–staff ratio:	9	(12.7)
Services & facilities/student:	30	(£1,227)
Expected completion rate:	17	(92.5%)
Good honours:	28	(68.8%)
Graduate prospects:	76	(60.9%)

maximum scores. Nevertheless, Lancaster is not just a ratings factory.

Lancaster is another of the campus universities of the 1960s which has always traded on its flexible degree structure. Most undergraduates can broaden their first-year studies by taking a second or third subject. The final choice of degree comes only at the end of that year. Combined degree programmes, with 200 courses to choose from, are especially popular. The degree portfolio now includes medicine, with students taking a five-year course following the Liverpool University curriculum.

The projected dropout rate of 7.5 per cent is lower than the average for the subjects on offer. Lancaster also exceeds expectations for the recruitment of state-school students, but the proportion from working-class homes and disadvantaged areas are both marginally below the benchmark for the university's courses.

The previously uninspiring campus has benefited from recent developments, which have included refurbished lecture theatres, sports facilities and residences. The university is a ten-minute bus ride from Lancaster, three miles away. Students join one of nine residential colleges, which become the centre of most students' social life. Most house between 800 and 900 students in self-catering accommodation. Some 3,400 new and updated residential places came on stream in 2005 and more eco-friendly residences will open in 2008, where students can live in town houses with shared facilities and monitor their bills. As part of the developments, Cartmel and Lonsdale colleges have transferred to the New Alexandra Park area of the campus with enhanced social facilities.

The campus has a reputation for being one of the safest in the UK. Sports facilities are good and conveniently placed. There are plans for a new sports centre with climbing wall (built to Chancellor Chris Bonington's specifications.) For the outdoor life, the Lake District is within easy reach. Road and rail communications are good but, while Manchester and Liverpool are within easy reach, some students still find the immediate location more isolated than they expected.

Undergraduate Fees and Bursaries

- Fees for UK/EU students: £3,145
- International student fees: £8,750–£10,600
- Bursary on full grant: household income up to £18,360: £1,315 then £500
- Bursaries on partial grant: household income up to £27.8K: £500.
- Scholarships based on circumstances or by competition. For full details see the university's website: www.lancaster.ac.uk/ugfinance

Students

Undergraduates:	8,045	(5,810)
Postgraduates:	1,760	(1,795)
Mature students:	5.8%	
Overseas students:	9.1%	
Applications per place:	5.1	
From state-sector schools:	90.6%	
From working-class homes:	22.0%	

For detailed information about fees, grants and bursaries and how they work, see chapter 7.

Accommodation

Number of places and costs refer to 2007–08
University-provided places: 6,700 (does not include 600 university-managed houses)
Percentage catered: 0%
Self-catered costs: £57.00–£99.75 a week.
First years are usually accommodated but Insurance, Clearing and very late applicants are not guaranteed places.
International students are guaranteed accommodation throughout their studies.
Contact: CRO@lancaster.ac.uk

University of Leeds

The rise of Leeds as a clubbing mecca to rival Manchester has added to the attractions of a university which has long been one of the giants of the higher education system. It was the most popular university in Britain in 2003 and 2004, and has been second only to the recently merged Manchester University ever since, closing the gap significantly at the start of 2008. The university plans to invest £172 million in new buildings and bring in more than 100 senior academics over the next few years in order to break into the top 50 universities in the world. It is currently 80th in the world rankings published by *Times Higher Education* and QS.

An unusually wide range of degrees gives applicants more than 700 undergraduate programmes to choose from, with over 1,300 academic staff teaching 33,000 students.

The university occupies a 140-acre site, two thirds of which is designated a conservation area, within walking distance of the city centre. The buildings are a mixture of Victorian and modern, the latest of which has seen a £4 million investment in chemistry laboratories housed in a listed building. Other recent projects have extended the library, provided more space for biology and moved the business school into new £10-million premises.

The university had begun to spread its wings by merging with Bretton Hall College, near Wakefield, with its sculpture park and established reputation in the performing and visual arts. But it has already closed the campus and brought the new Faculty of Performing Arts and Cultural Industries back to Leeds, where there will be a £1.5-million development including a theatre, performance design studio and rehearsal space. Nine other colleges in various parts of the county offer Leeds courses, but handle their own admissions.

Further afield, Leeds is also part of a "Worldwide Network" which brings together four American and four British universities to collaborate initially on research, postgraduate degree programmes and continuing professional development. There was already a thriving European programme involving more than 100 Continental partners and a flow of students in both directions. A free-standing language unit caters for casual learners as well as specialists.

Leeds has followed the fashion for modular courses, enabling its students to take full advantage of a growing range of interdisciplinary degrees. Almost a quarter now take dual honours or combinations such as communications, women's studies or international studies. The university was chosen to house a national centre of

---

Leeds
West Yorkshire LS2 9JT
0113 343 2336
ask@leeds.ac.uk
www.leeds.ac.uk
www.luuonline.com

Edinburgh
Belfast
LEEDS
London
Cardiff

The Times Rankings
Overall Ranking: =31

Student satisfaction:	=39	(75%)
Research quality:	=29	(4.5)
Entry standards:	22	(385)
Student–staff ratio:	24	(14.6)
Services & facilities/student:	57	(£1,014)
Expected completion rate:	23	(92.1%)
Good honours:	20	(71.8%)
Graduate prospects:	48	(67.3%)

excellence in interdisciplinary teaching and another in assessment and learning in medical practice settings. Business and management is also increasingly popular, the business school having moved into the former Leeds Grammar School site.

Electrical and mechanical engineering, English, food science, Italian and town planning were all rated internationally outstanding for research in 2001, when Leeds had among the largest number of academics in the national assessment exercise. Teaching ratings were generally good, with education, philosophy, physics and healthcare studies awarded maximum points. Medical science and pharmacy produced by far the best results in the latest National Student Survey, which saw the university slip back after finishing in the top 20 in 2006.

Student facilities are generally first rate. Leeds teams regularly excel in competition and the university hosts one of five centres of cricketing excellence. The 8,000 computer workstations are among the most at any university and the library one of the biggest. Nearly a quarter of the undergraduates come from independent schools, and there is a low proportion of working-class students – less the one in five. But the projected dropout rate has improved and, at less than 8 per cent, is below the national average for the university's courses and entry grades. The already large students'

union, famous for its long bar and big-name rock concerts, has been extended to cope with the latest phase in the university's expansion. A £4.5-million upgrade has provided a new venue, more shops and catering facilities. Town–gown relations are generally good.

Undergraduate Fees and Bursaries

- Fees for UK/EU students: £3,145
- International student fees: £9,700–£12,600 £23,500 (clinical)
- Bursary on full grant: £1,500
- Bursaries on partial grant: household income up to £36K: sliding scale £1,300–£325.
- Scholarships based on circumstances or by competition. For full details see the university's website: www.leeds.ac.uk/students/fees/index.htm

Students

Undergraduates:	22,305	(2,205)
Postgraduates:	5,435	(3,370)
Mature students:	6.6%	
Overseas students:	6.3%	
Applications per place:	7.2	
From state-sector schools:	74.2%	
From working-class homes:	18.9%	

For detailed information about fees, grants and bursaries and how they work, see chapter 7.

Accommodation

Number of places and costs refer to 2008–09
University-provided places: 7,650
Percentage catered: 17%
Catered costs: £90–£140 a week.
Self-catered costs: £70–£124 a week.
Single first years are guaranteed a place provided conditions are met.
International students: guaranteed to full fee-paying undergraduates if conditions are met.
Contact: accom@leeds.ac.uk
www.leeds.ac.uk/accommodation/overview.htm

Leeds Metropolitan University

Leeds Met took the bold step of becoming the first university to set fees below the £3,000-a-year maximum allowed in 2006 and, having held them at £2,000 since then, it is by far the cheapest in England at which to take a full-time degree. Professor Simon Lee, the Vice-Chancellor, admitted that some of his colleagues considered him "crazy" because students might think the university's degrees were of lower quality than its competitors', but the move made a mark in a crowded market. Both applications and enrolments hit record levels and there was another 12 per cent rise in the demand for places in 2007. At the start of 2008, applications were again ahead of the national average. The rate inevitably limits the scope for bursaries for students from poor backgrounds, but the university considers that every student has the equivalent of a £1,100 bursary in low fees.

Leeds Met already had a reputation for widening participation in higher education: it is one of the largest providers of Foundation degrees and has more than 50,000 students (16,000 of whom are full-time undergraduates) since the incorporation of a large further education college in Harrogate. Four out of ten students come from the Yorkshire and Humberside region, and more than half are over 21 on entry. More than nine out of ten are state-educated and a third come from working-class homes. Partnerships with 14 colleges from Newcastle to Nottinghamshire are designed to produce the equivalent of an American state university system, enabling students to take Leeds Met courses locally.

More than 3,500 students come from 120 countries outside the UK. Just over half are taking conventional full-time degrees, such is the popularity of sandwich and part-time courses. The projected dropout rate of 15 per cent is significantly below the official benchmark. As part of its efforts to widen access, Leeds Met runs a course for sixth-formers from the region, awarding UCAS points for those who complete successfully. There is also a wide range of summer schools, including one for Asian women and one for Afro-Caribbean boys.

There are two bases in Leeds: the Civic Quarter Campus, close to the city centre, and the Headingley Campus, three miles away in the 100 acres of park and woodlands of Beckett Park. The latter boasts outstanding sports facilities, including the £2-million Carnegie Regional Tennis Centre, as well as teaching accommodation for education, informatics, law and business. Over 7,000 students take part in some form of sporting activity, and there is a range of £1,000 sports scholarships. The Civic Quarter campus is the subject of a £100-million development programme, which began with the opening in 2005 of a

Civic Quarter
Leeds
West Yorkshire LS1 3HE
0113 283 3113 (enquiries)
http://prospectus.
  leedsmet.ac.uk/main/
  enquiry.htm
www.lmu.ac.uk
www.lmusu.org.uk

Student satisfaction:	=99	(68%)
Research quality:	=92	(0.8)
Entry standards:	=77	(264)
Student–staff ratio:	110	(23.6)
Services & facilities/student:	=68	(£984)
Expected completion rate:	59	(82.7%)
Good honours:	74	(53.6%)
Graduate prospects:	=84	(59.4%)

new film school. A futuristic lecture theatre complex next to Leeds Civic Hall will house the business school from September 2009. The former BBC building has reopened as Old Broadcasting House, where new facilities are being developed for the Faculty of Arts and Society. And, in the first development of its kind, a new stand has been built at the Headingley rugby ground, with classrooms, coaching facilities and social space for use by the university and the two professional clubs. A media centre along similar lines is planned for the neighbouring Test and county cricket ground.

Business, management and economics achieved the best scores for teaching quality. Education and the large School of Health Sciences, with its 1,200 students, were close behind. Only 12 subjects were entered for the last Research Assessment Exercise, with librarianship and information management the only one to reach the top three categories of seven. However, an institutional audit by the Quality Assurance Agency in 2004 praised the university for "placing the student experience at the heart of the enterprise". Students are included on the committees that design and manage courses, although the impact has not been obvious in the first three National Student Surveys. Leeds Met was among the bottom five universities in the 2007 results.

There is a growing emphasis on educational technology, which was enhanced by a £20-million learning resources centre. More than 400 computers, audiovisual presentation studios and study areas are available all hours. Contacts with small and medium-sized businesses have been carefully fostered as part of the university's successful attempts to maintain a good record in graduate employment. Like its older neighbour, Leeds Met is benefiting from the city's growing reputation for nightlife, but it is making its own contribution with a famously lively entertainments scene. With 3,500 bed spaces, those who accept places before Clearing are guaranteed university accommodation.

Undergraduate Fees and Bursaries

- Fees for UK/EU students: £2,000
- International student fees: £7,500–£8,300
- Bursary on full grant: n/a
- Bursaries on partial grant: n/a
- Scholarships based on circumstances or by competition. For full details see the university's website: www.leedsmet.ac.uk/visiting/index_finance.htm

Students

Undergraduates:	16,095	(7,245)
Postgraduates:	1,450	(2,710)
Mature students:	25.0%	
Overseas students:	7.0%	
Applications per place:	5.0	
From state-sector schools:	93.5%	
From working-class homes:	33.3%	

For detailed information about fees, grants and bursaries and how they work, see chapter 7.

Accommodation

Number of places and costs refer to 2008–09
University-provided places: 3,500
Percentage catered: 0%
Self-catered costs: £62.70–£120.00 a week.
First years with Conditional Firm or Unconditional Firm offers guaranteed accommodation.
International students: guaranteed accommodation if conditions are met.
Contact: www.leedsmet.ac.uk/fm/accomm

University of Leicester

Leicester has started to take off, after many years living in the shadow of the big city universities. A string of excellent assessments for teaching and research have coincided with a £300-million campus development programme – one of the biggest in Britain – that has produced a buzz around the university. It has been in the top five in each of the first three National Student Surveys, with French, maths, biology, genetics and geology all recording the highest satisfaction levels in the country for their subject. Genetics recorded the most satisfied students of any department in any discipline in the UK. Leicester was also shortlisted for *The Times Higher Education Supplement*'s University of the Year in both of the award's first two years.

Rising demand for places, restored in 2007 after a dip in the first year of top-up fees, has led to many subjects raising their entrance requirements. Even at the start of 2008, when the switch from six choices per candidate to five reduced applications nationally, Leicester experienced a healthy demand for places.

Though the university celebrated its 80th anniversary in 2001, it is only now approaching the size of most of its traditional counterparts after growing by more than 60 per cent in recent years.

Such is the scale of the postgraduate and distance learning programmes that little more than half of the 18,500 registered students are full-time campus-based undergraduates. Professor Robert Burgess, the Vice-Chancellor, is focusing on strengthening research and has scaled down the university's initial enthusiasm for two-year Foundation degrees. But efforts continue to broaden Leicester's intake, for example through a summer school for local teenagers. Almost nine out of ten undergraduates come from state schools and a quarter come from working-class homes. The 7 per cent projected dropout rate is below the benchmark set according to the university's courses and entry grades.

Teaching ratings were generally good: the last dozen assessments all produced at least 22 points out of 24, with archaeology, ancient history, economics, education, museum studies and psychology recording full marks. It also hosts national centres of excellence for teaching and learning in geography, genetics and physics. The university is a leader in space science, with Europe's largest university-based space research facility, including the £52-million National Space Centre, and was heavily involved in the Beagle 2 mission to Mars.

The medical school registered one of the best teaching quality scores for the subject and allows graduates in the health

---

University Road
Leicester LE1 7RH
0116 252 5280 (admissions)
admissions@le.ac.uk
www.le.ac.uk
www.leicesterstudent.org

The Times Rankings
Overall Ranking: 14

Student satisfaction:	=2	(83%)
Research quality:	=29	(4.5)
Entry standards:	33	(360)
Student–staff ratio:	=22	(14.5)
Services & facilities/student:	23	(£1,329)
Expected completion rate:	16	(92.9%)
Good honours:	27	(69.0%)
Graduate prospects:	33	(72.3%)

and life sciences to qualify in four years. The school has among the most modern facilities in Britain, and the siting of a medically based interdisciplinary research centre at the university was another indication of growing strength. The genetics department, where DNA genetic fingerprinting was discovered, achieved the only 5* rating in the last research assessments. But a dozen subjects in the next category enabled Leicester to outperform a clutch of civic universities in terms of average grades per member of staff. According to Thomson Scientific, Leicester – a member of the 1994 Group of research-intensive universities – has the tenth highest number of highly cited researchers in the UK.

Other than clinical medicine which is taught at the city's three hospitals, all teaching and much residential accommodation is concentrated in a leafy suburb a mile from the city centre. Its location, adjacent to one of Leicester's main parks, is an attraction to students. A new biomedical sciences building opened in 2004 and a £31-million library extension, doubling its size and expanding its capacity to 1,500 seats, opened in 2008. The Richard Attenborough Centre has given Leicester a particular reputation for catering for disabled students.

Among a number of areas to have been refurbished recently is the students'

union, which has spruced up its main bar areas and runs one of the most popular university nightclubs, the Venue. Extensive residential accommodation includes a new £21-million 600-bed en-suite development. First years are guaranteed a residential place and many second and third-year students also live in hall; although the majority choose to live in the reasonably priced private accommodation available nearby. The main sports facilities are conveniently located; in 2008–09, students paid £50 a year to use them.

Undergraduate Fees and Bursaries
- Fees for UK/EU students: £3,145
- International student fees: £9,050–£21,995
- Bursary on full grant: £1,310
- Bursaries on partial grant: household income up to £39.3K: sliding scale £1,010–£100.
- Scholarships based on circumstances or by competition. For full details see the university's website: www.le.ac.uk/fees

Students		
Undergraduates:	7,495	(1,755)
Postgraduates:	2,045	(4,200)
Mature students:	12.3%	
Overseas students:	11.7%	
Applications per place:	6.4	
From state-sector schools:	87.9%	
From working-class homes:	25.3%	

For detailed information about fees, grants and bursaries and how they work, see chapter 7.

Accommodation
Number of places and costs refer to 2008–09
University-provided places: 4,188
Percentage catered: 34%
Catered costs: £94.12–£139.93 a week (30 weeks).
Self-catered costs: £69.09–£138.04 (42 weeks).
First-year students are guaranteed housing if conditions are met.
International students: as above, with priority to those returning.
Contact: www.le.ac.uk/accommodation

University of Lincoln

Eleven years ago, the opening of an impressive purpose-built campus alongside a marina in the centre of Lincoln brought about the most dramatic transformation of any university in recent times. Humberside University, as it then was, even gave its new location pride of place in its title. Five years later it went a step further, selling the previous headquarters campus in Hull and becoming Lincoln University. While not moving out of Hull entirely, the university is concentrating its activities on a much smaller city-centre site.

The switch has paid undoubted dividends, helping to attract high-quality academics. The number of professors grew from eight to 87 in four years. Student applications increased for five years in a row before the introduction of top-up fees, despite rising admission requirements, and the upward trend resumed with a 14 per cent rise at the start of 2007.

New science laboratories, sports facilities, an architecture school, a new library in a converted warehouse and a students' union and entertainment venue in a former railway engine shed have taken the cost of the development in Lincoln to over £100 million, and another £30 million has been committed to complete the main campus. The latest developments are a

£6-million performing arts centre, including a 450-seat theatre and three large studio spaces, and the Human Performance Centre – a regional facility for excellence in sport, coaching and exercise science.

The various projects have won two regeneration awards. The campus now has around 1,000 beds, while purpose-built private developments in close proximity to the university now provide well over 2,000 further residential places. Only the School of Health and Social Care remains in Hull, following the transfer of art and design degree provision in the city to Hull College.

Lincoln initially concentrated on social sciences, but the university now has a wider range of courses. Following the acquisition of former art and design and agriculture colleges from De Montfort University in 2001, the university now has more than 8,000 students in and around Lincoln. The School of Architecture has over 400 students. Art and design is based in the city centre, while animal, biological and equine studies are at Riseholme Park, a 1,000-acre site ten minutes outside Lincoln. Riseholme has been chosen as one of the training centres for equine events ahead of the 2012 Olympic Games.

Poor performances in both teaching and research assessments account for Lincoln's low position in *The Times*

Brayford Pool
Lincoln LN6 7TS
01522 882000 (enquiries)
www.lincoln.ac.uk/home/
  enquiries/index.htm
www.lincoln.ac.uk
www.lincolnsu.com

The Times Rankings
Overall Ranking: =103

Student satisfaction:	=93	(70%)
Research quality:	=99	(0.7)
Entry standards:	=80	(261)
Student–staff ratio:	111	(23.7)
Services & facilities/student:	89	(£842)
Expected completion rate:	=54	(83.9%)
Good honours:	76	(52.9%)
Graduate prospects:	110	(50.3%)

ranking, although results improved in the later years of the cycle. Education achieved maximum points for teaching quality and two recent institutional audits have been complimentary. Only 21 per cent of the academics were entered for the last research ratings, when no subjects reached the top three categories of seven, but twice as many academics are now engaged in research and the income from this activity is much increased. A top priority is to achieve a high-profile return in the Research Assessment Exercise in 2008 to match a sharp rise in the university's research income over recent years.

All students take the Effective Learning Programme, which uses computer packages backed up by weekly seminars to develop necessary study skills and produce a detailed portfolio of all their work. Some degrees can be taken as work-based programmes, with credit awarded for relevant aspects of the jobs.

Lincoln was the first university to win a Charter Mark for exceptional service, although this was not reflected in the initial rounds of the National Student Survey. Results in the survey improved considerably in 2007, with media studies performing especially well. More than a third of the undergraduates come from working-class homes and the projected dropout rate of 14 per cent is both an improvement on previous years and better than the average for the subjects on offer, given the entry standards. Only three universities devote as much of their tuition fee income to bursaries and scholarships as Lincoln. The city is adapting to its new student population with new bars and clubs, although the social scene there is not the prime draw for students.

Undergraduate Fees and Bursaries

- Fees for UK/EU students: £3,145
- International student fees: £8,524–£9,038
- Bursary on full grant: £600
- Bursaries on partial grant: up to £599 based on size of maintenance grant.
- Scholarships based on circumstances or by competition. For full details see the university's website: www.lincoln.ac.uk/fees

---

Students

Undergraduates:	8,510	(2,785)
Postgraduates:	485	(885)
Mature students:	16.9%	
Overseas students:	6.5%	
Applications per place:	3.3	
From state-sector schools:	96.9%	
From working-class homes:	35.6%	

For detailed information about fees, grants and bursaries and how they work, see chapter 7.

Accommodation

Number of places and costs refer to 2007–08
University-provided places: Hull, 200; Lincoln, 1,037; Riseholme Park, 180
Percentage catered: 13% (Riseholme Park only)
Catered costs: £91–£129 a week (half-board)
Self-catered costs: £85–£95 a week.
Student accommodation prioritised by distance. International students are given detailed information and assistance.
Contact: accommodation@lincoln.ac.uk
www.lincoln.ac.uk/accommodation

University of Liverpool

Liverpool is investing £200 million to improve its 100-acre precinct for a student population that has reached 22,000. The dozen projects include a £19-million library scheme, a £36-million restructuring of the Faculty of Engineering, and the transformation of the redbrick Victoria Building into a public gallery and museum during Liverpool's year as the Capital of Culture, in 2008. A new headquarters building houses a one-stop shop for student services and sports facilities have been renovated and extended. A new small animal teaching hospital opened in 2007, bringing all veterinary science clinical teaching onto one site. A £50-million fundraising drive aims to establish world-class centres of excellence in management, law, medicine, engineering, veterinary science and architecture.

The university is continuing to modernise its portfolio of courses while preserving a well-established reputation for research. Liverpool is among the top 15 recipients of research funds, with outside income increasing dramatically in recent years. And there has been substantial investment in new educational technology, helping to cope with the demands of extra undergraduates. The main library is now open 24 hours and the top-rated medical school has also been expanded to take another 50 medics and 32 dentists, who will train at Lancaster and Central Lancashire universities respectively. The university has been awarded a national centre of excellence to develop professionalism in medical students. Full-time numbers throughout the university are almost exactly balanced between the sexes.

A series of excellent ratings in the early teaching assessments took time to repeat, but philosophy, veterinary science, medicine and physics all achieved perfect scores. Veterinary students were the most satisfied in the country in the National Student Survey published in 2007. Physiology, mechanical engineering and English recorded 5* ratings for research in the last Research Assessment Exercise, when more than half of the academics entered for assessment were in departments placed in one of the top two categories. There has been considerable investment in the recruitment of world-renowned academics in advance of the next assessments in 2008, with a particular focus on chemistry.

Liverpool prides itself on strength across the board and opened a new university in Suzhou, China, in partnership with Xi'an Jiatong University, in 2006. Liverpool is popular with international students, 93 per cent of

Liverpool L69 3BX
0151 794 5927 (enquiries)
ugrecruitment@liv.ac.uk
www.liv.ac.uk
www.liverpoolguild.org.uk

Edinburgh
Belfast
LIVERPOOL
London
Cardiff

The Times Rankings
Overall Ranking: 34

Student satisfaction:	=39	(75%)
Research quality:	28	(4.6)
Entry standards:	25	(377)
Student–staff ratio:	=13	(13.3)
Services & facilities/student:	58	(£1,013)
Expected completion rate:	28	(90.0%)
Good honours:	=32	(67.6%)
Graduate prospects:	39	(70.7%)

whom say they would recommend Liverpool to their friends. Applications from home and overseas were up by more than 10 per cent in 2007, but the university suffered more than most from the switch from six choices per applicant to five for courses beginning in 2008. New courses for 2009 include Irish studies and politics and a combined diploma in dental hygiene and therapy. One of Europe's largest facilities for training dentists opened in 2007, marking the start of a £6-million investment programme following the award of another 125 dental places from 2009.

Liverpool was among the first traditional universities to run access courses for adults without traditional academic qualifications. The projected dropout rate of nearly 9 per cent is below the national average for the courses and entry grades. Even before the introduction of top-up fees, the university was awarding record numbers of scholarships and bursaries to widen opportunities further. They include five in memory of the Hillsborough disaster victims and thirty in memory of John Lennon, mainly for Merseyside residents. Other access initiatives include a week-long summer school and the opening of a purpose-built children's centre to help mature students and staff, with 68 subsidised places. The proportion of state-educated students is higher than at the other civic universities and nearly a quarter of the undergraduates are from working-class homes.

Both the university and the city have a loyal following among students, and Liverpool's status as Capital of Culture should add to the attractions. The 3,357 places in halls of residence, self-catering flats and houses are more than enough to guarantee accommodation to all first years. The suburban setting of the main halls complex and the focus of social life on the guild of students means that there is less integration than at some other civic universities, but there is no shortage of nightlife.

Undergraduate Fees and Bursaries

- Fees for UK/EU students: £3,145
- International student fees: £9,100–£11,650 £18,000 (medicine)
- Bursary on full grant: household income up to £17,910: £1,330, then £1,025.*
- Bursaries on partial grant: household income £17,911–£38,330: £1,025.*
- Scholarships based on circumstances or by competition. For full details see the university's website: www.liv.ac.uk/study/undergraduate/money/

* Figures for 2007–08

Students

Undergraduates:	13,425	(3,380)
Postgraduates:	1,960	(1,895)
Mature students:	12.6%	
Overseas students:	8.4%	
Applications per place:	7.1	
From state-sector schools:	86.4%	
From working-class homes:	23.6%	

For detailed information about fees, grants and bursaries and how they work, see chapter 7.

Accommodation

Number of places and costs refer to 2008–09
University-provided places: 3,357
Percentage catered: 59%
Catered costs: £93.45–£106.40 a week.
Self-catered costs: £72.80–£82.60 a week.
First-year students are guaranteed accommodation if requirements are met.
International students: as above.
Contact: accommodation@liverpool.ac.uk
www.liv.ac.uk/accommodation

Liverpool Hope University

Liverpool Hope has opted out of this year's league tables after finishing at the bottom of last year's ranking in *The Times Good University Guide*. It might have moved up this year, having registered much higher satisfaction levels in the latest National Student Survey, but the university believes that the criteria used in league tables do not reflect its emphasis on widening participation in higher education. Only five universities had a lower score for graduate destinations in last year's table, and Hope was in the bottom ten for its students' projected completion rate.

Hope is a unique ecumenical institution formed from the merger of two Catholic and one Church of England teacher training colleges in 1980. The two churches' leading figures on Merseyside described the union as a "sign of hope", unintentionally providing the title for one of the nine new universities created in 2005. It describes itself as "teaching led, research informed and mission focused" and includes "taking faith seriously" among its five key values.

Students' levels of satisfaction have varied considerably in the three years of the National Student Survey. Hope was in the top 30 when the first results appeared in 2005, but only three universities had a lower overall score 12 months later. Although still in the bottom half, the results published in 2007 were much better, with media studies producing the best results. Theology was easily the top scorer for research, while management did best in the assessments of teaching quality, achieving full marks.

University status provided a bigger boost in demand for places than at any of the 2005 newcomers, although it is not clear whether this has continued since Hope has now also become the only institution to suppress the publication of its applications figures. Most students opt for combined subject degrees, choosing after the first year whether to give them equal weight or to go for a major/minor arrangement. Gaming technology and Irish studies is one of the more unusual combinations suggested; environmental management and dance another. Subjects are grouped into four "deaneries": arts and humanities; education; business and computing; sciences and social sciences.

Some 70 per cent of the students are over 20 on entry and female undergraduates outnumber their male counterparts by more than two to one. Hope comfortably exceeds all of the official benchmarks for widening participation in higher education. Almost all the undergraduates attended state schools or colleges, four out of ten are

---

Hope Park
Liverpool L16 9JD
0151 291 3295 (admissions)
admission@hope.ac.uk
www.hope.ac.uk
www.hopesu.co.uk

The Times Rankings
Liverpool Hope blocked the release of data from the Higher Education Statistics Agency and so we cannot give any ranking information.

from working-class families and almost a third are from areas with little tradition of higher education – the second-highest proportion in England. This is partly the result of the Network of Hope, which brings university courses to sixth-form colleges across the northwest of England, in areas where there is limited higher education. Combined honours, Foundation degrees and postgraduate teacher training courses are taught in Bury, Wigan and Blackburn. The downside of the university's access agenda is a projected dropout rate of more than 26 per cent, significantly more than the national average for the courses and entry qualifications and a figure exceeded by only three universities.

The university's own premises are now concentrated on two sites in Liverpool, with a residential outdoor education centre set in 20 acres of woodland in the heart of Snowdonia, North Wales. The main campus is three miles from the city centre in the suburb of Childwall, while the performing arts are based at the more central Everton campus, which also boasts a £15-million headquarters for community education activities. The £5-million main library, on the Hope campus, has 250,000 items and 700 study spaces, with electronic access from other sites.

Sports facilities have been improving and there are student union bars on both campuses. The university has a range of residential accommodation, some of it provided by a private firm, and is able to guarantee places for first years and all overseas students.

Undergraduate Fees and Bursaries

- Fees for UK/EU students: £3,145
- International student fees: £6,600
- Bursary on full grant: household income up to £17.5K: Year 1 £530, Year 2 £800, Year 3 £1,070; £17.5K–£25K: Year 1 £400, Year 2 £600, Year 3 £1,100.
- Bursaries on partial grant: household income £25K–£38K: £400 (same value for all three years).
- Scholarships based on circumstances or by competition. For full details see the university's website: www.hope.ac.uk/student-finance-2007-2008/money-for-your-course-2007-08.html

Students		
Undergraduates:	4,505	1,685
Postgraduates:	630	1,045
Mature students:	27.4%	
Overseas students:	9%	
Applications per place:	5.4	
From state-sector schools:	97.8%	
From working-class homes:	40.0%	

For detailed information about fees, grants and bursaries and how they work, see chapter 7.

Accommodation

Number of places and costs refer to 2008–09
University-provided places: 1,032
Percentage catered: 23% (optional catering package)
Optional catered costs: £81.11 a week.
Self-catered costs: £61.11–£88.75 a week.
First years are guaranteed accommodation, but it may not be on the main campus.
International students: housing is subject to availablility, but all needs are catered for.
Contact: accommodation@hope.ac.uk

Liverpool John Moores University

Naming itself after a football pools millionaire was just the start for one of the most innovative of the new universities. JMU was once accused of marketing itself more as a fun factory than a seat of learning, but the former polytechnic prefers to portray itself as "forward-thinking". Among the initiatives to its credit was Britain's first student charter, which became a template for others. It also launched the first degree in criminal justice and the first distance learning degree in astronomy. Now it is investing £100 million to transform its three campuses by 2012. A Design Academy is due to open in 2008, during Liverpool's tenure as the European Capital of Culture, and a £20-million science building is set to follow in 2009.

Before university status had even been confirmed, JMU set about transforming itself into a huge, futuristic multimedia institution. The two learning resource centres serving different academic areas and a state-of-the-art media centre are open all hours. Many lectures have been replaced by computer-based teaching, freeing academic staff for face-to-face tutorials. Student numbers increased substantially in the early years of the

decade and applications were up again by more than 10 per cent in 2007, having held steady against the national trend when top-up fees were introduced. Applications were still healthy when the official deadline passed for courses beginning in 2008.

Mainly concentrated in an area between Liverpool's two cathedrals, the university is now one of Britain's biggest with more than 21,000 students. Arts and science courses occupy separate sites within easy reach of the city centre, with the IM Marsh campus three miles away for education and community studies. JMU has retained a local commitment to higher education, with more than 60 per cent of the students drawn from the Merseyside area, some attracted by the range of diploma courses which still supplement the largely voca-tional degree programme. A "learning federation" embracing four further education colleges in St Helens, Southport and Liverpool itself adds to the regional flavour.

A growing research reputation is a source of particular pride, and is reflected in an unusually large number of postgraduates for a new university. JMU was one of only two new universities to have a subject rated internationally outstanding in the latest Research Assessment Exercise. Sports science made the step up from a grade 5 in 1996 and has now been marked out as a national

---

Roscoe Court
4 Rodney Street
Liverpool L1 2TZ
0151 231 5090
recruitment@livjm.ac.uk
www.livjm.ac.uk
www.l-s-u.com

Edinburgh
Belfast
LIVERPOOL
London
Cardiff

teaching centre. General engineering succeeded in holding onto grade 5 and four more subjects reached the next category. Astronomy has a growing reputation, with a part share in a telescope in the Canary Islands, which helped secure a Queen's Anniversary Prize in 2006. The International Centre for Digital Content, a partnership with Mersey Television, is developing a range of new courses, including masters programmes in computer games design and e-commerce. A £1.6-million maritime centre features the UK's most advanced 360-degree shiphandling simulator. The new science building will include the schools of Psychology and Sport and Exercise Sciences, allowing the university to concentrate most of its teaching and research in science and technology on one city centre site. The faciltities will include a 70-metre running track and specialist laboratories.

The impressive range of courses in hospitality, leisure, sport and tourism achieved a perfect score for teaching quality, as did physics and the healing and human development courses in the School of Health. JMU is one of the most popular of the new universities, judged in terms of applications per place. The university's efforts to extend access to higher education are successful: there are significantly more state-educated undergraduates than average for the subjects offered and more than a quarter come from areas where participation in higher education is low. Work-based degrees give students credit towards their final awards for experience in the workplace and encourage them to build study projects around their job, while the campus also build in work-related skills and experience. The university launched a curriculum review to address concerns about the dropout rate, which fell to 21 per cent in the latest projections – still higher than the official benchmark for the university.

Student facilities have been improving. The conversion of a city-centre hotel was one of a number of residential projects which have allowed the university to guarantee a place for young entrants from outside Merseyside, including those who enter through Clearing. The university now claims to have more accommodation than students requiring it.

Undergraduate Fees and Bursaries
- Fees for UK/EU students: £3,145
- International student fees: £13,190–£14,167
- Bursary on full grant: £1,050
- Bursaries on partial grant: household income £25–£50K: £420.
- Scholarships based on circumstances or by competition. For full details see the university's website: www.ljmu.ac.uk/StudyLJMU/Fees/

Students		
Undergraduates:	14,760	(5,510)
Postgraduates:	1,440	(2,660)
Mature students:	18.5%	
Overseas students:	8.2%	
Applications per place:	4.8	
From state-sector schools:	95.6%	
From working-class homes:	36.7%	

For detailed information about fees, grants and bursaries and how they work, see chapter 7.

Accommodation
Number of places and costs refer to 2007–08
University-provided places: 3,000 plus 15,000 through Liverpool Student Homes.
Percentage catered: 0%
Self-catered costs: £61–£89 a week.
All new students are guaranteed a place in university accommodation.
International students: as above
Contact: accommodation@ljmu.ac.uk;
www.ljmu.ac.uk/accommodation;
0151-231 4166

University of London

The federal university is Britain's biggest by far, despite the loss of Imperial College in 2007. Some other prestigious members have considered going their own way and applied for their own degree-awarding powers to hold in reserve, but they are bound together by the London degree, which enjoys a high reputation worldwide. Reforms to the university's governance have given the colleges more autonomy and look to have staved off further departures for now.

London students do have access to some joint residential accommodation, sporting facilities and the University of London Union. But most identify with their college.

The following colleges – some of which have dropped the word "college" from their title to underline their university status – have separate entries, and each also appears within the main university League Table.

Goldsmiths, University of London
King's College London
London School of Economics and Political
  Science
Queen Mary
Royal Holloway
School of Oriental and African Studies
University College London

Many of London's teaching hospitals have now merged with colleges of the university:

King's College now incorporates Guys and St Thomas's (the United Medical and Dental Schools of Guys and St Thomas's).

Queen Mary now incorporates St Bartholomew's and the Royal London School of Medicine and Dentistry.

University College now incorporates the Royal Free Hospital Medical School and the Eastman Dental Hospital.

In addition, the School of Slavonic and Eastern European Studies is now part of University College.

Eleven colleges do not have separate entries in the *Guide*. These are listed below and opposite, with useful postal, telephone, and electronic contacts.

Birkbeck College
Malet Street, London WC1E 7HX
0845 601 0174 (course enquries)
info@bbk.ac.uk
www.bbk.ac.uk
15,055 undergraduates, mainly part-time.
Apply direct, not through UCAS.

Senate House
Malet Street
London WC1E 7HU
020 7862 8360/61/62
enquiries@london.ac.uk
www.london.ac.uk
www.ulu.co.uk

Enquiries: to individual colleges, institutes or schools.

Central School of Speech and Drama
Embassy Theatre, Eton Avenue,
London NW3 3HY
020 7722 8183
enquiries@cssd.ac.uk
www.cssd.ac.uk
580 undergraduates. Acting ahd theatre
practice.

Courtauld Institute of Art
Somerset House,
London WC2R oRN
020 7848 2645
ugadmissions@courtauld.ac.uk
www.courtauld.ac.uk
155 undergraduates. History of art degree.

Heythrop College
Kensington Square,
London W8 5HQ
020 7795 4202 (admissions enquiries)
enquiries@heythrop.ac.uk
www.heythrop.ac.uk
335 undergraduates. Degrees in theology
and philosophy.

Institute of Education
20 Bedford Way,
London WC1H oAL
020 7612 6000
info@ioe.ac.uk
www.ioe.ac.uk
195 undergraduates; mainly postgraduate
education courses.

London Business School
Regent's Park.
London NW1 4SA
020 7000 7000
webenquiries@london.edu
www.london.edu
Postgraduate MBA and other courses.

London School of Hygiene and Tropical Medicine
Keppel Street,
London WC1E 7HT
020 7299 4646 (enquiries)
registry@lshtm.ac.uk
www.lshtm.ac.uk
Postgraduate medical courses.

Royal Academy of Music
Marylebone Road,
London NW1 5HT
020 7873 7373 (general office)
registry@ram.ac.uk
www.ram.ac.uk
320 undergraduates. Degrees in music.

Royal Veterinary College
Royal College Street,
London NW1 oTU
020 7468 5149 (undergraduate admissions)
registry@rvc.ac.uk
www.rvc.ac.uk
1,345 undergraduates. Degrees in veterinary
medicine.

St George's, University of London
Cranmer Terrace,
London SW17 oRE
020 8672 9944 (general enquiries)
www.sgul.ac.uk
3,460 undergraduates. Degrees in
medicine.

School of Pharmacy
29–39 Brunswick Square,
London WC1N 1AX
020 7753 5831 (enquiries)
registry@pharmacy.ac.uk
www.pharmacy.ac.uk
730 undergraduates. Degrees in pharmacy.

London Metropolitan University

London Met made its debut in our *Guide* five years ago, perilously close to the bottom of *The Times* League Table. It has not appeared since because it has blocked the release of data from the Higher Education Statistics Agency. Initially, senior officials argued that using figures relating to the two universities from which London Met was formed – London Guildhall and North London – would create a misleading impression of the new institution. This objection no longer applies, but the university is one of only two in Britain that chooses to keep its performance secret. Those statistics that are available paint a mixed picture: student satisfaction levels had increased in the last National Student Survey, for example, but the university remained in the bottom five.

London Met specialises in extending higher education boundaries to bring in groups who are under-represented at traditional universities. Since the merger, it has developed hundreds of new degree courses, described as both intellectual and vocational, and which allow students to study citizenship, ethics or enterprise alongside their main subject. Many prepare students for professional qualifications and give credit for work experience or volunteering.

Recent developments have seen four "business-related" departments join together to form the London Metropolitan Business School which, with 10,000 students and more than 100 courses, will be one of Europe's largest. An "international medical degree" is being launched in September 2008, through the University of Health Studies, in Antigua. The five-year programme will be based in London and graduates will complete the United States Medical Licensing Examination, enabling them to practise in America.

With over 28,000 students, 7,000 of whom are from other countries, it has become the biggest single institution in the capital. However, applications have been uneven: the university had its grant for 2005–06 reduced for failing to hit its enrolment targets and, while applications were up at the start of 2007, the 2.7 rise was much less than the national average. A 17.5 per cent decline at the start of 2008, when UCAS reduced the number of choices per applicant from six to five, was more than twice the national average. Fortunately, many students come through other routes and overseas recruitment has remained healthy. London Met has more undergraduates from other EU countries than any university.

The university's sites are centred on the City of London and north London's Holloway Road. A new graduate school,

31 Jewry Street
London EC3N 2EY
020 7133 4200 (enquiries)
admissions@londonmet.
  ac.uk
www.londonmet.ac.uk
www.londonmet
  su.org.uk

Edinburgh

Belfast

Cardiff

LONDON

designed by Daniel Libeskind, opened soon after the merger, and an impressive £30-million science centre followed in 2006. This features a "superlab" of 280 workstations that is Europe's largest, as well as a multipurpose gym and sports therapy facilities.

Among a variety of craft subjects, the silversmithing and jewellery courses are the largest in Britain, with facilities to match, while those in furniture restoration and conservation were the first of their kind in Europe.

Courses are also directed at the local community. More than a third of the students are Afro-Caribbean and the proportion of mature students is among the highest in England. The projected dropout rate has improved and, at 21 per cent in the latest statistics, is better than the national average for the university's courses and entry standards. One of London Met's first objectives was to improve student retention: student support services, from admission to careers advice, have been remodelled and there is a particular emphasis on academic and pastoral counselling on entry and at other key points of courses.

Quality assessments were patchy at the two predecessor universities. Economics and business studies scored well for teaching quality at Guildhall, while business and management achieved the only perfect score at North London. Research grades were generally low in the last assessments, but London Met has a long-term strategy to bring about improvement. Fewer than 100 Guildhall academics were entered for the latest Research Assessment Exercise, and only German reached the top three grades. American studies was the only subject to make the top three grades at North London.

Residential accommodation is limited, but many of London Met's students live at home. Sports facilities are still not extensive, although competitive teams are successful. However, the social scene is lively, particularly in north London.

Undergraduate Fees and Bursaries

- Fees for UK/EU students: £3,145
- International student fees: £8,200
- Bursary on full grant: household income up to £18K: £1,000 then sliding scale £975–£775.*
- Bursaries on partial grant: household income £25.2K–£40K: sliding scale £750–£300.*
- Scholarships based on circumstances or by competition. For full details see the university's website: www.londonmet.ac.uk/student-services/saifs

* Figures for 2007–08

Students		
Undergraduates:	14,800	7,160
Postgraduates:	2,600	4,260
Mature students:	51.0%	
Overseas students:	29.4%	
Applications per place:	7.1	
From state-sector schools:	97.5%	
From working-class homes:	40.9%	

For detailed information about fees, grants and bursaries and how they work, see chapter 7.

Accommodation

Number of places and costs refer to 2008–09
University-provided places: about 800
Percentage catered: 0%
Self-catered costs: £83–£103 a week.
First years and disabled students given priority, but the university cannot guarantee accommodation.
International students: first years given priority.
Contact: accommodation@londonmet.ac.uk

London School of Economics and Political Science

Always one of the big names of British higher education, the LSE was second only to Harvard University in the *Times Higher Education/QS* world rankings for social science in 2005 and only one place lower since then. Now it is planning 20 per cent more places, having seized the chance to tackle a longstanding shortage of teaching space by acquiring former Government buildings near the school's Aldwych headquarters.

The LSE took on a new lease of life under Professor Anthony Giddens, the academic face of Tony Blair's Third Way, as big names arrived from a variety of other top universities. Sir Howard Davies, his equally high-profile successor, is building on that progress, having made the move into academic life from the Financial Services Authority. The cosmopolitan feel that derives from the highest proportion of overseas students at any publicly funded university will continue and many of the new places will be for postgraduates, but there will be some increase in UK undergraduate places.

The LSE has produced 29 heads of state and 13 Nobel prizewinners in economics, literature and peace – including George Bernard Shaw, Bertrand Russell, Friedrich von Hayek and Amartya Sen. The nationals of more than 150 countries take up half of the places. At the undergraduate level, only the much larger Manchester University has more applications from overseas. Its international character not only gives the LSE global prestige but also an unusual degree of financial independence. Less than a fifth of its income is from the Higher Education Funding Council.

Only Oxford and Cambridge have higher entry standards. More than four British undergraduates in ten are from independent schools – one of the highest ratios in the country and much higher than the funding council's benchmark figure. Efforts are being made to attract a broader intake with Saturday classes and summer schools. The projected dropout rate of 3 per cent is among the lowest at any university. Scores in the National Student Survey slipped a little in 2007, but applications remained healthy at the official deadline for courses beginning in 2008.

Areas of study range more broadly than the name suggests. Law, management and history are among the subjects top-rated for teaching, and there is even a small contingent of scientists. Business, economics, psychology and mathematics all produced good results recently. Only Cambridge outperformed the LSE in the last research assessments, which saw half

---

Houghton Street
London WC2A 2AE
020 7955 7125
stu.rec@lse.ac.uk
(pre-application)
ug-admissions@lse.ac.uk
(post-application)
www.lse.ac.uk
www.lsesu.com

The Times Rankings
Overall Ranking: 4

Student satisfaction:	=55	(74%)
Research quality:	2	(6.3)
Entry standards:	4	(469)
Student–staff ratio:	=7	(12.6)
Services & facilities/student:	11	(£1,562)
Expected completion rate:	3	(96.9%)
Good honours:	12	(75.2%)
Graduate prospects:	3	(87.7%)

of the school's subjects rated internationally outstanding. The school entered the highest proportion of its academics, at 97 per cent, of any university and just one subject (statistics) slipped below the top two grades.

The LSE does not hide its light under a bushel: it describes itself as "the world's leading social science institution for teaching and research". A pan-European survey also showed the school's students to be more active in student associations, more entrepreneurial and more open to opportunities to work abroad than those at other leading universities. The students' union claims to be the only one in Britain to hold weekly general meetings at which every student may attend and vote, while the 120 student societies cover an unusually wide range of interests.

Improvements were being made to the campus long before the opportunity arose to expand. A £30-million Norman Foster-designed redevelopment of the Lionel Robbins Building now houses a much-improved library. The move was a welcome one since the number of books borrowed by LSE students is more than four times the national average, according to a recent survey. Additional buildings have been acquired, routes between buildings are being pedestrianised and a new student services centre has opened.

Partying is not the prime attraction of the LSE for most applicants, who tend to be serious about their subject, but London's top nightspots are on the doorstep for those who can afford them. The 3,650 residential places for 7,500 full-time students offer a good chance of avoiding central London's notoriously high private sector rents.

Undergraduate Bursaries and Scholarships

- Fees for UK/EU students: £3,145
- International student fees: £12,360–£13,872
- Bursary on full grant: £2,500 (England and Wales).
- Bursaries on partial grant: household income up to £38.3K payments on sliding scale.
- Scholarships based on circumstances or by competition. For full details see the university's website: www.lse.ac.uk/financialSupportOffice/

Students

Undergraduates:	3,785	(40)
Postgraduates:	4,235	(970)
Mature students:	3.4%	
Overseas students:	48.5%	
Applications per place:	13.4	
From state-sector schools:	59.4%	
From working-class homes:	17.5%	

For detailed information about fees, grants and bursaries and how they work, see chapter 7.

Accommodation

Number of places and costs refer to 2008–09
University-provided places: 3,650
Percentage catered: about 36%
Catered costs: from £65–£134 a week.
Self-catered costs: £70–£160 a week.
First years are guaranteed an offer of accommodation.
Policy for international students: same as above.
Contact: accommodation@lse.ac.uk
to apply online: www.lse.ac.uk/accommodation

London South Bank University

London South Bank ensured that there was no confusion about its location by adding the capital's name to its title in 2003, but there has been no change of direction. Once marketed as "the university without ivory towers", its mission statement underlines the point with an emphasis on wealth creation and the labour market. A study by PricewaterhouseCoopers found that a South Bank degree increased lifetime earnings by more than £185,000, which was nearly £26,000 more than the national average. Over 70 per cent of students are from the capital, most of them from south London and especially from the area's wide range of ethnic minorities. Of nearly 18,000 undergraduates, over a third are part-time and half of the undergraduates are on sandwich courses. Less than half enter with traditional academic qualifications.

Applications have been buoyant throughout the period surrounding the introduction of top-up fees and the switch from six choices per applicant to five barely dented the momentum at the start of 2008. The proportion of mature entrants is among the highest in Britain, encouraged by initiatives such as the summer school for local people to upgrade their qualifications. The Fast Track to Higher Education programme has been expanded to include numeracy, communication and study skills,

as well as the original mathematics. The courses, some of which are tailored to the needs of mature students and some for younger students, start at the end of June and are limited to 15 hours a week so as not to affect students' benefit entitlement.

London South Bank has stayed closer than most of the new universities to the technological and vocational brief given to the original polytechnics. Until the recent explosion in demand for health subjects, engineering was second only to business studies in terms of size. Diploma and degree courses run in parallel so that students can move up or down if they are better suited to another level of study. Education, hospitality and town planning produced the best scores in teaching assessments, but politics and health subjects also did well.

No subjects reached the top two categories in the last research assessments, but more than four out of ten researchers were in departments on the next rung of the ladder. Computer science, electronic engineering, town planning, social policy and English led the way. The results were considerably better than those in 1996 even though a higher proportion of academics entered. Specialist facilities, such as the Centre for Explosion and Fire Research, show that the vocational theme carries through into research.

London South Bank is in the midst of a

---

103 Borough Road
London SE1 0AA
020 7815 7815
enquiry@lsbu.ac.uk
www.lsbu.ac.uk
www.lsbsu.org

The Times Rankings
Overall Ranking: 113

Student satisfaction:	=73	(72%)
Research quality:	=73	(1.3)
Entry standards:	112	(193)
Student–staff ratio:	113	(25.2)
Services & facilities/student:	94	(£822)
Expected completion rate:	104	(72.0%)
Good honours:	=94	(48.4%)
Graduate prospects:	=95	(56.3%)

15-year programme to develop its campus in Southwark, near the Elephant and Castle, and not far from the South Bank arts complex. The nine-storey Keyworth Centre, which opened in 2003, has upgraded much of the teaching accommodation and provided a new focal point for the university. Construction of its flagship building "Keyworth II" is now underway. Upon completion in 2009, it will house the Faculty of Health and Social Care, provide facilities for the Department of Education and for Sports and Exercise Science, as well as providing more general teaching and social space.

Some health students are based on the other side of London, in hospitals in Romford and Leytonstone, where there are limited learning resources, supplementing those in Southwark. The university now trains 40 per cent of London's nurses.

The social scene suffers from the fact that the large numbers of mature students are more likely to spend their leisure time with their family or local community than their fellow-students. The capital's attractions are on the doorstep but, with more than 40 per cent of the students coming from working-class homes, many cannot afford them. The projected dropout rate has slipped back to more than a quarter after improvements earlier in the decade, a proportion exceeded by only one university in England.

A new hall of residence means that London South Bank now has residential places within 10 minutes' walk of the main campus. There are not enough to guarantee places for all first years, but the 2,000 overseas students are all given places if they want them. Sports facilities improved considerably with the extension of the campus sports centre and the launch in 2004 of the Academy of Sport, Physical Activity and Well-being. Representative teams have been quite successful in recent years and sports bursaries of £3,000 are available for elite performers.

Undergraduate Fees and Bursaries
- Fees for UK/EU students £3,145
- International student fees £8,120–£8,360*
- Bursary on full grant: Year 1 £500; Year 2 £750; Year 3 £750 (+ £250 graduation bonus for Hons graduates).*
- Bursaries on partial grant: Year 1 £500; Year 2 £750; Year 3 £750 (+ £250 graduation bonus for Hons graduates).*
- Scholarships based on circumstances or by competition. For full details see the university's website: www.lsbu.ac.uk/fees

*1 Figures for 2007–08

Students

Undergraduates:	8,985	(6,965)
Postgraduates:	2,060	(3,765)
Mature students:	58.1%	
Overseas students:	10.3%	
Applications per place:	4.8	
From state-sector schools:	98.0%	
From working-class homes:	41.9%	

For detailed information about fees, grants and bursaries and how they work, see chapter 7.

Accommodation
Number of places and costs refer to 2008–09
University-provided places: 1,400
Percentage catered: 0%
Self-catered costs: £86.50 (standard) – £106.00 (en suite) a week.
First-year UK students are not guaranteed accommodation, but high priority is given to those who live furthest away.
International students: first years are generally accommodated if conditions are met.
Contact: accommodation@lsbu.ac.uk

Loughborough University

Loughborough has had the most satisfied undergraduates of any conventional university in two of the first three National Student Surveys. In 2007, five of the university's subjects were ranked top in the UK – civil engineering; chemical, process and energy engineering; materials and minerals technology; information services; and other technological subjects. Loughborough also won the first two *Times Higher Education* awards for best student experience, after separate national polls of undergraduates. The message has begun to get through to sixth-formers with better than average applications in 2007 and 2008.

Still best known for its successes on the sports field, Loughborough has enhanced its academic reputation recently, consistently finishing well up *The Times* rankings and rivalling Oxbridge in its teaching quality ratings, which averaged no less than 22 points out of 24. The best results came in information science and human sciences. The Office for Standards in Education also rates Loughborough in its top category for teacher training in physical education, design and science. The built environment, sociology and sports science reached the top rung of the research assessment ladder in 2001, when almost half of the academics entered for

assessment were in the top two categories.

Loughborough merged with the neighbouring colleges of education and art and design, giving a more balanced mix between arts and science, and making the university less male-dominated. The university remains a major centre of engineering with more than 2,800 students in a £20-million integrated engineering complex. Aeronautical, automotive and civil engineering are particularly strong, although art and design, business and sports science now all have more students than any single branch of the discipline.

The original 216-acre campus has benefited from a construction programme which included a large student union extension and a new business school, as well as the gradual refurbishment of residential accommodation. Nearly 5,000 rooms now all have telephone and internet connections and another 1,300 rooms are on the way in four new halls, representing the biggest single investment in the university's history.

The size of the campus has been increased by 75 per cent following the purchase of the adjacent Holywell Park site. This will become the focus for research and collaboration with industry, including a £59-million BAE-sponsored Systems Engineering Innovation Centre. The university prides itself on a close

---

Ashby Road
Loughborough
Leicestershire LE11 3TU
01509 263171 (switchboard)
www.lboro.ac.uk/
prospectus/ug/index.htm
www.lboro.ac.uk
www.lufbra.net

The Times Rankings
Overall Ranking: 12

Student satisfaction:	=2	(83%)
Research quality:	=37	(4.3)
Entry standards:	=31	(361)
Student–staff ratio:	=53	(17.1)
Services & facilities/student:	27	(£1,293)
Expected completion rate:	14	(94.0%)
Good honours:	35	(67.4%)
Graduate prospects:	31	(73.2%)

relationship with industry, which accounts for its record haul of six Queen's Anniversary Prizes. Arts facilities are improving with the upgrading of the Cope Auditorium to serve the campus and local community. The business school is being extended and a £12.7-million building for Health, Exercise and Biological Sciences is under construction.

Most subjects are available either as three-year full-time or four-to-five-year sandwich courses, which includes a year in industry. This has helped to give graduates an outstanding employment record, as well a dropout rate of less than 5 per cent, which is particularly low for the subjects Loughborough offers. The university is a leader in the use of computer-assisted assessment, offering students the chance to gauge their own progress online.

Loughborough remains pre-eminent in British university sport, both in terms of facilities and performance. Representative teams have a record second to none and the programme of sports scholarships is the largest in the university system. The heavily oversubscribed School of Sport and Exercise Science moved into new premises in 2002, and in recent years the campus has acquired a 50-metre swimming pool, national academies for cricket and tennis, a gymnastics centre and a high-performance training centre for athletics. The university also opened the UK's only

centre for disability sport in 2005 and was shortlisted as a possible training camp for the British team ahead of the 2012 Olympics in London. Joining the Olympic effort will be a £15-million Sports Technology Institute, as well as enhanced research, innovation and enterprise in sport and leisure in the longer term.

Social activity is concentrated on the students' union. The relatively small town of Loughborough, a mile away, is never going to be a clubber's paradise, but both Leicester and Nottingham are within easy reach.

Undergraduate Fees and Bursaries

- Fees for UK/EU students: £3,145
- International student fees: £9,850–£12,800
- Bursary on full grant: £1,360
- Bursaries on partial grant: household income up to £34,750: £630.
- Scholarships based on circumstances or by competition. For full details see the university's website: www.lboro.ac.uk/admin/ar/funding/index.htm

Students

Undergraduates:	10,750	(305)
Postgraduates:	3,630	(2,330)
Mature students:	5.0%	
Overseas students:	8.8%	
Applications per place:	5.6	
From state-sector schools:	82.9%	
From working-class homes:	23.6%	

For detailed information about fees, grants and bursaries and how they work, see chapter 7.

Accommodation

Number of places and costs refer to 2008–09
University-provided places: 4,725
Percentage catered: 56%
Catered costs: £3,636.30–£4,926.60 (31 or 35 weeks)
Self-catered costs: £2,796.30–£5,070.00 (39 weeks)
First years are guaranteed accommodation.
International students: guaranteed accommodation for two years of their course.
Contact: SAC@lboro.ac.uk

University of Manchester

Always among the giants of British higher education, with 22 Nobel prizewinners to its credit, Manchester became larger and more powerful in 2004 through a merger with neighbouring UMIST. The largest conventional university in Britain has kept its familiar name, but is now headed by a Vice-Chancellor from the other side of the world. Professor Alan Gilbert arrived from the University of Melbourne shortly before the new institution was formed.

Some departments were already administered jointly with UMIST and the two institutions only separated fully in 1993, so the new institution has been able to avoid some of the problems associated with other university mergers. A £400-million building and refurbishment programme, the largest ever in UK higher education, will be complete by the end of 2009 and another £250 million of investment is planned by 2015. At the same time, a raft of new professors has been appointed. The aim is not only to break into higher education's "golden triangle" of Oxford, Cambridge and London, but to make Manchester one of the top 25 universities in the world by 2015. By then, the aim is to have at least five Nobel laureates on the staff. The first joined in 2006 and there have been other high-profile appointments, such as the novelist

Martin Amis as Professor of Creative Writing.

Manchester celebrated its 150th anniversary with its best ratings to date, and was already going from strength to strength before the merger. Seven of the last dozen subjects to be assessed achieved maximum points for teaching quality – a record that none of its rivals could match – while the twelve subject areas judged internationally outstanding for research in 2001 trebled the haul five years earlier. The successful departments were spread equally between the arts and sciences, with three-quarters of the academics entered for assessment placed in the top two categories.

The university has been climbing *The Times* rankings, as well as reclaiming its place as the university with the largest number of applicants. The demand for places had been increasing, but applications were down by almost twice the national average at the start of 2008, after UCAS had reduced the number of choices per candidate from six to five. One of the priorities in the new institution's founding strategy is to broaden the undergraduate intake, with a particular focus on increasing recruitment from the city and its surrounding area. However, in addition to the normal bursary package for British students, Manchester is aiming eventually to have 750 awards for students from

---

Oxford Road
Manchester M13 9PL
0161 275 2077
ug-admissions@
  manchester.ac.uk
www.manchester.ac.uk
www.umsu.
  manchester.ac.uk

The Times Rankings
Overall Ranking: 27

Student satisfaction:	=64	(73%)
Research quality:	=16	(5.1)
Entry standards:	13	(412)
Student–staff ratio:	=10	(12.8)
Services & facilities/student:	19	(£1,378)
Expected completion rate:	=20	(92.3%)
Good honours:	23	(70.5%)
Graduate prospects:	47	(67.4%)

educationally deprived backgrounds in developing countries.

UMIST's legacy is a strong reputation among academics and employers alike in its specialist areas of engineering, science and management. Two thirds of its academics reached one of the top two out of seven categories in the last research assessments. Materials technology and health subjects were both 5* rated. Teaching ratings, too, were good, especially in engineering, and its graduates enjoyed a consistently excellent employment record. Surveys of employers frequently placed UMIST among their favourite recruiting grounds, helping to produce an unrivalled network of industrial sponsorship. Employers have rated Manchester's careers service the best at any university .

The merger has produced the largest engineering school in the UK, with a £20-million budget and 1,200 students. A £14-million extension to the School of Chemistry, the second-largest in Britain, opened in 2007. There already was a federal business school, which is among the strengths of the merged institution, as is the medical school, which was rewarded for impressive teaching ratings with extra places in collaboration with Keele University. A new teaching block caters for the additional 230 places a year.

The city's famed youth culture and the university's position at the heart of a huge student precinct already help to ensure keen competition for places – and hence high entry standards in most subjects. Sports facilities, which were already first rate, have improved still further since the city hosted the Commonwealth Games. Students get discount rates at the aquatics centre opened for the games on campus, for example. The city's reputation for violent crime may be overstated, but the students' union (which has the largest premises in the country) runs late-night minibuses, self-defence classes, and regular safety campaigns. Students tend to be fiercely loyal both to the university and their adopted city.

Undergraduate Fees and Bursaries
- Fees for UK/EU students: £3,145
- International student fees: £10,500–£12,900 £23,500 (clinical)
- Bursary on full grant: £1,000
- Bursaries on partial grant: household income up to £27.8K: £1,000.
- Scholarships based on circumstances or by competition. For full details see the university's website: www.manchester.ac.uk/ undergraduate/funding/

Students

Undergraduates:	24,135	(3,175)
Postgraduates:	6,740	(5,110)
Mature students:	8.3%	
Overseas students:	13.6%	
Applications per place:	8.7	
From state-sector schools:	77.7%	
From working-class homes:	20.7%	

For detailed information about fees, grants and bursaries and how they work, see chapter 7.

Accommodation

Number of places and costs refer to 2007–08
University-owned places: 9,100
Percentage catered: 29%
Catered costs: £3,649–£4,981 (40 weeks)
Self-catered costs: £2,504–£4,561 (40 weeks); £2,644–£3,388 (37 week contract)
All unaccompanied students are guaranteed accommodation provided conditions are met.
International students paying overseas fees are guaranteed accommodation if conditions met.
Contact: accommodation@manchester.ac.uk

Manchester Metropolitan University

With over 33,000 students, including over 7,000 part-timers, Manchester Metropolitan is neck and neck with its recently merged neighbour for the title of the largest conventional higher education institution in Britain. But the giant institution boasts quality as well as quantity, as it demonstrated in 2001 with one of the first 5* ratings for research at a new university. Sports science was the area rated internationally outstanding, while seven other subjects were placed in the top three of seven categories.

Although the former polytechnic has not been able to sustain the lead it held briefly over Manchester University in applications, still only a handful of institutions are more popular. The demand for places has increased throughout most of the decade, although applications were down by more than the national average at the start of 2008, when the number of choices per applicant was cut from six to five. Longstanding commitments to extending access are being continued: even among the full-time undergraduates, a fifth are over 25 and a third come from working-class homes. Nearly one in five comes from an area without a tradition of higher education.

Almost 1,000 courses cover more than 70 subjects, with the menu of programmes including a growing range of two-year Foundation degrees. The university takes teaching seriously: small groups are used whenever possible and staff are encouraged to take a three-year MA in teaching. Many courses also involve work placements. MMU has more professionally accredited courses than any other university

Education courses have also fared well in the Teacher Training Agency's performance indicators, especially for primary training. The university trains more teachers than any other and has launched a Centre for Urban Education to develop its expertise further. Some 800 trainees and other students taking contemporary arts and sports science are at the former Crewe and Alsager College campuses, 40 miles south of Manchester and now rebranded as MMU Cheshire. The remaining education students are based at Didsbury, five miles out of the centre of Manchester, with those taking community studies. A single Institute of Education covers both centres.

The Crewe and Alsager campuses are six miles apart, but free transport is provided between the two. Although the rural location inevitably makes for a quieter life than in Manchester, Alsager has an arts centre with two theatres, a

---

All Saints Building
Oxford Road
Manchester M15 6BH
0161 247 6969 (admissions)
admissions@mmu.ac.uk
www.mmu.ac.uk
www.mmunion.co.uk

Edinburgh
Belfast
MANCHESTER
London
Cardiff

The Times Rankings
Overall Ranking: 92

Student satisfaction:	=84	(71%)
Research quality:	=76	(1.2)
Entry standards:	=67	(272)
Student–staff ratio:	=93	(20.2)
Services & facilities/student:	78	(£937)
Expected completion rate:	96	(75.2%)
Good honours:	82	(51.3%)
Graduate prospects:	=84	(59.4%)

dance studio and an art gallery, as well as extensive sports facilities. The Crewe campus, which has seen a district of the town rebranded as the University Quadrant, has its own nightclub. The university has begun to develop Crewe as its Cheshire base, adding sports facilities and residential accommodation, as well as more lecture theatres. The opening of a £30-million student village is the first piece of a rebuilding programme at Crewe, which will be home to academics and students in business and management, the arts, exercise and sport science, humanities and social studies, education and teacher training.

The five sites in Manchester will be reduced to two, leafy Didsbury in the southern suburbs and the extensive All Saints campus, close to the city centre and Manchester University. New science and engineering buildings at All Saints cost £42 million – part of a £300-million building programme for the university as a whole. The large business school will benefit from a new £62-million building next to the Mancunian Way, while health courses – including the recently incorporated Manchester School of Physiotherapy – will be centred on an enhanced Didsbury campus, and clothing, food and hospitality courses will be based at All Saints. Overseas links have expanded rapidly in recent years, offering exchange opportunities in Europe and farther afield, as well as establishing teaching bases abroad.

More than half of the students come from the Manchester area, easing the pressure on accommodation in a city of nearly 70,000 students. Some 85 per cent of hall places are reserved for first years, with priority going to the disabled and those who live furthest from the university. The city's attractions do no harm to recruitment levels, but much depends on where the course is based. Didsbury may offer the best of both worlds, with swift access to the city centre and a peaceful environment, but students at Crewe and Alsager can feel isolated. Some potential applicants are daunted by the sheer size of the university, but individual courses and sites usually provide a social circle.

Undergraduate Fees and Bursaries
- Fees for UK/EU students: £3,145
- International student fees: £7,595–£12,150*
- Bursary on full grant: household income up to £20.4K: £1,000 then sliding scale £900–£800.
- Bursaries on partial grant: household income up to £39.3K: sliding scale £700–£100.
- Scholarships based on circumstances or by competition. For full details see the university's website: www.mmu.ac.uk/studentfinance/index.php

*Figures for 2007–08

Students

Undergraduates:	23,605	(3,665)
Postgraduates:	2,480	(3,540)
Mature students:	20.3%	
Overseas students:	6.7%	
Applications per place:	5.3	
From state-sector schools:	94.0%	
From working-class homes:	34.0%	

For detailed information about fees, grants and bursaries and how they work, see chapter 7.

Accommodation
Number of places and costs refer to 2007–08
University-provided places: 5,100
Percentage catered: 6%
Catered costs: Manchester: £82 a week; Cheshire: £85.50 a week.
Self-catered costs: Manchester: £66.50–£96.00 a week; Cheshire: £60–£76 a week.
All new full-time students will be housed if requirements are met. Local restrictions apply. International students: as above.
Contact: accommodation@mmu.ac.uk

Middlesex University

Middlesex has been changing the character of its intake, reorganising its courses and becoming more international, and now physical changes are on the way. A £100-million building programme will concentrate the university on three sites in north London. The new package may help encourage a revival in recruitment among home students, which has been patchy in recent years. It was one of the few English universities to register a decline in applications through UCAS in 2007, although the figures for the start of 2008 were around the national average. Overseas recruitment has been Middlesex's salvation: foreign undergraduates make up 15 per cent of its intake. A longstanding commitment to Europe sees more than 1,000 students arriving from the Continent and even more come from further afield. There is a network of 11 regional offices, producing a student population drawn from 130 countries. Its successes in the overseas market won a Queen's Award for Enterprise and the university has now opened its own campus in Dubai offering business degrees and short courses in a variety of subjects.

Now almost 25,000 strong, including part-timers, the university aims to carry on growing. Partner colleges at home and abroad participate in exchanges and/or offer Middlesex qualifications. The university has reorgan-ised its schools to focus on its strengths in business, computing and the arts. Media students will benefit from a new Skillset Academy, in partnership with Top TV and the SAE Institute.

The highly flexible course system allows students to start many courses in January if they prefer not to wait until autumn, and offers the option of an extra five-week session in July and August to try out new subjects or add to their credits. An experiment bringing forward the start of the academic year to early September has been abandoned, with the result that the first assessments have reverted to after Christmas.

Nine out of ten students take vocational courses, many at postgraduate or sub-degree level. The business school is the biggest subject area, but almost half of the undergraduates are on multidisciplinary programmes. About 42 per cent are over 21 on entry and half of the full-timers come from London. Almost all of the British students are from state schools, 45 per cent of them from working-class homes. The dropout rate had been improving, but the latest projection of more than a quarter failing to complete their chosen course on time is significantly worse than the national average for the university's subjects and entry qualifications. Even

North London Business Park
Oakleigh Road South
London N11 1QS
020 8411 5555
enquiries@mdx.ac.uk
www.mdx.ac.uk
www.musu.mdx.ac.uk

The Times Rankings
Overall Ranking: 105

Student satisfaction:	=104	(67%)
Research quality:	=73	(1.3)
Entry standards:	=105	(219)
Student–staff ratio:	=106	(22.1)
Services & facilities/student:	17	(£1,412)
Expected completion rate:	105	(71.9%)
Good honours:	101	(47.3%)
Graduate prospects:	75	(61.2%)

before the introduction of top-up fees, Middlesex was attempting to attract better-qualified students by offering £1,000-a-year scholarships for UK entrants with 300 UCAS points (the equivalent of three Bs).

For some time, the university has been reducing the number of campuses dotted around London's North Circular Road. The latest to close will be Enfield in August 2008, its courses transferring to Hendon, where £50 million has already been invested in a library, learning resources centre and roofing in the main quadrangle to provide meeting space. New student facilities, including a fitness suite, expanded nursery and refectory will be available at Hendon for the new academic year to meet the demand from the extra students and staff. Hendon, which boasts one of the country's few Real Tennis courts, already housed the business school, but will now add sport and health subjects. The other locations include a picturesque country estate at Trent Park and an art and design campus at Cat Hill.

Nurses and other health students are based in four London teaching hospitals and on a campus at Archway which is shared with the University College and Royal Free Hospital medical schools. There is also a joint degree in veterinary nursing run with the Royal Veterinary College.

Middlesex did well in the first of the new institutional audits in 2003, but results from the first three National Student Surveys have been disappointing. It was near the bottom of the table in 2007. Philosophy secured the university's best score for teaching quality and has one of Middlesex's two grade 5 assessments for research, denoting nationally outstanding work and some of international excellence. History of art was the other top scorer.

The number of residential places is planned to double in the next few years from the current 1,900 beds. Sports facilities have been improving and will be better still when the Hendon development is complete.

Undergraduate Fees and Bursaries
- Fees for UK/EU students: £3,145
- International student fees: £9,200
- Bursary on full grant: £310
- Bursaries on partial grant: n/a
- Scholarships based on circumstances or by competition. For full details see the university's website: www.mdx.ac.uk/study/undergrad/moneymatters/index.asp

Students

Undergraduates:	11,990	(5,760)
Postgraduates:	1,690	(3,845)
Mature students:	36.3%	
Overseas students:	14.7%	
Applications per place:	7.3	
From state-sector schools:	98.2	
From working-class homes:	44.6%	

For detailed information about fees, grants and bursaries and how they work, see chapter 7.

Accommodation
Number of places and costs refer to 2007–08
University-provided places: 1,347
Percentage catered: 0%
Self-catered costs: £78.76–£93.90 a week.
Full-year international students have priority; age and residential restrictions apply.
International students are guaranteed a room provided requirements are met.
Contact: accomm@mdx.ac.uk

Napier University

Napier was Scotland's first and largest polytechnic, and also appointed the first woman to lead a university north of the border. Professor Joan Stringer moved from neighbouring Queen Margaret University College (as it then was) with the declared aim of making Napier "one of the leading modern universities in the United Kingdom". It is now in the midst of a £100-million redevelopment programme to help achieve that ambition.

Already an institution of more than 14,000 students, with 4,500 part-timers, it has continued to grow, largely thanks to increased recruitment from the Continent and further afield. Around 17 per cent of full-time undergraduates are from overseas. An International College, launched in 2007, offers them a dedicated service, with pastoral and recruitment activities, as well as support for Napier's many programmes in China, Hong Kong and Malaysia. The demand for places has remained buoyant at a time when it has faltered elsewhere in Scotland. A 12 per cent rise in applications in 2007 and near parity at the start of 2008 both represented the best figures north of the border.

Two new libraries, a purpose-built music centre and refurbishment of the science laboratories underlined Napier's ambitions, with a £5-million computing centre completing the first phase of the university's development plan at the university's headquarters in Merchiston, the student district of Edinburgh. This was followed by the £30-million transformation of the university's Craiglockhart campus, a one-time military hospital where Scotland's biggest business school has been built. It features a glass atrium housing a cyber café and two spherical lecture theatres with a total of 600 seats, and a new fitness suite was added in 2007.

Next on the list is the Sighthill campus, in the west of Edinburgh, which will be closed throughout 2009–10 while construction work takes place. Sighthill will become home to the Faculty of Health, Life and Social Sciences, bringing the faculty under one roof for the first time in a sustainable and well-equipped building for teaching and learning. New sports facilities are among the other improvements planned for the campus, complementing council proposals for an athletics arena nearby.

The university is named after John Napier, the inventor of logarithms. The tower where he was born still sits among the concrete blocks of the Merchiston campus. There are several smaller sites, mainly in the leafy south of Edinburgh, but the eventual aim is to have one campus for each of the three faculties.

Napier has been held up as a model to

Craiglockhart Campus
Edinburgh EH14 1DJ
08452 606040
www.napier.ac.uk/enquiries
www.napier.ac.uk
www.napierstudents.
  com

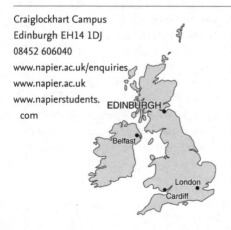

The Times Rankings
Overall Ranking: 64

Student satisfaction:	–	(–)
Research quality:	=92	(0.8)
Entry standards:	84	(257)
Student–staff ratio:	=61	(17.9)
Services & facilities/student:	82	(£915)
Expected completion rate:	102	(73.3%)
Good honours:	=47	(60.8%)
Graduate prospects:	9	(77.9%)

other universities trying to reduce wastage rates. There is a student mentoring scheme, "bridging programmes" offering pre-term introductions to staff and information on facilities, and summer top-up courses in a variety of subjects. The latest projected dropout rate of 16.5 per cent represents a big improvement on the previous figure, but is more than the UK average for the subjects on offer.

Computing and accounting achieved the highest possible scores in the teaching quality assessments carried out in Scotland between 2000 and 2002. Health subjects, general engineering, civil engineering and library and information management all did well in the 2001 Research Assessment Exercise. A new Skillset Screen Academy, run in partnership with Edinburgh College of Art, reflects the university's strong reputation in film education.

Most of the avowedly vocational courses include a work placement, and the close relationship with industry and commerce helps to produce consistently good graduate employment figures. Students are offered personal development programmes focusing on topics such as self awareness, empowering attitudes and building relationships. The modular course system allows movement between courses at all levels and has allowed students the option of starting courses in

February, rather than September. Links with a network of partner colleges encourage progression from further to higher education.

The dispersed nature of the university does nothing for the social scene, although Edinburgh is hardly dull. Despite improvements, some students find life too quiet in the evenings and at weekends.

Undergraduate Fees and Bursaries

- Scottish-domiciled and EU students: no fees payable.
- Non-Scottish UK-domiciled student fees: £1,775 a year.
- International student fees: £8,350–£9,690
- Scholarships based on circumstances or by competition. For full details see the university's website: www.napier.ac.uk/ napierlife/money/Pages/default.aspx/

Students		
Undergraduates:	8,960	(2,300)
Postgraduates:	1,045	(2,230)
Mature students:	40.6%	
Overseas students:	17.0%	
Applications per place:	3.2	
From state-sector schools:	94.0%	
From working-class homes:	33.9%	

For detailed information about fees, grants and bursaries and how they work, see chapter 7.

Accommodation

Number of places and costs refer to 2008–09
University-provided places: 904
Percentage catered: 0%
Self-catered costs: £80.36 average cost a week.
First years are guaranteed a place provided requirements are met. Residential restrictions apply.
International students are guaranteed a place as long as requirements are met.
Contact: accommodation@napier.ac.uk

Newcastle University

Major big-city universities seem to take it in turns to be fashionable – Manchester gave way to Nottingham, and then to Newcastle. However, four years of static or falling applications suggest that the mantle may have been passed on again. Scaling back numbers in the medical school prevented Newcastle from sharing in the general rise in applications in 2007 and the fall at the start of 2008, with the switch from six choices per applicant to five, was above the national average.

The university has embarked on a £200-million programme of investment in its campus and facilities. The first phase involves a five-story, glass-fronted building costing £35 million, which will house all the main student services, as well as a visitor centre, creating a welcoming "front door" to the university. A partnership with a private languages firm will also put £49 million into accommodation and teaching facilities for international students.

Science and engineering laboratories have already been upgraded, disabled access improved and thousands of students provided with internet connections in university flats and halls of residence.

Originally Durham University's medical school, Newcastle's excellence in that area was confirmed by maximum points for teaching in medicine, anatomy and physiology, pharmacology and pharmacy, reviewed jointly with molecular bio-sciences, psychology and its department of speech. Dentistry only just missed out on the same score. The medical school's reputation was confirmed by its selection as a national centre to disseminate best teaching practice in medicine. The school has gone back into partnership with Durham, with about a third of trainees spending their first two years at Durham's Stockton campus.

Newcastle has also been chosen to house a national centre of teaching excellence in music. Other academic developments include the creation of nine new research institutes, housed in new buildings costing over £30 million. Research grades improved in the last assessments, with biological sciences, clinical laboratory sciences, music and psychology all rated internationally outstanding. Six out of ten academics entered for the exercise were in departments placed in the top two categories.

New courses have included a Natural Sciences degree, complementing Newcastle's designation as a "Science City", Britain's first degree in folk and traditional music, and a four-year business and accounting degree, which provides a fast-track to professional qualifications. Newcastle already had a number of unusual features for a traditional university, such as a fine art degree which attracts up to 15

Kensington Terrace
Newcastle upon Tyne NE1 7RU
0191 222 5594 (enquiries)
www.ncl.ac.uk/forms/
 enquiries/www.ncl.ac.uk
www.unionsociety.co.uk

Edinburgh
Belfast
NEWCASTLE UPON TYNE
London
Cardiff

The Times Rankings
Overall Ranking: =20

Student satisfaction:	=39	(75%)
Research quality:	=33	(4.4)
Entry standards:	19	(394)
Student–staff ratio:	27	(14.9)
Services & facilities/student:	13	(£1,481)
Expected completion rate:	=20	(92.3%)
Good honours:	22	(71.1%)
Graduate prospects:	20	(75.3%)

applicants per place. It also has a longstanding reputation for agriculture, which recorded good scores for both teaching and research, with the benefit of two farms in Northumberland.

The campus is spacious and varied, occupying 45 acres close to the main shopping area, civic centre, Northumbria University and Newcastle United's ground. The university also boasts an expanded and refurbished theatre, an art gallery and three museums, which it hopes to bring together in a "cultural quarter" for the city.

The university expanded dramatically in the 1990s, and now has more than 17,000 full-time students. It has become popular with independent schools, whose applicants take almost a third of the places, but the university has stepped up its contacts with local state schools in order to broaden its intake. The 300 students recruited through the programme have been doing at least as well as those with higher entry grades. Alumni and other friends of the university have raised £6 million in two years to add to the bursaries available for students from less affluent backgrounds. Official performance indicators reveal a healthy 92 per cent completion rate – better than anticipated, given the subject mix.

Few students regret choosing Newcastle for a degree, even if southerners can find the winter temperatures a shock. The city's nightlife is legendary – eighth best in the world, according to one survey – and the university topped a student poll based on computer facilities and student services, as well as the social scene. The cost of living is reasonable and town–gown relations better than in many cities.

Sport is a particular strength, Newcastle claiming to be one of the top ten universities both in terms of performance and facilities. A £5.5-million sports centre opened on the campus in 2005, supplementing the two existing centres, which have refurbished fitness suites, massage clinics and all the normal indoor services. The main outdoor pitches are two miles from the university. Over £30,000 is awarded annually in sports bursaries for elite athletes.

Undergraduate Bursaries and Scholarships

- Fees for UK/EU students: £3,145
- International student fees: £9,915–£12,970
  £24,015 (clinical)
- Bursary on full grant: household income up to £18,360: £1,240 then £930.
- Bursaries on partial grant: household income £25K–£26,222: £930; £26,223–£31,466: £620.
- Scholarships based on circumstances or by competition. For full details see the university's website: www.ncl.ac.uk/undergraduate/finance

---

Students

Undergraduates:	13,940	(120)
Postgraduates:	3,470	(2,175)
Mature students:	8.4%	
Overseas students:	8.6%	
Applications per place:	6.2	
From state-sector schools:	68.4%	
From working-class homes:	20.3%	

For detailed information about fees, grants and bursaries and how they work, see chapter 7.

Accommodation

Number of places and costs refer to 2008–09
University-provided places: 4,200
Percentage catered: 31%
Catered costs: £93.10–£107.80 a week.
Self-catered costs: £65.45–£90.65 a week.
All single undergraduates are guaranteed a room in university-managed accommodation provided requirements are met. Local restrictions apply.
International students: as above.
Contact: accommodation-enquiries@ncl.ac.uk

University of Wales, Newport

Newport saw applications rise by 76 per cent in four years, starting with the biggest increase in applications anywhere in the UK following a change of status from college to university. But, as in the rest of Wales, there was a big drop at the beginning of 2008. All subjects had been experiencing increased demand for places, including areas such as computing, which are in decline nationally. Students have also been attracted by a range of new courses in areas such as creative sound and music, cinema studies and script-writing, computer games design and internet technologies.

Newport had already embarked on an ambitious expansion strategy before attaining full membership of the University of Wales. A futuristic riverside campus that will practically double the number of students has begun to take shape, housing the Business School and part of the School of Art, Media and Design. At the same time, Newport will pursue closer links with the University of Wales Institute Cardiff, which was already a partner in a number of subjects.

Art, media and design was awarded a grade 5 rating for research in the last assessments, but other research and teaching ratings were disappointing. However, both students and employers appear enthusiastic. Newport finished in the top ten in England and Wales in the first national student satisfaction survey, with the best results anywhere in finance and accounting, although it has slipped down the table subsequently. A poll of local employers was particularly positive about the university.

Just one academic in ten was entered for the latest Research Assessment Exercise, the lowest proportion in the university system. As a result, only one university finished below Newport for average grades per member of staff, although there has been a significant increase in research activity with the launch of a dedicated Research and Enterprise Department. Business and management was the most successful area in teaching quality assessments, but an overall audit by the Quality Assurance Agency in 2004 was positive. Estyn, the Welsh schools inspectorate, gave the best grades in Wales to the teacher-training courses, which also showed high levels of student satisfaction.

The university, which was previously Gwent College of Higher Education, now has over 9,000 students from 44 different countries. Virtually all the full-time undergraduates come from state schools and there is a higher proportion from working-class homes than at any other university institution in Wales. However,

---

Caerleon Campus
Lodge Road
Newport
South Wales NP18 3QT
01633 432030
admissions@newport.ac.uk
www.newport.ac.uk
www.newportunion.com

Edinburgh
Belfast
NEWPORT London
Cardiff

The Times Rankings
Overall Ranking: 96

Student satisfaction:	=84	(71%)
Research quality:	=107	(0.5)
Entry standards:	=105	(219)
Student–staff ratio:	92	(20.1)
Services & facilities/student:	85	(£890)
Expected completion rate:	97	(74.9%)
Good honours:	=84	(50.7%)
Graduate prospects:	80	(60.4%)

the projected dropout rate of more than 23 per cent is still higher than the benchmark set according to the subject mix. Newport operates a number of access schemes, including one offering students at local schools and colleges guaranteed places if they fulfil certain criteria.

The university is actively involved with a range of local businesses. It was rated the number one university in Wales for enterprise education by the Knowledge Exploitation Fund. Among its innovations is the Corus to Campus project for redundant steelworkers (previously employed by Corus), and it is also a leading player in the Community University of the Valleys. The university also hosts the International Film School Wales, whose graduates include double-BAFTA winner Asif Kapadia, and Justin Kerrigan, director of the cult movie *Human Traffic*.

There are currently two campuses. The smaller, Allt-Yr-Yn, campus focuses on engineering and computing, business and professional and social studies. The larger Caerleon campus is further out, with impressive views, and caters for humanities, science, education and art, media and design. This is also where the student village of 661 self-catered study bedrooms is located, and a new building for fashion and other subjects is under construction. Free buses link the two sites, which are officially among the safest in Britain: the college was the first educational establishment to pass an industry-standard security inspection.

A well-equipped sports centre at Caerleon has transformed facilities that previously compared unfavourably with those of other universities. The city of Newport has established a reputation for producing successful rock bands and has plenty of clubs and entertainment venues, but students in search of serious cultural or clubbing activity gravitate to nearby Cardiff.

Undergraduate Fees and Bursaries

- Welsh-domiciled student fees: £3,145, with grant of up to £1,890
- Non-Welsh UK domiciled and EU student fees: £3,145
- International student fees: £7,250–£8,250
- Welsh National Bursary for all UK students, means-tested with maximum of £310.
- Bursary on full grant: household income up to £20K: £1,000.
- Bursaries on partial grant: household income up to up to £30K: £600; up to £40K: £300.
- Scholarships based on circumstances or by competition.For full details see the university's website: www3.newport.ac.uk/displayPage.aspx?object_id=257&type=PAG

Students

Undergraduates:	3,250	(4,230)
Postgraduates:	465	(1,590)
Mature students:	38.1%	
Overseas students:	2.5%	
Applications per place:	4.2	
From state-sector schools:	99.2%	
From working-class homes:	39.3%	

For detailed information about fees, grants and bursaries and how they work, see chapter 7.

Accommodation

Number of places and costs refer to 2008–09
University-provided places: 661
Percentage catered: 0%
Self-catered costs: £56–£75 a week.
First years guaranteed accommodation if requirements met.
International students: same as above.
Contact: accommodation@newport.ac.uk

University of Northampton

Northampton had a university in the thirteenth century, but it took until 2005 to get it back after Henry III dissolved the original version – allegedly because his bishops thought it posed a threat to Oxford. More than 80 places separate the two universities in *The Times* League Table, but Northampton will hope to narrow that gap somewhat in years to come. It has already registered good results in the first three National Student Surveys, with sports science and physical geography, environmental science history producing the highest levels of satisfaction in 2007.

The modern university has its origins in teacher training and, as Nene College of Higher Education, lobbied unsuccessfully to become a polytechnic. The later campaign, to establish a university in one of the few counties without one, eventually bore fruit, but only after almost a decade. By then, it had incorporated vocational courses for the leather industry, occupational therapy, nursing and midwifery. All remain in a surprisingly broad portfolio of more than 100 degree and diploma courses. The business school is taking part in a national pilot to develop two-tear degrees and four-year work-based equivalents. Specialisms such as leather technology, fashion and waste management have helped to build up the recruitment of overseas students to some 700 a year from 100 different countries.

The university has two sites: an 80-acre campus on the edge of Northampton, where £73 million has been spent on improvements in recent years, and the smaller but more central Avenue campus, which specialises in art and design, media, technology and the performing arts. Both sites have new halls of residence, and the main Park Campus has also seen several new teaching developments, a management centre and a research centre. Another £80 million of investment is planned over the next ten years. In the first phase, new arts facilities at Avenue will form the centrepiece of the town's "cultural mile", while an innovative student centre on the Park Campus will provide administrative and support services both during and outside office hours. The university has taken over a school next to the Avenue campus, which will house the School of Education after a £9-million refurbishment.

Student numbers have been steady for several years, but are expected to rise from the current 10,500 to about 12,000 by 2010. Applications were up by more than 23 per cent at the start of 2007, having bucked the national trend with a small rise when top-up fees were introduced, and remained healthy at the start of 2008 in spite of the reduction in the number of choices

---

Park Campus
Boughton Green Road
Northampton NN2 7AL
0800 358 2232 (courses)
study@northampton.
  ac.uk
www.northampton.ac.uk
www.northampton
union.com

The Times Rankings
Overall Ranking: 84

Student satisfaction:	=26	(76%)
Research quality:	=86	(1.0)
Entry standards:	102	(225)
Student–staff ratio:	=75	(19.0)
Services & facilities/student:	99	(£786)
Expected completion rate:	73	(80.0%)
Good honours:	69	(55.2%)
Graduate prospects:	=95	(56.3%)

allowed in the UCAS process. Foundation degree students pay £1,100 a year less than the £3,145 fee for honours degrees. Business is the most popular area, but health subjects are not far behind. Art and design produced the best teaching quality score, while English and history were highly rated in the 2001 Research Assessment Exercise.

Northampton takes its mission to widen participation in higher education seriously: almost all the undergraduates attended state schools or colleges, while nearly 38 per cent come from working-class homes. The projected dropout rate had improved in the latest official figures, but still nearly one in five of those who began courses in 2004 will is not expected to complete in the expected time – marginally more than the national average for the university's courses and entry grades. Some of the degrees – such as podiatry and furniture design and manufacture – recruit from all over Britain (and farther afield) but in other subjects most of the students are from the region. As a result, the 1,620 residential places are enough to guarantee accommodation for all first years who make Northampton their first choice.

Sports enthusiasts have a Premier League rugby club and the home of the British Grand Prix on their doorstep, as well as a more modest football club and first-class cricket. The university has added a £100,000 gym to its sports facilities, which include a sports hall and outdoor pitches. The town of Northampton has a number of student-oriented bars, but the two campuses' union bars remain the hub of the social scene.

Undergraduate Fees and Bursaries

- Fees for UK/EU students: £3,145
- International student fees: £7,450–£8,250
- Bursary on full grant: £1,000
- Bursaries on partial grant: household income up to £30K: £700; up to £40K: £500.
- Scholarships based on circumstances or by competition. For full details see the university's website: www.northampton.ac.uk/study/fees/

Students		
Undergraduates:	6,885	(2,180)
Postgraduates:	475	(1,105)
Mature students:	35.4%	
Overseas students:	7.3%	
Applications per place:	5.9	
From state-sector schools:	97.3%	
From working-class homes:	37.5%	

For detailed information about fees, grants and bursaries and how they work, see chapter 7.

Accommodation
Number of places and costs refer to 2008–09
University-provided places: 1,620
Percentage catered: 0%
Self-catered costs: £37.50 (small twin) – £79.75 (en-suite single) a week.
First years are guaranteed accommodation provided requirements are met.
International students: as above.
Contact:
www.northampton.ac.uk/study/accommodation/

Northumbria University

Northumbria consistently ranks among the leading universities created out of the polytechnics and a £136-million investment in its city centre campus is gradually producing facilities to match. The first phase was completed in 2007, when 9,000 design, law and business students moved into the new City Campus East development, which is linked to the existing main campus by an iconic new footbridge spanning Newcastle's central motorway. The next phase, which will take until 2010, will turn the main site into the first fully pedestrianised, green campus in a city centre. The library has already had a £6-million refurbishment and the new development will include a £20-million sports centre, which is due to open in 2009.

There are now 27,000 UK students and 3,500 more taking franchised courses in other countries. More than half of the students are from the North of England. Northumbria was one of the few universities to see a significant increase in applications at the official for courses beginning in 2008, despite the cut in the number of choices per candidate. The demand for places has been growing for most of the decade.

Entry grades for those with A levels are among the highest in the new universities, but more than half of the students are admitted with other qualifications or on the strength of relevant work experience. Free one-day taster courses run between January and July to give local people an idea of what a university course would be like. There is also a network of feeder colleges encouraging applications from adults without traditional academic qualifications.

More than 20 per cent of students are from areas with little tradition of higher education, while almost a third come from working-class homes. The 16 per cent projected dropout rate is just above the benchmark for Northumbria's courses and entry grades.

Health subjects have now overtaken business studies in terms of student numbers and have been highly successful in teaching assessments: nursing achieved Northumbria's first maximum score and, like modern languages and physics, health subjects managed 23 points out of 24. Education also managed maximum points and followed up with a glowing report from the Office for Standards in Education, which places it in the top category for primary training and secondary design and technology. The university also has a national centre of excellence in assessment, building on Northumbria's attempts to give students more constructive feedback and teaching

---

Ellison Terrace
Newcastle upon Tyne NE1 8ST
0191 232 6002 (switchboard)
er.admissions@unn.ac.uk
www.unn.ac.uk
www.mynsu.co.uk

The Times Rankings
Overall Ranking: 73

Student satisfaction:	=64	(73%)
Research quality:	=82	(1.1)
Entry standards:	54	(292)
Student–staff ratio:	=102	(21.0)
Services & facilities/student:	=60	(£1,010)
Expected completion rate:	68	(80.7%)
Good honours:	=88	(49.9%)
Graduate prospects:	50	(66.4%)

Edinburgh
Belfast
NEWCASTLE UPON TYNE
London
Cardiff

them how to assess themselves as future professionals. The university has not been especially successful in the National Student Surveys, but physical geography and environmental science have produced some of the best scores for their subjects.

The majority of subjects will continue to be based in the city centre, with health, education and community studies on the Coach Lane campus on the outskirts of the city, where £18 million has been spent upgrading facilities. Coach Lane now incorporates a learning resources centre with a fully integrated library, a clinical skills centre and new sports facilities, as well as teaching and seminar rooms.

Northumbria's best-known feature is its School of Design, which scooped the top national award for fashion design in 2006, but 17 subjects reached the equivalent of an "excellent" rating in teaching assessments. Five of the university's academics have won National Teaching Fellowships. Research ratings improved in 2001, but only psychology and art and design reached the top three grades. Many degrees are available as sandwich courses, with placements of up to a year in business or industry. Law and business studies have the highest entrance requirements.

Sport plays a growing role: Northumbria is consistently among the top ten in the British Universities Sports Association rankings. The sports scholarship programme has supported over 200 athletes from over 40 sports in the past ten years, some going on to success at the highest level. All new first years are offered places in university accommo-dation if they apply "in good time", while others are assisted by the accommodation office. Two large residential developments with en-suite rooms opened in September 2005, bringing the total stock to 3,500 places, and there is a plentiful supply of privately rented flats and houses.

Undergraduate Fees and Bursaries

- Fees for UK/EU students: £3,145
- International student fees: £8,300–£8,700
- Bursary on full grant: £310
- Bursaries on partial grant: n/a
- Scholarships based on circumstances or by competition. For full details see the university's website: http://northumbria.ac.uk/brochure/studfees/

Students

Undergraduates:	16,685	(6,135)
Postgraduates:	3,055	(3,755)
Mature students:	25.2%	
Overseas students:	11.4%	
Applications per place:	4.2	
From state-sector schools:	91.7%	
From working-class homes:	31.6%	

For detailed information about fees, grants and bursaries and how they work, see chapter 7.

Accommodation

Number of places and costs refer to 2007–08
University-provided places: 3,500
Percentage catered: 8%
Catered costs: £84 or £94 a week.
Self-catered costs: £55–£84 a week.
First years who need accommodation can be offered rooms. Local restrictions apply.
International students: first years can be guaranteed accommodation if requirements met.
Contact:
  rc.accommodation@northumbria.ac.uk

University of Nottingham

Nottingham is the nearest Britain has to a truly global university, with campuses in China and Malaysia modelled on a headquarters that is among the most attractive in Britain. For many years it has been among the institutions with the stiffest competition for each place, and a striking new campus and extra courses made the university even more fashionable. Growth in applications has resumed after a two-year blip fuelled by media coverage of gun crime early in the decade.

The university has had a spectacular rise up the pecking order of higher education. In less than 20 years, it went from being a solid civic university to a prime alternative to Oxbridge. Currently in the top 70 in the world rankings published by *Times Higher Education* and QS, it seldom stands still.

The lifting of restrictions on student recruitment allowed the university to make room for 750 more students, but new undergraduates' average A-level grades have not dropped. Once in, they tend to stay the course – the dropout rate of 3 per cent is among the best in the country. But the university is trying to broaden an intake which has more independent school students and fewer from working-class homes than the national average for the subjects offered. There is a well-established summer school for state-school teenagers and a bursary scheme, which pre-dated top-up fees, for Nottinghamshire students with no family history of higher education.

The 30-acre Jubilee campus, which cost £50 million and includes 750 residential places, is barely a mile away from the original parkland site. Futuristic buildings clustered around an artificial lake house the schools of management and finance, computer science and education. An additional building for the fast-growing business school was added in 2004 and a new sports hall opened the following year. The campus is undergoing further £200-million expansion to accommodate an innovation park and will acquire a landmark sculpture towering over its buildings.

The adjoining medical school is also close to University Park, although its recently established graduate-entry outpost is in Derby. The biosciences and the new veterinary school are at Sutton Bonington, ten miles south of the city.

Nottingham describes itself as "research-led", with work carried out at the university winning two Nobel Prizes in 2003. Professor Peter Mansfield, who won the prize for medicine for research leading to the development of the MRI scanner, has spent almost all his academic career there. The university's record-breaking

University Park
Nottingham NG7 2RD
0115 951 5559 (enquiries)
undergraduate-enquiries@
  nottingham.ac.uk
www.nottingham.ac.uk
www.su.nottingham.ac.uk

The Times Rankings
Overall Ranking: =16

Student satisfaction:	=39	(75%)
Research quality:	=18	(5.0)
Entry standards:	=15	(403)
Student–staff ratio:	19	(13.8)
Services & facilities/student:	18	(£1,390)
Expected completion rate:	6	(96.2%)
Good honours:	11	(75.7%)
Graduate prospects:	18	(76.0%)

research contracts place it among the top four universities for private funding. However, the last research assessments were disappointing by the university's high standards, with only five subjects awarded the coveted 5* rating – American studies, German, Iberian languages, music and theology – with 26 more subjects on the next assessment grade.

The university has devoted about £70 million to a research recruitment initiative in advance of the 2008 assessments. It has filled 20 research chairs and invested in the equipment and support posts to accompany them. Recent developments include a £7-million biomedical sciences building on the main campus and a £10-million graduate-entry outpost for the medical school in Derby.

Most teaching assessments were excellent, with classics, economics and politics joining psychology and manufacturing engineering leading the way. Classics, languages and biology were the top scorers in the latest National Student Survey.

Nottingham has long-standing links with the Far East, which provides the majority of its 7,000 overseas students, and has a Chinese physicist, Professor Fujia Yang, as its Chancellor. The university has had a branch in Malaysia since 2000 and launched a new venture in Ningbo, China, in 2004. Purpose-built campuses with echoes of the Nottingham's distinctive clock tower opened in Ningbo and near Kuala Lumpur in September 2005. Students will have the opportunity to move between the three countries.

Both main campuses are within three miles of the centre of Nottingham, with a good selection of student-friendly clubs. However, halls of residence and the students' union tend to be the centre of social life for students in both locations. New bars, café facilities and a nightclub were included in a £1-million makeover of student facilities in 2007. Sports facilities are excellent and expanding.

Undergraduate Fees and Bursaries

- Fees for UK/EU students: £3,145
- International student fees: £10,200–£14,230 £24,500 (clinical)
- Bursary on full grant: £1,050
- Bursaries on partial grant: household income up to £33.5K: £1,050; £33.5K–£34.6K: £790; £34.6K–£42.5K: £525.
- Scholarships based on circumstances or by competition. For full details see the university's website: www.nottingham.ac.uk/prospectuses/ undergrad/introduction/finance/

Students

Undergraduates:	15,520	(3,120)
Postgraduates:	2,570	(2,700)
Mature students:	6.5%	
Overseas students:	5.7%	
Applications per place:	4.9	
From state-sector schools:	66.1%	
From working-class homes:	16.9%	

For detailed information about fees, grants and bursaries and how they work, see chapter 7.

Accommodation

Number of places and costs refer to 2007–08
University-provided places: 7,400
Percentage catered: 58%
Catered costs: £102.25–£162.25 a week.
Self-catered costs: £75.00–£113.75 a week.
First years are guaranteed accommodation if conditions are met.
International undergraduates: guaranteed for 3 years if conditions are met.
Contact: ugaccommodation@nottingham.ac.uk
www.nottingham.ac.uk/accommodation

Nottingham Trent University

Consistently among the leading new universities in *The Times* League Table, as well as being one of the biggest, Nottingham Trent has demonstrated high quality in an unusually wide range of disciplines. Best known for fashion and other creative arts, which have the largest number of students, it also recorded maximum scores in teaching assessments for physics and biosciences. The law school is one of Britain's largest, offering legal practice courses for both solicitors and barristers, and there is even a commercial farm and equestrian centre on a campus devoted to animal, rural and environmental studies.

Nottingham Trent has the highest entry grades of any new university and an employment record which regularly sees more than 95 per cent of graduates in work or further study within six months. It helps that the university has the third highest number of year-long placements in the UK through its working partnerships with more than 6,000 businesses and private sector organisations. Almost a third of the undergraduates come from working-class homes and over nine out of ten attended state schools or colleges, while the projected dropout rate had dropped below 10 per cent in the latest official statistics – significantly less than the national average for the university's courses and entry grades.

An ambitious research programme was amply rewarded in the last assessments, when Nottingham Trent had four subjects judged nationally outstanding, with much of their work considered internationally excellent. Only two other new universities matched the achievements of drama, dance and the performing arts, English, media studies and health subjects.

An annual opinion survey shows that most of the students are satisfied, although the university could have done better in the first three National Student Surveys. Nottingham Trent registered one of the biggest increases in applications at any university at the beginning of 2008, when others were hit by the cut in choices per candidates from six to five. It was the second successive 10 per cent increase, following a blip in 2006 following publicity over gun crime earlier in the decade.

There are now nearly 25,000 undergraduates, including a large contingent of part-timers. The extensive main city site boasts a mixture of Victorian and modern buildings. The schools of science and technology, education, and arts and humanities are five miles away on the Clifton campus. The Brackenhurst campus is 14 miles out and includes an equestrian centre with a

Burton Street
Nottingham NG1 4BU
0115 848 2814 (admissions)
admissions@ntu.ac.uk
www.ntu.ac.uk
www.trentstudents.org

The Times Rankings
Overall Ranking: 56

Student satisfaction:	=93	(70%)
Research quality:	=69	(1.4)
Entry standards:	=70	(269)
Student–staff ratio:	66	(18.0)
Services & facilities/student:	67	(£990)
Expected completion rate:	31	(89.1%)
Good honours:	=64	(56.4%)
Graduate prospects:	25	(74.0%)

purpose-built indoor riding area, a well-equipped veterinary nursing building and animal unit. Another 300 residential places were added there in 2006, following a £3-million renewal of the teaching facilities.

Art and design facilities on the city campus have been upgraded and both the Boots Library and the students' union refurbished. Computing and informatics have a new building on the Clifton campus and the university has launched a bus service linking Clifton and the city. A total of £130 million has been earmarked for building projects over the next six years starting with a £70-million regeneration of the Newton and Arkwright buildings to produce a first-class working environment and student support facilities by the autumn of 2009.

Teaching ratings were variable, but showed improvement towards the end of the cycle of assessment, with politics achieving the best score. The university was responsible for the largest programme of Foundation degrees when the two-year qualification was launched. Subjects ranging from forensic science to wildlife conservation saw a big increase in applications in 2008.

The student body is diverse, with large numbers of mature and overseas students. The university's residential stock has been increasing, with a £10-million development with 446 beds opening on the City campus in 2004. It still is not sufficient to house all first years, but new students are guaranteed "university-allocated" accommodation, which may be in the private sector. Social life varies between campuses, but all have access to the city's lively cultural and clubbing scene. A late-night bus service links the main campuses and the city's new tram system serves the university.

Undergraduate Fees and Bursaries

- Fees for UK/EU students   £3,145
- International student fees   £7,550–£10,800
- Bursary on full grant: £1,050
- Bursaries on partial grant: household income up to £40K: sliding scale £650–£350.
- Scholarships based on circumstances or by competition. For full details see the university's website: www.ntu.ac.uk/prospective_students/fees/index.html

Students		
Undergraduates:	20,455	(3,895)
Postgraduates:	4,465	(4,730)
Mature students:	12.5%	
Overseas students:	13.2%	
Applications per place:	6.6	
From state-sector schools:	91.8%	
From working-class homes:	31.8%	

For detailed information about fees, grants and bursaries and how they work, see chapter 7.

Accommodation

Number of places and costs refer to 2008–09
University-provided places: 3,800
Percentage catered: 0%
Self-catered costs: £62–£105 (40–48 weeks).
First years and new students are guaranteed accommodation if conditions are met.
International students: guaranteed accommodation if conditions are met.
Contact: www.ntu.ac.uk/accommodation

University of Oxford

After eight years of League Table frustration, Oxford finally toppled Cambridge from first place in *The Times* rankings in 2002, and has maintained its grip ever since. The university also moved up to join Cambridge in second place in world rankings published by *Times Higher Education* and QS in 2007. A package of far-reaching organisational reforms designed to safeguard Oxford's supremacy and compete more effectively on the international stage were rejected by the dons, but the university will not stand still. Gradually, there may be more research students and marginally fewer UK undergraduates, as well as changes in the relationship between the university and its fiercely independent colleges.

Oxford is the oldest and probably the most famous university in the English-speaking world, and it remains almost inseparable from Cambridge in terms of overall quality. Like Cambridge, it attracts world-class academics and takes its share of the brightest students. The pair are head and shoulders above the other non-specialist universities in *The Times* ranking and in the view of most experts.

Yet Oxford briefly slipped to third place in our table at the start of the decade, partly because of comparatively low central spending on facilities such as careers and sport. The college structure, which produces an enviable student environment, acted as a handicap. However, a fairer reflection of overall spending, endorsed by the Higher Education Statistics Agency, had a dramatic effect.

Applications held steady with the introduction of top-up fees and increased by more than the national average in 2007, although they were down marginally in the following year. The university is still struggling to broaden its intake and shake off allegations of social elitism. The long-term growth in demand for places (which is concentrated in the more job-oriented subjects) is due, at least partly, to more systematic attempts to get the message through to teenagers that Oxford is open to all who can meet the exacting entrance requirements. Student visits to comprehensive schools have been supplemented by summer schools, recruitment fairs and colleges' own initiatives, as well as tireless public statements of intent by the university.

For all the university's efforts to shed its "Brideshead Revisited" stereotype, however, official figures still show 46 per cent of Oxford's students coming from independent schools – the largest proportion at any university. Fewer than 12 per cent come from working-class homes, despite the introduction of £3,150 bursaries for all undergraduates who are eligible for full fee

University Offices
Wellington Square
Oxford OX1 2JD
01865 270000 (main
  switchboard)
undergraduate.admissions
  @admin.ox.ac.uk
www.ox.ac.uk
www.ousu.org

The Times Rankings
Overall Ranking: 1

Student satisfaction:	1	(84%)
Research quality:	3	(6.2)
Entry standards:	2	(502)
Student–staff ratio:	4	(11.6)
Services & facilities/student:	2	(£2,884)
Expected completion rate:	1	(98.6%)
Good honours:	1	(90.1%)
Graduate prospects:	4	(83.9%)

remission – well before the advent of top-up fees. Still higher bursaries introduced in 2006 may help broaden the mix. Only about one student in 70 drops out, the lowest proportion in the country.

Applications must be made by mid-October – a month earlier if you wish to be interviewed overseas. There are written tests for some subjects and you may be asked to submit samples of work. Selection is in the hands of the 30 undergraduate colleges, which vary considerably in their approach to this issue and others. Sound advice on academic strengths and social factors is essential for applicants to give themselves the best chance of winning a place and finding a setting in which they can thrive. Only a minority of candidates opt to go straight into the admissions pool without expressing a preference for a particular college. The choice is particularly important for arts and social science students, whose world-famous individual or small group tuition is based in college. Science and technology, which have benefited from Oxford's phenomenally successful fundraising efforts, are taught mainly in central facilities. All subjects operate on eight-week terms and assess students entirely on final examinations – a system some find too pressurised.

The development of a major new campus on the site of the Radcliffe Infirmary is likely to be the first fruit of a £1-billion fundraising campaign. Recent developments include a £60-million building to house the western world's largest chemistry department, as well as new premises for economics. A £21-million social sciences library followed, while animal facilities drew bitter (often illegal) protests from animal rights campaigners.

There was never much doubt about the strength of Oxford's research but, with 25 out of 46 subject areas rated internationally outstanding and 96 per cent of those entered for assessment placed in the top two categories, the latest grades confirmed the university's high standing. The university had the largest number of top-rated researchers and also attracts the largest amount of research income, at more than £200 million. Most teaching assessments were similarly impressive.

Undergraduate Fees and Bursaries

- Fees for UK/EU students: £3,145*
- International student fees: £9,605–£12,810†
  £23,475 (clinical)†
- Bursary on full grant: £3,150
- Bursaries on partial grant: household income up to £50K: sliding scale £3,150–£200.
- Scholarships based on circumstances or by competition. For full details see the university's website: www.oxfordopportunity.com

* UK & EU students eligible for tuition fee support not liable for College fees
† Plus College fees (£3,300–£4,900)

Students

Undergraduates:	11,530	(4,610)
Postgraduates:	6,630	(1,865)
Mature students:	4.5%	
Overseas students:	11.6%	
Applications per place:	4.1	
From state-sector schools:	53.7%	
From working-class homes:	11.4%	

For detailed information about fees, grants and bursaries and how they work, see chapter 7.

Accommodation

See chapter 10 for information about individual colleges.

Oxford Brookes University

Now firmly established as a leading new university in *The Times* League Table, Oxford Brookes was one of a handful of former polytechnics to have a subject rated internationally outstanding in the last Research Assessment Exercises. That the 5* rating in history placed the department ahead of its world-renowned neighbour can only have added to the sense of achievement. English and French reached the next grade. The biggest entry in any new university represented 41 per cent of the academic staff, and meant that overall results were unusually variable.

Applications have been steady, although the decline at the start of 2008, with the reduction in the number of choices from six to five per applicant was above average. The university's location has always been an advantage in student recruitment, but the quality of provision is the real draw. Its departments feature near the top of *The Times* rankings for several subjects. Town planning and economics achieved perfect scores for teaching quality and Brookes has been in the top 25 in the National Student Survey for the last two years. Philosophy, theology and social work achieved the best results in 2007. Ofsted rated primary teacher training outstanding.

The university houses national centres for hospitality, leisure and tourism, and the teaching of business and undergraduate research, as well as one for teacher training in partnership with Westminster University. The *Architect's Journal* rated the Department of Architecture the best outside London. Oxford Brookes, which has a consistently excellent record for graduate employment, is also partnering Warwick University in the Government's academy for gifted and talented schoolchildren.

More than a quarter of the undergraduates come from independent schools – by far the highest proportion among the new universities and twice the national average for the university's subjects and entry grades. However, 37 per cent of places go to students from working-class homes. The university has been trying to attract more students from state schools and has targeted areas in Oxfordshire.

Brookes made a leap in size in 2000, taking in Westminster College, a merger which added 2,000 students, mainly in teacher training and the humanities, and forming a £2.5-million Institute of Education. As a polytechnic, Oxford pioneered the modular degree system that has swept British higher education. After more than 20 years' experience, the scheme has now trimmed the 2,000 modules it once offered, but undergraduates can pair subjects as

---

Headington Campus
Gypsy Lane
Oxford OX3 0BP
01865 484848 (enquiries)
query@brookes.ac.uk
www.brookes.ac.uk
www.thesu.com

The Times Rankings
Overall Ranking: 55

Student satisfaction:	=26	(76%)
Research quality:	=63	(1.6)
Entry standards:	50	(300)
Student–staff ratio:	68	(18.2)
Services & facilities/student:	76	(£944)
Expected completion rate:	50	(84.9%)
Good honours:	55	(59.1%)
Graduate prospects:	=51	(65.9%)

diverse as history and biology, or catering management and environmental management. Each subject has compulsory modules in the first year and a list of others that are acceptable later in the course. Students are encouraged to take some subjects outside their main area of study, and there is a range of possible exit points.

There are four main sites, two of which are only a mile from the city centre and linked to each other by a footbridge. Some £150 million has been earmarked for improvements to the Headington, Wheatley and Harcourt Hill campuses over the next few years. Buildings on the original Gipsy Lane site, at Headington, dating from the 1950s and '60s will be replaced with flexible, functional buildings benefiting from the latest technology. A public consultation showed strong support for a contemporary architectural style and more green spaces for the new development. Students starting in 2009 will benefit from the first stages of the project. Maths and engineering have now joined computing and business five miles away at Wheatley. The new engineering building will support the university's status as a Government-designated regional centre for motorsport and high performance engineering. The Harcourt Hill campus at Botley focuses on teacher education, human development and learning.

A swimming pool and 18-hole golf course have been added to the already impressive sports facilities. Representative teams have a good record, with the rowers particularly successful and the cricketers now combining with Oxford University to take on county teams. The students' union runs the biggest entertainment venue in Oxford, a city that can be expensive, but which offers enough to satisfy most students. The university has 3,700 residential places, all with internet access – enough for all first-year undergraduates.

Undergraduate Fees and Bursaries
- Fees for UK/EU students: £3,145
- International student fees: £9,400–£10,900
- Bursary on full grant: household income up to £5K: £1,800; £5K–£21K: £1,560; £21K–£25K: £1,050.
- Bursaries on partial grant: household income up to £36K: sliding scale £1,050–£150.
- Scholarships based on circumstances or by competition. For full details see the university's website: www.brookes.ac.uk/studentfinance

Students

Undergraduates:	10,810	(2,835)
Postgraduates:	1,880	(3,240)
Mature students:	22.8%	
Overseas students:	13.9%	
Applications per place:	6.8	
From state-sector schools:	71.3%	
From working-class homes:	37%	

For detailed information about fees, grants and bursaries and how they work, see chapter 7.

Accommodation

Number of places and costs refer to 2007–08
University-provided places: 3,700
Percentage catered: 23%
Catered costs: £4,000–£4,700 a year.
Self-catered costs: £3,000–£5,140 a year.
All accommodation is allocated to first years by distance from Oxford Brookes.
International students: as above.
Contact: accomm@brookes.ac.uk

University of Plymouth

One of the first new universities to be awarded a medical school (in collaboration with Exeter University), Plymouth has been carrying out major restructuring to concentrate activities in its home city. The aim is to break into the research elite while still serving the region through teaching. The most controversial element of the plans involved the transfer to Plymouth of courses from the Seale-Hayne agricultural campus, near Newton Abbot, and the arts and humanities programme based in Exeter. Education courses from the Exmouth campus are also transferring to the main North Hill campus in September 2008.

The plans were part of an academic reorganisation which divided the university into six faculties and included a big programme of capital investment. It has seen the opening of a £30-million headquarters and a second teaching building for the Peninsula Medical School. The library has been extended and upgraded, with 24-hour study facilities, and the students' union has also been refurbished. A £35-million arts complex opened in 2007, housing the Faculty of Arts and the Plymouth Arts Centre, and providing an award-winning focal point for a "cultural quarter" around the university. Teaching facilities and

residential accommodation for the education courses transferring from Exmouth are costing another £25 million, while a £11-million building for the Faculty of Health and Social Work, overlooking the Drake Reservoir, will include sports facilities as well teaching space.

The Peninsula Medical School has quickly established itself with applicants and was the only successful bidder for a new dental school in the last national competition. The school, which will train 64 dentists a year, opened in 2007. With campuses in Plymouth, Exeter, Truro and Taunton, along with teaching facilities in Bristol, the university's Faculty of Health and Social Work is the largest provider of nurse, midwifery and health professional education and training in the southwest.

As a polytechnic, its title laid claim to the whole of the southwest of England, but although the university chose to name itself after its Plymouth base, it maintains a strong regional role. It is a partner in the Combined Universities in Cornwall (CUC) initiative, which aims to increase the provision of further and higher education in one of the few counties without its own university. Plymouth has also established a unique relationship with its 18 partner colleges, which spread from Cornwall to Somerset, through a faculty devoted entirely to serving their 5,300 students

---

Drake Circus
Plymouth
Devon PL4 8AA
01752 232137 (admissions)
admissions@
  plymouth.ac.uk
www.plymouth.ac.uk
www.upsu.com

The Times Rankings
Overall Ranking: 62

Student satisfaction:	=55	(74%)
Research quality:	=63	(1.6)
Entry standards:	63	(227)
Student–staff ratio:	=46	(16.4)
Services & facilities/student:	=63	(£1,000)
Expected completion rate:	66	(81.2%)
Good honours:	52	(60.2%)
Graduate prospects:	=100	(55.3%)

taking university courses. They have become the University of Plymouth Colleges, sharing £2 million in capital investment.

The intake reflects Plymouth's position as the working-class hub of the southwest, with nine out of ten students state-educated and almost a third from the poorest social classes. The projected dropout rate of 16 per cent is marginally below the national average for the courses and entry grades. Although the university is still best known for marine studies, with 160 researchers in a Marine Institute established in 2006, its top teaching scores came in civil engineering, building, psychology, nursing and hospitality, each of which narrowly missed out on full marks. Plymouth was chosen to house no fewer than four national teaching centres: in health and social care placements, experiential learning in environmental and natural sciences, institutional partnerships and education for sustainable development. It is also taking part in a national pilot of two-year degrees. No university has exceeded the nine National Teaching Fellowships won by its academics.

Plymouth also has a longstanding commitment to research. More than a third of the academics were entered for the last Research Assessment Exercise, with computer science, psychology and art

history all rated nationally outstanding with significant work of international excellence.

The university offers a lively social scene, with excellent and recently upgraded facilities for water sports as well as a thriving nightlife. An £850,000 fitness centre has improved the sports facilities, while a range of sports scholarships and bursaries will help support high-fliers. A £15-million scheme has also seen the construction of a 1,300-bed student village.

Undergraduate Fees and Bursaries

- Fees for UK/EU students: £3,145
- International student fees £8,250–£8,750
- Bursary on full grant: £1,015
- Bursaries on partial grant: household income £25K–£40K: £300.
- Scholarships based on circumstances or by competition. For full details see the university's website: www.plymouth.ac.uk/ugfees

---

Students

Undergraduates:	16,985	(7,505)
Postgraduates:	1,380	(4,670)
Mature students:	30.8%	
Overseas students:	4.9%	
Applications per place:	4.6	
From state-sector schools:	93.0%	
From working-class homes:	31.8%	

For detailed information about fees, grants and bursaries and how they work, see chapter 7.

Accommodation

Number of places and costs refer to 2007–08
University-provided places: over 1,795
Percentage catered: 0%
Self-catered costs: £69–£127 a week.
First years are guaranteed accommodation.
International students: accommodation is guaranteed providing conditions are met.
Contact: accommodation@plymouth.ac.uk

University of Portsmouth

Portsmouth has always been among the leaders of its generation of universities. Strength in teaching has been recognised with the award of two national centres of excellence and four subjects reached grade 5 of the last research assessments: biomedical and biomolecular studies, cosmology, European studies and Slavonic studies. No former polytechnic managed more, and three grade 4s in that exercise left 45 per cent of the researchers in the top three of the seven categories. Every faculty was involved in research, and the 38 per cent of academics entered for the assessment was among the most in the new universities.

Graduate employment is healthy, especially for a university where a high proportion of the students take arts subjects. Languages are Portsmouth's traditional strength – one student in five takes a language course at some level – and the facilities rival those of many traditional universities. About 1,000 Portsmouth students go abroad for part of their course, and at least as many come from the Continent. French achieved a near perfect teaching score and its research was rated internationally outstanding. However, it is in health subjects that the university's reputation has been growing most obviously. A national teaching centre

reflects the broader range of subjects available in recent years. The new School of Professionals Complementary to Dentistry is one example of this. A £4-million building houses one of the first new dental education facilities in England for 50 years. Other additions to the portfolio of degree courses include subjects as diverse as dental hygiene and dental therapy, counter fraud and criminal justice studies and watersports science.

Portsmouth leapt from halfway into the top 15 in the latest National Student Survey, with extremely high levels of satisfaction in history and archaeology, sports science and politics. Teaching quality assessments were variable, but there was a marked improvement in later years of the cycle. Pharmacy recorded a maximum score, while education and politics, radiography and psychology all came close. Portsmouth academics have won National Teaching Fellowships in three of the last six years and, in addition to the health centre, the university is to lead on the development of teaching Foundation degrees.

The main Guildhall campus, dotted around the city centre, has undergone extensive redevelopment with the establishment of a University Quarter. The £11-million library complex, integrated into its 1970s predecessor, was voted the best new building in the city. Earlier developments included the aluminium-clad St

---

Winston Churchill Avenue
Portsmouth
Hampshire PO1 2UP
023 9284 8484
info.centre@port.ac.uk
www.port.ac.uk
www.upsu.net

The Times Rankings
Overall Ranking: 61

Student satisfaction:	=39	(75%)
Research quality:	=58	(1.7)
Entry standards:	=67	(272)
Student–staff ratio:	=77	(19.4)
Services & facilities/student:	81	(£917)
Expected completion rate:	65	(81.4%)
Good honours:	91	(49.3%)
Graduate prospects:	53	(65.4%)

Michael's Building and the eco-friendly Portland Building, with its solar panels. The business school has moved into a new £12-million building on the main campus. Other new facilities include a £2.5-million sports science building that houses laboratories, a swimming flume and two British Olympic Medical Centre accredited climatic chambers. A fully equipped newsroom has been provided to service the new journalism course, as part of a wider extension and refurbishment of facilities for media studies and art and design.

Teaching in all subjects is now concentrated on the Guildhall campus, while much of the residential stock are a couple of miles away at Langstone. A £6.5-million student centre caters for the multicultural population of the university with alcohol-free areas, an international students' bar and a family area for students with children. Modernised sport, exercise and fitness facilities at St Paul's include resistance and cardiovascular training gyms, dance studios and a sports hall.

Applications were up by 5 per cent in 2007 and remained healthy in 2008, when other universities were hit by the cut in choices per candidate. More than a quarter of the undergraduates come from working-class homes, although this is still less than the national average for the subjects and entry qualifications. Efforts are being made to broaden the intake further through an award-winning membership club that introduces teenagers to higher education through workshops, holiday courses and access to university facilities. The projected dropout rate of nearly 18 per cent is only just above the university's benchmark.

Portsmouth has a larger working-class population and more deprivation than some applicants may realise. But the new 170-metre Spinnaker Tower is already a landmark and the city has a vibrant student pub and club scene to supplement a popular students' union. The cost of living is not as high as at many southern universities, and the sea is close at hand. Hall places are offered to 90 per cent of first years and the university runs "secure a home" days at the beginning of September to help the remaining new arrivals with house-hunting.

Undergraduate Fees and Bursaries
- Fees for UK/EU students: £3,145
- International student fees: £7,100–£9,650
- Bursary on full grant: £900
- Bursaries on partial grant: household income up to £32K: £600.
- Scholarships based on circumstances or by competition. For full details see the university's website: www.port.ac.uk/money

Students

Undergraduates:	12,970	(2,605)
Postgraduates:	1,575	(2,455)
Mature students:	13.8%	
Overseas students:	9.8%	
Applications per place:	5.0	
From state-sector schools:	93.8%	
From working-class homes:	28.0%	

For detailed information about fees, grants and bursaries and how they work, see chapter 7.

Accommodation

Number of places and costs refer to 2008–09
University-provided places: about 2,944
Percentage catered: 24.8%
Catered costs: £86–£110 a week (36 weeks).
Self-catered costs: £72–£113 a week (36 weeks).
First years are guaranteed accommodation, subject to terms and conditions.
International students: as above.
Contact: Student.housing@port.ac.uk

Queen Margaret University

Scotland's first new university of the 21st century got a new campus to match, when Queen Margaret University moved into gleaming new premises in Musselburgh, to the southeast of Edinburgh, in September 2007. The "campus in the park", as it has been dubbed, was designed in consultation with students, and is only six minutes by train from the city centre. The two main campuses from college days, in Corstorphine and Leith, are being sold, but drama courses will remain at Edinburgh's Gateway Theatre to ensure that the university retains a foothold in the city centre.

Named after Saint Margaret, the 11th-century Queen of Scotland, the institution dates back to 1875 and was originally a school of cookery for women. The college had been awarding its own degrees since 1992, but was too small to qualify for university status. Now that it has achieved that ambition, Queen Margaret is by no means out of place in its new company. Easily the best-placed of last year's new entrants, it finished higher in our League Table than many former polytechnics. Average entry scores are the highest among its peer group and the university registers a series of good scores on other measures.

With just over 5,200 students, Queen Margaret is the smallest university in Scotland and it says that it is likely to remain so. The strategic plan promises that the new university will be "smart, innovative and very clearly focused" to compensate for the limitations of size. Three quarters of the students are female, seven out of ten of them from north of the border. Nearly 3,000 students are in the health sciences faculty, with social sciences and media, followed in terms of size by business and enterprise, the other main areas. The smaller School of Drama and the Creative Industries combines the conservatoire and university traditions, providing training for aspiring performers, directors, administrators and critics.

Health is an area of particular strength: Queen Margaret achieved the highest research ratings in Scotland in this area and offers courses in an unusually broad range of subjects, from dietetics, podiatry and audiology, to art therapy, music therapy, and health psychology. There is also a specialism in international health care, with students in Angola, Guatemala, Uganda, Ethiopia, Gambia, India and Cuba. Other international programmes run in Singapore, Egypt, Saudi Arabia, Greece and Switzerland.

The granting of university status came too late to boost applications in 2007 – although there was a 2.4 per cent increase

---

Queen Margaret University Drive
Musselburgh EH21 6UU
0131 474 0000
admissions@qmu.ac.uk
www.qmu.ac.uk
www.qmusu.org.uk

The Times Rankings
Overall Ranking: =68

Student satisfaction:	–	(–)
Research quality:	=66	(1.5)
Entry standards:	58	(286)
Student–staff ratio:	=93	(20.2)
Services & facilities/student:	=91	(£831)
Expected completion rate:	83	(77.7%)
Good honours:	59	(58.5%)
Graduate prospects:	43	(69.8%)

in any case – but Queen Margaret might have hoped for better figures at the start of 2008. The projected dropout rate of nearly 20 per cent had worsened in the latest survey, having been better than average for Scotland and easily the best at the new universities north of the border in previous years. Almost one undergraduate in three comes from a working-class home and roughly one in five is from an area with little history of higher education. Over 30 per cent of first-year undergraduates are over the age of 21 and half of them are over 30.

There are 800 residential places on the new campus, 500 of them reserved for undergraduates. An impressive learning resource centre is open 24 hours a day, and other features include a student union building, indoor and outdoor sports facilities, a variety of catering outlets and landscaped gardens with a range of environmental features. Queen Margaret claims that the campus is the "greenest" at any new university in Scotland – a high priority among the students. The campus has already won an award for sustainable design.

Undergraduate Fees and Bursaries
- Scottish-domiciled and EU students: no fees payable.
- Non-Scottish UK-domiciled student fees: £1,775 a year.
- International student fees: £8,800–£9,700
- Scholarships based on circumstances or by competition. For full details see the university's website: www.qmu.ac.uk/ prospective_students/funding.htm

Students

Undergraduates:	3,075	(1,055)
Postgraduates:	420	(730)
Mature students:	31.9%	
Overseas students:	14.5%	
Applications per place:	6.6	
From state-sector schools:	91.9%	
From working-class homes:	28.4%	

For detailed information about fees, grants and bursaries and how they work, see chapter 7.

Accommodation

Number of places and costs refer to 2008–09
University-provided places: 800
Percentage catered: 0%
Self-catered costs: £3,640 (40 weeks) to £4,550 (50 weeks).
First years are guaranteed accommodation.
Residential and age restrictions apply.
International students: guaranteed housing.
Contact: accommodation@qmu.ac.uk
www.qmu.ac.uk/services/
student_accommodation.htm

Queen Mary, University of London

More than £150 million has been spent developing London University's East End base into a broadly based institution of 13,000 students. Professor Adrian Smith, Queen Mary's Principal, believes it has "punched below its weight" at times, and is trying to put that right with a higher profile and impressive new facilities. Queen Mary is ranked among the top 150 universities in the world by *Times Higher Education*/QS, and now has the capital's most extensive self-contained campus.

A new state-of-the-art learning resource centre with 24-hour access opened in 2003 and a new student village with almost 2,000 en-suite rooms followed in 2004. More residences and an arts quarter, containing research facilities, a conference centre, drama studio and teaching space, were completed in 2006. A £15-million humanities building is due to open in September 2008 and a biosciences innovation centre is already under construction, next door to the £44-million Blizard Building – the striking new home of Barts and The London School of Medicine and Dentistry, in Whitechapel.

The modern setting is a far cry from the People's Palace, which first used the site to bring education to the Victorian masses, but there is still a community programme as well as conventional teaching and research. The arts-based Westfield College and scientific Queen Mary came together in 1989, but it took time to mould the new institution and overcome financial difficulties. The sale of Westfield's Hampstead base released the necessary capital to begin to modernise the Mile End Road campus.

Already London University's fourth largest unit, Queen Mary is expected to carry on growing. It is one of London's designated points of expansion in the sciences, although its strength is more obvious on the arts side, which boasts a clutch of high-profile academics. The college is leading a national initiative to boost the number of maths graduates.

Applications rose by more than 7 per cent in 2006, despite top-up fees, and there was another increase at the start of the following year. There has been consistent success in attracting overseas students, who make full use of a unit specialising in English as a foreign language. A strategic alliance with City University covers teaching and research initiatives in areas such as engineering, health and history.

Teaching ratings improved after a patchy start. Dentistry produced the only perfect score, with politics and modern languages close behind. English, history

---

Mile End Road
London E1 4NS
0800 376 1800 (admissions)
admissions@qmul.ac.uk
www.qmul.ac.uk
www.qmsu.org

The Times Rankings
Overall Ranking: 37

Student satisfaction:	=39	(75%)
Research quality:	=24	(4.7)
Entry standards:	=38	(340)
Student–staff ratio:	=10	(12.8)
Services & facilities/student:	35	(£1,173)
Expected completion rate:	32	(88.5%)
Good honours:	=47	(60.8%)
Graduate prospects:	21	(75.1%)

and archaeology produced the best results in the first National Student Satisfaction survey, and the Quality Assurance Agency had already given the college a good overall report in its first institutional audit. Iberian and Latin American languages, law and linguistics were the only subjects rated internationally outstanding for research in the 2001 assessments, but another 13 reached grade 5, leaving almost half of the researchers in the top two categories of seven. The proportion of academics entered for the exercise, at nine out of ten, was among the highest at any university.

The majority of undergraduates take at least one course in departments other than their own, under the modular course system. Most degrees are organised in units to allow maximum flexibility. Interdisciplinary study has always been encouraged: for example, medics can choose selected modules in English and drama. The medical school is to house a national teaching centre for clinical and communications skills. There is a flourishing exchange programme, which includes universities in the United States and Japan, as well as Europe. Each student has an adviser to guide them through the possibilities. Language students can use the University of London Institute, in Paris, while students at Beijing's University of Posts and Telecommunications can take double degrees (awarded by their own institution and Queen Mary) without leaving China.

Queen Mary attracts a socially diverse intake: almost a third of the undergraduates come from the two lowest socio-economic classes, many of them from local ethnic groups. Social life centres on the campus, which features a newly refurbished students' union with a subsidised health and fitness centre and a new bar, and the West End is easily accessible by tube. Students welcome the relatively low prices (for the capital) in East London, which has more to offer than many expect when they apply.

Undergraduate Fees and Bursaries

- Fees for UK/EU students: £3,145
- International student fees: £8,850–£14,250 £23,350 (clinical)
- Bursary on full grant: £1,050
- Bursaries on partial grant: household income up to £34.6K: £839.
- Scholarships based on circumstances or by competition. For full details see the university's website: www.qmul.ac.uk/undergraduate/feesfinance

---

Students

Undergraduates:	9,255	(95)
Postgraduates:	2,045	(1,185)
Mature students:	17.1%	
Overseas students:	15.8%	
Applications per place:	6.7	
From state-sector schools:	83.6%	
From working-class homes:	32.4%	

For detailed information about fees, grants and bursaries and how they work, see chapter 7.

Accommodation

Number of places and costs refer to 2007–08
University-provided places: 2,506
Percentage catered: 8.9%
Catered costs: £117–£126 a week.
Self-catered costs: £83.72–£113.40 a week.
First years giving Queen Mary as first choice get priority, if terms and conditions are met. Residential restrictions apply.
International students given priority if conditions are met and includes distance.
Contact: residences@qmul.ac.uk

Queen's University, Belfast

Generally regarded as Northern Ireland's premier university, Queen's became a member of the Russell Group of leading UK research institutions in 2006. The university is investing £259 million in new staff and improved facilities to improve its research performance, raise entry standards and regain the international standing it enjoyed before the Troubles. Research grades improved in the last assessment exercise: although mechanical engineering was again the only subject rated internationally outstanding, 15 of the 40 subject areas reached the next grade. An expensive recruitment programme across all three faculties is designed to reap more rewards in 2008.

Almost £190 million is being spent on capital projects, the centerpiece of which will be a £45-million new library, said to be one of the most ambitious building projects in Northern Ireland, which is due for completion in 2009. The university's vision for the future also includes improvements in student facilities: a student village, also costing £45 million, has replaced the existing tower block residences with three-storey self-catering "villas". A new student guidance centre is bringing services together at the heart of the campus. The students' union has been refurbished and a £7-million extension to

the physical education centre opened in 2007.

Applications have been patchy in recent years: the demand for places rose in 2007, but there was a substantial fall at the official deadline for courses beginning in 2008. Queen's was one of four university colleges for the whole of Ireland in the 19th century, and still draws students from all over the island. The aim now is to revive demand from mainland Britain and increase the number of overseas students. A variety of international agreements have been forged in the United States, Malaysia, China and India.

Teaching assessments showed the university's all-round strength: none of the 18 areas inspected after 1996–97 yielded less than 21 points out of 24. Dentistry, economics, electronic engineering, pharmacy and psychology all achieved maximum points, as did education at St Mary's and Stranmillis colleges (both associated with Queen's). The university has done well in the first three National Student Surveys. It was on the fringe of the top 20 in 2007, with particularly good results in medical science and pharmacy.

The university district, which is among the most attractive in Belfast, is one of the city's main cultural and recreational areas. Queen's runs a highly successful arts festival each November, opened a new art gallery in 2001 and has the only full-time

---

University Road
Belfast BT7 1NN
028 9097 2727 (admissions)
admissions@qub.ac.uk
www.qub.ac.uk
www.qubsu.org

The Times Rankings
Overall Ranking: =31

Student satisfaction:	=18	(77%)
Research quality:	=37	(4.3)
Entry standards:	30	(364)
Student–staff ratio:	=31	(15.3)
Services & facilities/student:	31	(£1,222)
Expected completion rate:	41	(86.6%)
Good honours:	24	(70.3%)
Graduate prospects:	17	(76.1%)

university cinema in the UK – one of the best in Ireland. Another £2 million has been invested in arts facilities recently, the lion's share of the cash going into a new studio theatre. More teaching accommodation has been added, with better access for the disabled, and the university's great hall has had a £2.5-million refurbishment, courtesy of the university's own foundation.

Courses at Queen's are modular and semesters have been introduced. Students are encouraged to take language programmes from a unique "virtual" language laboratory, which provides online tuition from any computer in the university. IT facilities are good: Queen's was the first institution to meet the national target of providing at least one computer workstation for every five undergraduate students. An unusually large proportion of graduates go on to further study, which does Queen's no harm in the employment league.

Strictly non-denominational teaching is enshrined in a charter which has guaranteed student representation and equal rights for women since 1908. The charter even precluded the teaching of theology – this is done through a network of four associated colleges.

Nightlife has returned to the city centre, but the social scene is still concentrated on the students' union and the surrounding area. Sports facilities, which include a university hut in the Mourne mountains, are of a high standard and are being expanded. The university runs academies for rugby and Gaelic sports, which have strong external links. Numerous Queen's players are selected at club, provincial and national levels. First-years are guaranteed university accommodation and there is plenty of reasonably priced private housing for other years, although there have been tensions between students and residents of the most popular area.

Undergraduate Fees and Bursaries

- Fees for UK/EU students: £3,145
- International student fees: £8,550–£11,576
  £21,830 (clinical)
- Bursary on full grant: £1,125
- Bursaries on partial grant: household income up to £22.9K £600; up to £32K: £100 for sports or books.
- Scholarships based on circumstances or by competition. For full details see the university's website: www.qub.ac.uk/home/TuitionFeesandStudentSupportArrangements200809/

Students		
Undergraduates:	13,385	(5,310)
Postgraduates:	2,085	(3,355)
Mature students:	16.8%	
Overseas students:	5.0%	
Applications per place:	5.8	
From state-sector schools:	99.5%	
From working-class homes:	34.4%	

For detailed information about fees, grants and bursaries and how they work, see chapter 7.

Accommodation

Number of places and costs refer to 2008–09
University-provided places: over 2,000
Percentage catered: 0%
Self-catered costs: £60.00–£86.31 a week.
First-year students have priority.
International students are given priority.
Contact: accommodation@qub.ac.uk

University of Reading

Assessments in both teaching and research have demonstrated an all-round strength that may have surprised those who knew Reading primarily for its highly regarded agricultural and environmental courses. The university was ranked among the top 200 in the world in 2007 and previously achieved top scores for teaching in subjects as diverse as film, theatre and television studies, nursing, philosophy and psychology. There have been good results, too, in the first three National Student Surveys, putting Reading in the top 20 for satisfaction levels. English, the performing arts and physical geography and environmental science were the top performers in 2007.

Several of the successes came in subjects added when the university took in Bulmershe College, which provided a second campus near the original 320-acre parkland site on the outskirts of Reading. Facilities for meteorology, management, agriculture, archaeology and psychology were upgraded in the 1990s and the university continues to invest extensively in its infrastructure. A new School of Pharmacy opened in 2005 and sports facilities have been extended. A multi-million pound student services building, providing a one-stop-shop for student support and welfare, followed in 2007.

Reading was the only university established between the two world wars, having been Oxford's extension college for the first part of the last century, but the attractive main campus now has a modern feel. There are also 2,000 acres of university-owned farmland nearby for teaching and research in agricultural and plant sciences. The university's location, a bus ride away from Heathrow Airport, and an international reputation in key areas for developing countries have always ensured a healthy flow of overseas students. The creation of a new business school, through a forthcoming merger with Henley Management College, should bring a further boost.

Applications recovered in 2008 after two disappointing years. About one undergraduate in six is from an independent school and the proportion from areas without a tradition of higher education is among the lowest in the country, but the university is close to national averages for its subjects when its location is taken into account. The retention rate exceeds national norms, with just over 7 per cent of undergraduates who started courses in 2004 expected to leave without a qualification.

The university is involved with a number of centres of excellence in teaching and learning, including one focusing on career management skills.

Whiteknights
PO Box 217
Reading RG6 6AH
0118 378 8618/9
student.recruitment@
  reading.ac.uk
www.reading.ac.uk
www.rusu.co.uk

The Times Rankings
Overall Ranking: =31

Student satisfaction:	=12	(78%)
Research quality:	=21	(4.9)
Entry standards:	=38	(340)
Student–staff ratio:	41	(16.2)
Services & facilities/student:	59	(£1,012)
Expected completion rate:	24	(91.7%)
Good honours:	21	(71.7%)
Graduate prospects:	61	(63.3%)

All undergraduates take career management skills modules that contribute five credits towards their degree classification. The online system, which has 200 web pages of advice, exercises and information, has been bought by 30 other universities and colleges. Sessions are delivered jointly by academics and careers advisors, with input from alumni and leading employers.

Successes in the last Research Assessment Exercise were well spread. Archaeology, English, meteorology, Italian and psychology were all rated internationally outstanding for the second time in a row, with 58 per cent of the academics entered for assessment placed in the top two categories of seven.

The town – only a short walk from the campus – may not be the most fashionable, but it has plenty of nightlife and an award-winning shopping centre. It also offers plenty of temporary and part-time employment opportunities for students. London is easily accessible by train, but the cost of living is on a par with the capital. More than 4,500 residential places include a landscaped student village, while first-rate sports provision includes accessible rowing and sailing boathouses, scholar-ships and an academy. Teams have a good record in inter-university competitions and the campus has been chosen as a possible pre-Olympics training camp for basketball and fencing.

Students praise the social scene, although the high proportion from the South East means that many go home at the weekends. The large students' union had a £500,000 refit in 2007, improving and extending its popular main venue. The union has been voted among the best in Britain, and has won numerous awards including Best Bar None status for encouraging safe drinking. Students who live in town can make use of the free night bus service to take them back into Reading.

Undergraduate Fees and Bursaries

- Fees for UK/EU students: £3,145
- International student fees: £9,350–£11,300
- Bursary on full grant: £1,350
- Bursaries on partial grant: household income up to £35K: £900; up to £45K: £450.
- Scholarships based on circumstances or by competition. For full details see the university's website: www.rdg.ac.uk/studentfinance/

Students

Undergraduates:	8,610	(2,025)
Postgraduates:	1,955	(2,085)
Mature students:	11.2%	
Overseas students:	9.3%	
Applications per place:	5.5	
From state-sector schools:	83.6%	
From working-class homes:	24.0%	

For detailed information about fees, grants and bursaries and how they work, see chapter 7.

Accommodation

Number of places and costs refer to 2007–08
University-provided places: about 4,500
Percentage catered: 37%
Catered costs: £114–£153 (30 weeks).
Self-catered costs: £65–£115 (37 weeks).
First-year undergraduate students are guaranteed a place if conditions are met.
International students: given priority if conditions are met.
Contact: StudentHelp@reading.ac.uk

The Robert Gordon University

So close are links with the North Sea oil and gas industries that Robert Gordon has dubbed itself the Energy University, but nursing and the health sciences are now equally important. The university's mission statement has switched the emphasis from vocational to professional education; the creative industries are also a growth area.

There is a full portfolio of courses in business, health, design and engineering. Flexible programmes, with credit accumulation and transfer, make for easy movement in and out of the university for an often mobile local workforce. Work placements, lasting up to a year, are the norm, helping an employment record that has been Scotland's best for several years and consistently one of the leaders in the UK.

Efforts to extend access beyond the normal higher education catchment have produced a diverse student population, with more than a third of the undergraduates coming from working-class homes and almost a fifth from areas sending few students to higher education. The dropout rate has improved over recent years, but the 18 per cent projection in the latest survey is still higher than the UK average for RGU's subjects and entry qualifications.

Only two of the subjects assessed in the main rounds of teaching assessment were rated Excellent, but a majority of the rest were considered Highly Satisfactory. Just 120 academic staff were entered for the last Research Assessment Exercise and none of the subjects featured in the top three of the seven categories. But the university has committed itself to winning international recognition for applied research in the current decade.

There are now about 140 degrees to choose from. There was serious consideration of a merger with Aberdeen University in 2002. Although this was eventually abandoned, collaboration between the two institutions continues. Students from the city's two universities mix easily, and there is healthy academic rivalry in some areas, despite the obvious differences.

Named after an 18th-century philanthropist, Robert Gordon has two sites around the city and an attractive field study centre at Cromarty, in the Highlands. The historic Schoolhill site adjoins Aberdeen art gallery in the city centre, while Garthdee, where 70 per cent of undergraduates are taught, is a mile away overlooking the River Dee. The university has spent £100 million on its buildings and facilities, with Sir Norman Foster designing the business school, while other recent developments made room for art, architecture and the faculty of health and social care (with 3,000 students). Another £110 million of improvements is planned for Garthdee over the next few years.

Schoolhill
Aberdeen AB10 1FR
01224 262728 (enquiries)
admissions@rgu.ac.uk
www.rgu.ac.uk
www.rgunion.co.uk

ABERDEEN
Edinburgh
Belfast
London
Cardiff

Like most new universities, especially in Scotland, RGU recruits most of its students locally, 60 per cent of them female. However, overseas recruitment has been growing sharply and the overall demand for places has been stronger than at most universities north of the border. The Scottish Government has provided £500,000 in European funding to help more people from disadvantaged communities to take courses. The university already offers four-week intensive access programmes in mathematics, engineering, chemistry and computing during August and September for applicants who narrowly miss the entry requirements to top up their qualifications. If they prefer, prospective students may take access units in these subjects by distance learning, using study packs and with the support of an assigned tutor. The scheme, which runs all year round, is recommended for aspiring students without traditional academic backgrounds.

The university is pinning many of its hopes on new technology. An award-winning virtual campus was launched with an online course in e-business for postgraduates, again with European funding. It also enables management undergraduates to receive course materials via an intranet, and other degree and short courses are available.

Aberdeen is a long way to go for English students, but train and air links are excellent, and the city regularly features in the top ten for quality of life. An £11-million sports and leisure centre opened in 2005, providing a centre of excellence for the region in hockey, as well as a 25-metre swimming pool, three gyms, a climbing wall and bouldering room, a café bar, three exercise studios and a large sports hall. Although private accommodation can be expensive, low prices in the students' union partially compensate, and there are enough residential places to guarantee accommodation to first years from outside the local area.

Undergraduate Fees and Bursaries

- Scottish-domiciled and EU students: no fees payable.
- Non-Scottish UK-domiciled student fees: £1,775 a year.
- International student fees: contact university.
- Scholarships based on circumstances or by competition. For full details see the university's website: www.rgu.ac.uk/stud_finance

Students

Undergraduates:	6,720	(2,160)
Postgraduates:	1,405	(2,700)
Mature students:	23.1%	
Overseas students:	10.0%	
Applications per place:	4.1	
From state-sector schools:	93.5%	
From working-class homes:	38.2%	

For detailed information about fees, grants and bursaries and how they work, see chapter 7.

Accommodation

Number of places and costs refer to 2008–09
University-provided places: 1,328
Percentage catered: 0%
Self-catered costs: £65–£86 a week.
All first-year students are eligible to apply for student accommodation. Residential restrictions apply.
International students: accommodation guaranteed.
Contact: accommodation@rgu.ac.uk
www.rgu.ac.uk/accommodation

Roehampton University

Roehampton is now making its mark as a university in its own right, after four years in a federation with Surrey University. There have been record intakes, despite rising entry scores. Although applications were down by more than the national average at the start of 2008, with the reduction in choices per applicant, there were still four candidates for every place. The university had bucked the national trend with increases both when top-up fees arrived and in the following year.

Roehampton, fully independent since 2004, is continuing to collaborate with Surrey on research projects and joint pro-grammes. It comprises four distinctive colleges, which still maintain some of the traditional ethos of their religious founda-tions: the Anglican Whitelands, the Roman Catholic Digby Stuart, the Methodist Southlands, and the Froebel, which follows the humanist teachings of Frederick Froebel. Students need not follow any of these denominations to enrol in the colleges. The university also has a Jewish resource centre and Muslim prayer rooms.

All four colleges are based in a 26-hectare campus, with stunning parkland and lakes, on or adjacent to Roehampton Lane. Whitelands moved from Putney in 2004 to the 18th-century mansion, Parkstead House, overlooking Richmond Park, which also houses the School of Human and Life Sciences. The buildings have been refurbished with IT facilities, student accommodation, laboratories and teaching space. The colleges all have their own bars and other leisure facilities, although they are open to all members of the university.

A new dance and PE building opened on the main campus in 2005. The institute had already spent £20 million relocating Southlands, providing a new site for the social sciences. Recent projects include a £4-million facility for the School of Arts, which opened in 2006, and a new national centre of excellence for teaching on citizenship education, human rights and social justice. A 15-year programme will bring further improvements, designed to enhance the student experience and provide an environment that can be enjoyed by the local community.

The four schools of Arts, Education, Human and Life Sciences, and Business and Social Sciences encourage inter-disciplinary work. Themes such as "creativity", "childhood", "wellbeing" and "social justice" are explored in two or more schools and permeate many of the university's activities. In line with the university's origins, education remains the largest subject area, accounting for more than a quarter of the students.

Anthropology and history were rated

Erasmus House
Roehampton Lane
London SW15 5PU
020 8392 3232 (enquiries)
enquiries@
  roehampton.ac.uk
www.roehampton.ac.uk
www.roehampton
  student.com

The Times Rankings
Overall Ranking: =86

Student satisfaction:	=84	(71%)
Research quality:	57	(1.9)
Entry standards:	103	(224)
Student–staff ratio:	=102	(21.0)
Services & facilities/student:	25	(£1,308)
Expected completion rate:	77	(79.5%)
Good honours:	80	(52.1%)
Graduate prospects:	93	(56.9%)

internationally outstanding in the last research assessments, with dance in the next-highest category, the music and dance component achieving the best possible score. Having entered 45 per cent of its academics for assessment – a higher figure than at any of the former polytechnics – Roehampton outperformed all of its new peer group in terms of average grades per member of staff. The Quality Assurance Agency has complimented Roehampton on the accessibility of academic staff to students and the positive ways in which they responded to student needs. However, the results from the 2007 National Student Survey were disappointing.

Teaching grades were respectable, rather than spectacular. Despite the predominance of arts students, biological sciences produced the best score, with psychology and linguistics close behind. A Work and Study Scheme gives local employees credit towards their degree for relevant tasks performed in the workplace. The programme is designed to help employers recruit and retain key staff, as well as helping those who cannot afford to study full time.

Nine out of ten undergraduates were educated in state schools and more than a third come from working-class homes. The projected dropout rate had been coming down, but the latest figures suggest that 20 per cent of students will fail to graduate in the expected time – significantly more than average for the university's courses and entry grades.

About 80 per cent of first years who want a hall place are offered one, with priority going to those who make Roehampton their first preference. Two new residences opened in 2005, adding 300 places to the residential stock. Rents are not cheap for those who miss out on a place or prefer the private sector, but students like the proximity of central London and the lively and attractive suburbs around Roehampton.

Undergraduate Fees and Bursaries

- Fees for UK/EU students: £3,145
- International student fees: £8,875
- Bursary on full grant: £500
- Bursaries on partial grant: £500
- Scholarships based on circumstances or by competition. For full details see the university's website: www.roehampton.ac.uk/admissions/finance/index.html

---

Students

Undergraduates:	6125	(595)
Postgraduates:	1035	(775)
Mature students:	25.0%	
Overseas students:	6.6%	
Applications per place:	4.1	
From state-sector schools:	94.0%	
From working-class homes:	34.3%	

For detailed information about fees, grants and bursaries and how they work, see chapter 7.

Accommodation

Number of places and costs refer to 2008–09
University-provided places: 1,600
Percentage catered: 12.5%
Catered costs: £125 a week
Self-catered costs: £86 (standard) – £104 (en suite) a week.
First years are given priority if conditions met. Local restrictions apply.
International students: guaranteed for first year
Contact: accommodation@roehampton.ac.uk

Royal Holloway, University of London

London University's "campus in the country" occupies 135 acres of woodland between Windsor Castle and Heathrow. The 600-bed Founder's Building, modelled on a French chateau and opened by Queen Victoria, is one of Britain's most remarkable university buildings. The merger with Bedford College, and the sale of Bedford's valuable site in Regent's Park, enabled Royal Holloway to embark on a major redevelopment of the campus, which has since been extended with a £100-million building programme. Recent projects have included a major new auditorium, extensions to the School of Management and other academic buildings, an extension to the main library and new student residences, which have been praised for their comfort and eco-friendly features.

Other developments include an expanded academic staff, better student services and a portfolio of scholarships and bursaries that pre-dated top-up fees. One offers free places or reduced fees to those who stay on for a postgraduate degree. The conversion of the huge Victorian boilerhouse into a performance space for drama and the establishment of formal links with institutions such as New York, Sydney and Yale universities, demonstrate that progress has not just been a matter of bricks and mortar. Closer to home, another link allows music students to take lessons at the Royal College of Music.

Both partners in the merger which formed the college were originally for women only, their legacy commemorated in the Bedford Centre for the History of Women. The arts and humanities still account for most of the top ratings, but the gender balance in the student population is now roughly equal. French, German, geography and music were considered internationally outstanding in the latest research assessments, when three quarters of the academics entered for assessment were in departments rated in the top two of seven categories. The successes placed Royal Holloway in the top dozen research institutions and have helped cement a place in the top 30 of *The Times* League Table.

Royal Holloway is not just about the arts: the college offers a science foundation year at further education colleges in the region, and the balance of disciplines is gradually shifting. Psychology and biological sciences registered perfect scores in teaching assessments. All the sciences were judged nationally outstanding for research in 2001 and physics produced the best results in the

University of London
Egham
Surrey TW20 0EX
01784 443350 (admissions)
admissions@rhul.ac.uk
www.rhul.ac.uk
www.su.rhul.ac.uk

The Times Rankings		
Overall Ranking: 30		
Student satisfaction:	=55	(74%)
Research quality:	=12	(5.2)
Entry standards:	=31	(361)
Student–staff ratio:	=25	(14.7)
Services & facilities/student:	29	(£1,244)
Expected completion rate:	36	(88.2%)
Good honours:	36	(66.4%)
Graduate prospects:	49	(66.9%)

first National Student Survey. All 18 departments encourage inter-disciplinary work, which is facilitated by a modular course structure with examina-tions at the end of every year. An Advanced Skills Programme, covering information technology, communication skills and foreign languages, further encourages breadth of study.

Immediate expansion plans centre on the college's areas of excellence, as well as on distance learning and research. Royal Holloway already offers e-degrees in classics, history, business management and postgraduate courses in information security and management to add to its University of London external programme. It is spearheading the development of the University of London Institute in Paris, allowing students to spend part of their course in France.

Applications for courses beginning in 2007 were up by more than 14 per cent, following good results in the first two national surveys of student satisfaction. The latest survey showed the geography students to be the most satisfied in the country. The college still draws a quarter of its undergraduates from independent schools, although the proportion coming from working-class homes has been rising. However, the ethnic mix is above average and a rise in the projected dropout rate to almost 12 per cent may turn out to be temporary, after several years of much better figures.

Over 2,900 students are in halls of residence, many of them in the Founder's Building itself. The college's green belt location at Egham, Surrey, 35 minutes from the centre of London by rail, ensures that social life is concentrated on an extended students' union. However, the West End is close for those determined to seek the high life. Sports facilities are good and have been upgraded recently – Royal Holloway claims to be "the University of London's best sporting college". A high proportion of students come from London and the Home Counties, so many go home weekends, but the lively students' union puts on entertainment and activities seven days a week.

Undergraduate Fees and Bursaries

- Fees for UK/EU students: £3,145
- International student fees: £11,555–£12,785
- Bursary on full grant: £750
- Bursaries on partial grant: household income up to £39.3K: £750.
- Scholarships based on circumstances or by competition. For full details see the university's website: www.rhul.ac.uk/prospective-students/finance/ug_Bursaries.html

Students

Undergraduates:	5,805	(155)
Postgraduates:	1,445	(925)
Mature students:	8.1%	
Overseas students:	26.2%	
Applications per place:	5.5	
From state-sector schools:	74.7%	
From working-class homes:	22.2%	

For detailed information about fees, grants and bursaries and how they work, see chapter 7.

Accommodation

Number of places and costs refer to 2007–08
University-provided places: 2,932
Percentage catered: 37%
Catered costs: £67–£112 a week.
Self-catered costs: £60–£120 a week.
First years are prioritised for accommodation provided conditions are met.
International students: non-EU students guaranteed accommodation.
Contact: Accommodation-Office@rhul.ac.uk

University of St Andrews

St Andrews was one of a handful of Scottish universities to join the National Student Survey in 2006 – and the impact has been dramatic. By registering one of the highest satisfaction levels at any university in *The Times* League Table, the results have helped restore the university's position as the leading institution north of the border and secure a place in the top five overall.

As the oldest Scottish university and the third oldest in Britain, St Andrews has long been both well known and fashionable among a mainly middle-class clientele. Applications were down by only 2.5 per cent at the official deadline for courses beginning in 2008, when the UK average, with the reduction in choices per applicant, was more than 7 per cent. Earlier increases – including a 44 per cent rise in one year – mean that are still more than eight applicants for every place.

With about 35 per cent of the students coming from south of the border, St Andrews has earned the nickname of Scotland's English university. But another 30 per cent come from 90 countries farther afield, giving the university a cosmopolitan feel. Fee concessions and exchange schemes have boosted applications, particularly in the United States, which provides nearly a quarter of first-year students on its own.

Peer assessments have shown that there is top quality behind the prestige. St Andrews has the best teaching and research grades in Scotland, as well as the lowest dropout rate. Uniquely, every subject assessed has been rated either Excellent or Highly Satisfactory for teaching, demonstrating quality across the board. Psychology and English were the only starred research departments, but 15 subjects on the next rung of the ladder put the university into the top ten in terms of the average per member of staff.

Nearly four in ten undergraduates come from independent schools, when the UK average for the university's courses and entry scores is less than a quarter. A dedicated Access Centre has been trying to broaden the intake, and a successful fundraising campaign is building up a bank of £3,000-a-year scholarships for students from poor homes. Only Oxford and Cambridge have a lower proportion of students from working-class backgrounds.

The town of St Andrews is steeped in history, as well as being the centre of the golfing world. The university at its heart accounts for about a third of the 18,000 inhabitants. There are close relations between town and gown, both cultural and social. New students ("bejants" and "bejantines") acquire third and fourth-year "parents" to ease them into university life, and on Raisin Monday give their academic

---

College Gate
North Street
St Andrews, Fife KY16 9AJ
01334 462150
admissions@
  st-andrews.ac.uk
www.st-andrews.ac.uk
www.yourunion.net

guardians a bottle of wine in return for a receipt in Latin, which can be written on anything. Another unusual feature is that all humanities students are awarded an MA rather than a BA.

Many of the main buildings date from the 15th and 16th centuries, but sciences are taught at the modern North Haugh site a few streets away. Everything is within walking distance, but bicycles are common. Although small, St Andrews offers a wide range of courses. The university's reputation has always rested primarily on the humanities, which acquired a £1.3-million research centre recently. An £8-million headquarters for the School of International Relations opened in 2006, with Europe's first Centre for Syrian Studies, an Institute of Iranian Studies and a Centre for Peace and Conflict Studies. St Andrews has the largest mediaeval history department in Britain and has now added film studies and sustainable development. But a full range of physical sciences is offered, with sophisticated lasers and the largest optical telescope in Britain.

An academic partnership with Dundee University is being developed in order to expand teaching and research in areas of common interest. A joint degree in electronics and optoelectronics was the first project, followed by shared teaching in medical education and health sciences, and the launch of a course pooling St Andrews'

excellence in art history and Dundee's flair for design.

Students do not come to St Andrews for the nightclubs, but there is no shortage of parties in a tight-knit community. The sports facilities are excellent and more than half of all students live in halls of residence, the latest of which was opened by Gordon Brown in 2007, providing self-catering accommodation for 920 students during term and three-star accommodation for golfers and other tourists in vacations. Features such as the grass roof, which acts as a heat insulator during the winter and a natural cooler during the summer months, made it the first university residence to be awarded the Green Tourism Business Scheme's Gold Award.

Undergraduate Bursaries and Scholarships

- Scottish-domiciled and EU students: no fees payable.
- Non-Scottish UK-domiciled student fees: £1,775 a year (£2,825 medicine).
- International student fees: £10,950; £17,300 (medicine)
- Scholarships based on circumstances or by competition. For full details see the university's website: www.st-andrews.ac.uk/ scholarships

---

Students

Undergraduates:	5,875	(1,065)
Postgraduates:	1,535	(490)
Mature students:	4.4%	
Overseas students:	30.0%	
Applications per place:	8.5	
From state-sector schools:	60.9%	
From working-class homes:	15.2%	

For detailed information about fees, grants and bursaries and how they work, see chapter 7.

Accommodation

Number of places and costs refer to 2007–08
University-provided places: 3,481
Percentage catered: 49%
Catered costs: £124–£169 a week.
Self-catered costs: £56–£122 a week.
Accommodation guaranteed for single entrant undergraduates if conditons are met.
Policy for international students: as above.
Contact: studacc@st-andrews.ac.uk

University of Salford

In the last five years, Salford has begun to slip below some of the new universities in *The Times* League Table. But consistently good graduate employment rates, carefully targeted courses and an emphasis on the university's location close to the centre of Manchester appeal to students. Applications were up by almost 9 per cent in 2007 and remained healthy the following year, in spite of the reduction in the number of choices allowed for each applicant.

The university is investing £150 million in new buildings and facilities, including upgraded libraries and new catering facilities in the students' union. Salford Law School opened in 2007 in a £10-million building featuring a Law Society-approved library. New acoustic laboratories opened in the same year, with a reverberation room capable of transforming the quality of sound and an anechoic chamber, which is said to be the quietest place in the world. Also new is the £22-million Mary Seacole building, which houses the Faculty of Health and Social Care.

Salford stresses its business links and modern portfolio of courses, including two-year Foundation degrees. The university does well on the Government's access measures: more than a third of the undergraduates come from working-class homes and almost a quarter are from areas sending few students to higher education. But the projected dropout rate has slipped again, to more than a quarter, in the latest statistics – well above the national average for the subjects and students' qualifications. A new Student Services Division has been charged with improving every aspect of student life, even planning events for students staying at Salford over the Christmas holiday closure.

Teaching quality grades improved ratings in the latter years of the cycle, with perfect scores for politics and biological sciences. Business and health subjects are now big recruiters. The university's growing involvement in health has seen the establishment of a national centre for prosthetics and orthotics, and a high reputation for the treatment of sports injuries. Another innovation was the launch of Europe's first nursing course for deaf students. There is also a degree in traditional Chinese medicine, with an acupuncture clinic, and a BA in journalism and war studies – the only undergraduate degree in the UK to combine the two disciplines.

Engineering is the university's traditional strength, attracting many of the 3,000 overseas students. Two thirds of courses offer work placements, half of them abroad and almost all counting towards degree classifications. The tradition of sandwich courses always

---

Salford
Greater Manchester M5 4WT
0161 295 4545
course-enquiries@
 salford.ac.uk
www.salford.ac.uk
www.salfordstudents.com

Edinburgh
Belfast
SALFORD
London
Cardiff

The Times Rankings
Overall Ranking: 83

Student satisfaction:	=84	(71%)
Research quality:	56	(2.1)
Entry standards:	=70	(269)
Student–staff ratio:	=69	(18.4)
Services & facilities/student:	80	(£923)
Expected completion rate:	103	(73.2%)
Good honours:	73	(54.1%)
Graduate prospects:	60	(63.5%)

serves Salford well in terms of graduate employment. A business enterprise support programme helps students set up their own businesses, providing entrepreneurship training and business skills, as well as a business mentor.

Online degrees have been introduced and the university has also made headlines with more unusual innovations, such as degrees in business economics with gambling studies, not to mention the appointment of Britain's first Professor of Pop Music. The university launched Salford Business School in 2006, formed from the merger of four existing schools and has several areas of expertise such as information management, operational research and gambling studies. Salford's extended range of courses meant that fewer than 40 per cent of the academics were entered for the latest Research Assessment Exercise, when the built environment and information management were the only areas considered internationally outstanding. European studies – another longstanding strength – again reached the second rung of the ladder and will benefit from a £1-million languages centre.

The university remains committed to research: it has established nine interdisciplinary research centres and a graduate school. It also led the way in formally recognising interaction with business and industry as of equal importance to teaching and research.

The modern landscaped campus, a haven of lawns and shrubberies along the River Irwell, is less than two miles from Manchester city centre and has a mainline railway station. The university also has its own TV and radio studios. The School of Media, Music and Performance plans to take full advantabe of the move by the BBC of production facilities to nearby Salford Quays.

Students like the friendly atmosphere and most of the residential places are either on campus or in a student village 15 minutes' walk away. This is important in an area where security is a big issue, one which the university has been addressing with the police and local authority.

Undergraduate Fees and Bursaries

- Fees for UK/EU students: £3,145
- International student fees: £8,400–£10,500
- Bursary on full grant: £310
- Bursaries on partial grant: subject and academic bursaries available.
- Scholarships based on circumstances or by competition. For full details see the university's website: www.salford.ac.uk/study/fees

Students

Undergraduates:	12,185	(3,320)
Postgraduates:	1,510	(2,875)
Mature students:	32.5%	
Overseas students:	7.5%	
Applications per place:	4.5	
From state-sector schools:	96.7%	
From working-class homes:	34.3%	

For detailed information about fees, grants and bursaries and how they work, see chapter 7.

Accommodation

Number of places and costs refer to 2008–09
University-provided places: 2,696 plus 541 managed by a specialist company
Percentage catered: 0%
Self-catered costs: £56.04–£78.57 (en suite); managed accommodation: £84–£90.
First years are guaranteed accommodation (terms and conditions apply).
International students: as above.
Contact: www.accommodation.salford.ac.uk/

School of Oriental and African Studies, London

As the major national centre for the study of Africa and Asia, SOAS has a global reputation in subjects relating to two thirds of the world's population. Originally only a specialist Oriental college, the school now covers a much wider range of subjects. The library, with nearly one million volumes, periodicals and audiovisual materials in 400 languages, attracts scholars from around the world. It is in the top 50 in the *Times Higher Education/QS* world rankings for the arts and humanities and has been strengthening its academic staff in a variety of disciplines.

The 4,000 students come from some 110 countries, although two thirds are from Britain and the rest of the EU – and the proportion is higher still among the undergraduates. However, the school has a much wider portfolio of courses than its name would suggest, with 300 degree combinations on offer. Degrees are available in familiar subjects such as law, music, history or the social sciences, but with a different emphasis. There is also a more limited portfolio of Foundation degrees and language courses. Over 5,000 students (from inside and outside SOAS) take language courses at a variety of levels.

Student recruitment is on the rise, especially among independent school candidates, who account for almost a third of the British undergraduates. An increase in student numbers of 33 per cent was one of the largest at any university in 2005 and this was followed by another rise of nearly 18 per cent as top-up fees arrived, but applications were down by more than the national average at the official deadline for courses beginning in 2008. The main growth area is postgraduate courses, which have helped to tackle a financial deficit. In addition, more than 2,400 students are now taking distance learning courses, mainly outside the UK. Numbers have risen with the transfer of University of London postgraduate programmes previously taught by Imperial College, making SOAS one of the world's largest providers of distance learning at this level.

Postgraduates are attracted by a research record which saw history rated internationally outstanding in the last assessments. Seven of the 11 subject areas were placed in the top two categories. Teaching assessments have also been good, a maximum score for history of art leading the way, with East and South Asian studies close behind. The final assessments produced solid results in politics and economics.

Nearly all students take advantage of the unique opportunities for learning one

---

Thornhaugh Street
Russell Square
London WC1H 0XG
020 7898 4301/4306
study@soas.ac.uk
www.soas.ac.uk
www.soasunion.org

The Times Rankings
Overall Ranking: 24

Student satisfaction:	=84	(71%)
Research quality:	=10	(5.3)
Entry standards:	28	(368)
Student–staff ratio:	3	(10.5)
Services & facilities/student:	5	(£1,746)
Expected completion rate:	52	(84.4%)
Good honours:	17	(73.4%)
Graduate prospects:	45	(68.0%)

of the 50 languages on offer. There is also an option of spending one, two or three terms of a degree course in one of the school's many partner universities in Africa or Asia. The school was chosen to house a national teaching centre for languages. More than a fifth of the British undergraduates come from working-class homes – less than the national average for the school's subjects. The dropout rate has fluctuated over recent years, but was back down to less than 16 per cent in the latest statistics, just above the UK average for the subjects and entry qualifications at SOAS.

The school is located in Bloomsbury, but in 2001 opened a second campus at Vernon Square, Islington. Less than a mile from the main Russell Square site, and adjacent to the student residences, it provides student-orientated facilities such as an internet café. The centrepiece of the main campus is an airy, modern building with gallery space as well as teaching accommodation, a gift from the Sultan of Brunei. There is no separate students' union building, although the students do have their own bar and catering facilities. The well-equipped and under-used University of London Union is close at hand, with swimming pool, gym and bars. The West End is also on the doorstep.

The 769 residential places, which accommodate first-year students, are within 15 minutes' walk of the school.

Another 119 places are planned in flats in Vernon Square. However, the school has few of its own sports facilities and the outdoor pitches are remote, with no time set aside from lectures. The ethnic and national mix has led to inevitable tensions at times, but SOAS is small enough for most students to know each other, at least by sight, and the atmosphere is normally friendly. Students tend to be highly committed – not surprising since many will return to positions of influence in developing countries – and the variety of cultures makes for lively debate.

Undergraduate Fees and Bursaries

- Fees for UK/EU students: £3,145
- International student fees: £11,460
- Bursary on full grant: £740
- Bursaries on partial grant: household income £25K–£39.3K: £420.
- Scholarships based on circumstances or by competition. For full details see the university's website: www.soas.ac.uk/soasnet/adminservices/registry/scholarships/

Students

Undergraduates:	2,600	(80)
Postgraduates:	1,225	(825)
Mature students:	22.4%	
Overseas students:	37.4%	
Applications per place:	6.5	
From state-sector schools:	70.1%	
From working-class homes:	20.9%	

For detailed information about fees, grants and bursaries and how they work, see chapter 7.

Accommodation

Number of places and costs refer to 2007–08
University-provided places: 769 (Sanctuary Management Services); 167 (intercollegiate)
Percentage catered: 10%
Catered costs: £108.01–£132.44 a week.
Self-catered costs: £119.54–£141.89 a week.
First years cannot be guaranteed accommodation.
International students: as above, although they are a high priority.
Contact: student@sanctuary-housing.co.uk

University of Sheffield

Sheffield has slipped out of the top 20 in *The Times* League Table after losing the benefit of some of the best grades in the early rounds of teaching assessment, but its stock remains high both in the academic world and among students. Student numbers rose by 14 per cent in three years, to more than 24,000, and there has been a corresponding increase in academic staff across all seven faculties. A major new learning facility, the £23-million Information Commons, opened in 2007 and operates 24 hours a day, providing 1,300 study spaces and 500 computers linked to the campus network, as well as 110,000 books and periodicals.

Only one subject (medicine) scored fewer than 20 points out of 24 for teaching quality, while three quarters of the staff assessed for the last Research Assessment Exercise were placed in the top two categories. Nine starred departments were spread around medicine, science, engineering and social science. The top performers were electrical and electronic engineering, the biosciences, politics and Russian, each of which achieved maximum scores for both teaching and research. The university houses national teaching centres for the arts and social sciences and for enterprise learning. The medical school was allocated more places after a re-inspection found improvements, and it is now the most popular in Britain in terms of applications per place and was the best performer in the first National Student Survey. Sheffield produced some of the best results among the big city universities in 2007, with students in the biological and physical sciences particularly satisfied.

Research excellence, which takes pride of place in Sheffield's mission statement, has boosted the university's facilities: £100 million for biological and physical sciences, medicine, engineering and social sciences, and £15 million on an advanced manufacturing research centre in which Boeing is the senior partner, which forms the hub of a technology park. The university is the lead institution for systems engineering, smart materials and stem-cell technology in a research network of European, American and Chinese universities.

Sheffield has always enjoyed a high ratio of applications to places, despite expanding through much of the 1990s. There are more than 3,500 overseas students from 128 countries. But the overall number of applicants rose by a modest 2.7 per cent in 2007 and dropped by more than the national average when the number of choices per applicant was cut in 2008.

The academic buildings are concentrated in an area about a mile from the city centre on the affluent west side of Sheffield, with most university flats and halls of

---

Western Bank
Sheffield S10 2TN
0114 222 1255 (enquiries)
www.shef.ac.uk/asksheffield
www.shef.ac.uk
www.shef.ac.uk/union

The Times Rankings
Overall Ranking: 22

Student satisfaction:	=26	(76%)
Research quality:	=29	(4.5)
Entry standards:	=15	(403)
Student–staff ratio:	=22	(14.5)
Services & facilities/student:	42	(£1,140)
Expected completion rate:	=18	(92.4%)
Good honours:	19	(71.9%)
Graduate prospects:	=28	(73.7%)

residence a little further into the suburbs. Recent developments mean that the main university precinct now stretches into an almost unbroken mile-long "campus". The former Jessop Hospital, an imposing building at the heart of the campus, has been purchased by the university for use by academic departments, while another new site adjacent to the engineering departments will house high-tech multidisciplinary facilities.

The intake is more diverse than at most leading universities – nearly 84 per cent come from state schools or colleges – and more than one undergraduate in five comes from a working-class home. A famously lively social scene is based on the student union's extended facilities – twice voted the best in Britain – but also takes full advantage of the city's burgeoning club life. In addition to its own popular facilities, the union owns a pub in the western suburb where most students live. Town–gown relations are much better and the crime rate lower than in most big cities. The university claims the highest proportion of graduates staying in the city after completing their studies.

Residential accommodation is plentiful, with most university-owned places within walking distance of lectures, and private housing reasonably priced. First years from outside Sheffield are guaranteed accommodation. The main halls of

residence are being replaced by a student village in a phased programme, which is due for completion in 2009. A second development will take spending on accommodation to £200 million and provide rooms for 4,000 students.

The university's excellent sports facilities have been the subject of a £6-million makeover, which includes a 170-station fitness centre and a third Astroturf pitch specifically for soccer and rugby. Top-notch facilities were built by the city for the 1991 World Student Games and a £25-million regional centre for the English Institute of Sport opened in 2003. A five-year student sports strategy was launched in 2007, aiming to boost participation at various levels of the sport and recreation.

Undergraduate Fees and Bursaries

- Fees for UK/EU students: £3,145
- International student fees: £9,920–£13,050 £23,580 (clinical)
- Bursary on full grant: household income up to £16,784: £680; up to £25K: £420.
- Bursaries on partial grant: household income up to £34.6K: £420 (subject and academic bursaries available).
- Scholarships based on circumstances or by competition. For full details see the university's website: www.shef.ac.uk/bursaries/

Students

Undergraduates:	16,405	(2,070)
Postgraduates:	4,785	(2,440)
Mature students:	8.2%	
Overseas students:	8.0%	
Applications per place:	7.4	
From state-sector schools:	83.8%	
From working-class homes:	21.3%	

For detailed information about fees, grants and bursaries and how they work, see chapter 7.

Accommodation

Number of places and costs refer to 2008–09
University-provided places: 5,846
Percentage catered: 32%
Catered costs: £3,798.48–£5,444.88 (42 weeks).
Self-catered costs: £2,940.00–£4,586.46 (42 weeks).
First years are guaranteed accommodation if conditions are met. Local restrictions apply.
International students: as above.
Contact: studentoffice@sheffield.ac.uk
www.shef.ac.uk/housing

Sheffield Hallam University

Sheffield Hallam has been undergoing a physical transformation designed to alter its image and cater for an even bigger student population. Its main site is in the heart of Sheffield and when the Faculty of Arts, Technology, Engineering and Sciences sets up home bordering the city's cultural industries quarter in 2008, there will be only two campuses. Development has been continuing apace, with £81 million already spent on teaching and learning facilities and as much again earmarked for projects due for completion by 2010. They will support key areas for the university, including creative and digital disciplines, health and social care.

An atrium provides social space for staff and students, and innovative library developments take pride of place on both campuses. Business and management courses, which account for easily the biggest share of places, have their own city-centre headquarters. The Collegiate Crescent campus, a former teacher training college, houses education, health and community studies. The students' union has taken over the spectacular but ill-fated National Centre for Popular Music, with facilities described by the former higher education minister Kim Howells as the best he had seen.

While most of the development has been on the main campus, adjoining the main bus and rail stations, the latest stage has seen the opening of a new social centre on the Collegiate Crescent site. The £14-million development that opened in 2005 has allowed the Faculty of Health and Wellbeing to almost double in size, as extra provision is made for nursing, radiotherapy, physiotherapy and social work. The Centre for Sport and Exercise Science, with its £6-million research facility, won glowing praise from inspectors, and is one of Europe's largest centres of its kind, with more than 2,000 students.

Teaching grades improved steadily after a disappointing start, with physics, psychology and hospitality, sport, leisure and tourism recording perfect scores. Physics has since been dropped as an undergraduate subject, but a new science learning centre is among a series of developments in this area. Maths and geography were the top performers in the 2007 National Student Survey.

Research in art and design, history and materials were all rated nationally outstanding with significant work of international standard in the last research assessments. The university has since recruited a sports engineering group, which gained the top rating in that exercise. Sheffield Hallam traces its origins in art and design back to the 1840s and celebrated the centenary of education and teacher training in 2005.

City Campus
Sheffield S1 1WB
0114 225 5555
admissions@shu.ac.uk
www.shu.ac.uk
www.hallamunion.com

The Times Rankings
Overall Ranking: 76

Student satisfaction:	=73	(72%)
Research quality:	=82	(1.1)
Entry standards:	=70	(269)
Student–staff ratio:	=90	(19.9)
Services & facilities/student:	77	(£938)
Expected completion rate:	=48	(85.0%)
Good honours:	60	(58.1%)
Graduate prospects:	=77	(60.6%)

It is now one of the largest of the new universities, with more than 30,000 students, including high proportions of part-time and mature students, and more than 1,000 taught on franchised courses in further education colleges. Business and industry are closely involved in the development hundreds of courses, with almost half of the students taking sandwich course placements with employers. More than 200 "specialist flexible courses" mix part-time study, distance learning and work-based learning.

The university leads two national teaching centres, one for fostering employability and the other promoting autonomous learning. It is also a partner in a third, led by Coventry University, on e-learning in the professions. A "virtual campus" offers students e-mail accounts and cheap equipment to access the growing volume of online courses, assignments and discussion groups provided by the university, even when they are at home or on work placements.

A third of undergraduates come from working-class homes and almost one in five from areas that send few students to higher education. The projected dropout rate of almost 13 per cent is among the lowest in the new universities and is significantly better than the national average for the subjects offered and the students' entry qualifications.

Such is Sheffield Hallam's size that it is not possible to guarantee all first years university-owned accommodation, although the large local intake means that many live at home. Sports facilities are supplemented by those provided by the city for the World Student Games. The impressive swimming complex, for example, is on the university's doorstep.

Undergraduate Fees and Bursaries

- Fees for UK/EU students: £3,145
- International student fees: £7,500–£9,345
- Bursary on full grant: £700
- Bursaries on partial grant: household income up to £700 payable to students receiving at least £1K in maintenance grant.
- Scholarships based on circumstances or by competition. For full details see the university's website: www.shu.ac.uk/study/ug/money.html

---

Students

Undergraduates:	17,280	(4,635)
Postgraduates:	2,585	(4,910)
Mature students:	20.9%	
Overseas students:	5.4%	
Applications per place:	4.9	
From state-sector schools:	95.5%	
From working-class homes:	32.6%	

For detailed information about fees, grants and bursaries and how they work, see chapter 7.

Accommodation

Number of places and costs refer to 2007–08
University-provided places: 4,090
Percentage catered: 10%
Catered costs: £89.90 a week (39 weeks).
Self-catered costs: £58–£92 (42–44 weeks).
All first years offered university owned, managed, partnership or private housing.
International students: as above, providing conditions are met.
Contact: accommodation@shu.ac.uk
www.shu.ac.uk/accommodation

University of Southampton

Southampton celebrated its 50th anniversary in 2002, but it has really taken off in the course of the last decade. During that time, student numbers have shot up, and the university has expanded onto new sites and invested heavily in its infrastructure. A five-year, £250-million programme to further develop teaching and research facilities is now under way. The university's 2001 research grades were among the top ten in Britain, while the last five teaching assessments all produced perfect scores. Southampton receives over six applications for every place and has been in the top ten in the National Student Survey for the last two years.

Although the percentages of students from working-class homes and areas with little tradition of university education are lower than the national average for the subjects offered, the statistics agency concluded that this was largely a matter of location. Students act as ambassadors, associates and mentors in local schools and colleges, as part of the university's effort to broaden its intake. A range of Foundation degrees carefully tailored to industry needs offers students flexible ways of learning.

The proportion of income derived from research at Southampton is among the highest in Britain. The 2001 assessments saw the number of subjects rated internationally outstanding shoot up from two to eight, including all branches of engineering. Physics, computer science, European studies, law and music were the other top-scorers. Economics, education and politics, philosophy and archaeology all scored maximum points for teaching quality.

The medical school, too, enhanced its reputation with a maximum score for teaching quality in a set of assessments that saw more variation than most. The school features an innovative common core curriculum for the pre-registration programmes of over 3,000 medical, nursing and other health students from entry to internship. Twice Southampton's medics have come out as the most satisfied in the country, according to the National Student Survey. Law, English and European languages also did well in the results published in 2007, which saw the university finish ahead of the other non-collegiate members of the Russell Group of leading research universities.

The main Highfield campus, in an attractive location two miles from the city centre, adjoining Southampton Common, has been the focus of recent development to cater for the expansion in numbers. Education, engineering, nursing, chemistry, electronics and computer science have all benefited. The library has

---

University Road
Southampton SO17 1BJ
023 8059 4732 (admissions)
admissns@soton.ac.uk
www.soton.ac.uk
www.susu.org

Edinburgh
Belfast
Cardiff London
SOUTHAMPTON

The Times Rankings
Overall Ranking: =16

Student satisfaction:	=10	(79%)
Research quality:	=8	(5.4)
Entry standards:	20	(389)
Student–staff ratio:	=42	(16.3)
Services & facilities/student:	14	(£1,479)
Expected completion rate:	26	(90.7%)
Good honours:	14	(74.8%)
Graduate prospects:	=35	(71.8%)

been greatly extended and the campus now has is an e-science centre, as well as a commercial services hub. A new student services centre provides learning support and other advisory facilities – all of which are backed up online for students in other areas of the university.

The Waterside Campus, in the city's revitalised dock area, houses the National Oceanography Centre, Southampton. A £49-million joint project with the Natural Environment Research Council, it is considered Europe's finest, encompassing teaching, research and knowledge transfer facilities. The Avenue campus, near the main site, is home to most of the arts departments. Clinical medicine is based at Southampton General Hospital, where a new research centre opened in 2007.

Winchester School of Art, which has been part of the university since 1996, has also enjoyed significant recent investment in new facilities. New programmes include degrees in graphic arts and heritage studies for museums and galleries. The arts are well represented in Southampton, too, with three nationally renowned arts centres: the Turner Sims Concert Hall, the Nuffield Theatre and the John Hansard Gallery all based at Highfield.

Social facilities for students have been expanded and refurbished, with the addition of a popular new nightclub. Sports facilities were upgraded, with the opening in 2004 of an £8.4-million indoor sports complex and swimming pool next to the students' union and a £4.5-million development of the outdoor facilities, with grass and synthetic pitches, a new pavilion, bar and meeting rooms. Student accommodation is plentiful and was improved in 2006 with the £20-million renovation of three halls of residence.

Undergraduate Fees and Bursaries

- Fees for UK/EU students: £3,145
- International student fees: £9,380–£12,000
  £21,800 (clinical)
- Bursary on full grant: £1,000
- Bursaries on partial grant: household income up to £32K: £500.
- Scholarships based on circumstances or by competition. For full details see the university's website: www.soton.ac.uk/study/feesandfunding/

Students

Undergraduates:	14,390	(2,730)
Postgraduates:	4,720	(2,895)
Mature students:	15.4%	
Overseas students:	8.3%	
Applications per place:	6.7	
From state-sector schools:	82.7%	
From working-class homes:	20.0%	

For detailed information about fees, grants and bursaries and how they work, see chapter 7.

Accommodation

Number of places and costs refer to 2007–08
University-provided places: 5,200
Percentage catered: 20%
Catered costs: £96.95–£134.05 a week.
Self-catered costs: £62.30–£104.65 a week.
All first years are offered accommodation if conditions met.
International students: single, fee-paying, non-EU students are guaranteed accommodation.
Contact: accommodation@soton.ac.uk
www.soton.ac.uk/accommodation

Southampton Solent University

The largest of the nine new universities created in 2005, Southampton Solent also has the broadest range of programmes, stretching from Foundation courses for those without the qualifications to begin degrees, to PhDs. The 10,000 students embrace civil and mechanical engineering, as well as media, arts and business, with a separate maritime centre capitalising on the coastal location. The subject mix explains why the former Southampton Institute is now one of the few universities with a majority of male students.

The newly rebranded Solent Curriculum plays to the university's strengths in vocational courses, with an eye to maintaining a good graduate employment record. There is a strong representation of "non-traditional" disciplines, such as yacht and powercraft design, computer and video games, and comedy writing and performance. A new range of courses for 2008 included degrees in fashion management, television and music production, and coaching and sport development. A Graduate Enterprise Centre provides advice and rent-free offices for those hoping to start their own businesses, while the Warsash Maritime Centre is an internationally renowned training and research facility for the shipping and offshore oil industries.

Teaching quality assessments generally went well, but research grades were low in the last assessments. Social work produced by far the highest levels of satisfaction in an otherwise disappointing set of National Student Survey results published in 2007. Applications shot up by 24 per cent in 2007 and were close to the national average at the official deadline for courses beginning in 2008.

Demand for places remains especially strong in marine-based courses. The university is higher education's premier yachting institution, with a world champion student team that has won the national championships four times in six years. Three new boats will support courses at the new, purpose-built Watersports Centre, where some of the activities are targeted on disadvantaged young people in the area. The centre now boasts seven powerboats, nine dinghies and three keelboats.

Almost a third of the students come from Hampshire and there has been a substantial increase in the proportion with working-class roots, taking it above the national average for the university's subjects and entry qualifications. Solent's 17 per cent projected dropout rate is also better than the university's "benchmark". About 11 per cent come from overseas, while 100 are enrolled on research degrees. There is a special link with the

---

East Park Terrace
Southampton SO14 0YN
023 8031 9000
  (main switchboard)
ask@solent.ac.uk
www.solent.ac.uk
www.solentsu.co.uk

The Times Rankings
Overall Ranking: 97

Student satisfaction:	=84	(71%)
Research quality:	=107	(0.5)
Entry standards:	101	(229)
Student–staff ratio:	98	(20.5)
Services & facilities/student:	70	(£980)
Expected completion rate:	82	(78.2%)
Good honours:	110	(43.1%)
Graduate prospects:	98	(55.7%)

Channel Island of Guernsey, which has no higher education of its own. Colleges on the island (and in various parts of the south of England) bring students for taster courses and provide evidence of academic potential that can lead to entry on criteria other than A level.

The main campus has few architectural pretensions, but is conveniently based in the city centre within walking distance of the station. Recent investment has included a new Centre for Professional Development in Broadcasting and Multimedia Production, which includes an online editing suite, digital television studio and gallery, for use by under-graduates as well as community groups and professionals. Media, arts and society courses now attract almost as many students as the consistently popular business school.

Other recent additions include the Centre for Health, Exercise and Sports Science, which enables sports science students to conduct the latest types of fitness testing, including ergonomic and biomechanical movement analysis. New music studios feature an industry-standard recording complex, while a per-formance space and dance studio, opened in 2008, includes a dance floor, tiered seating and a technical viewing gallery.

Students like the location, close to the city's growing complement of bars and nightclubs, as well as to the main shopping area. There are more than 2,300 hall places close to the campus, most of which are allocated to first years and almost half of which are en suite. A landlord accreditation scheme helps to guarantee standards of accommodation for those who rely on the private sector. Away from the water, there is the usual range of sports facilities, with a sports hall and fitness suite on campus and outdoor pitches, tennis and netball courts four miles away. Students living in hall and members of university sports clubs get free fitness classes and gym use.

Undergraduate Fees and Bursaries

- Fees for UK/EU students: £3,145
- International student fees: £6,100–£7,990
- Bursary on full grant: household income up to £18.3K: £1,050; up to £23K: £750; up to £25K: £500.
- Bursaries on partial grant: household income up to £39.3K: sliding scale £500–£250.
- Scholarships based on circumstances or by competition. For full details see the university's website: www.solent.ac.uk/fees/info.aspx

---

Students

Undergraduates:	8,435	(1,555)
Postgraduates:	285	(365)
Mature students:	22.3%	
Overseas students:	11.2%	
Applications per place:	3.2	
From state-sector schools:	96.0%	
From working-class homes:	35.5%	

For detailed information about fees, grants and bursaries and how they work, see chapter 7.

Accommodation

Number of places and costs refer to 2007–08
University-provided places: 2,340 (85% are offered to first years).
Percentage catered: 0%
Self-catered costs: £68.25–£93.80 a week.
First years are guaranteed accommodation if conditions are met.
International students: some accommodation is set aside.
Contact: Accommodation@solent.ac.uk

Staffordshire University

Staffordshire describes itself as a "university in the community" but it is increasingly reliant on overseas students, both at home and abroad. There are 5,000 students taking Staffordshire courses outside Britain, almost half of them located around the Pacific Rim, as well as a growing cohort of foreign students in the university's domestic campuses. There are more than 12,000 UK students and, while the demand for places held steady with the arrival of top-up fees, Staffordshire was one of the few universities where applications fell in 2007. There was a further decline at the start of 2008, with the reduction in the number of choices per applicant.

The university is based on two main sites: the headquarters in Stoke and the other 12 miles away in Stafford. A £1.5-million media centre opened at Stoke in 2005, while the large business school straddles the two campuses in an attempt to foster links with the private sector. The first phase of plans for a 400-acre University Quarter will see the construction of a science centre.

The rural Stafford site features the purpose-built Octagon Centre, in which lecture theatres, offices and walkways surround one of the largest university computing facilities in Europe. A £2.4-million New Technologies Centre, opened in 2003, has helped develop popular courses such as film production technology and a broadcast-standard television studio has now been added. Health, engineering and technology are all based at Stafford, while Stoke specialises in the arts, sciences and social sciences.

A new campus in Lichfield houses an integrated further and higher education centre, developed in partnership with Tamworth and Lichfield College, in the first purpose-built institution of its kind. The main aim is to act as a resource centre for local businesses. The School of Health has branches in Telford, Shrewsbury and Oswestry, but franchised courses spread the university's net much further afield. Staffordshire courses are taken in China, Malaysia, Singapore, Hong Kong, Pakistan, India, Sri Lanka, Greece, Spain and France.

The university also runs courses for more than 1,000 students at further education colleges in its own region, as well as offering incentives for local people to apply. A priority applications scheme guarantees a place to under-21s from Staffordshire, Shropshire or Cheshire as long as they meet the minimum requirements for their chosen course, while mature students are guaranteed at least an interview if they join one of the range of access courses. Even before the advent of top-up fees, the university was offering £500 awards to disadvantaged students from

College Road
Stoke-on-Trent ST4 2DE
01782 294000 (main switchboard)
admissions@staffs.ac.uk
www.staffs.ac.uk
www.staffsunion.com

The Times Rankings
Overall Ranking: 67

Student satisfaction:	=26	(76%)
Research quality:	=82	(1.1)
Entry standards:	91	(251)
Student–staff ratio:	59	(17.6)
Services & facilities/student:	=63	(£1,000)
Expected completion rate:	=74	(79.8%)
Good honours:	78	(52.5%)
Graduate prospects:	104	(53.8%)

Shropshire, Cheshire and Staffordshire. The policy has been working – more than a third of the students are from the local area and a programme, run in conjunction with Keele University, aims to increase the numbers further. An extensive portfolio of Foundation degrees has continued to expand, with the addition of telecommunications and management, and communications and networks courses developed in collaboration with BT/Accenture. Many programmes are available with a January start, a popular arrangement with overseas students who take English language courses before beginning a degree.

Staffordshire is in the top three universities for secondary teacher training courses, and was among the leading new universities in the 2007 National Student Survey, with sociology and social policy students emerging as the most satisfied in the country. In the last Research Assessment Exercise, a relatively low proportion of academics was entered and, although no subjects reached the top two grades, media studies and art and design were in the next category.

With 98 per cent of its undergraduates state-educated and more than a third coming from working-class homes, Staffordshire comfortably exceeds all the benchmarks set by the funding council for widening access to higher education. There is good provision for the 700 students with disabilities. The projected dropout rate of 19 per cent is only slightly higher than average for the university's courses and entry qualifications.

Stoke is not the liveliest city of its size, but the campus is close to the railway station, within easy reach of the centre and has a buzzing union. Stafford is much the more attractive setting and offers the best chance of a residential place, but the town is quiet and the campus is a mile and a half outside it. Sports facilities are good, especially in Stafford, where there is a new £1.4-million sports centre and all-weather pitches. Sports scholarships and good coaching have helped attract some outstanding athletes, who have access to a sports performance centre to help with training schedules, psychological support and dietary assessments.

Undergraduate Fees and Bursaries

- Fees for UK/EU students: £3,145
- International student fees: £5,375–£8,650
- Bursary on full grant: household income up to £20.8K: £1,000; up to £25K: £850.
- Bursaries on partial grant: household income up to £30.8K: £500.
- Scholarships based on circumstances or by competition. For full details see the university's website: www.staffs.ac.uk/marketingservices/cost/

Students

Undergraduates:	8,340	(3,455)
Postgraduates:	1,150	(2,245)
Mature students:	24.6%	
Overseas students:	7.6%	
Applications per place:	5.0	
From state-sector schools:	97.7%	
From working-class homes:	36.6%	

For detailed information about fees, grants and bursaries and how they work, see chapter 7.

Accommodation

Number of places and costs refer to 2008–09
University-provided places: 1,200 (Stoke); 776 (Stafford)
Percentage catered: 0%
Self-catered accommodation: £52.50–£85.00 a week (38 weeks).
First years have priority, if conditions met.
International students: have priority, if conditions are met.
Contact: Accommodation_stoke@staffs.ac.uk
Accommodation_stafford@staffs.ac.uk

University of Stirling

One of the most beautiful campuses in Britain features low-level, modern buildings in a loch-side setting beneath the Ochil Hills on the historical Airthrey Estate, two miles from the centre of Stirling. Even after a 20 per cent expansion over four years, largely due to the incorporation of three nursing colleges at Falkirk, Inverness and Stornoway, in Lewis, the university remains a relatively small institution of 9,000 students with a community feel. There are no faculties, but five "core areas" have been identified: health and well-being, culture and society, environment, enterprise and economy, and sport.

Although highly rated in some research fields, there were no starred departments in the last research assessments. However, ten out of the 22 subject areas reached grade 5, denoting national excellence and significant work of international standard. Excellent teaching ratings for economics, sociology, theology, business studies, psychology and English show Stirling's strength in the arts and social sciences. Among the sciences, only environmental science matched this feat, its success reflected in a new School of Biological and Environmental Sciences, with substantially refurbished facilities for both teaching and research. Sports studies are particularly

popular, as are film and media studies, which acquired a £40,000 high-tech newsroom in 2004. International exchanges are common, with many students going to American, Asian and European universities each year.

Stirling was the British pioneer of the semester system, which has now become so popular in other universities. The academic year is divided into two 15-week terms, with short mid-semester breaks. Students have the option of starting courses in February, rather than September. Successful completion of six semesters will bring a General degree; eight semesters, honours. The emphasis on breadth is such that there are no barriers to movement between departments. Undergraduates can switch the whole direction of their studies, in consultation with their academic adviser, as their interests develop. The modular scheme allows students to speed up their progress on a Summer Academic Programme, which squeezes a full semester's teaching into July and August. Full-time students are not allowed to use the programme to reduce the length of their course, but part-timers can use it to make rapid progress.

The level of competition for places was steady at the start of 2007, following a small decline in the previous year. The intake is surprisingly diverse, with 92 per

---

Stirling FK9 4LA
01786 467044 (admissions)
admissions@stir.ac.uk
www.stir.ac.uk
www.susaonline.org.uk

STIRLING
Edinburgh
Belfast
London
Cardiff

The Times Rankings
Overall Ranking: 40

Student satisfaction:	–	(–)
Research quality:	=47	(3.9)
Entry standards:	=55	(288)
Student–staff ratio:	=34	(15.4)
Services & facilities/student:	74	(£964)
Expected completion rate:	29	(89.9%)
Good honours:	31	(67.9%)
Graduate prospects:	=35	(71.8%)

cent of undergraduates state-educated and more than a quarter coming from working-class homes. Large numbers come from areas that send few students to higher education, and three-quarters are from north of the border.

Sports facilities are excellent and have been extended and refurbished recently. As well as enhancing recreational provision, the programme has enhanced training opportunities for students and visiting athletes, swimmers and tennis players, as well as providing dedicated facilities for teaching and research. The national tennis and swimming centres are both based on the campus, the latter in a 50-metre pool, and there is even a nine-hole golf course. A golf centre, opened in 2004, has three target greens, a practice area, indoor facilities and a synthetic putting green. A new football academy opens in 2008. Sports bursaries worth between £900 and £2,000, according to performance, are open to overseas students, as well as Britons. The campus also houses the new headquarters of the Scottish Institute of Sport.

Students appreciate the individual attention that a small campus university can offer, although some find the atmosphere claustrophobic. The original campus buildings are now being refurbished, upgrading teaching, learning and accommodation facilities. Stirling is

not the top choice of nightclubbers, but the students' union has been named the best in Scotland, winning "Best Bar None" status in 2005, 2006 and 2007, and there is a lively social programme. The £6.3-million refurbishment of the MacRobert Arts Centre has transformed cultural activities on campus, while the surrounding scenery offers its own attractions for walkers.

The Highland campus, for nurses and midwives, moved to the new state-of-the-art Centre for Health Science in Inverness in January 2007. The Western Isles campus is located in Stornoway, where the teaching accommodation is an integral part of the recently built Lewis Hospital.

Undergraduate Fees and Bursaries
- Scottish-domiciled and EU students: no fees payable.
- Non-Scottish UK-domiciled student fees: £1,775 a year.
- International student fees: £9,100–£11,200
- Scholarships based on circumstances or by competition. For full details see the university's website: www.external.stir.ac.uk/undergrad/financial_info/index.php

---

Students

Undergraduates:	6,810	(905)
Postgraduates:	1,365	(1,430)
Mature students:	13.0%	
Overseas students:	9.2%	
Applications per place:	6.4	
From state-sector schools:	91.7%	
From working-class homes:	26.2%	

For detailed information about fees, grants and bursaries and how they work, see chapter 7.

Accommodation

Number of places and costs refer to 2007–08
University-provided places: 2,799
Percentage catered: 0%
Self-catered costs: £59.00–£82.40 a week.
All first years are guaranteed suitable housing arranged by the University.
International students: as above.
Contact: Accommodation@stir.ac.uk

University of Strathclyde

Even as Anderson's Institution in the 18th century, Strathclyde concentrated on "useful learning". Some Glaswegians still refer to it as "the tech". The nickname does less than justice to the current portfolio of courses, but the university has never shrunk from its technological and vocational emphasis. Strathclyde aims to offer courses that are both innovatory and relevant to industry and commerce – hence product design and innovation, or international business with modern languages.

Traditional science degrees have continued to prosper, however, with a series of top ratings. All but two of the 26 subjects assessed under Scotland's original system of grading teaching quality were considered Excellent or Highly Satisfactory. Its careers service is also rated among the best, having four times won a Government charter mark for customer service. No department reached the top grade of the last research assessments, but ten of the 33 subject areas reached the next rung of the ladder, accounting for 90 per cent of those entered.

Strathclyde's main strength, however, is in the top-rated business school, which is one of the largest in Europe and the only one in Scotland to be accredited by the European Quality Improvement System.

Business studies students follow an "integrative studies" programme, which is designed to place them in a realistic business environment from day one and involves work with a range of major companies. The scheme is now being piloted in other faculties. The engineering faculty is also the largest in Scotland, and has linked with Glasgow University to provide a joint department of naval architecture and marine engineering.

European focus is evident throughout the university, which has encouraged all departments to adapt their courses to the needs of the single market. Many students combine business or engineering with European studies or languages to give themselves an edge in the job market. Mature students account for a fifth of the places and have a special organisation to look after their interests. With over 20,000 students, including part-timers, Strathclyde is the third-largest university in Scotland, but its numbers swell to 60,000 including short courses and distance learning programmes.

Strathclyde actively promotes wider access, comfortably exceeding national averages for state-educated students, the share of places going to applicants from working-class homes and those from areas sending few students to higher education. Its efforts are underpinned by fundraising for a scholarship programme to aid

16 Richmond Street
Glasgow G1 1XQ
0141 552 4400 (main switchboard)
scls@mis.strath.ac.uk
www.strath.ac.uk
www.strathstudents
.com

GLASGOW
Edinburgh
Belfast
London
Cardiff

The Times Rankings
Overall Ranking: 35

Student satisfaction:	=26	(76%)
Research quality:	51	(3.6)
Entry standards:	29	(367)
Student–staff ratio:	=51	(16.8)
Services & facilities/student:	32	(£1,219)
Expected completion rate:	64	(81.8%)
Good honours:	16	(74.6%)
Graduate prospects:	=14	(76.4%)

students from poor homes. However, a projected dropout rate of more than 16 per cent is well above the UK average for the university's subjects and entry qualifications.

The main John Anderson campus is in the centre of Glasgow, behind George Square and near Queen Street station. Apart from the Edwardian headquarters, the buildings are mostly modern. The site of a former maternity hospital in the centre of the campus will eventually provide extra teaching accommodation, but a £73-million refurbishment programme is taking priority. Strathclyde has a second campus on the west side of the city, acquired from a merger with Jordanhill College of Education, Scotland's largest teacher training institution, in 1993. The 67-acre parkland site houses the faculty of education, which is breaking new ground with Scotland's first part-time teacher training degree and also offers courses in speech and language pathology, community arts, social work, sport and outdoor education. The university plans to sell the site and move the courses onto the main campus, but this is unlikely to take place before the end of the decade.

Strathclyde is losing its image as a "nine-to-five" university, thanks to a student village on the main campus, complete with pub, which has increased the number of residential places. Over 1,400 of these are on campus, all with network access, and another 500 are nearby. The Millennium Student project has delivered full network access from every study bedroom on campus and it is planned to make extensive high-speed dial-up facilities into the university network available for all students in the Glasgow area. The ten-floor union building attracts students from all over Glasgow with its reputation for hard-drinking revelry. For those with more sophisticated tastes, there are several theatres and the city's own variety of cultural venues.

Undergraduate Fees and Bursaries

- Scottish-domiciled and EU students: no fees payable.
- Non-Scottish UK-domiciled student fees: £1,775 a year.
- International student fees: £8,695–£11,025*
- Scholarships based on circumstances or by competition. For full details see the university's website: www.strath.ac.uk/feenews

* Figure for 2007–08

Students

Undergraduates:	11,840	(4,345)
Postgraduates:	3,665	(6,155)
Mature students:	14.8%	
Overseas students:	5.3%	
Applications per place:	5.2	
From state-sector schools:	92.5%	
From working-class homes:	28.9%	

For detailed information about fees, grants and bursaries and how they work, see chapter 7.

Accommodation

Number of places and costs refer to 2007–08
University-provided places: 1,979
Percentage catered: 7%
Catered costs: £81 a week.
Self-catered costs: £57–£85 a week.
First years are offered accommodation.
International students: as above.
Contact:
student.accommodation@mis.strath.ac.uk

University of Sunderland

The university doubled in size in four years, and has taken advantage of urban regeneration programmes in one of Britain's newest cities to expand its facilities and create among the newest university campuses. The main campus, in the city centre, now has a well-appointed science complex and a new design centre. The Sir Tom Cowie campus at St Peter's, an award-winning 24-acre site by the banks of the Wear, initially housed the business school and the informatics centre. To these is being added a £20-million arts, design and media centre, the first phase of which opened in 2003. An £8.5-million redevelopment of the city campus is now complete, having added the Gateway, a one-stop shop for students bringing together a wide range of services.

Developments have been planned with an eye to history, for example incorporating a working heritage centre for the glass industry at the heart of the new campus, which is built around a 7th-century abbey described as one of Britain's first universities. The glass and ceramics design degree carries on a Sunderland tradition – the National Glass Centre was one of the features of the new campus – while the courses in automotive design and manufacture serve the region's new industrial base. The large pharmacy department is another strength and the well-equipped School of Computing and Technology is one of the largest in the UK with over 3,000 students.

Teaching assessments improved after a poor start. The biosciences recorded the university's only perfect scores, but nursing and anatomy and physiology came close to joining them. The last research assessments were more impressive, registering a big improvement on 1996 and representing the best performance of any new university in terms of average grades per member of staff. Although no subjects reached the top two grades, the 44 per cent of academics entered for assessment was the most in any former polytechnic, and art and design, English and history all managed grade 4. The successes made the university particularly resentful of the Government's plans to concentrate research funding further.

Sunderland is making the most of the opportunity to link up with the multi-national companies that have arrived on its doorstep. The Institute for Automotive and Manufacturing Advanced Practice has a team of 40 researchers and consultants working with local businesses, while nearby Nissan played an important role in designing a course in automotive product development. The Sony media centre provides students with excellent television and video production facilities.

Chester Road
Sunderland SR1 3SD
0191 515 3000 (course helpline)
student-helpline@
 sunderland.ac.uk
www.sunderland.ac.uk
www.sunderlandsu
 .co.uk

Edinburgh
Belfast
SUNDERLAND
London
Cardiff

The Times Rankings
Overall Ranking: 82

Student satisfaction:	=64	(73%)
Research quality:	=58	(1.7)
Entry standards:	95	(249)
Student–staff ratio:	40	(16.1)
Services & facilities/student:	104	(£737)
Expected completion rate:	=86	(77.0%)
Good honours:	=97	(47.7%)
Graduate prospects:	87	(59.3%)

The university has a determinedly local focus, aiming to double the number of students coming from an area which has little tradition of sending students to higher education. Nearly four undergraduates in ten now come from "low participation neighbourhoods" – by far the largest proportion at any English university and more than twice the national average for the subjects on offer. A pioneering access scheme offers places to mature students without A levels, as long as they reach the required levels of literacy, numeracy and other basic skills. The Learning North East initiative, based on Sunderland's successful pilot for the University for Industry, even offers free taster courses to take at home.

Over 40 per cent of the undergraduates have a working-class background, and the projected dropout rate has dropped from more than a quarter to less than one in five in recent years. Provision for disabled students is excellent, with award-winning information produced for those with disabilities, trained support staff in every academic school as well as in the libraries and special modules to help dyslexics. The campus also houses the North East Regional Access Centre, which assesses the learning support requirements of students with disabilities and specific learning difficulties. There is special provision among the 2,200 residential places.

Sunderland itself is fiercely proud of its identity and has the advantage of a coastal location but, despite the city title, with the exception of the impressive new football ground, it has the leisure facilities of a medium-sized town. Those in search of big cultural events or serious nightlife head for Newcastle, which is less than half an hour away by Metro.

Undergraduate Fees and Bursaries

- Fees for UK/EU students: £3,145
- International student fees: £8,150
- Bursary on full grant: £525
- Bursaries on partial grant: household income up to £39,305: £525.
- Scholarships based on circumstances or by competition. For full details see the university's website: www.welcome. sunderland.ac.uk/fees.asp

---

Students

Undergraduates:	7,820	(9,200)
Postgraduates:	1,995	(1,200)
Mature students:	29.2%	
Overseas students:	16.8%	
Applications per place:	4.8	
From state-sector schools:	97.4%	
From working-class homes:	41.7%	

For detailed information about fees, grants and bursaries and how they work, see chapter 7.

Accommodation

Number of places and costs refer to 2008–09
University-provided places: 1,392 beds in halls; 129 (Managed Houses/Head Tenancy scheme).
Percentage catered: 0%
Self-catered costs: £1,650 (twin) – £3,100 a year (40–50 week contracts).
First-year students are given priority.
International students: as above.
Contact: residentialservices@sunderland.ac.uk
www.sunderland.ac.uk/residential services

University of Surrey

Surrey has been one of the recent success stories of the university world, remaining true to the technological history while building a strong research base and a degree of financial independence envied by its peers. Even some of the arts degrees carry a BSc and are highly vocational: four out of five undergraduates in all subjects undertake work experience. Placements of one (or two half) years, often taken abroad, mean that most degrees last four years. The format and the subject balance combine to keep Surrey at the head of the graduate employment league, as well as producing a healthy research income. Indeed, it has taken to describing itself as the "University for Jobs" to ram the point home. Recent expansion in healthcare, human sciences and performing arts has added to the traditional strengths in science and engineering.

The mix has been proving popular: the 37 per cent growth in applications in 2007 was almost the biggest at any university and Surrey was one of the few to register an increase at the start of 2008, despite the switch from six choices to five per applicant. The 12 per cent rise was again among the highest at any university. The growth in demand for places has come at an opportune time: the university is planning to boost its numbers by 40 per cent, partly through overseas ventures. An internation-

al institute in the Chinese city of Dalian, in partnership with Dongbei University, will be the first of these. Nearer home, Surrey is taking in the Guildford School of Acting and launching its first degree in English literature in 2008.

All students are encouraged to enrol for a course at the European language centre, and a growing number of degrees, including a new range in engineering, have a language component. The cosmopolitan feel is enhanced by one of the largest proportions of overseas students at any university – a feat which won Surrey a Queen's Award for Export Achievement. The 2,700 foreign students come from 140 different countries.

Scores improved from a low base in the 2007 National Student Survey, with social policy, sociology and anthropology producing the highest levels of satisfaction. Teaching assessments were impressive, with near-perfect scores for economics, education, physics and astronomy, and electrical and electronic engineering, one of Surrey's three top-rated research areas. Health and sociology also won 5* research grades, leaving a third of the researchers in departments considered internationally outstanding – a proportion bettered by only four universities in Britain. Six out of ten reached one of the top two grades. Another indication of the university's research strength lies in the growing proportion of

---

Guildford
Surrey GU2 7XH
01483 300800 (main switchboard)
ug-enquiries@surrey.ac.uk
www.surrey.ac.uk
www.ussu.co.uk

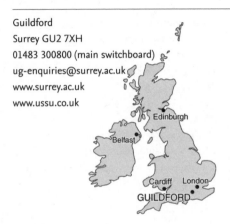

Edinburgh
Belfast
Cardiff London
GUILDFORD

income derived from sources other than Government grants: up from 10 per cent to about 70 per cent in little over a decade. The Surrey Research Park is one of only three science parks still owned, funded and managed by the university that opened it, helping Surrey to amass one of the highest proportions of private funding at any British university.

Both the proportions of undergraduates from working-class homes and from areas without a tradition of higher education are lower than the benchmark figures, which take account of the subject mix and entry standards. But the statistics agency has acknowledged that the explanation lies largely in the university's location. The projected dropout rate of 10.5 per cent is better than the national average.

The compact campus is a ten-minute walk from the centre of Guildford. Most of the buildings date from the late 1960s, but the new business school and the gleaming European Institute of Health and Medical Sciences offer a striking contrast. Shaped like a giant ship's prow, the steel and glass building houses the large nursing and midwifery departments. A £12-million management building and an Advanced Technology Institute opened in 2002. The campus includes two lakes, playing fields and enough residential accommodation to enable all first-years to live in. A second campus, adjacent to the Stag Hill

headquarters, is now being developed. The new postgraduate medical school is intended to be the first stage in the development of a health campus, which will also contain more residential places for students and staff, as well as other academic buildings, leisure and sporting facilities.

Guildford has plenty of cultural and recreational facilities, but riotous nightclubs are not encouraged. The campus is the centre of social life, and has seen recent improvements to leisure facilities. The proximity of London is an attraction to many students, but also helps account for the high cost of living, which is not mitigated by the allowances available in the capital.

Undergraduate Fees and Bursaries

- Fees for UK/EU students: £3,145
- International student fees: £8,300–£10,700
- Bursary on full grant: household income up to £10K: £2000, then sliding scale to £750.
- Bursaries on partial grant: household income up to £35K: sliding scale £600–£500.
- Scholarships based on circumstances or by competition. For full details see the university's website: www.surrey.ac.uk/undergraduate/fees/bursaries/

Students

Undergraduates:	7,375	(2,225)
Postgraduates:	2,810	(3,300)
Mature students:	18.6%	
Overseas students:	12.5%	
Applications per place:	4.5	
From state-sector schools:	88.6%	
From working-class homes:	22.5%	

For detailed information about fees, grants and bursaries and how they work, see chapter 7.

Accommodation

Number of places and costs refer to 2008–09
University-provided places: 4,080
Percentage catered: 0%
Self-catered accommodation: £57.00–£98.70 a week.
All first years are guaranteed a place.
International students designated overseas for fees are guaranteed accommodation.
Contact: www.surrey.ac.uk/Accommodation

University of Sussex

Sussex's all-round academic reputation has seldom been higher. The university is close to the top 100 in the world rankings published by *Times Higher Education/QS*, and rates higher still for the arts and social sciences. Sir Harry Kroto won the 1996 Nobel Prize for Chemistry and Professor Anthony Leggett took the 2003 Physics prize for work carried out at Sussex. Although no subject was considered internationally outstanding in the last Research Assessment Exercise, more than half were placed in the next category. No subject dropped below grade 4, despite a high proportion of academics entered for assessment.

The university now generates more than a third of its income from private sources, largely in research contracts. Philosophy and sociology scored maximum points for teaching quality, with politics and inter-national relations, mathematics and American studies – a long-established strength – the best of the rest.

The demand for places has been strong, especially in subjects such as such as social work, environmental science, and even physics. With the university taking more postgraduates in recent years, the result has been increasing competition for degree places. But this trend came to a sudden halt at the start of 2008, with a 20 per cent drop in applications, exacerbated by the switch from six choices per applicant to five. The decline was more than twice the national average.

Sussex's earlier successes in attracting applicants was said to be due partly to targeting schools in London and the South East, as well as to innovations such as weekly campus tours for prospective applicants and drop-in arrangements for mature students. A revised portfolio of arts subjects seems to have helped, but a similar exercise for the sciences in 2006 caused bitter controversy with plans (later reversed) to drop chemistry.

The interdisciplinary approach that has always been Sussex's trademark has been re-examined to adapt this 1960s concept for the 21st century. The eleven schools have been reduced to five and students are being offered a clearer framework so that they are fully aware of the combinations available to them. Student support is being improved through a revamped personal tutor system and a 50 per cent increase in the number of student advisers. Arts and social science students are still in the majority, but the life sciences are not far behind. Sussex is committed to taking candidates with no family tradition of higher education and has much larger numbers of mature students than most of its peer group of institutions. The

Sussex House
Falmer
Brighton BN1 9RH
01273 678416 (admissions)
ug.admissions@
   sussex.ac.uk
www.sussex.ac.uk
www.ussu.info

proportion of working-class students and the share of places going to those from areas with little tradition of higher education are both lower than the statistics agency's benchmark figures, but this is attributed to the university's south coast location. The projected dropout rate of more than 11 per cent is around than the national average for the subjects on offer. The university was only just outside the bottom ten in the 2007 National Student Survey, when other campus universities had many of the most satisfied students in the country. However, an earlier survey of graduates five years after leaving Sussex showed an enviable employment record.

The university is based in an 18th-century park at Falmer, close to the South Downs and four miles from the centre of Brighton. Sir Basil Spence's original buildings have been supplemented by new developments. The library has been extended and the language centre recently refurbished. Relations with neighbouring Brighton University are good. The two institutions succeeded in a joint bid for a medical school, which opened in 2003 and has since recorded big increases in applications. The Brighton and Sussex Medical School is split between the Royal Sussex County Hospital and the two universities' Falmer campuses.

Undergraduates can take a year abroad in many subjects. Some courses offer joint qualifications with Continental universities, and those returning from a year abroad are given priority, with first years, for more than 3,000 residential places on campus, and more accommodation is being built. Sports facilities are good, and the university has launched initiatives in basketball and hockey to entice top performers.

Sussex has always attracted overseas students in large numbers and has seen big increases recently, but a high proportion of the remainder are from the London area, where many return at weekends. As a result, the well-appointed campus can be quiet, although there is no shortage of social events, and Brighton has plenty to offer.

Undergraduate Fees and Bursaries

- Fees for UK/EU students: £3,145
- International student fees: £9,500–£12,150
- Bursary on full grant: £1,000
- Bursaries on partial grant: n/a
- Scholarships based on circumstances or by competition. For full details see the university's website: www.sussex.ac.uk/scholarships_and_bursaries.html

---

Students

Undergraduates:	6,995	(2,280)
Postgraduates:	1,850	(1,325)
Mature students:	17.1%	
Overseas students:	8.9%	
Applications per place:	7.1	
From state-sector schools:	84.8%	
From working-class homes:	20.0%	

For detailed information about fees, grants and bursaries and how they work, see chapter 7.

Accommodation

Number of places and costs refer to 2007–08
University-provided places: 3,430
Percentage catered: 0%
Self-catered costs: £47.50–£104.00 a week.
First-year students are guaranteed accommodation if conditions are met.
International students: given priority providing conditions are met.
Contact: housing@sussex.ac.uk

Swansea University

Swansea became independent of the University of Wales in 2007, although its students will continue to receive the federal university's degrees for the foreseeable future. As the student union president noted, most people already used the new title of Swansea University, but independence is intended to reflect confidence in the future, as well as helping with international recruitment and research partnerships.

The university's attractive coastal location and accessibility to students from outside Wales already made it a natural alternative to the Welsh capital for thousands of applicants – so much so that in a poll of 10,000 students, Swansea won the *Times Higher Education Supplement*'s inaugural award for the best student experience in the UK. The university also did well in the first three national student satisfaction surveys, finishing in the top 20 in 2007. Education and sports science students were among the most satisfied in the country.

Applications were healthy until the beginning of 2008 when, in common with the rest of Wales, the university saw a big decline with the switch from six choices per candidate to five. A wide variety of new courses have been introduced as part of a development plan stressing language combinations. There are now about 500

degree courses in the modular scheme, and undergraduates are encouraged to stray outside their specialist area in their first year. Swansea takes its European interests seriously, with links to more than 90 Continental institutions. The new law school offers options in European and international law, while both arts and science students can undertake some of their studies abroad.

Swansea has won European funding for some of its projects, including Graduate Opportunities Wales, which steers students towards small firms through industrial placements and vacation jobs. The most important academic development, however, has come with the opening of the Swansea Clinical School, more than 30 years after the first attempt to secure approval for a medical school. The university already had a postgraduate school, but collaboration with University of Wales College of Medicine and Swansea NHS Trust saw the Welsh Assembly back plans for 50 undergraduates to begin training in 2001. The "fast track" programme will allow 70 graduates to qualify as doctors in four years rather than five.

About half of the subjects assessed for teaching quality received Excellent ratings. Swansea counts physical sciences, management and languages among its strengths, and all branches of engineering are highly rated. Civil engineering was the

---

Singleton Park
Swansea SA2 8PP
01792 295111
admissions@swansea.ac.uk
www.swan.ac.uk
www.swansea-union.co.uk

Edinburgh
Belfast
London
SWANSEA Cardiff

The Times Rankings
Overall Ranking: 48

Student satisfaction:	=18	(77%)
Research quality:	=33	(4.4)
Entry standards:	53	(295)
Student–staff ratio:	30	(15.1)
Services & facilities/student:	=60	(£1,010)
Expected completion rate:	=34	(88.3%)
Good honours:	=88	(49.9%)
Graduate prospects:	73	(61.4%)

only top-rated subject in the last research assessments, but a third of the researchers were placed in one of the top two grades. Despite its international links, Swansea has not forgotten its local responsibilities. A Community University of the Valleys offers part-time courses for mature students as part of the effort to regenerate the area. Compacts with the region's schools encourage students in areas of economic disadvantage to aspire to higher education.

The immediate locality is far from depressing, however. The attractive parkland campus two miles from the centre of Swansea overlooks the sea and offers ready access to the Gower Peninsula, the UK's first area of outstanding natural beauty. Apart from Singleton Abbey, the neo-Gothic mansion which houses the administration, most of the buildings are modern. The newest is the £50-million six-storey Institute of Life Science, the research arm of the School of Medicine, which is home to the IBM "Blue C" Supercomputer, one of the fastest computers in the world dedicated to life science research. Another recent addition is the £4.3-million Digital Technium Building, housing the media and communication studies department.

Swansea makes a particular effort to cater for disabled students, which are coordinated through a £250,000 assessment and training centre. Other access measures have been successful: more than a quarter of the undergraduates come from working-class homes, while the 15 per cent from areas sending few students to higher education and the 92 per cent share of places going to applicants from state schools and colleges are both higher than the funding council's benchmark for the institution. The projected dropout rate is a respectable 11 per cent.

Sports facilities are good. An Olympic-sized swimming pool, a new athletics track, all-weather pitches and gym are all helping to attract top performers. The 1,800 computers available for student use represent one of the best ratios at any university. Another 350 hall places opening in September will take the total over 3,000 . The city has a reasonable range of leisure facilities, but the campus itself is the focus of social life.

Undergraduate Fees and Bursaries

- Welsh-domiciled student fees: £3,145, with grant of up to £1,890
- Non-Welsh UK domiciled and EU student fees: £3,145
- International student fees: £9,010–£11,460
- Welsh National Bursary for all UK students, means-tested with maximum of £310.
- Scholarships based on circumstances or by competition. For full details see the university's website: www.swansea.ac.uk/scholarships

Students

Undergraduates:	8,770	(2,600)
Postgraduates:	1,285	(1,460)
Mature students:	20.5%	
Overseas students:	6.9%	
Applications per place:	4.3	
From state-sector schools:	92.4%	
From working-class homes:	26.8%	

For detailed information about fees, grants and bursaries and how they work, see chapter 7.

Accommodation

Number of places and costs refer to 2008–09
University-provided places: about 3,400
Percentage catered: 11%
Catered costs: £93.50–£104.50 a week.
Self-catered costs: £62–£93 a week.
First-year students holding a firm offer are guaranteed accommodation if conditions are met.
International students: offered up to 3 years.
Contact: accommodation@swansea.ac.uk

Swansea Metropolitan University

The newest university in this year's *Guide* can trace its history back more than 150 years, although its change of status came only in January 2008. However, it does not appear in the main League Table or in any of the subject tables because the university instructed the Higher Education Statistics Agency not to release data on its performance. Early drafts of the main ranking suggest that it would have appeared in the bottom ten places, last of the nine institutions in Wales.

Swansea Met is divided into three faculties: Applied Design and Engineering, Art and Design, and Humanities. Of around 5,600 students, just more than half are full-time undergraduates, almost half of whom are studying education or the humanities and a third of whom are over 21 on entry. Surprisingly, given the mix of subjects, more of them are male than female. Two thirds of the undergraduates come from within 45 miles of Swansea, but there is also a long-established tradition of overseas recruitment, which accounts for almost 7 per cent of the places.

Based around the centre of Swansea, the new university is gradually developing an urban campus. There are four sites close to the city centre and another high above the city, overlooking Swansea Bay, for education and the humanities. The main Mount Pleasant campus is the largest in terms of student numbers, hosting design and engineering, business and leisure courses. Its automotive engineering degrees – especially those focused on motorsport – are probably now the best-known feature of the university.

The nearby Dynevor site has seen the most recent development, with an impressive new building for art, design and media, which was rated excellent in the now dated teaching quality assessments. All the faculty's students undertake an "external project" with a company or outside organisation, which has improved employment prospects in a notoriously difficult group of subjects. The two smaller sites are the former college of art, which focuses on the university's internationally rated work on architectural stained glass, and the former BBC building, where the music technology degree is located.

Grades in the 2001 Research Assessment Exercise were the lowest at any institution in this year's *Guide*, but the university is hoping for better in 2008. Every faculty has a research director and a series of research centres is planned.

University status arrived at an opportune moment for, while other universities in Wales were experiencing a

---

Mount Pleasant
Swansea SA1 6ED
01792 481010
enquiry@sihe.ac.uk
www.sihe.ac.uk
www.metsu.org

The Times Rankings
Swansea Metropolitan blocked the release of data from the Higher Education Statistics Agency and so we cannot give any ranking information.

serious downturn in applications at the beginning of 2008, the decline at Swansea Met was less than 3 per cent. Comfortably the best performance in the Principality following the switch from six choices per applicant to five, this represented substantial real-terms growth in demand for places. Teacher training produced the best results in a generally disappointing set of student satisfaction ratings published in 2007.

Efforts to widen participation in higher education are high on the new university's agenda. More than a third of the undergraduates have a working-class background and almost a quarter come from areas with little tradition of higher education – significantly more than the UK average for Swansea Met's subjects and entry qualifications. However, the projected dropout rate is also well over that average, with almost a quarter not expected to complete their course in the expected time.

There are only 300 residential places – not enough for all first years – but private housing is plentiful and reasonably priced. The city has seen considerable develoment recently and has a good range of pubs and clubs. The university's sports facilities are not extensive, but the nearby Gower Peninsula, officially an area of outstanding natural beauty, is a prime location for surfers and walkers.

Undergraduate Fees and Bursaries
- Welsh-domiciled student fees: £3,145, with grant of up to £1,890
- Non-Welsh UK domiciled and EU student fees: £3,145
- International student fees: £6,950
- Welsh National Bursary for all UK students, means-tested with maximum of £310.
- Bursary on full grant: £500 if living more than 45 miles from University.
- Bursaries on partial grant: £500 if living more than 45 miles from University (UK and EU students only).
- Scholarships based on circumstances or by competition. For full details see the university's website: www.sihe.ac.uk/sihe/bursaries/bursaries.htm

Students

Undergraduates:	3,040	(1,375)
Postgraduates:	470	(740)
Mature students:	31.3%	
Overseas students:	6.8%	
Applications per place:	3.5	
From state-sector schools:	97.8%	
From working-class homes:	37.9%	

For detailed information about fees, grants and bursaries and how they work, see chapter 7.

Accommodation
Number of places and costs refer to 2008–09
University-provided places: 318
Percentage catered: 0%
Self-catered costs: £49 (twin) – £65 (en suite) a week.
First years cannot be guaranteed accommodation. Residential restrictions apply.
International students: guaranteed if conditions met and application received by 31 August.
Contact: accommodation@smu.ac.uk;
01792 482082

University of Teesside

Teesside used to describe itself as the Opportunity University, stressing its open access and customer-oriented approach. But its latest mission statement stresses "pursuing excellence" to suggest that there will be no compromise on quality. The formula is popular with undergraduates, who have placed the university on the fringes of the top 20 in the first three National Student Surveys. Only one former polytechnic finished higher in the results published in 2007, when Teesside's nursing students were the most satisfied in the country. Health subjects, art and design, history and law also did well.

Teesside has long been among the leading new universities for the proportion of leavers going into graduate-level jobs or further training and teaching ratings improved sharply in the later years of assessment. Health subjects were among the top scorers for teaching quality, as well as computer science, design and nursing. The 7,500 health students are now by far the largest group in the university. The last set of research grades were an improvement on 1996, with history rated as outstanding, but the overall results still left Teesside among the bottom ten universities. It has since announced a £1.5-million research investment plan.

Official performance indicators also show the university well ahead of the access benchmarks calculated by the Higher Education Statistics Agency. Few English institutions draw a larger proportion of undergraduates from areas of low participation in higher education, while more than 45 per cent of the students come from working-class homes. The projected dropout rate has improved, partly because of a European-funded programme on supporting non-traditional students, and is now below the national average for the courses and entry qualifications.

Although Middlesbrough has never been considered a fashionable student destination, the demand for places has been sustained at a time when some new universities were having recruitment problems. There was a big drop in applications for degree courses at the beginning of 2008, but increases in Foundation degrees and nursing diplomas kept the total close to the national average. There are now more than 21,000 undergraduates, over half of them taking part-time courses and more than a third over 21 on entry. Teesside is particularly strong in niche markets such as computer games design and animation, sport and exercise, forensic science and health-related courses like physiotherapy and radiography.

Over 2,000 students are taking Teesside courses at local further education colleges, which are also involved in the growing

---

Borough Road
Middlesbrough TS1 3BA
01642 218121 (switchboard)
enquiries@tees.ac.uk
www.tees.ac.uk
www.utsu.org.uk

The Times Rankings
Overall Ranking: 88

Student satisfaction:	=18	(77%)
Research quality:	=99	(0.7)
Entry standards:	=89	(253)
Student–staff ratio:	=79	(19.5)
Services & facilities/student:	102	(£750)
Expected completion rate:	99	(74.4%)
Good honours:	86	(50.2%)
Graduate prospects:	91	(57.3%)

range of full-time and part-time two-year Foundation degrees. The university has opened its first higher education centre attached to one of the colleges in Darlington. The Passport scheme offers help and guidance to students considering going to university. However, the university's best-known access initiative targets a much younger age group. The prize-winning Meteor scheme gives primary school-children a taste of higher education, with university students acting as mentors while earning some useful extra cash and gaining experience of working in schools.

More than £100 million has been spent in recent years on the town-centre campus. The latest additions are a £10-million centre for creative technologies, for computing, media and design students, and a £12-million Institute of Digital Innovation, which supports digital business enterprises. Over 100 new graduate business have been incubated on campus since 2000. Computer provision is generous, with 1,800 PCs and specialist facilities for those studying computer games design, animation and digital media.

Middlesbrough has more nightlife than sceptics might imagine, and the booming student population has attracted new pubs, cafés and student-orientated shops in and around the Southfield Road area. The cost of living is another attraction: university rents are among the lowest in the country and the lively students' union has twice won the title of students' union of the year. Outdoor sports facilities include a £1.5-million watersports centre on the River Tees, which is shared with Durham University.

Undergraduate Fees and Bursaries

- Fees for UK/EU students: £3,145
- International student fees: £8,000–£8,500
- Bursary on full grant: £1,000
- Bursaries on partial grant: n/a
- Scholarships based on circumstances or by competition. For full details see the university's website: www.tees.ac.uk/funding www.tees.ac.uk/sections/fulltime/fees.cfm

Students

Undergraduates:	8,470	(12,405)
Postgraduates:	1,210	(1,455)
Mature students:	34.1%	
Overseas students:	4.6%	
Applications per place:	5.1	
From state-sector schools:	98.5%	
From working-class homes:	45.6%	

For detailed information about fees, grants and bursaries and how they work, see chapter 7.

Accommodation

Number of places and costs refer to 2008–09
University-provided places: 1,168
Percentage catered: 0%
Self-catered costs: £44.24–£70.27 a week (residences, 37 weeks); £40–£44 (managed housing, 38 weeks)
University managed residences are reserved exclusively for first years.
International students: as above.
Contact: 01642 342255;
accommodation@tees.ac.uk

Thames Valley University

Having survived a tumultuous period in which the university's academic standards were criticised, the Vice-Chancellor resigned and demand for places collapsed, Thames Valley has embarked on a new future as a much larger institution spanning further and higher education. A merger with Reading College, at the start of 2004, has produced a university of almost 60,000 students, including 36,000 part-timers, where more than half of the places are on further education courses and there is even a sixth-form academy. Armed with a £6.7 million "strategic development grant", it is aiming to become the country's leading university for employer engagement, with an accent on the creative industries and entrepreneurship.

A new campus in Brentford, West London, opened fully in 2006, with 850 residential places as well as extensive teaching accommodation for the largest healthcare faculty in Britain. One of the two campuses in Reading is being completely redeveloped and £9.5 million is being invested in improving the original campus at Ealing. Another £3 million has already been spent on the Slough campus, with more to come.

It is all a far cry from the end of the 1990s, when barely 30 degrees were left.

Although the aftermath of that period has left the university in the lower reaches of *The Times* League Table, the university is virtually unrecognisable from those dark days and it has started to climb the rankings. The finances are under control, a quality audit has produced a clean bill of health, and even before the merger, there were plans for renewed growth. However, after a big increase in 2005, applications have been dropping again. There was a 26 per cent decline in demand for places at the start of 2008, following the switch from six choices per applicant to five.

Courses are now concentrated in four faculties – arts, music and design; health and human sciences; professional studies; and technology. Many further education programmes are being extended into degrees or professional qualifications. Among the casualties of the reorganisation, however, were the two top-rated subjects, sociology and linguistics, which also achieved one of the few grade 5 research assessments in the new universities in 1996.

Amid the reconstruction, new honours degrees have been launched in areas such as video production, 3D design, entrepreneurship, and web and e-business computing. The portfolio of two-year Foundation degrees is growing, with employers such as Compaq, Ealing Studios and the Savoy Hotel Group helping to

---

St Mary's Road
Ealing
London W5 5RF
020 8579 5000
learning.advice@
 tvu.ac.uk
www.tvu.ac.uk
www.tvusu.co.uk

The Times Rankings
Overall Ranking: 112

Student satisfaction:	=104	(67%)
Research quality:	=111	(0.4)
Entry standards:	=107	(212)
Student–staff ratio:	=99	(20.6)
Services & facilities/student:	103	(£747)
Expected completion rate:	106	(69.5%)
Good honours:	=94	(48.4%)
Graduate prospects:	=66	(62.7%)

provide courses. Some are run in conjunction with Stratford-upon-Avon College –
one of a number of partner institutions.
The university also has 17 outreach centres
in and around Reading, at Southall and
even Heathrow Airport.

A policy of open access puts the
university at a disadvantage in rankings
such as ours. TVU also has the worst
research record in the university system,
having entered only 75 academics for the
latest assessments. Three quarters of the
students are over 25, and 60 per cent are
female. More than a third of the undergraduates come from working-class
homes, and the latest projected dropout
rate is back above one in five, although
this is still fractionally less than the
national average for the university's
courses and entry grades.

Some of the vocational courses have a
strong reputation. Nursing courses are
popular and well regarded, while the
School of Tourism, Hospitality and
Leisure Management is recognised by
the Académie Culinaire de France for its
culinary arts programmes. The school
achieved a good score in the final round of
teaching assessment, but linguistics and
sociology were the only other subjects to
manage 22 points out of 24 for teaching
quality. TVU made big strides in the last
National Student Survey, with accountancy
students easily the most satisfied, after

finishing second from bottom in 2006.

The town-centre sites in Ealing,
Reading and Slough are linked by a free
bus service. The business-oriented campus
in Slough consists mainly of 1960s
buildings, but has been enhanced by an
award-winning learning resources centre
designed by Sir Richard Rogers. The
busier Ealing base was suffering from
overcrowding before retrenchment took
place. Almost half of the students are from
London or Berkshire, despite an
unexpectedly large contingent of overseas
students. Residential accommodation is
growing and the new Paragon building, in
Brentford, won *Building* magazine's Major
Housing Project of the Year award.
However, students who rely on private
housing find the cost of living high. The
Slough campus boasts an impressive gym,
but otherwise sports facilities are limited.

Undergraduate Fees and Bursaries

- Fees for UK/EU students: £3,145
- International student fees: £7,600–£8,900
- Bursary on full grant: £1,030
- Bursaries on partial grant: household income £25K–£40K: £515.
- Scholarships based on circumstances or by competition. For full details see the university's website: www.tvu.ac.uk/students/ undergraduate/Scholarships_and_bursaries. jsp

Students

Undergraduates:	8,905	(8,295)
Postgraduates:	650	(1,290)
Mature students:	56.9%	
Overseas students:	14.7%	
Applications per place:	4.2	
From state-sector schools:	96.2%	
From working-class homes:	36.7%	

*For detailed information about fees, grants and
bursaries and how they work, see chapter 7.*

Accommodation

Number of places and costs refer to 2007–08
University-provided places: about 911
Percentage catered: 0%
Self-catered costs: £87–£152 a week.
First years are prioritised for accommodation at
Ealing if conditions are met; accommodation at
Reading is allocated on a distance
from campus basis.
International students: same as above.
Contact: uas@tvu.ac.uk
reading.homes@tvu.ac.uk

University of Ulster

Ulster remains one of the most popular universities in Britain, in spite of a 16 per cent fall in applications at the start of 2008, when the number of choices per applicant was cut from six to five. The university – the only one in Britain with a charter stipulating that there should be courses below degree level – would like to expand but is constrained by Government policy. UU has had to pull out of its most ambitious project: the proposed "peaceline campus" linking Belfast's two communities after years of on/off negotiations. But there are plans to improve and expand all four main sites, at a cost of £200 million, during the current decade.

With more Irish students now choosing to stay in the Province to study, there is plenty of scope for expansion, despite the fact that UU already has more than 20,000 students. The main sites in and near Belfast have never been busier, while Magee attracts students from both sides of the border. High technology brings the university together for teaching purposes, but the sites are 80 miles apart at their farthest point and very different in character. Jordanstown, seven miles outside Belfast, has the most students, concentrating on engineering, health and social science. Numbers are being limited to prevent overcrowding and more building is

planned. The isolated original university campus, at Coleraine, follows the style of the 1960s, and is the most traditional in outlook, with a focus on science and the humanities. There is a new £11-million Centre for Molecular Biosciences, and further building is in the pipeline. The small Belfast site has always specialised in art and design, but a £30-million redevelopment will see its range of subjects expand.

Recent development has focused mainly on the Magee campus in Londonderry, although Jordanstown has acquired improved library and computing facilities. Once the poor relation of the university, confined to adult education, Magee is now a thriving centre. Student numbers are expected to grow to about 7,500, including part-timers, with new schools of performing arts, computing and electronics, as well as improved provision for education, nursing and Irish studies. The Institute for Legal and Professional Studies will allow graduates to train as barristers and solicitors. The historic Foyle Arts Centre has become part of the university and a postgraduate medical school is planned

Although often overshadowed by Queen's University, Ulster's community consciousness has worked to its advantage. Almost half the students come from working-class homes – far more than the

---

Cromore Road
Coleraine
Co. Londonderry BT52 1SA
08700 400 700
enquiry via website
www.ulster.ac.uk
www.uusu.org

The Times Rankings
Overall Ranking: 53

Student satisfaction:	=39	(75%)
Research quality:	55	(2.4)
Entry standards:	62	(278)
Student–staff ratio:	=46	(16.4)
Services & facilities/student:	16	(£1,462)
Expected completion rate:	=86	(77.0%)
Good honours:	53	(60.1%)
Graduate prospects:	=69	(62.1%)

UK average – and the student profile mirrors the religious balance in the wider population. Mature students are well catered for, with access courses for those who lack the necessary entry qualifications, a nursery and three playgroups in the university. There has never been a big representation from mainland Britain, but its contingent of international students include those from the Republic of Ireland as well as further afield. The Campus One programme provides an alternative mode of study, with a range of courses available online to students all over the world.

Teaching ratings were mainly sound, rather than spectacular, although business and management registered maximum points. Research is not Ulster's principal strength, but grades improved in the latest assessments, with Celtic studies and biomedical sciences rated internationally outstanding. Sociology and social policy did best in the first three national student satisfaction surveys, with sports science also producing good results in 2007. However, the latest projected dropout rate was more than 22 per cent – considerably more than the "benchmark" calculated according to the university's subjects and entry grades.

As with any split-site university, the student experience varies according to the location. Some courses offer lectures on more than one campus, but for the most part students are based on a single site throughout their university life. Jordanstown, for example, hosts the Sports Institute for Northern Ireland and the university's own High Performance Centre, but there are no on-site sports facilities at the Belfast campus. With more than half of the students living with their parents or at their own home, the university is not always the focus of social life. The exception is Coleraine, a classic campus university, where there are fewer home-based students, although many gravitate towards the nearby seaside towns of Portrush and Portstewart.

Undergraduate Fees and Bursaries

- Fees for UK/EU students: £3,145
- International student fees: £8,540
- Bursary on full grant: up to £18,360: £1,040; up to £21K: £620; up to £25K: £310.
- Bursaries on partial grant: household income up to £39.3K: £310.
- Scholarships based on circumstances or by competition. For full details see the university's website: http://prospectus.ulster.ac.uk/geninfo/how-much-does-it-cost.html

---

Students

Undergraduates:	15,325	(3,845)
Postgraduates:	1,255	(3,310)
Mature students:	18.2%	
Overseas students:	9.1%	
Applications per place:	8.0	
From state-sector schools:	99.9%	
From working-class homes:	46.8%	

For detailed information about fees, grants and bursaries and how they work, see chapter 7.

Accommodation

Number of places and costs refer to 2008–09
University-provided places: 2,400
Percentage catered: 0%
Self-catered costs: £45–£95 a week.
First-year students are guaranteed accommodation if conditions are met.
International students: same as above.
Contact: accommodation@ulster.ac.uk

University of the Arts London

The London Institute resisted the temptation to apply for university status after it was formed in 1986 because the art, design, fashion and media colleges that had come together for administrative purposes were world-famous in their own right. But the arrival as rector of Sir Michael Bichard, previously Permanent Secretary at the Department for Education and Skills, prompted a rethink. The resulting University of the Arts London got in ahead of the recent wave of universities in order to ensure that it had a research remit and is already becoming a powerful "brand".

The five component colleges became six when Wimbledon College of Art joined in 2006. The founding members, which continue to use their own names and enjoy considerable autonomy, were Camberwell College of Arts, Central Saint Martins College of Art and Design, Chelsea College of Art and Design, London College of Fashion and London College of Communication (formerly the London College of Printing). Together, they boast a total of more than 20,000 students spread around 20 sites around central London, representing the biggest concentration of art, design and creative arts in Europe.

Teaching and research grades for the Institute barely did justice to the eminence of the colleges. Although Camberwell and what was then the College of Printing achieved near-perfect scores for teaching quality in art and design, the other colleges' grades in this category and those for business and management, materials technology and media studies were strong but not spectacular. Chelsea and London College of Fashion were jointly awarded a national teaching centre for the arts, focusing on practice-based teaching and learning. Wimbledon brings an international reputation for excellence in theatre design, boasting the UK's largest school of theatre. Teaching quality assessors liked the heavy use of often eminent visiting lecturers, who do about half of the teaching, as well as the close links with industry and the broad range of courses, which stretch from further education to postgraduate. But the university as a whole has been bottom of rankings in the last two National Student Surveys. Art and design students are among the least satisfied nationally, but the university was also in the bottom ten for those subjects alone.

The figures have not affected applications, which have risen every year since the university was established. The 9 per cent rise at the beginning of 2008 was one of the few increases at any university. A number of two-year Foundation degrees have been introduced, including one in interactive games production and another in fashion styling and photography. Students have

---

65 Davies Street
London W1K 5DA
020 7514 6000
info@arts.ac.uk
www.arts.ac.uk
www.suarts.org

The Times Rankings
Overall Ranking: 75

Student satisfaction:	106	(62%)
Research quality:	=33	(4.4)
Entry standards:	49	(304)
Student–staff ratio:	101	(20.8)
Services & facilities/student:	87	(£870)
Expected completion rate:	38	(87.1%)
Good honours:	=56	(58.8%)
Graduate prospects:	107	(51.5%)

access to the largest art and design specialist careers information centre in the country, while the pioneering Emerging Artists Programme continues to support graduates in the early years of their careers.

The projected dropout rate was down to 12 per cent in the latest survey, which is better than average for the subjects on offer. The university has been running weekend classes and summer schools in an attempt to broaden the intake, as well as organising a national event to help students with their portfolios, and the proportion of undergraduates from working-class homes is now a quarter.

Big changes were already under way before the change of title was agreed: a £70-million development programme has produced prestigious new premises for Chelsea College next door to the Tate Gallery, on Millbank, with extensive work-shop facilities, studios and an impressive new library. Another £32 million has been spent on new headquarters for the College of Communication at the Elephant and Castle, south of the Thames, where a newly built Special Archives and Collections Centre will include the archives of the filmmaker Stanley Kubrick. The college now has Film Academy status. The next big project will bring Central St Martins together on one site for the first time, when it moves to the new King's Cross development in 2011.

A £2-million information technology system links all the sites. The colleges vary considerably in character and facilities, although a single students' union serves them all and a new Student Hub has brought all student services together at the university's central London headquarters. The university is not overprovided with residential accommodation, although there are 11 residences spread around the colleges, providing more than 2,200 beds. House-hunting workshops help those who have to rely on what is inevitably an expensive private housing market. Somewhat stereotypically, the university owns no sports facilities, although it has arranged student discounts with a number of providers.

Undergraduate Fees and Bursaries

- Fees for UK/EU students: £3,145
- International student fees: £10,400
- Bursary on full grant: £310
- Bursaries on partial grant: considered for £1,000 University Access Bursary.
- Scholarships based on circumstances or by competition. For full details see the university's website: www.arts.ac.uk/money

---

Students

Undergraduates:	11,785	(670)
Postgraduates:	1,600	(850)
Mature students:	26.5%	
Overseas students:	31.0%	
Applications per place:	4.7	
From state-sector schools:	94.3%	
From working-class homes:	25.0%	

For detailed information about fees, grants and bursaries and how they work, see chapter 7.

Accommodation

Number of places and costs refer to 2008–09
University-provided places: 2,244
Percentage catered: 0%
Self-catered costs: £76.25–£166.60 a week.
First-year students are offered accommodation if conditions (including age and distance) are met. Priority for disabled or special needs students.
International students: guaranteed if conditions met and application received by 31 August.
Contact: www.arts.ac.uk/housing/

University College London

Such is the breadth and quality of provision at University College London (UCL) that, even without being a university in its own right, it can fairly describe itself as one of the top multifaculty institutions in England. Its position in *The Times* rankings has regularly confirmed this and, in 2007, it broke into the top ten universities in the world in the global rankings published by *Times Higher Education* and QS. UCL's excellence is built on a history of pioneering subjects that have become commonplace in higher education: modern languages, geography and fine arts among them.

Already comfortably the largest of London University's colleges, UCL took in a number of specialist schools and institutes at the end of the 1990s. Most were medical or dental, and UCL's medical school is now a large and formidable unit. Its credentials have been strengthened still further with the announcement that UCL will be the main university partner in the new national medical research centre to be constructed adjacent to St Pancras Station. The centre will undertake cutting-edge research to advance understanding of health and disease.

The various acquisitions mean that there are now outposts in several parts of central and north London, but the main activity remains centred on the original impressive Bloomsbury site. There have been discussions with Camden Council on the creation of a university quarter, linking UCL's buildings and the neighbouring University College Hospital buildings, together with neighbouring parts of the University of London.

Chemical engineering, several languages, pharmacology, psychology, anthropology, economics and chemistry are among 13 areas rated internationally outstanding for research. One academic in three was in a top-rated department in the last assessments but, although almost nine out of ten were in the top two categories, the results did not quite match the high benchmark set in 1996. Economics, health-related subjects, history of art and organismal biosciences all recorded maximum points for teaching, but most subjects scored well. UCL has done better than most London universities in the first three National Student Surveys, although the 2007 results did not quite match the previous year's.

A growing number of degrees take four years, and most are organised on a modular basis.

About 6,000 of UCL's students are from overseas, more than half of them postgraduates and a third of them from other EU countries, reflecting the college's high international standing. The

---

Gower Street
London WC1E 6BT
020 7679 3000 (Study
   Information Centre)
contact via website
www.ucl.ac.uk
www.uclu.org

The Times Rankings
Overall Ranking: 7

Student satisfaction:	=26	(76%)
Research quality:	=6	(5.5)
Entry standards:	8	(434)
Student–staff ratio:	1	(9.1)
Services & facilities/student:	6	(£1,702)
Expected completion rate:	13	(94.3%)
Good honours:	13	(75.1%)
Graduate prospects:	=5	(81.5%)

proportion is likely to rise further in the coming years. Most departments interview suitably qualified British applicants and, once accepted, many first-year students are helped to make the academic and social adjustment to university life through UCL's Transition Programme, which includes a variety of activities such as peer mentoring and workshops. UCL stresses its commitment to teaching in small groups, especially in the second and subsequent years of degree courses. The approach seems to work: almost three quarters leave with a first or upper second. The projected dropout rate of less than 6 per cent is below the national average for the courses and entry grades.

UCL is conscious of its traditions as a college founded to expand access to higher education, but the 38 per cent share of places going to independent school students is one of the highest in Britain. Less than one undergraduate in five has a working-class background and just 6.4 per cent come from an area without a tradition of higher education. Concerted attempts are being made to broaden the intake with summer schools for state school students, outreach activities and campus-based programmes. UCL is sponsoring a new academy, which it sees as part of its contribution to the local community.

The academic pace can be frantic but, close to the West End and with its own theatre and recreational facilities, there is no shortage of leisure options. Students also have immediate access to London University's underused central students' union facilities. Residential accommodation is plentiful and of a good standard. Indoor sports facilities are close at hand, but the main outdoor pitches, though good enough to attract professional football clubs, are a coach ride away in Hertfordshire. Hockey players have access to Astroturf pitches at the Old Cranleighans ground, in Thames Ditton.

Undergraduate Fees and Bursaries

- Fees for UK/EU students: £3,145
- International student fees: £11,810–£15,460 £23,060 (clinical)
- Bursary on full grant: household income up to £15.8K: sliding scale £2,700–£1,600, then at least 50% of maintenance grant.
- Bursaries on partial grant: at least 50% of maintenance grant.
- Scholarships based on circumstances or by competition. For full details see the university's website: www.ucl.ac.uk/prospective-students/ undergraduate-study/fees-and-costs/ www.ucl.ac.uk/scholarships

Students

Undergraduates:	11,085	(720)
Postgraduates:	5,040	(2,545)
Mature students:	13.4%	
Overseas students:	26.8%	
Applications per place:	8.7	
From state-sector schools:	62.4%	
From working-class homes:	17.5%	

For detailed information about fees, grants and bursaries and how they work, see chapter 7.

Accommodation

Number of places and costs refer to 2008–09
University-provided places: 4,197 (including 500 intercollegiate places)
Percentage catered: 30%
Catered costs: £101.71–£144.97 a week.
Self-catered costs: £68.60–£145.18 a week.
First years are guaranteed accommodation if conditons are met.
International students: as above.
Contact: Residences@ucl.ac.uk
www.ucl.ac.uk/admission/accommodation

University of Warwick

The most successful of the first wave of new universities, Warwick was derided by many in its early years for its close links with business and industry. Few are critical today. Gordon Brown described it as "one of the great universities, absolutely central to the industrial, scientific and technological future of our country." Both teaching and research are very highly rated, but the university's mission statement still stresses the extension of access to higher and continuing education and community links.

There is a smaller proportion of independent school students than at most of the leading universities – less than a quarter – although this does not translate into large numbers of working-class undergraduates. The share of places going to students from the lowest social classes and the representation from areas sending few young people to higher education are both lower than the national average for Warwick's subjects and entry qualifications. But the mix helps to produce one of the lowest dropout rates in Britain. Warwick puts almost a third of its income from top-up fees into bursaries and financial support – one of the highest proportions among the old universities.

Teaching assessments were outstanding, with seven maximum scores, and the university's one appearance in the National Student Survey produced respectable results. Language students were the most satisfied. The university was awarded a national teaching centre in theatrical performance, in partnership with the Royal Shakespeare Company, and is collaborating with Oxford Brookes University on another centre to "reinvent" undergraduate research. Six subjects were rated internationally outstanding for research: business, economics, English, theatre studies and applied mathematics and statistics. Nine out of ten academics entered for assessment were placed in the top two categories, preserving Warwick's place among the top five research universities. The science park, one of the first in Britain, is among the most successful.

While other leading universities were trying to cover the whole range of academic disciplines, Warwick pursued a selective policy. Without the expense of medicine, dentistry or veterinary science to bear, the university invested shrewdly in business, science and engineering. However, the temptation of medicine has proved too much to bear, and the university now has a thriving graduate entry medical school, with more than 2,000 students. The university is to lead a new regional health sciences centre, which will include an anatomy training and clinical skills centre for Warwick students and local surgeons.

Another deviation has seen the university embracing the Government's

Coventry CV4 7AL
024 7652 3723 (admissions)
ugadmissions@warwick.ac.uk
www.warwick.ac.uk
www.warwicksu.com/
Default.aspx

Edinburgh
Belfast
COVENTRY
Cardiff
London

The Times Rankings
Overall Ranking: 6

Student satisfaction:	=26	(76%)
Research quality:	5	(5.6)
Entry standards:	5	(448)
Student–staff ratio:	17	(13.6)
Services & facilities/student:	4	(£1,881)
Expected completion rate:	4	(96.7%)
Good honours:	7	(79.4%)
Graduate prospects:	=23	(74.9%)

two-year Foundation degrees. One of the few leading universities to offer the vocational programmes, Warwick is running three courses in education and community enterprise, the latter taught by a local further education college.

With around ten applicants for every place on conventional degree courses, many departments stick rigidly to offers averaging more than an A and two Bs at A level. Applications have been buoyant, holding steady at the start of 2008, when the number of choices per applicant was cut from six to five. Warwick has been building up its numbers in science and engineering, as other universities have struggled to fill their places. The business school has also been growing rapidly, with a new £15-million extension now complete, while computer science has acquired new, upgraded facilities.

Hundreds of millions of pounds have been spent on the campus, which has often resembled a building site. However, students are about to welcome a second significant extension to union facilities. Work is almost complete on a new £12.5-million building to house a "digital laboratory" for manufacturing and engineering research and a new indoor tennis centre opened in 2008. A suite of new plant science labs and a new base for the partnership with Royal Shakespeare Company will follow shortly.

The 750-acre campus is three miles south of Coventry, where many students choose to live, and three times as far from Warwick. University accommodation is plentiful and the Arts Centre is one of the largest of its type in Britain. The sports facilities are both extensive and conveniently placed on campus, where there is a new sports centre with 25-metre swimming pool and a range of other facilities.

Undergraduate Fees and Bursaries

- Fees for UK/EU students: £3,145
- International student fees: £10,250–£13,350
- Bursary on full grant: £1,800
- Bursaries on partial grant: household income up to £36K: £1,800.
- Scholarships based on circumstances or by competition. For full details see the university's website: www.warwick.ac.uk/go/WUAP

Students

Undergraduates:	10,635	(9,740)
Postgraduates:	3,535	(6,405)
Mature students:	10.7%	
Overseas students:	15.9%	
Applications per place:	8.9	
From state-sector schools:	76.0%	
From working-class homes:	18.7%	

For detailed information about fees, grants and bursaries and how they work, see chapter 7.

Accommodation

Number of places and costs refer to 2008–09
University-provided places: 5,722 (on campus); 1,650 (head leasing)
Percentage catered: 0%
Self-catered costs: £70–£115 a week (30, 39, 50 week contracts).
All first-year undergraduates are guaranteed accommodation (terms and conditions apply). International students as above (terms and conditions apply).
Contact: www.warwick.ac.uk/accommodation

University of the West of England, Bristol

West of England (UWE) is the largest provider of higher education in the south-west of England and one of the most popular post-1992 universities, both in terms of total applications and the proportion – one in four – who subsequently choose to study there. Applications were ahead of the national average at the official deadline for courses beginning in 2008, following several years of increases earlier in the decade. The university has sometimes found itself in trouble for missing its benchmarks for widening access to higher education, but official reports now accept that this is largely due to its location. The proportion of independent school entrants has dropped to less than 12 per cent – still a figure exceeded by only one new university – while the share of places going to students from working-class homes is approaching three in ten. UWE has one of England's largest bursary schemes, with its top rate of £1,250 going to over a third of its students.

UWE boasted the best teaching quality record in the new universities and has always been regarded among the leaders in its peer group. Perfect scores for education and in the joint assessment for biology and biomedical sciences represented the best results, but in the last five years of assessments, every subject was given at least 20 out of 24 points. The projected dropout rate has been coming down but, at more than 18 per cent, is still above the national average for the university's subjects and entry qualifications.

Unusually, the university trains and pays its 900 student representatives – the biggest such network in the country. More than half of the students come from the West Country and there are close links with local business and industry. These provide guest lecturers, professors involved in practice and thousands of part-time jobs and work placements for students. A network of 15 colleges stretches into Somerset and Wiltshire, offering UWE programmes. Hartpury College, near Gloucester, has become an associate faculty of the university, specialising in agriculture, equine studies and other land-based courses, and there are university centres in hospitals in Bath and Swindon.

A tradition of vocational education regularly helps the university to a healthy graduate employment record. The entrance system credits vocational qualifications and practical experience equally with traditional academic results. Law received a commendation from the Legal Practice Board and the degree in architecture and planning won a similar accolade from the Royal Town Planning Institute for bringing

Frenchay Campus
Coldharbour Lane
Bristol BS16 1QY
0117 328 3333 (admissions)
admissions@uwe.ac.uk
www.uwe.ac.uk
www.uwesu.org/ez

The Times Rankings
Overall Ranking: 65

Student satisfaction:	=55	(74%)
Research quality:	=63	(1.6)
Entry standards:	=80	(261)
Student–staff ratio:	74	(18.8)
Services & facilities/student:	83	(£906)
Expected completion rate:	=69	(80.6%)
Good honours:	67	(55.9%)
Graduate prospects:	=55	(64.4%)

together the two disciplines in one joint-honours course giving dual professional qualifications. UWE is one of just four universities recognised by the Forensic Science Society for the quality of courses in the subject.

Among the new universities, only Oxford Brookes entered a larger proportion of academics than UWE's 40 per cent in the 2001 Research Assessment Exercise. The results were an improvement on 1996, with accounting and finance rated nationally outstanding with much work of international standards. However, the scale of the entry also produced more low grades than the university would have wished.

There are four sites in Bristol itself, mainly around the north of the city, with regional centres in Bath, and Swindon concentrating on the growth area of nursing. Only Bower Ashton, which has new studio space and media suites for its art, media and design students, is in the south. The main campus at Frenchay, close to Bristol Parkway station but four miles out of the city centre, has by far the largest number of students and includes the Student Services Department, which brings together the various non-academic services. The St Matthias campus (for social sciences and humanities) and Glenside (for midwifery, nursing, physiotherapy and radiography) are more attractive but less lively.

Bristol is a hugely popular student centre: an attractive and lively city, but not cheap. University accommodation has become more plentiful in recent years, with over 4,000 places available, including nearly 2,000 in a new £80-million student village on the Frenchay campus. Sports facilities were a bone of contention for students, but a new sports complex opened in 2006 as part of a £200-million investment programme, which is one of the largest in UK higher education. It has been chosen as a pre-Olympics training site for baminton, fencing, table tennis, indoor volleyball and wrestling.

Undergraduate Fees and Bursaries

- Fees for UK/EU students: £3,145
- International student fees: £8,250–£8,700
- Bursary on full grant: household income up to £18,360: £1,250 then £750.
- Bursaries on partial grant: household income £25K–£27K: £750.
- Scholarships based on circumstances or by competition. For full details see the university's website: www.uwe.ac.uk/money

---

Students

Undergraduates:	17,500	(6,430)
Postgraduates:	2,195	(3,480)
Mature students:	22.8%	
Overseas students:	6.6%	
Applications per place:	4.6	
From state-sector schools:	88.3%	
From working-class homes:	28.6%	

For detailed information about fees, grants and bursaries and how they work, see chapter 7.

Accommodation

Number of places and costs refer to 2007–08
University-provided places: 4,066
Percentage catered: 0%
Self-catered costs: £55–£110 a week.
First-year students are guaranteed accommodation provided requirements are met.
International students are offered accommodation where possible.
Contact: accommodation@uwe.ac.uk

University of the West of Scotland

A merger between Paisley University and Bell College, in Hamilton, has produced Scotland's largest new university, with more than 18,000 students and the largest School of Health, Nursing and Midwifery north of the border. The university is planning £150 million of improvements to its four campuses, with local provision within reach of 40 per cent of Scots. However, the figures in this year's tables apply to Paisley alone, since the new university declined to release data on Bell College.

Bell, which offered courses in business, science and technology, health and social studies, was the only higher education presence in Lanarkshire. The new institution's four bases are in Paisley, Ayr, Dumfries and Hamilton. Among the first developments will be a new campus in Ayr, costing more than £75 million, to be completed by 2010; £5.5 million of library and student support services in Dumfries; and a £2-million engineering centre at Hamilton. A new computing laboratory and an employment centre for students have already opened at Paisley.

Both Paisley and Bell saw applications rise in 2007. Paisley had enjoyed surges in popularity in the early years of the decade as students flocked to a new range of degree subjects such as computer animation, commercial music, computer games technology, sports studies and music technology. The demand for places on the education and media campus in Ayr grew by 50 per cent in a year.

The two parent institutions had proud records in attracting under-represented groups onto courses. Paisley had the highest proportion of students from areas without a tradition of higher education of any university in Britain and, at nearly 47 per cent, Bell's was even higher. Unfortunately, however, Paisley's projected dropout rate of more than 23 per cent was also the highest in Scotland and Bell's was well above average for its subjects and entry qualifications. Paisley introduced a range of measures to address the problem, including a personal tutor system, strengthened counselling support and attendance monitoring. Access measures are continuing, with hundreds of youngsters aged 14 and 15 attending the "University Experience" and sampling a week of student life.

Paisley is Scotland's largest town, while Hamilton is the fifth-largest. Both are within a dozen miles of Glasgow and draw a high proportion of the students from the local area, many on part-time courses. Numbers at Paisley have grown rapidly in recent years, but staffing levels compare favourably with most new universities. There are around 1,100 international

Paisley Campus
Paisley
Renfrewshire PA1 2BE
0141 848 3000
  (switchboard)
info@uws.ac.uk
www.uws.ac.uk
www.upsa.org.uk

PAISLEY
Edinburgh
Belfast
London
Cardiff

The Times Rankings
Overall Ranking: =103

Student satisfaction:	–	(–)
Research quality:	=99	(0.7)
Entry standards:	87	(255)
Student–staff ratio:	=77	(19.4)
Services & facilities/student:	49	(£1,099)
Expected completion rate:	=108	(68.7%)
Good honours:	105	(46.1%)
Graduate prospects:	68	(62.3%)

students, thanks to long-established links with over 40 EU institutions and a growing number of Chinese and Indian nationals.

Courses are strongly vocational, with business, multimedia and health subjects by far the most popular choices. There are close links with business and industry and all students are offered hands-on computer training. Paisley was the first UK university approved by Microsoft, Macromedia and Cisco, and has the status of Microsoft Academic Professional Development Centre. A games development laboratory, supported by Sony, is part of a £300,000 package of investment in multimedia and games facilities.

A majority of Paisley's subjects were rated Highly Satisfactory for teaching quality. Under the later assessment system, accounting and finance have achieved good results and the university received the highest-possible rating in an institutional review. The university pioneered credit transfer in Scotland, giving credit for non-academic achievement, and its modular course system covers day, evening and weekend classes. Most students either take sandwich degrees or have work placements built into their courses, earning an average of £10,000 in the process, but the impact on graduate employment has not been as great as in some other universities. Research grades improved in the last assessments, with accountancy achieving the only grade 5

in any new university in Scotland, but still the majority of entrants were placed in the bottom three grades.

Paisley has invested over £9 million in student facilities in recent years. The main campus, 20 acres in the town centre, has seen substantial development, including a new library and learning resource centre. The Ayr campus has seen the establishment of a management centre in an 18th-century mansion. The Dumfries (Crichton) campus, operated in partnership with Bell and Glasgow University, has over 400 students.

The main centres – industrial Paisley and seaside Ayr – could hardly be more different, and social life varies accordingly. Leisure facilities have been improving, with the opening of a new students' union in Ayr and a £5-million union building in Paisley. Sports provision has also been upgraded: £1.5 million was spent recently on Paisley's indoor and outdoor facilities.

Undergraduate Fees and Bursaries
- Scottish-domiciled and EU students: no fees payable.
- Non-Scottish UK-domiciled student fees: £1,775 a year.
- International student fees: £7,500–£8,300
- Scholarships based on circumstances or by competition. For full details see the university's website: www.uws.ac.uk/schoolsdepts/studentservices/fundingadvice/fundsource.asp

---

Students

Undergraduates:	11,640	(4,370)
Postgraduates:	790	(990)
Mature students:	42.7%	
Overseas students:	3.6%	
Applications per place:	3.4	
From state-sector schools:	98.1%	
From working-class homes:	42.9%	

For detailed information about fees, grants and bursaries and how they work, see chapter 7.

Accommodation

Number of places and costs refer to 2007–08
University-provided places: 887 (628 at Paisley; 103 at Ayr, 156 at Hamilton)
Percentage catered: 0%
Self-catered costs: £52–£63 a week.
First-year students can apply for housing if conditions are met. Residential restrictions. International students: single non-EU students are guaranteed accommodation.
Contact: www.uws.ac.uk/about/facilities/accommodation.asp

University of Westminster

Westminster has completed a ten-year modernisation of its four sites, costing £130 million, and has since added new gym facilities, a £1-million venue and a vast underground exhibition space. The £33-million transformation of the former Harrow College, in north London was Europe's largest university construction project and the redevelopment of one of the three central sites, opposite Madame Tussauds, was even more costly. The large business school acquired a "cloistered environment" creating more space for teaching and research. The last phase saw the redevelopment of the New Cavendish Street site, near the BT Tower.

The greenfield Harrow campus boasts a high-tech information resources centre with good facilities for the highly rated media studies courses. Computing and design are also based on a site designed for 7,500 students. The West End sites provide the perfect catchment area for part-time undergraduates, who account for about a third of the 18,000 places. Only the Open University has more. By no means all the students are Londoners, however: over 15 per cent come from abroad – among the highest proportions among the new universities – and Westminster has the largest number of ethnic minority students in Britain. Westminster courses

are also taught in nine overseas countries, from Oman to the United States, a characteristic which won the university a Queen's Award for Enterprise.

The historic headquarters building, near Broadcasting House, in central London, houses social sciences and languages. Westminster claims to offer the largest number of languages of any British university, and French and Chinese scored particularly well in teaching assessments. Science and health courses are concentrated on the Cavendish campus. The univer-sity's growing interest in health includes degrees from the British College of Naturopathy and Osteopathy and a range of courses in complementary medicine, including a BSc in acupuncture. There are degrees in herbal medicine, homeopathy and nutritional therapy, and a diploma in the traditional Chinese massage technique of Qigong.

Westminster achieved a series of good teaching quality scores. Psychology and tourism lead the way with maximum points, with media studies, Chinese, community care and primary health all close behind. The university weaves work-related skills into its degree programmes, but scores in the 2007 National Student Survey were among the lowest in the country for the second successive year.

Westminster's haul of four subjects on grade 5 in the last assessment exercise was

---

309 Regent Street
London W1B 2UW
020 7911 5000 (enquiries)
course-enquiries@
    westminster.ac.uk
www.westminster.ac.uk
www.uwsu.com

Edinburgh
Belfast
Cardiff
LONDON

The Times Rankings
Overall Ranking: =101

Student satisfaction:	=99	(68%)
Research quality:	=76	(1.2)
Entry standards:	88	(254)
Student–staff ratio:	=46	(16.4)
Services & facilities/student:	101	(£763)
Expected completion rate:	=71	(80.5%)
Good honours:	90	(49.6%)
Graduate prospects:	109	(51.0%)

the best of any new university, although the decision to enter fewer than 30 per cent of academics limited both the funding rewards and the impact on the university's ranking. Asian studies, law, linguistics and media studies were all rated nationally outstanding with much work of international quality. Larger numbers will be entered in 2008, following a research drive that has seen the establishment of several interdisciplinary programmes.

More than four out of ten undergraduates are from working-class homes – a much higher proportion than the national average for the subjects offered. The university also exceeds its benchmark for the admission of students from state schools and colleges, although the central London location reduces the share of places going to students from areas without a tradition of higher education. The scholarship programme is the largest of its kind, with £4.3 million being awarded annually to over 500 home and overseas students. The university won the *Times Higher Education* award for its support for overseas students in 2005. Over 70 per cent of British undergraduates qualify for a cash bursary of £310 per year, as recipients of maintenance or special support grants at any level. The dropout rate has been improving and is now below average for the university's subjects and entry standards.

Westminster's students, like those at all the London universities, complain of the high cost of living, particularly for accommodation. The university has added considerably to its residential stock in recent years, with the opening of a £6-million block of halls in Harrow to be followed by the refurbishment of its Marylebone halls in time for the September 2008 intake, but there is no way round the capital's inflated housing market at some stage. The Harrow campus is lively socially, but those based on the other sites tend to be spread around the capital. Sports facilities are also dispersed, with playing fields and a boathouse in Chiswick, west London.

Undergraduate Fees and Bursaries

- Fees for UK/EU students: £3,145
- International student fees: £9,450
- Bursary on full grant: £310
- Bursaries on partial grant: £310
- Scholarships based on circumstances or by competition. For full details see the university's website: www.wmin.ac.uk/funding

---

Students

Undergraduates:	11,645	(6,205)
Postgraduates:	2,815	(4,045)
Mature students:	29.2%	
Overseas students:	16.2%	
Applications per place:	5.0	
From state-sector schools:	94.7%	
From working-class homes:	42.0%	

For detailed information about fees, grants and bursaries and how they work, see chapter 7.

Accommodation

Number of places and costs refer to 2008–09
University-provided places: nearly 1,500
Percentage catered: 0%
Self-catered costs: £73.08 (small single) –
£138.04 (en suite) a week.
First-year students have priority. Residential restrictions apply.
International students: as above.
Contact: www.wmin.ac.uk/unilet

University of Winchester

Winchester celebrated the arrival of university status in 2005 by making the shortlist for *The Times Higher Education Supplement*'s inaugural award of Univer-sity of the Year. It was quite an achievement for an institution that still has only 3,500 full-time students and which was a univer-sity college for only a year, but a place among the top 20 universities in the first National Student Survey suggested that the accolade was deserved. The novelty has since worn off a little, with the university slipping down the student satisfaction table, but applications were still ahead of the national average at the official deadline for courses beginning in 2008. Dance students were the most satisfied in the country and there were good results in education and English.

The university traces its history as an Anglican foundation back to 1840 and has occupied its King Alfred campus since 1862. The compact site is on a wooded hillside overlooking the cathedral city, ten minutes walk away, and with views of the surround-ing countryside. A second centre, which opened in 2003, occupies a large 18th-century rectory in nearby Basingstoke and concentrates on lifelong learning. It offers Foundation degrees in community and creative industries, cultural studies, education and social sciences.

Known as King Alfred's College until 2004, the university is still best-known for teacher training, which accounts for about a third of the places. It is one of the largest providers of primary school training in England, but courses on the main campus also span business, arts, health and social care, and social sciences. Degrees range from choreography and dance, through social work, business, media and teacher training to ethics and spirituality. Law will be introduced in 2008, along with design for digital media, social work, and childhood, youth and community studies. Street arts, global tourism, sustainable development management, philosophy and health and wellbeing are to follow in 2009.

The later teaching quality assessments were excellent, with maximum scores in archaeology and education, and a near-miss in theology and religious studies. Winchester also outscored many of the former polytechnics in the last Research Assessment Exercise, when an impressive 40 per cent of the academics were entered and both history and theology reached the fifth of the seven categories.

The university is particularly proud of its low dropout rate. At 12 per cent, the last official projection was below the national average for the subjects and entry grades, but the university puts the actual figure lower still. More than 95 per cent of the British students are state-educated and nearly a third are from working-class

Winchester
Hampshire SO22 4NR
01962 827234
course.enquiries@
  winchester.ac.uk
www.winchester.ac.uk
www.winchester
  students.co.uk

The Times Rankings
Overall Ranking: 66

Student satisfaction:	=39	(75%)
Research quality:	=66	(1.5)
Entry standards:	=74	(267)
Student–staff ratio:	=61	(17.9)
Services & facilities/student:	97	(£796)
Expected completion rate:	51	(84.5%)
Good honours:	61	(57.4%)
Graduate prospects:	111	(49.7%)

homes. Male undergraduates are heavily outnumbered and there are about 150 overseas students from a range of countries. Winchester students can take advantage of exchange schemes with American universities in Maine, Oregon and Wisconsin, as well as with Beppu University in Japan.

The main campus is well equipped, with its own theatre, sports hall and fitness suite. Outdoor pitches and a modern sports pavilion are not far away. Joint funding with local authorities and Sport England will soon add an eight-lane athletics track, an all-weather pitch and floodlighting. A four-storey University Centre opened in September 2007, transforming the students' union, adding a nightclub, cinema, catering facilities, a bookshop and a supermarket at a cost of £9 million. A "learning café" creates an informal working space with networked PCs and wireless Internet access. An award-winning extension to the library had already made room for 200,000 books, 450 study spaces and 150 computers.

A £12-million student village provides nearly 1,000 residential places – enough to guarantee accommodation for all first years, as well as those from overseas. Like most of the newest universities, Winchester makes a virtue of its small size. Professor Joy Carter, the vice-chancellor, will be anxious not to endanger this in the process of capitalising on the institution's enhanced status. Students value the close-knit atmosphere and find the city livelier than its staid image might suggest, with a number of bars catering to their tastes. London is only an hour away by train and Southampton less than half that for those who hanker after the attractions of a bigger city.

Undergraduate Fees and Bursaries

- Fees for UK/EU students: £3,145
- International student fees: £7,549
- Bursary on full grant: £820
- Bursaries on partial grant: household income up to £39.3K: £410.
- Scholarships based on circumstances or by competition. For full details see the university's website: www.winchester.ac.uk/?page=6891

Students		
Undergraduates:	3,420	(830)
Postgraduates:	115	(930)
Mature students:	19.0%	
Overseas students:	3.8%	
Applications per place:	4.4	
From state-sector schools:	96.0%	
From working-class homes:	31.7%	

For detailed information about fees, grants and bursaries and how they work, see chapter 7.

Accommodation

Number of places and costs refer to 2007–08

University-provided places: 956

Percentage catered: 21%

Catered costs: £102.20 a week (30 weeks).

Self-catered costs: £78.61–£86.17 a week (40 weeks).

First years are guaranteed accommodation if conditions are met.

International fee-paying students are guaranteed places provided conditions are met.

Contact: housing@winchester.ac.uk

University of Wolverhampton

Wolverhampton's record for widening participation in higher education is such that it is the only university in Britain where a majority of undergraduates come from working-class homes. Almost all the students are from state schools and more than a quarter come from areas of low participation in higher education. Strongly regional in outlook, the university draws two thirds of its 24,000 students from the West Midlands, although there is a growing contingent from overseas – the university has offices in China, India, Poland and Nigeria. One in three enters as a mature student and the campuses have a cosmopolitan feel, with about the same proportion coming from the region's ethnic minorities.

Wolverhampton pioneered the high street "higher education shop" and more recently, a dedicated Student Finance Support Unit and Student Gateway Service, bringing all student support together in one convenient location. Big outreach programmes take courses into the workplace. The four campuses each have their own learning centres and are linked by a free bus service. Two are in the city, while sport and performance, education and part of the School of Health are based in Walsall. The original site is in the heart of the city centre. A purpose-built campus in Telford focuses on business and engineering for a county with no higher education institution of its own.

The university has been investing millions of pounds in an infrastructure programme known as "New Horizons", which is due to be completed in 2008. The project has seen the completion of the £26-million development of the City Campus, including the flagship Millennium City Building, an extension of the Harrison Learning Centre, a new technology centre with 600 PCs and a teaching and administration building. A 350-bed student village has opened on the Walsall campus, together with a Lottery-supported sports hall offering elite training facilities for judo and a Sports Science and Medicine Centre that are being used to train Olympic contenders. At Telford the £7-million e-Innovation Centre has already won awards for the incubation and support it offers to e-businesses.

The latest statistics show an improvement in the projected dropout rate, but still more than one in five of those who entered in 2004 may fail to complete their courses in the expected time. Wolverhampton insists that the actual dropout rate is much lower. The university runs a national teaching centre focusing on retention, progression and achievement. Teaching assessments

---

Wulfruna Street
Wolverhampton WV1 1SB
01902 321000
enquiries@wlv.ac.uk
www.wlv.ac.uk
www.wolvesunion.org

The Times Rankings
Overall Ranking: 107

Student satisfaction:	=73	(72%)
Research quality:	=104	(0.6)
Entry standards:	111	(197)
Student–staff ratio:	=71	(18.6)
Services & facilities/student:	75	(£945)
Expected completion rate:	100	(73.9%)
Good honours:	112	(41.1%)
Graduate prospects:	94	(56.8%)

improved after a poor start, with philosophy achieving a perfect score and business and education only one point behind. Teacher training courses are rated in the top four in the country by Ofsted, and Wolverhampton academics have been awarded four National Teaching Fellowships by the Higher Education Academy.

The university claims a number of firsts for its academic programmes, pioneering interactive multimedia communication degrees, as well as offering the only degree in British sign language and one of the first in virtual reality design and manufacturing. It was the first university to be registered under the British Standard for the quality of its all-round provision. Wolverhampton was also the first to open a student employment bureau with an online jobs vacancy service that has since been adopted by many other institutions. The university stresses innovation and enterprise in its work with students and businesses, encouraging student "start up" companies and leading a project to develop student placements in their own companies for those who wish to become entrepreneurs.

Research is mainly applied and aimed at technology transfer, as well as underpinning teaching at all levels. The main strengths are in applications of computing and biomedical science, including ground-breaking work on brain tumours. History and Spanish achieved the best results in the last Research Assessment Exercise, but overall scores were among the lowest in the university system, with no subjects in the top two of the seven categories.

Social facilities vary considerably between sites. Wolverhampton has a growing nightlife and the university has been voted the friendliest in the West Midlands. The cost of living is reasonable and the attractions of Birmingham are now only a metro tramride away.

Undergraduate Fees and Bursaries

- Fees for UK/EU students: £3,145
- International student fees: £8,200 or £8,350
- Bursary on full grant: £500
- Bursaries on partial grant: household income up to £35K: £300.
- Scholarships based on circumstances or by competition. For full details see the university's website: www.wlv.ac.uk/default.aspx?page=6949

Students

Undergraduates:	12,585	(6,350)
Postgraduates:	1,075	(3,460)
Mature students:	29.7%	
Overseas students:	12.0%	
Applications per place:	4.4	
From state-sector schools:	99.0%	
From working-class homes:	50.0%	

For detailed information about fees, grants and bursaries and how they work, see chapter 7.

Accommodation

Number of places and costs refer to 2008–09
University-provided places: 2,048
Percentage catered: 0%
Self-catered costs: £2,246–£3,245 (37 weeks).
First-year students are offered accommodation provided requirements are met. Residential restrictions apply.
International students: same as above.
Contact: residences@wlv.ac.uk

University of Worcester

Worcester has the most ambitious development plans of all the new universities created in 2005. It is spending £120 million on a second campus in the city centre and another £60 million on a unique library and history centre that will be the first joint public and university library in Britain. Work is already under way on the second campus to cater for an additional 4,000 students over the next five years. Some 200 student residences are due to open in September 2009 in restored Georgian buildings and the project is due for completion by 2011.

The impact of university status is still being felt – applications were up by almost 10 per cent at the start of 2008, when the switch from six choices per applicant to five resulted in a decline elsewhere. But numbers had expanded in each of the last five years before the new title arrived. The demand for business courses has been particularly strong and there have been big increases, too, in physical education, sports studies, forensic science, marketing, pre-hospital and emergency care, journalism, social work and advertising.

First as a post-war emergency teacher training college and later as a university college, the institution has always been the only provider of higher education in Hereford and Worcester. The university remains strong in education and also in nursing and midwifery – a mix that explains an overwhelmingly female student population. Jacqui Smith, the Home Secretary, trained as a teacher there. But the six academic departments also cover applied sciences, geography and archaeology, a business school and arts, humanities and social sciences. Degrees range from animal biology to sports coaching and computing.

Education secured the best scores in an otherwise sound but unspectacular set of teaching assessments. Research grades were less impressive, although there are pockets of excellence such as the National Pollen and Aerobiology Research Unit, which produces all Britain's pollen forecasts. Results in the first three National Student Surveys have been generally positive. Worcester was in the top 40 in 2007, its best score coming in education. More than a third of the undergraduates come from working-class homes, but the projected dropout rate of nearly 19 per cent is higher than the national benchmark for the subject mix and entry grades. As well as the normal range of bursaries, the university offers £1,000 scholarships for academic achievement in the first year of a course and extra-curricular activities such as voluntary work.

The existing campus occupies a parkland site ten minutes walk from the

---

Henwick Grove
Worcester WR2 6AJ
01905 855111 (admissions)
admissions@worc.ac.uk
www.worcester.ac.uk
www.worcsu.com

The Times Rankings
Overall Ranking: 81

Student satisfaction:	=26	(76%)
Research quality:	=92	(0.8)
Entry standards:	98	(245)
Student–staff ratio:	85	(19.7)
Services & facilities/student:	95	(£814)
Expected completion rate:	67	(80.8%)
Good honours:	106	(45.6%)
Graduate prospects:	=66	(62.7%)

city centre. Recent improvements have included a £1-million digital arts centre and drama studio, and another 182 residential places will be added in a £10-million development that is due to open in September 2009. Sport plays an important part in university life: a well-appointed sports centre also provides employment opportunities for students, while competitive teams are successful and the facilities for casual participants extensive. A mobile 3-D motion analysis laboratory has been used by the England Cricket Board. Sports scholarships are offered in partnership with Worcestershire County Cricket Club and Worcester Wolves Basketball Club, as well as in hockey. The basketball team have been national champions for three years in succession.

The new campus, which is being developed with the aid of regional and central Government grants, will occupy the site of the old Worcester Royal Infirmary. It will include teaching, residential and conference facilities, as well as the new library and learning centre. The university has undertaken to continue improving the existing St John's campus, which will still be the place of study for two thirds of the university when the new development is completed. It contains three halls of residence with a total of 589 rooms, most of which are allocated to first years. There will be shuttle buses and a cycle route between the two sites. The university also has a number of partner colleges around the region offering Worcester courses.

Social life revolves around the students' union, which also has a "job pod" to help members find work experience and part-time jobs. The cathedral city is not large, but is safer than many university locations and has its share of pubs and clubs that cater for a growing student clientele.

Undergraduate Fees and Bursaries

- Fees for UK/EU students: £3,145
- International student fees: £8,000
- Bursary on full grant: £750
- Bursaries on partial grant: £750; if not eligible for maintenance grant: £500.
- Scholarships based on circumstances or by competition. For full details see the university's website: www.worc.ac.uk/student/finance/809.html

Students

Undergraduates:	3,885	(2,255)
Postgraduates:	450	(1,160)
Mature students:	35.0%	
Overseas students:	2.8%	
Applications per place:	4.6	
From state-sector schools:	96.8%	
From working-class homes:	34.9%	

For detailed information about fees, grants and bursaries and how they work, see chapter 7.

Accommodation

Number of places and costs refer to 2008–09
University-provided places: 589 university-owned; 119 university-managed places
Percentage catered: 0%
Self-catered costs: £65–£95 a week
First year are accommodated on a first come, first served basis. Generally all are housed. International students are accommodated provided requirements are met.
Contact: accommodation@worc.ac.uk

University of York

Never out of the top ten in *The Times* rankings, York has built a reputation in less than 50 years that places it among the top 75 universities in the world. But the university has decided that, with little more than 12,000 students, it is too small to maintain that standing, play a leading role in the economy of the region and contribute to the national agenda for higher education. In an audacious move for a highly selective university, York has begun to develop a second campus to accommodate a 50 per cent increase in student numbers.

The aim is for the first buildings on the Heslington East site, close to the existing campus, to be occupied by October 2009, but the development will take 10 to 15 years to complete. The first cluster of buildings will include computer science and a new department of theatre, film and television, as well as residential accommodation and a central "hub" providing social facilities and teaching space. Eventually, there will be housing for 3,300 students, as well as more academic buildings, sports facilities and a performing arts and community complex.

Expansion into new subjects has already started, with the first law students arriving in 2007. The first undergraduates will follow in 2008 with the first intake in writing, directing and performance in theatre, film and television. The university believes that, with eight applicants for every place, other departments can grow at the same time as retaining or achieving a place in the top ten for their subject. Applications for degree courses were down by much more than average at the start of 2008, when UCAS cut the number of choices per applicant from six to five. There had also been a small decline in the previous year, when most universities had seen rising demand for places.

Medicine was introduced in 2003 in partnership with Hull University. There were over 1,200 applications for 140 places at the Hull York Medical School for courses beginning in 2008. York also runs its own nursing and midwifery programmes, which came fourth in our table for these subjects this year. No university had a better record in the teaching quality assessments. Half of the subjects assessed between 1995 and 2001 achieved perfect scores. It has also done well in the National Student Survey, finishing in the top 20 in all three years of polling, with physics and biology doing particularly well in the 2007 results.

Entrance requirements are high and the dropout rate of less than 5 per cent is among the lowest in the country. Although nearly eight out of ten undergraduates are state educated, only 17 per cent come from

---

Heslington
York YO10 5DD
01904 433533 (admissions)
admissions@york.ac.uk
www.york.ac.uk
www.yusu.org

The Times Rankings
Overall Ranking: 9

Student satisfaction:	=18	(77%)
Research quality:	=6	(5.5)
Entry standards:	12	(423)
Student–staff ratio:	12	(13.1)
Services & facilities/student:	24	(£1,313)
Expected completion rate:	10	(95.2%)
Good honours:	15	(74.7%)
Graduate prospects:	=40	(70.5%)

working-class homes. Every student has a supervisor responsible for their academic and personal welfare. Extra-curricular courses include language and computer literacy training, as well as courses on personal effectiveness, financial management, active citizenship and introduction to accounting. The business community is involved at every level. Undergraduates can also take the "York Award", comprising a range of courses, work placements and voluntary activities which aim to prepare students for the world of work. Over 600 students work as volunteer teaching assistants in local schools.

Computer science, psychology and English were all rated internationally outstanding in the last Research Assessment Exercise, which placed 84 per cent of the academics in the top two of seven categories. The results placed York among the top six universities, as it is for the proportion of research funding that it attracts.

The current campus occupies 200 acres of parkland, a mile outside the picturesque city centre. Students join one of eight colleges, which mix academic and social roles. Most departments have their headquarters in one of the colleges, but the student community is a deliberate mixture of disciplines, years and sexes. Nursing apart, only archaeology and

medieval studies are located off campus, sharing a medieval building in the centre of the city.

Social life on campus is lively. There are two newspapers, television and radio stations, as well as several magazines, to keep students abreast of campus issues. Sports facilities are good, and include a 50-station fitness suite, four sports halls, and dance studio. Extensive playing fields are on campus and the River Ouse fosters a strong rowing tradition. Cultural events abound in the city, which is also famous for a high concentration of pubs. The club scene has improved, but students still head for Leeds for the top names.

Undergraduate Fees and Bursaries

- Fees for UK/EU students: £3,145
- International student fees: £9,510–£12,555
- Bursary on full grant: £1,400
- Bursaries on partial grant: household income up to £35K: £700; up to £40K: £350.
- Scholarships based on circumstances or by competition. For full details see the university's website: www.york.ac.uk/studentmoney/

Students		
Undergraduates:	7,745	(1,360)
Postgraduates:	2,900	(1,270)
Mature students:	8.1%	
Overseas students:	9.8%	
Applications per place:	7.7	
From state-sector schools	77.9%	
From working-class homes:	17.1%	

For detailed information about fees, grants and bursaries and how they work, see chapter 7.

Accommodation

Number of places and costs refer to 2008–09
University-provided places: 4,077
Percentage catered: 0%
Self-catered costs: £75.74–£91.07 a week.
First-year single undergraduates are provided with accommodation if terms and conditions are met.
International students: as above.
Contact: accommodation@york.ac.uk
www.york.ac.uk/admin/accom

York St John University

One of the four universities designated in 2005, York St John is a Church of England foundation that dates back more than 160 years. The eight-acre site faces York Minster across the city walls and is a five-minute walk from the city centre. Now serving over 6,000 students, the campus has seen £50 million of development in recent years and more is planned. The Fountains Learning Centre, which has 500 computer workstations, an internet café and lecture theatre, provides a striking entrance. Another new teaching development, mainly for health and life sciences, will open in 2008–09 and is intended to be a signature building linking the university quarter with the city centre.

York Diocesan Training School opened in 1841 with one pupil on the register, in whose honour the current students' union is named. Divided between York and Ripon for most of its existence, the institution diversified beyond teacher training in the 1980s and decided to concentrate all its teaching on York from the start of the decade. Almost three quarters of the students are female and only about half come straight from school.

Education and theology remains the biggest faculty, with 1,700 students taking programmes in teacher education, education studies, theology and religious studies, theology and ministry and evangelism studies. Health and life sciences are not far behind in terms of size, with 1,600 full-time students and 200 part-timers studying health, psychology and sport. The large faculty of business and communication has a high proportion of joint honours, while the faculty of arts, which was established in 2001, is expanding, particularly in media subjects.

The university was awarded a national centre for excellence in creativity, based on its work in English and theatre studies, which is working an enriched curriculum in the creative arts. The C4C Centre, based in a renovated Victorian Gothic chapel, provides facilities for students, staff, and creative partners to work together. Another music technology suite has been added, and a refurbishment programme has begun in the design and technology block.

Occupational therapy achieved the best score in a mainly undistinguished set of teaching quality assessments. But recent reports from the Quality Assurance Agency have been positive. Languages and philosophy, theology and religious studies had the highest levels of satisfaction in the National Student Survey results published in 2007. Applications were up by more than 10 per cent at the official deadline for entry in that year, following the award of the university title, and were close to the national average at the official deadline for

New Mayor's Walk
York YO31 7EX
01904 876598 (admissions)
admissions@yorksj.ac.uk
www.yorksj.ac.uk
www.ysjsu.com

Edinburgh
Belfast
YORK
London
Cardiff

courses beginning in 2008. Almost 95 per cent of students attended state schools of colleges, while three in ten are from working-class homes. The projected dropout rate of 13 per cent is better than the national average for York St John's courses and entry qualifications.

The university was one of a handful that set undergraduate charges below the £3,000 maximum when top-up fees were introduced. It charged £2,560 a year for degrees in 2007, but York St John joined almost all other universities on fees of £3,145 in 2008. Fees for Foundation degrees remain at the standard level of £1,225 a year.

Relatively high numbers of locally based mature students ease the pressure on residential accommodation. As a result, all first years who want to live in university-owned accommodation are able to do so. More self-catering accommodation for 230 students, costing £10 million, will open in September 2008. Sports facilities are not extensive, but York is popular as a student city with a growing range of clubs as well as, supposedly, a pub for every day of the year.

Undergraduate Fees and Bursaries

- Fees for UK/EU students: £3,145
- International student fees: £7,800–£10,800
- Bursary on full grant: household income up to £18,360: £1,570; up to £20,970: £1,050; up to £25K: £525.
- Bursaries on partial grant: n/a
- Scholarships based on circumstances or by competition. For full details see the university's website: www.yorksj.ac.uk/bursaries

Students

Undergraduates:	4,040	(1,470)
Postgraduates:	245	(685)
Mature students:	18.4%	
Overseas students:	2.8%	
Applications per place:	4.3	
From state-sector schools:	94.3%	
From working-class homes:	31.4%	

For detailed information about fees, grants and bursaries and how they work, see chapter 7.

Accommodation

Number of places and costs refer to 2008–09
University-provided places: 1,125
Percentage catered: 14.5%
Catered costs: £103.40 (10-meal package) a week.
Self-catered costs: £65.17–£118.00 a week (44–48 weeks).
First years are guaranteed accommodation.
Residential and age restrictions apply.
International students: guaranteed housing.
Contact: accommodation@yorksj.ac.uk

Colleges of Higher Education

This listing gives contact details for higher education institutions not mentioned elsewhere within the book. All the institutions of the University of London which do not have their own entry are listed under the main entry for the University of London. All the institutions listed below offer degree course, some providing a wide range of courses while others are specialist colleges with a limited range of courses and a small intake. Those marked with a * are members of GuildHE (www.guildhe.ac.uk).

The Arts Institute at Bournemouth*
Wallisdown, Poole, Dorset BH12 5HH
01202 533011
general@aib.ac.uk
www.aib.ac.uk

Bishop Grosseteste University College, Lincoln*
Lincolnshire LN1 3DY
01522 527347
info@bishopg.ac.uk
www.bishopg.ac.uk

Conservatoire for Drama and Dance
c/o London Contemporary Dance School
The Place, 17 Duke's Road,
London WC1H 9PY
020 7121 1111
lcds@theplace.org.uk
www.theplace.org.uk
and **Royal Academy of Dramatic Arts**
62–64 Gower Street, London WC1E 6ED
020 7636 7076
www.rada.org

Dartington College of Arts*
Dartington Hall Estate
Totnes, Devon TQ9 6EJ
01803 862224
enquiries@dartington.ac.uk
www.dartington.ac.uk

Edinburgh College of Art
Lauriston Place, Edinburgh EH3 9DF
0131 221 6000
registry@eca.ac.uk
www.eca.ac.uk

Glasgow School of Art
167 Renfrew Street,
Glasgow G3 6RQ
0141 353 4500
registry@gsa.ac.uk
www.gsa.ac.uk

Harper Adams University College*
Newport, Shropshire TF10 8NB
01952 820280
admissions@harper-adams.ac.uk
www.harper-adams.ac.uk

Leeds Trinity and All Saints College*
Brownberrie Lane, Horsforth,
Leeds LS18 5HD
0113 283 7100
enquiries@leedstrinity.ac.uk
www.leedstrinity.ac.uk

Liverpool Institute of Performing Arts*
Mount Street
Liverpool LI 9HF
0151 330 3000
admissions@lipa.ac.uk
www.lipa.ac.uk

Newman University College*
Genners Lane, Bartley Green,
Birmingham B32 3NT
0121 476 1181
registry@newman.ac.uk
www.newman.ac.uk

North East Wales Institute of Higher Education
Plas Coch Campus, Mold Road,
Wrexham, N. Wales LL11 2AW
01978 290666
sid@newi.ac.uk
www.newi.ac.uk

Northern School of Contemporary Dance
98 Chapeltown Road
Leeds LS7 4BH
0113 219 3000
info@nscd.ac.uk
www.nscd.ac.uk

Norwich School of Art and Design*
Francis House, 3–7 Redwell Street
Norwich, Norfolk NR2 4SN
01603 610561
info@nsad.ac.uk
www.nsad.ac.uk

Ravensbourne College of Design and Communication*
Walden Road
Chislehurst, Kent BR7 5SN
020 8289 4900
info@rave.ac.uk
www.rave.ac.uk

Rose Bruford College*
Burnt Oak Lane
Sidcup, Kent DA15 9DF
020 8308 2600
contact from website
www.bruford.ac.uk

Royal Agricultural College*
Stroud Road, Cirencester
Gloucestershire GL7 6JS
01285 652531
admissions@rac.ac.uk
www.royagcol.ac.uk

Royal College of Art
Kensington Gore, London SW7 2EU
020 7590 4444
admissions@rca.ac.uk
www.rca.ac.uk

Royal College of Music
Prince Consort Road, London SW7 2BS
020 7589 3643
admissions@rcm.ac.uk
www.rcm.ac.uk

Royal College of Nursing
20 Cavendish Square
London W1G 0RN
020 7409 3333
distance.learning@rcn.org.uk
www.rcn.org.uk

Royal Northern College of Music
124 Oxford Road, Manchester M13 9RD
0161 907 5200
info@rncm.ac.uk
www.rncm.ac.uk

Royal Scottish Academy of Music and Drama
100 Renfrew Street, Glasgow G2 3DB
0141 332 4101
registry@rsamd.ac.uk
www.rsamd.ac.uk

Royal Welsh College of Music and Drama
Castle Grounds, Cathays Park
Cardiff CF10 3ER
029 2034 2854
music.admissions@rwcmd.ac.uk
drama.admissions@rwcmd.ac.uk
www.rwcmd.ac.uk

St Mary's University College*
Waldegrave Road
Twickenham, Middlesex TW1 4SX
020 8240 4000
enquiry@smuc.ac.uk
www.smuc.ac.uk

St Mary's University College
191 Falls Road
Belfast BT12 6FE
028 9032 7678
contact via website
www.stmarys-belfast.ac.uk

Stranmillis University College
Stranmillis Road
Belfast BT9 5DY
028 9038 1271
registry@stran.ac.uk
www.stran.ac.uk

Trinity College Carmarthen
College Road, Carmarthen
Wales SA31 3EP
01267 676767
registry@trinity-cm.ac.uk
www.trinity-cm.ac.uk

Trinity Laban
King Charles Court, Old Royal Naval Court,
Greenwich, London SE10 9JF
020 8305 4300
info@trinitylaban.ac.uk
www.trinitylaban.ac.uk

University College Birmingham*
Summer Row, Birmingham B3 1JB
0121 604 1000
marketing@ucb.ac.uk
www.ucb.ac.uk

University College for the Creative Arts*
contact via website
www.ucreate.ac.uk
New Dover Road, Canterbury, Kent CT1 3AN
01227 817302
Ashley Road, Epson, Surrey KT18 5BE
01372 728881
Falkner Road, Farnham, Surrey GU9 7DS
01252 722441
Oakwood Park, Maidstone, Kent ME16 8AG
01622 620000
Fort Pitt, Rochester, Kent ME1 1DZ
01634 888702

University College Falmouth*
Woodlane, Falmouth
Cornwall TR11 4RH
01326 211077
admissions@falmouth.ac.uk
www.falmouth.ac.uk

University College Plymouth St Mark and St John* **(Marjon)**
Derriford Road, Plymouth, Devon PL6 8BH
01752 636700
admissions@marjon.ac.uk
www.marjon.ac.uk

University of the Highlands and Islands
UHI Millennium Institute
Ness Walk
Inverness IV3 5SQ
01463 279000
eo@uhi.ac.uk
www.uhi.ac.uk

Writtle College*
Chelmsford
Essex CM1 3RR
01245 424200
info@writtle.ac.uk
www.writtle.ac.uk

Index